*International Review of
Industrial
and Organizational
Psychology
1989*

International Review of Industrial and Organizational Psychology 1989

Edited by

Cary L. Cooper
and
Ivan T. Robertson

*University of Manchester
Institute of Science & Technology UK*

JOHN WILEY & SONS
Chichester · New York · Brisbane · Toronto · Singapore

Copyright © 1989 by John Wiley & Sons Ltd.

All rights reserved.

No part of this book may be reproduced by any means, or transmitted, or translated into a machine language without the written permission of the publisher.

The Library of Congress has cataloged this serial publication as follows:

International review of industrial and organizational psychology.
  —1986– —Chichester; New York: Wiley, c1986–
    v.: ill.; 24 cm.
  Annual.
  ISSN 0886-1528 = International review of industrial and organizational psychology

  1.Psychology, Industrial—Periodicals. 2.Personnel management—Periodicals.
  [DNLM: 1.Organization and Administration—periodicals. 2.Psychology, Industrial—periodicals.   W1IN832U]
  HF5548.7.I57   158.7'05—dc19   86-643874
                                    AACR 2   MARC-S
  Library of Congress   [8709]

British Library Cataloguing in Publication Data:

International review of industrial and organizational
  psychology 1989.
  1. Industrial psychology
  I. Cooper, Cary L. (C Lynn), *1940–* II. Robertson,
  Ivan T.
  15877

ISBN 0 471 92174 2

Typeset by Input Typesetting Ltd, London
Printed and bound in Great Britain by Anchor Press Ltd, Tiptree, Essex

CONTRIBUTORS

Cary L. Cooper **Editor**	*Manchester School of Management, University of Manchester Institute of Science and Technology, UK*
Ivan Robertson **Editor**	*Manchester School of Management, University of Manchester Institute of Science and Technology, UK*
Terry A. Beehr	*Department of Psychology, Central Michigan University, USA*
Michael T. Brannick	*Department of Psychology, University of South Florida, USA*
Laura R. Burris	*Department of Psychology, University of Illinois at Chicago, USA*
Michael D. Coovert	*Department of Psychology, University of South Florida, USA*
Marcelline R. Fusilier	*Department of Management, University of Nebraska at Lincoln, USA*
Daniel C. Ganster	*Department of Management, University of Nebraska at Lincoln, USA*
Ricky W. Griffin	*Department of Management, College of Business Administration, Texas A & M University, USA*
Lawrence R. James	*School of Psychology, Georgia Institute of Technology, USA*
Lois A. James	*School of Psychology, Georgia Institute of Technology, USA*
Tony Keenan	*Department of Business Organisation, Heriot-Watt University, UK*
Robert G. Lord	*Department of Psychology, University of Akron, USA*
Karen J. Maher	*Department of Psychology, University of Akron, USA*
Jyuji Misumi	*Department of Social Psychology, Nara University, Japan*
Glenda Y. Nogami	*The Pennsylvania State University College of Medicine, USA*

Ann Marie Ryan	*Department of Psychology, Bowling Green State University, USA*
Paul R. Sackett	*Industrial Relations Center, University of Minnesota, USA*
Arie Shirom	*Department of Labor Studies, Tel-Aviv University, Israel*
Peter B. Smith	*School of Social Sciences, University of Sussex, UK*
Paul E. Spector	*Department of Psychology, University of South Florida, USA*
Siegfried Streufert	*The Pennsylvania State University College of Medicine, USA*
Jean Talaga	*Department of Psychology, Central Michigan University, USA*
David D. Van Fleet	*Department of Management, College of Business Administration, Texas A & M University, USA*

CONTENTS

Editorial Foreword		ix
1.	Selection Interviewing Tony Keenan	1
2.	Burnout in Work Organizations Arie Shirom	25
3.	Cognitive Processes in Industrial and Organizational Psychology Robert G. Lord and Karen J. Maher	49
4.	Cognitive Style and Complexity: Implications for I/O Psychology Siegfried Streufert and Glenda Y. Nogami	93
5.	Coaching and Practice Effects in Personnel Selection Paul R. Sackett, Laura R. Burris and Ann Marie Ryan	146
6.	Retirement: A Psychological Perspective Jean Talaga and Terry A. Beehr	186
7.	Quality Circles: A Review and Suggested Future Directions David D. Van Fleet and Ricky W. Griffin	213
8.	Control in the Workplace Daniel C. Ganster and Marcelline R. Fusilier	235
9.	Job Analysis Paul E. Spector, Michael T. Brannick and Michael D. Coovert	281
10.	Japanese Management — A Sun Rising in the West? Peter B. Smith and Jyuji Misumi	330
11.	Causal Modelling in Organizational Research Lawrence R. James and Lois A. James	372
Index		405

EDITORIAL FOREWORD

This fourth volume of the *International Review of Industrial and Organizational Psychology* contains eleven chapters, written by distinguished colleagues, in current areas of significance within the industrial, occupational, and organizational psychology fields.

This volume extends the range of topics covered in the series (see contents pages for earlier volumes, at the back of the book), without so far having to deal with a topic area more than once. For the fifth year, we will be covering another set of new topics. After five years, we hope the *International Review* will have established itself as an essential resource in I/O psychology. We expect, after our fifth anniversary, that the field will have developed to such an extent that in future volumes we will be including a mixture of further reviews of established topics, as well as coverage of new areas and issues.

Topics scheduled for inclusion in the 1990 volume are:

Vocational Guidance
Feedback Systems in Organizations
Decision-Making in Organizations
Psychology of Groups
Management Development
Ethical Behavior at Work
Cross-Cultural Psychology
Laboratory v. Field Experiments in I/O Psychology
Psychological Aspects of Pay and Reward Systems at Work
Organizational/Environmental Psychology

CLC
ITR
July 1988

Chapter 1
SELECTION INTERVIEWING

Tony Keenan
Department of Business Organisation
Heriot-Watt University
UK

Despite over half a century of criticism by researchers, the interview continues to be an extremely popular method of selection even among organizational psychologists. A recent survey of the individual assessment practices of industrial/organizational psychologists in America (Ryan and Sackett, 1987) reported that 94 per cent used the interview as part of their assessment. In Britain, also, the popularity of the interview is unabated. Robertson and Makin (1986) found that over 80 per cent of a sample of 108 organizations always used the interview in selection.

There are undoubtedly many reasons for this continued popularity, not all of which are as irrational as the research evidence would seem to suggest. The essence of the research criticism is that the interview lacks reliability and validity (Mayfield, 1964; Ulrich and Trumbo, 1965; Schmitt, 1976). Leaving aside the question of whether more recent studies are as pessimistic about validity as their predecessors, it is worth pointing out that there are other criteria, in addition to validity, for assessing the practical usefulness of a selection device. One of these is fairness of impact in terms of minority groups (Reilly and Chao, 1982). Muchinsky (1986) suggests two additional considerations. The first is applicability. This refers to the extent to which the particular selection method can be applied across the full range of job and applicant types. Many techniques which apparently have higher validity than the interview, such as assessment centres, are much less flexible in this respect. The other consideration suggested by Muchinsky is cost effectiveness. Interviews are relatively cheap and easy to carry out compared with a number of other techniques. This is particularly important where the selection ratio is such that large numbers of applicants have to be screened out for a small number of vacancies (Keenan, 1988). There may be few alternatives to the interview for this kind of initial screening. It is also important to distinguish between the interview as a selection device in the sense of discriminating among several candidates to decide who is most appropriate for the job, and as a recruitment tool, the purpose of which is to enhance the attractiveness of the organization and the probability of job offer acceptance. Many would see the interview as indispensable for the latter purpose.

It appears then that, notwithstanding the findings of validity studies carried out by researchers, the interview is here to stay. Quite simply, most practising managers find that in dealing with the real-life selection problems which confront them, there is often no practical way in which the interview can be excluded from the selection process. Of course, the validity of any selection method, including the interview, is an extremely important consideration. Consequently this issue is examined in some detail below.

RELIABILITY AND VALIDITY

It is generally accepted that it is highly desirable that interviews should be both reliable, in the sense that interviewers agree with each other in their judgements, and valid, in that these judgements are predictive of job performance. In an early review, Wagner (1949) located 106 articles related to interviews but only 25 of these contained empirical data. He concluded from his review that, in general, the interview lacked both reliability and validity. However, reliability estimates varied considerably ranging from .23 to .97 with a median of .57. Validity coefficients ranged from .09 to .94 with a median of .27. Mayfield (1964) and Ulrich and Trumbo (1965) drew a similar conclusion to Wagner, suggesting that the interview was lacking in both reliability and validity.

Subsequent reviews by Wright (1969) and Schmitt (1976) showed a decline in the number of reliability and validity studies, presumably reflecting a general pessimism about the likely outcome. This period also saw an increasing focus on micro-analytic studies of interviewing processes, particularly decision making. Arvey and Campion (1982), in the most recent review of research on the interview, were a little more optimistic about the validity issue. They cited one study of a panel interview where validity coefficients ranging from .26 to .34 were obtained (Landy, 1976). Anstey (1977) reported a validity of .35 for Civil Service selection using interview panels. When the coefficient was corrected for restriction of range it rose to .66.

Latham, Saari, Purcell, and Campion (1980) reported promising results for the situational interview. They used the critical incident technique to produce a series of job situations. Candidates were then asked to indicate how they would react if confronted with these situations. They reported an internal consistency of .71 and inter-observer reliability of .76. Validity coefficients were .33 and .39. Latham and Saari (1984) carried out a follow-up study, in this case using subjects currently in post as volunteers. There was a correlation of .42 between the situational interview and supervisors' ratings of performance. One limitation with this approach was the use of existing employees, who presumably would have less motivation to give socially desirable answers than 'real' applicants. If the responses obtained were indeed more authentic than would be the case with real applicants, one potential effect of this might well be to produce artificially high validity coefficients. Latham and Saari also reported the results of a validity study using real candidates where a validity coefficient of only .14 was found. However, a *post hoc* analysis revealed that interviewers were not recording the answers to individual questions, as is required for the situational interview procedure, but merely recorded overall judgements. Latham and Saari gave this as the reason for the low validity.

The Latham technique identifies critical job behaviours, then asks subjects to predict how they *might* react if confronted with them. A variant of this approach is contained in the work of Janz (1982). He also used the critical incident technique to identify job situations but, rather than asking candidates to discuss how they might respond, the interviewer asked candidates for information about how they had actually behaved when confronted with similar incidents in the past. This behaviour description interview had a validity coefficient of .54 compared with .07 for a standard interview. Orpen (1985) carried out a similar study to that of Janz but with some methodological improvements. Validity coefficients of .42 and .62 were obtained against two criterion measures. This compared wth correlations of .07 and .09 for an unstructured interview.

Arvey, Miller, Gould, and Burch (1987) reported a study of selection of sales clerks in retailing. The correlation between interview judgements and performance in year one was .34. After range restriction correction this increased to .42. Results for performance in the second year produced a validity coefficient of .51 which, after correction for range restriction, was estimated to be .61. Arvey *et al.* (1987) suggest that this higher than usual validity may be due to the fact that the job in question required considerable face-to-face contact and that interviewers may be able to assess the social skills which are relevant to such interactions effectively. In support of this, Gifford, Ng, and Wilkinson (1985) asked subjects to rate social skill and motivation in videotaped recordings of real interviews. The interviewees also provided self-assessments of social skill and motivation. There was evidence that social skill, using self-assessment of applicants as the criterion, was to an extent judged accurately. It appeared that judges used inferences from non-verbal cues to evaluate social skill.

While recent validity studies are encouraging, they must still be seen against the background of the majority of investigations over many years which suggest a lack of validity for the interview. Schmitt and Hunter (1977) point out that the results of these primary research studies are distorted by artefacts which make it difficult to estimate the size of the effects and to compare size effects across studies. Meta analysis (Schmitt and Hunter, 1977) endeavours to correct for some of these defects and to provide better estimates of average validities across studies. Hunter and Hirsch (1987) quote both published and unpublished meta analytical studies of the interview. The meta analysis conducted by Hunter and Hunter (1984) yielded average validities of .10. However, a more extensive meta analysis by McDaniel *et al.* (1986) covered many more studies. Although the majority of validities were low, a minority of validities were higher. However, the standard deviations were high. The average validity against performance ratings was .29 and against training success was .25. They found that the type of interview made little difference to the prediction of training success but there was some difference in the prediction of supervisory ratings. The validity of job-related interviews against supervisory ratings was .30 compared with .21 for the psychological interview. However, as they point out, these comparisons are very difficult because of the high standard deviations. The difference between structured and unstructured job interviews was small with an average of .32 for structured versus an average of .26 for unstructured interviews. However, this is somewhat at variance with the results of Weisner and Cronshaw (1986) who found a validity of .13 for unstructured interviews compared to .40 for structured interviews. McDaniel *et al.* (1986) did not find a significant moderating effect when interviews were divided into those where the jobs required social skill and those where the jobs did not require social skill. They interpreted this as being non-supportive of the suggestion that the interview measures social skill. On the other hand, they found that interviewer evaluations were correlated with general cognitive ability and suggest that this relationship is a priority area for future research.

These high variations in validities may simply reflect the fact that, far from being uniform procedures, interviews are highly varied in purpose and content and in what they are attempting to measure. If this is the case, it would seem to be essential to go beyond questions of interview validity in general, and to analyse the nature and process of interviewing itself.

A SIMPLIFIED MODEL OF THE INTERVIEWING PROCESS

It seems reasonable to suppose that the initial stage in any selection process is one of identification of appropriate selection criteria against which to judge applicants. Conventionally, this would involve systematic job analysis to identify the abilities needed for effective job performance. The unanswered question about many of the early validity studies in particular, is the extent to which such procedures were carried out and how they influenced the conduct of the interviews.

Once the necessary skills and abilities have been identified, the next stage presumably is to obtain information relevant to these within the interview itself. This information is of two main types. First, there is the verbal content of the interview which is a function of the questioning techniques used and the interviewee's subsequent answers. Secondly, there is information arising from the non-verbal interplay between interviewer and candidate.

The third element within the interview cycle is decision making. This involves not only processes associated with assimilation of information, but also retention and integration of information to form a judgement about the candidate.

Within this overall framework, it could be suggested that individual differences affect outcomes and consequently influence validity. Both common sense and practical experience would suggest that there are large individual differences among interviewers, both in their skill in obtaining information from candidates, and in the way in which they process that information to reach decisions. These could either be enduring characteristics of the individual, such as personality or cognitive ability, or less enduring attributes, such as interview training or experience.

Individual differences among candidates could also influence interview outcomes. The concern here is with attributes which, while they may influence outcomes, are not directly relevant to job performance. Once again, it is useful to treat enduring attributes, such as personality or minority group membership, as conceptually distinct from less enduring ones, such as experience of interviews or strategies adopted in the interview situation.

The remainder of this chapter will review recent research evidence relating to the interview in terms of the model of interviewing processes set out above. It will build on earlier reviews by Schmitt (1987) and Arvey and Campion (1982), to which the reader is referred.

JOB ANALYSIS, CRITERIA, AND CONTENT OF INTERVIEWS

Verbal Content

Although the process of development of selection criteria through job analysis is conceptually and procedurally distinct from the information gathering stage of the interview, in practice very few research studies have reported on one without discussing the other. This is because job analysis and criteria development tend only to be reported in any detail in those cases where they have been used to provide a framework for the interview content. Of course job analysis also has implications for decision making, since judgements should really be made against a set of pre-established selection criteria. However, few decision-making studies have directly addressed the issue of criteria development, and consequently they are treated separately in this review.

As mentioned above, relatively few of the early validity studies made explicit reference to job analysis or selection criteria. Where selection criteria were mentioned, there was a tendency to focus on traits or trait-like concepts. The present author has argued elsewhere that selecting against traits can seriously mislead interviewers and lead to poor decision making (Keenan 1988). This is primarily because the use of traits frequently leads to problems of ambiguity of meaning and encourages recruiters to make unsubstantiated assumptions, both about the intercorrelation of behaviours presumed to constitute traits, and about the relationship between these traits and job performance. Keenan (1988) has argued that a direct focus on job behaviours would be a more fruitful approach.

The argument that judgement of traits is problematic is supported by a recent review of the practice of industrial/organizational psychologists in which practitioners were asked what they found most difficult to assess accurately in the interview (Ryan and Sackett, 1987). Many of the qualities reported as difficult, such as personality, self-insight, and leadership, are clearly trait-type concepts. It is interesting that the qualities the practitioners reported as being relatively easy to assess tended to be those where judgements could be made by direct observation in the interview, e.g. verbal ability and communication skill. This is not to say of course that such observations are necessarily valid in that they generalize to the work situation itself. It is arguable whether the interview should be used in this way as a kind of work sample, as opposed to being a vehicle for analysing past achievements along the lines suggested by Janz (1982), especially in view of the failure of a major meta analysis study to support the argument that the interview can measure social skill effectively (McDaniel et al., 1986).

In the Ryan and Sackett (1987) study practitioners were also asked the extent to which they conducted systematic job analysis before carrying out selection. The results indicated that job analysis was not the norm. One wonders how these interviewers could obtain relevant information from the candidates in the absence of systematic data on the skills and abilities needed to perform the job effectively.

Despite its obvious importance, there have been relatively few investigations of the verbal content of interviews. Keenan and Wedderburn (1980) investigated graduate recruitment interviews. They found that interviewers spent a disproportionate amount of time discussing their own organization and candidates' reasons for making an application, compared with the amount of time they spent discussing candidates' past achievements. This is interesting in the light of the commonly held view that one of the best predictors of future achievement is the analysis of past achievements. The findings were interpreted as a preference on the part of the interviewer for topics with which they themselves were most familiar, e.g. their own organization.

Taylor and Sniezek (1984) took the approach of Keenan and Wedderburn (1980) a stage further. They asked interviewers of college students to rate topics of conversation for importance and also asked candidates which topics were emphasized in interviews conducted by these individuals. They found that recruiters showed little agreement among themselves about the importance of topics. Also, according to the reports of candidates about what took place in the interview, individual recruiters failed to cover topics they believed were important. In line with the Keenan and Wedderburn (1980) findings, several of the areas recruiters regarded as important were either future oriented, such as 'long-term career goals', or were very general such as 'ability to get on with others'.

A number of recent studies have explicitly used job analysis to determine interview content and it is notable that these have shown encouraging evidence of validity. Included here are the investigations of Latham *et al.* (1980) and Latham and Saari (1984) on the situational interview, and those of Janz (1982) and Orpen (1985) on the behaviour description interview. As indicated above, both took critical incident analysis as the starting point, but the approach of the Latham group was to ask people to describe what they would do when placed in hypothetical situations. The Janz technique, on the other hand, focused on behavioural events relevant to the critical incidents which candidates had actually experienced. One approach is based on the assumption that a person's intentions will predict his or her behaviour, while the other assumes that future behaviour is predicted by past behaviour. At present, the evidence is simply not available to indicate which is the most fruitful approach and well-controlled studies comparing the two are clearly needed. In any event these two methods of obtaining information in an interview are obviously not mutually exclusive, and ultimately the best interviews may involve a combination of both. It is worth mentioning in passing that both the Janz (1982) and Orpen (1985) investigations used standard interviews for control purposes. The questions asked in these were rather reminiscent of the questioning areas which were favoured by interviewers in the real-life interview study reported by Keenan and Wedderburn (1980). Both Janz (1982) and Orpen (1985) reported negligible validities for these standard interviews.

The idea of identifying specific examples of past effective job behaviour has also been used in a variant of the biodata approach. Hough (1984) used critical incidents of effective behaviour of attorneys to develop an accomplishment record inventory. She developed eight behavioural dimensions and individuals were asked to describe, in written form, specific accomplishments in these areas. These written reports correlated .25 with a measure of job performance.

Schmitt and Ostroff (1986) addressed a limitation of techniques which focus on specific job behaviours. Candidates need to have some relevant job knowledge to be able to answer the questions meaningfully and consequently the technique cannot be used for many entry-level positions. Schmitt and Ostroff (1986) describe a procedure for translating critical incidents into questions about which even inexperienced candidates would have sufficient knowledge to produce meaningful responses.

Although interview content ought to be related to selection criteria identified through job analysis, the interview is a dynamic situation and it is to be expected that the verbal content will fluctuate according to the circumstances. Sackett (1982) studied the influence of initial impressions in determining interview content. Evidence from the person perception literature suggested that individuals seek information to confirm initial hypotheses or preconceptions. He investigated whether subjects used such confirmatory strategies in the interview. Subjects in an interview simulation were given information designed to lead them to expect that candidates would be either extraverted or introverted. The confirmatory hypothesis would suggest that introvert-oriented questions would be asked of the introverted candidate, the reverse being the case for the extravert candidates. However, in both circumstances, extravert questions predominated. Sackett argued that interviewers see extraversion as a favourable characteristic and, because they seek favourable information about candidates in the interview, extravert-oriented questions predominate. The study was repeated with an acceptable/non-acceptable pre-interview set and again the evidence did not support a confirmatory hypothesis strategy. Here, also, there was a tendency to choose questions designed to elicit favourable, rather than unfavourable, information. McDonald and Hakel (1985) carried out a similar investigation and once again interviewers did not engage in confirming strategies.

The suggestion that interviewers seek favourable information in their questioning strategies is supported by the results from an unpublished study by the author. Students taking part in real-life interviews were asked to describe how interviewers behaved when they presented a strength compared with when they presented a weakness. When candidates presented a strength (as perceived by them) there was a high level of follow-up probing. However, when a weakness emerged, there were relatively few attempts at follow-up probing on the part of interviewers. These findings are of particular relevance in view of the evidence from studies of decision making that interviewers are more heavily influenced by negative than by positive information (Springbett, 1958). It would seem that the interviewer searches for favourable information in terms of content, but focuses on unfavourable data when the information is being processed. This apparent contradiction highlights the need for research into the relationship between information gathering in the interview and subsequent processing of that information at the decision-making stage.

Non-verbal Behaviour

The role of non-verbal behaviour in interviews has been the focus of a number of research studies. Arvey and Campion (1982), after reviewing research on non-verbal behaviour in interviews, concluded that it appears to influence the evaluations made by interviewers. They suggested that the research indicated that, in general, high levels of immediacy in terms of eye contact, frequent head nodding, and so on, were associated with more favourable evaluations. However, a number of the studies they reviewed were simulations, using experimental designs which held verbal content and other extraneous variables constant. This makes it difficult to estimate the importance of non-verbal behaviour in naturalistic situations where these other variables are free to influence interviewers. In this respect, Arvey and Campion (1982) concluded that the effect of non-verbal behaviour is generally less than that of the verbal content of the interview.

More recent investigations have attempted to assess the influence of non-verbal behaviour when compared directly with other variables using multivariate analysis. For example, Parsons and Liden (1984), using multiple regression and discriminant analysis, concluded that non-verbal cues added significantly to the rating of applicant quality, even after controlling for the influence of objective information. They also reported relationships between non-verbal behaviour and race and sex of applicant. Rasmussen (1984) compared the influence of application forms, verbal behaviour, and non-verbal behaviour on interviewer judgements. He found a significant main effect for the application form, with no discernible interactions, indicating that a good application form was always favourable for the candidate irrespective of the verbal and non-verbal content of the interview. However, a significant interaction was found between verbal content and non-verbal behaviour, with verbal content appearing to be the dominant effect. When the verbal content was positive, high levels of non-verbal behaviour enhanced perceived favourability. However, when the verbal content was poor, high levels of non-verbal behaviour actually reduced favourability. It seems that non-verbal behaviour enhances the magnitude but not the direction of the effects of verbal content.

Little is known about whether non-verbal behaviour increases or decreases the accuracy of interviewer judgements. Gifford, Ng, and Wilkinson (1985) compared interviewers' perceptions of candidate non-verbal behaviour and their judgements about the candidate's level of motivation and social skill. They used applicant self-rating as the measure of motivation and social skill. There was evidence that social skill but not motivation was to an extent accurately judged and that this was done partly using non-verbal cues. The main significant effects were time spent talking and applicant gestures. Smiling, facial regard, and postural attitude were not predictive of self-assessed social skill.

Finally, Rynes and Miller (1983) investigated the role of interviewer non-verbal behaviour and its influence on candidates. High levels of interviewer non-verbal behaviour were consistently interpreted by subjects as a signal regarding the possibility of the candidate being given a job offer. It also affected perceptions of the desirability of the job, but only where there was limited information about job attributes.

In summary, research evidence about the verbal content of interviews is very limited. The evidence continues to support the view that non-verbal behaviour can influence interviewer perceptions. Also, more recent research does nothing to alter the conclusion drawn by Arvey and Campion (1982) that verbal behaviour is probably more influential than non-verbal behaviour in influencing interviewer perceptions. Finally, the finding of an interaction between verbal and non-verbal behaviour, where high levels of non-verbal behaviour augmented the effects of verbal behaviour in a positive or negative direction, dependent on verbal content, is important and deserving of further study.

INFORMATION PROCESSING AND DECISION MAKING

It is evident from the reviews of research on the interview carried out by Mayfield (1964), Ulrich and Trumbo (1965), Wright (1969), Schmitt (1976), and Arvey and Campion (1982), that decision making has been a major focus of research interest in interviewing for over two decades. Much of this work has used the hypothetical applicant method which requires subjects, who are often students, to rate 'paper' people. More recent research has seen a decline in the popularity of this method and an increase in the use of more realistic stimulus situations such as videotaped interviews.

Research on decision making in the 1960s and 1970s identified a number of apparent biases in interviewer judgements. For example, it seems that negative information is more heavily weighted than positive information (Springbett, 1958; Hollman, 1972). Studies of the temporal placement of information have generally highlighted the importance of early impressions. However, Farr and York (1975) found that, where interviewers had to make repeated judgements, recency rather than primacy effects occurred. There is also evidence that attitudinal and racial similarity affects evaluations of candidates (Rand and Wexley, 1975; Wexley and Nemeroff, 1974). A number of pencil-and-paper studies found evidence of contrast effects, where judgements were influenced by the quality of the preceding candidates (Schmitt, 1976). Contrast effects have also been shown using videotaped interviews (Kopelman, 1975; Schuh, 1978).

Much of the more recent research on decision making has elaborated on previous work, although some new directions are also evident. Paunonen, Jackson, and Oberman (1987) followed up the work of Tucker and Rowe (1979), who gave students either a favourable or an unfavourable letter of reference before asking them to read transcripts of interviews. The unfavourable letter resulted in candidates being given less credit for successes and being held more responsible for failures. Paunonen *et al.* (1987) investigated the joint effect on judgements of personality and reference information about the competence of the candidate. They found that the competence information had a much stronger effect than personality. The experimental manipulation of personality consisted of constructing candidates whose attributes were either congruent or incongruent with characteristics of job incumbents. These were determined by the responses of individuals in the occupational categories used to the Strong Vocational Interest Blank. When the competence manipulation was weakened in a second experiment, an effect of personality was found such that respondents preferred candidates with congruent personalities. It appears that the respondents in the Paunonen *et al.* (1987) study, who were college students, were differentially attributing personality attributes to particular occupational groups. There is evidence from a study by Jackson, Peacock, and Holden (1982) that similar processes occur in professional interviewers. They asked employment interviewers how typical twenty personality characteristics were of fifteen occupations.

In a study of the effects of early information, Dipboye, Fontenelle, and Garner (1984) investigated the influence of previewing the application form on the conduct of interviews and on decision making. Previewing the application had little impact on how the interviews were conducted although those who saw the application form showed a tendency to recall more non-application form information. Previewing the application also had little effect on assessment of the candidates. Another study, conducted by Dipboye and his colleagues (Dipboye, Stramler, and Fontenelle, 1984), used a different methodology where subjects observed videotaped interviews, having previously seen either favourable or unfavourable application form information about the applicants. The results indicated that the application form resulted in biased recall of information. When evaluating applicants with unfavourable application form information, subjects recalled less favourable information from the interview itself and rated the candidate's performance in answering the questions as poorer.

Beehr and Gilmore (1982), in a follow up of previous studies which had suggested that candidate attractiveness positively influenced judgements (Carlson, 1967; Dipboye, Arvey, and Terpstra, 1977; Dipboye, Fromkin and Wibeck, 1978), investigated the effect of applicant attractiveness depending on whether or not attractiveness was job relevant. Attractiveness was defined as job relevant where the job involved a high frequency of face-to-face contact. They found a significant interaction between relevance and attractiveness, such that attractive people were evaluated more highly when attractiveness was relevant to the job, as defined above. However, none of the effects encountered was responsible for as much as 10 per cent of the variance. More recently, Gilmore, Beehr, and Love (1986) failed to find an interaction between attractiveness and whether or not attractiveness was job relevant. They did, however, report a main effect for attractiveness. In an investigation which could be construed as the influence of a different type of attractiveness, Baron (1983) compared the effects of the applicant wearing perfume on male and female interviewers. There was an interaction between wearing perfume and sex of interviewer. Male interviewers reacted negatively to the presence of artificial scent regardless of the sex of the interviewee, whereas female interviewers reacted in the opposite fashion.

To summarize, the study of interviewer decision processes has identified a number of biases. For practical purposes, it is important to distinguish between those biases which are unique to the individual, compared to those which affect all interviewers in more or less the same manner. The effects of the former can probably be reduced by using panel interviews, which may partly explain the promising validity data for panel interviews (Landy, 1976; Anstey, 1977,

Rothstein and Jackson, 1980; Weisner and Cronshaw, 1986). Obviously, group biases cannot be so readily dealt with.

INDIVIDUAL DIFFERENCES

Interviewers

Individual differences among interviewers could play an important role in determining the effectiveness of interviews. While this is an intuitively appealing suggestion, relatively few studies have looked at this issue and the evidence is far from complete.

Schmitt (1976) reviewed studies of individual differences in the weight given to individual items of information in reaching decisions. There is evidence that individual interviewers weight individual items of information differently (Valenzi and Andrews, 1973). However, this begs the question as to whether individual interviewers are consistent in their rating strategies across applicants. If interviewers are consistent, this then raises the further question as to whether or not some weighting strategies result in more valid assessments than others.

Zedeck, Tziner, and Middlestadt (1983) criticized the earlier studies of information integration for the use of the hypothetical applicant method and argued for the study of interviewers making real-life decisions. They investigated the weighting strategy of ten interviewers in live interviews, using regression analysis. There were individual differences in weighting strategies, with interviewers using different dimensions in formulating decisions. However, individual interviewers were consistent in their use of information. On the basis of these findings Zedeck et al. (1983) argued for an ideographic approach to interview research. Dougherty, Ebert, and Callender (1986) took this approach a stage further by including validity data in their study. They investigated the decision strategies of three interviewers and, like Zedeck et al. (1983), found differences between interviewers but a high level of intra-interviewer consistency. When the judgements were aggregated across the three interviewers, as is the case in the typical validity study, validity coefficients were negligible. However, for one of the three interviewers, there was evidence of acceptable validity with ratings on nine out of the ten performance dimensions rated being significantly correlated with supervisors' judgements. There was also evidence that training improved the validity of judgements for two of the three interviewers.

Although it seems likely that interviewers will differ in their susceptibility to the various decision-making biases, there are only a handful of published studies in this area. London and Poplawski (1976) reported sex differences in rating, with females generally giving more favourable ratings to hypothetical candidates than males. Raza and Carpenter (1987), in a study of real-life interviews, also found a tendency for female interviewers to give more favourable ratings than males. There was also evidence from the Raza and Carpenter (1987) investigation that male interviewers were more susceptible to age bias in so far as there was a negative correlation between hiring recommendation and applicant age, but the effect held only for male interviewers. However, while these effects were statistically significant, Raza and Carpenter (1987) concluded that the influence of these demographic factors was modest compared with other more job-relevant variables, such as skill.

Interviewer experience is intuitively appealing as a moderating factor in interviews. A number of studies have compared the judgement processes of professional interviewers with those of students. The impetus for these studies was presumably a concern that the use of students in experiments might produce findings which would not apply to experienced, professional, interviewers.

Bernstein, Hakel, and Harlan (1975) reviewed six studies of decision making and concluded that the only difference between students and real interviewers was that college students were more lenient in their ratings. Dipboye, Fromkin, and Wibach (1973) and McGovern, Jones, and Morris (1979) also found few differences between professional interviewers and college students. However, these studies were largely confined to the judgement component of the interview, often using the highly artificial hypothetical applicant method.

Studies comparing students with professional interviewers do not address the issue of whether or not the effectiveness of professional interviewers will vary with the amount of their interviewing experience. Keenan (1978a) compared the decision making of interviewers who regarded interviewing as a substantial part of their duties (classified as experienced) with those who only carried out the function occasionally (classified as inexperienced). Keenan found a correlation between personal liking for the candidate and judged suitability for both categories of interviewer. This was interpreted as a form of bias (Keenan, 1977). However, the bias was stronger for experienced interviewers ($r = .66$) compared with their less experienced colleagues ($r = .35$). The author was only able to find one study which investigated interviewer experience in relation to information gathering techniques. Taylor and Sniezek (1984) reported that interview experience had no influence on the extent to which the recruiters' declared importance of interviewing topics correlated with applicants' perception of the extent to which these had been emphasized in the interview itself.

Despite the plethora of training courses for interviewers, there have been few published studies of the impact of interview training programmes. Arvey and Campion (1982) reviewed a number of studies concerned with training in relation to interviewer judgements. Some of these reported positive effects of training on interview rating techniques (Wexley, Sanders, and Yukl, 1973; Latham, Wexley and Purcell, 1975; Vance, Kihnert, and Farr, 1978). The investigation described above by Keenan (1978a) into the relationship between liking and perceived suitability in real-life interviews also compared interviewers who had been on a formal training course with those who had not. He found that the relationship was lower for those who had been trained. These studies have concentrated on judgements to the exclusion of information gathering processes. Yet many practical interview training programmes place heavy emphasis on information gathering. The studies reported by Howard and Dailey (1979) and Howard, Dailey, and Galanick (1979) are an exception to this general trend, since they evaluated the effects of a training programme which included information gathering in the form of videotaped practice interviews and presentations. They found significant effects of training in six areas including questioning techniques, techniques of rapport, and listening skills.

The Janz (1982) study, described briefly above, is of some interest in a training context. He trained two groups of interviewers in different interviewing styles which he called the standard interview and the behaviour description interview. The former focused on establishing rapport, the impact of body language, the use of probing, and so on. The behaviour description interview training was directed much more towards techniques of focusing the individual on specific examples of relevant past behaviour. Content analysis of what happened in the interview showed marked differences. In the standard interview self-perceptions were commonly explored, whereas in the behaviour description interview the emphasis was much more on past behaviour. As mentioned above it is interesting that there were marked differences in validity coefficients in favour of the group subjected to behaviour description interview training.

Applicants

It would be strange indeed if applicant characteristics had no effect whatsoever on interview outcomes. Where such characteristics are job relevant, this could be seen as contributing to interview validity. However, this would not be the case if it could be shown that applicant characteristics which have no relevance for job performance influence interview outcomes. Applicant characteristics can be divided into two overlapping types. First there are enduring characteristics, such as age, sex, race, and personality. The last of these may be relevant to the job in some circumstances but not in others. Second, there are applicant strategies. These could range from rather specific factors such as interview preparation techniques, to more general self-presentation styles such as authenticity versus impression management. Some of these strategies might be a function of underlying enduring characteristics, while others could be a result of coaching or experience of interviews.

Considering enduring characteristics first, Arvey (1979) reviewed a number of studies of the effects of applicant sex on interview evaluations. He concluded that females were generally given lower evaluations than males with similar or identical qualifications. In addition, females were usually given lower ratings for jobs regarded as typically 'masculine', whereas the reverse was true where the jobs were considered to be typically 'feminine' (Cohen and Bunker, 1975; Cash, Gillen, and Burns, 1977). In a more recent review, Arvey and Campion (1982) reported further studies of sex bias. On the whole these studies supported the findings of the earlier work, but there was an increasing tendency for investigators to consider effects of sex in conjunction with other variables, such as attractiveness. For example, Heilman and Saruwatari (1979) found that attractive females were rated more highly for clerical jobs but were given low ratings for management jobs. Arvey and Campion (1982) concluded that contextual and other personal variables need to be considered in combination with sex and that the situation is more complex than had previously been realized.

In his earlier review, Arvey (1979) had concluded that, when sex was considered in combination with other variables, its effect tended to be relatively small. This has been confirmed in more recent studies. Thus, Arvey *et al.* (1987) found that females were marginally preferred to males for the female oriented job of retail sales clerk. McDonald and Hakel (1985) found significant effects for both sex and race, but the amount of variance was so small as to be of no practical significance. Parsons and Liden (1984) reached a similar conclusion regarding both sex and race.

The last two studies mentioned above addressed the issue of applicant race. In his 1979 review, Arvey reported that the few studies of race of applicant that had been done up until that time had found that minority racial applicants were given more favourable evaluations. These studies would seem to contradict everyday experience, where many believe that discrimination against minority racial groups occurs in the interview. Perhaps there is a serious methodological flaw with many of these studies. Most of them were simulations of one type or another. If the experimental subjects were aware of employment legislation regarding race discrimination and/or responded in a socially acceptable way to the stimulus materials, they might well have reacted by favouring the minority group. Perhaps simulations are inappropriate for answering questions about race bias in interviews. Arguably, demand characteristics could also have affected the results of some of the simulation studies of sex bias described above.

There is evidence from studies using pencil-and-paper stimulus material that younger candidates receive higher evaluations than older candidates (Avalio, 1982; Haefner, 1977; Rosen and Jerdee, 1976). Gordon, Rozelle, and Baxter (1988), using a videotape simulation, found that young applicants were viewed more favourably than older applicants. Increasing subjects' accountability increased the amount of age bias. Raza and Carpenter (1987) found that older applicants were given lower hiring recommendations in real-life interviews, but the effect held only for male interviewers. Contrary to most studies, Arvey *et al.* (1987) found that older workers were slightly favoured for retailing sales posts. This latter finding suggests that, as has been found for sex effects, age stereotypes may interact with the type of job for which the applicant is being considered.

It seems likely that some applicants will adopt strategies in the interview in an attempt to achieve a successful outcome. Assuming such strategies are unrelated to job performance, to the extent that they are successful they are likely to attenuate validity. Despite this, there has been little research on this particular issue. Harlan, Kerr, and Kerr (1977) asked college students whether their chances of employment would be enhanced by emphasizing intrinsic or extrinsic factors in the interview. Subjects believed that it would be best to emphasize intrinsic factors. However, no evidence was presented as to whether subjects actually adopted this strategy in interviews. In a follow-up of this investigation, Giles and Field (1982) assumed that these beliefs would be reflected in candidate strategies. They argued that, if candidates regularly emphasize intrinsic factors, then interviewers would eventually come to believe that job candidates actually possess higher needs for intrinsic satisfaction than is in fact the case. Students attending the placement service of a university were asked to rank a series of job characteristics in terms of relative importance to them. Interviewers were also asked to predict how important each characteristic was for the typical student. Interviewers were found to overestimate the importance of intrinsic factors compared with extrinsic factors.

Keenan and Scott (1985) quesioned undergraduates about how they typically prepared for interviews and about the tactics they used in the interviews themselves. Their responses were then correlated with their success in obtaining jobs. For most respondents, the main preparation consisted of reading the company brochure. The length of time reading it varied from less than five minutes to over 40 minutes (only 3.6 per cent were in this last category). Length of time reading the brochure was significantly associated with success. Indeed, when several predictors were included in a multivariate analysis, time spent reading the literature was the second largest contributor of unshared variance after class of degree obtained. Neither attempting to guess questions and prepare answers in advance, nor reviewing strengths and weaknesses before the interview, had any influence on outcomes. As far as tactics in the interview itself were concerned, those who adopted a strategy of giving answers to please the interviewer regardless of their own views, and those who tried to present middle of the road views on issues were less successful in obtaining job offers.

Little is known about what determines a candidate's strategy in an interview. Perhaps motivation to succeed in the interview affects strategy in the sense that a candidate is likely to try harder to impress for a job he or she particularly wants compared with one he or she is indifferent about. Keenan (1978b) found a curvilinear relationship when self-reported motivation to succeed in the interview was correlated wth interviewer judgements in real-life interviews. Both those who had little motivation to succeed and those who were highly motivated to succeed were judged less favourably than candidates whose level of motivation was intermediate. It seems then that in the interview, as in other areas of life, wanting something too much can actually reduce one's chances of attaining it!

It is possible that personality characteristics are a factor in influencing candidate strategies. However, there is little evidence about the role of candidate personality in interviews. Keenan (1978c, 1982) found that graduates who were high on the personality traits of Machiavellianism and Intolerance of Ambiguity performed relatively poorly in selection interviews. However, level of difficulty in coping with everyday social situations and Locus of Control were not significantly associated with interview outcomes (Keenan, 1982).

RECRUITMENT

Selecting suitable applicants is not the sole function of the interview. It also provides an opportunity for applicants to make judgements about the organization generally, and about the job on offer in particular. There would seem to be two main ways in which interviewers are capable of influencing the perceptions of candidates. First, there is the potential influence of the interviewers' personality and general interviewing style. Secondly, there is the possible effect of the amount and quality of information about job attributes that the interviewer provides to the candidate.

Before attempting to estimate the relative effect of these two factors, it is worth asking whether there is any evidence that interviewers actually influence perceived desirability of jobs and the likelihood of accepting offers. Most of the relevant studies have been concerned with undergraduates who typically have little job experience, and the extent to which these findings can be generalized to more experienced candidates is unknown. Glueck (1973) interviewed business and engineering students and found that more than one-third cited the recruiter as the main reason for selecting a particular employer. In the Keenan (1978b) study described above (unpublished data), candidates were asked to estimate their likelihood of accepting a job offer immediately before and immediately after interviews. Approximately half of the candidates changed their mind to some degree as a result of the interview experience. Liden and Parsons (1986) carried out a field study of young job applicants and concluded that those who responded more favourably to the interviewer were more positive about taking a job in the organization.

A study by Schmitt and Coyle (1976) supported the view that the personal characteristics of the interviewer affect the likelihood of job acceptance. They found that perceived interviewer personality and manner of deliver influenced the interviewee's evaluations of the interviewer. Harn and Thornton (1985) found that the perceived listening skills of interviewers were related to applicant willingness to accept a job offer. Keenan and Wedderburn (1975) found interviewer style in the form of non-verbal behaviour influenced candidates' impressions.

None of these studies directly compared the effect of interviewer style with that of information about the nature of the job. Powell (1984) compared interviewer recruiting practices with information about job attributes and found that only the latter influenced likelihood of acceptance.

Rynes and Miller (1983), in a videotape simulation, compared non-verbal behaviour of the interviewer with the amount of positive information about job attributes. Non-verbal behaviour was interpreted by subjects as an indicator of the likelihood of their chances of getting a job offer. However, recruiter non-verbal behaviour only influenced perceived desirability of the job when there was limited information about job attributes. Rynes, Heneman, and Schwab (1980) have pointed out that studies of the impact of recruiters on candidates have tended to use cross-sectional designs and to focus on the early stages of recruitment, such as the initial interview. Yet applicants often receive only minimal information on job attributes at the initial stages (Herriot and Rothwell, 1981). In an attempt to overcome these limitations, Taylor and Bergman (1987) carried out a longitudinal field study. Recruitment practices, including interviewer style, had some influence on applicant reactions, but only at the initial interview stage. Job attributes had significant impact on applicant reactions at all stages of the recruitment process.

Of course, the provision of job attribute information by interviewers will only influence candidates if it is perceived to be credible. Fisher, Ilgen, and Hoyer (1979), in a survey of undergraduates, investigated the effect of information favourabilty and the credibility of the source of information on job offer acceptance. The results indicated that interviewers were the least credible source of information and that, while giving negative job information enhanced credibility, it decreased the probability of job offer acceptance.

In summary, it appears that both interviewer style and information about job attributes influence candidate perceptions and likely acceptance of offers. The relative importance of each will depend critically on the amount of job-relevant information provided and its perceived credibility. Where a significant amount of job-attribute information is provided by a credible source, this is likely to be the dominant factor. Whether this is typically achieved in real-life interviews is as yet an unanswered question.

SUMMARY AND CONCLUSIONS

There is now a considerable amount of evidence that the selection interview lacks validity. However, recently, more promising evidence of validity has emerged, especially where the interview has focused on either past behaviour or predicted behaviour in hypothetical situations.

Lack of validity could be a result of the selection criteria used. It seems likely that behavioural criteria, based on careful job analysis, will prove to be an improvement on earlier, trait-based, approaches. Little is known about the content of interviews in general or the information gathering techniques used by interviewers, despite the fact that this is central to the whole issue of what construct the interview is trying to measure. There is an urgent need for research in this area. There is now a considerable amount of information on various decision-making biases. However, as yet we know little about how far these can be minimized by appropriate training programmes.

Despite the intuitively appealing suggestion that interview outcomes are influenced by characteristics of both interviewers and candidates, there is little research evidence available. This is particularly true of the role of candidate strategies in interviews. A return to the study of real-life interviews, as opposed to simulations, might stimulate research on this issue.

Evidence continues to accumulate on the role of the interviewer in influencing candidate reactions. Recent studies suggest that information on job attributes may be more influential in this respect than the general style of the interviewer, although more research is necessary before a definitive conclusion can be reached on this issue.

REFERENCES

Anstey, E. (1977) A 30-year-follow-up of the CSSB procedure, with lessons for the future. *Journal of Occupational Psychology*, **50**, 149–159.

Arvey, R.D. (1979) Unfair discrimination in the employment interview: Legal and psychological aspects. *Psychological Bulletin*, **86**, 736–765.

Arvey, R.D., and Campion, J.E. (1982) The employment interview: A summary and review of recent research. *Personnel Psychology*, **35**, 281–322.

Arvey, R.D., Miller, H.E., Gould, R., and Burch, P. (1987) Interview validity for selecting sales clerks. *Personnel Psychology*, **40**, 1–12.

Avalio, B.J. (1982) Age stereotypes in interview evaluation contexts. *Dissertation Abstracts International*, **42**, 3020B.

Baron, R.A. (1983) 'Sweet smell of success'? The impact of pleasant artificial scents on evaluation of job applicants. *Journal of Applied Psychology*, **68**, 709–713.

Beehr, T.A., and Gilmore, D.C. (1982) Applicant attractiveness as a perceived job-relevant variable in selection of management trainees. *Academy of Management Journal*, **25**, 607–617.

Bernstein, V., Hakel, M.D., and Harlan (1975) The college student as interviewer: A threat to generalizability. *Journal of Applied Psychology*, **60**, 266–288.

Carlson, R.E. (1967) Selection interview decisions: The relative influence of appearance and factual written information on an interviewer's final rating. *Journal of Applied Psychology*, **51**, 460–468.

Cash, T.F., Gillen, B., and Burns, D.S. (1977) Sexism and 'beautyism' in personnel consultant decision making. *Journal of Applied Psychology*, **62**, 301–307.

Cohen, S.L., and Bunker, K.A. (1975) Subtle effects of sex role stereotypes on recruiters' hiring decisions. *Journal of Applied Psychology*, **60**, 566–572.

Dipboye, R.L., Arvey, R.D., and Terpstra, D.E. (1977) Sex and physical attractiveness of raters and applicants as determinants of resumé evaluations. *Journal of Applied Psychology*, **62**, 288–294.

Dipboye, R.L., Fontenelle, G.A., and Garner, K. (1984) Effects of previewing the application on interview process and outcomes. *Journal of Applied Psychology*, **69**, 118–128.

Dipboye, R.L., Fromkin, H.L., and Wiback, K. (1975) Relative importance of applicant sex, attractiveness, and scholastic standing in evaluation of job applicant resumés. *Journal of Applied Psychology*, **60**, 39–43.

Dipboye, R.L., Stramler, C.S., and Fontenelle, G.A. (1984) The effects of the application on recall of information from the interview. *Academy of Management Journal*, **27**, 561–575.

Dougherty, T.W., and Ebert, R.J., and Callender, J.C. (1986) Policy capturing in the employment interview. *Journal of Applied Psychology*, **71**, 9–15.

Farr, J.L., and York, C.M. (1975) Amount of information and primary-recency effects in recruitment decisions. *Personnel Psychology*, **28**, 233–238.

Fisher, C.D., Ilgen, D.R., and Hoyer, W.D. (1979) Source credibility, information favorability, and job offer acceptance. *Academy of Management Journal*, **22**, 94–103.

Gifford, R., Ng, C.F., and Wilkinson, M. (1985) Non-verbal cues in the employment interview: links between applicant qualities and interviewer judgements. *Journal of Applied Psychology*, **70**, 729, 736.

Giles, W.F., and Field, H.S. (1982) Accuracy of interviewers' perceptions of the importance of intrinsic and extrinsic job characteristics to male and female applicants. *Academy of Management Journal*, **25**, 148–157.

Gilmore, D.C., Beehr, T.A., and Love, K.G. (1986) Effects of applicant sex, applicant physical attractiveness, type of rater and type of job on interview decisions. *Journal of Occupational Psychology*, **59**, 103–109.

Glueck, W. (1973) Recruiters and executives: How do they affect job choice? *Journal of College Placement*, **34**, 77–78.

Gordon, R.A., Rozelle, R.M., and Baxter, J.C. (1988) The effect of applicant age, job level, and accountability on the evaluation of job applicants. *Organizational Behavior and Human Decision Processes*, **41**, 20–33.

Haefner, G.E. (1977) Race, age, sex and competence as factors in employment selection of the disadvantaged. *Journal of Applied Psychology*, **62**, 199–202.

Harlan, A., Kerr, J., and Kerr, S. (1977) Preference for motivator and hygiene factors in a hypothetical interview situation: Further findings and some implications for the employment interview. *Personnel Psychology*, **30**, 557–566.

Harn, T.J., and Thornton, G.C. III (1985) Recruiter counselling behaviours and applicant impressions. *Journal of Occupational Psychology*, **58**, 57–65.

Heilman, M.E., and Saruwatari (1979) When beauty is beastly: The effects of appearance and sex on evaluation of job applicants for managerial and non-managerial jobs. *Organizational Behavior and Human Performance*, **23**, 360–372.

Herriot, P., and Rothwell, C. (1981) Organizational choice and decision theory: Effects of employer's literature and selection interview. *Journal of Occupational Psychology*, **54**, 17–31.

Hollman, D.T. (1972) Employment interviewers' errors in processing positive and negative information. *Journal of Applied Psychology*, **56**, 130–134.

Hough, L.A. (1984) Development and evaluation of the 'accomplishment record' method of selecting and promoting professionals. *Journal of Applied Psychology*, **69**, 135–146.

Howard, G.S., and Dailey, P.R. (1979) Response-shift bias: A source of contamination of self-report measures. *Journal of Applied Psychology*, **64**, 144–150.

Howard, G.S., Dailey, P.R., and Galanick, N.A. (1979) The feasibility of informed pretests in attenuating response-shift bias. *Applied Psychological Measurement*, 3, 481–494.
Hunter, J.E., and Hirsh, H.R. (1987) Applications of meta-analysis. In C.L. Cooper and I.T. Robertson (eds), *International Review of Industrial and Organizational Psychology*, New York: Wiley.
Hunter, J.E., and Hunter, R.F., (1984) Validity and utility of alternative predictors of job performance. *Psychological Bulletin*, 96, 72–98.
Jackson, D.N., Peacock, A.C., and Holden, R.R. (1982) Professional interviewers' trait inferential structures for diverse occupational groups. *Organizational Behavior and Human Performance*, 26, 1–19.
Janz, T. (1982) Initial comparisons of patterned behaviour description interviews versus unstructured interviews. *Journal of Applied Psychology*, 67, 577–580.
Keenan, A. (1977) Some relationships between interviewers' personal feelings about candidates and their general evaluation of them. *Journal of Occupational Psychology*, 50, 275–283.
Keenan, A. (1978a) Selection interview outcomes in relation to interviewer training and experience. *The Journal of Social Psychology*, 106, 249–260.
Keenan, A. (1978b) The selection interview: Candidates' reactions and interviewers' judgements. *British Journal of Social and Clinical Psychology*, 17, 201–209.
Keenan, A. (1978c) Selection interview performance and intolerance of ambiguity. *Psychological Reports*, 42, 353–354.
Keenan, A. (1982) Candidate personality and performance in selection interviews. *Personnel Review*, 11, 20–22.
Keenan, A. (1988) Decision making in occupational selection. Unpublished manuscript.
Keenan, A., and Scott, R.S. (1985) Employment success of graduates: Relationships to biographical factors and job-seeking behaviours. *Journal of Occupational Behaviour*, 6, 305–311.
Keenan, A., and Wedderburn, A.A.I. (1975) Effects of non-verbal behaviour of interviewers and candidates' impressions. *Journal of Occupational Psychology*, 48, 129, 132.
Keenan, A., and Wedderburn, A.A.I. (1980) Putting the boot on the other foot: Candidates' descriptions of interviewers. *Journal of Occupational Psychology*, 53, 81–89.
Kopelman, M.D., (1975) The contrast effect in the selection interview. *British Journal of Educational Psychology*, 45, 333–336.
Landy, F.J. (1976) The validity of the interview in police officer selection. *Journal of Applied Psychology*, 61, 193–198.
Latham, G.P., and Saari, L.M. (1984) Do people do what they say? Further studies on the situational interview. *Journal of Applied Psychology*, 69, 569, 573.
Latham, G.P., Saari, L.M., Russell, E.P., and Campion, M.A. (1980) The situational interview. *Journal of Applied Psychology*, 65, 422–427.
Latham, G.P., Wexley, K.M., and Purcell, E.D. (1975) Training managers to minimise rating errors in the observation of behaviour. *Journal of Applied Psychology*, 60, 550–555.
London, M., and Poplawski, J.R. (1976) Effects of information on stereotype development in performance appraisal and interview contexts. *Journal of Applied Psychology*, 17, 239–260.
Liden, R.L., and Parsons, C.K. (1986) A field study of job applicant interview perceptions, alternative opportunities, and demographic characteristics. *Personnel Psychology*, 39, 109–122.

Mayfield, E.C. (1964) The selection interview: A re-evaluation of published research. *Personnel Psychology*, 17, 239–260.
McDaniel, M.A., Whetzel, D.L., Schmidt, F.L., Hunter, J.E., Maurer S., and Russell, J. (1986) The validity of employment interviews: A review and meta meta-analysis. Unpublished Manuscript, Washington, DC: US Office of Personnel Management.
McDonald, T., and Hakel, M.D. (1985) Effects of applicant race, sex, suitability, and answers on interviewers' questioning strategy and ratings. *Personnel Psychology*, 38, 321–334.
McGovern, T.V., Jones, B.W., and Morris, S.E. (1979) Comparison of professional versus student ratings of job interviewer behavior. *Journal of Counselling Behavior*, 26, 176–179.
Muchinsky, P. (1986) Personnel selection decisions. In C.L. Cooper and I.T. Robertson (eds), *International Review of Industrial and Organizational Psychology*, New York: Wiley.
Orpen, C. (1985) Patterned behaviour description interviews versus unstructured interviews: A comparative validity study. *Journal of Applied Psychology*, 70, 774–776.
Parsons, C.K., and Liden, R.C. (1984) Interviewer perceptions of applicant qualifications: A multivariate field study of demographic characteristics and nonverbal cues. *Journal of Applied Psychology*, 69, 557–568.
Paunonen, S.V., Jackson, D.J., and Oberman, S.V. (1987) Personnel selection decisions: Effects of applicant personality and the letter of reference. *Organizational Behavior and Human Decision Processes*, 40, 96–114.
Powell, G.N. (1984) Effects of job attributes and recruiting practices on applicant decisions: A comparison. *Personnel Psychology*, 37, 721–731.
Rand, T.M., and Wexley, K.N. (1975) Demonstration of the 'similar to me' effect in simulated employment interviews. *Psychological Reports*, 36, 535–544.
Rasmussen, K.G. (1984) Nonverbal behavior, verbal behavior, resumé credentials, and selection interview outcomes. *Journal of Applied Psychology*, 69, 551–556.
Raza, S.M., and Carpenter, B.N. (1987) A model of hiring decisions in real employment interviews. *Journal of Applied Psychology*, 72, 596–603.
Reilly, R.R., and Chao, G.T. (1982) Validity and fairness of some alternative employee selection procedures. *Personnel Psychology*, 35, 1–61.
Robertson, I.T., and Makin, P.J. (1986) Management selection in Britain: A survey and critique. *Journal of Occupational Psychology*, 59, 45–57.
Rosen, B., and Jerdee, T.H. (1976) The nature of job-related age stereotypes. *Journal of Applied Psychology*, 61, 180–183.
Rothstein, M., and Jackson, D.N. (1980) Decision making in the employment interview: An experimental approach. *Journal of Applied Psychology*, 65, 271–283.
Ryan, A.M., and Sackett, P.R. (1987) A survey of individual assessment practices by I/O psychologists. *Personnel Psychology*, 40, 455–488.
Rynes, S.L., Heneman, H.G. III, and Schwab, D.P. (1980) Individual reactions to organizational recruiting: A review. *Personnel Psychology*, 33, 529–542.
Rynes, S.L., and Miller, H.E. (1983) Recruiters' job influences on candidates for employment. *Journal of Applied Psychology*, 68, 147–154.
Sackett, P.R. (1982) The interviewer as hypothesis tester: the effects of impressions of an applicant on interviewer questioning strategy. *Personnel Psychology*, 35, 789–804.
Schmidt, F.L., and Hunter, J.E. (1977) Development of a general solution to the problem of validity generalizations. *Journal of Applied Psychology*, 62, 529–540.
Schmitt, N. (1976) Social and situational determinants of interview decisions: Implications for the employment interview. *Personnel Psychology*, 29, 79–101.

Schmitt, N., and Coyle, B.W. (1976) Applicant decisions in the employment interview. *Journal of Applied Psychology*, **61**, 184–192.

Schmitt, N., and Ostroff, C. (1986) Operationalizing the 'behavioral consistency' approach: Selection test development based on a content-orientated strategy. *Personnel Psychology*, **39**, 91–107.

Schuh, A.J. (1978) Contrast effect in the interview. *Bulletin of the Psychonomic Society*, **11**, 195–196.

Springbett, B.M. (1958) Factors affecting the final decision in the employment interview. *Canadian Journal of Psychology*, **12**, 13–22.

Taylor, M.S., and Bergman, T.J. (1987) Organizational recruitment activities and applicants' reactions at different stages of the recruitment process. *Personnel Psychology*, **40**, 261–285.

Taylor, M.S., and Sniezek, J.A. (1984) The college recruitment interview: Topical content and applicant reactions. *Journal of Occupational Psychology*, **57**, 157–168.

Tucker, D.H., and Rowe, P.M. (1979) Relationship between expectancy, causal attributions, and final hiring decisions in the employment interview. *Journal of Applied Psychology*, **64**, 27–34.

Ulrich, L., and Trumbo, D. (1965) The selection interview since 1949. *Psychological Bulletin*, **63**, 100–116.

Valenzi, E., and Andrews, I.R. (1973) Individual differences in the decision process of employment interviewers. *Journal of Applied Psychology*, **58**, 49–53.

Vance, R.J., Kuhnert, K.W., and Farr, J.L. (1978) Interview judgments: using external criteria to compare behavioral and graphic ratings. *Organizational Behavior and Human Performance*, **22**, 279–294.

Wagner, R. (1949) The employment interview: A critical summary. *Personnel Psychology*, **2**, 17–46.

Weisner, W.H., and Cronshaw, S.F. (1986) The moderating impact of interview format and degree of structure on interview validity. Unpublished manuscript. Guelph, Canada: University of Guelph.

Wexley, K.N., and Nemeroff, W.F. (1974) The effects of racial prejudice, race of applicant, and biographical similarity on interviewer evaluations of job applicants. *Journal of Social and Behavioral Sciences*, **20**, 66–78.

Wexley, K.N., Sanders, R.E., and Yukl, G.A. (1973) Training interviewers to eliminate contrast effects in employment interviews. *Journal of Applied Psychology*, **57**, 233–236.

Wright, O.R. (1969) Summary of research on the selection interview since 1964. *Personnel Psychology*, **22**, 391–413.

Zedeck, S., Tziner, A., and Middlestadt (1983) Interviewer validity and reliability: An individual analysis approach. *Personnel Psychology*, **36**, 355–370.

Chapter 2
BURNOUT IN WORK ORGANIZATIONS[1]

Arie Shirom
Department of Labor Studies
Tel-Aviv University
Israel

INTRODUCTION

The term burnout appeared in print in the early 1970s (Freudenberger, 1974) to denote a certain combination of chronic, long-lasting emotional exhaustion, physical fatigue, absence of job involvement, dehumanization of the recipients of one's services, and lowered job accomplishments. It apparently filled a void in labelling a hitherto unnamed, but prevalent, phenomenon. The term burnout has caught the attention of researchers (primarily in I/O psychology and neighbouring disciplines), consultants, and practitioners (see Maslach, 1982b). This happened first in the context of the helping professions, like nursing and social work. Soon, the initial focus expanded to cover all other people occupations — that is, occupations whose members deal extensively with other people on their job. Employees in the uniformed services, teachers, managers, and also clerical and service employees were included in samples studied by burnout researchers.

There are several reasons for the popularity and widespread publicity given to the term burnout. First, unlike other attitudinal concepts describing affective states, such as depression or anxiety, it carried with it a minimal stigmatizing burden. Its use to communicate with burned out employees was, therefore, conducive to more effective diagnostic and intervention efforts. Second, burnout, unlike labels such as incompetent or inept, did not imply that the one who admits to being afflicted by it is necessarily the one to be blamed for it. Thus, when we describe ourselves as burned out, we are using a socially acceptable label. Other reasons had to do with macro level socioeconomic changes, characteristic of many industrialized countries in the West (Cherniss, 1980b). Among these changes has been the continuous decline in public funds

---
[1] Preparation of this chapter was assisted by a grant from the Ford Foundation (Ford Grant No. 11) received through the Israel Foundation Trustees.

to support services provided by people occupations. This fall of the budgetary axe coincided, in several countries, with a growth in public demand for the same services, and with a rise in politicians' expectations that the providers of these services would amend society's social ills (Farber, 1983; Paine, 1982).

An indication of the rising popularity of burnout research is the fact that between 1980 and 1985, more than 300 articles in refereed periodicals, and about a dozen books, were published on this subject (Roberts, 1986). In recent additions to the research literature, a growing diversity of the applications of the term burnout is evident (Pines and Aronson, 1988). To illustrate, it has been used to denote early deterioration of exceptional natural abilities among adolescents (Solano, 1987), loss of motivation among college students (Meier and Schmeck, 1985), advanced pathology of schizophrenic patients (McGinness, 1987), and the process of dissipation of intimacy and love in marital relationships (Pines, 1987, 1988). This review will cover only burnout of employees in work organizations, excluding research which exclusively deals with this phenomenon in other, non-employment-related settings, such as in the above examples.

As noted, early research on burnout was confined to employees in the helping professions, such as social workers, nurses, probation officers, ministers, and poverty lawyers (much of this early research is referenced by Maslach, 1982b, pp. 168–84; and Cherniss, 1980b). This early tradition has continued unabated, as illustrated by recent studies of social workers (Brookings, Bolton, Brown, and McEvoy, 1985; Leiter and Meachem, 1986; Wade, Cooley, and Savicki, 1986); public service lawyers (Jackson, Turner, and Brief, 1987); nurses (Bartz and Maloney, 1986; McCarthy, 1985; McCranie, Lambert, and Lambert, 1987); teachers (Anderson and Iwanicki, 1984; Cedoline, 1982; Kyriacou, 1987); and physicians (Keinan and Melamed, 1987; Lemkau, Rafferty, Purdy, and Rudisill, 1987). Since there was no theoretical rationale for limiting the applicability of burnout to the helping professions (Maslach and Jackson, 1984), researchers directed their attention to its study in a variety of other occupational categories, wherein jobs involve primarily interactions with people, such as prison guards (Shamir and Drory, 1982); military officers and policepersons (Burke and Deszca, 1986; Ezrahi and Shirom, 1986; Jones, 1985; Whitehead and Lindquist, 1986); managers (Cahoon and Rowney, 1984; Glogow, 1986); park attendants (Rosenthal et al., 1983); rehabilitation clinicians (Ursprung, 1986a); correctional officers (Dignam, Barrera, and West, 1986); and librarians (Birch, Marchant, and Smith, 1986). Increasingly, however, one finds indications that burnout has been investigated in samples of blue-collar employees like service workers (Ursprung, 1986b) or of employees in the tertiary sector, not oriented towards people, like athletes (Smith, 1986) and secretaries (Nagi, 1985). The wide spectrum of occupational categories covered by burnout research, as exemplified above, necessarily entails adapting a broad frame of reference in reviewing this research.

This chapter was not intended to be an exhaustive review of existing literature on burnout. I have chosen, instead, to highlight specific key issues that appeared crucially important if we are to make our research in this area theoretically more meaningful and practically more significant. The issues on which this review focus are indicated in the chapter's structure. Excluding the introductory and concluding sections, there are three sections to the chapter. The first section discusses the conceptual meaning of burnout, in an attempt to identify its unique content and theoretical underpinnings. In the second section, I consider a few epidemiological aspects of burnout. Burnout among teachers is taken as a case in point, offering tentative generalizations which may apply to other people occupations. The third section covers the issues of the causes and consequences of burnout. In it, I outline the major findings of the few longitudinal studies which have been undertaken in this field of study. The concluding part details recommended directions for future research, to enhance our understanding of burnout.

THE CONSTRUCT VALIDITY OF BURNOUT

Unlike other behavioural science concepts, the term burnout was adopted by researchers from its lay use by respondents, to describe a certain group of negative attitudes they had towards their jobs (Maslach and Jackson, 1984). The use of respondents' jargon does have clear advantages in field research, such as establishing immediate rapport with respondents. However, one of its shortcomings has been the diverse ways of defining burnout conceptually and operationally. The conceptual vagueness and over-inclusiveness of burnout was described by the progenitor of the term, Freudenberger (1983), as a situation whereby burnout became a buzzword used to convey an almost unlimited variety of social and personal problems. There are indications that some researchers regard burnout as a pseudoscientific jargon, devoid of substance (as an example, it did not appear at all in a massive handbook covering theoretical and clinical aspects of stress — Goldberger and Breznitz, 1982). Others, while acting in a gate-keeper's role, would reject outright any paper dealing with burnout (Maslach and Jackson, 1984, reported having had these experiences). It is therefore incumbent upon a reviewer to demonstrate that, beyond the different definitional approaches, there is a shared meaning unique to the concept of burnout, providing it with scientific legitimacy.

To provide readers with a sense of the field's development over time, the major definitional approaches in it will be described below, in their order of appearance in print. A more detailed discussion of definitional approaches to burnout may be found in Maslach (1982a, 1982b), Paine (1982), Shinn (1982), and Farber (1983).

Definitional Approaches

Maslach's MBI

Probably the earliest, and the most widely referenced approach towards the conceptualization of burnout is that which resulted from the work of Maslach and her associates. She defined burnout as a syndrome, consisting of the symptoms of emotional exhaustion, depersonalization (referring to a detached, cynical, and callous response to clients) and reduced personal accomplishment (Maslach, 1982b). To gauge burnout, a standardized measure called the Maslach Burnout Inventory (MBI) was constructed (Maslach, 1982a). MBI comprises 22 items, giving three scales, each purportedly designed to operationalize a burnout component. The MBI and practically all other burnout measures were constructed by performing factor analysis on correlation matrices of questionnaire items. These items, in turn, were derived from observational and interview data culled in pilot studies of employees in helping professions. It should be noted that MBI's emotional exhaustion scale, on which I shall focus, actually includes more items tapping physical fatigue than emotional exhaustion, and includes items reflecting overload (Maslach and Jackson, 1981, p. 102). The MBI has been the most widely used measure of burnout in research (Maslach, 1982b, p. 8). With few exceptions (e.g. Golembiewski, Munzenrider, and Carter, 1983), it has been applied primarily to the study of burnout in the helping professions. Independently of the group of researchers who constructed the MBI, its factor structure was replicated in samples of teachers (Belcastro, Gold, and Hays, 1983; Gold, 1984; Iwanicki and Schwab, 1981), nurses (Bartz and Maloney, 1986; Dolan, 1987), managers (Golembiewski and Munzenrider, 1983), university students (Powers and Gose, 1986), and secretaries (Nagi, 1985).

Pines et al. BI

Yet another major approach towards the conceptualization of burnout has been suggested by Pines and her colleagues (e.g. Pines, Aronson, and Kafry, 1981). In it, burnout was defined as a response to stress, represented by a combination of the following symptoms: (1) emotional, physical, and mental fatigue; (2) feelings of helplessness, hopelessness, and entrapment; (3) lack of enthusiasm about work and about life in general; and (4) low self-esteem, or the negation of one's life (Pines *et al.*, 1981, pp. 3, 34–5, 202–3). This group of researchers constructed yet another measure to gauge burnout, referred to in this review as the Burnout Index (BI). It comprises 21 items (evaluated on a seven-point frequency scale), whose mean value is calculated to derive the overall score of a respondent (Pines *et al.*, 1981, pp. 202–4).

BI has been applied to a wide variety of occupations, including managerial ones, in several industrialized Western Countries, (e.g. Etzion and Pines, 1986; Kafry and Pines, 1980; Pines *et al.*, 1981). Initially, this group of researchers proposed to limit the term burnout to the helping professions and to use the term tedium to refer to the same phenomenon in other people occupations (Kafry and Pines, 1980). However, this distinction was not followed up. Scores of the BI, and of the MBI's emotional exhaustion and depersonalization scales, were found in two studies (Corcoran, 1985; Stout and Williams, 1983), to be moderately correlated (i.e. r's .50), suggesting that the two instruments were measuring some amount of the same phenomenon.

Chrniss's developmental model

In the burnout literature, there are several attempts to conceptualize it as a process. Sometimes it is regarded as the final step in a progression of unsuccessful attempts to cope with negative stress conditions (e.g. Farber, 1984). Others view it as a process developing from job impoverishment — lack of motivators (Ezrahi, 1987). Cherniss (1980a) and his associates constructed a developmental model, which has partly been supported by empirical evidence (Wolpin, 1988). They interviewed 28 beginning professionals in helping professions several times over about a two-year period of time. The model was based on data gathered in intensive interviews held with these new professionals. In this model, burnout is viewed as a series of negative attitude changes that occur over time, particularly in self-interest, work alienation, emotional detachment, and perceiving oneself as not responsible for the outcome of the helping process.

Cherniss further developed and extended his thinking on the process of burnout in a summary of research on burnout published in the same year (1980b). In it, he integrated his process model with the area of stress at work, and proposed three distinct stages characterizing burnout. The first stage is perceived stress, that subsequently leads to physical fatigue and emotional exhaustion as well as to anxiety (Cherniss, 1980b, pp. 17–18). The third stage of the transactional process is defensive coping, by which Cherniss referred to a number of attitudinal and behavioural changes, including cynicism towards clients, withdrawal, and emotional detachment. An attempt to validate Cherniss's model, in a longitudinal design, was recently reported by Burke (1987).

Edelwich and Brodsky's (1980) model

This is somewhat akin to the above, in that it described a stage model of the occurrence of disillusionment in the helping professions. These authors argued that most employees in the helping professions start their work career with idealistic enthusiasm, then experience inevitable frustrations in their organizations, such as failure to respond to clients' needs, powerlessness, and sexism. Subsequently, a process of demoralization, or burnout, unfolds. The fourth stage of burnout consisted of retreat into apathy, or emotional withdrawal. In both of these process models, burnout is that stage of the transactional process in which a previously committed helping professional disengaged from his or her work in response to stress and frustration experienced on the job. Especially in Edelwich and Brodsky's (1980) book, but to some extent in other process models of burnout, there exists an unfortunate tendency to view burnout as an unavoidable, contagious, and negative emotional experience.

Golembiewski's eight-phase model

Golembiewski and his colleagues (Golembiewski and Munzenrider, 1984; Golembiewski, Munzenrider, and Carter, 1983; Golembiewski, Munzenrider, and Stevenson, 1985) pioneered in proposing the existence of eight progressive phases of burnout. Each of the three components of burnout in the MBI was hypothesized to be sequentially prepotent, with the sequence following from depersonalization to lack of personal accomplishment to emotional exhaustion.

The phases were found to be progressively virulent, but individuals did not necessarily pass through each phase. Golembiewski and his associates (1985) claimed that their results supported the view that individuals at different phases of burnout also differ on antecedents and consequences of burnout. Therefore, different interventions should be planned for individuals in each of the major groups of phases. There is some research which has validated the existence of progressive phases of burnout by systematically comparing individuals in the various phases (Golembiewski, Munzenrider, and Stevenson, 1985; Burke, 1987).

There are several additional developmental models of burnout. Thus Blase (1982) followed a group of 43 teachers for a school year and used several methods to assess burnout. He proposed a distinction between the process of burning out and the state of burnout. During the process of burning out, there is a gradual and progressive erosion of a teacher's coping resources.

Blase's (1982) model may be used to demonstrate a common feature of most development models of burnout: during the early stages all identify burnout with a gradual and progressive depletion of a respondent's coping resources. All identify the central symptoms of burnout, during these early development stages, to be physical fatigue and emotional exhaustion.

Concurrent and Discriminant Validity

Does the new label of burnout stand for a social psychological construct with a unique theoretical content, not overlapping the conceptually established domains of anxiety, hopelessness, helplessness, meaninglessness, self-estrangement, and depression? Several researchers sought to establish the concurrent and discriminant validity of burnout.

Following the work of Russell (1980, 1983) on the structure of affective states, Ezrahi and Shirom (1986) hypothesized that three affective components would underlie the BI: anxiety, depression, and physical and emotional exhaustion — the only component hypothesized to be uniquely associated with the concept of burnout. In their research, Ezrahi and Shirom used questionnaire responses of 704 senior army officers in the Israeli defence forces. Following the results of dimensional analyses, they constructed three unidimensional scales out of the pool of items in the BI, labelled depression, anxiety, and burnout. Regressions of each scale on four measures of stress lent considerable support to their concurrent validity. The major implication of this research is that a unidimensional approach towards the conceptualization of burnout (as operationalized in Pines *et al.* (1981) BI) would lead one to identify physical fatigue and emotional exhaustion as its unique content.

Maslach and Jackson (1984) culled findings of five studies in which the MBI was used to measure burnout in diverse samples. Twenty-eight work-related variables (mostly perceived job or organization characteristics) were correlated with each of the three MBI scales. The non-significant correlations obtained were 18, 54, and 64 per cent for the three scales of emotional exhaustion, depersonalization, and lack of personal accomplishment, respectively. A very similar pattern of findings emerged in subsequent large-scale studies in which the MBI was used (e.g. Friesen, 1986; Ezrahi, 1987; Wolpin, 1988). I interpret this trend as evidence that only emotional exhaustion is significantly associated with the work context variables examined, and as an indication that the other two factors might be related to personality types (Garden, 1987), or might be more fruitfully studied from the theoretical perspective of learned helplessness or depression possibly resulting from an advanced state of burnout.

The last point is further buttressed by Meier's (1984) study. He found that burnout measures, including a summary score on MBI, correlated highly and significantly with depression measures, thereby weakening support for burnout's discriminant validity, as measured by MBI. There is evidence indicating that the emotional exhaustion scale of the MBI is contaminated by items measuring a separate construct, frustrations and discouragements about work, a construct which was found to be highly correlated with generalized professional depression among helping professionals (Firth, McIntee, and McKeown, 1985). Thus the operationalization of emotional exhaustion in the MBI might account for this scale overlapping with depression, as depicted in Meier's (1984) study.

Convergent Validity

Yet another group of validation efforts focused on the convergent validity of burnout, primarily by comparing independent methods of measuring it. Thus a study of 'objective' versus 'subjective' burnout compared self-reports of police officers to their spouses' reports of behaviour of the officers at home (Maslach and Jackson, 1981), using MBI. Emotionally exhausted police officers were described by their wives as coming home upset and anxious. The other two MBI scales were unrelated to behaviour at home, as perceived by the spouses. However, MBI proponents could argue that depersonalization is best observed by clients, and further that self-reports of lack of personal accomplishment should be validated against peer or superior assessments.

This indeed was done in two other studies. Rafferty, Lemkau, Purdy, and Rudisill (1986) provided support for the validity of the emotional exhaustion scale of the MBI. They did that by reporting that it significantly correlated with psychologists' and resident directors' assessments in a sample of 67 family practice physicians. The same authors failed to validate similarly the depersonalization and lack of personal accomplishment scales of the MBI (with one exception: resident directors' assessments correlated .22 with self-assessed frequency of lack of personal accomplishment). In a similar vein, but using a more elaborate design, Ezrahi (1987) compared self-reported burnout scores (using MBI) with the investigator's structured observations of teachers' classroom behaviour, and with superior assessment of burnout, in a sample of fifteen schools. Again, only the emotional exhaustion scale in the MBI was validated by the observational study and by the superior assessments.

Burnout's Core Meaning

What are the major implications of the above validation efforts? It appears that at this juncture the field of burnout is ready for an identification of the boundaries and content of this concept. I shall first chart the boundaries, namely the location of the concept in the domain, and subsequently describe what I consider to be its unique content.

There are several common features to the conceptualizations of burnout reviewed above. First, all relate to an individual level phenomenon. None relate to it as a group or organization level property. Second, it is viewed as a negative emotional experience. Yet a third feature is that the burnout is seen as a chronic, ongoing feeling. According to the cognitive theory of emotions, developed by Lazarus and Folkman (1984, pp. 273-4, 284-5), cognitions and emotions are theoretically separable. In nature, they tend to appear conjoined, mutually affecting each other over time. But for the purpose of conceptual analysis, appraisals of stress may be viewed as leading to emotional experiences (Lazarus and Folkman, 1984). The majority of past conceptualizations of burnout viewed it as a negative affective response to stress (e.g. Cherniss, 1980b; Meier, 1983, 1984; Perlman and Hartman, 1982; Shinn, Rosario, March, and Chestnut, 1984; Ursprung, 1986a). While researchers did not identify the type (or types) of stress involved (e.g. daily hassles, critical job events, or continuous role stresses), stress as a cause of burnout is frequently defined in a broad sense, including instances wherein an employing organization failed to provide employees with expected job rewards like positive feedback and opportunities for self-determination (Maslach, 1982b; Freudenberger, 1980). The conceptualization of burnout as a chronic, ongoing affective response makes it distinct from a temporary state of fatigue which passes after a resting period. Burnout, however, may occur in the very early stages of an employee's work career, decline after the initial socialization and entry period, and rise up again in a curvilinear fashion (Shirom and Mazeh, in press).

In line with the conceptual approach towards burnout recommended by Paine (1982) and Shinn (1982), the position taken here is that it should be narrowly defined to cover a specific, coherent set of stress-related negative experiences which are job related. The major conclusion which may be drawn from past validation efforts is that the unique content of burnout has to do with the depletion of an individual's energetic resources. Specifically, burnout refers to a combination of physical fatigue, emotional exhaustion, and cognitive weariness. This is the dimension of the burnout experience for which there is most support in the validation efforts. This is the dimension identified in longitudinal research on burnout (Jackson, Schwab, and Schuler, 1986), and, by most burnout scale constructors, as the predominant component of this concept (Freudenberger, 1983; Garden, 1987; Pines et al., 1981; Maslach, 1982a). The depletion of energetic resources, denoted now by the term burnout, does not overlap any other established behavioural science concept. Not surprisingly, several researchers already used only this primary dimension of burnout to operationalize it in field research (Cunningham, 1983; Shirom, 1986; Garden, 1987). The additional components that several authors sought to add to this core negative emotional experience, involving the depletion of energetic resources, often confounded it with an antecedent coping behaviour (e.g. depersonalization, in the MBI), or with a personality trait accompanying it (like low self-esteem, in the BI), or with some of its sequels (like reduced levels of personal accomplishments and job performance, in the MBI).

There are several underlying assumptions often made by burnout researchers that need to be discarded if one accepts the core definition of burnout. Thus it is evident that physical fatigue, emotional exhaustion, and cognitive weariness, the three facets of the general process involving gradual depletion of coping resources, are quite common in the world of work. They need not, and should not, be restricted to individuals whose work requires large amounts of contact with people in need of aid (Maslach and Jackson, 1984). Therefore, a theory of burnout must not allow itself to be exclusively concerned with the people occupations. Yet another assumption often made by burnout researchers (e.g. Jackson, Schwab, and Schuler, 1986) is that the term exhaustion means that the burnout syndrome is most relevant for job holders whose work is very involving. In fact, most studies reported moderate negative correlations between burnout and work involvement or commitment (Farber, 1984). A third assumption found in burnout research is that it is often preceded by high levels of arousal (Maslach, 1982b; Edelwich and Brodsky, 1980). Again, this is not necessarily implied by the above core definition.

ON BURNOUT'S EPIDEMIOLOGY

Has, in fact, the problem of burnout reached serious proportions? It appears that its prevalence and incidence, in different social categories, is a largely uncharted terrain in this field (Maslach and Jackson, 1984). Therefore, answers to basic questions, such as the per cent of people in specific occupations who were found to be in advanced stages of burnout, are not directly available from the literature. Very few studies explored sociodemographic or personality differences in the prevalence of burnout. There are very few exceptions: gender differences were found (e.g. Pines and Kafry, 1981; Izraeli, 1988), cultural differences in it were described (e.g. Etzion and Pines, 1986), and some attention was directed to personality traits which might predispose the development of burnout (Garden, 1987; Keinan and Melamed, 1987).

Few researchers did report prevalence data on burnout. In the preceding section, the eight-phase model of burnout proposed by Golembiewski and his colleagues was discussed. In their research (Golembiewski, Munzenrider, and Stevenson, 1985) they found that in 26 different samples, the phases, which they designated as the advanced burnout phases, contained an average of 45 per cent of all respondents.

To provide an assessment of the prevalence of burnout, a decision was made to select, for an in-depth study, a people profession characterized by relatively moderate levels of burnout. Teachers in regular schools (excluding administrators, superintendents, and special education teachers) were selected. There are several studies that documented moderate levels of burnout among teachers in comparison with other occupational groups (Kyriacou, 1987). Pines et al. (1981), using the BI, provided comparative data on mean levels of burnout across 30 different occupational groups. Teachers' mean level (3.2) was a bit below the grand mean (3.3) found for all occupations combined. Anderson and Iwanicki (1984), who used the MBI, derived the percentile rank on the Emotional Exhaustion (frequency) scale for 800 teachers in their sample by referring to MBI normative data. The percentile rank found (47), indicated that, in comparison with a fairly large body of burnout data for human service professionals, the level of burnout among teachers was moderate. Using a very similar procedure, other researchers (Alexander, Adams, and Martray, 1983; Belcastro, Gold, and Hays, 1983) reached much the same conclusion.

A plausible approach to the determination of the proportion of burned out teachers would be to classify as 'significantly burned-out' all those whose mean score exceeded the value of 4 on the BI or MBI ('sometimes' in the BI, or 'a few times a month' in the MBI frequency scale). This approach is based on the view that burnout tends to be under-reported, either because of social desirability effects, negative acquiescence effects (due to the primacy of negatively phrased statements in these popular burnout measures), or both. However, the counter-argument against this approach is that there is little evidence supporting the existence of the above biasing problems in self-report measures of affective reactions to jobs (Spector, 1987). Thus, the MBI was found not to be influenced by a social desirability response set (Maslach and Jackson, 1981). Therefore, a more conservative measure of burnout was derived, in which only teachers whose mean burnout scores were 5.0 or above, were defined as burned out. In practice, it means that a burned out teacher reported experiencing the symptoms often, usually, or always, if the BI was used, or every week, a few times a week, and every day, if the MBI was used.

Farber (1984) investigated burnout in a sample of 693 public school teachers in New York State, in the academic years 1980/81 and 1981/82. Burnout was measured by a modified version of the MBI, adapted for use with teachers. Using the decision rule described above, 22 per cent of urban teachers (but only about 10 per cent of suburban teachers) in his sample were burned out. Shirom (1986) estimated the prevalence of burnout on the basis of responses of 1044 high school teachers in academic year 1982/83, drawn from a representative sample of Israeli high schools. He found, using a modified version of BI, and applying the same decision rule, that 23 per cent of his respondents were burned out. Nagi and Davis (1985) and Whiteman, Young, and Fisher (1985), who respectively used the MBI and the BI, estimated that close to one-third of their samples of teachers (junior high and elementary school teachers) were highly burned out. However, the latter researchers used a different decision rule than the one adopted above.

In general, the evidence on teachers' burnout supports the proposition that in several Western industrialized countries the problem of burnout is more than faddish, and has, in fact, reached a serious proportion. This proportion may range from 10 per cent to 30 per cent of all teachers. Given the pattern of the findings reported above, the problem of burnout is probably affecting in the neighborhood of 20 per cent of all teachers. Assuming that one can extrapolate from the results obtained for teachers to other people occupations, then it is clear that a substantial minority of employees are burned out.

As noted above, there appears to be a growing interest among researchers in identifying gender differences in burnout. An established finding, in the literature on gender differences, is that, in response to stress, women report more physical symptoms, but less physiological illness, than men (Jick and Mitz, 1985; Baruch, Biener, and Barnell, 1987). Most investigators who dealt with gender differences, reported a higher mean burnout level for employed women relative to men (Freudenberger, 1983). This recurrent finding, in the nexus of increasing rates of women employees in the helping professions, brought about in-depth explorations of the dynamics of burnout among them (e.g. Freudenberger, 1983; Izraeli, 1988).

CAUSES AND CONSEQUENCES OF BURNOUT

Both the scientific community and the public at large, have shown a substantial amount of interest in the causes and consequences of burnout, especially among professionals engaged in helping people. This interest is indicated by the space provided for these topics in popular magazines of the helping professions, and in those professions' scientific periodicals (see Pines and Aronson, 1988). In this section, I shall first discuss theoretical models which have been offered to unravel the causal chain in which burnout is a link, and then proceed to summarize empirical research on the precursors and sequels of it. In both types of scientific contributions, the conceptual confusion which surrounds the definition of burnout reappears. To exemplify, the sparse research on the relationships of burnout to job performance is plagued by the definitional problem: items measuring performance-related behaviour are sometimes incorporated into measures of burnout, such as in Jones's (1981) Staff Burnout Scale for Health Professionals, or in the personal accomplishment scale of the MBI. However, the definitional problems of burnout, and their methodological implications, have already been addressed in the first section of this review and will not be reiterated here.

The theoretical literature on the causes and consequences of burnout often enumerate a variety of different hypothesized antecedents and consequences of this phenomenon. Hypothesized causes have included employee characteristics like age or gender, job features like amount of control and autonomy, management practices like closeness of supervision, organizational culture and structure, and variety of societal characteristics (Jackson, Schwab, and Schuler, 1986).

This diversity might be illustrated by the following example. An elaborate diagnostic model of the causes of burnout was developed by Carroll and White (1982). They have extended to the explanation of burnout the Lewinian Person–Environment Fit theory, as further developed by interactional and community psychologists (such as J.R.P. French and R.H. Moos), to explain how stress at work leads to psychological and physiological strain. These authors argued that it is the joint, interactive impact of certain personal factors and job-context and environmental characteristics that produce burnout. Examples of the former factors are inadequate, client-focused socialization process, overly specific or narrow job skills, and incompetency in the utilization of available social supports. Job-context and environmental characteristics were described as task/role-person mismatches. Carroll and White's (1982) theoretical perspective did not inspire systematic empirical studies. This is partly due to the exhaustiveness of their diagnostic model, in which the major proposition appears to be that any obstacle, in every element of an individual life space, that impedes this individual's effort to accomplish objectives may lead to the burnout experience (Carroll and White, 1982, p. 52).

An entirely different theoretical approach to diagnose the causes of burnout was developed by Etzion (1987). She proposed that the causes of burnout may not be perceived by those afflicted by it. The reasoning she offered was that burnout results from employees being exposed to relatively small, unnoticed and almost unrecognizable, but pervasive and enduring stresses on the job. Gradual erosion of coping resources occurs when these insidious job-related stresses perpetrate, unhindered, the radar screen of an individual employee's buffers and defences. This process of erosion can go on undetected, because most of the small stresses arise from barely perceptible and generally denied mismatches between personal characteristics and the environment. Thus, much like Carroll and White (1982), Etzion (1987) drew upon the Person–Environment Fit perspective for the diagnosis of the causes of burnout. However, she reached dissimilar diagnostic conclusions. Etzion's (1987) pictorial portrayal of the antecedents of burnout invokes, as explanatory constructs, subconscious processes. However, Etzion (1987) correctly indicated that hassles (Lazarus, 1984) as a class of job-related stresses, have not yet been incorporated as possible predictors in burnout research. Yet another class of job-related stresses, critical job events, also awaits consideration by burnout researchers (for an exception, see Justice, Gold, and Klein, 1981).

The typical empirical study of the causes of burnout was aptly described by Shamir (1986). He found, in most books reporting quantitative research on the antecedents of burnout, a laundry list approach. Practically, this approach meant that every conceivable negative feature of the job environment, including lack of positive job features, appeared as a correlate of burnout. Predominantly, research in this field has been correlational, using cross-sectional designs. As an illustration, Shamir (1986) located, in Pines *et al.*'s (1981) research-based volume on burnout, reports of findings relating burnout to 32 antecedent conditions. All were found to be significantly associated with burnout. These correlates included role-related stresses, deprivations of various kinds of organizational rewards, diverse characteristics of organizational climate, and variety of personal factors.

This type of empirical research runs the danger of arriving at simplistic conclusions, which might be quite misleading. Researchers often overlooked the possibilities that the effects of stress on burnout might be moderated by personality characteristics, such as hardiness (Kobasa and Puccetti, 1983; Rich and Rich, 1987), or by situational characteristics, such as available social support from superiors and peers (Etzion, 1984). Predisposing factors, such as constitutional vulnerability, were often not controlled for or even considered. In this type of correlational research, which has been predominant in the burnout area, the identified associations between stress and burnout, or between burnout and its sequels, do not support causal propositions. Significant correlations reported to have been found may be spurious, accounted for by high intercorrelations among the stresses used as potential predictors.

While the emphasis has been on the literature covering hypothesized precursors, or empirically supported antecedent conditions of burnout, it should be noted that the theoretical literature and empirical studies on the consequences of burnout are equally diverse (see Cherniss, 1980b; Lazaro, Shinn, and Robinson, 1985; and Jackson, Schwab, and Schuler, 1986), and suffer from the same limitations noted above.

It is thus apparent that neither burnout theory, nor past correlational research on the antecedents of burnout would be helpful points of departure for an adequate coverage of the topic. Therefore, a decision was made to limit the review in this section to longitudinal research only. Very few longitudinal studies of burnout have been undertaken. Their respective contributions, to our understanding of the causal chain which includes burnout as a major link, are described below.

Not all longitudinal studies employed a design which allowed researchers to make causal statements. Sometimes, the analytic procedure of simple hierarchical regression was used to test hypotheses about the antecedents and consequences of burnout. A case in point is Jackson, Schwab, and Schuler's (1986) research on 249 teachers who were mail-surveyed twice, a year apart. MBI was used to gauge burnout. The major findings about hypothesized antecedents can be summarized briefly as follows: unmet expectations about the job did not predict burnout, but role conflict was a powerful predictor of emotional exhaustion. Principal and colleague social support were important predictors of personal accomplishment, yet another dimension of the MBI.

Regarding the hypothesized consequences of burnout, then Jackson et al. (1986) found that burnout scores, predominantly those obtained from the emotional exhaustion scale of the MBI, significantly predicted their respondents' (a) preferred job statuses, (b) subsequent thoughts about leaving their jobs, and (c) actual job leaving. They interpreted the results as supporting the conclusion that emotional exhaustion predicted subsequent turnover.

In one of the samples studied by Golembiewski and his colleagues (1985), burnout was measured longitudinally over a one-year period. They found that about three-quarters of the respondents retained their original burnout phase assignments. This finding led the researchers to conclude that advanced burnout seems widespread and lasts for long periods.

Yet another study which employed a relatively weak design is that of Wade, Cooley and Savicki (1986). They conducted a one-year, longitudinal study of burnout, involving 46 helping professionals in different human service facilities. They found that burnout levels, gauged by the MBI, were quite stable over one year. Respondents who moved towards higher (n = 18) and lower (n = 15) burnout levels were compared on a set of potential predictors of burnout.

The former group was found to experience less social support in the workplace, was less involved, and reported having less control and more economic stress relative to the latter group. This study was based on a relatively small sample size: it is reported because its findings about the role of social support in decreasing levels of burnout buttress those of several correlational studies (Shinn et al., 1984; Etzion, 1984).

Wolpin (1988) used questionnaires, completed one year apart, to measure the levels of burnout, and a number of its presumed predictors and outcomes, among 245 school-based educators in Canada. Burnout was measured by the MBI and by Cherniss's Negative Attitude Change (Cherniss, 1980a). Multivariate analyses showed that somatic symptoms were more likely to be caused by burnout rather than the reverse. Inconclusive findings were obtained about the location of job dissatisfaction in the causal chain considered here. Burnout turned out to be a precursor of stress perceptions; teachers who moved up on the burnout ladder had experienced higher levels of job impoverishments.

In yet another major longitudinal research on stress–burnout relationship (Shirom, 1986), the directionality of causal influence between stress and burnout, on the one hand, and burnout and somatic complaints, job dissatisfaction, and intention to leave work, on the other hand, were investigated. Respondents were teachers (n = 404) in a representative sample of Israeli high schools. Burnout was operationalized as emotional exhaustion and physical fatigue, and a variant of the BI was administered. Respondents completed questionnaires about one month after the beginning of the school year in 1983 (time 1) and about one month before it ended (time 2). Structural regression analysis was used in this investigation. Since teachers face instruction-related stress on a continuous basis, it was expected that over the school year, their adaptive resources would become increasingly depleted. In fact, it was found that, on the average, teachers were similarly burned out at both times of measurement.

The results of the structural regressions did not provide support to the traditional causal chain leading from stress at work to burnout; in fact, with respect to two stress indices out of five, the reverse appeared to hold. There was strong support for the view that burnout at time 1 leads to higher levels of job dissatisfaction, somatic complaints, and intention to leave the teaching profession at time 2.

Several common features and recurrent findings can be identified in the reviewed longitudinal studies. To the extent that they reported cross-lagged correlations between specific stresses and burnout, only about 5 per cent of their respective variance was found to be shared. Cross-lagged correlations of similar magnitude were obtained by other researchers of stress–strain relationships (e.g. Frese, 1985). This, however, may cast a serious doubt on the practical utility and theoretical fruitfulness of linking stress and burnout. However, burnout is probably related to stresses in life domains other than work; hassles and critical job events, as potential stressors, were not measured at all in these studies; only moderate reliabilities were obtained for the indices measuring stress and burnout, thus restricting the range of the correlations obtained; and finally, for the extremes of the sample, even small amounts of shared variance may be highly important.

In most studies, correlations of above .50 were obtained between the two measurements of burnout. This may be interpreted as representing a relative stability or chronicity of the investigated phenomenon. However, it is evident that substantial minorities of respondents went up and down on the burnout ladder in practically all the studies. There is a strong indication that, for the respondents who reported a downward movement, social support resources, notably from their superiors, were more abundantly available, relative to other categories of respondents.

In most of the reviewed studies, burnout induced higher levels of somatic complaints rather than the reverse. The fact that there is evidence implicating burnout in bringing about somatic complaints, and possibly depression (whose measurement scales tend to include items tapping psychosomatic complaints), provides support for the developmental models of burnout, described in the first section. Clearly, burnout, conceptualized as a psychological strain, behaved differently relative to other strains, not only in that it predicted somatic complaints. In a clear departure from the predominant theoretical approach in stress research, these longitudinal studies have cast doubts on the view that stress, and especially interpersonal types of stress, produce burnout. Could it be that this traditional and widely accepted view about the antecedents of burnout is inadequate, and that respondents' reports about depleted energetic resources are associated with subsequent elevated levels of perceived stress? This appears to be a major challenge for future research.

It was not clear from the studies reviewed here whether or not burnout behaved differently from job dissatisfaction. Both strains responded similarly to personal control: the higher the control, the lower tended to be the psychological strain. However, overload, or case load, tended to predict burnout, and to a significantly lesser extent, job dissatisfaction. Overall, the longitudinal studies support and augment the evidence coming from cross-sectional designs (Lazaro et al., 1984) linking burnout to job withdrawal behaviours such as turnover.

In sum, the few longitudinal studies that were undertaken on the burnout phenomenon provide sufficient support to past developmental models and justify additional research. However, the strategy guiding any additional research should be carefully considered thus to reflect lessons learnt, like from inadequate past conceptualization and operationalization of burnout. The next section outlines recommended ingredients of future research strategy on burnout.

CONCLUSIONS: DIRECTIONS FOR FUTURE RESEARCH

This concluding section addresses some of the broader issues raised by the burnout literature. In particular, the following two issues are considered. (1) What are the implications for theory building and empirical research on burnout, of the core-concept proposed in the first section? (2) If future research is to advance our understanding of burnout, what directions should it follow?

The unidimensional view of burnout, referring to a combination of physical fatigue, emotional exhaustion, and cognitive weariness, has several advantages, relevant for future theory building in this area. A major theoretical approach in stress research views stress as a perceived disruption of an existing balance between demands and resources, and views the response to stress, that is, strain, as representing a range of dysfunctional adaptation to stress (Lazarus and Folkman, 1984). Inherent in this view is the assumption that individuals seek to preserve demands–resources balance, or maintain homeostasis. Recently, Hobfoll (in press) has constructed an alternative theoretical model, based upon the underlying assumptions that individuals seek to maximize growth, and have a basic need to protect and enhance that which they value. From this notion, Hobfoll (in press) developed the model of conservation of resources. According to this model, when individuals experience actual loss of resources, they respond by attempting to limit the loss of resources and by maximizing gain of resources. To do this, we must usually employ other resources. Applying these notions to burnout, then it can be argued that individuals experience burnout when they perceive a net loss, which cannot be replenished, of valuable personal resources, specifically physical vigorousness, emotional robustness, and cognitive agility. This net loss is experienced in response to external demands (stressors), and cannot be compensated for by expanding other resources, or borrowing, or in other ways replenishing the original loss. A burned out person may exacerbate his or her losses by entering an escalating spiral of losses. Then, he or she may reach an advanced stage of burnout, wherein hopelessness, helplessness, depression, and anxiety become the predominant emotions.

There are several ways in which the model of conservation of resources can contribute to advance theory building in burnout research. To illustrate, it can be used to differentiate theoretically between the phases of burnout. Thus, in the early stages of burnout, active and direct coping, to enhance and protect an individual's resources, is the characteristic coping behaviour. However, in the more advanced stages, wherein burnout appears coupled with depression and apathy, indirect and inactive coping behaviour prevails.

What are some of the implications of the proposed conceptualization of burnout to field research? First on my agenda is an exploration of the relationships among chronic physical fatigue, emotional exhaustion, and cognitive weariness. Each of these components has been studied in the past from a different disciplinary perspective. The study of physical fatigue has a long history in ergonomics (Gran Jean, 1981), while cognitive weariness has been studied by cognitive scientists with an interest in the effects of stress conditions (especially overload) on erroneous decision making (Fisher, 1984, pp. 130–44). Emotional exhaustion has thus far been studied almost exclusively by students of burnout. There is an urgent need to explore the nomological net of physical fatigue, emotional exhaustion, and cognitive weariness. Ezrahi's (1985) findings, in his study of burnout among high-ranking military officers in the Israeli defence force, suggest that for this group of respondents, physical fatigue and emotional exhaustion are closely intertwined, part and parcel of the very same construct, but not so cognitive weariness. This result could be sample specific, and possibly reflect the responsibilities of these senior decision makers and the far reaching consequences of admitting a chronic weariness of their cognitive resources. Cognitive weariness would appear to be centrally important in occupations such as air traffic controllers and police radio dispatchers, whose job duties require them to maintain continued vigilance (Kirmeyer, in press). An elucidation of the nature of the relationships among the physical, emotional, and cognitive components of burnout appears to be a necessary precondition to future enquiries involving the consequences of burnout and the role played by a variety of moderators, personal and situational, in the causal chain linking stress, burnout, and its sequels.

Having elucidated the connectedness among the three components of burnout, researchers may turn their attention to its consequences. Here, several possible linkages to work currently done in other disciplines suggest themselves. Of prime importance is a link with researchers in behavioural medicine, who have only recently reported (Appels, Mulder, and Hoopener, in press) that chronic physical fatigue, subjectively reported, was a potent predictor of myocardial infarctions, in several prospective studies of the aetiology of cardiovascular diseases. By way of explanation: one of the major problems of preventive cardiology stems from the fact that more than half of those who suffer a myocardial infarction (or die suddenly because of it) visited a doctor in the weeks prior to the coronary event, but their disease went undiagnosed because of the vague symptoms they described to their physicians (Salomon, 1969). In prospective investigations, syndromes of fatigue, vital exhaustion, and depression were found to be premonitory symptoms of later cardiac disease (Appels, 1986). As an example, in a serendipitous finding of the series of prospective studies called the Farmingham Study, the single questionnaire item: 'at the end of the day, I am exhausted both mentally and physically' had a high predictive power of subsequent myocardial infarction (Appels, 1986). Incidentally, this item is remarkably similar to items which appear in the emotional exhaustion scale of the MBI and in other burnout measures. Indeed, researchers in industrial medicine (e.g. Simonson, 1971) have long shown that chronic physical fatigue is a concomitant of physical ill-health and accident proneness.

Yet another major recommended avenue for future research on burnout emerges when one considers this phenomenon from the theoretical perspective of open systems approach (Miller, 1978; Matteson, 1987). The literature on burnout has dealt almost exclusively with individual employee burnout, overlooking the theoretical possibilities of defining burnout at other, alternative levels of analysis, like those of the group, organizational unit or total organization. This appears to be a natural extension, given open systems approach postulates of dynamic interplay and interconnectedness among elements of any given system. This recommended extension should be carried out with caution and reservedness, for the more inclusive the level of analysis, the higher the system's complexity (cf. Staw, Sandelands, and Dutton, 1981). While open systems approach has been used in theorizing on burnout (e.g. Carroll and White, 1982), heretofore it was applied only at the individual level of analysis.

An individual employee may be viewed as an element of an organization. At the individual level stress may be defined as occurring when demands addressed to him or her exceed his or her resources (Neale, Singer, and Schwartz, 1987). Because elements in the system are interrelated, a change in any one affects others. Thus a stress experienced by many employees may be defined as a system-wide stress, potentially leading to organizational-wide burnout. The application of an ecological perspective in the study of job stress and its consequences has been suggested elsewhere (Hobfoll, in press). However, the phenomenon of organizational burnout, signifying a chronic state of depleted resources, fatigue, and exhaustion in responding to environmental cues demanding reaction from the organization, has not been subjected to empirical study except in the context of organizational decline (Jick, 1985).

Hopefully, this review will encourage new, more theory based research concerning burnout. I have attempted to reconceptualize burnout in a new way that, to my assessment, better reflects current understanding of this phenomenon and recent findings of empirical research. Especially in this section, it has been my goal to cross disciplinary borders and make the concept of burnout meaningful to physicians, epidemiologists, sociologists, health educators, and business managers, to name a few. An effort was made to show that burnout has merits when viewed from a multidisciplinary (or new interdisciplinary) perspective.

REFERENCES

Alexander, L., Adams, R.D., and C.R. Martray (1983, April) Personal and professional stresses associated with the teacher burnout phenomenon. Paper presented at the annual meeting of the American Educational Research Association, Montreal, Quebec, Canada.

Anderson, M.B.G., and Iwanicki, E.F. (1984) Teacher motivation and its relationship to burnout. *Educational Administration Quarterly*, **20**, 109–132.

Appels, A. (1986) Tiredness before myocardial infarction. In J.H. Lacky and D.A. Stungeon (eds), *Proceedings of the Fifteenth European Conference on Psychomatic Research*. London: John Libbey & Co., pp. 184–189.

Appels, A., Mulder, P., and Hoopener, P. (in press) Vital exhaustion as a precursor of myocardial infarction and other serious diseases. *International Journal of Cardiology*.

Bartz, C., and Maloney, J.P. (1986) Burnout among intensive care nurses. *Research in Nursing & Health*, **3**, 147–153.

Baruch, G.K., Biener, L., and Barnell, R.C. (1987) Women and gender in research on work and family stress. *American Psychologist*, **42**, 130–136.

Belcastro, P.A., Gold, R.S., and Hays, L.C. (1983) Maslach Burnout Inventory factor structure for samples of teachers. *Psychological Reports*, **53**, 364–366.

Birch, N., Marchant, M.P., and Smith, N.N. (1986) Perceived role conflict, role ambiguity, and reference librarians burnout in public libraries. *Library and Information Sciences Review*, **8**, 53–65.

Blase, I.J. (1982) A social psychological grounded theory of teacher stress and burnout. *Educational Administration Quarterly*, **18**, 93–113.

Brookings, F.B., Bolton, B., Brown, C.E., and McEvoy, A. (1985) Self-reported job burnout among female human service professionals. *Journal of Occupational Behavior*, **6**, 143–150.

Burke, R.J. (1987) Issues and implications for health care delivery systems: A Canadian perspective. In J.C. Quick, R.S. Bhagat, J.E. Dalton, and J.D. Quick (eds), *Work Stress: Health Care Systems in the Workplace*. New York: Prager pp. 27–49.

Burke, R.J., and Deszca E. (1986) Correlates of psychological burnout phases among police officers. *Human Relations*, **39**, 487–502.

Cahoon, A.R., and Rowney, J.I.A. (1984) Managerial burnout: a comparison by sex and level of responsibility. *Journal of Health and Human Resources Administration*, **7**, 249–264.

Carroll, J.F.X., and White, W.L. (1982) Theory building: integrating individual and environmental factors within an ecological framework. In W.S. Paine (ed.), *Job Stress and Burnout*. Beverly Hills, CA: Sage, pp. 41–60.

Cedoline, A.J. (1982) *Job Burnout in Public Education*. New York: Teachers College Press, Columbia University.

Cherniss, C. (1980a) *Professional Burnout in Human Service Organizations*. New York: Prager.

Cherniss, C. (1980b) *Staff Burnout: Job stress in the human services*. Beverly Hills, CA: Sage.

Corcoran, K.J. (1985) Measuring burnout: A reliability and conversant validity study. *Journal of Social Behavior and Personality*, **1**, 107–112.

Cunningham, W.G. (1983) Teacher burnout-solutions for the 1980s. A review of the literature. *Urban Review*, **15**, 37–51.

Dignam, J.T., Barrera, M. Jr., and West, S.G. (1986) Occupational stress, social support and burnout among correlational offices. *American Journal of Community Psychology*, **14**, 177–193.

Dolan, N. (1987) The relationship between burnout and job satisfaction in nurses. *Journal of Advanced Nursing*, **12**, 3–12.

Edelwich, J., and Brodsky, A. (1980) *Burnout: Stages of disillusionment in the helping professions*. New York: Human Services Press.

Etzion, D. (1984) The moderating effect of social support on the relationship of stress and burnout. *Journal of Applied Psychology*, **69**, 615–622.

Etzion, D. (1987) Burnout: The hidden agenda of human distress. (Working paper No. 930/87). Tel Aviv: Tel Aviv University, Faculty of Management.
Etzion, D., and Pines, A. (1986) Sex and culture as factors explaining coping and burnout among human service professionals: A social psychological perspective. *Journal of Cross Cultural Psychology*, **17**, 191–209.
Ezrahi, Ch. (1987) What is burnout? The relationships among subjective burnout, objective burnout, and personality traits. Unpublished master's thesis, The Hebrew University School of Education, Jerusalem, Israel.
Ezrahi, Y. (1985) Burnout in military officers ranks: A construct validation. Unpublished Doctoral dissertation, Tel Aviv University, Tel Aviv, Israel.
Ezrahi, Y., and Shirom, A. (1986, July) Construct validation of burnout. A paper presented at the 21st Congress of the International Association of Applied Psychology, Jerusalem, Israel.
Farber, B.A. (1983). Introduction: A critical perspective on burnout. In B.A. Farber (ed.), *Stress and Burnout in the Human Service Professions*. New York: Pergamon, pp. 1–22.
Farber, B.A. (1984) Teacher burnout: assumptions, myths and issues. *Teachers College Record*, **86**, 321–338.
Firth, H., McIntee, J., and McKeown, P. (1985). Maslach Burnout Inventory factor structure and norms for British nursing staff. *Psychological Reports*, **57**, 147–150.
Fisher, S. (1984) *Stress and the Perception of Control*. London: Lawrence Earlbaum.
Frese, M. (1985) Stress at work and psychosomatic complaints: a causal interpretation. *Journal of Applied Psychology*, **70**, 314–328.
Freudenberger, H.J. (1974) Staff burnout. *Journal of Social Issues*, **30**, 159–164.
Freudenberger, H.J. (1980) *Burnout: The high costs of high achievement*. New York: Anchor Press.
Freudenberger, H.J. (1983) Burnout: Contemporary issues, trends, and concerns. In B.A. Farber (ed.), *Stress and Burnout*. New York: Pergamon, pp. 23–28.
Friesen, D. (1986, April) Overall stress and job satisfaction as predictors of burnout. Paper presented at the annual meeting of the American Educational Research Association, San Francisco, CA.
Garden, A.M. (1987) Depersonalization: A valid dimension of burnout? *Human Relations*, **40**, 545–560.
Glogow, E. (1986) Research note: Burnout and loss of control. *Public Personnel Management*, **15**, 79–83.
Gold, Y. (1984) Factorial validity of the Meslach Burnout Inventory in a sample of California elementary and junior high school classroom teachers. *Educational and Psychological Measurement*, **44**, 1009–1010.
Goldberger, L., and Breznitz, S. (eds) (1982) *Handbook of Stress*. New York: The Free Press.
Golembiewski, R.T., and Munzenrider, R. (1983) Testing three phases model of burnout: Mapping of worksite descriptors. *Journal of Health and Human Resources Administration*, **5**, 374–393.
Golembiewski, R.T., and Munzenrider R. (1984) Active and passive reactions to psychological burnout: toward greater specificity in a phase model. *Journal of Health and Human Resources Administration*, **7**, 264–268.
Golembiewski, R.T., Munzenrider, R., and Carter, D. (1983). Phases of progressive burnout and their work-site covariants. *Journal of Applied Behavioral Science*, **13**, 461–482.
Golembiewski, R.T., Munzenrider, R., and Stevenson, J. (1985) *Stress in Organizations*. New York: Prager.

Gran Jean, E. (1981) *Fitting the Task to the Man: an ergonomic approach*. London: Taylor & Prancis.

Hobfoll, S.E. (in press) *The Ecology of Stress*. Washington, DC: Hemisphere Publishing Co.

Iwanicki, E.F., and Schwab, R.L. (1981) A cross validation study of the Maslach Burnout Inventory. *Educational and Psychological Measurement*, 41, 1167–1174.

Izraeli, D. (1988) Burning out in medicine: A comparison of husbands and wives in dual-career couples. Unpublished manuscript, Bar-Ilan University, Dept. of Sociology, Ramat-Gan, Israel.

Jackson, S.E., Schwab, R.L., and Schuler, R.S. (1986) Toward an understanding of the burnout phenomenon. *Journal of Applied Psychology*, 71, 630–640.

Jackson, S.E., Turner, J.A., and Brief, A.P. (1987) Correlates of burnout among public service lawyers. *Journal of Occupational Behavior*, 8, 339–349.

Jick, T.D. (1985) As the axe falls: Budget cuts and the experience of stress in organizations. In T.A. Beeher and R.S. Bhagat (eds), *Human Stress and Cognition in Organizations: An integrated perspective*. New York: Wiley, pp. 83–117.

Jick, T.D., and Mitz L. (1985) Sex differences in work stress. *Academy of Management Review*, 10, 408–420.

Jones, J.W. (1981) Diagnosing and treating staff burnout among health professionals. In J.W. Jones (ed.), *The Burnout syndrome: Current research, theory, interventions*. Park Ridge, IL: London House Press, pp. 107–126.

Jones, J.W. (ed.) (1985) *Burnout in Policing*. IL: London House Press.

Justice, B., Gold, R.S., and Klein, J.P. (1981). Life events and burnout. *Journal of Psychology*, 108, 219–226.

Kafry, D., and Pines, A. (1980) Life and work tedium. *Human Relation*, 33, 477–503.

Keinan, G., and Melamed, S. (1987) Personality characteristics and proneness to burnout: A study among internists. *Stress Medicine*, 3, 307–315.

Kirmeyer, S.L. (in press) Coping with competing demands: Interruption and the Type A pattern. *Journal of Applied Psychology*.

Kobasa, S.C., and Puccetti, M.C. (1983) Personality and social resources in stress resistance. *Journal of Personality and Social Psychology*, 48, 839–850.

Kyriacou, C. (1987) Teacher stress and burnout: an international review *Educational Research*, 22, 146–152.

Lazaro, L., Shinn, M., and Robinson, P.E. (1985) Burnout, performance, and job withdrawal behavior. *Journal of Health and Human Resources Administration*, 7, 213–234.

Lazarus, R.S. (1984) Puzzles in the study of daily hassles. *Journal of Behavioral Medicine*, 7, 375–389.

Lazarus, R.S., and Folkman, S. (1984) *Stress, Appraisal, and Coping*. New York: Springer.

Leiter, M.E., and Meachem, K.A. (1986) Role structure and burnout in the field of human services. *Journal of Applied Behavioral Science*, 22, 47–52.

Lemkau, J.P., Rafferty, J.P., Purdy, R.R., and Rudisill, J.R. (1987) Sex role stress and burnout among family practice physicians. *Journal of Vocational Behavior*, 31, 81–90.

Maslach, C. (1982a) Understanding burnout: definitional issues in analyzing a complex phenomenon. In U.S. Paine (ed.), *Job Stress and Burnout*. Beverly Hills, CA: Sage, pp. 29–41.

Maslach, C. (1982b) *Burnout: the cost of caring*. Englewood Cliffs, NJ: Prentice Hall.

Maslach, C., and Jackson, S. (1981) The measurement of experienced burnout. *Journal of Occupational Behavior*, 2, 99–115.

Maslach, C., and Jackson, S.E. (1984) Burnout in organizational settings. In S. Oskamp (ed.), *Applied Social Psychology Annual*, Vol. 5. Beverly Hills, CA: Sage, pp. 133–153.

Matteson, M.T. (1987) Individual organizational relationships: implications for preventing job stress and burnout. In J.C. Quick, R.S. Bhagat, J.E. Dalton, and D. Quick (eds), *Work Stress: Health care systems in the workplace*. New York: Praeger, pp. 156–171.

McCarthy, P. (1985) Burnout in psychiatric nursing. *Journal of Advanced Nursing*, **10**, 305–310.

McCranie, E.W., Lambert, V.A., and Lambert, C.E. Jr. (1987) Work stress, tardiness, and burnout among hospital staff nurses. *Nursing Research*, **36**, 374–378.

McGinness, J. (1987) Free radicals and the developmental pathology of schizophrenic burnout. *Integrative Psychiatry*, **5**, 288–301.

Meier, S.T. (1983) Toward a theory of burnout. *Human Relations*, **36**, 899–910.

Meier, S.T. (1984) The construct validity of burnout. *Journal of Occupational Psychology*, **57**, 211–219.

Meier, S.T., and Schmeck, R.R. (1985) The burned-out college student: A descriptive profile. *Journal of College Students Personnel*, **26**, 63–69.

Miller, J.G. (1978) *Living Systems*. New York: McGraw-Hill.

Nagi, S. (1985) Burnout and selected variables as components of occupational stress. *Psychological Reports*, **56**, 195–200.

Nagi, S., and Davis, L.G. (1985) Burnout: A comparative analysis of personality and environmental variables. *Psychological Reports*, **57**, 1319–1328.

Neale, M.S., Singer, J.A., and Schwartz, G.E. (1987) A systems assessment of occupational stress: Evaluating a hotel during contract negotiations. In A.W. Riley and S.J. Zaccaro (eds), *Occupational Stress and Organizational Effectiveness*. New York: Prager, pp. 167–203.

Paine, W.S. (1982) Overview: Burnout stress syndromes and the 1980s. In W.S. Paine (ed), *Job Stress and Burnout: Research, theory and intervention perspectives* (pp. 11–29). Beverly Hills, CA: Sage.

Perlman, B., and Hartman, E.A. (1982) Burnout: Summary and future research. *Human Relations*, **35**, 283–305.

Pines, A. (1987) Marriage burnout: a new conceptual framework for working with couples. *Psychotherapy in Private Practice*, **5**, 31–43.

Pines, A. (1988). *Keeping the Spark Alive: Preventing burnout in love and marriage*. New York: St Martin's Press.

Pines, A., and Aronson, E. (1988) *Career Burnout: causes and cures*, 2nd ed. New York: The Free Press.

Pines, A., Aronson, E., and Kafry, D. (1981) *Burnout: from tedium to personal growth*. New York: The Free Press.

Pines, A., and Kafry D. (1981) Tedium in the life and work of professional women as compared with men. *Sex Roles*, **7**, 117–134.

Powers, S., and Gose, K.F. (1986) Reliability and construct validity of the Maslach Burnout Inventory in a sample of university students. *Educational and Psychological Measurement*, **46**, 251–5.

Rafferty, J.P., Lemkau, J.P., Purdy, R.R., and Rudisill, J.R. (1986) Validity of the Maslach Burnout Inventory for family practice physicians. *Journal of Clinical Psychology*, **42**, 488–492.

Rich, V.L., and Rich, A.R. (1987) Personality hardiness and burnout in female staff nursing. *Image: Journal of Nursing Scholarship*, **10**, 63–66.

Roberts, C.A. (1986) Burnout: Psychobabble, or a valuable concept? *British Journal of Hospital Medicine*, **36**, 194–197.

Rosenthal, D., Teague, M., Retish, P., West J., and Vessell, R. (1983) The relationship between work environment attributes and burnout. *Journal of Leisure Research*, **15**, 125–135.

Russell, J.A. (1980) A circumplex model of affect. *Journal of Personality and Social Psychology*, **39**, 1161–1178.

Russell, J.A. (1983) Pancultural aspects of the human conceptual organization of emotions. *Journal of Personality and Social Psychology*, **45**, 1281–1288.

Salomon, H. (1969) Prodrama in acute myocardial infarction. *Circulation*, **46**, 463–471.

Shamir, B. (1986, July) Some arguments against the use of burnout as a broadly applied development variable. Paper presented at the 21st Congress of the International Association of Applied Psychology, Jerusalem, Israel.

Shamir, B., and Drory, A. (1982) Occupational tedium among prison officers. *Criminal Justice and Behavior*, **9**, 79–99.

Shinn, M. (1982) Methodological issues: Evaluating and using information. In W.S. Paine (ed.), *Job Stress and Burnout* London: Sage, pp. 61–82.

Shinn, M., Rosario, M., March, H., and Chestnut, D.E. (1984) Coping with job stress and burnout in the human services. *Journal of Personality and Social Psychology*, **46**, 864–876.

Shirom, A. (1986, July) Does stress lead to affective strain, or vice versa? A structural regression test. Paper presented at the 21st Congress of the International Association of Applied Psychology, Jerusalem, Israel.

Shirom, A., and Mazeh, T. (in press) Periodicity in seniority — job satisfaction relationship. *Journal of Vocational Behavior*.

Simonson, E. (1971) *Physiology of Work Capacity and Fatigue*. Springfield, IL: Charles C. Thomas.

Smith, R.E. (1986) Toward cognitive–affective models of athletic burnout. *Journal of Sport Psychology*, **8**, 36–50.

Solano, C.H. (1987) Stereotypes of social isolation and early burnout in the gifted: do they still exist? *Journal of Youth and Adolescence*, **16**, 527–541.

Spector, P. (1987) Method variance as an artifact in self-regard and perceptions at work: Myth or significant problem? *Journal of Applied Psychology*, **72**, 438–443.

Staw, B.M., Sandelands, L.E., and Dutton, J.E. (1981) Threat–rigidity effects in organizational behavior: A multilevel analysis. *Administrative Science Quarterly*, **28**, 501–524.

Stout, J.K., and Williams, J.M. (1983) Comparison of two measures of burnout. *Psychological Reports*, **53**, 283–289.

Ursprung, A.W. (1986a) Burnout in the human services: a review of the literature. *Rehabilitation Counseling Bulletin*, **29**, 190–199.

Ursprung, A.W. (1986b) Incidence and correlates of burnout in residential service settings. *Rehabilitation Counseling Bulletin*, **25**, 225–239.

Wade, D.C., Cooley, E., and Savicki, V. (1986) A longitudinal study of burnout. *Children and Youth Services Review*, **8**, 161–173.

Whitehead, J.T., and Lindquist, C.A. (1986) Correctional officer job burnout: a path model. *Journal of Research in Crime and Delinquency*, **23**, 23–42.

Whiteman, J. L., Young, J.C., ad Fisher, M.L. (1985) Teacher burnout and the perception of student behavior. *Education*, **105**, 299–305.

Wolpin, J. (1988) *Psychological burnout among Canadian teachers: A longitudinal study*. Unpublished Ph.D. dissertation, York University, Toronto, Canada.

Chapter 3
COGNITIVE PROCESSES IN INDUSTRIAL AND ORGANIZATIONAL PSYCHOLOGY

Robert G. Lord
and
Karen J. Maher
Department of Psychology
University of Akron
USA

During the last decade there has been a large increase in the extent to which I/O psychologists have utilized cognitive or information processing approaches to guide research and practice. As an illustration of this trend, we found 18 journal articles in 1977 that adopted a cognitive perspective, 27 in 1982, and 56 articles in 1986. These sources varied widely in terms of topic and the conditions under which information processing was studied. For example, cognitive perspectives have been applied to areas such as human factors, performance appraisal, learning, leadership, and motivation. In addition to normal work or laboratory situations, conditions under which cognitive processes have been studied include fatigue or stress, night shifts, sleep deprivation, sky diving, cold water immersion, extremes of heat and altitude, vibrations, emergency airline situations, underwater performance, and space travel.

This eclectic view of the cognitive I/O literature was derived from a computer search of the international psychological and business literature (PSYCINFO and ABI/INFORM databases). This search identified cognitive processing research of the past decade (1976 to 1986), yielding 428 citations. We supplemented the computer search by examining the major I/O journals (*Academy of Management Journal, Academy of Management Review, Administrative Science Quarterly, Journal of Applied Psychology*, and *Organizational Behavior and Human Decision Processes*) for additional and current citations. Because this combined procedure yielded over 500 citations, this review is necessarily selective. In the following sections we will review literature pertaining primarily to social perceptions and interpersonal ratings, social processes, problem solving, and decision making. We exclude all literature dealing with man–machine interfaces, human factors, communication networks, motivation, and macro topics such as group behavior or organizational design. We also exclude the literature on individual differences in cognitive processing, but much of this is covered in the chapter on cognitive style and complexity by Streufert (1989) (Chapter 4 in this volume).

Our purpose in reviewing the cognitive processing work in these areas is to go beyond accurate summaries of existing literature. We hope to identify trends as well as neglected topics, and provide helpful suggestions for future research. We will also comment on the methodologies typically used by I/O psychologists to study cognitive processing.

Before reviewing the literature, it is necessary to explain our conceptualization of cognitive process research. We include research that attempts to explain how people acquire, store, retrieve, or use information during typical work-related activities. We exclude 'cognitive research' that merely posits mental antecedents to work activities without linking such antecedents to information processes. For example, we will exclude the goal-setting research because it merely identifies goals as determinants of behavior, ignoring for the most part how goals affect information processing.

PERFORMANCE APPRAISAL

Theorists have attempted to apply cognitive processing principles to the area of performance appraisal more than any other substantive area in I/O psychology. Several conceptual articles published in the early 1980s acknowledged the need to consider the cognitive processes involved in rating behavior. Landy and Farr (1980), in their widely cited review of performance ratings, noted that cognitive processes of the rater are integral to the rating process. Landy and Farr viewed the performance appraisal context as a specific instance of person perception, where implicit personality theories were thought to play a large role. Cooper (1981a), in a review of halo research, noted that the literature has underestimated the role of raters' cognitive distortions as a source of illusory covariance. In one of the most clearly explicated cognitive models of the rating process, Feldman (1981) acknowledged the central role of categorization processes in performance ratings. Feldman suggested that the rating process is characterized by a dual process system. Automatic processes may operate where ratees are categorized without conscious monitoring. This automatic process may be superseded, however, by controlled processes characterized by causal attributions. Both types of processing result in the assignment of a target person to a category based on a prototype matching process. Categorization affects the information that is attended to, stored, or recalled from memory. This basic categorization model of rater processes was expanded and presented as a function of the organizational context and the self-presentation behavior of the ratee by Ilgen and Feldman (1983). DeNisi, Cafferty, and Meglino (1984) similarly outlined a cognitive model of the performance rating process based on the social cognition literature and presented a series of testable propositions. In this model, the rater is viewed as an active seeker of information, who is partially influenced by preconceived notions about the ratee and appraisal purpose.

These models will not be reviewed in detail here. We will note, however, that all models assume the rating process is characterized by cognitive distortion affecting all stages of the information processing sequence: attention and encoding, storage, retrieval, and judgement. Moreover, the models have assigned particular importance to certain contextual factors. The relevance of these contextual factors will be reviewed in a later section. Below, we will review the empirical work conducted on the cognitive processes involved in several areas related to performance appraisal: illusory correlation, categorization and rater bias, temporal factors, and purpose.

Sources of Illusory Correlation

Illusory correlation, or halo, is present when observed halo exceeds true halo among dimensions (Cooper, 1981a). Halo error has been one of the most widely researched topics in the application of information processing research to performance appraisal. Several studies have investigated likely sources of illusory halo error. A rater's implicit notion of covariation, or conceptual similarity schema, is thought to be one source of illusory correlation. Raters' encoding, storage, and retrieval of information is biased in the direction of their conceptual similarity schema (implicit theories of dimensional covariance), resulting in illusory correlation, or halo.

Three studies have investigated the conceptual similarity schemata of job dimensions. Cooper (1981b) had subjects rate the perceived similarity of job dimensions for three jobs. The ratings were then compared to dimension intercorrelation data from prior studies. Mean conceptual similarity ratings correlated significantly with job performance ratings, illustrating that raters could approximate the relationships among the job dimensions. However, in a second analysis, Cooper compared data from a fourth study to normative conceptual similarity data. This comparison showed that conceptual similarity ratings were inferior to actual behavior in predicting rated behaviors. Though these results are equivocal, Cooper concluded that conceptual similarity of job dimensions is a likely source of illusory correlation.

Using real-world baseball players as ratees, Kozlowski, Kirsch, and Chao (1986) examined the effects of job knowledge and ratee familiarity on raters' conceptual similarity schemata. Results indicated that those raters with high job (baseball) knowledge were sensitive to actual job dimension covariation when familiar with ratees, but tended to rely on conceptual similarity schemata when unfamiliar with ratees. Those raters low in job knowledge relied on conceptual similarity schemata to form ratings regardless of the degree of ratee familiarity. Halo was greatest for raters with low job knowledge and decreased with increasing job and ratee familiarity. Kozlowski and Kirsch (1987) obtained a similar pattern of results with an individual-level analysis. When familiar ratees were evaluated, raters with more job knowledge relied less on conceptual similarity schemata, and exhibited less halo and greater accuracy than raters with low job knowledge. However, for raters unfamiliar with ratees, those with high job knowledge exhibited more halo, a decrease in accuracy, and relied more on conceptual similarity schemata. Those low in job knowledge showed less reliance on conceptual similarity schemata in forming ratings. Interestingly, Jacobs and Kozlowski (1985) found that halo increased with greater ratee familiarity. These results are somewhat inconsistent with the findings of Kozlowski and Kirsch (1987), who found that halo was greater for unfamiliar ratees. Taken together, these results suggest that raters have schemata regarding job dimension covariation which may lead to illusory halo in performance ratings. However, this relationship appears to be affected by the extent of ratee and/or job familiarity in an inconsistent manner. These contradictory findings may be due to different operationalizations of familiarity between studies.

Shared distinctiveness between salient group characteristics and performance has also been thought to be a source of illusory correlation. London and Poplawski (1976) presented subjects with information on two groups of hypothetical workers which varied in the amount and favorability of information. The hypothesis that the co-occurrence of distinctive events (low amount of total information and low number of unfavorable or favorable statements) would lead to the development of differential stereotypes for each group was not confirmed. Similarly, Feldman, Camburn, and Gatti (1986) suggested that shared distinctiveness between group membership and group behaviors would lead to development of a prototype of the distinctive group. Hypotheses were not supported, and it was concluded that the development of illusory correlation based only on shared distinctiveness is unlikely to occur. However, both of these studies were conducted under highly artificial laboratory conditions. As Feldman et al. (1986) noted, it is likely that these effects depend on prior categorization and cannot be produced in the laboratory in the absence of prior information.

Jacobs and Kozlowski (1985) note that proponents of the conceptual similarity explanation for halo implicitly assume that ratings on conceptually similar dimensions elicit consistency in evaluation, resulting in halo error. However, an alternative view holds that an overall evaluation of the ratee invokes consistency in the dimension ratings. Categorization models of rater bias exemplify this latter perspective.

Categorization as a Source of Rater Bias

Nathan and Lord (1983) compared two models of cognitive processing thought to underlie halo in performance rating. The traditional model, outlined by Borman (1978), holds that raters can store information in independent dimensional schemata and retrieve the information in this form. An alternative model is based on cognitive categorization and holds that information is stored as part of a prototype-based category. Dimension ratings result from the recall of a prototype of the category in which the ratee has been classified. In the Nathan and Lord study, subjects observed one of two videotapes of a lecturer, exhibiting either good or poor performance. Subjects rated the performance of the target person and completed a behavioral questionnaire. Results indicated that raters were generally able to distinguish among performance dimensions, consistent with the traditional model. However, for some dimensions true behavioral differences were suppressed by a general impression, consistent with a categorization model. It was concluded that neither model alone is sufficient to describe the rating process. Raters are able to use information that has been integrated into distinct dimensions, but ratings are also influenced by one's global impression of the ratee.

Nathan and Alexander (1985) discussed the importance of categorization processes and the covariation among behaviors in their inferential accuracy model. They suggested that accuracy is a function of the category and the prototype to which persons are compared. Contrary to the prevailing view, categorization processes can lead to *increased rating accuracy*. They maintain that accuracy is a function of observed performance, the rater's sensitivity to the covariation among target behaviors, and the rater's threshold for making inferences of the presence or absence of traits or behaviors. This threshold can differ with time, raters' predispositions, and levels of a ratee's performance. Thus, rating accuracy can vary regardless of the opportunity to observe relevant behavior, depending on the threshold for inference.

Two empirical studies provided support for Nathan and Alexander's (1985) proposition that categorization can *increase* accuracy. Mount and Thompson (1987), in a field survey, had subordinates assess the degree to which managers' behavior was congruent with how the subordinate thought the managers should behave. They found that ratings of managers were more accurate, had more halo, and were more lenient to the extent they were perceived as congruent with a desired categorization schema. Murphy and Balzer (1986) investigated the relationship between halo and accuracy. Subjects viewed four videotapes of target individuals and completed both behavioral questionnaires and performance evaluations. Subjects rated two tapes immediately after viewing them and rated the remaining tapes the following day. Results indicated that interdimension correlations were higher in the delayed rating condition (greater halo). However, ratings obtained in the delayed condition were more accurate than in the immediate rating condition. It was concluded that raters depend on their general impressions of ratees to form ratings. Moreover, distortion in the correlational structure of ratings does not necessarily lead to decreased accuracy.

Murphy and associates investigated other determinants of accuracy. The relationship between the accuracy of *observation* and the accuracy of *rating* was investigated by Murphy et al. (1982). Subjects viewed videotaped lectures and were asked to evaluate performance and behavioral frequency. Correlations between the corresponding elevation, differential elevation, and differential accuracy scores (Cronbach, 1955) on each rating task (performance evaluation and behavioral frequency ratings) were significant. Most models treat observation and rating as distinct stages of the rating process. Results of this study generally indicated that accuracy in observation is related to accuracy in evaluation.

Cognitive biases are likely to operate regardless of the rating format. Murphy, Martin, and Garcia (1982) found that behavioral observation scales measure general impressions rather than specific behaviors. Similarly, Murphy and Constans (1987) found that the use of behavioral anchors in BARS rating formats may bias ratings. When BARS contained anchors that were actually observed, but not representative of overall performance, ratings were biased in the direction of the unrepresentative anchors. Balzer (1986) predicted that initial impressions would have a biasing effect on the recording of incidents in behavioral diaries. Results indicated that raters were more likely to record information that was incongruent with initial impressions than incidents congruent with initial impressions. Implications of this finding are that behavioral diaries, while designed to minimize bias in performance ratings, are themselves subject to cognitive distortion. Nathan and Alexander (1985) argued that both BARS and BOS yield ratings based on cognitive structures rather than observable behaviors. These studies suggest that cognitive biases operate regardless of the rating format used. From this perspective, user acceptance and practicality may be more important issues when deciding on a format (Napier and Latham, 1986).

Temporal Factors and Performance Ratings

Several studies have investigated the effects of previous decisions or prior observations of performance on ratings. These studies are important, because they address the dynamic nature characteristic of ongoing performance appraisals in organizations. Bazerman, Beekun, and Schoorman (1982), following the escalation of commitment literature, hypothesized that raters would be more likely to rate poor performing employees higher when the rater had previously promoted the ratee, than when another rater made the promotion decision. Results indicated that those who had previously given the promotion to a subordinate gave more favorable evaluations to the subordinate than those who did not promote the individual. Murphy, Balzer, Lockhart, and Eisenman (1985) investigated the effects of *previous* performance on evaluations. Subjects either rated two tapes depicting good lecture performance, followed by average performance, or two tapes depicting poor lecture performance, followed by the same average tape. A contrast effect was found, such that the average tape in the poor performance condition was rated higher than the same average tape in the good performance condition. To determine whether memory or encoding biases were operating to produce the contrast effect, a second study investigated the effects of a memory delay on ratings of the average tape. After a one-day delay, there were no differences in ratings of the average tape between the two conditions. It was concluded that memory biases cannot explain the contrast effect found in the first study. In a related study, the effects of *subsequent* performance on ratings were investigated by Murphy, Gannett, Herr, and Chen (1986). In this study a tape showing average performance was viewed, followed by either two tapes depicting poor performance or two tapes depicting good performance of the stimulus lecturer. Any effects on rating the average tape would have to be due to biases in memory. Subjects either rated behavior and performance on the three tapes immediately after viewing them, or one day later. For the behavior ratings only, there was a larger difference between the two conditions for the delayed ratings, with the average tape in the poor condition rated lower than the average tape in the good condition, demonstrating an assimilation effect. Behavioral ratings were more strongly influenced by memory biases than were performance judgements. It was concluded that memory biases are the cause of this effect. In considering the results of both of these studies, Murphy et al. (1986) concluded that conditions that minimize memory biases and maximize encoding biases may produce contrast effects. Conditions that place increased demands on memory may produce assimilation effects.

These studies are valuable because they acknowledge that previous decisions about a ratee's performance and observations of differing levels of performance may affect ratings. However, in the studies conducted by Murphy (Murphy et al., 1985, 1986), subjects rated each tape separately. It might be more interesting to assess the effects of changes in performance over time on global ratings of performance across all tapes, as these are most similar to ratings found in organizations.

Purpose of Rating

Williams, DeNisi, Blencoe, and Cafferty (1985) examined the effects of rating purpose on raters' cognitive processes, using an attribution theory framework. Subjects rated written vignettes which contained performance, consensus, consistency, and distinctiveness information for eight target employees. Two general types of performance appraisal outcomes were manipulated: deservedness (how deserving each target was for promotion, training referral, or raise) or designation (selecting one employee for promotion or training, or determining how large a raise each employee should receive). Subjects in the deservedness condition gave higher ratings overall than subjects in the designation outcome condition. A second study by Williams et al., (1985) addressed the types of information raters seek for different purposes. Overall, distinctiveness information was sought most by raters. Designation outcomes resulted in greater requests for consensus information, while deservedness outcomes resulted in greater requests for distinctiveness information. These results indicated that raters process information differently depending on the type of appraisal outcome. Williams, DeNisi, Meglino, and Cafferty (1986) showed videotapes of carpenters performing work tasks, either grouped by workers or grouped by tasks. Deservedness or designation decisions were made for the target ratees. Two days later subjects were asked to rate from memory the performance of each worker. Results indicated that the way in which information was presented (grouped by task or worker) did not affect decisions made immediately after viewing the tape. However, higher ratings were given by those making designation decisions on the delayed ratings.

Murphy, Philbin, and Adams (in press) similarly examined the effects of purpose on rating. Raters who observed videotaped behavior for the purpose of rating the performance of the lecturer were more accurate than those who observed the videotapes to learn the content of the lecture. However, these differences decreased with a greater delay between observation and rating. Interestingly, subjects in the performance appraisal condition more accurately recognized behaviors when the memory delay was short, but were less accurate the longer the delay. These differences over time were not apparent for those who viewed the tapes to learn lecture content. The results of these studies make it clear that the purpose of the appraisal can affect how information is sought and processed by raters.

Comments

Several comments can be made about the performance appraisal literature as a whole. First, despite several compelling theoretical arguments for the importance of investigating rater cognitive processes (e.g. Feldman, 1981; Landy and Farr, 1980), relatively little systematic empirical work has been conducted to test these theories. Many of the studies of rater cognitive processing have been characterized by *post-hoc* information processing explanations — few studies have been designed explicitly to assess the *process* of performance rating. Feldman (1981) outlined several guidelines for research in the area, but the field has not followed many of these suggestions. Many studies have concluded that performance ratings are influenced by cognitive categories and a prototype matching process (e.g. Mount and Thompson, 1987), following Feldman's (1981) theory, yet no research has explicitly investigated the structure of these categories, or the characteristics of prototypical members of the categories. We find it surprising that researchers in the performance appraisal arena have ignored these issues, particularly since systematic research has been conducted in the area of leadership perception along these lines (Lord, Foti, and DeVader, 1984; Lord, Foti, and Phillips, 1982).

A second comment involves the role of organizational context and purpose in performance appraisal. All of the models cited in the introduction of this section acknowledged the importance of both cognitive processes and contextual factors in the study of performance appraisal. Feldman (1981) addressed the importance of dispositional, situational, and time-related factors in categorization processes. Landy and Farr (1980) found it 'appalling' that research has not addressed the effect of positional and organizational characteristics, including rating purpose, on rating behavior. Rating purpose is also integral to the model proposed by DeNisi, Cafferty, and Meglino (1984). Ilgen and Feldman (1983) recognize the relevance of studying ratee characteristics in person perception. We agree with Landy and Farr and find it equally alarming that few studies have addressed these contextual factors in conjunction with cognitive factors in performance appraisal. Some recent work (Murphy et al., in press; Williams et al., 1985, 1986) is an important step in addressing contextual issues involved in the rating process. We think research should continue along these lines. A preliminary line of research would be the investigation of how these various contextual variables impact on the development of raters' categories and prototypes.

Third, Banks and Murphy (1985) cautioned that an increasing focus on cognitive processing research may widen further the gap between research and practice. These authors point out that cognitive processing research may not tell us much about actual rating behavior. Raters may be influenced by biases at various stages of the processing sequence, yet make inaccurate or irrelevant ratings due to motivational or organizational constraints. We agree with this line of thinking. Performance ratings may be characterized more by a manager's or organization's needs than by any attempt on the part of the rater to incorporate performance information accurately. The appraisal process may be highly influenced by political variables where accuracy is not a relevant concern (Longenecker, Gioia, and Sims, 1987). Researchers must also consider future interaction and interdependence between rater and ratee (Ilgen and Favero, 1985). These factors are likely to influence the types of rating that are given, yet are not reflective of actual performance. Given these various organizational constraints, Banks and Murphy (1985) suggest that the rater's willingness to provide accurate ratings may lie outside the domain of cognitive processing research.

Though we agree that the cognitive processes involved in forming rating-relevant judgements are distinct from actual rating behavior, we believe there is still a place for cognitive processing research in the performance appraisal realm. We assume that raters make conscious decisions regarding promotions, raises, etc., that are *then* reflected in performance ratings. In other words, performance evaluations are likely to be characterized by on-line versus memory-based processing (Hastie and Park, 1986). When information is processed on-line, evaluations are made automatically at the time information is encoded. Under this assumption, the process underlying initial impression formation and categorization in person perception may become all the more important. The study of expectancy confirmation behavior may be an appropriate focus (Darley and Fazio, 1980; Feldman, 1986). Raters' first impressions likely determine how subsequent rating-relevant information is processed. Affective reactions towards ratees, for example, may influence rating behavior irrespective of objective performance (Cardy and Dobbins, 1986; Tsui and Barry, 1986).

A common finding of the studies reviewed in this section is that raters tend to rely on their general impressions of ratees and infer behavior from these impressions. It then becomes very important to identify those behaviors that are considered to be characteristic of effective performance. These categories likely vary from organization to organization, or from department to department. Borman (1987) found that managers very knowledgeable about a particular job can articulate categories of subordinate effectiveness. Recent work on rater training has shown that giving raters a common frame of reference for what is considered effective performance can lead to increased rating accuracy (Athey and McIntyre, 1987; Bernardin and Buckley, 1981; Bernardin and Pence, 1980; McIntyre, Smith, and Hassett, 1984; Pulakos, 1984). We believe this line of research should receive continued attention. Identifying organization-specific categories of effectiveness, and teaching raters what these categories are, should increase levels of relevant rater accuracy.

LEADERSHIP PERCEPTION

The study of leadership perceptions is one of the more fully explicated cognitive approaches to social perceptions in I/O psychology. Early work focused on implicit leadership theories, which arose out of work on group performance ratings and attribution theory. More recently, categorization theory has provided a more general model of leadership perception.

Implicit Theories of Leadership

In a pivotal study, Staw (1975) found that general knowledge of group task performance served as a cue by which group members attributed characteristics to their work groups. Group members were given bogus performance feedback indicating that their work group either performed well or poorly, though actual task performance of the two groups was equivalent. Members in the high performance condition rated their groups as being more cohesive and motivated, and having greater communication and influence than subjects who rated low performing groups. This study illustrated that knowledge of performance had a significant effect on perceptions of group characteristics. Staw suggested that this *performance cue effect* (PCE) stemmed from individuals having distinct stereotypes, or implicit theories, of effective and ineffective group performance. In a follow-up study (Staw, 1975), subjects who were not actually members of a group rated characteristics of hypothetical groups which subjects imagined had performed well or poorly. Results were consistent with the first study. Assuming only a general performance level, the high performing group was rated higher in cohesiveness, influence, communication, and motivation than the low performing group.

Three other studies investigated PCEs and ratings of group characteristics. DeNisi and Pritchard (1978) suggested that reliance on implicit theories to form ratings of group characteristics would decrease as more information about the group was provided. To test this hypothesis, subjects worked together in groups for two meetings prior to the experimental manipulation. As expected, these authors found that with increased familiarity of group characteristics, PCEs were minimized. However, Downey, Chacko, and McElroy (1979), in a direct replication of the Staw (1975) study, and Binning and Lord (1980) also investigated the effects of the degree of group familiarity on the strength of the performance cue manipulation. Results of these studies indicated that performance information affected group characteristics ratings when groups were somewhat familiar (Binning and Lord, 1980) or highly familiar, with a twelve-week work history (Downey et al., 1979). In short, three studies found spport for the PCE in members' perceptions of their task group. DeNisi and Pritchard (1978) found conflicting results, but their study suffered methodological difficulties as discussed by Binning and Lord (1980). McElroy and Downey (1982) also demonstrated PCEs for group members with varying levels of task and group involvement. Levels of involvement had no impact on the strength of the PCE.

Taken as a whole, this research indicates that PCEs appear consistently in ratings of group characteristics under varying degrees of group familiarity. We find it somewhat disconcerting, however, that this line of research investigating PCEs on *group* perceptions has received little recent attention. In light of the interest in quality circles and other group processes, we believe this avenue of research should be renewed. However, the value of this line of research lies partially in its application to leadership perception, which we will now address.

Mitchell, Larson, and Green (1977) directly extended Staw's (1975) research to leadership perceptions. They suggested that much of the leadership research was also confounded by an attributional process whereby group members use the group's performance as a cue to describe the group *leader's* behavior. A series of three studies was conducted in which subjects were presented with a stimulus of a group problem-solving meeting. The stimuli were a tape recording, a video recording, and actual participation in the group, in the three studies, respectively. The results of the first two studies were consistent with predictions. Subjects who were told the group performed well attributed more initiating structure and consideration behaviors (as measured by the Leader Behavior Description Questionnaire — LBDQ) to the leader than those told the group performed poorly on the task. In the last study, results though not significant, were in the expected direction.

Most of the research summarized to this point has explained PCEs within an attribution theory framework, where subjects attribute causality to group and/or leader characteristics based on performance information. However, attribution theory offers an incomplete model for explaining the underlying *cognitive* mechanisms of performance cue effects. Subsequent research on PCEs focused on *implicit leadership theories* as an explanatory mechanism and provided a more cognitive orientation to this phenomenon. Implicit leadership theories refer to knowledge structures, common across individuals, that reflect patterns of behaviors and traits thought to be characteristic of effective and ineffective leaders.

Two studies examined the effects of implicit leadership theories on leadership questionnaire ratings. Eden and Leviatan (1975) had subjects complete a questionnaire measure of leadership and were given general information about a fictitious organization with no information about leaders in the organization. The factor structure of the questionnaire scales was highly similar to the factor structure obtained under normal conditions (i.e. rating one's own supervisor), even with no information on supervisory behavior. Rush, Thomas, and Lord (1977) found similar results with the LBDQ. Subjects were provided only with a brief written vignette describing a leader and the general performance level of his or her department. Rush *et al.* (1977) also replicated these findings with three groups of subjects who had increasing levels of familiarity with a leader's behavior. Results indicated that the factor structures of LBDQ responses obtained under varying levels of leader familiarity were congruent with the factor structure in the limited information condition. Furthermore, results of the performance cue manipulation showed that performance information affected mean leadership behavior ratings. Subjects told the leader's department performed well assigned higher ratings on leadership dimensions than those told the leader's department performed poorly.

It is apparent from these studies that the factor structure of leadership questionnaires can be replicated in situations where minimal behavioral and performance information is given. These findings are taken as evidence that raters possess implicit leadership theories and infer leader characteristics based on these knowledge structures. These results also call into question the use of questionnaires such as the LBDQ. Ratings on such instruments may reflect not only actual behavior but also raters' implicit theories of leadership (Rush et al., 1977).

Lord, Binning, Rush, and Thomas (1978) manipulated actual leader *behavior* in a stimulus videotape by coaching the designated leader to exhibit few or many structuring behaviors. Consistent with other studies, the questionnaire ratings in the high performance condition were greater than in the low performance condition. Moreover, a non-significant interaction between the performance cue and leader behavior indicated that the degree to which the leader exhibited structuring behavior did not affect adjustments in ratings caused by the performance manipulation. It was concluded that subjects independently used behavioral and performance information to form ratings of leader behavior.

Rush and Beauvais (1981) attempted to minimize PCE on LBDQ ratings by asking subjects to rate only those items they felt could be rated accurately. It was hypothesized that PCEs would be diminished when subjects restricted ratings to unambiguous items. However, even those items subjects felt they had sufficient information to rate were affected by performance cues. The effects of a temporal delay between viewing the leadership stimulus and making ratings were investigated by Rush, Phillips, and Lord (1981). Because raters rely on implicit theories to reconstruct likely behaviors, it was hypothesized that a 48-hour delay would cause an increased reliance on inferences derived from implicit leadership theories. Results indicated the effects of the performance manipulation did increase, while the effects of the behavioral manipulation (as in Lord et al., 1978) remained stable. It was concluded that raters form a general leadership impression based on *both* behavior and performance information, and rate leaders based on this impression.

A series of two studies by Larson and his colleagues (Larson, 1982; Larson, Lingle, and Scerbo, 1984) investigated encoding and retrieval mechanisms underlying PCEs. Larson (1982) had subjects view a videotape of a problem-solving group. Subjects were told the group performed well or poorly either before or after viewing the tape. Subjects then rated the leader of the group on the consideration and initiating structure scales of the LBDQ. Group performance information had the same impact on ratings whether it was introduced before or after the tape was viewed, therefore it was concluded that implicit theories were most influential at the time of rating. In a further investigation of this issue, Larson et al. (1984) manipulated performance cues *both* prior to and after observation of the stimulus videotape in a within-subjects design. Subjects were told prior to observation that the group performed well or poorly. After the tape was shown, however, subjects were informed that the experimenter inadvertently showed the wrong tape. Half the subjects were told that the group they had just watched performed opposite to what they had been told before viewing the tape. In addition to the LBDQ, behavioral questionnaires were developed that asked subjects to identify *specific* behaviors that did or did not occur on the tape. Using these questionnaires, a signal detection analysis was conducted. Results showed support for a dual-process model of PCEs. Implicit theories of leadership guide the information that is *encoded and stored in memory* when performance information is provided before viewing the stimulus. After observation, performance cues invoke a *response bias*, such that a rater's implicit theories lead to inferences of what behaviors probably occurred. These dual processes combine additively to produce PCEs. The studies conducted by Larson and his colleagues are quite important because they represent efforts to move beyond the identification of boundary conditions of PCEs, by determining at what stages of information processing implicit theories may have the greatest impact on leadership ratings.

From the studies summarized to this point it is clear that PCEs are a robust phenomenon in ratings of leader behavior. Moreover, numerous studies have shown that implicit leadership theories are likely responsible for these effects. Individuals possess implicit theories of effective and ineffective leadership. These cognitive structures determine, in part, how information in the form of leader behavior is observed, encoded, and recalled. Though results appear unequivocal, there are several limitations to this line of research. The most obvious limitation is that all of the studies were conducted in the laboratory, thus placing severe constraints on the generalizability of these findings to real-world raters and leaders. Other limitations are related to the rather myopic use of the performance cue experimental paradigm to investigate implicit leadership theories. If implicit theories are common across individuals, there should be other methods of eliciting them besides manipulation of group performance levels. Also of interest is the impact of various contextual factors, such as group composition and organizational constraints, on the effects of performance cues. For example, one study (Butterfield and Powell, 1981) found a PCE for hypothetical managers with the same management styles (e.g. consideration) and for both male and female leaders. These contextual issues deserve further investigation. Finally, though implicit leadership theories have served as explanatory constructs for PCEs, implicit theories themselves are not strongly grounded in any theoretical base. Categorization theory, however, provides a model of cognitive processing that explains the mechanisms for findings described above, it offers a more general framework for the study of social perception that can be extended beyond the performance manipulation paradigm.

Categorization Theory

A complete discussion of categorization theory and its application to leadership is presented in Lord, Foti, and Phillips (1982). The categorization model of leadership perception is based on the object categorization model of Rosch (1978) and the person perception work of Cantor and Mischel (1979). An important feature of the categorization model is that it explains the underlying cognitive structure of implicit theories. Individuals are placed into meaningful, pre-existing categories which reduce the complexity of incoming information. The categorization model also explains how leadership categories affect ratings at different stages of the cognitive process: attention, encoding, storage, retrieval, and judgement (Lord, 1985). Categorization judgements are made by comparing a stimulus person to a leadership prototype, which is thought to be a critical component of implicit leadership theories. Therefore, under conditions of limited information, raters can classify a stimulus person into an existing leadership category. Raters then need only recall the category label (leader), and rely on the prototype of a leader to make judgements of likely behaviors and traits.

The categorization model of leadership perception has received considerable empirical support. Phillips and Lord (1982) showed subjects a videotape of a problem-solving group where the leader had been coached to exhibit instances of prototypically effective, prototypically ineffective, and non-prototypical behaviors. Group performance levels were also manipulated. They found that subjects displayed greater accuracy in identifying the presence of non-prototypic behaviors than the prototypically effective items. There was no discriminability in detecting the presence or absence of prototypically ineffective behaviors. When subjects were told the group performed well, behavioral ratings of prototypical items were distorted in the direction consistent with an effective leader prototype. However, the non-prototypical items did not demonstrate PCEs. These findings suggest that raters recalled only the category prototype of an effective or ineffective leader and inferred likely behaviors when making judgements. Binning, Zaba, and Whattam (1986) replicated Phillips and Lord (1982) and found that performance cues affected global performance ratings more strongly than specific behavioral ratings. However, PCEs were significant for both types of ratings.

Phillips (1984) investigated the effects of a temporal delay on raters' accuracy in remembering prototypical and non-prototypical behaviors. Results indicated that there was a greater decrement over time in accuracy for the non-prototypical behaviors relative to the prototypical behaviors. The initial category label applied to the leader (effective, ineffective) led subjects to retrieve information consistent with this prototype. Memory for non-prototypical behaviors, which were unrelated to a category, was adversely affected by the delayed ratings.

In a study of political leaders, Foti, Fraser, and Lord (1982) investigated the hierarchical nature of leadership categories. Prototypicality ratings were obtained from Gallup Poll surveys of political leaders. It was found that subjects identified significant differences between prototypes at the superordinate level (leader) and prototypes at the basic level (political leader), thus supporting the hierarchical nature of leadership perception. Furthermore, only those traits prototypical of political leader changed when overall leadership ratings changed, congruent with the notion that perceptions of leaders are centered around prototypes. In a separate investigation of political leaders, Foti, Lord, and Dambrot (in press) compared descriptions of two gubernatorial and two mayoral candidates one week before and one week after the election. Results indicated that prototypical item ratings increased after the election for the winner, while ratings of prototypical items decreased for the loser.

The structure of leadership categories was directly tested in three studies by Lord, Foti, and DeVader (1984). They found that the prototypicality of a specific leadership trait was related to its distinctiveness and the extent of overlap among basic level leader categories. These results provide further support for the centrality of leadership prototypes to leadership perception. The second study showed that items predetermined to have greater prototypicality yielded faster reaction times in assessing the extent to which they characterized a good leader. These findings are important because they suggest that prototypical leader attributes may be more available in raters' memories than non-prototypical attributes.

Several studies have investigated the interrelationship of attribution theory and categorization theory in the formation of leadership perceptions. According to Calder (1977) and Pfeffer (1977), attributional processes are central to leadership perceptions. However, categorization theory suggests that leadership perceptions are based primarily on the categorization process. To contrast these two perspectives, Phillips and Lord (1981) manipulated the salience of the leader and the perceived existence of other causes of behavior, both fundamental variables in attribution theory. They also manipulated group performance information. It was concluded that leadership perceptions did not depend on the existence of causal attributions, and in fact, categorization and the attribution of causality may operate independently. Lord et al. (1984) found that the prototypicality of leader attributes also predicted attributions of leader responsibility for successful outcomes. Thus, causal attributions may be the result of prior categorization. Similar conclusions were reached by Lord and Alliger (1985) in a comparison of several information processing models of leadership perception. Cronshaw and Lord (1987) contrasted the two theories by manipulating consensus (attribution theory) and prototypicality (categorization theory). They found that categorization processes, as opposed to attribution processes, determined leadership perceptions. These results taken together suggest that causal attributions may not be involved in the formation of leadership perceptions. Rather, they suggest that *both* causal attributions and categorization processes are involved. Leadership can be *inferred* from events or outcomes which may be dependent on causal analyses. Leadership can also be *recognized* through direct exposure to a leader's behaviors or traits, and need not involve explicit causal analysis (Lord, 1985). Leadership perceptions are a product of both of these processes.

Comments

We believe an integration of attribution theory and categorization theory can provide a viable model of social perception. Lord and Maher (1989) provide a detailed explication of the distinction between the inferential and recognition-based models that illustrates how both processes are involved in leadership perception. A similar model could be developed for the performance appraisal area. However, there are still many unanswered questions about the development and maintenance of leadership perceptions. Recent theorizing in the area of expert/novice differences suggests that experts and novices may have different leadership prototypes within specific contexts. Preliminary research on this topic (Baumgardner and Forti, 1988) suggests this may be the case. Also of interest is how leadership perceptions change as one moves from novice to expert. No studies have addressed this issue. Differences in subordinate characteristics may also affect perceptions of leadership. Cashman and Snyder (1980) found that the factor structure of leader perceptions varied depending on the amount of subordinates' self-reported role ambiguity and work competence. Stable individual differences may also impact on the formation of leadership perceptions. Weiss and Adler (1981), however, found no differences in implicit theories of leadership across varying levels of cognitive complexity. Though no definitive conclusions can be drawn from these two studies, we believe more efforts should be undertaken to investigate how various contextual factors and individual difference variables affect social perceptual processes. Other avenues for further investigation include the effects of social norms and task demands on leadership perceptions (Lord and Alliger, 1985).

SOCIAL PROCESSES

Superior–Subordinate Interaction

Green and Mitchell (1979) developed a cognitive theory of leader–member interactions based on Kelley's (1973) attribution theory principles. According to the Green and Mitchell model, leaders operate much like scientists in seeking and using attributional information about subordinates. They posit that careful causal analyses mediate between subordinate behavior and a superior's response to that behavior. This basic theoretical perspective has been tested in a series of well-controlled laboratory experiments which generally provide support for the theory. Ilgen and Knowlton (1980) found that superiors in *ad hoc* laboratory work groups altered their feedback to subordinates as a function of attributions as well as subordinate performance level. Mitchell and Wood (1980) showed that nursing supervisors reacted to written case histories in a manner consistent with attribution theory predictions. Poor work histories and serious negative incidents produced greater assessments of subordinate causality and a greater willingness to direct responses at nurses rather than aspects of the situation. Their direct manipulation of causal attributions in a second study supported causal attributions as a mediating variable. Mitchell and Kalb (1981) also investigated reactions to hypothetical cases, finding that negative outcomes produced more internal attributions and greater responsibility judgements than benign outcomes.

Two studies which created somewhat more natural situations by using short-term work groups also found support for attribution theory predictions. Knowlton and Mitchell (1980) examined the effect of ability attributions (manipulated by giving subjects who acted as supervisors aptitude scores for their subordinates) and effort attributions (manipulated through the behavior of confederates who acted as subordinates) on evaluations of subordinates. Effort attributions produced more extreme evaluations of subordinates for both high and low performance conditions. Importantly, effort effects occurred through supervisors' sensitivity to subordinates' *behavior* not to experimenter provided *information* as is usually the case in attribution theory studies. Though the work period was short in this experiment (one hour), this study demonstrates supervisors' potential to extract attributional information from natural work situations. Mitchell and Kalb (1982) investigated the effects of actor–observer biases in causal attributions in a two-hour proofreading laboratory task in which supervisors and subordinates switched places after the first hour. Major findings were that experienced supervisors (those who had worked as subordinates prior to their supervisory session) were more likely to see environmental factors as causes for poor performance than were inexperienced supervisors (who were supervisors for the first rather than the second session). Mitchell and Kalb also reported similar results using field data from a small military sample. They found a strong correlation between a superior's experience on a subordinate's job and external attributions for poor subordinate performance. Mitchell and Kalb's findings have practical importance since leader experience with subordinate tasks can serve as a 'cognitive antidote' to the frequently demonstrated actor–observer biases in attributional research. The effects of experience are also theoretically interesting since they demonstrate that actor–observer biases have a cognitive (prior task knowledge) as well as a perceptual component (the differential salience to actors and observers of person and situational information).

Martinko and Gardner (1987) provide a highly elaborate attribution theory model which shows how attributions of both leaders and members can form the basis for dyadic interactions. They also explain how attributional biases may produce conflict between leaders and subordinates over the interpretation of poor performance. Though interesting, this work may overemphasize the *cognitive* relative to the *social* aspects of leader–member interactions. Wood and Mitchell (1981) explored the social nature of leader attributions, arguing that subordinates actively manage the attributions that leaders make by providing accounts, justifications, and apologies for performance outcomes. In two separate studies in which subjects made judgements and recommendations based on written stimulus materials, these impression management factors affected both attributions of causality and whether employee focused or situational responses were rated as being appropriate. This line of reasoning foreshadowed a more involved role-playing study by Gioia and Sims (1986), which showed that superiors often asked subordinates to assess causality for them. Thus, both the Wood and Mitchell and the Gioia and Sims studies highlight the *social* aspects of attributional processes.

Relying on socially communicated information may be an important way to reduce the informational and cognitive requirements of otherwise burdensome causal analyses implied by most of the attributional research. Three other means of simplification are to use less complicated processes for assessing causality (see Lord and Smith, 1983), to rely on pre-existing knowledge structures such as scripts which already contain causal information (Read, 1987), or to conceptualize causal assessment and superior reactions as dynamic rather than static processes (Green, Fairhurst, and Snavely, 1986). Given the multiple tasks and time pressures common to management, we think these four means to reduce the information processing requirements of attributional assessments should be given increased attention by future research. They may well provide more externally valid models of the cognitive processes actually used by managers in reacting to their subordinates.

Comments

We think the programmatic line of research initiated by the Green and Mitchell (1979) theory provides a good example of how cognitive approaches can help us understand specific substantive areas in the I/O field. However, we also think further development of this area is needed. The contrived nature of many attributional situations suggests obvious external validity problems. Also, though attributions are conceptualized as mediators between subordinate behavior and superior reactions, no studies provide any statistical analysis of the hypothesized mediating processes.

Turning to a broader issue, we think the conceptual model laid out by Green and Mitchell may be overly restrictive as a general model for superior–subordinate interactions. Causal attributions may well be produced by processes other than the quasi-scientific model suggested by Kelley (1973). Also, causal analyses may follow superior reactions to subordinates as a means to rationalize their reaction, rather than being a rational antecedent to superior reactions. Finally, as suggested by Feldman's (1981) work in performance appraisal, superiors can react to subordinates without any assessment of causality.

Two related topics where we think a cognitive approach should be applied are in understanding the evolution of superior–subordinate roles and in understanding superior attempts to motivate or train subordinates. Graen's vertical dyad linkage model of leadership (Graen and Cashman, 1975), which has had a predominantly behavioral orientation, could benefit from analysis in terms of the cognitive processes of both superiors and subordinates. This could be accomplished by an extension of Feldman's (1981) categorization approach or by more reciprocal cognitive models (see Lord and Maher, 1989). For example, superiors may evaluate subordinates' fit with a 'good subordinate' prototype as a partial determinant of leader–member exchanges; similarly, subordinates may evaluate the extent to which superiors fit 'effective leader' prototypes. Since prototypes can also guide behavior, it follows that dyads with similar prototypes of good superiors (or good subordinates) would be more likely to develop high quality dyadic relationships. Such effects might help explain the frequently noted facilitative effects of superior–subordinate cognitive or perceptual similarity (see Pulakos and Wexley, 1983), by linking cognitive similarity to similarity in interpersonal (or self) evaluative processes.

Much of the work in the leadership field has been concerned with leaders' motivational effects on subordinates. Such work is frequently based in reinforcement theory with its natural focus on a leader's use of rewards and punishments (Podsakoff, 1982). Alternative perspectives focus on cognitive effects such as clarifying paths to goals (see Ashour, 1982, for an approach integrating both of these perspectives). However, we think such work needs to be extended by viewing leaders as important informational sources for subordinates. Work along these lines has been initiated by Larson (1984, 1986), who was concerned primarily with factors that affect whether superiors provide feedback to subordinates. Such work should be integrated with explanations that focus on the feedback-seeking behavior of subordinates (Ashford and Cummings, 1983), but more importantly they need to be integrated with models that explain how subordinates use information to guide their own behavior (e.g. Lord and Hanges, 1987; Taylor, Fisher, and Ilgen, 1984). In other words, such cognitively based models of *subordinate* motivation may provide rich models for deductive reasoning concerning how superiors impact on the motivations of their subordinates. Such models would also have natural ties to currently popular topics such as self-leadership (Manz and Sims, 1987).

In short, the leadership field has made substantial strides in understanding how cognitions *can* affect the relations between leaders and subordinates. This work is encouraging, but we think more attention needs to be given to the descriptive accuracy of such models in real work situations. Borrowing McElroy's (1982) terminology, we think the field should move from experimentally plausible cognitive models, to descriptive process models, and ultimately to prescriptive process models. In addition, cognitive models need to be applied to more general issues than leader responses to poor subordinate performance.

Social Information Processing and Task Perceptions

One of the more interesting applications of a social information processing perspective was spawned by Salancik and Pfeffer's (1978) work on task design. In this groundbreaking and widely influential article, they argued that job attitudes and behavior resulted from the way workers processed information. Thus, they conceptualized job satisfaction as resulting from workers' cognitive processes, and they emphasized the similarity between job attitudes and needs, arguing that both were personal constructs resulting from contextually based information processes. By context they meant both the *social context* in which behavior occurred and the enactment or *behavioral context* created by an individual's interpretation of his or her past behaviors. Salancik and Pfeffer argued that, because people are limited information processors, they rely on social and behavioral cues to help them form task perceptions and affective reactions, rather than using all possible task information. Using such cues may distort task perceptions; however, Salancik and Pfeffer's theory did not imply that people *ignored* task characteristics in forming job attitudes, as much of the subsequent research has suggested.

Salancik and Pfeffer developed a fairly complex information processing theory that applied to insufficient justification, intrinsic and extrinsic motivation, organizational climate, and job attitudes. Subsequent research has focused primarily on job attitudes, but researchers concerned with the other three topics would surely benefit from carefully studying Salancik and Pfeffer's SIP theory. Their SIP theory maintains that social processes can directly influence attitudes based on co-workers' overt statements. Influence can also be indirect, operating through attentional processes, interpretation of environmental cues, or interpretation of personal needs. Unfortunately, subsequent research has investigated only direct social influences. SIP Research has also largely ignored the contextual effect associated with an individual's interpretation of his or her past behavior.

Several articles support Salancik and Pfeffer's basic proposition that direct social cues affect perceptions of job characteristics and task satisfaction (Griffin, 1983; Griffin, Bateman, Wayne, and Head, 1987; Kilduff and Regan, 1988; O'Connor and Barrett, 1980; O'Reilly and Caldwell, 1979; Vance and Biddle, 1985; Weiss and Shaw, 1979; White and Mitchell, 1979; White, Mitchell, and Bell, 1977). In fact, given the different formats of social cues (written, co-worker statements, superior statements, information on training tapes), timing of cues (before, during, and after task activities), and different samples (actual workers in field studies or subjects in laboratory studies) this consistent support for the effects of social cues on job descriptions and satisfaction is surprising. Equally robust are the effects of job enrichment on job descriptions and satisfaction. As noted by Griffin *et al.* (1987), it is clear that *both* objective task characteristics and social cues affect job descriptions, and that both of these factors need to be considered in designing jobs and in interpreting the meaning of descriptive measures of job characteristics. The three studies examining the effects of social cues on performance have been less consistent, showing some significant effects (White and Mitchell, 1979; White, Mitchell, and Bell, 1977) and some non-significant effects (Griffin, 1983).

SIP theory has implications for the validity of questionnaires designed to measure job perceptions and job redesign approaches based on these measures. Such issues have been discussed in three excellent reviews (Blau and Katerberg, 1982; Shaw, 1980; Thomas and Griffin, 1983) so they will be only briefly mentioned here. The logical extension of Salancik and Pfeffer's contextual theory is that, to the extent that job descriptions reflect contextual effects rather than the effects of actual job characteristics, then job redesign based on such descriptions *may* be inappropriate. In considering the external validity of these predominantly laboratory studies, several factors are important. First, individual differences do seem to moderate social cue effects (see Thomas and Griffin, 1983), social cue effects may be weaker for individuals having more task experience (Vance and Biddle, 1985), and social cues may predict job descriptions better than job choice (Kilduff and Regan, 1988). Nevertheless, Griffin's (1983) field experiment demonstrated very large social cue effects explaining between 29 and 40 per cent of the variance in descriptions of core task attributes. Social cue effects also generalized to descriptions of non-manipulated social interactions, suggesting a very strong halo effect as well.

Other non-experimental field studies provide support for various aspects of SIP theory, showing the influence of work groups on job descriptions. Dean and Brass (1985) showed that social interactions affected job descriptions in real work groups, producing a convergence with more objective outside observers' perceptions of jobs. Such effects were greater for individuals who were central in communication networks, suggesting social interaction can lead to *more* accurate job descriptions. O'Reilly and Caldwell (1985) found that the intensity of group norms affected perceptions of job characteristics using data from 21 different work groups. Also, consistent with work on social influence, group cohesiveness enhanced the effects of group norms for perceptions of some task characteristics (e.g. significance). In a three-month study, Thomas (1986) found that various social groups (supervisors, doctors, instructors, family members, and patients) affected the job perceptions of nurses. The influence of these various groups changed over time, and differed for student nurses as compared to working nurses. Working nurses reported that co-workers were an important source of information about job perceptions, but student nurses indicated that co-workers were among the *least* important sources of information about jobs. These findings suggest that SIP researchers should adopt a broader conceptualization of relevant social groups. Finally, O'Reilly, Parlette, and Bloom (1980) found that job tenure and strength of professional identity affected the 'frames of reference' used in describing jobs. All these findings are consistent with the general SIP framework provided by Salancik and Pfeffer.

More sophisticated causal analyses of field data show some surprising results. Glick, Jenkins, and Gupta (1986) used latent variable analysis of job descriptions and affective ratings provided by both observer and job incumbents. They found that job characteristics could predict some dependent variables independently of method variance. However, prediction of satisfaction was at least five times as great when method variance was included (see their Table 6). Although their results cannot completely rule out what is generally referred to as the job characteristics model, a SIP model which includes social and methodological factors provides a much stronger explanation of dependent variables. One potential explanation for such 'method bias' is that workers' satisfaction levels affect their ratings of job characteristics. Adler, Skov, and Salvemini (1985) tested this reverse causality notion in a laboratory experiment by providing bogus satisfaction feedback to subjects doing a simulated work task. They found significant effects on perceptions of all five JDS task dimensions, leading them to question the proper interpretation of cross-sectional data relating perceptions of job characteristics to affective ratings. A second field study, using confirmatory structural equation modelling (Hogan and Martell, 1987), found that 'a single-factor model, with that factor interpretable either as common method variance or generalized affect, explains these data at least as well as any traditional variation on job characteristics theory' (p. 242). In short, though one can find 'pure' effects of job characteristics on descriptions of job characteristics and affective ratings, the support for social context effects and common method variance (which undoubtedly involves more than social context effects) is so overwhelming that it would be foolish to ignore such factors in designing real jobs.

Comments

Though practically important, when evaluated from a cognitive perspective, we find most of the experimental SIP literature to be uninformative. The major focus of most researchers has been on comparing social cue effects to job enrichment effects (an issue which research soon realized cannot be adequately resolved based on laboratory data). In fact, despite Salancik and Pfeffer's focus on social information processing, all of the experimental studies could be more appropriately classified as social influence or attitude change research rather than information processing studies. For the most part, these studies do not develop or test any cognitive theory, nor do they measure any cognitive processes. In fact, we would not label them as cognitive studies at all if we rigorously applied the definition of cognitive processes developed in the introduction. Field research, particularly the studies using sophisticated causal analysis, indicate a clear need for a better understanding of what job descriptions actually measure. We think answering such measurement related questions may well be the best I/O application of an information processing approach.

One final point concerning the SIP literature on job design should be made. The most basic point of Salancik and Pfeffer's (1978) argument was that the effects of job characteristics on affective and behavioral reactions depended on the *contextual* interpretation provided by workers. To us it seems unfortunate that such a broadly relevant perspective has been investigated primarily within the narrow objectives of competitively testing the SIP and job characteristics models. Our concern is that the I/O field may tire of SIP research before researchers ever focus on the most fundamental insights Salancik and Pfeffer had to offer.

PROBLEM SOLVING

Problem solving generally refers to a comprehensive process involving the recognition and representation of a problem, generation of possible solutions, choice of a particular solution, and its effective implementation. Decision making is usually only concerned with these last two steps. Thus, the initial steps in problem solving apply to the ill-structured situations that often characterize managerial information processing, while the latter two components pertain to the more structured situations typically investigated in earlier studies of decision making (Ungson, Braunstein, and Hall, 1981). We begin with work on problem recognition and representation.

Problem Recognition and Representation

Several recent theorists have offered conceptual frameworks that emphasize perceiver factors as opposed to stimulus properties in explaining problem recognition (Billings, Milburn, and Schaalman, 1980; Cowan, 1986; Kiesler and Sproull, 1982). These models are similar in that they all posit an event-related triggering mechanism involving the comparison of environmental information to some standard based on level of aspiration or past experience. Discrepancies between standards and feedback from the environment result in problem recognition. From this point, the models differ in several interesting ways. Billings *et al.* posit that discrepancies lead to evaluations of the expectancy and value of possible loss in crisis perception, suggesting a fairly sophisticated and logical process. Kiesler and Sproull, on the other hand, emphasize managers' limited processing capacity. For them, limitations in selective attention, constructing meaning, and retaining information are crucial in explaining why potentially important problems may not be perceived. Cowan (1986) emphasizes the role of evoked schemata in theorizing about problem recognition. He maintains that people can recognize problems relatively automatically if they have experience and a familiar schema that can be applied; alternatively, novel situations for which appropriate schemata are lacking can still be perceived as problems if managers use more controlled processes.

Cowan also stresses the role of categorization processes in helping managers determine whether noticed discrepancies are problems or can safely be ignored. Categorization processes have also been used by Dutton and Jackson (1987) to help explain how strategic issues are interpreted. They argue that classifying an issue as a 'threat' or an 'opportunity' affects subsequent information processing and motivational processes of managers, impacting substantially on the eventual actions that are chosen. Moreover, they posit that differences in categorization affect where in an organization decisions will be made, whether actions will be internally or externally directed, and how extreme responses are likely to be.

Interestingly, all four of these theoretical works conceptualize initial stages in problem solving as being based on the fit between stimulus events and cognitive constructs of managers. This line of reasoning is quite consistent with Pound's (1969) earlier work on problem recognition. It can be extended by theoretical developments which help explain how 'fit' is evaluated (Lord and Hanges, 1987; Mervis and Rosch, 1981). However, perhaps the greatest need is for empirical investigation using data from actual organizational problems.

Two empirical studies of problem definition and interpretation observed extensive discussions relevant to a specific problem and applied novel methodologies to interpreting the data. Sapienza (1987) investigated the impact of imagery on the definition and response to problems by groups of managers in two organizations. Her linguistic analysis based on observations and transcripts from six months of meetings of top managers indicated that problems were *socially* defined by: managers' discussions of their perceptions; development of common vocabularies, syntax, and images; and by the emergence of a reigning (salient) image with strategic implications. Donnellon, Gray, and Bougon (1986) extensively investigated the communications pertaining to a behavioral simulation of an organization. They expected that communications would forge a common interpretation of the situation, providing a cognitive basis for collective action. Instead, they found that different members constructed *different* meanings and interpretations for the same collective action. Interestingly, Ross and Staw (1986) depicted a similar process, albeit on a much larger scale, in their development of an escalation prototype based on Expo 86. What they described is that over time, social–political processes resulted in many different meanings being attached to the same action (Expo 86). These multiple meanings provided a basis for co-opting different groups and justifying increased costs. All three of these studies showed that the definitions and interpretations of problems which *developed over time* were crucial in understanding the development of and commitment to alternatives. They demonstrate that there is a *social as well as a cognitive* link between problem conceptualization, schematic or linguistic representation, and actions chosen.

Descriptive Models of Problem Solving

Several other studies have attempted to model decision processes based on extensive interviews with key organizational members. These studies are noteworthy in two respects. First, they provide *descriptive* data on important organizational decisions, which are needed to help guide our theory development. Second, they often sample from many organizations, lending some generality to findings. For example, in an influential study of strategic decision making Mintzberg, Raisinghani, and Theoret (1976) modelled strategic decision-making processes in 25 organizations. They found that decision processes could be organized into three phases — *problem identification, solution development, and solution selection*. These phases were composed of a number of subroutines and were supported by a number of other dynamic processes. Thus, the decision processes they represented were hierarchically organized, and complexity was handled by a number of smaller processes that were common to many organizations.

Mintzberg *et al.*'s study revealed a number of interesting aspects of organizational decision making with important implications for understanding information processing. First, key organizational decisions are multi-person processes that unfold over long periods of time, with most decisions taking more than a *year* to make. Second, although the phases identified seemed to agree with common models of decision making — moving from problem identification, to solution generation, to choice of an appropriate solution — there was no support for the idea that solutions were made by a linear progression from one phase to the next. Phases were often reordered as when solution generation helped define a problem or when implicit choices were made prior to developing a solution. Also, there was extensive cycling back to prior phases as when the selection phase required a redefinition of a problem. Third, and perhaps most surprising, was a lack of support for any of the normative literature suggesting that choices were made by analytic procedures (p. 258). In more than 75 per cent of the cases, evaluative processes could not be distinguished from choice processes, contradicting rational models where evaluation precedes choice. In fact, Mintzberg *et al.* noted that despite the emphasis on evaluation–choice processes in the literature on strategic decisions, '. . . this routine seems to be far less significant in many of the decision processes we studied than diagnosis or design' (p. 257). Fourth, though they developed a general model of decision making based on the major subroutines they discovered, Mintzberg *et al.* found that special cases (paths) of this general model, which ignored key subroutines (such as skipping the solution development routine), described most of the cases they examined. In other words, decision makers seemed to be simplifying the general decision routine by skipping one or more parts.

Nutt (1984) reported similar findings in a study of decision-making processes associated with projects in 78 different organizations. Using interview data from multiple individuals in each organization, Nutt compared reported decision-making processes to an ideal model involving five stages: problem formulation, conceptual development (which generates alternative approaches), detailing (refining) alternatives, evaluation, and implementation. He found that 'Nothing remotely resembling the normative methods described in the literature was carried out' (p. 446). The usual simplifications involved very abbreviated search (Stage 2) and limited evaluation (Stage 4) procedures. Problem solving was generally solution centered, with a very early commitment to action. However, only a minority of the problems (25 per cent) were initiated by the availability of solutions as might be implied by 'garbage can' models of decision making (Cohen, March, and Olsen, 1972). Instead, consistent with other work on problem recognition, most problems (62 per cent) were evoked by performance gap information, and executives tended to look for ready-made solutions rather than developing a novel response to their particular problem.

An interesting supplement to the descriptive work on actual organizational problems is work that explores problem solving based on experimenter-provided case material. Isenberg (1986) compared twelve experienced managers and three novice business students, coding their problem-solving protocols into seventeen different categories. He found that compared to students, managers, particularly effective managers, tended to use knowledge gained through their experience to generate appropriate actions. They did not rely on extensive analysis of facts provided in the case. Though information search often was severely restricted, an opportunistic orientation coupled with past experience still permitted effective problem solving. On the surface, Isenberg's findings are consistent with earlier works that emphasized bounded rationality (March and Simon, 1958) and limited search (Cyert and March, 1963) in problem solving. However, Isenberg's results suggested that *experienced* managers are still effective when using such simplified processes.

DECISION MAKING

Decision-making models can be separated into *structural models*, which are concerned with the relation between stimulus inputs and output responses, and *process models*, which focus on the transformation processes that occur between input and output (Abelson and Levi, 1985). Our emphasis will be on process models, since they are more congruent with an information processing framework. In contrast to the descriptive work from applied settings, much of the laboratory work on decision making has been more closely tied to rational or normative models. The general finding is that, even in controlled laboratory settings, decision makers do not optimize and normative models do not describe accurately the processes used to make decisions. These general findings have resulted in three lines of research. One is carefully to reconsider what we mean by rationality in the first place (Einhorn and Hogarth, 1981). A second line of research is to examine certain types of mistakes such as base rate fallacies in Bayesian decision making (Fischoff and Beyth-Marom, 1983); the use of simplifying heuristics (Tversky and Kahneman, 1974); or more recently, the framing of decisions (Kahneman and Tversky, 1979; Tversky and Kahneman, 1981). The third approach has been to incorporate decision making or information processing costs into definitions of rationality. This latter approach is particularly interesting. It suggests that not only will *quantitative* changes occur — decision makers trade off accuracy to reduce decision-making costs as in limited search conditions – but also *qualitative* changes will be made — decision makers may use low cost intuitive procedures in some situations and high cost analytic procedures in other situations. Qualitative changes, which vary decision strategies and processes to match expected benefits, suggest that decision makers are fairly sophisticated even though they may not be 'rational' in a formal sense.

Contingent Decision Making

This notion of rationality based on cost-guided, qualitative changes in decision-making processes is consistent with work on contingent decision making. For example, Klein (1983) suggests that decision makers choose heuristic strategies based on problem characteristics so as to enhance the utility of the decision outcome. This basic idea that the nature of decision processes will change with the nature of the problem or situations was also suggested by Payne (1982). It is a critical insight in terms of understanding information processing which raises entirely new research agendas incorporating contingency factors.

Beach and Mitchell's (1978) work represents the most extensive research program on contingent decision making. They hypothesized that decision makers choose different strategies when dealing with different problems. Subsequent research has generally supported their initial theorizing. McAllister, Mitchell, and Beach (1979) conducted three laboratory studies which demonstrated that subjects used more effortful analytic strategies as: (1) decisions became more significant; (2) decisions could not be reversed; and (3) decision makers were more accountable for their actions. Their first two studies, which used within-subjects designs, provided strong support for all three factors. However, their third study, which used a between-subjects design, found strong effects for accountability, marginal effects for significance, and non-significant effects for reversibility. In a follow-up study Waller and Mitchell (1984) had accounting students select from one of five accounting information systems to be used in a managerial role-playing problem. They found that more analytic (and more reliable) strategies were used as problem uncertainty and significance increased.

Christensen-Szalanski (1978) extended this line of thinking developing a more explicit cost/benefit formulation for selecting the decision strategy with the maximum net expected gain. This formulation was tested in two laboratory experiments which manipulated cost functions (through fatigue) and expected benefit functions (by changing the payoff function for correct solutions). In the first study, increasing the payoff function increased the time subjects spent, their confidence, and the accuracy of their solutions. Cost curves were marginally shifted by fatigue. The second study focused on strategy choice as an intervening mechanism by having the experimenter choose the strategy. More complex strategies increased subjects' confidence in their solution, independent of the level of benefits (accuracy effects). In a follow-up, Christensen-Szalanski (1980) found that short time deadlines caused subjects to use less preferred strategies, decreasing the confidence they had in their solutions. A second study using 'art and English majors who lacked mathematical skills' found higher cost curves, lower confidence, and less accuracy as compared to business students. However, there was no difference from business students in the strategy selection process. As a whole, these studies show that the cost of thinking is an important factor in modelling human decision processes, although it should not be assumed that decision makers consciously make the calculations implied by the cost/benefit model.

Comments

A very important contribution of this contingency decision-making research is the recognition that people can do things differently at different times and in different contexts. This finding complicates information processing research in general, for it suggests that not just one but several models of information processing should be explored. It also implies that there is no single 'correct' information processing model in any theoretical domain (e.g. problem solving, decision making, social perceptions, attribution theory, etc.) or in any type of situation. Such conclusions indicated a need for integrating theoretical and external validity issues.

However, the work on contingent decision making is weakest in terms of external validity issues. A crucial question is whether people will be equally rational in using information processing costs and expected benefits to select strategies when: (1) strategies are not provided to problem solvers; (2) non-university subject populations are used; (3) real problems rather than hypothetical problems are solved; and (4) problem solving occurs in a work rather than an experimental/laboratory context. This external validity issue is best illustrated by Waller and Mitchell's (1984) discussion of accounting strategies actually used by managers when investigating cost variances. Namely, that despite the existence of a range of analytic approaches that could be applied, managers in practice shun the more analytic strategies and prefer simpler decision strategies (p. 402).

The use of simple decision processes can be particularly interesting when they occur in an organizational context with high norms for rationality. Staw (1980) suggests that under such circumstances rationality may be *retrospective*, occurring after a decision as a means to justify the prior choice, rather than being *prospective* as normative models of rationality would require. Staw's emphasis in explaining retrospective rationality is motivational, with organizational demands for rationality or individuals' needs for self-justification being the main underlying causal factors. O'Reilly (1983) adopts a more cognitive perspective identifying a number of biases in acquiring and processing information that may occur once a decision maker is committed to an alternative. O'Reilly's perspective is noteworthy because it also emphasizes organizational and social factors that limit the number of alternatives that are considered *prior* to making decisions. Argyris (1983) adopts a somewhat different perspective by noting that the reasoning processes used to generate and guide actions may be very different (disconnected) from the reasoning processes used to diagnose and invent actions. Research on post-decision rationalization also suggests that reasoning processes and actual decision processes may not be tightly connected. Moreover, much of the reasoning may occur *after decisions are made*. One way to integrate such work with other areas of decision making is to recognize that the *time* dimension is a crucial *contingency* factor in explaining information processing, but that the point of choice in making decisions should be placed in the middle rather than at an end of this dimension. In other words, decision making, especially decision making in real-world contexts, occurs over time, and the point at which decisions are made does not conclude the processing of relevant information. It does, however, provide an important focal point which may indicate that a shift in the type of information processing is likely.

Cybernetic Decision Making

Hogarth (1981) criticizes much of the literature on judgement and decision making for focusing on discrete events, particularly since much human judgement involves continuous adaptation to cope with complex and changing environments. This criticism applies to the I/O work on decision making as well. Hogarth notes that most decision-making work gives insufficient attention to the effects of feedback between an organism and the environment. Further, he argues that many of the heuristic processes which seem suboptimal in the context of discrete choices, may be very functional in a continuous environment. In fact, such a perspective defines rationality in terms of an evolutionary adaptation, in which *both actions and benchmarks by which actions are evaluated* change over time (p. 211). A continuous perspective also emphasizes factors that affect our ability to interpret feedback and learn over time as key determinants of effectiveness in judgements.

The potential utility of a cybernetic perspective is shown by the work of Kleinmuntz and Thomas (1987). They compared action- versus judgement-oriented decision strategies in a dynamic medical decision-making task. Their study manipulated factors relevant to each decision strategy: one factor, the provision of a Bayesian decision-making aid to integrate information from diagnostic tests, was designed to facilitate judgement-oriented strategies; whereas the second factor, minimal risk from selecting the wrong medical treatment, was designed to facilitate the action-oriented strategy. They found that most subjects used a judgement-oriented strategy, which was enhanced by the provision of a decision-making aid. However, they also found that under conditions of low risk, *the best subjects barely reached the performance levels of a random, action-oriented benchmark procedure* (p. 354). Thus, their study showed that under appropriate conditions, 'low power' action-oriented procedures can be very effective. They also showed that, at least in this context, subjects did not use action-oriented strategies as much as they should, preferring a 'diagnose and then act' to an action-first approach. This latter finding was explained in terms of the existence of ineffective 'metadecision' heuristics, ineffective rules-of-thumb for deciding what strategies to use. Their results can also be explained by a learning failure noted by Hogarth (1981, p. 203). Subjects do not learn about the effectiveness of strategies (or actions) which are not chosen, and feedback may even reinforce ineffective strategies or behaviors.

Learning failures are also characteristic of another line of research which is cybernetic in nature—escalation research. Based on a seminal study by Staw (1976), over a dozen studies have investigated the tendency to escalate commitment to a course of action. Staw (1981) reviewed some of this research and concluded that escalation involved a complex process which involved self-justification of prior decisions, social norms which favored consistency, and retrospective as opposed to prospective rationality. Others have explained escalation in terms of prospect theory (Whyte, 1986) which sees escalation as resulting from framing choices in terms of a comparison of a sure loss (costs already incurred) and a possible loss (if commitment of additional resources turns out to be profitable). Framing in terms of losses produces more risky choices than framing in terms of gains. Ross and Staw (1986) have recently suggested a more comprehensive framework which emphasizes institutional, as well as self-justification and information processing explanations of commitment.

An escalation study by McCain (1986) adopted a much more continuous approach, investigating allocation of resources over ten trials in which multiple alternatives were available. He found that whereas subjects who had personally chosen failing divisions invested more money in that division initially, they ceased funding that division *sooner* than subjects who were not responsible for initial allocation to a failing division. McCain's perspective emphasizes factors that affect learning in the course of repeated investments, explaining his results in terms of attribution theory principles (consensus). We think exploring escalation from a learning perspective involving many trials is very useful. For example, McCain's results could also be explained in terms of hindsight bias (Davies, 1987) or factors which facilitate learning from feedback such as having a specific outcome goal (Kernan and Lord, in press).

Two key requirements for cybernetic models of decision making are that they explain the interpretation of and learning from feedback, and the incorporation of a temporal perspective into decision making. Control theory (Lord and Hanges, 1987; Powers, 1973) provides a general model relevant to both of these objectives. It has been used to explain when organizational feedback will be effective (Taylor, Fisher, and Ilgen, 1984). Lord and Kernan (1987) have also suggested that with repetitive tasks, feedback (particularly feedback indicating substandard performance) will often cause shifts from automatic to controlled information processing. They suggest that learning is most likely to occur when controlled processes are used to assimilate information into pre-existing, goal-based, cognitive structures.

Control theory has also been used to explain how standards change over time (Campion and Lord, 1982; Hanges, Alexander, and Herbert, 1986) which incorporates a temporal perspective. Interestingly, different patterns of standard changes can produce hysteresis effects, which have been successfully modelled using catastrophe theory (Hanges, 1986). Hysteresis effects simply imply that the effects of using a particular standard (goal) vary as a function of the direction from which it is approached (moving *over time* from lower to higher performance versus moving from higher to lower performance). This basic idea is very similar to the *static* notions of prospect theory (Kahneman and Tversky, 1979) which suggest that choices framed as possible losses are evaluated very differently from choices framed as possible gains. In fact, we are struck by the functional similarity between framing effects in prospect theory (Kahneman and Tversky, 1979, Fig. 1, p. 454) and fold catastrophe models that reflect the effects of changes in standards over time (Stewart and Peregoy, 1983, Fig. 10, p. 343).

CONCLUSIONS

This survey of the work on cognitive processes in the I/O field can be best integrated in terms of several general conclusions and suggestions, which are organized in terms of methodology and theory in the following sections.

Methodology

For the most part, the literature we have covered has been unbalanced in terms of methodology. The work is predominantly laboratory in nature with many areas lacking even a single field study designed from an information processing perspective (e.g. performance appraisal, leadership perceptions, SIP work on task perceptions). The mixture of descriptive to theoretical work is also highly skewed. The handful of descriptive studies occurred mainly in the decision-making and problem representation areas. These studies are rich in insight and use atypical but laudable methodologies (e.g. protocol analysis). Almost any substantive area would benefit from more descriptive work.

It is surprising that most of the work covered does not measure any cognitive processes. An exception is the work by Mitchell and colleagues on attribution theory explanations of superior evaluations of subordinate performance. Further, when processes are measured, their mediating role is not assessed. Research is largely input–output research, rather than input–process–output research. The cognitive perspective serves mainly as a rich source for generating either hypotheses or *post hoc* explanations. Though measuring cognitive processes is difficult (Lord and Carpenter, 1986; Srull, 1984), it seems to us to be a *requirement* for reaping the benefits of a cognitive perspective.

A third methodological observation is that little attention has been paid to level of aggregation issues. Interestingly, most of the descriptive work pertains to single decisions made either by individuals or single organizations. This work (Mintzberg *et al.*, 1976; Nutt, 1984) characterized cognitive processes as being heuristic, simplified, and cyclical. Most experimental work, however, compares data from subjects in different treatment groups. Such data often provide support for more rational models (e.g. cost/benefit models of decision making or attributional models of subordinate perceptions). Yet, these studies may not adequately model the cognitive processes of *any* specific individuals. It is very possible that less rational, idiosyncratic processes are cancelled out through aggregation procedures, producing a distorted view of typical information processing. A similar argument can be made in terms of investigating rating behavior. Though aggregation across items in a rating scale may be desirable for psychometric purposes, such aggregation may obscure important cognitive processes. Analysis of cognitive effects on responses to single items may be required to understand adequately rater information processing.

Finally, there is often an overemphasis on practical relevance versus theoretical refinement as a guiding principle for research. Many interesting theoretical ideas in widely cited works have never been investigated. For example, Feldman's (1981) suggestion that we research the underlying structure of prototypes has never been investigated, despite the numerous works on performance appraisal which cite his study in connection with cognitive categorization. Similarly, the richer aspects of Salancik and Pfeffer's (1978) SIP theory have been eschewed for the more applied issue of whether perceptions of task characteristics reflect social influences or objective task properties.

Theory

Although reference to information processing or social cognitions provides an aura of theoretical legitimacy, we find no common theoretical perspective to underlie cognitive work in the I/O literature. Different researchers mean different things when referring to cognitive or social–cognitive theory. Sometimes the work is closely tied to basic cognitive research and theory (e.g. Feldman, 1981). At other times, the linkage is more tenuous. As with hand-me-down clothes, there is often a poor fit between the body of empirical work and the theory to which it relates. For example, though clothed in information processing terms, we found the research based on Salancik and Pfeffer's (1978) SIP model to be better characterized as social influence or attitude change research.

A second theoretical problem is that much of the theoretical work ignores the potentially important role of context. This problem stems in part from the relatively 'pure' perspective that can be developed in laboratory as opposed to field research. However, work on contingent decision making (Payne, 1982; Beach and Mitchell, 1978), leadership perceptions (Lord et al., 1984), performance appraisal (Longenecker et al., 1987), escalation (Ross and Staw, 1986), and framing (Kahneman and Tversky, 1979) illustrate the importance of context. Cognitive process researchers should keep in mind that all applications take place within a social, temporal, and behavioral context. A pressing need is for theoretical work that integrates contextual and information processing effects. We have provided some suggestions along these lines in our discussions of performance appraisal and cybernetic models of decision making.

A third theoretical issue pertains to the definition of limited information processing capacity. This issue is important because much of our IP research attempts to explain or minimize the effects of limited information processing capacity. Though the term *limited capacity* is usually used in a generic sense, there are actually two principal types of information processing capacity limitations: limitations in working memory (which includes short-term memory) and limitations in long-term memory. Working memory limitations pertain to the capacity to manipulate or transform information. Working memory limitations make multiplication much more difficult than addition, and they make heuristic processes desirable compared to more computationally demanding optimization procedures. Limitations of long-term memory, on the other hand, involve storage and accessing difficulties, not limitations in capacity. Long-term memory capacity is generally thought to be extremely large. Storage and retrieval difficulties are largely a function of the amount of time available, encoding procedures, and retrieval cues. The effects of cognitive categories on performance ratings or leader behavior ratings, would most likely operate through memory limitations (biased retrieval or generic encoding). Our basic point is that more precision is needed when we refer to limited information processing capacity. Working memory and long-term memory limitations are quite different.

A final theoretical issue pertains to the lack of a common theoretical perspective. This state reflects the existence of a multiplicity of IP models which are often implicitly adopted by researchers in our field. (See Lord and Maher, 1988, for a thorough discussion of this issue.) In this review we have found work which is clearly tied to rational models of information processing (Mitchell's work on superior evaluations of subordinates, research on contingent decision making), limitations in working memory (descriptive work on problem solving, escalation, and framing), limitations in long-term memory (performance appraisal, leader behavior ratings, SIP theory), and cybernetic models (problem recognition, problem solving, cybernetic decision making). Our initial search of the field also identified many studies of expert information processing, which we chose to skip because of space limitations. Much of the IP work in the I/O area has centered on contrasting rational and limited capacity IP models. However, we think that other contrasts are equally useful. For example, rationality on discrete tasks may be very different from rationality using a cybernetic perspective; alternatively, capacity limitations may be very different for experts (who have vast stores of organized information which minimize long-term memory limitations) as compared to novices (who exhibit both working memory and long-term memory limitations). We think the field would benefit greatly from more attention to the underlying IP model and assumptions which implicitly guide work. We believe that these different IP models have important implications for theoretical development and applied practice (see Lord and Maher, 1988).

REFERENCES

Abelson, R.P., and Levi, A. (1985) Decision making and decision theory. In G. Lindzey and E. Aronson (eds), *Handbook of Social Psychology*, Vol. 1. New York: Random House, pp. 231–309.

Adler, S., Skov, R.B., and Salvemini, N.J. (1985) Job characteristics and job satisfaction: When cause becomes consequence. *Organizational Behavior and Human Decision Processes*, 35, 266–278.

Argyris, C. (1983) Action science and intervention. *The Journal of Applied Behavioral Science*, 19, 115–140.

Ashford, S.J., and Cummings, L.L. (1983) Feedback as an individual resource: Personal strategies of creating information. *Organizational Behavior and Human Performance*, 32, 370–398.

Ashour, A.S. (1982) A framework of a cognitive-behavioral theory of leader influence and effectiveness. *Organizational Behavior and Human Performance*, 30, 407–430.

Athey, T.R., and McIntyre, R.M. (1987) Effect of rater training on rater accuracy: Levels-of-processing theory and social facilitation theory perspectives. *Journal of Applied Psychology*, 72, 567–572.

Balzer W.K. (1986) Biases in the recording of performance-related information: The effects of initial impression and centrality of the appraisal task. *Organizational Behavior and Human Decision Processes*, 37, 329–347.

Banks, C.G., and Murphy, K.R. (1985) Toward narrowing the research–practice gap in performance appraisal. *Personnel Psychology*, 38, 335–345.

Baumgardner, T.L., and Forti, J.C. (1988) The implications of experience for leadership categorization theory: A field study. Unpublished manuscript, University of Akron.

Bazerman, M.H., Beekun, R.I., and Schoorman, F.D. (1982) Performance evaluation in a dynamic context: A laboratory study of the impact of a prior commitment to the ratee. *Journal of Applied Psychology*, 67, 873–876.

Beach, L.R., and Mitchell, T.R. (1978) A contingency model for the selection of decision strategies. *Academy of Management Review*, 3, 439–449.

Bernardin, H.J., and Buckley, M.R. (1981) Strategies in rater training. *Academy of Management Review*, 6, 205–212.

Bernardin, H.J., and Pence, E.C. (1980) Effects of rater training: Creating new response sets and decreasing accuracy. *Journal of Applied Psychology*, 65, 60–66.

Billings, R.S., Milburn, T.W., and Schaalman, M.L. (1980) A model of crisis perception: A theoretical and empirical analysis. *Administrative Science Quarterly*, 25, 300–316.

Binning, J.F., and Lord, R.G. (1980) Boundary conditions for performance cue effects on group process ratings: Familiarity versus type of feedback. *Organizational Behavior and Human Performance*, 26, 115–13.

Binning, J.F., Zaba, A.J., and Whattam, J.C. (1986) Explaining the biasing effects of performance cues in terms of cognitive categorization. *Academy of Management Journal*, 29, 521–535.

Blau, G.J., and Katerberg, R. (1982) Toward enhancing research with the social information processing approach to job design. *Academy of Management Review*, 7, 543–550.

Borman, W.C. (1978) Exploring upper limits of reliability and validity in job performance ratings. *Journal of Applied Psychology*, 63, 135–144.

Borman, W.C. (1987) Personal constructs, performance schemata, and 'folk theories' of subordinate effectiveness: Explorations in an army officer sample. *Organizational Behavior and Human Decision Processes*, 40, 307–322.

Butterfield, D.A., and Powell, G.N. (1981) Effect of group performance, leader sex, and rater sex on ratings of leader behavior. *Organizational Behavior and Human Performance*, 28, 129–141.

Calder, B.J. (1977) An attribution theory of leadership. In B.M. Staw and G.R. Salancik (eds), *New Directions in Organizational Behavior*. Chicago: St Clair Press.

Campion, M.A., and Lord, R.G. (1982) A control systems conceptualization of the goal-setting and changing process. *Organizational Behavior and Human Performance*, 30, 265–287.

Cantor, N., and Mischel, W. (1979) Prototypes in person perception. In Berkowitz (ed.), *Advances in Experimental Social Psychology*. New York: Academic Press.

Cardy, R.L., and Dobbins, G.H. (1986) Affect and appraisal accuracy: Liking as an integral dimension in evaluating performance. *Journal of Applied Psychology*, 71, 672–678.

Cashman, J.F., and Snyder, R.A. (1980) Perceptions of leaders' behavior: Situational and personal determinants. *Psychological Reports*, 46, 615–624.

Christensen-Szalanski, J.J.J. (1978) Problem solving strategies: A selection mechanism, some implications, and some data. *Organizational Behavior and Human Performance*, 22, 307–323.

Christensen-Szalanski, J.J.J. (1980) A further examination of the selection of problem-

solving strategies: The effects of deadlines and analytic aptitudes. *Organizational Behavior and Human Performance*, 25, 107–122.
Cohen, M.D., March, J.G., and Olsen, J.P. (1972) A garbage can model of organizational choice. *Administrative Science Quarterly*, 17, 1–25.
Cooper, W.H. (1981a) Ubiquitous halo. *Psychological Bulletin*, 90, 218–244.
Cooper, W.H. (1981b) Conceptual similarity as a source of illusory halo in job performance ratings. *Journal of Applied Psychology*, 66, 302–307.
Cowan, D.A. (1986) Developing a process model of problem recognition. *Academy of Management Review*, 11, 763–776.
Cronbach, L. (1955) Processes affecting scores on 'understanding of others' and 'assumed similarity'. *Psychological Bulletin*, 52, 177–193.
Cronshaw, S.F., and Lord, R.G. (1987) Effects of categorization, attribution, and encoding processes on leadership perceptions. *Journal of Applied Psychology*, 72, 97–106.
Cyert, R.M., and March, J.G. (1963) *A Behavioral Theory of the Firm*. Englewood, Cliffs, NJ: Prentice-Hall.
Darley, J.M., and Fazio, R.H. (1980). Expectancy confirmation processes arising in the social interaction sequence. *American Psychologist*, 35, 867–881.
Davies, M.F. (1987) Reduction of hindsight bias by restoration of foresight perspective: Effectiveness of foresight-encoding and hindsight-retrieval strategies. *Organizational Behavior and Human Decision Processes*, 40, 50–68.
Dean, J.W., and Brass, D.J. (1985) Social interaction and the perception of job characteristics in an organization. *Human Relations*, 38, 571–582.
DeNisi, A.S., Cafferty, T.P., and Meglino, B.M. (1984) A cognitive view of the performance appraisal process: A model and research propositions. *Organizational Behavior and Human Performance*, 33, 360–396.
DeNisi, A.S., and Pritchard, R.D. (1978) Implicit theories of performance as artifacts in survey research: A replication and extension. *Organizational Behavior and Human Performance*, 21, 358–366.
Donnellon, A., Gray, B., and Bougon, M.G. (1986) Communication, meaning, and organized action. *Administrative Science Quarterly*, 31, 43–55.
Downey, H.K., Chacko, T.I., and McElroy, J.C. (1979) Attribution of the 'causes' of performance: A constructive, quasi-longitudinal replication of the Staw (1975) study. *Organizational Behavior and Human Performance*, 24, 287–299.
Dutton, J.E., and Jackson, S.E. (1987) Categorizing strategic issues: Links to organizational action. *Academy of Management Review*, 12, 76–90.
Eden, D., and Leviatan, U. (1975) Implicit leadership theory as a determinant of the factor structure underlying supervisory behavior scales. *Journal of Applied Psychology*, 60, 736–741.
Einhorn, H.J., and Hogarth, R.M. (1981) Behavioral decision theory: Processes of judgment and choice. In M.R. Rosenzweig and L.W. Porter (eds), *Annual Review of Psychology*, Vol. 32. Palo Alto, CA: Annual Reviews, Inc., pp. 53–88.
Feldman, J.M. (1981) Beyond attribution theory: Cognitive processes in performance appraisal. *Journal of Applied Psychology*, 66, 127–148.
Feldman, J.M. (1986) A note on the statistical correction of halo error. *Journal of Applied Psychology*, 71, 173–176.
Feldman, J.M., Camburn, A., and Gatti, G.M. (1986) Shared distinctiveness as a source of illusory correlation in performance appraisal. *Organizational Behavior and Human Decision Processes*, 37, 34–59.
Fischoff, B., and Beyth-Marom, R. (1983) Hypothesis evaluation from a Bayesian perspective. *Psychological Review*, 90, 239–260.

Foti, R.J., Fraser, S.L., and Lord, R.G. (1982) Effects of leadership labels and prototypes on perceptions of political leaders. *Journal of Applied Psychology*, **67**, 326–333.

Foti, R.J., Lord, R.G., and Dambrot, F. (in press) The effect of election outcomes on perceptions and descriptions of political leaders. *Journal of Applied Social Psychology*.

Gioia, D.A., and Sims, H.P., Jr. (1986) Cognition–behavior connections: Attribution and verbal behavior in leader–subordinate interactions. *Organizational Behavior and Human Decision Processes*, **37**, 197–229.

Glick, W.H., Jenkins, G.D., and Gupta, N. (1986) Method versus substance: How strong are underlying relationships between job characteristics and attitudinal outcomes? *Academy of Management Journal*, **29**, 441–464.

Graen, G., and Cashman, J.F. (1975) A role-making model of leadership in formal organizations: A developmental approach. In J.G. Hunt and L.L. Larson (eds), *Leadership Frontiers*. Kent State University, pp. 143–497.

Green, S.G., Fairhurst, G.T., and Snavely, B.K. (1986) Chains of poor performance and supervisory control. *Organizational Behavior and Human Decision Processes*, **38**, 7–27.

Green, S.G., and Mitchell, T.R. (1979) Attributional processes of leaders in leader–member interactions. *Organizational Behavior and Human Performance*, **23**, 429–458.

Griffin, R.W. (1983) Objective and social sources of information in task redesign: A field experiment. *Administrative Science Quarterly*, **28** 184–200.

Griffin, R.W., Bateman, T.S., Wayne, S.J., and Head, T.C. (1987) Objective and social factors as determinants of task perceptions and responses: An integrated perspective and empirical investigation. *Academy of Management Journal*, **30**, 501–523.

Hanges, P.J. (1986) A catastrophe model of control theory's decision mechanism, the effects of goal difficulty, task difficulty, goal direction, and task direction on goal commitment. Unpublished doctoral dissertation, University of Akron.

Hanges, P.J., Alexander, R.A., and Herbert, G.R. (1986) Using regression analysis to empirically verify catastrophe models. Paper presented at the Conference of the Society of Industrial/Organizational Psychology, Chicago, IL.

Hastie, R., and Park, B. (1986) The relationship between memory and judgment depends on whether the judgment task is memory-based or on-line. *Psychological Review*, **93**, 258–268.

Hogan, E.A., and Martell, D.A. (1987) A confirmatory structural equations analysis of the job characteristics model. *Organizational Behavior and Human Decision Processes*, **39**, 242–263.

Hogarth, R.M. (1981) Beyond discrete biases: Functional and dysfunctional aspects of judgment heuristics. *Psychological Bulletin*, **90**, 197–217.

Ilgen, D.R. and Favero, J.L. (1985) Limits in generalization from psychological research to performance appraisal processes. *Academy of Management Review*, **10**, 311–321.

Ilgen, D.R., and Feldman, J.M. (1983) Performance appraisal: A process focus. In B.M. Staw and L.L. Cummings (eds), *Research in Organizational Behavior*, Vol. 5. Greenwich, CT; JAI Press, pp. 141–197.

Ilgen, D.R., and Knowlton, W.A., Jr (1980) Performance attributional effects on feedback from superiors. *Organizational Behavior and Human Performance*, **25**, 441–456.

Isenberg, D.J. (1986) Thinking and managing: A verbal protocol analysis of managerial problem solving. *Academy of Management Journal*, **29**, 775–788.

Jacobs, R., and Kozlowski, S.W.J. (1985) A closer look at halo error in performance ratings. *Academy of Management Journal*, **28**, 201–212.

Kahneman, D., and Tversky, A. (1979) Prospect theory: An analysis of decision under risk. *Econometrica*, **47**, 263–291.

Kelley, H.H. (1973) The processes of causal attribution. *American Psychologist*, **28**, 107–128.
Kernan, M.C., and Lord, R.G. (in press) The effects of goals and specific feedback on escalation processes. *Journal of Applied Social Psychology*.
Kiesler, S., and Sproull, L. (1982) Managerial responses to changing environments: Perspectives on problem sensing from social cognition. *Administrative Science Quarterly*, **27**, 548–570.
Kilduff, M., and Regan, D.T. (1988) What people say and what they do: The differential effects of information cues and task design. *Organizational Behavior and Human Decision Processes*, **41**, 83–97.
Klein, R.M. (1983) Utility and decision strategies: A second look at the rational decision maker. *Organizational Behavior and Human Performance*, **31**, 1–25.
Kleinmuntz, D.N., and Thomas, J.B. (1987) The value of action and inference in dynamic decision making. *Organizational Behavior and Human Decision Processes*, **39**, 341–364.
Knowlton, W.A., and Mitchell, T.R. (1980) Effects of causal attributions on a supervisor's evaluation of subordinate performance. *Journal of Applied Psychology*, **65**, 459–466.
Kozlowski, S.W.J., and Kirsch, M.P. (1987) The systematic distortion hypothesis, halo, and accuracy: An individual level analysis. *Journal of Applied Psychology*, **72**, 252–261.
Kozlowski, S.W.J., Kirsch, M.P., and Chao, G.T. (1986) Job knowledge, ratee familiarity, conceptual similarity and halo error: An exploration. *Journal of Applied Psychology*, **71**, 45–49.
Landy, F.J., and Farr, J.L. (1980) Performance rating. *Psychological Bulletin*, **87**, 72–107.
Larson, J.R., Jr (1982) Cognitive mechanisms mediating the impact of implicit theories of leader behavior on leader behavior ratings. *Organizational Behavior and Human Performance*, **29**, 129–140.
Larson, J.R., Jr (1984) The performance feedback process: A preliminary model. *Organizational Behavior and Human Performance*, **33**, 42–76.
Larson, J.R., Jr (1986) Supervisor's performance feedback to subordinates: The impact of subordinate performance valence and outcome dependence. *Organizational Behavior and Human Decision Processes*, **37**, 391–408.
Larson, J.R., Jr, Lingle, J.H., and Scerbo, M.M. (1984) The impact of performance cues on leader–behavior ratings: The role of selective information availability and probabilistic response bias. *Organizational Behavior and Human Performance*, **33**, 323–349.
London, M., and Poplawski, J.R. (1976) Effects of information on stereotype development in performance appraisal and interview contexts. *Journal of Applied Psychology*, **61**, 199–205.
Longenecker, C.O., Gioia, D.A., and Sims, H.P., Jr (1987) Behind the mask: The politics of employee appraisal. *Academy of Management Executive*, **1**, 183–193.
Lord, R.G. (1985) An information processing approach to social perceptions, leadership and behavioral measurement in organizations. In B.M. Staw and L.L. Cummings (eds), *Research in Organizational Behavior*, Vol. 7. Greenwich, CT: JAI Press.
Lord, R.G., and Alliger, G.M. (1985) A comparison of four information processing models of leadership and social perception. *Human Relations*, **38**, 47–65.
Lord, R.G., Binning, J.F., Rush, M.C., and Thomas, J.C. (1978) The effect of performance cues and leader behavior on questionnaire ratings of leadership behavior. *Organizational Behavior and Human Performance*, **21**, 27–39.

Lord, R.G., and Carpenter, M. (1986) Measuring cognitive processes. Paper presented at the Academy of Management Convention, Chicago, IL.

Lord, R.G., Foti, R.J., and DeVader, C.L. (1984) A test of leadership categorization theory: Internal structure, information processing, and leadership perceptions. *Organizational Behavior and Human Performance*, 34, 343–378.

Lord, R.G., Foti, R.J., and Phillips, J.S. (1982) A theory of leadership categorization. In J.G. Hunt, U. Sekaran, and C. Schriesheim (eds), *Beyond Establishment Views*. Carbondale: Southern Illinois University Press, pp. 104–121.

Lord, R.G., and Hanges, P.J. (1987) A control system model of organizational motivation: Theoretical development and applied implications. *Behavioral Science*, 32, 161–178.

Lord, R.G., and Kernan, M.C. (1987) Scripts as determinants of purposeful behavior in organizations. *Academy of Management Review*, 12, 265–277.

Lord, R.G., and Maher, K.J. (1988) Alternative information processing models and their implications for theory, research, and practice. Manuscript submitted for publication.

Lord, R.G., and Maher, K.J. (1989) Perceptions of leadership and their implications in organizations. In J. Carroll (ed.), *Applied Social Psychology in Business Organizations*, Hillsdale, NJ: Erlbaum.

Lord, R.G., and Smith, J.E. (1983) Theoretical, information processing, and situational factors affecting attribution theory models of organizational behavior. *Academy of Management Review*, 8, 50–60.

Manz, C.C., and Sims, H.P., Jr (1987) Leading workers to lead themselves: The external leadership of self-managing work teams. *Administrative Science Quarterly*, 32, 106–128.

March, J.G., and Simon, H.A. (1958) *Organizations*. New York: Wiley.

Martinko, M.J., and Gardner, W.L. (1987) The leader/member attribution process. *Academy of Management Review*, 12, 235–249.

McAllister, D.W., Mitchell, T.R., and Beach, L.R. (1979) The contingency model for the selection of decision strategies: An empirical test of the effects of significance, accountability, and reversibility. *Organizational Behavior and Human Performance*, 24 228–244.

McCain, B.E. (1986) Continuing investment under conditions of failure: A laboratory study of the limits to escalation. *Journal of Applied Psychology*, 71, 280–284.

McElroy, J.C. (1982) A typology of attribution leadership research. *Academy of Management Review*, 7, 413–417.

McElroy, J.C., and Downey, H.K. (1982) Observation in organizational research: Panacea to the performance-attribution effect? *Academy of Management Journal*, 25, 822–835.

McIntyre, R.M., Smith, D.E., and Hassett, C.E. (1984) Accuracy of performance ratings as affected by rater training and perceived purpose of rating. *Journal of Applied Psychology*, 69, 147–156.

Mervis, C.B., and Rosch, E. (1981) Categorization of natural objects. In M. R. Rosenzweig and L.W. Porter (eds), *Annual Review of Psychology*, Vol. 32. Palo Alto, CA: Annual Reviews, Inc., pp. 89–115.

Mintzberg, H., Raisinghani, D., and Theoret, A. (1976) The structure of unstructured decision processes. *Administrative Science Quarterly*, 21 246–275.

Mitchell, T.R., and Kalb, L.S. (1981) Effects of outcome knowledge and outcome valence on supervisors' evaluations. *Journal of Applied Psychology*, 66, 604–612.

Mitchell, T.R., and Kalb, L.S. (1982) Effects of job experience on supervisor attributions for a subordinate's poor performance. *Journal of Applied Psychology*, **67**, 181–188.

Mitchell, T.R., Larson, J.R., Jr. and Green, S.G. (1977) Leader behavior, situational moderators, and group performance: An attributional analysis. *Organizational Behavior and Human Performance*, **18**, 254–268.

Mitchell, T.R., and Wood, R.E. (1980) Supervisors' responses to subordinate poor performance: A test of an attributional model. *Organizational Behavior and Human Performance*, **25**, 123–138.

Mount, M.K., and Thompson, D.E. (1987) Cognitive categorization and quality of performance ratings. *Journal of Applied Psychology*, **72**, 240–246.

Murphy, K.R., and Balzer, W.K. (1986) Systematic distortions in memory-based behavior ratings and performance evaluations: Consequences for rating accuracy. *Journal of Applied Psychology*, **71**, 39–44.

Murphy, K.R., Balzer, W.K., Lockhart, M.C., and Eisenman, E.J. (1985) Effects of previous performance on evaluations of present performance. *Journal of Applied Psychology*, **70**, 72–84.

Murphy, K.R., and Constans, J.I. (1987) Behavioral anchors as a source of bias in rating. *Journal of Applied Psychology*, **72**, 573–577.

Murphy, K.R., Gannett, B.A., Herr, B.M., and Chen, J.A. (1986) Effects of subsequent performance on evaluations of previous performance. *Journal of Applied Psychology*, **71**, 427–431.

Murphy, K.R., Garcia, M., Kerkar, S., Martin, C., and Balzer, W.K. (1982) Relationship between observational accuracy and accuracy in evaluating performance. *Journal of Applied Psychology*, **67**, 320–325.

Murphy, K.R., Martin, C., and Garcia, M. (1982) Do behavioral observation scales measure observation? *Journal of Applied Psychology*, **67**, 562–567.

Murphy, K.R., Philbin, T.A., and Adams, S.R. (in press) Effect of purpose of observation on accuracy of immediate and delayed performance ratings. *Organizational Behavior and Human Decision Processes*.

Napier, N.K., and Latham, G.P. (1986) Outcome expectancies of people who conduct performance appraisals. *Personnel Psychology*, **39**, 827–837.

Nathan, B.R., and Alexander, R.A. (1985) The role of inferential accuracy in performance rating. *Academy of Management Review*, **10**, 109–115.

Nathan, B.R., and Lord, R.G. (1983) Cognitive categorization and dimensional schemata: A process approach to the study of halo in performance ratings. *Journal of Applied Psychology*, **68**, 102–114.

Nutt, P.C. (1984) Types of organizational decision processes. *Administrative Science Quarterly*, **29**, 414–450.

O'Connor, E., and Barrett, G.V. (1980) Information cues and individual differences as determinants of subjective perceptions of task environments. *Academy of Management Journal*, **23**, 697–716.

O'Reilly, C.A. (1983) The use of information in organizational decision making: A model and some propositions. In B.M. Staw and L.L. Cummings (eds), *Research in Organizational Behavior*, Vol. 5. Greenwich, CT: JAI Press.

O'Reilly, C.A., and Caldwell, D.F. (1979) Information influence as a determinant of perceived task characteristics and job satisfaction. *Journal of Applied Psychology*, **64**, 157–165.

O'Reilly, C.A., and Caldwell, D.F. (1985) The impact of normative social influence and cohesiveness on task perceptions and attitudes: A social information processing approach. *Journal of Occupational Psychology*, **58**, 193–206.

O'Reilly, C.A., Parlette, G.N., and Bloom, J.R. (1980) Perceptual measures of task

characteristics: The biasing effects of differing frames of reference and job attitudes. *Academy of Management Journal*, **23**, 118–131.
Payne, J.W. (1982) Contingent decision behavior. *Psychological Bulletin*, **92**, 382–402.
Pfeffer, J. (1977) The ambiguity of leadership. *Academy of Management Review*, **2**, 104–112.
Phillips, J.S. (1984) The accuracy of leadership ratings: A cognitive categorization perspective. *Organizational Behavior and Human Performance*, **33**, 125–138.
Phillips, J.S., and Lord, R.G. (1981) Causal attributions and perceptions of leadership. *Organizational Behavior and Human Performance*, **28**, 143–163.
Phillips, J.S., and Lord, R.G. (1982) Schematic information processing and perceptions of leadership in problem-solving groups. *Journal of Applied Psychology*, **67**, 486–492.
Podsakoff, P.M. (1982) Determinants of a supervisor's use of rewards and punishments: A literature review and suggestions for further research. *Organizational Behavior and Human Performance*, **29**, 58–83.
Pound, W. (1969) The process of problem finding. *Industrial Management Review*, **11**, 1–19.
Powers, W.T. (1973) Feedback: Beyond behaviorism. *Science*, **179**, 351–356.
Pulakos, E.D. (1984) A comparison of rater training programs: Error training and accuracy training. *Journal of Applied Psychology*, **69**, 581–588.
Pulakos, E.D., and Wexley, K.N. (1983) The relationship among perceptual similarity, sex, and performance ratings in manager–subordinate dyads. *Academy of Management Journal*, **26**, 129–139.
Read, S.J. (1987) Constructing causal scenarios: A knowledge structure approach to causal reasoning. *Journal of Personality and Social Psychology*, **52**, 288–302.
Rosch, E. (1978) Principles of categorization. In E. Rosch and B.B. Lloyd (eds), *Cognition and Categorization*. Hillsdale, NJ: Erlbaum.
Ross, J., and Staw, B.M. (1986) Expo 86: An escalation prototype. *Administrative Science Quarterly*, **31**, 274–297.
Rush, M.C., and Beauvais, L.L. (1981) A critical analysis of format-induced versus subject-induced bias in leadership ratings. *Journal of Applied Psychology*, **66**, 722–727.
Rush, M.C., Phillips, J.S., and Lord, R.G. (1981) Effects of a temporal delay in rating on leader behavior descriptions: A laboratory investigation. *Journal of Applied Psychology*, **66**, 442–450.
Rush, M.C., Thomas, J.C., and Lord, R.G. (1977) Implicit leadership theory: A potential threat to the internal validity of leader behavior questionnaires. *Organizational Behavior and Human Performance*, **20**, 93–110.
Salancik, G.R., and Pfeffer, J. (1978) A social information processing approach to job attitudes and task design. *Administrative Science Quarterly*, **23**, 224–253.
Sapienza, A.M. (1987) Imagery and strategy. *Journal of Management*, **13**, 543–555.
Shaw, J.B. (1980) An information processing approach to the study of job design. *Academy of Management Review*, **5**, 41–48.
Srull, T.K. (1984) Methodological techniques for the study of person memory and social cognition. In R.S. Wyer and T.K. Srull (eds), *Handbook of Social Cognition*, Vol. 2. Hillsdale, NJ: Erlbaum, pp. 1–72.
Staw, B.M. (1975) Attribution of the 'causes' of performance: A general alternative interpretation of cross-sectional research on organizations. *Organizational Behavior and Human Performance*, **13**, 414–432.
Staw, B.M. (1976) Knee deep in the big muddy: A study of escalating commitment to a chosen course of action. *Organizational Behavior and Human Performance*, **16**, 27–44.
Staw, B.M. (1980) Rationality and justification in organizational life. In B.M. Staw and

L.L. Cummings (eds), *Research in Organizational Behavior*, Vol. 2. Greenwich, CT; JAI Press, pp. 45–80.
Staw, B.M. (1981) The escalation of commitment to a course of action. *Academy of Management Review*, **6**, 577–588.
Stewart, I.N., and Peregoy, P.L. (1983) Catastrophe theory modeling in psychology. *Psychological Bulletin*, **94**, 336–362.
Streufert, S. (1989) Cognitive style and complexity: Implications for I/O psychology. In C.L. Cooper and I.T. Robertson (eds), *International Review of Industrial and Organizational Psychology*, Vol. 4. London: Wiley.
Taylor, M.S., Fisher, C.D., and Ilgen, D.R. (1984) Individuals' reactions to performance feedback in organizations: A control theory perspective. In K.M. Rowland and G.R. Ferris (eds), *Research in Personnel and Human Resources Management*, Vol. 2. Greenwich, CT: JAI, pp. 81–124.
Thomas, J.G. (1986) Sources of social information: A longitudinal analysis. *Human Relations*, **39**, 855–870.
Thomas, J.G., and Griffin, R. (1983) The social information processing model of task design: A review of the literature. *Academy of Management Review*, **8**, 672–682.
Tsui, A.S., and Barry, B. (1986) Interpersonal affect and rating errors. *Academy of Management Journal*, **29**, 586–598.
Tversky, A., and Kahneman, D. (1974) Judgment under uncertainty: Heuristics and biases. *Science*, **185**, 1124–1131.
Tversky, A., and Kahneman, D. (1981) The framing of decisions and the rationality of choice. *Science*, **211**, 453–458.
Ungson, G.R., Braunstein, D.N., and Hall, P.D. (1981) Managerial information processing. *Administrative Science Quarterly*, **26**, 116–134.
Vance, R.J., and Biddle, T.F. (1985) Task experience and social cues: Interactive effects on attributional reactions. Organizational Behavior and Human Decision Processes, **35**, 252–265.
Waller, W.S., and Mitchell, T.R. (1984) The effects of context on the selection of decision strategies for the cost variance investigation problem. *Organizational Behavior and Human Performance*, **33**, 397–413.
Weiss, H.E., and Shaw, J.B. (1979) Social influence on judgments about tasks. *Organizational Behavior and Human Performance*, **24**, 126–140.
Weiss, H.M., and Adler, S. (1981) Cognitive complexity and the structure of implicit leadership theories. *Journal of Applied Psychology*, **66**, 69–78.
White, H.M., and Mitchell, T.R. (1979) Job enrichment versus social cues: A comparison and competitive test. *Journal of Applied Psychology*, **64**, 1–9.
White, S.E., Mitchell, T.R., and Bell, C.H., Jr (1977) Goal setting, evaluation apprehension, and social cues as determinants of job performance and job satisfaction in a simulated organization. *Journal of Applied Psychology*, **62**, 665–673.
Whyte, G. (1986) Escalating commitment to a course of action: A reinterpretation. *Academy of Management Review*, **11**, 311–321.
Williams, K.J., DeNisi, A.S., Blencoe, A.G., and Cafferty, T.P. (1985) The role of appraisal purpose: Effects of purpose on information acquisition and utilization. *Organizational Behavior and Human Decision Processes*, **35** 314–339.
Williams, K.J., DeNisi, A.S., Meglino, B.M., and Cafferty, T.P. (1986) Initial decisions and subsequent performance ratings. *Journal of Applied Psychology*, **71**, 189–195.
Wood, R.E., and Mitchell, T.R. (1981) Manager behavior in a social context: The impact of impression management on attributions and disciplinary actions. *Organizational Behavior and Human Performance*, **28**, 356–378.

Chapter 4

COGNITIVE STYLE AND COMPLEXITY: IMPLICATIONS FOR I/O PSYCHOLOGY

Siegfried Streufert
and
Glenda Y. Nogami
*The Pennsylvania State University College of Medicine
USA*

WHERE DO STYLE AND COMPLEXITY FIT INTO I/O PSYCHOLOGY?

Industrial/organizational psychologists must be concerned with the appropriateness of employee actions. For example, we would want to know whether employees on an assembly line handle all (required) activities correctly. We would want to know whether managerial decisions are likely to have the desired outcome. Most often, we assume that knowledge of, or familiarity with, demands of the job, whether gained through training, experience or some other means, are decisive in the selection of 'correct' or 'appropriate' actions.

Organizations may fail where too many faulty actions and decisions prevail. As a result, much theory and research in I/O psychology has been concerned with creating, enhancing or maintaining the 'appropriate' knowledge base of employees. To improve performance, we have delved into the content of employee perceptions. We have explored their attitudes and their motivations and have prescribed, counted, and evaluated their actions. We endeavor to assess whether potential new employees possess the appropriate knowledge base. We train them to externally defined criteria. We monitor whether actions are sufficiently correct to ensure the organization's success.

In assembly line operations, such an approach may work adequately. Unfortunately, it may not work as well as an employee rises through the organization. With increasing and more varied job demands, it is not always possible to discern what a 'correct' action or decision might be. Uncertainty, insufficient information and fluidity of many task environments can interfere with the identification of single 'correct' responses. Even where tasks are relatively simple, people who recently responded 'appropriately' to demands may suddenly respond differently or unreliably. Worst of all, actions or responses that were appropriate yesterday may turn out to be inappropriate tomorrow.

The problem is especially severe at advanced levels, e.g. in many management positions. Very few meaningful differences in level of training, intelligence and experience exist for most senior executives. Yet, some continue to do well in assignment after assignment or in job after job while others fail when transferred or when task situations change drastically. What is the basis of these differences? Are there some consistent characteristics of individuals which hold across task and settings: differences that distinguish between those who are and those who are not likely to succeed?

Individual difference variables that govern a person's response to a variety of different tasks, that result in consistent types of action despite diverse situational demands, must be relatively independent of *content*, i.e. independent of task-specific variables. For example, such consistent individual differences would not relate directly to concerns with the 'accuracy' of specific responses to a particular setting. Rather, these variables must reflect stable cognitive and action tendencies that are applied across tasks. Rather than attitudes, specific knowledge or practiced skills which a person might apply to some given job, these 'personality' variables must reflect a characteristic style which an individual might employ across tasks and settings. They are variables which control how a person *in general* perceives, processes, and organizes information and how that person would act (e.g. Messick, 1976; Witkin, Oltman, Raskin, and Karp, 1971). In contrast to cognitive content, such pervasive personality variables are considered to be aspects of *cognitive structure*. Individual differences on variables included in the structure family have often been identified with *cognitive styles* or with *cognitive complexity*. In subsequent sections of this review, we will use the term structure when we wish to identify cognitive styles and cognitive complexity within the same category.

ORIENTATION OF THIS REVIEW

This chapter explores *individual differences* in cognitive styles and in cognitive complexity. We will not dwell on the overall impact of cognition on human functioning in organizations. Without question, that topic is of importance. Chapter 3 by Lord and Maher in the present volume explores that topic. The present chapter is limited to a concern with structural differences among individuals and with the effect of these differences upon human functioning in the I/O context.

The scientific literature concerned with styles and complexity is extensive. Much of it is not or is only tangentially related to I/O psychology. Consequently, not all efforts related to styles and complexity will be reviewed. We have ignored work focused on mental illness, on the development of both styles and complexity in children, the application of instructional styles (except where relevant to training procedures in I/O settings) and similar areas of theory and research. On the other hand, research by theorists and researchers from personality, social psychology, political science and other sciences has been included where relevance to the I/O context appeared evident. We have chosen to emphasize primarily, but not exclusively, research data collected during the last decade.

COGNITIVE STYLE

Styles, Controls, and Abilities

Messick (1984) provided an excellent review of the diverse conceptualizations of cognitive styles and their relationships to cognitive controls, stylistic abilities and abilities *per se*. His recent review is, in some part, based on his own earlier statements (e.g. 1978) and on prior reviews of Gardner (1962) and Gardner, Jackson, and Messick (1960). While a complete recapitulation of Messick's views would require too much space, we will provide a short summary. Messick views 'cognitive styles' as characteristic *consistencies* of information processing. Styles tend to have opposing extremes, each of which may have its own value in some specific situation. Styles, according to Messick, function in pervasive ways: they are applied across a wide range of situations and tasks and are not subject to easy modification. They tend to function as controlling mechanisms of attention, impulse, thought, and action *across diverse areas* (cf. also Gardner *et al.*, 1959; Gardner, Jackson, and Messick, 1960; Messick, 1972, 1973; Klein, 1958, 1970). Messick (1982) would include cognitive complexity in the style category. Somewhat related views have been expressed by Kogan (1973) and Santostefano (1978).

Styles may be distinguished from other aspects of cognitive functioning that affect human behavior in I/O settings, e.g. abilities and cognitive controls. 'Abilities' refer to the mastery of content, e.g. the *level* of cognition. Abilities are task specific. They are 'enabling' variables, facilitating task performance within some specific area. Styles, in contrast, cut across abilities. There can be a zero level on an ability scale, yet the opposing endpoint of that scale defies precise specification. Ability scales measure a *single* phenomenon which occurs at various levels. Positive value is associated with only one end of the scale. If a maximum endpoint on an ability scale could be defined, it would only reflect a different *level* (not a different kind) of cognition when compared to the zero point. In the case of styles, however, both endpoints may be equally valued, but in different situations. For example, the field independent person is considered more analytic; the field dependent person more socially sensitive — each has its unique value.

According to Messick, 'cognitive controls' (a concept initially introduced by Klein, 1954) represent a mixed breed. Controls reflect consistent functioning across some tasks or situations. To that extent they are similar to styles. However, controls typically do not have opposing endpoints with disparate value. Further, they are more likely *domain* specific: they affect some aspect of our experience, thought, and action but would leave other (unrelated) aspects (domains) untouched. As a result (and despite their name), they do not control thinking and behavior as pervasively as do styles. In this latter respect, they hold some similarity to ability.

Messick's views, while often accepted as the standard in the realm of cognitive styles, are certainly not without detractors or without alternatives proposed by other theorists. Kogan (1976), for example, provides a different categorization of styles versus abilities and Goldstein and Blackman (1978b) consider many of the earlier style concepts under the rubric of cognitive controls.

Unambiguous definitions of the concepts 'style' and 'control' were possible when the number of proposed styles were limited and applications of the style concept to complex human functioning (e.g. in organizations) was of little interest. Most early style concepts were simply concerned with modes of perception. A host of additional structural characteristics have since been proposed, including many new 'styles' and 'controls'. For example, Messick in his 1970 review listed nine styles (with cognitive complexity included) but refers to nineteen style categories by 1976. Likely, that author excluded yet many others that had been suggested prior to that time. Several additional styles that have been proposed since (e.g. Kirton's, 1976, adaptor v. innovator distinction) are directly relevant to this field. Unfortunately, many of the newcomers are less easily characterized as styles, controls or abilities. Messick points out that some supposed styles fall into categories where there is considerable overlap. In the view of the present authors, that overlap is, in part, due to diverse conceptualizations of 'style' by different authors and, in part, due to an actual blurring among the various segments of cognitive structure. The components of human cognitive functioning are not as differentiated as some psychologists (who happen to be blessed with a highly analytic, i.e. field independent style) might like.

In effect, individuals may, under some circumstances, combine some styles or some aspects of available styles, controls, and abilities (intentionally or unintentionally) to provide a unique and, at times, temporary framework for perception, cognition, and performance. Several writers have already recognized the adaptive 'cognitive strategy' which is involved. For example, Pask (1976) speaks of 'versatile' learners and Hudson (1966) discusses intellectual 'labiles'. Entwistle (1982) sees considerable advantages in such adaptive capabilities, described as 'systematic alternation of complementary stylistic functioning', similar to the 'bicognitive' terminology of Ramirez and Castaneda

(1974). Such adaptive combinations of styles and levels of styles would most likely be task, situation or environment specific.

Nonetheless, the reliable application of a person's particular style can also have considerable task relevant value: where a person reliably engages in the same task, a particular static level on a stylistic (bipolar) dimension might be desirable. For example, the social sensitivity of a field dependent person would aid an employee who has been assigned to a job that primarily requires a socio-emotional leader. Where task assignments are relatively fixed, we might find specific levels of ability as well as specific levels on some stylistic dimensions that jointly (assuming motivation, etc., is given) optimize performance (e.g. Federico and Landis, 1979). On the other hand, where task demands are complex, multifaceted and fluid, a successful employee should possess a number of abilities and may have to apply *varied* stylistic orientations in a flexible adaptive fashion. Conventional theory which views styles as pervasive and necessarily consistent across areas of cognitive functioning would tend to deny that such a flexible use of an individual's style is possible. The present review would place that assumption in doubt.

How Many Styles?

Lack of clarity among the distinctions between styles, controls and, to some extent, abilities (cf. Kagan and Kogan, 1970), amplified by the discrepant views of various writers (e.g. Messick, 1984, v. Goldstein and Blackman, 1978a), have given rise to claimed style status for a wide variety of constructs. Some of them overlap; others have found their way into well-known measurement techniques employed in I/O psychology (e.g. in the Myers–Briggs instrument). Still others have been proposed and have generated neither research nor many proponents. By necessity, we will have to limit our review to some of those concepts of style that have been relatively widely accepted.

Initially, styles were seen as organizers of perception, the way an individual filters and processes stimuli to generate meaning from the environment (Harvey, 1963) or as learned strategies, programs or transformations that translate objective stimuli into meaningful dimensions (Bieri, 1971). Such processes would allude to styles such as field dependence/independence (Witkin *et al.*, 1962), impulsivity/reflection (Kagan *et al.*, 1964), levelling/sharpening (Gardner *et al.*, 1959), constricted/flexible control (Gardner *et al.*, 1959), breadth of categorization (Pettigrew, 1958), focusing/scanning (Gardner and Long, 1962a, 1962b), tolerance for unrealistic experiences (Gardner *et al.*, 1959), and conceptual orientation (or differentiation; Gardner, 1953). Even early versions of cognitive complexity with their perceptual social orientation could be (and were, by some writers) classified as styles. These early styles were not only perceptual in their focus, they also fulfilled the demand of assigning different characteristics and values to the two ends of the stylistic dimension.

Later additions to the style category, often for good reason ignored by those who wish to maintain the 'purity' of the style concept, have varied widely. The restriction to perception was given up rather early. Distinctions between cognitive styles and controls have also been ignored, resulting in the addition of concepts such as 'dogmatism' (Rokeach, 1960). Dogmatism functions as a perceptual filter that tends to eliminate incongruent information. The resulting 'closed mindedness' may restrict an employee's capacity to adapt or absorb changes in information patterns (Chandrasekaran and Kirs, 1986) and may generate extremity of judgement (Malhotra, Jain, and Pinson, 1983). Without question, closed mindedness would be detrimental to performance in organizations that are functioning in complex and fluid environments. Nonetheless, at least some writers would wish to eliminate dogmatism from any list of styles: Rokeach's concept of dogmatism assigns clear 'value' to the absence of dogmatic thinking, i.e. to only one end of the dimension.

Another 'style' that has gained considerable popularity during the last decade is 'Type A', a description of the coronary prone behavior pattern (e.g. Friedman and Rosenman, 1974; Rosenman, 1978). The Type A person is viewed as an individual who tends to be hostile, sets unrealistic deadlines, is time urgent and so forth. While that style is supposedly pervasive, it does not become evident in the absence of social challenge. In other words, it is restricted to a specific subset of (competitive) settings. To some extent (at least in females), the Type A style may be reflected in the impulsivity component of the reflective–impulsive style (Blumenthal, McKee, Williams, and Haney, 1981).

A number of other concepts frequently employed in I/O psychology have also been identified with style, e.g. the sensing — intuition and the thinking — feeling scales of the Myers–Briggs assessment (Schweiger, 1985). Even Fiedler's (1964) Least Preferred Co-worker (LPC) approach has sometimes been considered as a style. However, as was the case with dogmatism, its negative valence on one end of the dimension places it into the doubtful category.

Measurement

Each style concept does, of course, have an associated measurement technique. In some cases, two or three quite discrepant measures may be used. For example, field dependence/independence is assessed with the Room Adjustment Test and the Rod and Frame Test, both evaluating three-dimensional physical perception against expectations, and with the two-dimensional Embedded Figures Test where subjects seek to discover figures hidden in a complex set of lines.

Too many measures of too many styles have been proposed to describe and evaluate all of them in this chapter. Prior reviews of style have done an excellent job by considering both measurement techniques and shortcomings associated with at least the most important (or most frequently researched) cognitive styles. The interested reader is especially referred to Goldstein and Blackman (1978b), Messick (1981), Robey and Taggart (1981), and Schweiger (1983). The latter two papers include considerations of two measures of management styles that are not discussed in this paper (Huysmans, 1970; Keen, 1973).

We will briefly consider some of the characteristics of three style measures that have produced more research data than any of the others: field dependence/independence, reflection/impulsivity, and scales from the partially stylistic Myers–Briggs Type Indicator.

Use of the Rod and Frame Test for field dependence/independence is, to say the least, cumbersome. Consequently, most researchers have employed the Embedded Figures Test (EFT) (Witkin *et al.*, 1971), typically in its group administration format. The test consists of geometric figures in which other figures are 'hidden'. It is the subjects' task to find as many of the hidden figures as possible. Scoring is based on figures identified and time to identification. Field independent persons find it easier to separate figures from ground.

Reliability and validity of the EFT is viewed favorably by some authors (Witkin *et al.*, 1971) but has been questioned by others (e.g. Guilford, 1980; Kogan, 1976). The most serious concern focuses on validity. Questions have been raised whether the Embedded Figures Test is able to measure cognitive style in its true sense (cf. the comments of Guilford, 1980; Kogan, 1976; Widiger, Knudson, and Rorer, 1980). Worse, the test probably assesses, at least in part, some component of ability rather than style (cf. Schweiger, 1983). For example, Widiger *et al.* (1980) found that the measure loads highly on an ability factor (together with other measures of ability) but does not converge with other measures of style. The problem will become evident to the reader in the following section: several researchers have obtained significant correlations of the Embedded Figures Test with measures of ability, especially measures of general intelligence. In other words, interpretations of field dependence/independence data requires some caution. Any use of the measure to predict variables of interest to I/O psychologists should be preceded by the question whether the same (or better) predictions might be possible through the use of pure measures of ability.

Reflection/impulsivity has been previously reviewed by Messer (1976). It is generally assessed with the Matching Familiar Figures Test (MFFT; Kagan *et al.*, 1964). A number of figures are presented. The respondent has to select one that is exactly identical to a standard. Dissimilarities, where present, tend to be small and may involve considerable detail; in other words, the task is difficult. Rapid selection of one of the alternatives without careful study of the detail may produce error. The test is concerned with the assessment of consistencies in speed and accuracy with which alternative hypotheses are formulated and information is processed. Impulsive individuals tend to choose the first answer that occurs to them; reflective individuals often ponder various possibilities before reaching any conclusion. Impulsive responses may be valued for their speed but are potentially inaccurate. Reflective responses may be slow but are more likely accurate since they are based on the detailed consideration of multiple alternatives.

MFFT reliability scores for speed are excellent. Reliability for errors tends to be moderate. Moreover, error scores tend to correlate with intelligence at levels approaching error score reliability. None the less, the error score is often used in addition to the latency score since it allows researchers to distinguish among persons who are error-prone quick responders and others who maintain relative accuracy despite higher response speed (cf. Messer, 1976). Further, reflection is not entirely independent of field independence. The MFFT may share some of the same ability components that affect performance on the EFT.

The Myers–Briggs (MBTI) measure (Myers, 1962) employs the Jungian concepts of sensation, thinking, intuition, and feeling (in addition to others) which have at times been viewed as stylistic (pervasive) concepts. The measure uses a forced choice format which requires respondents to indicate their style of functioning. By pairing the various style combinations with each other, a typology is obtained. Some research has successfully matched managers' styles with their preferences and/or behaviors (e.g. Henderson and Nutt, 1980; Behling, Gifford, and Tolliver, 1980). The quality of reliability and validity of the measure has received somewhat mixed reviews (e.g. Carlyn, 1977; Coan, 1978; Mendelsohn, 1970; Sundberg, 1970).

Research Data

While considerable research has been reported in the literature, the implications of the accumulated results in general and for I/O psychology specifically are still restricted. First of all, the vast majority of research has focused on a single style: field dependence versus independence. Some additional (but less extensive) data are available on reflection versus impulsivity. Beyond these two points of focus, however, information on the impact of styles begins to be rather limited. A second problem is due to the proliferation of style concepts: a number of efforts with potential relevance to I/O psychology have introduced style concepts that are limited to the interest of a single author and, in addition, may be poorly defined. Where sufficient information is available, the research is discussed in separate sections below.

Perception

With the origin of style theory firmly rooted in perception, it is not surprising that differences in cognitive styles are related to a wide range of perceptual characteristics, varying, for example, from diverse views of business environments (Wolfe and Chacko, 1980) to color discrimination (Fine, 1983; Fine and Kobrick, 1980). Generally, field independent individuals perceive their environments more correctly (or appropriately) than their field dependent counterparts (e.g. Sarmany, 1979). Even though it is usually argued that field dependent people depend more on environmental cues (e.g. Goodenough, Cox, Sigman, and Strawderman, 1985), their external orientation does not aid the development of a more accurate cognitive representation of the environment. Internal cues, especially those stored prior to information receipt, appear to be of considerable importance in generating more veritable impressions of the physical and the social task environment.

Interpersonal functioning

It has been repeatedly argued that field dependent persons are more self-disclosing and more socially sensitive to another person. Research data generally confirm that notion, especially where the other person is present or is at least visually represented (Sahoo, 1982). These findings hold even in non-verbal communication settings (Sabatelli, Dreyer, and Buck, 1979). In contrast, communication in the absence of the other person is handled more effectively by field independent individuals. The reason for the discrepancy in these findings may be due to greater 'social intelligence' of field independent persons, contrasted with greater 'social orientation' of their field dependent counterparts (Erez, 1980). As a consequence, modes of social interaction as well as leadership styles of field dependent and independent persons may differ widely. Erez, for example, has argued that an employee centered leadership style would be associated with field independence and a *cognitive* social orientation.

Acceptance of a leader's views and/or recommendations may also be controlled by the employee's style. While some research has not shown any relationship between field dependence/independence and persuasability (Imam, 1986), other data (e.g. Heesacker, Petty, and Cacioppo, 1983) suggest that field dependent persons are greatly influenced by the credibility of a source, even when that source is presenting counter-attitudinal arguments. In contrast, field independent persons tend to respond to the quality of arguments *per se* (cf. also Weiss and Nowicki, 1981). In the absence of a highly credible source, field dependent individuals are more resistant to attitude change (Davies, 1985), i.e. show some tendencies reminiscent of dogmatism (cf. Chandrasekaran and Kirs, 1986).

In contrast to the 'employee centered' leadership style of field independent persons, Erez (1980) suggested that a 'job centered' leadership style reflects field dependence, lower social intelligence but considerable sensitivity to environmental demands. Some data would indeed suggest that greater social sensitivity (social orientation) of field dependent persons (e.g. competitiveness of the task setting) will specifically impact on their task relevant behavior (Bolocofsky, 1980).

Data obtained with the Myers–Briggs inventory indicate that higher employee scores on the sensing/intuition components of that inventory predict better supervisor ratings and greater supervisor satisfaction with employee performance (Handley, 1982). Considerable research has pointed to several advantages of personality and/or attitudinal similarity (e.g. Byrne, 1971) for both interpersonal relationships and task group performance. Several researchers have explored the effects of similarity in cognitive style. Their findings suggest that stylistic similarities can generate greater satisfaction (e.g. Renninger and Snyder, 1983), better performance (e.g. McDonald, 1984) and less effort and time to completion of a task (e.g. Frank and Davis, 1982).

Task performance

Prior reviews have indicated that field independence and reflective (rather than impulsive) cognitive styles tend to generate better performance across a range of settings (e.g. Blackman and Goldstein, 1982). While some research, often relevant to specific task settings, has failed to support that conclusion (e.g. Avolio, Kroeck and Panek, 1985, with traffic accidents and Wolfe and Chacko, 1980, with business game performance), most researchers report significant differences. For example, field independent individuals excel in academic performance (Leino and Puurula, 1983), foreign language skills (Hansen and Stansfield, 1982), efficient handling of reports (Lusk and Kersnick, 1979), tracking tasks (Marincola and Long, 1985), speed of task completion (Debiasio, 1986; Frank and Noble, 1984), diagnostic troubleshooting (Moran, 1986), and a variety of other activities that require cognitive effort. Moreover, field independent persons find it easier to organize disorganized task settings. They tend to view difficult tasks as simpler and complete them sooner than their field dependent counterparts (Frank and Noble, 1984). In addition, field independent individuals (especially if they are also tolerant of ambiguity) are more confident in actions they have taken or in decisions they have made (e.g. Gul, 1984; Gul and Zaid, 1981).

Task performance has also been studied on the basis of the impulsive/reflective style. Most of the data tend to favor reflection. For example, reflectives made fewer errors in simulated diagnostic tasks (Rouse and Rouse, 1982), and in a judgement setting (Schwabisch and Drury, 1984) and did better on conditional reasoning tasks (Overton, Byrnes, and O'Brien, 1985). However, they take more time to complete their tasks because more alternatives are considered and evaluated (Kendall, Hooke, Rymer, and Finch, 1980). While both field dependence/independence and impulsivity/reflection differences are predictive of performance, styles assessed by Myers–Briggs scores may not relate to performance differences (Zmud, 1979) or may produce only limited effects (e.g. differences in risk perception; Henderson and Nutt, 1980).

Training and learning

Prior reviews of cognitive styles and training or learning (e.g. Davis and Frank, 1979; Kogan, 1980) again point to the superiority of field independent learners. It is often assumed that their higher levels of performance are generated by an ability to conduct 'combinatorial analysis'. As workload increases, differences between persons identified by the two ends of this dimension become more pronounced (cf. Davis and Frank, 1979).

Findings that failed to obtain differences between field dependent versus independent learners or trainees tend to be rare (e.g. Mueller and Fisher, 1980). The majority of results point towards greater trainability of field independent persons and, in some cases, identify the basis of the enhanced capacity to absorb new and potentially incongruent or unexpected information. For example, field independent persons appear to take better notes and organize new material better, resulting in higher levels of post-training recall (e.g. Frank, 1984). In contrast, field dependent persons do well when structure is already (externally) provided (Kiewra and Frank, 1986). More effective post-training recall and recognition by field independent individuals extends to a variety of learning/training tasks and settings such as computer based instruction (Roberts and Park, 1984), acquisition of gross motor skills — for males only (Swinnen, Vandenberghe, and VanAssche, 1986), memory for written material (Adejumo, 1983), recall of categories within learned material (Reardon, Jolly, McKinney, and Forducey, 1982) and even memory of non-verbal and non-visual material (Walker, O'Leary, Chaney, and Fauria, 1979). Some writers have suggested that these differences are indicative of active (field independent) versus passive (field dependent) learning styles. A consideration of data in the literature would place some doubt upon such an assumption. More likely, the divergent results may reflect differences in the capacity to organize and reorganize cognitive space.

Learning and training have also been investigated with other styles, especially reflection versus impulsivity. While some authors (e.g. Swinnen *et al.*, 1986) obtained no differences, most data have tended to favor reflective functioning (Overton *et al.*, 1985). More isolated research on focusing/scanning points to scanning as more useful in learning and training environments (Meredith, 1985).

Creativity

While the available paper-and-pencil measurement techniques for assessing creativity leave much to be desired, they may at least provide us with some estimate of the creative potential of individuals. A variety of creativity tests (or subtests) have identified the field independent person as more creative (e.g.

Chadha, 1985; Noppe, 1985). Such results survive even where the research controls for the impact of intelligence (Gundlach and Gesell, 1979).

Intelligence

The repeated superiority of field independent (and to some extent reflective) individuals suggests contributions of ability to the effect of a pure style, for example a potential interrelationship of field independence with intelligence. A number of researchers have focused on this problem — generally, some limited relationship between intelligence and field dependence/independence may exist. While some researchers have, once again, failed to obtain a significant association (e.g. Gonzales and Roll, 1985), others report a significant association of field independence with some subtests of IQ (see, for example, the work of Robinson, 1983, with the WAIS).

Repeated findings of such a nature have led some writers (e.g. Cooperman, 1980) to argue that one or more cognitive styles are, in fact, equivalent to intelligence. Views of this nature may be exaggerated since most of the obtained significant interrelations appear to be of low order (e.g. Shore, Hymovitch, and Lajoie, 1982). None the less, some impurity of measurement, especially for field dependence versus independence, is evident. To assure that data cannot be predicted by ability (e.g. intelligence) alone, research should follow the example of those prior efforts that introduced controls for ability.

Sources of stylistic differences

If some style(s) may be related to intelligence, we might question whether measured behaviors reflect learned modes of functioning or whether they are due to one or more innate factors. While no final answer to that question can yet be obtained, some available data may be suggestive. Research with field dependence/independence in twins suggests no differences between sets of monozygotic and dizygotic twins (Martin and Gross, 1979). Members of the same family tend to be quite similar on several measures of style (Reiss and Oliveri, 1983). Age differences throughout adolescence (Flexer and Roberge, 1983) and throughout adult middle and older age (the 40s, 50s and 60s) appear to have little impact on field dependence/independence (Lee and Pollack, 1980) but may reduce both intelligence and field independence in older persons (Larsen, 1982). In sum, there seems to be no clear support for innate origin of the style.

A number of researchers have obtained differences among people that might be ascribed to cultural experience. For example, urban residents in India tend to be more field independent than rural residents (Chatterjea and Paul, 1981; Pandey and Pandey, 1985). Mexican Americans are more field dependent than Anglo-Americans but third generation Mexican Americans are more field independent than their first generation counterparts (Saracho, 1983). Field independence may also increase with business experience or may be associated with specific jobs. For example, established accountants have been shown to be less field dependent than business students (Pincus, 1985).

Males, in general, tend to be more field independent than females (e.g. Pandey and Pandey, 1985), a finding that some writers have ascribed to prior experience or area of training (Johnson, Flinn, and Tyer, 1979). However, Hughes (1981) was unable to relate greater male field independence to sex role characteristics (or, for that matter, to anxiety levels). Thomas (1982) has attempted to explain differences between males and females via a mathematical model which assumes a recessive gene as productive of field independence. While Thomas's model may explain most previous relevant research on gender differences, its value has yet to be tested prospectively.

Physiological concomitants

Considerable research has focused on left versus right brain hemisphere functioning or dominance and its correspondence to cognitive styles (e.g. the work of Federico, 1984; Mintzberg, 1976; and the research of Gordon, Charms, and Sherman, 1987, with managerial performance). Other researchers have measured the relationship of right- versus lefthandedness or symmetry/asymmetry in left versus right movements (e.g. Sousa, Rohrberg, and Mercure, 1979). Yet others have considered such diverse variables as EEG and circadian rhythms (e.g. Sarmany, 1985). At present the available information on the physiological concomitants of styles is too preliminary to provide a summary of results or to draw meaningful conclusions.

How Useful Are Styles in I/O Psychology?

As suggested earlier, only limited implications can be drawn at this time. We have learned much about the impact of field independence and some about the effect of reflection. Both, in general, would be more valuable in most employment categories than field dependence or impulsivity. We may expect that field independent (and probably reflective) employees would be more accurate in their task performance. We would expect them to be more open to instructions and to information in general (even if the information is incongruent) and we would expect them to deal more effectively with others. However, their task performance would likely be slower than for reflective individuals. They may be more creative and may respond better to training.

However, as explained earlier, each end of a stylistic dimension supposedly has its own value. There are, after all, possible tasks where the field dependent and the impulsive styles might be of greater value. Where tasks require little cognitive effort, where consistency is of value, where a restructuring of thought is not necessarily useful or may even be undesirable, and where quick action is important, we might prefer employees that are field dependent and/or impulsive.

Let us return, for a moment, to an earlier suggestion. We indicated that styles *may*, in some individuals, be less than fixed: such persons may employ a 'cognitive strategy' to adapt specific styles and/or specific levels of these styles to a task at hand. At present we know that persons who have the capacity for stylistic adaptation do exist. However, research on cognitive styles fails to tell us how common they are and whether the use of cognitive strategy can be trained. We will deal with that problem in the last section of this chapter. None the less, it appears obvious that such individuals would be most useful to organizations that must adapt frequently, i.e. organizations that have to function in complex, fluid, and uncertain environments.

COGNITIVE COMPLEXITY

The Concept of Cognitive Complexity

The prior section of this chapter has provided a relatively unambiguous definition of 'cognitive style'. We will not be able to do the same for cognitive complexity. Unfortunately, stated views of cognitive complexity have tended to vary. Most apparent differences among theorists can, however, be resolved when discrepancies in terminology are clarified (cf. Streufert and Streufert, 1978).

While several of the complexity theories contain unique aspects, a core of common orientations exists as well. Complexity theorists and researchers have been concerned with the *dimensionality* of human cognition. Conceptualizations of cognitive complexity necessarily focus on differentiation, i.e. the number of bipolar dimensions that are used to conceptualize, organize, and understand the perceived world. Some theories go beyond differentiation to focus on discrimination on single dimensions (shades of grey between two opposites) and/or on integration (the often temporary association of differentiated dimensions to 'make sense' of incoming information). Integration cannot occur where it has not been preceded by differentiation.

Diverse theorists define their terms somewhat differently. Yet all would agree that a consistent, i.e. unchanging, response despite contrary information would suggest that information has been processed in unidimensional fashion. For example, if 'John' were always categorized as a 'bad' person, regardless of context, task or situation, unidimensional (undifferentiated) cognition would be implied. The unidimensional individual has learned (or has experienced) that 'John' is bad and applies that attitude across all realms of experience.

Unidimensional response reliability to specific task demands can be trained or acquired by experience. In those organizational settings where highly consistent responses are of value, unidimensional action (reflecting cognitive simplicity) would be useful. However, where tasks or situations are fluid, requiring potentially adaptive adjustments to concurrent conditions, multidimensionality, i.e. cognitive complexity would be more useful. Both differentiation and integration should be applied. In fact, cognitive complexity is needed wherever uncertainty and situational flux prevail, especially where multifaceted task components and environmental demands require frequent re-adaptation.

Is 'cognitive complexity' yet another cognitive style? Opinions on that topic appear to vary somewhat. Most reviewers of cognitive styles have included complexity/simplicity as one of those styles. However, their focus has generally been limited to differentiation as measured by the REP test. On the other hand, Messick (1978) would include *both* differentiation and integration within a style of cognitive simplicity versus complexity. However, that author specifically emphasizes dimensionality, articulation (a term used by Scott, 1959, 1969) which suggests the discrimination of points on single dimensions and *hierarchic* integration. Hierarchic integration would suggest a complex but relatively fixed and consistent mode of processing information, a mode that would fall within the limits of earlier definitions of the style concept. Other theorists and researchers, however, would either deny the hierarchic aspect of cognitive complexity or would relegate hierarchic complexity to one among several possible forms of complex information processing (e.g. Driver, 1979; Streufert and Streufert, 1978). Most would emphasize 'flexible complexity', the capacity to reintegrate with change in relevant information as the primary form of more advanced human information processing. The latter would hardly fit the definition of a style. Moreover, some writers would question the pervasive (reliable) application of complexity across domains (e.g. Scott, Osgood, and Peterson, 1979) or even across tasks and situations within the same domain (Streufert and Swezey, 1986). Whether one wishes to see such a flexible application of differentiation, integration, and other components of cognitive complexity by 'complex' (but not by 'simple') individuals as a lack of reliability or as an application of cognitive strategy, the observed behaviors do not match restrictive definitions of 'style'.

Different authors have taken various approaches in more recent attempts to classify cognitive complexity/simplicity. Harrison (1966) would still assign cognitive complexity to the style category, with the addendum that 'value' (levels of performance quality) can be attributed to that style (cf. Goldstein and Blackman, 1978a, 1978b). Others (e.g Streufert and Streufert, 1978; Streufert and Swezey, 1986) are more cautious. While the latter authors do not exclude the impact of a stylistic basis (or component) for cognitively complex behavior, they consider possible contributions from ability (likely innate but not based on standard IQ) and even effects of a preference for complexity as well. Their views of possible contributions of ability find some parallel in recent observations by Sternberg (e.g. 1980, 1984) whose triarchic conceptualization of intelligence provides two components (not normally assessed with IQ tests) that seem to overlap considerably with cognitive complexity. Such a possible convergence is supported by the absence of meaningful correlations between standard measures of IQ and cognitive complexity for both normal and above normal intelligence ranges.

Some writers have used complexity-like concepts but have left their specific unspecified. For example, Isenberg (1984) discusses the 'intuitive' basis of managerial success. 'Intuition' implies 'seeing patterns in the chaos'. The behaviors which emerge from his intuitive cognitive process hold considerable similarity to integrative performance measured by proponents of the complexity concept. Isenberg has successfully predicted optimal managerial functioning on the basis of his intuition concept. Translated into complexity theory we would conclude that his cognitively complex (more intuitive) managers are more effective than their less cognitively complex counterparts.

An extensive exploration of concepts that are related to complexity theory (such as those of Isenberg and Sternberg) would be very useful. In view of limited space, however, that exploration will have to wait. For the present purposes, we will continue with a review of published theory, of measurement, and of results that have emerged from an interest in cognitive complexity *per se*.

Theory

An extensive review of theory has recently been presented by Streufert and Swezey (1986). While some theoretical advances have been published since that review was written, those advances tend to include other concepts beyond cognitive complexity. The last section of this chapter will be concerned with those advances. The more extensive summaries and comments on complexity theory by Streufert and Streufert (1978) and Streufert and Swezey (1986) will not be repeated here. Rather, a brief summary will be presented.

Early cognitive complexity theory, with roots in concepts of Werner (1957), Piaget (1952), and others began with the contributions of Kelly (1955). His Personal Constructs Theory considered consistent individual differences in the interpretation of events. Based on Kelly's more clinically oriented work, Bieri (1961, 1968) focused on dimensions of social judgements and social versatility. Bieri's views provided the basis for today's theories of cognitive complexity: the greater the number of dimensions available to a person, the greater his or her cognitive complexity. However, the efforts of Kelly, Bieri, and their associates tended to focus only on differentiation (the orthogonal use of multiple dimensions). As was the case for early theories of style, Bieri's theory was generally limited to a concern with perceptions (here of other persons).

Harvey, Hunt, and Schroder (1961) introduced a concern with cognitive development towards complexity. Their 'Conceptual Systems Theory' assumed four stages of development from 'concrete' to 'abstract'. Not all persons would reach the abstract stage of thinking. Some of the stages tended to confound structural style with beliefs and attitudes (i.e. cognitive content rather than structure). The views of these authors, especially in the developmental context, have been further expanded by Hunt (e.g. 1966).

Schroder, Driver, and Streufert (1967) proposed an Interactive Complexity Theory. On the basis of considerable exploratory research, these authors concluded that cognitive complexity includes a number of pervasive processes: differentiation (number of dimensions), integration (interrelationships among differentiated dimensions), and discrimination (shades of grey on single dimensions). Moreover, these authors attempted to clarify the interactive effects between complexity in the environment and the cognitive complexity of individuals. The interaction was visualized as a family of inverted U-shaped curves. Optimal differentiative and integrative functioning was assumed to occur at some intermediate level of environmental complexity. That optimum was assumed to be somewhat higher for cognitively complex individuals. Further, the greater someone's cognitive complexity, the higher the differentiative and integrative capacity that would be achieved under those optimal conditions. In contrast, individual differences would emerge to a lesser degree or disappear where the environment is highly unfavorable (e.g. stressful overload or deprivation). Predictions based on this theory extended beyond social perception to perceptions in general and to a number of attitudinal and performance attributes.

Interactive Complexity Theory was later refined by Streufert (1978) and Streufert and Streufert (1978) who suggested that optimal environmental levels would not differ for comparisons of more versus less cognitively complex individuals. The revised theory extended predictions to cover a variety of cognitions, attitudes, attributions, and other behaviors. Predictions with clear relevance to the I/O context emerged for the first time.

Streufert and associates have discussed the potential for flexible adaptation to existing environmental (task or interpersonal) conditions. Managers who possess the capacity to differentiate and integrate and are able to apply these capacities in a flexible mode are, in many cases, able to adjust their functional level of cognitive complexity to meet the demands of a present situation, generating more optimal responses to the specific task at hand.

Another change in interactive complexity theory was proposed by Driver (1979). Focusing specifically on managerial behavior, Driver identified decision styles based on two dimensions: (a) use of a single or a multiple focus; and (b) quantity of information sought and employed. Combining the four endpoints results in four modes of functioning: (1) decisive (single focus, low use of information); (2) flexible (multiple focus, low use of information); (3) hierarchic (single focus, high use of information); and (4) integrative (multiple focus, high use of information).

Scott (1969; see also Scott, Osgood, and Peterson, 1979), based a theoretical approach on the work of Zajonc (1960) and (to some extent) on the concepts of Lewin (1936) and Heider (1946). Scott developed a theory which, similar to that of Schroder et al., focused on a number of diverse cognitive functions that are subsumed as part of cognitive complexity. Although different in terminology, Scott's components of cognitive complexity reflect differentiation, integration, and discrimination. In addition, Scott discusses domain-specific complexity, i.e. suggests that people do not necessarily respond in similar ways when they deal with diverse experience. In other words, Scott limits the pervasiveness of cognitive complexity. While he maintains the view that some level of complexity will be common within a domain, other levels of cognitive complexity may exist in unrelated cognitive domains of the same individual.

Finally, Streufert and Swezey (1986) apply a modified version of Streufert and Streufert's (1978) complexity theory to the specific concerns of I/O psychology, especially to managerial functioning in organizations. Both the cognitive complexity of individuals as well as the complexity levels of their organizations are considered. The theory provides about 100 propositions about the effects of managerial and organizational complexity. Some of these propositions remain yet untested. Data in support of others are reviewed by the authors.

Measurement

Since cognitive complexity supposedly generates a pervasive (even though potentially domain restricted) approach to various kinds of work tasks and situations, its measurement is relevant to several concerns of industrial and organizational psychology. Attitudes towards superiors and peers, motivations, perceptions of the task environment, insights into the potential strategy of a competitor, solutions to complex problems and strategic plans for the organization are just some of the topics that are potentially modified by a manager's cognitive complexity.

Techniques designed to assess individual differences in cognitive complexity differ from most familiar measurement methods. Most 'quick and easy' measures employed to assess a host of characteristics are based on the assumption that people can (and, if approached correctly, will) tell us *what* they think or know. However, cognitive complexity (in common with other styles) is not concerned with '*what*' people think; rather, it focuses on '*how*' people think (Streufert et al., 1988). Unfortunately, most individuals have never considered the 'how' of their own cognitive processes and would, consequently, find it very difficult to answer direct questions about that topic (cf. Streufert, 1986). Social desirability, acquiescent response set and other confounds likely distort responses to direct assessment. In fact, many attempts to develop and validate paper-and-pencil questionnaires designed to measure cognitive complexity directly have failed.

The solution to the measurement problem requires that individuals engage in a task which encourages the use of cognitive complexity (where it is available to an individual). The degree to which complexity (and its differentiation, integration, etc., components) is employed is then assessed through performance indicators. Kelly's Role Concept Repertoire Test (REP Test) provides a rather elegant method of obtaining a quick estimate of complexity. Various formats of the test have been developed by a number of researchers, some of them remaining close to the original in both design and scoring, others deviating considerably (e.g. Crockett's Role Category Questionnaire, 1965).

The REP Test has good reliability and validity (Schneier, 1979b). However, it is limited to the perceptual social domain. Within that domain, derivations of the test have found worldwide use in organizational assessment (e.g. Dunn, Pavlak, and Roberts, 1987; Hersey and Blanchard, 1982a, 1982b; Petrovskii, 1986). Fortunately, there appears to be little support for occasional claims that the test is able to measure cognitive efforts extending beyond differentiation.

A number of other paper-and-pencil measures of complexity that assess performance have been developed by Scott and associates (e.g. 1962, 1966, 1969; based on information theory, Attneave, 1959). The measures employ sorting tasks where different (non-overlapping) groups are said to represent cognitive dimensions. Somewhat related procedures have also been reported by Wyer (1964).

Streufert and associates (Streufert, Pogash, and Piasecki, 1988) employ a quasi-experimental simulation technology which assesses cognitive complexity evident in decision making. Individuals (or groups) participate in an all-day computer assisted task. The simulation allows the introduction of fixed events at specified points in time to assure continuing comparability among different participants. The technique measures a number of cognitive (stylistic) attributes in addition to cognitive complexity. High levels of (alternate form) reliability and predictive validity (job success) have been established (Streufert, Pogash, and Piasecki, 1988).

A number of researchers have attempted to design measures which are not as clearly founded on the *direct* assessment of performance. Streufert and Driver (1967) based their Impression Formation Test on earlier work with primacy and recency (Asch, 1946). The test is limited to the assessment of differentiation and integration in the interpersonal perceptual domain. Scoring of the subjective responses requires trained raters. Reliability and validity (within that domain) are excellent.

Harvey's (cf. Harvey *et al.*, 1961) 'This I Believe' measure consists of a number of incomplete sentences that suggest cognitive conflict. The measure was later modified by Schroder and Streufert (1963) and, in various versions, became known as the 'Sentence Completion Test' or 'Paragraph Completion

Test'. For example, a sentence stem from that test states: 'When someone disagrees with me it usually means. . . '. The respondent writes a paragraph length response to several such stems. The sentences are then scored for both differentiation and integration, i.e. for cognitive process, not for the content of statements.

Despite their subjective nature, all of these tests have excellent reliability (if scored by trained raters) and have predicted a wide range of cognitive and behavioral functions. The Sentence Completion Test has been modified by Suedfeld to analyze existing (often historical) textual material. Suedfeld's technique is used to assess the complexity of persons who are no longer alive or who may be unwilling to respond to questionnaires (e.g. Suedfeld and Rank, 1976).

Some attempts have been made to develop rating or alternate choice paper-and-pencil tests. The most commonly used appear to be versions of the Situational Interpretation Test (SIT) and the Conceptual Systems Test (CST, e.g. Harvey, 1967). Earlier forms of the SIT measure were extensively employed by Schroder et al. (1967) and have continued to be used by Hunt (1966) and his associates. Tuckman's (1966) Interpersonal Topical Inventory (ITI) also had its basis in the same techniques. Its simpler format allows responses by a broader range of individuals. Unfortunately, assessments obtained with all of these paper-and-pencil inventories can be, to some extent, confounded with the content of respondents' attitudes, beliefs, and so forth. Quite in contrast to performance based measures of cognitive complexity which typically fail to correlate with measures of ability, some of the paper-and-pencil measures have been less independent (e.g. of IQ). Despite the experienced difficulties, attempts to develop objective measures of cognitive complexity have continued (e.g. Driver and Mock, 1974). For example, Driver and associates have employed the Driver Decision Style Exercise (DDSE) and the Driver-Streufert Complexity Index (DSCI). The use of the latter measures has generally been restricted to single research groups.

Despite differences in measurement technology and only moderate intercorrelations among the measures, the various measures of cognitive complexity have tended to produce similar results when more versus less cognitively complex individuals were compared on a variety of dependent variables. It may well be that the various tests assess diverse components of cognitive complexity which jointly or interactively produce common cognitive outcomes (cf. Streufert and Streufert, 1978; Streufert and Swezey, 1986). Because of their similar impact on various measures, we will, in general, discuss research results (below) without specific reference to the measurement instruments that were employed to select subjects. The relevant complexity measure will be mentioned only where consistent differences in obtained data imply that discrepant components of cognitive complexity (e.g. differentiation versus integration) may have diverse effects.

Research Data

Only a limited proportion of published data derive directly from research in I/O psychology. Data are especially rare from efforts that were carried out within industrial and organizational settings or with employees from such settings. None the less, much laboratory or field research on adults appears to be somewhat relevant to present concerns. Fortunately, evidence for the applicability of more basic research on cognitive complexity to industrial and organizational settings does exist (e.g. Levin, Louviere, Schepanski, and Norman, 1983; Streufert and Swezey, 1986).

In general, research suggests that individual differences in cognitive complexity affect a range of human functioning. By comparison, very few negative findings (i.e. indicating the absence of predicted relationships between cognitive complexity and behavior) have been reported (e.g. Bernardin, Cardy, and Carlyle, 1982; Goldsmith, 1985; Weiss and Adler, 1981; Wolfe and Chacko, 1980). In most of the cases where predictions based on complexity theory were not confirmed, research subjects were selected into more versus less complex samples on the basis of the REP Test (or similar measurement formats). While the REP Test provides an excellent assessment of perceptual complexity in interpersonal settings, it is not an adequate predictor of integrative functioning and it is not an effective measure beyond the interpersonal sphere. Failure to obtain significance has generally occurred where the REP Test was employed to predict behavior beyond interpersonal perception. Of course, another (rarely considered) reason for the limited number of negative findings may reflect a general bias inherent in the pursuit of science: negative results in the absence of a contradicting theory are more difficult to publish than data which confirm prominent theories or hypotheses. We will again consider research results under a number of subheadings.

Interpersonal perception

Interpersonal perception was the first field which researchers in cognitive complexity emphasized. Data tend to show that the perceptions of individuals scored as more versus less cognitively complex differ considerably. Perceptions of other persons, especially where their behavior includes apparent inconsistencies, tend to be more accurate and more balanced in cognitively complex individuals (Leventhal and Singer, 1964; Miller, 1969). In contrast, where resolutions of apparent inconsistencies are externally provided, less complex individuals appear to accept those resolutions better than more complex individuals (Ackerman, 1984) who likely developed their own resolutions. Moreover, less complex individuals tend to conceive of others in terms of external attributes while more complex persons see counterparts at least partly in terms of internal motivational aspects (Holloway and Wolleat, 1980; Schneier, 1979a).

As a result, judgements about others by less complex individuals are often more extreme (Campbell, 1960; Malhotra *et al.*, 1983; Supnick, reported by Crockett, 1965).

Accuracy of perception would prove of value when it is necessary to predict the behavior of another. Again, complex persons tend to exceed less complex individuals in this capacity (Bieri, 1955; Campbell, 1960; Leventhal, 1957). Adequate perception of others appears to be especially limited in less cognitively complex individuals when information contains inconsistencies (Crano and Schroder, 1967; Domangue, 1978; Harvey and Ware, 1967; Janicki, 1964; Millimet and Brien, 1980, Nidorf, 1961; Nidorf and Crockett, 1965; Press, Crockett and Rosenkrantz, 1969; Scott, 1963; Ware and Harvey, 1967; Wojciszke, 1979).

Limits in the capacity to handle, i.e. integrate, conflicting information about other persons has direct implications for a variety of other functions. For example, less complex individuals tend to show less consideration for others (Bruch, Heisler, and Conroy, 1981), are more likely to categorize them into simple 'good' versus 'bad' groupings or may engage in attitude polarization (Campbell, 1960; O'Keefe and Brady, 1980; O'Keefe and Delia, 1978). Less cognitively complex individuals tend to form impressions on the basis of one-sided information even where opposing information is presented (e.g. Mayo and Crockett, 1964). As a result, judgements of cognitively complex persons by those who are less complex tend to be inaccurate. This finding is not surprising when one considers that the judgement of complex individuals is more difficult to begin with (Adams-Webber, 1973).

In contrast, the quality and quantity of hypotheses about the behavior of others tends to be greater in more complex individuals (cf. Streufert and Driver, 1965). Complexity also generates more questions about the underlying causes of others' behavior (Holloway and Wolleat, 1980). The greater accuracy of predictions about others' (as well as a respondent's own future) behavior by cognitively complex individuals is especially pronounced where familiarity with the other person is somewhat limited (Neimeyer, Neimeyer, and Landfield, 1983). With time and greater familiarity, the less complex individuals may increase their accuracy. Cognitively complex females seem to handle the empathic functions somewhat better than do males (Brook, 1981; Zalot and Adams, 1977).

Some recent research suggests that the perceptual limitations which less cognitively complex persons experience are by no means limited to the interpersonal sphere. For example, Robertson and Meshkati (1985) showed that complex individuals perceived changes in a computer operated mental workload task more accurately than their less complex counterparts.

Differences in perceptual characteristics have been extended beyond the realm of individuals. For example, Thompson, Mann, and Harris (1981) report that spatial task performance (in males) is positively related to cognitive complexity. Similar results were reported by Meltzer (1982) in a visual perception task. Cognitively complex subjects apparently prefer more complex geometric stimuli (e.g. Lilli, 1973) and generate more physiological arousal in response to such stimuli (Bryson and Driver, 1969, 1972).

Of particular interest to I/O psychology is a study by Jones and Butler (1980) who predicted the dimensional perception of the work environment by 907 enlisted naval personnel who had just completed courses in electricity and electronics. On the average, less complex individuals perceived their task environment on only four dimensions while their more complex counterparts were aware of six dimensions.

Information orientation

Of course, differentiation or integration is impossible if information is absent or seriously limited. Research by Streufert and associates (e.g. Streufert and Driver, 1965) has shown that perceptual complexity requires a minimum of information but is detrimentally affected by information overload. Information can and often is obtained by individuals through their own action. In other words, individuals would be able to optimize their capacity for differentiative and integrative information processing *if* they were able to organize their information search activities optimally. Neither cognitively complex persons nor their less complex counterparts achieve that goal adequately. However, research suggests that less complex individuals are more directly responsive to the quantity of information present in the environment, i.e. they search more when information is inadequate and less when information overload exists (Streufert, Suedfeld, and Driver, 1965; Suedfeld and Streufert, 1966; cf. also Karlins and Lamm, 1967; Karlins, Coffman, Lamm, and Schroder, 1967; Tuckman, 1964). This sensitivity to environmental conditions is independent of the relevance of the information (Streufert, S.C., 1973). In other words, their search tends to be controlled by their environment.

In contrast, cognitively complex individuals are more actively information oriented (e.g. Karlins, 1967; Sieber and Lanzetta, 1964; Streufert, Suedfeld, and Driver, 1965). Their search activities are more a function of information need than of environmental conditions. This finding remains stable even if other potentially important variables are partialed out (Hussy, 1979). They are also better able to search for and maintain near-adequate amounts of relevant information (Schneider and Giambra, 1971; Streufert *et al.*, 1965). While the prior data were drawn from research with general populations, Hendrick (1979) confirmed these findings for a sample of managers. Moreover, cognitively complex persons tend to search for diverse (not only confirmatory) information (e.g. Watson, 1976) and are more sensitive to and more able to utilize minimal cues that might have been obtained through search (Harvey, 1966). These cues often form the basis for differentiative and integrative efforts that associate prior knowledge, information, and actions with new information to generate more effective strategic planning (Streufert *et al.*, 1965). All of these findings apply to *active* search activity. Where search can be delegated to others, less complex individuals are quite willing to request much more information from outside sources (Streufert and Castore, 1971) even under overload and even when it is impossible to assimilate that information because of extant load levels.

Impression formation

Considerable research on impression formation has presented sequential sets of information which were internally consistent within each set but inconsistent among sets. Cognitively complex subjects are able to integrate inconsistent sets of information while their less complex counterparts tend to focus on either the earlier or the later set (e.g. Petronko and Perin, 1970; Raphael, Moss, and Rosser, 1979; Streufert and Driver, 1967). Higher quality and better organization of the impressions (Fertig and Mayo, 1970; Raphael *et al.*, 1979) correlates with cognitive complexity. In contrast, differences in performance at lower levels are predicted by measures of intelligence (Raphael *et al.*, 1979).

Communication

More adequate perception of others and of the task environment would likely aid in the capacity to communicate. However, communication skills towards co-workers, superiors, and persons under one's supervision would require additional skills as well. How do more versus less complex persons fare in this domain?

Applegate (1982) has related impression formation to communication. The data suggest that higher levels of cognitive complexity result in more persuasive strategies, in more listener adaptive strategies, and in more complex perceptual impressions of communication partners (cf. also Hale, 1986; Sypher, Witt, and Sypher, 1986). Higher levels of persuasive capacity by cognitively complex individuals are not a function of verbal ability (Hale, 1980) but may be associated with less apprehension about communicating (Neuliep and Hazleton, 1985), more assertiveness and less unfavorable views of self, factors that themselves are related to complex cognitions (e.g. Raphael *et al.*, 1979).

Attitudes and attributions

In general, research suggests that attitudes towards others as well as attitudes towards one's (work) environment shift more readily (but less severely) in cognitively complex individuals (e.g. Bhutani, 1977). The resulting attitudes tend to be more moderated (Linville and Jones, 1980; O'Keefe and Brady,

1980). In contrast, attitude changes in less complex persons, when they occur, tend towards an 'all or nothing' orientation (Streufert, 1966). Differences in the effects of communications upon attitudes are of considerable importance, especially in marketing settings and where employee attitudes and satisfaction are of concern.

The cognitive complexity of the target of an advertising message affects subsequent product-relevant attitudes and actions (e.g. Durand, 1979; Durand and Lambert, 1979; Mizerski, 1978). In the absence of a significant communication, less complex persons tend to maintain invariant attitudes while their more complex counterparts respond with greater sensitivity to lesser cues in their environment (Streufert and Streufert, 1969). Major environmental cues have greater impact on the attitudinal orientations of cognitively less complex persons (Heslin and Streufert, 1968). Similar data obtained by Harvey (1965) indicated that communications presented in public and directed towards less complex persons tended to modify their attitude, while more complex individuals were more sensitive to private communications.

Attributions by complex versus less complex individuals tend to follow attitudinal differences. Less complex individuals tend to attribute success to themselves and failure to outside sources (Muneno and Dembo, 1982; Streufert and Streufert, 1969). Their positive attitudes towards themselves and negative attitudes towards 'blamed' external sources match those attribution patterns. More complex individuals generate both moderated attributions and attitudes.

Byrne and associates (e.g. Byrne, 1971) have demonstrated that similar attitudes result in attraction. With one exception (Black, 1971), research would suggest that the same appears to hold for cognitive complexity (Johnston and Centers, 1973; Streufert, Castore, Kliger, and Driver, 1967; Streufert, Bushinsky and Castore, 1967). Extremely close relationships such as marriage are no exception to that rule (Crouse, Karlins, and Schroder, 1968; Neimeyer, 1984).

Flexibility and creativity

Both flexibility and some components of creativity (cf. Messick, 1978) are implied in the functioning of cognitively complex individuals. Some writers would consider other variables such as tolerance for ambiguity, tolerance for diversity and open mindedness (e.g. Harvey, 1966) as part of complexity as well. In fact, considerable data suggest a moderate relationship among several of these variables (cf. Driver, 1979; Harvey, 1966; Kershner and Ledger, 1985). For example, persons engaged in creative endeavors (creative writing) scored higher on cognitive complexity than others (Quinn, 1980). Remote Associates Test (a measure of creativity developed by Mednick, 1963) scores correlated with integrative complexity (e.g. Karlins, 1967). Less complex individuals tend to be more rigid and less creative than their cognitively complex counterparts (Adams, Harvey, and Heslin, 1966; Scott, 1962).

Adaptation and adjustment to task demands

Greater flexibility and openness to information may aid adjustments to changing demands of the task environment. Research indicates that such adjustments are easier for complex persons. Merron, Fisher, and Torbert (1987) have shown that cognitively complex managers are more likely to redefine problems rather than accept them exactly as presented. Generally, they more easily adjust to unstructured tasks than do their less complex counterparts but do equally well in structured settings (Amerie and Beechy, 1984; Holloway and Wampold, 1986).

Complex individuals are better able to adapt their communications to the situation at hand. For example, it is known that election rhetoric by candidates tends towards more cognitively simple statements which can be easily understood by the electorate. In contrast, post-election statements by politicians designed to explain actions tend towards greater complexity (cf. Tetlock, 1981). Cognitively complex politicians accomplish this 'switch' better than their less complex counterparts. Similarly, managers must be able to 'adapt' their management style to tasks and persons at hand (Thorne, 1986). Cognitively simple managers find it more difficult to accomplish such a readjustment.

Leadership

Cognitively complex leaders tend to focus on somewhat different aspects of the leadership role than do their less complex counterparts. For example, Streufert, Streufert, and Castore, (1968) found that simple leaders are more production oriented while complex leaders focus on a different variety of leadership components, including both task oriented and socio-emotional aspects. Managers with greater cognitive complexity are more capable of collaborative leadership (Merron *et al.*, 1987) and make more use of feedback cues (Nydegger, 1975). Possibly as a result of such differences, complex leaders tend to receive more favorable ratings from followers (e.g. Nydegger, 1975). Groups with complex leaders tend to outperform groups with less complex leaders (Mitchell, 1971).

Suggestions that complexity might be related to Fiedler's LPC scale have only found mixed support (cf. Arnett, 1978; Mitchell, 1970; Schneier, 1978; Vecchio, 1979; Weiss and Adler, 1981). While some relationship might exist, other variables might intervene to modify or control potential interactions.

Task performance

The relationship between performance and cognitive complexity has been investigated across a wide variety of task settings. As already implied above, performance differences between more and less cognitively complex individuals would be less likely to emerge in highly structured, in simple or excessively overloading task settings. Differences would more likely emerge in unstructured settings with normal (relatively comfortable) work and information loads (Astley *et al.*, 1982; Streufert, 1970). None the less, some differences have even been obtained in relatively simple settings. For example, limited but significant performance differences for cognitively more versus less complex US Navy enlisted personnel were reported by Jones and Butler (1980). Complex persons performed better in a simulated artillery target practice task (Robertson and Meshkati, 1985). Similarly, cognitive complexity predicted greater success in a fault diagnosis task (Rouse and Rouse, 1979; cf. also 1982), was related to risk-taking differences by drivers (Von Eye and Hussy, 1979) and to strategy in a visual–motor setting (Streufert, Streufert, and Denson, 1985).

A wealth of data indicate the value of cognitive complexity in managerial tasks involving uncertainty and change. Hendrick (1979) employed a problem-solving setting and found that cognitively complex managers interacted at a faster pace, were better at cue utilization, and finished their task in half the time. Several researchers have reported that integrative capacity is an aid in information processing and decision making (e.g. the work of Lundberg, 1972, with a management simulation). A series of simulation-based efforts by Streufert (cf. Streufert, 1978; Streufert and Swezey, 1986) clearly established the greater effectiveness of cognitively complex individuals in strategic and planning activities. Even in betting decisions at horse races, cognitive complexity is of considerable value (Ceci and Liker, 1986, 1987). Moreover, such results appear to be independent of intelligence (Ceci and Liker, 1986).

Part of the more effective performance of complex individuals is generated by their information search and information utilization styles. Even when faced with large amounts of complex information, appropriate use of cognitive simplification processes (cf. Schwenk, 1984) by more cognitively complex individuals would likely permit some differentiation and integration. The less complex individuals, in contrast, would tend to simplify to avoid incongruity. For them, unidimensional solutions — which are often ineffective in managerial settings — would be a more likely outcome.

A series of very interesting efforts by Suedfeld, Tetlock, and associates have focused on historical events (e.g. Levi and Tetlock, 1980; Porter and Suedfeld, 1981; Raphael, 1982; Suedfeld and Tetlock, 1977; Tetlock, 1980; Tetlock, Bernzweig, and Gallant, 1985; Suedfeld, 1985; Tetlock, Hannum, and Micheletti, 1984). The studies consider individual or organizational functioning under diverse or changing task settings. For example, Suedfeld and associates found that military decision making and success, even against unfavorable odds (Robert E. Lee, Ulysses S. Grant, and others) is enhanced by cognitive complexity (Suedfeld, Corteen, and McCormick, 1986). Other data indicate that scientists whose statements reflect more cognitive complexity are viewed as more eminent by their peers (Suedfeld, 1985). Stress in the environment or simplification of topics under discussion can lead to less complex and, consequently, less effective functioning, e.g. Japan's decision to enter the Second World War (Tetlock, 1980) or the repeated initiation of war in the Middle East (Suedfeld, Tetlock, and Ramirez, 1977). Problems due to simplification and their effects extend to deliberations of the US Senate (Tetlock, Hannum, and Micheletti, 1984) and Supreme Court (Tetlock, Bernzweig and Gallant, 1985). In part, such simplifications are generated by environmental stresses or lack of control over one's environment: while simplification may result in war, war may produce yet additional simplifications of cognitive functioning, even in literary figures (Porter and Suedfeld, 1981) or professionals (Suedfeld, 1985).

Training for greater cognitive complexity

With evident advantages of cognitive complexity, at least in many settings, one obviously would raise the question whether complexity can be trained. If cognitive complexity were viewed as a style, i.e. a relatively lasting and pervasive approach to task environments, one would have to conclude that training must be difficult or, at least, slow in progress. If, on the other hand, complexity reflects an innate ability, training success would be unlikely or severely limited. Fortunately, such implied dire predictions are not accurate, at least not for many individuals.

As Scott and associates have suggested, cognitive complexity can vary widely across domains. In other words, evidence for absence or limited complexity in some cognitive domain does not imply that a person is generally incapable of differentiation and/or integration. The capacity for cognitively complex functioning may be present but may not have been 'activated' in other domains. Training certainly can enhance that activation process.

While some efforts to train individuals have met with little success (Sauser and Pond, 1981), others have successfully trained many individuals. Cronen and Lafleur (1977) used a rather massive communication attack on assumed 'truisms' to generate more complex functioning. Streufert *et al.* (1988) employed a variety of computer based procedures to increase differentiation and integration in simulated managerial task performance. In other words, it appears that successful training for many individuals is possible, even though specifically designed or adapted procedures may be required (cf. Stabell, 1978).

Age and cognitive complexity

The development of cognitive complexity through childhood and adolescence has been reviewed elsewhere (e.g. Streufert and Streufert, 1978) and is of less interest for present purposes. Although it had been assumed that complexity would increase from childhood to adulthood (DePaulo and Rosenthal, 1979) but would remain relatively stable over the years of adulthood, recent research has placed considerable doubt upon that notion.

Porter and Suedfeld (1981) found that cognitive complexity continues to increase during the adult years but drops a few years prior to death (cf. also Suedfeld, 1985). Brook (1981) found that cognitive complexity tends to increase from young to middle age but is diminished as persons reach older age. Streufert (1987) compared teams of managers drawn from younger (28–35 years old), middle aged (45–55) and older (65–75) age groups on a number of performance criteria. Differences between the younger and middle aged managers were minimal. Slight deteriorations in performance by middle aged teams were compensated by lesser impulsivity and the benefits of greater experience. Older teams functioned at much lower levels on a large number of performance indicators. Moreover, they were not aware of their low levels of performance. While some impact of generational differences in these comparisons cannot be completely excluded, the strength of the obtained data suggest that serious deterioration (even in still active managers) may often set in at more advanced ages. Fortunately, some training in cognitive complexity might aid in restoring at least part of the ability to differentiate and integrate.

Stress effects

A number of researchers have been interested in the effects of stress upon complexity. Stressors employed have included interpersonal conflict, physical or work overload, information or general stimulus deprivation, failure, uncontrollable aversive stimulation and more. Stressful environments, beyond an optimal level, are known to diminish cognitive complexity and its secondary effects (e.g. Harris and Highlen, 1982; Sillars and Parry, 1982; Streufert, 1970; Streufert and Driver, 1965; Streufert and Schroder, 1965; Streufert, Streufert, and Castore, 1969). While stress affects both more and less complex individuals, more cognitively complex persons maintain successful functioning at higher stress levels (e.g., Streufert, 1970) and recover more quickly from the stress experience (e.g. White, 1977). They are also less subject to 'learned helplessness' as defined by Seligman (1975).

Considerable research by Suedfeld has exposed complex individuals to sensory deprivation. The introduction of a persuasive message near the termination of 24 hours' deprivation had much greater impact on less complex individuals (Suedfeld, 1964). Less cognitively complex respondents find deprivation less pleasant than their more complex counterparts. When offered a reward during deprivation, complex individuals complied more but internalized the obtained information less.

Physiological concomitants

In addition to preliminary evidence for the impact of brain laterality on the cognitive complexity of individuals (e.g. Doktor, 1978; Doktor and Bloom, 1977; Domangue, 1984), some data are beginning to accumulate which suggest that a momentary state of human physiology may play a significant part in determining the level of a person's cognitive complexity. Several studies have associated a variety of cardiovascular or central nervous system changes (e.g. during stress experience) with diminished cognitive or performance indicants (e.g. Hancock and Meshkati, 1988; Hancock, Meshkati, and Robertson, 1985; Meshkati and Loewenthal, 1988; Robertson and Meshkati, 1985). While such research may confound stressors and physiological state as direct antecedents of behavioral functioning, other research employing prescription drug treatment might aid in identifying the cause of deteriorations in cognitive complexity. Streufert and associates (e.g. Streufert, et al., 1988a) investigated drug and performance interaction effects in hypertensive subjects. Drug treatment changed physiological state (e.g. it decreased heart rate which is often increased during stress experience) and increased the quality of differentiative and integrative performance in a complex managerial simulation, even in the presence of stress. In other words, the differences obtained by Meshkati and associates may well be due to direct changes in CNS functioning. Some research evidence based on EEG records may also suggest that central nervous system functioning of cognitively complex persons differs significantly from that of less complex persons (Federico, 1985).

How Useful is Cognitive Complexity in I/O Psychology?

The research on cognitive complexity clearly points to more effective functioning of the cognitively complex individual, at least in advanced, e.g. managerial, positions. Perceptions of the task and interpersonal environment in the organization would likely be more accurate and more detailed. Empathy would be available, including the kind of empathy that might aid in the 'discovery' of an opponent's strategy. Communications with others would likely be adaptive to the others' needs of capacity to understand. Leadership characteristics would include both social and task components. Information search activities might be more rational, i.e. determined by actual needs. Creativity and flexibility would be more likely applied and, where present, would lead to better adaptation to changed task demands. Performance, especially of complex tasks or with moderate stress would likely be better.

On the surface, it would appear that organizations should actively search for cognitively complex employees and ignore all candidates that are not. Such a notion would be too simplistic. First of all (cf. Streufert and Streufert, 1978), cognitively complex persons are in the minority, and highly complex individuals may not make up more than 10 per cent of the population. Should organizations then go out to train all their employees towards achieving greater complexity?

While training towards greater complexity is possible for many individuals, it may not serve an organization well in all cases. There are, after all, advantages that may be ascribed to the less complex (cognitively simple) person. Since correlations with ability tend to be absent, the less complex person is equally likely to be knowledgeable and generally competent. Moreover, he or she will more likely perform tasks in a reliable fashion, despite changes in information patterns. Interpersonal perceptions and communications will be predictable and consistent. For example, we would not have to be concerned about well-hidden agendas or other subtle strategies that might work against the organization. This employee will not be flexible and not likely creative, but, if motivated, will do the job in a consistent and reliable fashion. Performance will not likely deteriorate as much with age as would be the case for the more cognitively complex counterpart. If placed into a position of leadership, the cognitively less complex individual will more likely emphasize task orientation.

Of course, many individuals would be classified somewhere between cognitively complex and cognitively simple. The specific advantages they might have for the organization might be determined by their specific levels of complexity. Diverse jobs generate diverse demands. For those, however, who are likely promoted or transferred into varied, complex and fluid task settings, cognitive complexity would be of considerable advantage, even if their present job hardly requires differentiation and/or integration. We are often 'surprised' when an excellent employee, especially at managerial levels, fails to perform after a transfer to a new and different job. After all, this employee might have fulfilled the apparent preconditions for continued excellence: intelligence, experience, motivation, and more. That employee might now fail because of lacking cognitive complexity: capacities inherent in cognitively simple functioning might have been adequate to do the last job well. However, applying all the techniques that worked at the last job may not work on the new one: a multidimensional adaptive flexibility which allows the needed reorientation may be missing.

APPLYING MULTIPLE STYLES AND COMPLEXITY IN I/O PSYCHOLOGY

Today's fluid organizational environments often contain varied and multiple task demands. Especially at higher levels, e.g. for middle and upper level managers, personnel must repeatedly adjust their actions to match the demands of concurrent events and situations. Without question, abilities (such as intelligence) and experience can help managers deal with these various and changing demands (Fiedler, 1984). However, ability and experience are hardly enough. Both cognitive style and cognitive complexity are of considerable significance.

A focus on a single style or one or two aspects of complexity may not be adequate to predict overall managerial success. Consider the case of the mid- or upper level manager in a complicated, fluid, and uncertain task environment who may have to deal with multiple decisions, plans and strategies, and at the same time, must maintain an effective team of co-workers. Such a manager may need simultaneously to apply multiple styles. In contrast to the familiar propositions of style theory, he or she may have to differentiate among styles, i.e. be capable of selecting and applying the *appropriate* style, for a specific set of purposes, at the *appropriate* time. Further, such a manager may best adapt various combinations of styles to specific situations, persons and more. In other words, the effective manager may have to 'stretch' something that complexity theorists have called 'integrative flexibility' to apply not only to specific areas of thought and action but also to the selected application of cognitive styles themselves. Actions that employ the 'cognitive strategies' that were mentioned earlier might be especially helpful.

Attempts to expand predictions of style and complexity theories towards multiple applications have come from two theorists. Their theoretical developments occurred simultaneously and independently of each other. The theories contain significant differences as well as considerable similarities. This section will consider these two approaches in somewhat greater detail.

Schroder

Schroder developed a list of managerial competencies, based in part on complexity theory. The competencies were assumed to predict team success wherever leaders are accomplished in several of these competencies. Measurement involves behavioral observations by trained raters. Scoring is based on manuals which identify the specific behavioral indicators of competency: (1) *information search*, gathering a rich variety of information from many different sources; (2) *concept formation*, linking information to form new meaning, identifying strategies, methods, improvements, and changes; (3) *conceptual flexibility*, comparing different options for maximal use of opportunity; (4) *interpersonal search*, finding out what others are thinking and feeling, listening to subordinates, supervisors, peers, customers, etc.; (5) *managing interaction*, building cohesive teams of members who are committed to improving organizational performance and who take more and more responsibility; (6) *developmental orientation*, holding high expectations about the potential of people, providing them with resources, feedback, coaching, and training they need to exercise responsibility; (7) *self-confidence*, having positions of one's own and believing in the success of positions taken by one's teams or organizations; (8) *presentation*, presenting one's own and others' views so that the message gets across clearly; (9) *impact*, success in getting others to behave in ways that are consistent with goals; (10) *proactive orientation*, initiating ideas and taking responsibility for the implementation of plans; (11) *achievement orientation*, setting challenging standards for oneself and one's teams, measuring and providing feedback about success.

A careful look at the competencies suggests that structure, i.e. cognitive style and cognitive complexity, play a large but not an exclusive part. A manager who would be able to apply the appropriate styles and the appropriate components of cognitive complexity at the right time and the right place should have a team that excels. However, the eleven competencies are, in another part, content oriented, i.e. they focus on 'what' a manager should best do.

While Schroder's success predictions for teams that are led by managers scoring high on several competencies held in many cases, he noted some clear exceptions. Upon further analysis, Schroder partly changed focus from characteristics of individual leaders to their impact on those led. He concluded that behavior of high performing leaders is not solely based on the number of competencies they possess and that leadership development is not solely a function of overcoming limitations by moving these competencies into the strength column. That is, 'They [high performing leaders] don't have to be perfect in competency acquisition. They expand their strengths and compensate for limitations by building perfect teams of members with complementary strengths.'[1]

The emphasis on a 'leadership' component in addition to the usual 'cognition and performance' emphasis of complexity theorists, allowed Schroder to propose four *values* that should be associated with high performing versus poorly performing manager-leaders: (1) understanding the job demands of current complex organizations and viewing the pursuit of these demands as challenging goals; (2) understanding the managerial behavior involved, the resulting contributions of the eleven competencies and when those competencies should be used; (3) becoming aware of and accepting the competencies one possesses as strengths and limitations through a valid and objective process which maximizes accuracy; and (4) designing and implementing a developmental plan for expanding the contributions based on one's strengths, for building competency balance into the teams one leads and for compensating for one's limitations by capitalizing on the complementary strengths of others. Schroder's values incorporate the competencies listed earlier but transfer their functioning, in some part, to the team.

On first reading, the four values may not sound as though they would reflect individual differences that are either 'stylistic' in nature or would be based on

---

[1] Personal communication, May 1988, drawn from the book Schroder, H.M. *High Performing Leaders*, in preparation.

complexity theory approaches. None the less, they are closely related. We have already considered the structural relevance of the competencies. The values merely provide a vehicle for leader and task group members to apply the competencies. Moreover, the adaptive use of the competencies and the integrative application of 'values' require the capacity to apply both differentiation and integration at a metacontextual level.

Schroder's approach has considerable advantages. First, the described attributes and values are relatively close to concepts which already exist in this field, yet they provide a needed theoretical framework based partly on cognitive structure. Detractors may argue that the attributes and values are 'impure' because they 'confound' content with cognitive structure. However, those 'confounds' may, in effect, have applied value: after all, managerial behavior (and effectiveness) is based on both stylistic *and* content components.

Secondly, the approach of Schroder permits an integration of earlier complexity and style theories with the work of others, e.g. the efforts of Boyatzis (1982) and of Huff, Lake, and Schaalman.[2] Both Boyatzis and Huff *et al.* provided lists of managerial orientations that are considered antecedents of success. Existing validity data collected for these latter theoretical positions may enrich our understanding of the general effects of structural variables on managerial performance.

Streufert

Streufert developed his Meta-Complexity Theory on the basis of two influences. One of them derived from research data and extensive discussions with executives. The second impact was based on experience with two highly realistic but experimentally controlled simulations that have shown substantial validity for the prediction of managerial success (Streufert, Pogash, and Piasecki, 1988). The meta-complexity approach incorporates the major style, control, and cognitive complexity concepts that form the basis for this review. The theory attempts to join the various cognitive processes (styles, controls, cognitive complexity, etc.) into a single (parsimonious) theoretical structure.

It was Streufert's intent to develop a theoretical foundation that might provide encompassing predictions of managerial success. While earlier complexity theories focused only on single *judgemental dimensions*, meta-complexity theory applies discrimination, differentiation, and integration (as well as some other concepts drawn from prior complexity theories) at three different levels of human functioning: (1) to judgemental dimensions of individuals (i.e. cognitive complexity); (2) to cognitive processes such as styles, controls, abilities, and cognitive complexity (process complexity); and, finally, (3) to dimensions of organizational functioning (organizational complexity). In

[2] Cited in Schroder, *High Performing Leaders*, in preparation.

addition, the theory seeks to elucidate the interplay among these three levels towards optimal managerial and organizational behavior.

Since prior research has established that discrimination, differentiation, and integration are pervasive modes which describe wide ranging differences in overall human functioning, their application at higher (process) levels and their transfer to interpersonal (organizational) levels seems appropriate (e.g. Streufert, 1986, 1987; Streufert et al., 1988b; Streufert, Pogash, and Piasecki, 1988; Streufert and Swezey, 1986). For example, where 'differentiation' in cognitive complexity refers to the application of several dimensions to a single target object or person (for example, some degree of goodness versus badness plus some degree of profitability), differentiation in process complexity may reflect the simultaneous handling of a stimulus via a certain level of field dependence plus some specific level of cognitive complexity. Finally, differentiation in an organizational setting may reflect the formal or informal components of the organization which process information impinging upon that organization. Similar parallels at the three levels can be drawn for discrimination, integration, etc.

Earlier interactive complexity theory had emphasized two determinants of information processing: (a) the degree of (cognitive) complexity available to an individual and (b) the environmental constraints within which that complexity would emerge. Meta-complexity theory also focuses on both of these components (albeit at three levels). However, the interplay between individual (or the organization) and environment is conceived as bidirectional. While environmental extremes *may* limit the degree of discrimination, differentiation, and integration available to a person or an organization, environmental conditions (especially where they involve rapid or substantial change in managerial or organizational response), they may also produce a range of (hopefully adaptive) adjustments in managerial or organizational behavior. These adjustments can reflect adaptive modifications of judgemental dimensionality (i.e. changes in cognitive complexity) or adaptive changes of process complexity, i.e. in the level and use of styles, controls, abilities and of cognitive complexity, etc. (a process that has sometimes been called 'cognitive strategy'). Some changes in the environment may even generate adjustments in the dimensionality of organizational functioning (organizational complexity).

Meta-complexity theory holds that some (but certainly not all) managers are able to adapt their cognitive complexity and/or their process complexity to certain (but likely not all) changes in situational task demands. Similarly, some (but certainly not all) organizations can apply certain latitudes of complexity to sudden or major environmental change (with organizational culture a major stumbling block). The theory specifies the characteristics of managers, organizations, and their environments (and interactions among them) which can generate more versus less effective managerial and organizational functioning across a range of tasks and despite rapid flux in the environment.

In Streufert's view, *abilities* of individuals (and cognitive resources of organizations) tend to remain more or less stable for some time but can be applied to extant tasks at appropriate levels. In contrast, styles, controls, and characteristic cognitive complexity levels of individuals *may* remain rather stable or, in other persons, may be adaptively employed at various (potentially contrasting) levels to handle current task requirements. For example, for many individuals, cognitive processes (such as field dependence or cognitive simplicity) may remain highly stable across time, tasks, and situations. Managers who are characterized by fixed cognitive and process complexity may be able to handle some tasks well, but only when task requirements are relatively stable.

Other persons might adapt their style to be more field dependent in a social empathy task and more field independent in an analytic decision-making task. Similarly, they may apply cognitive simplicity combined with limited information search to situations which require decisive reactions to an emergency while they would employ differentiation and high levels of integration (cognitive complexity) when involved in strategic planning. Such managerial behavior reflects greater process complexity. (Of course, meta-complexity theory is not limited to a consideration of only field dependence/independence and cognitive complexity. These two — most commonly used — cognitive processes were only employed as examples. Any style, control, ability or any aspect of cognitive complexity which remains generally *independent* of others can — and should — be integrated into this theoretical structure.)

Individuals capable of considerable process complexity are better able to adapt to the fluid, uncertain, and multifaceted organizational settings that have become more and more common in the last few decades. They are also at an advantage when transferred or hired into new and widely differing assignments. None the less, their adaptive capacity is rarely perfect. Similarly, an adaptive 'organizational complexity' rarely reaches an optimum. Fortunately, especially for those individual managers who have some capacity for cognitive or process capacity, extensions of adaptive functioning into new realms of experience (via training) is possible.

Streufert assesses managerial functioning in quasi-experimental simulations that provide the complexity, fluidity, uncertainty, and workload that are typical of managerial settings. The simulation system assesses performance on more than 40 measures. Several of the measures are excellent predictors of managerial success, predicting such indicators as income at age, job level at age, number of promotions during the last ten years, and number of persons supervised (Streufert, Pogash, and Piasecki, 1988).

SUMMARY

The advent of both cognitive style theory and complexity theory about 40 years ago had little initial impact on I/O psychology. Theories and associated research generated a flurry of activity that was, however, primarily restricted to human perception. During an interim period following the initial years of rapid theoretical development, additional theoretical growth was relatively slow. Similarly, there appeared to be relatively little interest in styles and complexity except from psychologists involved in perception or cognition. In part, the lack of interest by applied scientists may have been due to the 'discouraging' news that people's pervasive styles cannot be changed. Where cognitive styles and cognitive complexity were considered relevant to I/O psychology, assumptions of fixed structural characteristics would, at best, have allowed I/O psychologists to use cognitive structure as a basis for selection and classification of employees.

Another limitation of earlier approaches to cognitive structure has been the restricted research focus on *single* stylistic concepts or on a *few* concepts that were restricted to complexity theory. Most applied psychologists, for example, did not think it particularly relevant that field dependent persons are more social, that field independent persons are more analytic, and so forth. The organizational context ideally requires a focus on many simultaneous concerns: i.e. individual differences on a single variable may not appear very relevant.

Fortunately, recent efforts have begun to view concepts from style and complexity theories as they interact with each other, with abilities and with job content, i.e. as they combine to create more versus less effective actions, for example in managers. This approach has placed style and complexity approaches into the context of other applied research and theory which is not related to concerns with cognitive structure. The effect of this 'marriage' has added considerable predictive capacity within the organizational context.

Data which indicate that training can and does change aspects of cognitive structure, moreover that those changes can be accomplished with relative ease (at least in some situations and for many individuals), have also made variables concerned with cognitive structure more attractive to both basic researchers and to those who wish to apply research data. The development of the more encompassing views by both Schroder and Streufert is an example of this new focus.

Yet, we are only at the very beginning of another integration, the 'integration' of styles and complexity with the main concerns of I/O psychologists. The possible contribution of several among the styles to variables of interest to I/O psychology has yet to be explored. The joint effect of styles, controls and complexity, together with ability, on human functioning in organizations promises to increase greatly our understanding of the sources for individual or organizational success and failure. Finally, increasing knowledge of how a flexible application of styles, of complexity, and of other structural components can modify outcomes *and* can be trained promises to be a major benefit to I/O psychology.

REFERENCES

Ackerman, B.P. (1984) Storage and processing constraints on integrating story information in children and adults. *Journal of Experimental Child Psychology*, 38, 64–92.

Adams, D.K., Harvey, O.J., and Heslin, R.E. (1966) Variation in flexibility and creativity as a function of hypnotically induced past histories. In O.J. Harvey (ed.), *Experience, Structure and Adaptability*, New York: Springer.

Adams-Webber, J.R. (1973) The complexity of the target as a factor in interpersonal judgment. *Social Behavior and Personality*, 1, 35–38.

Adejumo, D. (1983) Effect of cognitive style on strategies for comprehension of prose. *Perceptual and Motor Skills*, 56, 859–863.

Amerie, J.H., and Beechy, T.H. (1984) Accounting students performance and cognitive complexity. *Accounting Review*, 59, 300–313.

Applegate, J.L. (1982) The impact of construct system development on communication and impression formation in persuasive contexts. *Communication Monographs*, 49, 277–289.

Arnett, M.D. (1978) Least preferred co-worker score as a measure of cognitive complexity. *Perceptual and Motor Skills*, 47, 567–574.

Asch, S.E. (1946) Forming impressions of personality. *Journal of Abnormal and Social Psychology*, 41, 258–290.

Astley, W.G., Axelsson, R., Butler, R.J., Hickson, D.J., and Wilson, D.C. (1982) Complexity and cleavage: Dual explanations of strategic decision making. *Journal of Management Studies*, 19, 357–375.

Attneave, F. (1959) *Applications of Information Theory to Psychology*. New York: Holt.

Avolio, B.J., Kroeck, K.G., and Panek, P.E. (1985) Individual differences in information processing ability as a predictor of motor vehicle accidents. *Human Factors*, 27, 577–587.

Behling, O., Gifford, W.E., and Tolliver, J.M. (1980) Effects of grouping information on decision making under risk. *Decision Sciences*, 11, 272–283.

Bernardin, H.J., Cardy, R.L., and Carlyle, J.J. (1982) Cognitive complexity and appraisal effectiveness: Back to the drawing board? *Journal of Applied Psychology*, 67, 151–160.

Bhutani, K.A. (1977) A study of the effect of some cognitive and personality factors on attitude change. *Indian Educational Review*, 12, 50–60.

Bieri, J. (1955) Cognitive complexity–simplicity and predictive behavior, *Journal of Abnormal and Social Psychology*, 51, 263–268.

Bieri, J. (1961) Complexity–simplicity as a personality variable in cognitive and preferential behavior. In D.W. Fiske and S.R. Maddi (eds.), *Functions of Varied Experience*. Homewood, IL: Dorsey.

Bieri, J. (1965) Cognitive Complexity: Assessment issue in the study of cognitive structure. Unpublished manuscript.

Bieri, J. (1968) Cognitive complexity and judgment of inconsistent information. In R.P. Abelson, E. Aronson, W.J. McGuire, T.M. Newcomb, M.J. Rosenberg, and P.H. Tannenbaum (eds), *Theories of Cognitive Consistency*. Chicago: Rand McNally.

Bieri, J. (1971) Cognitive structures in personality. In H.M. Schroder and P. Suedfeld (eds), *Personality Theory and Information Processing*. New York: Ronald Press.

Black, H.K. (1971) The relationship of cognitive complexity–simplicity and affective stimuli in interpersonal attraction and differentiation. Unpublished doctoral dissertation, Pennsylvania State University.

Blackman, S., and Goldstein, K.M. (1982) Cognitive styles and learning disabilities. *Journal of Learning Disabilities*, 15, 106–115.

Blumenthal, J.A., McKee, D.C., Williams, R.B., and Haney, T. (1981) Assessment of conceptual tempo in the Type A (coronary prone) behavior pattern. *Journal of Personality Assessment*, **45**, 44–51.

Bolocofsky, D.N. (1980) Motivational effects of classroom competition as a function of field dependence. *Journal of Educational Research*, **73**, 213–217.

Boyatzis, R.E. (1982) *The Competent Manager*. Somerset, NJ: Wiley.

Brook, J. (1981) An exploratory study using repertory grid approach for measurement of cognitive complexity. *Perceptual and Motor Skills*, **53**, 827–831.

Bruch, M.A., Heisler, B.D., and Conroy, C.G. (1981) Effects of conceptual complexity on assertive behavior. *Journal of Counselling Psychology*, **28**, 377–385.

Bryson, J.B., and Driver, M.J. (1969) Conceptual complexity and internal arousal. *Psychonomic Science*, **17**, 71–72.

Bryson, J.B., and Driver, M.J. (1972) Cognitive complexity, introversion, and preference for complexity. *Journal of Personality and Social Psychology*, **23**, 320–327.

Byrne, D. (1971) *The Attraction Paradigm*. New York: Academic Press.

Campbell, V.N. (1960) Assumed similarity, perceived sociometric balance and social influence. Unpublished doctoral dissertation, University of Colorado; cited in J. Bieri, Complexity–simplicity as a personality variable in cognitive and preferential behavior. In D.W. Fiske and S. Maddi (eds), *Functions of Varied Experience*. Homewood, IL: Dorsey Press.

Carlyn, M. (1977) An assessment of the Myers–Briggs type indicator. *Journal of Personality Assessment*, **41**, 461–473.

Ceci, S.J., and Liker, J.K. (1986) A day at the races: A study of IQ, expertise and cognitive complexity. *Journal of Experimental Psychology: General*, **115**, 255–266.

Ceci, S.J., and Liker, J.K. (1987) A day at the races: A study of IQ, expertise and cognitive complexity. *Journal of Experimental Psychology: General*, **116**, 90.

Chadha, N.K. (1985) Creativity and cognitive style. *Psycho-Lingua*, **15**, 81–88.

Chandrasekaran, G., and Kirs, P.J. (1986) Acceptance of management science recommendations: The role of cognitive styles and dogmatism. *Information and Management*, **10**, 141–147.

Chatterjea, R.G., and Paul, B. (1981) Ecology, field independence and geometrical figure recognition: A study in intelligence controlled condition. *Personality Study and Group Behavior*, **1**, 1–10.

Coan, R.W. (1978) Critique of the Myers–Briggs type indicator. In O.K. Buros (ed.), *The Eighth Mental Measurement Yearbook*, Vol. 1. Highland Park, NJ: Gryphon, pp.973–975.

Cooperman, E.W. (1980) Field differentiation and intelligence. *Journal of Psychology*, **105**, 29–33.

Crano, W.D., and Schroder, H.M. (1967) Complexity of attitude structure and processes of conflict reduction. *Journal of Personality and Social Psychology*, **5**, 110–114.

Crockett, W.H. (1965) Cognitive complexity and impression formation. In B.A. Maher (ed.), *Progress in Experimental Personality Research*, Vol. 2. New York: Academic Press.

Cronen, V.E., and laFleur, G. (1977) Inoculation against persuasive attacks: A test of alternative explanations. *Journal of Social Psychology*, **102**, 255–265.

Crouse, B., Karlins, M., and Schroder, H.M. (1968) Conceptual complexity and marital happiness. *Journal of Marriage and the Family*, **30**, 643–646.

Davies, M.F. (1985) Cognitive style differences in belief persistence after evidential discrediting. *Personality and Individual Differences*, **6**, 341–346.

Davis, J.K., and Frank, B.M. (1979) Learning and memory of field independent–dependent individuals. *Journal of Research in Personality*, **13**, 469–479.

Debiasio, A.R. (1986) Problem solving in triads of varying numbers of field dependent and field independent subjects. *Journal of Personality and Social Psychology*, **51**, 749–754.

DePaulo, B.M., and Rosenthal, R. (1979) Age differences in nonverbal decoding skills: Evidence for increasing differentiation, *Merrill-Palmer Quarterly*, **25**, 145–150.

Doktor, R.H. (1978) Problem solving styles of executives and management scientists. *TIMS Studies in the Management Sciences*, **8**, 123–134.

Doktor, R.H., and Bloom, D.M. (1977) Selective lateralization of cognitive style related to occupation as determined by EEG alpha asymmetry. *Psychophysiology*, **14**, 385–387.

Domangue, B.B. (1978) Decoding effects of cognitive complexity, tolerance of ambiguity, and verbal–nonverbal inconsistency. *Journal of Personality*, **46**, 519–535.

Domangue, B.B. (1984) Hemisphere dominance, cognitive complexity, and nonverbal sensitivity. *Perceptual and Motor Skills*, **58**(1), 3–20.

Driver, M.J. (1979). Individual decision making and creativity. In S. Kerr (ed.), *Organizational Behavior*. Columbus, Ohio: Grid Publishing, pp.59–91.

Driver, M.J., and Mock, T.J. (1974) Human information processing, decision style theory and accounting information systems. Working paper No. 39, Graduate School of Business, University of Southern California.

Dunn, W.N., Pavlak, T.J., and Roberts, G.E. (1987) Cognitive performance appraisal — Mapping managers category structures using the grid technique, *Personnel Review*, **16**, 16–19.

Durand, R.M. (1979) Cognitive complexity, attitudinal affect, and dispersion in affect ratings for products. *Journal of Social Psychology*, **107**, 209–212.

Durand, R.M., and Lambert, Z.V. (1979). Cognitive differentiation and alienation of consumers. *Perceptual and Motor Skills*, **49**, 99–108.

Entwistle, N. (1982) Approaches and styles: Recent research on students' learning. *Educational Analysis*, **4**, 43–54.

Erez, M. (1980) Correlates of leadership style: field-dependence and social intelligence vs. social orientation. *Perceptual and Motor Skills*, **50**, 231–238.

Federico, P.A. (1984) Event-related-potential (ERP) correlates of cognitive styles, abilities and aptitudes. *Personality and Individual Differences*, **5**, 575–585.

Federico, P.A. (1985) Cognitive complexity and cerebral sensory interaction. *Personality and Individual Differences*, **6**, 253–261.

Federico, P.A., and Landis, D.B. (1979) Predicting student performance in a computer-managed course using measures of cognitive styles, abilities, and aptitudes. US Navy Pesonnel Research & Development Center Technical Report, August, pp.79–130.

Fertig, E.S., and Mayo, C. (1970) Impression formation as a function of trait consistency and cognitive complexity. *Journal of Experimental Research in Personality*, **4**, 190–197.

Fiedler, F.E. (1964) A contingency model of leadership effectiveness. In L. Berkowitz (ed.), *Advances in Experimental Social Psychology*. New York: Academic Press, pp.149–190.

Fiedler, F.E. (1984) Effects of intellectual ability and military experience on leadership performance. Paper presented at the Army Research Institute Conference, Georgetown University.

Fine, B.J. (1983) Field dependence and color discrimination ability in females. *Perceptual and Motor Skills*, **57**, 983–986.

Fine, B.J., and Kobrick, J.L. (1980) Field dependence, practice and low illumination as related to the Farnsworth–Munsel 100-Hue Test. *Perceptual and Motor Skills*, **51**, 1167–1177.

Flexer, B.K., and Roberge, J.J. (1983) A longitudinal investigation of field dependence-

-independence and the development of formal operational thought. *British Journal of Educational Psychology*, **53**, 195–204.
Frank, B.M. (1984) Effect of field independence–dependence and study technique on learning from a lecture. *American Educational Research Journal*, **21**, 669–678.
Frank, B.M., and Davis, J.K. (1982) The effect of field-independence match or mismatch on a communication task. *Journal of Educational Psychology*, **74**, 23–31.
Frank, B.M., and Noble, J.P. (1984) Field dependence–independence and cognitive restructuring. *Journal of Personality and Social Psychology*, **47**, 1129–1135.
Friedman, M., and Rosenman, R.H. (1974) *Type A Behavior and Your Heart*. New York: Knopf.
Gardner, R.W. (1953) Cognitive styles in categorizing behavior. *Journal of Personality*, **22**, 214–233.
Gardner, R.W. (1962) Cognitive controls in adaptation: Research and measurement. In S. Messick and J. Ross (eds), *Measurement in Personality and Cognition*. New York: Wiley.
Gardner, R.W., Holzman, P.S., Klein, G.S., Linton, H.B., and Spence, D. (1959) Cognitive control: A study of individual consistencies in cognitive behavior. *Psychological Issues*, **1**, Monograph 4.
Gardner, R.W., Jackson, D.N., and Messick, S. (1960). Personality organization in cognitive controls and intellectual abilities. *Psychological Issues*, **2**, Monograph 8.
Gardner, R.W., and Long, R.I. (1962a) Cognitive controls of attention and inhibition: A study of individual consistencies. *British Journal of Psychology*, **53**, 381–388.
Gardner, R.W., and Long, R.I. (1962b) Control, defense and centration effect: A study of scanning behavior. *British Journal of Psychology*, **53**, 129–140.
Goldsmith, R.E. (1985) Adaptation — innovation and cognitive complexity. *Journal of Psychology*, **119**, 461–467.
Goldstein, K.M., and Blackman, S. (1978a) Assessment of cognitive style. In P. McReynolds (ed.), *Advances in Psychological Assessment*, **4**, 462–525. San Francisco: Jossey-Bass.
Goldstein, K.M., and Blackman, S. (1978b) *Cognitive Style: Five approaches and relevant research*. New York: Wiley.
Gonzales, R.R., and Roll, S. (1985) Relationship between acculturation, cognitive style and intelligence. *Journal of Cross-Cultural Psychology*, **16**, 190–205.
Goodenough, D.R., Cox, P.W., Sigman, E., and Strawderman, W.E. (1985) Cognitive style conceptions of the field-dependence dimension. *Cahiers de Psychologie Cognitive*, **5**, 687–705.
Gordon, H.W., Charns, M.P., and Sherman, E. (1987) Management success as a function of performance on specialized cognitive tests. *Human Relations*, **40**, 671–698.
Guilford, J. (1980) Cognitive styles: What are they? *Psychological Measurement*, **40**, 715–735.
Gul, F.A. (1984) The joint and moderating role of personality and cognitive style on decision making. *Accounting Review*, **59**, 264–277.
Gul, F.A. and Zaid, O. (1981) Field dependence and accountants' confidence in decisions. *Psychological Reports*, **49**, 949–950.
Gundlach, R.H., and Gesell, G.P. (1979) Extent of psychological differentiation and creativity. *Perceptual and Motor Skills*, **48**, 319–333.
Hale, C.L. (1980) Cognitive complexity — simplicity as a determinant of communication effectiveness. *Communication Monographs*, **47**, 304–311.
Hale, C.L. (1986) Impact of cognitive complexity on message structure in a face-threatening conflict. *Journal of Language and Social Psychology*, **5**, 135–143.

Hancock, P.A., and Meshkati, N. (1988) *Human Mental Workload.* Amsterdam: North-Holland.

Hancock, P.A., Meshkati, N., and Robertson, M.M. (1985) Physiological reflections of mental workload. *Aviation, Space and Environmental Medicine,* **56,** 1110–1114.

Handley, P. (1982) The relationship between supervisors' and trainees' cognitive styles and the supervision process. *Journal of Counseling Psychology,* **29,** 508–515.

Hansen, J., and Stansfield, C. (1982) Student–teacher cognitive styles and foreign language achievement: A preliminary study. *Modern Language Journal,* **66,** 263–273.

Harris, R.M., and Highlen, P.S. (1982) Conceptual complexity and susceptibility to learned helplessness. *Social Behavior and Personality,* **10,** 183–188.

Harrison, R. (1966) Cognitive change and participation in a sensitivity training laboratory, *Journal of Consulting Psychology,* **30,** 517–520.

Harvey, O.J. (1963) *Cognitive Determinants of Role Playing.* University of Colorado: ONR Technical Report No. 3.

Harvey, O.J. (1965) Some situational and cognitive determinants of dissonance resolution. *Journal of Personality and Social Psychology,* **1,** 349–355.

Harvey, O.J. (1966) System structure, flexibility and creativity. In O.J. Harvey (ed.), *Experience, Structure and Adaptability.* New York: Springer.

Harvey, O.J. (1967) Conceptual systems and attitude change. In C.W. Sherif and M. Sherif (eds), *Attitude, Ego Involvement and Change.* New York: Wiley.

Harvey, O.J., Hunt, D., and Schroder, H.M. (1961) *Conceptual Systems and Personality Organization.* New York: Wiley.

Harvey, O.J., and Ware, R. (1967) Personality differences in dissonance resolution. *Journal of Personality and Social Psychology,* **2,** 227–230.

Heesacker, M., Petty, R.E, and Cacioppo, J.T. (1983) Field dependence and attitude change: source credibility can alter persuasion by affecting message relevant thinking. *Journal of Personality,* **51,** 653–666.

Heider, F. (1946) Attitudes and cognitive organization. *Journal of Psychology,* **21,** 107–112.

Henderson, J.C., and Nutt, P.C. (1980) The influence of decision style on decision making behavior. *Management Science,* **26,** 371–386.

Hendrick, H.W. (1979) Differences in group problem-solving behavior and effectiveness as a function in abstractness. *Journal of Applied Psychology,* **64,** 518–525.

Hersey, P., and Blanchard, K.H. (1982a) Grid principles and situationalism: Both a response to Blake and Mouton. *Group and Organization Studies,* **7,** 207–210.

Hersey, P., and Blanchard, K.H. (1982b) Leadership style: Attitudes and behaviors. *Training and Development Journal,* **36,** 50–52.

Heslin, R., and Streufert, S. (1968) Task familiarity and reliance on the environment in decision making. *Psychological Record,* **18,** 629–637.

Holloway, E.L., and Wampold, B.E. (1986) Relation between conceptual level and counseling-related tasks: A meta-analysis. *Journal of Counseling Psychology,* **33,** 310–319.

Holloway E.L., and Wolleat, P.L. (1980) Relationship of counselor conceptual level to clinical hypothesis formation. *Journal of Counseling Psychology,* **27,** 539–545.

Hudson, L. (1966) *Contrary Imaginations.* New York: Schocken.

Hughes, R.N. (1981) Sex differences in group embedded figures test performance in relation to sex-role, state and trait anxiety. *Current Psychological Research,* **1,** 227–234.

Hunt, D.E. (1966) A conceptual systems change model. In O.J. Harvey (ed.), *Experience, Structure and Adaptability.* New York: Springer.

Hussy, W. (1979) Analysis of the need for information during a modified prisoner's dilemma game. *Zeitschrift fur Experimentelle und Angewandte Psychologie,* **26,** 561–572.

Huysmans, J.H. (1970) *The Implementation of Operation Research*. New York: Wiley-Interscience.
Imam, A. (1986) Field dependency and persuasibility. *Journal of Personality and Clinical Studies*, **2**, 117–121.
Isenberg, D.J. (1984) How senior managers think (and what about). *Harvard Business Review*, 81–90.
Janicki, W.P. (1964) Effects of disposition on resolution of incongruity. *Journal of Abnormal and Social Psychology*, **69**, 575–584.
Johnson, S., Flinn, J.M., and Tyer, Z.E. (1979) Effect of practice and training in spatial skills on embedded figure scores of males and females. *Perceptual and Motor Skills*, **48**, 975–984.
Johnston, S., and Centers, R. (1973) Cognitive systemization and interpersonal attraction. *Journal of Social Psychology*, **90**, 95–103.
Jones, A.P., and Butler, M.C. (1980) Influences of cognitive complexity on the dimensions underlying perceptions of the work environment. *Motivation and Emotion*, **4**, 1–19.
Kagan, J., and Kogan, N. (1970) Individual variation in cognitive processes. In P.H. Mussen (ed.), *Charmichaels Manual of Child Psychology*, Vol. 1. New York: Wiley.
Kagan, J., Rosman, B.L., Day, D., Albert, J., and Phillips, W. (1964) Information processing in the child: Significance of analytic and reflective attitudes. *Psychological Monographs*, **78**, Whole No. 578.
Karlins, M. (1967) Conceptual complexity and remote associate proficiency as creativity variables in a complex problem solving task. *Journal of Personality and Social Psychology*, **6**, 264–278.
Karlins, M., Coffman, T., Lamm, H., and Schroder, H.M. (1967) The effect of conceptual complexity on information search in a complex problem-solving task. *Psychonomic Science*, **7**, 137–138.
Karlins, M., and Lamm, H. (1967) Information search as a function of conceptual structure in a complex problem solving task. *Journal of Personality and Social Psychology*, **5**, 456–459.
Keen, P.G. (1973) The implication of cognitive style for individual decision making. Harvard University: Unpublished doctoral dissertation.
Kelly, G.A. (1955) *The Psychology of Personal Constructs*, Vol. 1. *A theory of personality*. New York: W.W. Norton.
Kendall, P.C., Hooke, J.F., Rymer, R., and Finch, A.J. (1980) Cognitive style in adults: Task alternative, task strategy and time estimation. *Journal of Personality Assessment*, **44**, 175–181.
Kershner, J.R., and Ledger, G. (1985) Effect of sex, intelligence and style of thinking on creativity. *Journal of Personality and Social Psychology*, **48**, 1033–1040.
Kiewra, K.A., and Frank, B.M. (1986) Cognitive style: Effects of structure at acquisition and testing. *Contemporary Educational Psychology*, **11**, 253–263.
Kirton, M. (1976) Adaptors and innovators: A description and measure. *Journal of Applied Psychology*, **61**, 622–629.
Klein, G.S. (1954) Need and regulation. In M.R. Jones (ed.), *Nebraska Symposium on Motivation*. Lincoln: University of Nebraska Press.
Klein, G.S. (1958) Cognitive control and motivation. In G. Lindzey (ed.), *Assessment of Human Motives*. New York: Holt, Rinehart and Winston.
Klein, G.S. (1970) *Perception, Motives and Personality*. New York: Knopf.
Kogan, N. (1973) Creativity and cognitive style: A lifespan perspective. In P.B. Baltes and W.P. Schaie (eds), *Life-Span Developmental Psychology: Personality and socialization*. New York: Academic Press.

Kogan, N. (1976) *Cognitive Style in Infancy and Early Childhood.* Hillsdale, NJ: Lawrence Erlbaum Associates.

Kogan, N. (1980) Cognitive styles and reading performance. *Bulletin of the Orton Society,* **30,** 63–78.

Larsen, W.W. (1982) The relationship of reflection–impulsivity to intelligence and field dependence in older adults. *Journal of Psychology,* **111,** 31–34.

Lee, J.A., and Pollack, R.H. (1980) The effects of age on perceptual field dependence. *Bulletin of the Psychonomic Society,* **15,** 239–241.

Leino, A.L., and Puurula, A. (1983) *Admission to Teacher Education and Two Cognitive Styles.* Research Bulletin, Department of Education, University of Helsinki, Finland No. 61.

Leventhal, M. (1957) Cognitive processes and interpersonal prediction. *Journal of Abnormal and Social Psychology,* **55,** 176–180.

Leventhal, H., and Singer, D.L. (1964) Cognitive complexity, impression formation and impression change. *Journal of Personality,* **32,** 210–226.

Levi, A., and Tetlock, P.E. (1980). A cognitive analysis of Japan's 1941 decision for war. *Journal of Conflict Resolution,* **24,** 195–211.

Levin, I.P., Louviere, J.J., Schepanski, A.A., and Norman, K.L. (1983) External validity tests of laboratory studies of information integration. *Organizational Behavior and Human Performance,* **31,** 173–193.

Lewin, K. (1936) *Principles of Topological Psychology.* New York: McGraw-Hill.

Lilli, W. (1973) Active and passive preference of complex stimuli depending on cognitive differentiation of judgment. *Psychologissche Beitrage,* **15,** 291–300.

Linville, P.W., and Jones, E.E. (1980) Polarized appraisals of out-group members. *Journal of Personality and Social Psychology,* **38,** 689–703.

Lundberg, O.H. (1972) An empirical examination of relationships between cognitive style and complex decision making. *Dissertation Abstracts International,* **33,** No. 72-19341.

Lusk, E.J., and Kersnick, M. (1979) The effect of cognitive styles and report format on task performance. *Management Science,* **25,** 787–798.

Malhotra, N.K., Jain, A.K., and Pinson, C. (1983) Extremity of judgment and personality variables: Two empirical investigations. *Journal of Social Psychology,* **120,** 111–118.

Marincola, L.B., and Long, G.M. (1985) Perceptual style and dual task performance as a function of task difficulty and task emphasis. *Perceptual and Motor Skills,* **61,** 1091–1105.

Martin, T.O., and Gross, R.B. (1979) A comparison of twins for degree of closeness and field dependency. *Adolescence,* **14,** 739–745.

Mayo, C.W., and Crockett, W.H. (1964) Cognitive complexity and primacy–recency effects in impression formation. *Journal of Abnormal and Social Psychology,* **68,** 335–338.

McDonald, E.R. (1984) The relationship of student and faculty field dependence/independence congruence to student academic achievement. *Educational and Psychological Measurement,* **44,** 725–731.

Mednick, S.A. (1963) The associative basis of the creative process. In M.T. Mednick and S.A. Mednick (eds), *Research in Personality.* New York: Holt, Rinehart & Winston.

Meltzer, L.J. (1982) Visual perception: Stage one of a long-term investigation into cognitive components of achievement. *British Journal of Educational Psychology,* **52,** 144–154.

Mendelsohn, G.E. (1970) Critique of the Myers–Briggs type indicator. In O.K. Buros (ed.), *The Sixth Mental Measurement Yearbook*. Highland Park, NJ: Gryphon.
Meredith, G.M. (1985) Transmitter–facilitator teaching style and focus–scan learning style in higher education. *Perceptual and Motor Skills*, 6, 545–546.
Merron, K., Fisher, D., and Torbert, W.R. (1987) Meaning making and management action. *Group and Organizational Studies*, 12, 274–286.
Meshkati, N., and Loewenthal, A. (1988) The effects of individual differences in information processing behavior on experiencing mental workload and perceived task difficulty. In P.A. Hancock and N. Meshkati (eds), *Human Mental Workload*. New York: North Holland.
Messer, S.B. (1976) Reflection–impulsivity: A review. *Psychological Bulletin*, 83, 1026–1052.
Messick, S. (1970) The criterion problem in the evaluation of instruction. In M.C. Wittrock and D.W. Wiley (eds): *The Evaluation of Instruction: Issues and Problems*. New York: Holt, Rinehart and Winston.
Messick, S. (1972) Beyond structure: In search of functional modes of psychological process. *Psychometrica*, 37, 357–375.
Messick, S. (1973) Multivariate models of cognition and personality. In J.R. Royce (ed.), *Multivariate Analysis and Psychological Theory*. New York: Academic Press.
Messick, S. (1976) *Individuality in Learning: Implications of cognitive styles and creativity for human development*. San Francisco: Jossey-Bass.
Messick, S. (1978) Personality consistencies in cognition and creativity. In S. Messick & Associates (eds), *Individuality in Learning*. San Francisco: Jossey-Bass.
Messick, S. (1981) Constructs and their vicissitudes in educational and psychological measurement. *Psychological Bulletin*, 89, 575–588.
Messick, S. (1982) Developing abilities and knowledge: Style in the interplay of structure and process. *Educational Analysis*, 4, 105–121.
Messick, S. (1984) The nature of cognitive styles: Problems and promise in educational practice. *Educational Psychologist*, 19, 59–74.
Miller, A.G. (1969) Amount of information and stimulus valence as determinants of cognitive complexity. *Journal of Personality*, 37, 141–157.
Millimet, C.R., and Brien, M. (1980) Cognitive differentiation and interpersonal discomfort: An integration theory approach. *Journal of Mind and Behavior*, 1, 211–225.
Mintzberg, H. (1976) Planning on the left side and managing on the right. *Harvard Business Review*, 54, 49–58.
Mitchell, T.R. (1970) Leader complexity and leadership style. *Journal of Personality and Social Psychology*, 16, 166–174.
Mitchell, T.R. (1971) Cognitive complexity and group performance. *Journal of Social Psychology*, 86, 35–43.
Mizerski, R.W. (1978) Causal complexity: A measure of consumer causal attribution. *Journal of Marketing Research*, 15, 220–228.
Moran, A.P. (1986) Field independence and proficiency in electrical fault diagnosis. *IEEE Transactions on Systems, Man and Cybernetics*, SMC-16, 162–165.
Mueller, J.H., and Fisher, D.M. (1980) Field independence and input grouping in free recall. *Bulletin of the Psychonomic Society*, 16, 397–400.
Muneno, R., and Dembo, M.H. (1982) Causal attributions for student performance: Effects of teachers' conceptual complexity. *Personality and Social Psychology Bulletin*, 8, 201–207.
Myers, I.B. (1962) *The Myers–Briggs Type Indicator*. Palo Alto, CA: Consulting Psychologists Press.

Neimeyer, G.J. (1984) Cognitive complexity and marital satisfaction. *Journal of Social and Clinical Psychology*, **2**, 258–263.

Neimeyer, R.A., Neimeyer, G.J., and Landfield, A.W. (1983) Conceptual differentiation, integration and empathic prediction. *Journal of Personality*, **51**, 185–191.

Neuliep, J.W., and Hazleton, V. (1985) Cognitive complexity and apprehension about communication: A preliminary report. *Psychological Reports*, **57**, 1224–1226.

Nidorf, L.J. (1961) Individual differences in impression formation. Unpublished doctoral dissertation, Clark University.

Nidorf, L.J., and Crockett, W.H. (1965) Cognitive complexity and the integration of conflicting information in written impressions. *Journal of Social Psychology*, **66**, 165–169.

Noppe, L.D. (1985) The relationship of formal thought and cognitive styles to creativity. *Journal of Creative Behavior*, **19**, 88–96.

Nydegger, R.V. (1975) Information processing complexity and leadership status. *Journal of Experimental Social Psychology*, **11**, 317–328.

O'Keefe, D.J., and Brady, R.M. (1980) Cognitive complexity and the effects of thought on attitude change. *Social Behavior and Personality*, **8**, 49–56.

O'Keefe, D.J., and Delia, J.G. (1978) Construct comprehension and cognitive complexity. *Perceptual and Motor Skills*, **46**, 548–550.

Overton, W., Byrnes, J.P., and O'Brien, D.P. (1985) Developmental and individual differences in conditional reasoning. *Developmental Psychology*, **2**, 692–701.

Pandey, A.K., and Pandey, A.K. (1985) A study of cognitive styles of urban and rural college students. *Perspectives in Psychological Research*, **8**, 38–43.

Pask, G. (1976) Styles and strategies of learning. *British Journal of Educational Psychology*, **46**, 128–148.

Petronko, M.R., and Perin, C.T. (1970) A consideration of cognitive complexity and primacy–recency effects in impression formation. *Journal of Personality and Social Psychology*, **15**, 151–157.

Petrovskii, A.V. (1986) 'Contrasting position grid' as a diagnostic measure of the level of development of interpersonal relations. *Soviet Psychology*, **24**, 43–54.

Pettigrew, T.F. (1958) The measurement and correlates of category width as a cognitive variable. *Journal of Personality*, **26**, 532–544.

Piaget, J. (1952) *The Origins of Intelligence in Children*. New York: International Universities Press.

Pincus, K.V. (1985) Group embedded figures test: Psychometric data for a sample of accountants compared to student norms. *Perceptual and Motor Skills*, **60**, 707–712.

Porter, C.A., and Suedfeld, P. (1981) Integrative complexity in the correspondence of literary figures: Effects of personal and societal stress. *Journal of Personality and Social Psychology*, **40**, 321–330.

Press, A.N., Crockett, W.H., and Rosenkrantz, P.S. (1969) Cognitive complexity and the learning of balanced and unbalanced social structures. *Journal of Personality*, **37**, 541–553.

Quinn, E. (1980) Creativity and cognitive complexity. *Social Behavior and Personality*, **8**, 213–215.

Ramirez, M., and Castaneda, A. (1974) *Cultural Democracy: Bicognitive development and education*. New York: Academic Press.

Raphael, D. (1982) Integrative complexity theory and forecasting international crises: Berlin 1946–1962. *Journal of Conflict Resolution*, **26**, 423–450.

Raphael, D., Moss, S.W., and Rosser, M.E. (1979) Evidence concerning the construct validity of conceptual level as a personality variable. *Canadian Journal of Behavioural Science*, **11**, 327–339.

Reardon, R., Jolly, E.J., McKinney, K.D., and Forducey, P. (1982) Field dependence--independence and active learning of verbal and geometric material. *Perceptual and Motor Skills*, **55**, 263–266.

Reiss, D., and Oliveri, M.E. (1983) Sensory experience and family process: Perceptual styles tend to run in but not necessarily run families. *Family Process*, **22**, 289–308.

Renninger, K.A., and Snyder, S.S. (1983) Effects of cognitive style on perceived satisfaction and performance among students and teachers. *Journal of Educational Psychology*, **75**, 668–676.

Roberts, F.C., and Park, O.C. (1984) Feedback strategies and cognitive style in computer based instruction. *Journal of Instructional Psychology*, **11**, 63–74.

Robertson, M.M., and Meshkati, N. (1985) Analysis of the effects of two individual differences classification models on experiencing work load in a computer generated task. *Proceedings of the 29th Annual Meeting of the Human Factors Society*, 178–182.

Robey, D., and Taggart, W. (1981) Measuring managers' minds: The assessment of style in human information processing. *Academy of Management Review*, **3**, 375–383.

Robinson, D.L. (1983) The structure of Witkin's embedded figures test. *Perceptual and Motor Skills*, **57**, 119–125.

Rokeach, M. (1960) *The Open and Closed Mind*. New York: Basic Books.

Rosenman, R.H. (1978) The interview method of assessment of the coronary-prone behavior pattern. In T.M. Dembroski, S.M. Weiss, and J.L. Shields (eds), *Coronary Prone Behavior*. New York: Springer.

Rouse, S.H., and Rouse, W.B. (1982) Cognitive style as a correlate of human problem solving performance in fault diagnosis tasks. *IEEE Transactions on Systems, Man and Cybernetics*, **12**, 649–652.

Rouse, W.B. and Rouse, S.H. (1979) Measures of complexity of fault diagnostics tasks. *IEEE Transactions on Systems, Man and Cybernetics*, **SMC-9**, 720–727.

Sabatelli, R.M., Dreyer, A.S., and Buck, R. (1979) Cognitive style and sending and receiving of facial cues. *Perceptual and Motor Skills*, **49**, 203–212.

Sahoo, F.M. (1982) Affective sensitivity and cognitive style. *Indian Psychologist*, **1**, 57–65.

Santostefano, S. (1978) *A Biodevelopmental Approach to Clinical Child Psychology*. New York: Wiley.

Saracho, O.N. (1983) Cultural differences in the cognitive style of Mexican American students. *Journal of the Association for the Study of Perception*, **18**, 3–10.

Sarmany, I. (1979) Field dependence–independence in relation to loads tolerance. *Studia Psychologica*, **21**, 125–131.

Sarmany, I. (1985) Interacting features of cognitive style and operator's simulated work during a 24-hour cycle: III. *Studia Psychologica*, **27**, 283–290.

Sauser, W.I., and Pond, S.B. (1981) Effects of rater training and participation on cognitive complexity: An exploration of Schneier's cognitive reinterpretation. *Personnel Psychology*, **34**, 563–577.

Schneider, G.A., and Giambra, L.M. (1971) Performance in concept identification as a function of cognitive complexity. *Journal of Personality and Social Psychology*, **19**, 261–273.

Schneier, C.E. (1978) The contingency model of leadership: An extension to emergent leadership and leader's sex. *Organizational Behavior and Human Performance*, **21**, 220–239.

Schneier, C.E. (1979a) Cognitive structure and preference for constructs in impression formation: A field experiment. *Psychological Reports*, **45**, 459–467.

Schneier, C.E. (1979b) Measuring cognitive complexity: Developing reliability, validity,

and norm tables for a personality measurement. *Educational and Psychological Measurement*, **39**, 599-612.
Schroder, H.M., Driver, M.J., and Streufert, S. (1967) *Human Information Processing*. New York: Holt, Rinehart & Winston.
Schroder, H.M., and Streufert, S. (1963). The measurement of four systems of personality structure varying in level of abstractness: sentence completion method. Princeton University. ONR Technical Report 11.
Schwabisch, S.D., and Drury, C.G. (1984). The influence of the reflective-impulsive cognitive style on visual inspection. *Human Factors*, **26**, 641-647.
Schweiger, D.M. (1983) Measuring managers' minds: A critical reply to Robey and Taggart. *Academy of Management Review*, **8**, 143-151.
Schweiger, D.M. (1985) Measuring managerial cognitive styles: On the logical validity of the Myers-Briggs type indicator. *Journal of Business Research*, **13**, 315-328.
Schwenk, C.R. (1984) Cognitive simplification processes in strategic decision making. *Strategic Management Journal*, **5**, 111-128.
Scott, W.A. (1959) Cognitive consistency, response reinforcement and attitude change. *Sociometry*, **22**, 219-229.
Scott, W.A. (1962) Cognitive complexity and cognitive flexibility. *Sociometry*, **25**, 405-414.
Scott, W.A. (1963) Cognitive complexity and cognitive balance. *Sociometry*, **26**, 66-74.
Scott, W.A. (1966) Brief report: Measures of cognitive structure. *Multivariate Behavioral Research*, **1**, 391-395.
Scott, W.A. (1969) Structure of natural cognitions. *Journal of Personality and Social Psychology*, **12**, 261-278.
Scott, W.A., Osgood, D.W., and Peterson, C. (1979) *Cognitive Structure: Theory and measurement of individual differences*. Washington, DC and New York: V.H. Winston & Sons and Halsted Division, Wiley.
Seligman, M. (1975) *Helplessness*. San Francisco, CA: Freeman.
Shore, B.M., Hymovitch, J., and Lajoie, S.P. (1982) Processing differences in relations between ability and field independence. *Psychological Reports*, **50**, 391-395.
Sieber, J.E., and Lanzetta, J.T. (1964) Conflict and conceptual structure as determinants of decision making behavior. *Journal of Personality*, **32**, 622-641.
Sillars, A., and Parry, D. (1982) Stress, cognition, and communication in interpersonal conflicts. *Communication Research*, **9**, 201-226.
Sousa, P.J.F., Rohrberg, R., and Mercure, A. (1979) Effects of type of information and field dependence on asymmetry of hand movements during speech. *Perceptual and Motor Skills*, **48**, 1323-1330.
Stabell, C.B. (1978) Integrative complexity of information environment perception and information use: An empirical investigation. *Organizational Behavior and Human Performance*, **22**, 116-142.
Sternberg, R.J. (1980) Sketch of a componential subtheory of human intelligence. *Behavioral and Brain Sciences*, **3**, 573-614.
Sternberg, R.J. (1984) Toward a triarchic theory of human intelligence. *Behavioral and Brain Sciences*, **7**, 269-315.
Streufert, S. (1966) Conceptual structure, communicator importance and interpersonal attitudes toward conforming and deviant group members. *Journal of Personality and Social Psychology*, **4**, 100-103.
Streufert, S. (1970) Complexity and complex decision making. *Journal of Experimental Social Psychology*, **6**, 494-509.
Streufert, S. (1978) The human component in the decision making situation. In B. King, S. Streufert and F. Fiedler (eds), *Managerial Control and Organizational Democracy*.

Washington, DC: Victor H. Winston & Sons and Halsted Division, John Wiley & Sons, pp.215–230.
Streufert, S. (1986) How top managers think and decide. *Executive Excellence*, 3(8), 7–9.
Streufert, S. (1987) Age and executive competence: When is a manager too old? *International Management*, No. 12, 50–52.
Streufert, S., Bushinsky, R.G., and Castore, C.H. (1967) Conceptual structure and social choice: a replication under modified conditions. *Psychonomic Science*, 9, 227–228.
Streufert, S., and Castore, C.H. (1971) Information search and the effects of failure: A test of complexity theory. *Journal of Experimental Social Psychology*, 7, 125–143.
Streufert, S., Castore, C.H., Kliger, S.C., and Driver, M.J. (1967) Conceptual structure and interpersonal attraction. ONR Technical Report No. 4.
Streufert, S., DePadova, A., McGlynn, T., Piasecki, M., and Pogash, R. (1988a) Impact of B-blockade on complex cognitive functioning. *American Heart Journal*, 116, 311–318.
Streufert, S., and Driver, M.J. (1965) Conceptual structure, information load and perceptual complexity. *Psychonomic Science*, 3, 249–250.
Streufert, S., and Driver, M.J. (1967) Impression formation as a measure of the complexity of conceptual structure. *Educational and Psychological Measurement*, 27, 1025–1039.
Streufert, S., Nogami, G.Y., Swezey, R.W., Pogash, R.M., and Piasecki, M.T. (1988b) Computer assisted training of complex managerial performance. *Computers in Human Behavior*, 4, 77–88.
Streufert, S., Pogash, R.M., and Piasecki, M.T. (1988) Simulation based assessment of managerial competence: Reliability and validity. *Personnel Psychology*, 41, 537–555.
Streufert, S., and Schroder, H.M. (1965) Conceptual structure, environmental complexity and task performance, *Journal of Experimental Research in Personality*, 1, 132–137.
Streufert, S., and Streufert, S.C. (1969) Effects of conceptual structure, failure and success on attribution of causality and interpersonal attitudes. *Journal of Personality and Social Psychology*, 11, 138–147.
Streufert, S., and Streufert, S.C. (1978) *Behavior in the Complex Environment*. Washington, DC and New York, NY: V.H. Winston & Sons and Halsted Division, John Wiley and Sons.
Streufert S., Streufert, S.C., and Castore, C.H. (1968) Leadership in negotiations and the complexity of conceptual structure. *Journal of Applied Psychology*, 52, 218–223.
Streufert, S., Streufert, S.C., and Castore, C.H. (1969) Complexity, increasing failure and decision making. *Journal of Experimental Research in Personality*, 3, 293–300.
Streufert, S., Streufert, S.C., and Denson, A.L. (1985) Effects of load stressors, cognitive complexity and Type A coronary prone behavior on visual–motor task performance. *Journal of Personality and Social Psychology*, 48, 728–739.
Streufert, S., Suedfeld, P., and Driver, M.J. (1965) Conceptual structure, information search and information utilization. *Journal of Personality and Social Psychology*, 2, 736–740.
Streufert, S., and Swezey, R.W. (1985) Simulation and related research methods in environmental psychology. In A. Baum and J.E. Singer (eds), *Advances in Environmental Psychology*, Vol. 5. Hillsdale, NJ: Lawrence Erlbaum Associates, pp.99–117.
Streufert, S., and Swezey, R.J. (1986) *Complexity, Managers and Organizations*. New York: Academic Press.

Streufert, S.C. (1973) Effects of information relevance on decision making in complex environments. *Memory and Cognition*, **1**, 224–228.

Suedfeld, P. (1964) Attitude manipulation in restricted environments: 1. Conceptual structure and response to propaganda. *Journal of Abnormal and Social Psychology*, **68**, 242–247.

Suedfeld, P. (1985) APA presidential addresses: The relation of integrative complexity to historical, professional and personal factors. *Journal of Personality and Social Psychology*, **49**, 1643–1651.

Suedfeld, P., Corteen, R.S., and McCormick, C. (1986) The role of integrative complexity in military leadership: Robert E. Lee and his opponents. *Journal of Applied Social Psychology*, **16**, 498–507.

Suedfeld, P., and Rank, A.D. (1976) Revolutionary leaders: Long-term success as a function of changes in conceptual complexity. *Journal of Personality and Social Psychology*, **34**, 169–178.

Suedfeld, P., and Streufert, S. (1966) Information search as a function of conceptual and environmental complexity. *Psychonomic Science*, **4**, 351–352.

Suedfeld, P., and Tetlock, P.E. (1977) Integrative complexity of communications in international crisis. *Journal of Conflict Resolution*, **21**, 169–184.

Suedfeld, P., Tetlock, P.E., and Ramirez, C. (1977) War, peace and integrative complexity: UN speeches on the middle east problem. *Journal of Conflict Resolution*, **21**, 427–441.

Sundberg, N.D. (1970) Critique of the Myers–Briggs type indicator. In O.K. Buros (ed.), *The Sixth Mental Measurement Yearbook*. Highland Park, NJ: Gryphon, 1127–1130.

Swinnen, S., Vandenberghe, J., and VanAssche, E. (1986) Role of cognitive style constructs field dependence–independence and reflection–impulsivity in skill acquisition. *Journal of Sport Psychology*, **8**, 51–69.

Sypher, H.E., Witt, D.E., and Sypher, B.D. (1986) Interpersonal cognitive differentiation measures as predictors of written communication ability. *Communication Monographs*, **53**, 376–382.

Tetlock, P.E. (1980) A cognitive analysis of Japan's 1941 decision for war. *Journal of Conflict Resolution*, **24**, 195–211.

Tetlock, P.E. (1981) Pre- to postelection shifts in presidential rhetoric: Impression management or cognitive adjustment. *Journal of Personality and Social Psychology*, **41**, 207–212.

Tetlock, P.E., Bernzweig, J., and Gallant, J.L. (1985) Supreme Court decision making: Cognitive style as a predictor of ideological consistency and voting. *Journal of Personality and Social Psychology*, **48**, 1227–1239.

Tetlock, P.E., Hannum, K.A., and Micheletti, P.M. (1984) Stability and change in the complexity of senatorial debate: Testing the cognitive vs. rhetorical style hypotheses. *Journal of Personality and Social Psychology*, **46**, 979–990.

Thomas, H. (1982) A strong developmental theory of field dependence–independence. *Journal of Mathematical Psychology*, **26**, 169–178.

Thompson, E.G., Mann, I.T., and Harris, L.J. (1981) Relationships among cognitive complexity, sex, and spatial task performance in college students. *British Journal of Psychology*, **72**, 249–256.

Thorne, P. (1986) Management style: Can you change yours at will? *International Management*, **41**, 62.

Tuckman, B.W. (1964) Personality structure, group composition and group functioning. *Sociometry*, **27**, 469–487.

Tuckman, B.W. (1966) Integrative complexity: its measurement and relation to creativity. *Educational and Psychological Measurement*, 26, 329–382.

Vecchio, R. (1979) A test of the cognitive complexity interpretation of the least preferred co-worker scale. *Educational and Psychological Measurement*, 39, 523–526.

Von Eye, A., and Hussy, W. (1979) On the contribution of variables of cognitive complexity to the identification of risk groups in traffic. *Schweizerische Zeitschrift fur Psychologie und ihre Anwendungen*, 38, 58–70.

Walker, R.D., O'Leary, M.R., Chaney, E.F., and Fauria, T.M. (1979) Influence of cognitive style on an incidental memory task. *Perceptual and Motor Skills*, 48, 195–198.

Ware, R., and Harvey, O.J. (1967) A cognitive determinant of impression formation. *Journal of Personality and Social Psychology*, 1, 38–44.

Watson, S.R. (1976) Counselor complexity and the process of hypothesizing about a client. Unpublished doctoral dissertation, University of California.

Weiss, H.M., and Adler, S. (1981) Cognitive complexity and the structure of implicit leadership theories. *Journal of Applied Psychology*, 66, 69–78.

Weiss, H.M., and Nowicki, C.E. (1981) Social influence on task satisfaction: Model competence and observer field dependence. *Organizational Behavior and Human Performance*, 27, 345–366.

Werner, H. (1957) *Comparative Psychology of Mental Development*. New York: International Universities Press.

White, C.M. (1977) Cognitive complexity and completion of social structures. *Social Behavior and Personality*, 5, 305–310.

Widiger, T.A., Knudson, R.M., and Rorer, L.G. (1980) Convergent and discriminant validity of measures of cognitive styles and abilities. *Journal of Personality and Social Psychology*, 39, 116–129.

Witkin, H.A., Dyk, R.B., Faterson, H.F., Goodenough, D.R., and Karp, S.A. (1962) *Psychological Differentiation*. New York: Wiley.

Witkin, H.A., Oltman, P.K., Raskin, E., and Karp, S.A. (1971) *A Manual for the Embedded Figures Test*. Palo Alto, CA: Consulting Psychologists Press.

Wojciszke, B. (1979) Affective factors in organization of cognitive structures in the context of interpersonal perception. *Polish Psychological Bulletin*, 10, 3–13.

Wolfe, J., and Chacko, T.I. (1980) Cognitive structures of business game players. *Simulations and Games*, 11, 461–476.

Wyer, R.S. (1964) Assessment and correlates of cognitive differentiation and integration. *Journal of Personality*, 32, 495–509.

Zajonc, R.B. (1960) The process of cognitive tuning in communication. *Journal of Abnormal and Social Psychology*, 61, 159–167.

Zalot, G., and Adams, W.J. (1977) Cognitive complexity in the perception of neighbors. *Social Behavior and Personality*, 5, 281–283.

Zmud, R.W. (1979) Perceptions of cognitive styles: Acquisition exhibition and implications for information system design. *Journal of Management*, 5, 7–20.

Chapter 5

COACHING AND PRACTICE EFFECTS IN PERSONNEL SELECTION

Paul R. Sackett
Industrial Relations Center
University of Minnesota
Laura R. Burris
Department of Psychology
University of Illinois at Chicago
and
Ann Marie Ryan
Department of Psychology
Bowling Green State University
USA

Consider the following events taking place in various organizations:

1) Company policy permits an applicant failing a pre-employment test to retake the test after a one-week interval.
2) A police department prepares a test preparation guide outlining the content domain of an upcoming promotional exam for the job of sergeant.
3) A firm places an advertisement in the local paper offering to prepare job applicants to 'beat' a pre-employment polygraph exam.
4) Employees who have previously gone through a management assessment center offer advice based on the feedback received about their performance to co-workers about to attend.
5) An entrepreneur compiles a booklet made up of past examinations for a position, which are now a matter of public record, and sells it as a 'score-it-yourself practice guide' for the position in question.
6) A college student seeking summer work applies at a number of retail stores and finds that she is asked to complete virtually identical personality inventories by several of the stores.
7) Two weeks before a scheduled exam, an organization gives applicants a test orientation guide focusing on general principles of test taking.

8) A school of business requires all MBA students to attend a job seeking skills seminar in which students undergo multiple practice interviews, which are videotaped and on which the students receive detailed feedback.

The purpose of this chapter is to examine theory and evidence regarding coaching and practice effects in employee selection. The above examples illustrate only a few of the ways that coaching and practice can occur in selection settings. In this chapter we will review evidence regarding the effects of coaching and practice on performance on a number of commonly used selection devices, including cognitive ability tests, psychomotor ability tests, personality measures, assessment centers, and interviews.

DEFINITIONAL ISSUES

The terms 'coaching' and 'practice' are not clearly defined and differentiated in the psychological testing literature. Anastasi (1981) identified three types of interventions: (1) coaching, defined as intensive drill on items similar to those included on a test; (2) test-taking orientation, designed to eliminate differences in test sophistication, or general test-taking skills, among examinees; and (3) education, defined as attempts to develop widely applicable intellectual skills, work habits, and problem-solving strategies. The intent is to change not only test performance, but also criterion performance. Anastasi noted that these distinctions are not routinely made, and that each of these has been labelled 'coaching'. Thus attempts to evaluate coaching effects should be examined carefully to determine the actual nature of the intervention.

Messick (1981) also recognized that a range of activities fall under the label of 'coaching'. He conceptualized a continuum from practice on sample tests to intensive instruction aimed at skill development. He also noted that where interventions fall on this continuum tends to be linked to the type of test involved. For example, coaching for scholastic ability tests tends to focus on practice and test-taking strategies, while coaching for achievement tests tends to emphasize content-oriented review and instruction. Messick noted that there are competing schools of thought as to whether instruction ought to be included under the rubric of coaching. He concluded that rather than arguing as to where the line should be drawn as to what should and should not be included, an inclusive definition is preferred. Thus he defined coaching as any intervention specifically undertaken to improve test scores, regardless of whether the focus is on improving only the score or on improving the skill underlying the score.

A distinction between coaching and practice is incorporated in definitions offered by Kulik and his colleagues (Kulik, Bangert-Drowns, and Kulik, 1984; Kulik, Kulik, and Bangert, 1984). Their differentiation between coaching and practice focused on whether or not there is an external intervention: practice involves learning from one's own experience with alternate forms of a test while coaching involves active teaching. This distinction between practice and coaching is useful when examining the experimental designs used in coaching studies. With a pre–post control group design, any difference in experimental group mean scores from pre-test to post-test potentially reflects both a practice effect and a coaching effect. Mean pre–post differences for the control group reflect a practice effect; thus the control group effect size estimate is subtracted from the experimental group effect size estimate to produce an estimate of the coaching effect.

We will not attempt an integrated definition; the important lesson in our opinion is simply that there are a variety of activities that can fall under the labels of coaching and practice and attempts to interpret the results of coaching and practice studies should be made with care. We will use Kulik's distinction between coaching (any external intervention designed to improve scores) and practice (learning from one's own experience with the same or alternate forms of a test) as a basis for broadly differentiating between the two. However, regardless of the label used by the authors of the work we are reviewing, we will attempt to specify clearly the nature of the phenomenon being studied. In the following paragraphs we will elaborate on the range of issues that should be taken into account in examining coaching and practice effects in the employment setting.

FORMS OF COACHING AND PRACTICE

In the practice domain, we see six issues as important. First, does practice involve the same or an alternate form of the selection device in question? While a single organization with a retesting policy may use alternate forms, it is not inconceivable that an applicant applying for many jobs in a single field may encounter multiple employers using precisely the same test. Also, development of alternate forms may not be easily accomplished for some selection devices, such as assessment centers. Thus re-assessment may involve going through the same set of assessment exercises.

Second, the number of practice trials involved appears likely to affect the size of a practice effect. While the effect of a single practice trial is likely to be of most interest, as the setting of most concern is likely to be the applicant requesting a retest, there are certainly settings where multiple practice trials are possible. For example, an organization may allow applicants to re-apply for employment an unlimited number of times, requiring simply the passage of a certain period of time between application.

Third, the time interval between trials is likely to be important. A retest reliability study done for research purposes with a one-week interval may or may not offer useful information to an organization requiring unsuccessful applicants to wait six months before re-applying.

Fourth, whether or not feedback is provided is likely to be important, as it is likely to influence whether or not an applicant changes his or her response strategy upon retesting. This seems particularly important when one moves out of the maximum performance domain (e.g. ability tests), where there are clearly correct and incorrect responses, and into the typical performance domain (e.g. personality tests, interviews), where the response pattern sought by the organization may not be apparent to the applicant. In the typical performance domain, the examinee may adopt an explicit self-presentation strategy in responding to the selection device based on a hypothesis about what the employer is looking for in an applicant. On retest that strategy may be the same if no feedback about earlier test performance has been received, or if positive feedback has been received. However, if feedback is negative, an applicant may alter the hypothesis about what the employer is looking for and respond very differently upon retesting. The extent to which this occurs may depend on the specificity of the feedback. If an applicant is simply told that he or she did not score satisfactorily, the applicant is left to his or her own devices to generate alternative response strategies. If, on the other hand, the applicant receives explicit feedback, such as 'your score on the extraversion scale was too low', there is a clear basis for revising one's strategy.

Fifth, distinguishing between practice effects obtained in operational settings and in research settings is likely to be useful. In research settings, one can hypothesize greater likelihood of boredom or waning interest upon retest than may be the case in operational settings. The degree to which feedback about initial performance is sought, or is attended to when received, is likely to be greater in operational settings.

Sixth, differential effects on high and low scoring applicants are possible. Operationally, applicants seeking a retest are among the lower scoring applicants: those not initially scoring at or above an organization's cut-off. However, studies of practice effects done in research settings may focus on the full score range. The question is whether applicants throughout the score range are equally able to profit from the opportunity to retest.

Within the domain of coaching, broadly conceptualized as referring to external interventions intended to affect test scores, we see interventions falling into five basic categories. The distinctions among these are not always easy to make, and many interventions include elements of more than one category; none the less, we feel that they are conceptually useful.

The first type of coaching involves intensive drill on items similar to those on the actual selection device. This differs from the above discussion of practice in that it involves effects above and beyond those produced simply by a retest. The second type involves instruction in principles of test taking, unrelated to the specific content of the selection device in question. The third involves an orientation to the specific selection device, typically including issues such as the purpose of the device, what it is intended to measure, and a limited sample of items. The fourth involves providing principles for dealing effectively with the content of a specific selection device (e.g. pre-interview advice to 'try to appear calm and relaxed', or 'emphasize your strengths and don't dwell on your weaknesses'). The fifth involves specific behavioral advice for how to respond to a specific selection device. Telling an applicant to read the potential employer's annual report prior to an interview is an example of this type of coaching. An assessment center example may help clarify the distinction between this and the previous category. Telling an applicant prior to an in-basket that 'planning ahead is important' is an example of a principle; telling an applicant to 'be sure to read all of the in-basket items before responding to any of them' is specific behavioral advice.

The first three categories — intensive drill, general test-taking principles, and orientation to a specific selection device — typically are part of formal coaching programs, which may or may not be run by or sanctioned by the employer. The last two categories involve giving advice to candidates; these types of coaching may occur informally as well as occurring as part of a coaching program. Individuals who have been through a selection process (e.g. an assessment center) may pass on information to others about to encounter the process. This seems more likely in the case of internal selection processes than with external selection processes, as employees are routinely in contact with one another in the normal course of their work; however, it certainly can occur as well in instances where applicants and current employees know one another. These last types of coaching are most likely to be more brief than the more formal forms of coaching, though length of coaching is a variable of interest across all categories. These last types of coaching are also more likely than the others to be inaccurate, as they are often based on information flowing informally through the grapevine. The advice passed on from one individual to another about how to succeed on a selection device may in fact be totally incorrect.

REASONS FOR EXAMINING COACHING AND PRACTICE: VALIDITY AND FAIRNESS

Having outlined various forms of coaching and practice that may occur in organizations in some detail, some discussion of the reasons why organizations should be concerned about coaching and practice effects is in order, prior to moving to a review of the coaching and practice literature. Two major concerns surface in the literature: a concern for fairness to all applicants and a concern for the validity of descriptive statements about an applicant's standing on the characteristic being measured and subsequently about the validity of predictions made from applicants' scores (Messick, 1981).

The fairness issue focuses on differential access to coaching. This is a pressing and well-publicized concern in the educational arena, given the number of commercial ventures focusing on preparing candidates for tests like the Scholastic Aptitude Test or the Law School Admission Test. Given the cost of such programs, they will be more accessible to individuals able to afford them. If these programs are effective, regardless of whether the effects are on test scores alone or on the examinee's standing on the construct measured by the test, lack of access to coaching programs can hinder the educational opportunities of disadvantaged groups. While commercial coaching programs are not as common in the employment setting, they certainly do exist. Commercial test preparation programs are advertised for various government civil service jobs. Firms offering assistance with resumé preparation and coaching on interviewing skills are common. Thus the differential access issue is relevant in employment settings as well as in educational settings.

The validity issue concerns the effect of coaching and practice on the accuracy with which a score describes an individual's standing on the characteristic being measured (construct validity) and on the accuracy of predictions made from the scores (predictive validity). These two effects need to be viewed separately: if a coaching intervention adds a constant to the scores of all applicants and is provided to all applicants, the relative standing of applicants and thus the predictive validity of the test (i.e. the correlation with a criterion of interest for this group of applicants) is unchanged. However, the construct validity of the scores is affected, as inferences about the amount of the characteristic being measured possessed by each applicant are inflated as a result of the intervention. If the coaching intervention is not provided to all applicants, or if the effects of the intervention are not constant across all levels of the characteristic in question, then the predictive validity is affected as well. Thus differential access affects both fairness and validity in situations in which coaching or practice affects test scores but not true scores.

Messick (1981) differentiates between three ways in which coaching can affect scores. The first, as discussed in the above paragraph, is to increase scores without increasing an applicant's standing on the construct in question. Messick feels that this is a relatively minor problem with well-constructed tests. Improvements which do not improve true scores typically involve 'tricks' for responding to multiple choice items when one does not know the answer (e.g. looking for variations in length and specificity of the response alternatives), and well-constructed tests are developed with a careful eye to avoiding such problems. While this may be the case for standardized tests such as the SAT, the possibilities for artificially increasing scores are likely to be quite different for various selection devices, such as interviews for which a coaching program may provide applicants with specific responses to various anticipated questions.

The second is to increase scores by eliminating any artificial deficit in test scores resulting from lack of experience with the testing situation or from test anxiety. Increases of this sort would eliminate a source of error in measuring the characteristic in question, and thus would increase the construct validity of test scores and, subsequently, influence the predictive validity of the test. The third is genuinely to improve the applicant's standing on the characteristic in question. This would have no effect on either construct or predictive validity.

While the above discussion has focused on coaching, practice could also affect scores in any of these three ways. For example, an improved score obtained after going through an assessment center a second time could reflect artificial enhancement due to familiarity, it could reflect elimination of a deficit caused by anxiety accompanying the first pass through the center, or it could reflect actual improvement in managerial skills resulting from the experience of going through the assessment center and receiving feedback.

We have now reviewed definitional issues regarding coaching and practice, outlined various forms of coaching and practice that should be carefully differentiated in examining the coaching and practice literature, and considered reasons why organizations should be concerned about understanding the potential influence of coaching and practice. In the following section we will summarize existing reviews of the coaching and practice literature.

SUMMARY OF EXISTING REVIEWS OF THE COACHING AND PRACTICE LITERATURE

Existing reviews focus on aptitude and achievement tests, primarily in educational settings. In addition to their substantive conclusions, these reviews are of value in highlighting methodological issues to be considered in evaluating coaching and practice research. Recent meta-analytic reviews of the coaching literature (Kulik, Bangert-Drowns, and Kulik, 1984; Powers, 1986) and the practice literature (Kulik, Kulik, and Bangert, 1984) incorporate literature included in earlier reviews; we will summarize these meta-analytic reviews.

Kulik, Bangert-Drowns, and Kulik (1984) located 38 studies of the effects of coaching interventions. Their inclusion criteria were that the study have a control group and that, regardless of the label used by the original researchers, the study be one of coaching (a specific intervention designed to improve test performance), rather than of practice (examinees learning from their own experience with an earlier test administration) or actual instruction (programs aimed at skill acquisition and not at improving performance on a specific test). For each study, an effect size measure was computed as the difference between the mean test scores of the experimental and control groups, divided by the standard deviation of the test. Meta-analytic procedures developed by Glass,

McGaw, and Smith (1981) were used. Twenty study characteristics were coded and effect size differences as a function of study characteristics were examined. Note that this approach to meta-analysis differs from the Schmidt–Hunter approach (Hunter, Schmidt, and Jackson, 1982) which is dominant in industrial/organizational psychology. The Schmidt–Hunter approach estimates the extent to which variations in effect size can be explained by statistical artefacts, such as sampling error, prior to searching for substantive moderator variables. Kulik, Bangert-Drowns, and Kulik (1984) do not report sample sizes; thus we could not readily assess the extent to which apparent variability in study findings could be attributable to sampling error.

The most striking finding concerned the difference between studies of the SAT ($N = 14$) and studies using other tests ($N = 24$). As the studies differed both in study characteristics (e.g. grade level of examinees) and in effect sizes, the two sets of studies were analyzed separately.

All of the SAT studies used a pre-test/post-test design. Improvements from pre-test to post-test averaged .36 standard deviations (SD) for the experimental groups and .21 SD for the control groups. Thus a .21 SD mean improvement was obtained simply due to retesting, with an additional .15 SD improvement due to coaching. None of the study characteristics was significantly related to the effect size measures. However, the studies were quite homogeneous with regard to many characteristics, thus making the detection of moderators less likely. For example, only one of the fourteen studies involved test orientation only. While the effect size for that study was .05 and the mean effect size for the eleven studies focusing on drill on test items was .16, the difference is not significant. The appropriate conclusion is that the effectiveness of an orientation program has not been adequately studied, not that orientation and drill-focused coaching programs do not produce different effects. Similarly, eleven of the fourteen studies were categorized as 'long' (more than 9 hours), none of the fourteen included an anxiety-reduction component, thirteen of the fourteen included a drill component and ten of the fourteen did not involve random assignment to experimental or control groups (and effect sizes averaged .21 for the studies with random assignment and .12 for those with non-random assignment). On the other hand the studies were nearly evenly divided as to whether or not skill-oriented instruction was involved; no differences in effect size were found. Thus virtually no strong statements about which characteristics do or do not influence the effectiveness of SAT coaching programs can be made.

Twenty-four studies examined aptitude tests other than the SAT (e.g. Stanford-Binet, Otis-Lennon, Differential Aptitude Test, Graduate Record Exam, Medical College Admission Test, a variety of teacher-made tests). While the SAT studies tended to be homogeneous, these were quite heterogeneous as to grade level of examinees (ranging from kindergarten to college graduate), duration, and inclusion or exclusion of a testwiseness component, a drill component, or a content component.

Seventeen studies used a pre-test/post-test design, with the experimental groups showing a mean improvement of .76 SD and the control group a mean improvement of .25 SD. Thus a .51 SD mean effect was obtained due to coaching and a .25 SD effect due to retesting. Seven studies did not use a pre-test; these studies showed a .27 SD mean improvement, which can be directly interpreted as a coaching effect. The use of a pre-test proved to be the only study feature significantly related to effect size measures.

Again, the failure to find significant differences due to study characteristics may be due in part to a lack of power to detect differences. In addition, the relatively small number of studies forced Kulik, Bangert-Drowns, and Kulik (1984) to look at study characteristics one at a time. While we might be interested, say, in studies done with post-high-school examinees randomly assigned to conditions and done in operational testing situations rather than laboratory studies, such a combination might be present in only a single study.

Kulik, Bangert-Drowns, and Kulik (1984) are not able to explain the substantial differences between the SAT studies and the others. Obvious possibilities such as differences in program length prove unable to account for the differences; in fact, the SAT coaching programs are typically substantially longer in duration than the others. Both seem equally prone to methodological problems, such as failure to assign examinees to conditions randomly. Also puzzling is the difference between studies using a pre-test/post-test design and those using a post-test-only design: independent of the effects of a retest, studies with a pre-test produced a mean effect size .24 SD higher than those without a pre-test. Kulik *et al.* suggest the possibility of pre-test sensitization as an explanation.

A meta-analysis by Powers (1986) offers some insight into the variability of findings across studies. Powers identified ten studies, nine of aptitude tests used for post-secondary admissions and one of an aptitude test used for employment, which reported effects separately by item type (e.g. sentence completion, logical reasoning, issues and facts, supporting conclusions). Length of the directions given for each item type was measured by simply counting the number of words in the directions. Complexity of the directions and the task represented by an item type was measured by ratings by two experts in measurement. Both of these variables were found to correlate significantly with effect size measures for studies of both coaching and practice, indicating that more complex items are more susceptible to coaching and practice.

Kulik, Kulik, and Bangert (1984) conducted a meta-analysis of the practice literature for aptitude tests. Forty studies were located; for each study an effect size measure was computed as the difference between mean initial score and mean retest score, divided by the standard deviation of the initial scores. Inclusion criteria were that the study either used an age-normed test, used a retest interval of two months or less, or used an adult non-school population, regardless of the retest interval. In addition, studies with alternative forms were eliminated if there was any information to suggest lack of equivalence of the forms, as equating errors can either artificially increase or decrease an examinee's gain score. Five study characteristics were coded and related to study outcomes.

Effect size measures were found to be higher when the identical test was used for both test administrations (.42 SD, 19 studies) than when parallel forms were used (.23 SD, 21 studies). These results are based on comparing a first administration with a second; some studies also administered either the identical test or a parallel form more than twice. For identical tests, mean effect sizes continued to increase as the number of administrations increased (.70 SD for 3 administrations: .96 for 4; 1.35 for 5; up to 1.89 for 8). A similar progression was found for alternate forms (.32 for 3 administrations; .35 for 4; .47 for 5; up to .74 for 8).

Kulik, Kulik, and Bangert (1984) rated the ability level of the sample used in each study as low, middle, or high. They found that effect sizes differed significantly, with lower effect sizes for low ability samples (.17 SD for identical tests; .07 SD for parallel tests) than for middle or high ability samples (.40 SD and .82 SD respectively for identical tests; .26 SD and .27 SD respectively for parallel tests). They found no significant differences for grade level or year of publication.

These findings are consistent with those of the coaching meta-analysis discussed above. Many studies in that review used a pre-test/post-test design, and the control group in that design produces an interpretable practice effect. Most of the SAT studies in the coaching meta-analysis were not included in the practice meta-analysis, probably because the retest interval exceeded two months. In the coaching study, the mean practice effect sizes were .15 SD for the SAT studies and .25 SD for the studies using tests other than the SAT, in comparison with the .23 SD for alternative forms in the practice meta-analysis.

As many of the studies in both meta-analyses involved post-high-school subjects, they have implications for cognitive ability tests used in employment settings. The difference in effect sizes for coaching studies using the SAT versus studies using other tests makes it difficult to speculate as to the magnitude of coaching effects that is possible in the employment setting. The practice effects are more directly interpretable: scores were about a quarter of a standard deviation higher on retest if parallel forms were used; larger effects were found for retesting with identical tests. However, the fact that substantially smaller effects were found for low ability examinees may prove relevant when the issue is a retesting program for applicants who fail to meet an organization's standards. Also, the continued increase in scores with repeated administrations has implications for policy decisions about the number of retests that should be permitted.

ABILITY AND ACHIEVEMENT TESTING IN EMPLOYMENT SETTINGS

Two strategies were used to search for studies of coaching and practice effects on ability and achievement tests in employment settings. First, a computer search of *Psychological Abstracts* was undertaken. Second, a convenience sample of test manuals was examined to determine whether unpublished research was presented. An exhaustive survey would have been ideal; however, we did not have the resources to purchase large numbers of test manuals. We obtained manuals for 24 ability tests designed for use in employment settings. Tests included the Armed Services Vocational Aptitude Battery, the Crawford Small Parts Test, the Detroit Mechanical Aptitude Examination, the Engineering and Physical Sciences Aptitude Test, the Flanagan Aptitude Classification Test, the General Aptitude Test Battery, the MacQuarrie Test for Mechanical Ability, the Minnesota Clerical Test, the Personnel Selection and Classification Test, the Prognostic Test of Mechanical Abilities, the Purdue Pegboard, the Retail Selling Inventory, the Revised Minnesota Form Board, the Short Tests of Clerical Ability, the SRA Clerical Aptitudes Test, the Stenographic Aptitude Test, the Survey of Mechanical Insight, the Survey of Object Visualization, the Survey of Space Relations Ability, the Survey of Working Speed and Accuracy, the Test of Mechanical Comprehension, the Thurstone Employment Tests, the Watson–Glaser Critical Thinking Appraisal, and the Wesman Personnel Classification Test. As this list makes clear, a variety of different types of tests are included here: cognitive ability, spatial and perceptual ability, and psychomotor ability.

We found no studies of coaching effects on ability tests in employment settings, and only a small number of practice studies. We had anticipated that the test manuals would be a rich source of information about practice effects, as retest reliability studies are reported in a high proportion of the manuals. However, most reliability studies do not report means and standard deviations for the two administrations, but merely report the correlation between the two sets of test scores. Practice studies were found for the General Aptitude Test Battery (GATB), the Armed Services Vocational Aptitude Battery (ASVAB), the Professional and Career Examination (PACE), and two spatial ability tests used by the US Air Force. Findings are summarized in Table 1 and discussed on pp. 156–7.

Eight practice studies are reported for the GATB (Droege, 1966; United States Department of Labor, 1970). Three studies investigated practice effects when the same test was retaken after an interval of two weeks. These three studies differed only in the form of the GATB that was administered. Two of these studies were replicated with an interval of three months. The final three studies were investigations of practice effects when alternate forms of the GATB

Table 1 — Practice Effects for Ability Tests
General Aptitude Test Battery (GATB)

Subtest	2 weeks Identical (N = 156)	Alt. (N = 354)	13 weeks Alt. (N = 325)	1 year Alt. (N = 302)	2 years Alt. (N = 288)	3 years Alt. (N = 306)
Intelligence	.44	.15	.15	.21	.21	.24
Verbal	.32	.15	.14	.19	.18	.30
Numerical	.33	.16	.16	.21	.20	.18
Spatial perception	.50	.33	.29	.22	.21	.19
Form perception	.74	.39	.34	.13	.17	.20
Clerical perception	.71	.55	.49	.38	.29	.23
Motor coordination	—	.44	.33	.41	.38	.23
Finger dexterity	.72	.54	.41	.40	.44	.26
Manual dexterity	.69	.52	.31	.28	.50	.31

Armed Services Vocational Aptitude Battery (ASVAB)

Subtest	1 day (N = 57)	2 days (N = 57)
Coding speed	.48	.92
Numerical operation	.24	.69
Math knowledge	−.03	.33
Mechanical comprehension	−.13	.13
Auto and shop information	.11	.30
General science	−.14	−.14
Word knowledge	−.05	.02
Electronics information	−.08	.20
Arithmetic reasoning	−.13	.10
Paragraph comprehension	−.56	.03

Professional and Career Examination (PACE)

Subtest	Total score (# right/# items)	# Attempted score (# right/# items)
Verbal—Vocabulary (N = 14 190)	.00	.00
Verbal—Reading comprehension (N = 14 190)	.08	.09
Induction—Letter series (N = 13 050)	.39	.31
Induction—Geometric classifications (N = 13 050)	.29	.22
Deduction—Tabular Completion (N = 13 085)	.22	.15
Deduction—Inference (N = 13 085)	.32	.19
Number—Computation (N = 13 033)	.18	.03
Number—Arithmetic reasoning (N = 13 033)	.34	.10

Table 1 — continued

Air Force Spatial Relations Tests

Subtest	Identical form 10 min. (N = 32)	7 hr. (N = 32)	Alternate form 10 min. (N = 32)	7 hr. (N = 32)	Alternate form 10 min. (N = 32)	7 hr. (N = 32)
Information comp. test	1.05	.70	.65	.63	−.05	−.29
Flight orientation test	.93	1.03	1.17	1.07	−.07	.08

Note All values are effect size measures in standard deviation units. Identical = identical test administered. Alt. = alternate form of test administered.

were administered. The time intervals between the two administrations were 1 day, 1 week, 2 weeks, 6 weeks, 13 weeks, 26 weeks, 1 year, 2 years, and 3 years. We have chosen representative conditions to report in Table 1 in order to demonstrate general trends. The first two columns in Table 1 under the GATB heading compare practice effects for a study of identical tests with one of parallel tests with a two-week interval (United States Department of Labor, 1970). As this contrast indicates, improvements were found for all subtests, with larger effect sizes for identical tests than for parallel forms. The cognitive scales (general, verbal, numerical) show smaller effects than the perceptual scales (spatial, form perception, clerical perception). The identical form study did not include the motor coordination scale. The alternate form study included all nine scales, and found the largest effects for the psychomotor scales and the smallest effects for the cognitive scales. The third column in Table 1 presents information from this alternative form study for an interval of 13 weeks. Comparing columns two and three demonstrates that practice effects decline over time. The final three columns are gleaned from an alternative form study performed by Droege (1966). This study involved retesting three samples of current employees at intervals of one, two, and three years respectively. Although practice effects still exist after time periods as long as three years, the increment in score is not as great as can be expected when the retest interval is shorter.

A practice study was reported using the ASVAB (McCormick, Dunlap, Kennedy, and Jones, 1983). Fifty-seven paid volunteers took alternate forms of the ASVAB on five consecutive days. From means and standard deviations reported by the authors, we computed effect size measures for the day 1–day 2 comparison and the day 1–day 5 comparison. Findings, shown in Table 1, are mixed, with small and often negative effects for many scales and substantial positive effects for a few scales. An issue emphasized by the authors is the problem of examinee motivation, as the incentive to improve one's score that is likely to be present in the job application setting was not present in this setting. Also, examinees were told that their score on the first administration could be used to determine their eligibility for enlistment in the armed forces if they so desired, thus resulting in the possibility of a different motivational set across trials. In addition, the sample was made up of individuals who were not employed, but were participating in a job core training program. Their scores on the first administration were more than a full standard deviation below ASVAB means reported for normative samples. Recall that the metaanalysis of practice effects by Kulik, Kulik, and Bangert (1984) found smaller practice effects for low ability samples.

A large-scale practice study using the PACE was reported by Wing (1980). An alternative form of one of the PACE subtests was administered along with the operational PACE; samples of about 4000 per form were obtained for two alternate forms of each subtest. As some subtests were made up of markedly different types of items, practice effects were examined for each item type. As very similar findings were reported for different orders of administration (e.g. form A followed by form B versus form B followed by form A), effect size measures were averaged for presentation in Table 1. Hypothesizing that speediness may be a factor contributing to practice effects, scores were computed both as proportion of items correct and proportion of attempted items correct. Smaller practice effect size measures for the proportion of attempted items correct score would suggest that speediness is a factor for the subtest in question. As Table 1 shows, the size of practice effects varied across subtests. Wing noted that effects were larger for item types solvable by systematic application of general problem-solving skills (e.g. letter series, arithmetic reasoning) than for item types requiring application of previously acquired information (e.g. vocabulary). The results also provide some insight into how practice affects scores in the case of speed tests. For a number of subtests, practice had very little effect on the proportion of attempted items correct, but did have an effect on the total number of items correct, suggesting that practice makes examinees better able to make use of the time available to them.

Practice effects on two spatial aptitude tests used by the US Air Force were investigated by Krumboltz and Christal (1960). Air Force Reserve Officer Training Corps student officers took either the identical test, an alternative form, or another spatial relations test at either a ten-minute or a seven-hour interval. Control groups took only one test. The tests were the Instrument Comprehension Test, requiring examinees to choose which picture of an airplane in flight best matches information from aircraft instrument dials, and the Flight Orientation Test, requiring the examinee to examine two ground views taken from an aircraft cockpit and identify which flight maneuver has taken place between the two photographs. We computed effect size measures from information in the article by subtracting the control group mean from the retest mean and dividing by the control group standard deviation. As Table 1 indicates, large practice effects were found for both identical tests and alternative forms for both retest intervals. Taking one test (e.g. Flight Orientation) did not have a consistent impact on performance on the other test (e.g. Instrument Comprehension).

The series of studies reviewed above illustrates the procedural variations in practice effect studies that we outlined in the introduction of this chapter. Studies varied in their use of the same versus alternative form, in the number of practice trials, in the time interval between trials, in the use of operational testing settings versus research settings, and in the ability level of examinees. One issue not touched on in any of the studies was that of whether or not subjects received feedback on initial test performance prior to retest. Unfortunately, each of these procedural variations is represented by only one or two studies, thus making strong conclusions premature. However, the research does offer some useful information to test users. First, practice effects are found fairly consistently for a variety of test types and for a wide range of retest intervals, thus indicating that the practice issue should not be taken lightly by organizations using ability tests. Second, the studies identify a number of hypotheses meriting further investigation, such as the finding that certain item types appear more amenable to practice effects than others, and that psychomotor tests and spatial ability tests produce larger practice effects than cognitive ability tests.

One final note concerns the effect of practice on validity. The question of whether practice increases or decreases the predictive validity of the test has largely been ignored. One study has addressed this issue and preliminary results suggest that validity decreases with retesting (Smith, Wing, and Arabian, 1985). Further investigations of this issue would be informative.

PERSONALITY TESTS IN THE EMPLOYMENT SETTING

The same search strategy described above for ability tests was was followed for personality tests, namely a computer search for *Psychological Abstracts*, and a search of a convenience sample of test manuals. Test manuals were obtained for the Adjective Check List, the California Psychological Inventory, the California Test of Personality, the Edwards Personal Preference Schedule, the FIRO Awareness Scales, the Gordon Personal Profile, the Guilford–Zimmerman Temperament Survey, the Hand Test, the Jackson Personality Inventory, the Myers–Briggs Type Indicator, the Personality Research Form, the Study of Values, the Survey of Interpersonal Values, and the 16PF Questionnaire.

We found no coaching studies using personality tests, and no practice studies in an employment setting. Retest reliability studies reporting means and standard deviations for both test administrations using student samples were found in the manuals of the FIRO Awareness Scales, the Jackson Personality Inventory, the Myers–Briggs Type Indicator, and the Survey of Interpersonal Values. These studies report very small differences in means from test to retest, averaging less than .10 standard deviations. Note, though, that all of these studies were done in research settings. The effect of practice in an employment setting remains an open question. As noted in the introduction, the question of the effects of feedback on an examinee's response strategy upon retest is an issue of particular interest for typical performance measures, where self-presentation issues are of more concern than was the case with maximum performance measures.

COACHING AND PRACTICE IN ASSESSMENT CENTERS

We found no studies reporting interpretable assessment center practice effects. The major problem is the lack of standardization. Studies which assess a single group of individuals at two points in time are hard to interpret, as it is not clear that a rating of '3' carries the same behavioral meaning in the two assessment centers. A research design comparing retest performance to that of a control group not previously assessed would be needed to yield meaningful practice effects; no such studies were found.

Both formal and informal coaching programs are of interest with regard to assessment centers. Most organizations provide some type of orientation to the assessment center, and some offer formal coaching programs which involve participation in exercises similar to those in the actual assessment center. We note the existence of a workbook containing such practice exercises (Frank, Sefcik, and Jaffee, 1983).

As such formal programs are offered to all individuals scheduled to attend an assessment center, such programs are less of a concern to assessment center users than is informal 'grapevine' coaching by individuals who have previously been through the assessment center. Thus our review of coaching studies will highlight this concern for informal coaching.

Assessment Centers and Grapevine Coaching

Assessment center experiences, particularly in organizations where assessment center performance is a major determinant of one's future career, are a likely topic of grapevine discussion. Studies designed to look at coaching effects on assessment center performance should reflect what one would hear through the grapevine. In passing on information to a potential assessee, an individual's assessment center experience is likely to be recast as strategy suggestions and specific hints on how to tackle exercises. Prior assessees would base their statements about the 'correct way' to approach exercises on the feedback they had received after participating in an assessment center. This would naturally be somewhat anecdotal with emphasis on those behaviors on which the assessee received more extensive feedback.

Sackett and Dreher (1982) analyzed assessment ratings from several organizations and found that the underlying factors in assessment center ratings represented exercises rather than dimensions. Feedback to assessment center participants may be organized along dimensions but is often of the form 'in X exercise you did Y. This was good/bad.' It seems quite plausible that grapevine coaching discussions would center on exercises rather than dimensions. Clearly, all organizations provide some type of orientation prior to the assessment center; all forms of orientation might be considered coaching. For the present, we simply mention these formal coaching programs; we will discuss them further near the conclusion of this section.

Does grapevine coaching actually exist in organizations? Although no concrete evidence is available to show that previous assessees and assessors do coach others, Dodd (1977) reports survey results which indicate that many former assessment center candidates believe others possess 'inside' information. A survey conducted by the Public Service Commission of Canada found that 62 per cent of 63 respondents disagreed on a five-point Likert scale that others had 'inside' information. However, 93 per cent of 61 respondents claimed not to have inside information themselves. Thirty-four per cent felt that advance knowledge would help participant performance. At IBM where the assessment center process was long-standing, a survey found that only 14 per cent of approximately 700 respondents disagreed that others had inside knowledge about exercises and 74 per cent disagreed that they themselves had inside information. Only 37 per cent felt that such knowledge would aid performance.

Dulewicz, Fletcher, and Wood (1983) used a questionnaire with the same five-point response scale as Dodd's to assess attitudes of 81 participants who attended seven assessment centers: 69 per cent of respondents disagreed and 14 per cent agreed that other participants had inside information.

A study of participant reactions to assessment centers conducted by Teel and DuBois (1983) involved interviews with prior assessees from four organizations which utilized the assessment center for various purposes. Interviews were conducted with 37 assessees — 19 high scorers and 18 low scorers; moderate scorers were excluded. One agree–disagree statement used in the interviews was 'Came to center with as much knowledge as others about objectives and content'. Fifty-eight per cent of high-scoring individuals and 61 per cent of low scorers agreed with this statement.

Cohen (1978) states that it is common that candidates discuss their experiences with other candidates or future candidates. He suggests developing parallel forms of exercises to be used to offset possible candidate prior knowledge of a particular exercise.

Dodd concludes that assessment center programs, particularly long-standing ones, need to be concerned with the dissemination of exercise information which might be perceived as giving an unfair advantage to some participants. He suggests that a thorough orientation to the assessment center will offset this perception. What constitutes a 'thorough orientation' is not specified.

Assessment center programs differ widely in the extent of orientation given to participants, so an assessment of the adequacy or effectiveness of orientation given to assessees is difficult.

The value of survey findings such as those reported is somewhat limited: perceptions of what constitutes 'inside' information may vary greatly across participants. Some may not regard advice given by a prior assessee as 'inside' information. For the 7 per cent at the Public Service Commission and 26 per cent at IBM who stated that they had 'inside' information, it is unknown what the content of this information was, how it was obtained, or most importantly, how, if at all, it affected assessment center performance.

Does grapevine coaching have a significant effect on assessment center performance? Since assessment centers are used for developmental purposes or as training exercises it is assumed that the required performance can be taught and is not just innate ability. Whether or not this performance can be coached in a short time period and in a relatively informal manner needs to be examined.

Burroughs, Rollins, and Hopkins (1973) found that managers from certain departments performed better in an assessment center than those from other departments. Naturally, organizational members will have differential access to developmental experiences and/or self-select into positions which provide greater opportunities for development. However, this is seen as affecting true managerial ability; grapevine coaching may not have any broadly applicable or long-lasting effects on an individual's ability in any of the dimensions assessed.

Byham (1977) comments that knowing what skills are being measured and how they are being measured does not guarantee skill performance. It is likely that informal coaching consists less of information concerning what is being rated and more concerning 'what to do' types of advice.

Studies conducted thus far of coaching effects on assessment center performance have shown varying results, largely due to differing methodologies and the presence of methodological flaws. An important question to consider in examining these studies is that of determining what constitutes a significant gain from coaching. In practical terms, coaching effects are of concern when coaching is differently available and when the classification or selection of assessment center participants is affected by an appreciable rise (or drop) in performance ratings without a corresponding improvement (or decrease) in the assessee's underlying abilities.

Coaching and the Leaderless Group Discussion

Coaching effects on the Leaderless Group Discussion (LGD) were first discussed by Klubeck and Bass in 1954. A study was conducted to demonstrate that brief training could affect leadership status. One hundred and forty sorority girls volunteered as subjects. The discussions dealt with questions such as, 'Should co-eds marry while still in college?' and 'On what bases should sorority pledges be selected?' It was assumed that the questions were general enough so that all participants had equal knowledge prior to the discussion.

Each participant went through two LGDs. A half-hour private training session in between the LGDs was given to those who ranked third and sixth in the first discussion. The training consisted of two phases: an establishment of rapport and motivation to be trained and a lecture on leadership behaviour. The lecture centered on general dimensions; the participants were not told how to apply the leader qualities in a given situation.

Results showed that brief training was profitable for those with high initial rankings. Those with low leadership ratings did not profit or lose from training. In their discussion of results, Klubeck and Bass dismissed the possibility that increased scores were due merely to increased motivation.

In conclusions, Klubeck and Bass suggested that coaching ought to increase the validity of the LGD as a measure of leadership ability by increasing individual differences in LGD performance. They mentioned that the opinion that one cannot cram for the LGD (Harris, in Klubeck and Bass, 1954) is probably valid for those with low leadership potential, but cramming may benefit those of high potential.

Bass (1954) reports an unpublished study in which Pruitt and Bass replicated the above study. Training in this instance consisted of fifteen minutes of coaching with participants assembled as a group just prior to undergoing the LGD. Results supported Harris's (in Klubeck and Bass, 1954) hypothesis — trained groups performed considerably more poorly, appearing to be more nervous and tense. However, few data are provided on the study, preventing an examination of its design.

Clearly, one can find many grounds for questioning the generalizability of the above studies to LGDs used in assessment centers. The effects of training and experience may have been confounded, i.e. it cannot be said that those with high initial rankings improved because of the training program, the experience gained in the first LGD, or both. The subjects utilized in this study, sorority girls, are not representative of the 'typical' assessment center participant in terms of business knowledge and experience. It is unlikely that volunteer subjects are as motivated to do well as are assessment center participants whose future careers depend upon their performance. Finally, the discussion questions were general ones for which many highly differing opinions are acceptable and no real consensus was necessary. Most LGDs used in assessment centers deal with questions of a highly different nature. However, the studies also attempted to control for many other important factors which later studies neglected, such as initial leadership potential.

Another point that is particularly relevant is that training in both studies was concerned with general traits and not situational applications. The content of grapevine conversations might be more situational than trait oriented. The question of whether or not coaching should be directed at general dimensions or specific exercises is a relevant one.

Almost twenty years passed after Klubeck and Bass's study before the issue of coaching was again addressed. Burroughs *et al.* (1973) attempted to assess the effects of prior rater experience on LGD performance. Twenty-seven male volunteers were shown a videotape of a School Board LGD and given a list of variables and definitions on which to rate performance. These, along with a control group of fifteen, participated in a Town Council LGD. Results showed that viewing an LGD, having access to dimension definitions and serving as a rater was unrelated to better performance in a similar LGD.

Burroughs *et al.* generalized this finding to assessors in industry who later participate in assessment centers. Byham (1977) states there is no indication that serving as an assessor will help a person who becomes a participant. However, Lorenzo (1984), using simulation exercises, found that experienced assessors were more proficient than other managers in interviewing another individual, verbally presenting and defending information about others, and communicating this information in written reports.

Struth, Frank, and Amato (1980) compared the overall and dimension ratings received between subjects who had served as assessors for lower level positions and a group that had no previous exposure to the process. The previous assessors performed no better than the control on any of the evaluation categories.

These studies appear to indicate that assessor training has no effect on subsequent performance as an assessee, but may increase proficiency in certain managerial skills. The question of whether or not a prior assessor could be a source of useful information for a potential assessee remains unanswered. On conceptual grounds, it is clear that a prior assessor has access to far more relevant strategic information than a prior assessee due to the intensity and duration of his or her contact with the assessment center process. Thus, any concerns raised about informal coaching by assessees are also applicable to coaching by assessors.

Petty (1974) attempted to look at both experience and training effects on the LGD. One hundred ROTC students were assigned to four treatments: LGD participation and fifteen-minute lecture on the LGD, LGD participation only, lecture only, neither lecture nor participation. Groups consisting of subjects from each of the treatments then dealt with an offensive tactics problem which had previously been assigned in class. The assessors were students given a ten-minute briefing on rating error. The lack of assessor training and assessee prior knowledge of the discussion problem may have influenced results obtained.

The training effect was significant across all criterion measures while the experience effect failed to reach significance in any of the criterion measures. Petty attributes the incongruence with Bass's (1954) findings to the specificity of the training content. The training lecture dealt with the history, development, research concerning and rating instruments of the LGD. Subjects were told what was expected and how their score could be maximized. Petty cautions against generalizing results to industry but questions possible effects of 'grapevine' information in organizations.

The fact that this study uses exercise-specific training is significant. Other studies which had found coaching to have no effect on LGD performance based training content on leadership dimensions, not exercises.

Denning and Grant (1979) presented undergraduates with written information on dimensions that they would be rated on in an assigned role LGD (ARLGD). The information consisted of a 'clear and simply worded definition and suggested behavioral correlates, and a description of the scale on which they would be rated'. This information was given directly prior to the experiment, along with the materials for the exercise. The control subjects were given only a general description of assessment centers. No significant differences in ratings on any dimension between the groups were found. Denning and Grant state that the results of this study support the widespread belief that increased knowledge of assessment center methodology will not serve to increase performance ratings. They suggest that specific instructions should be given to all candidates as is done with other standardized tests.

The written information regarding dimensions provided participants in this study was brief and general and contained few behavioral correlates. One might conclude that this is representative of the information received through the 'grapevine' in an organization. It would be interesting to compare the amount and the specificity of the behavioral examples given here with those given to assessors in training as examples of good performance and with the type of information one might receive as feedback after participating in an assessment center. However, methodological issues other than coaching content cause one to question the generalizability of study results to organizational contexts: coaching was written and from an unidentified although presumably credible source, the coaching was included as part of the LGD preparation materials, and subject motivational level and lack of organizational experience may have affected their ability to profit from coaching.

McIntyre (1980) looked at how feedback might affect subsequent assessment center performance. Twenty-four assessees from a civil service promotional assessment center were re-assessed after receiving oral and written feedback. The time interval between assessments was not reported. These assessees demonstrated significantly higher scores on seven of the twelve categories in the re-assessment. The study lends support to the notion that certain dimensions are less coachable, since no improvement was found on the more stable, less exercise-dependent traits, such as work standards and sensitivity. Skills such as problem analysis and management control, which seem to be most dependent on the content of the exercises, showed the most improvement. Sixty-seven per cent of the overall ratings were improved.

This study points to the possibility that an assessee who has received feedback may have helpful information to pass on to those about to undergo an assessment center. McIntyre also states that motivation may have been responsible for some of the results obtained, since those who had initially received 'Not presently qualified' scores did the best in the re-evaluation.

Note that it is unclear whether this study is best classified as one of coaching or practice. Viewing feedback as an intervention puts it into the realm of coaching; viewing feedback as a naturally occurring event not directly aimed at score improvement puts it into the realm of practice.

The most recent study on coaching effects on ARLGDs examined both full (2 hour) and errant (7.5 minute) coaching (Kurecka, Austin, Johnson, and Mendoza, 1982). Female undergraduates were used as both assessors and assessees. Errant coaching consisted of listening to a tape of a biased account of a personal ARLGD experience. The control group heard a tape on the history of the LGD. The full coaching condition was given examples of good performance and actual practice in an LGD with feedback.

Results showed that those receiving full coaching performed significantly better than the control group. No difference was found between the control group and the errant coaching condition which had been designed to reproduce grapevine coaching. Kurecka et al. feel that conclusions cannot be drawn regarding the errant coaching since it was very brief and may not have been an accurate representation of true grapevine coaching. The authors of the study also point out that in much of the previous research 'coaching' was only on dimensions and effects were not found.

In sum, many of these studies failed to attend to variables found to be important in coaching studies in other settings. However, studies which involved feedback on previous LGD performance (McIntyre, 1980; Kurecka et al., 1982) found effects. Other studies which dealt with giving specific behavioral information (Petty, 1974; Denning and Grant, 1979) had varying results. The nature and behavioral specificity of information provided may have a major role in determining the results of coaching studies.

Coaching and the in-Basket

Only one study has been conducted related to coaching effects on in-basket performance (Jaffee and Michaels, 1978). One group of male students, the control group, was given the in-basket. An interview was conducted to assess why an individual took certain actions in the in-basket, but no feedback was given to the participants concerning their performance. Each was told 'to attempt to enhance the performance of the subject they were coaching by telling him any information that he felt would be of value to the subject in taking the exercise'. Fifteen minutes were given for coaching those in another group. No other instructions or feedback was provided. After a one-week delay the control group coached a second group. By using those with in-basket experience and delaying coaching, Jaffee and Michaels attempted to create grapevine coaching as it might exist in organizations.

In-baskets were scored and the control group was divided into high and low skilled. Jaffee and Michaels (1978) grouped the control subjects in this manner under the expectation that high scorers would have better quality information and would pass this on to those coached. This expectation is certainly questionable since the subjects were given no feedback on whether they had performed well or poorly or on which of the actions they had taken were good or bad.

In addition, the labels of high skill and low skill refer to the individual's performance on the in-basket exercise, not their skill in coaching. It is not reported whether the high-skill and low-skill coaches differed in the style and content of their coaching, a potentially important variable.

Performance did not differ significantly between the group coached by the high-skilled coaches, the group coached by low-skilled coaches, or the original group. The absence of feedback leads one to question whether coaches had recognized the positive and negative in their own performance so that they could impart this knowledge.

The research conducted thus far contains a number of limitations. First, studies have varied widely in the content of their coaching with few attempting to simulate what one would hear through the organizational grapevine.

Second, none of the studies has looked at the entire assessment center process or even at more than one exercise. Perhaps some exercises are subject to greater coaching effects than others. For example, many assessment centers include paper-and-pencil aptitude tests which may be subject to coaching effects, specific business games and case studies which some candidates may be familiar with, and some type of interview.

Also, as some studies appear to indicate, the possibility that certain dimensions of performance are more 'coachable' also exists. In an unpublished study Gill (in Dulewicz and Fletcher, 1982) found that coaching, in the form of instruction and discussion, had significant effects on performance in the areas of establishing priorities and decision making.

Third, an individual difference factor may play a role in coaching having an effect, as well as affecting self-selection into coaching. One consideration is the relationship of specific kinds of experience and assessment center performance. Dulewicz and Fletcher (1982) found that experience in making presentations or writing letters was unrelated to performance in the related exercises. However, planning experience was related to performance in a business plan presentation exercise. Since it cannot be determined how much of the prior experience had been coupled with constructive feedback, the results of this study must be considered tentative. Dulewicz and Fletcher recommend that either experience information be taken into account in rating, or participants be equated in experience prior to undergoing an assessment center.

In most cases, previous management experience as a biasing factor may not be an issue. If the previous experience has led to skill enhancement and that skill is being evaluated there is no problem. Concern should only arise if experience gives a participant an unfair advantage on a specific exercise, regardless of the participant's actual skill level. Although this point seems apparent, it is not always attended to in evaluating experience effects on assessment center performance.

COACHING AND PRACTICE EFFECTS IN THE EMPLOYMENT INTERVIEW

Studies investigating the effects of coaching on interviewing performance fall into three categories. These categories are descriptive case studies, multiple baseline quasi-experimental studies, and experimental studies. Within this broad classification system, however, the studies may be differentiated along a number of further dimensions. For example, while every study involves a program which is targeted at diagnosing and changing interview behavior, the program particulars may be vastly different across studies. Typically, the program involves one or more of the following change techniques: modelling, behavior rehearsal, roleplay, lecture, discussion, programmed materials, videotaped feedback and verbal feedback. The program may be designed for a group or an individual. The interviewing behaviors of interest range from the general (enthusiasm) to the specific (head nods). As always, the length of the program is important. A single 20-minute session is not likely to have the same effect as a series of six 90-minute sessions. Finally, the subjects may be drawn from a typical interviewee population, such as college seniors, or from a population with special needs, such as former patients in a psychiatric hospital. This list is not exhaustive.

Before summarizing the literature, it may be useful to discuss briefly the issues of conceptual clarity and validity as they apply to interview coaching. Furthermore, the generalizability of some studies may be severely restricted and the study characteristics contributing to this restriction should be highlighted.

Conceptual clarity involves distinguishing among coaching and practice effects and differentiating among the various forms of coaching. The effect of interest in these studies is a coaching effect. The investigators are not interested in unintentional improvements in interview behavior resulting from prior participation in an interview. Nevertheless, many of the interventions do involve practice. In fact, in the course of a coaching program an individual might participate in many interviews. Furthermore, the experimental studies often involve a pre-intervention interview and a post-intervention interview. If a control group is included the practice effect can be determined and controlled.

We found three studies providing data on the change in performance between pre-test interview and post-test interview for a control group. Barbee and Keil

(1973) reported mean change in ratings received for a number of interview behaviours as well as for apparent level of job skill, amount of adaptability, and likelihood of hiring. Although data were not presented in such a way that effect size could be determined, the control group showed improvement from pre-test to post-test. In fact, for some dimensions, this group showed greater absolute improvement than a group exposed to a videotape of the pre-test interview with no verbal feedback; however, this reversal was never significant. Venardos and Harris (1973) described two measures of pre-test/post-test improvement for the control group. Judges were asked to rate overall performance change on a seven-point scale (1 = much worse and 7 = significantly improved). The control group had a mean of 3.9 whereas both experimental groups had a mean exceeding 6. Assumedly, a score of 4 indicated no change. In addition, ratings of critical interview behaviors were made for each interview and a difference score was calculated. This score did not differ significantly from zero for the control group. Hollandsworth, Dressel, and Stevens (1977) presented mixed results. The change between pre-interview scores and post-interview scores was calculated. These change scores were not tested for significance so only directional trends can be examined; measures of effect size could not be determined. A self-report measure of anxiety decreased in absolute magnitude from pre-interview to post-interview for the control group. A measure of length of eye contact also showed improvement. Performance worsened with regard to length of speaking, affect, number of speech disturbances, number of positive self-statements, skill explanation, and honesty. Voice loudness showed a slight negative change but the direction in which this measure was expected to change was not stated. Two additional studies utilized pre-test/post-test control group designs but did not provide information with which to determine practice effects (Keil and Barbee, 1973; Speas, 1979). From this limited amount of data, it is impossible to suggest the magnitude of a practice effect. The Venardos and Harris (1973) study provided the most direct test but the sample size was small (N = 8).

These conflicting results may have been due to the unclear response pattern expectations inherent in interviewing. In some studies, subtle clues might have been available to control group subjects, leading to accurate assessments of response pattern expectations. In other settings, clues might have provided erroneous or irrelevant information. Furthermore, response pattern expectations may actually change from setting to setting — some patterns being more intuitive than others. In any event, it appears that practice effects are inconsistent in interview coaching.

Close inspection of the interview coaching literature reveals that the coaching interventions have usually involved a combination of types of coaching. Intense practice has been combined with prescriptive behavioral feedback as well as general tips. What has varied across workshops, as noted above, were the various technologies utilized to obtain similar coaching objectives. As such, the various types of coaching effects cannot be differentiated.

The effect of coaching on interview validity may be expected to depend upon the thrust of the intervention program. In order to investigate this issue, interview true score must be defined. It would seem that the true score is whether the individual will ultimately prove to be a satisfactory performer. The observed score is the recommendation for hire. In this scenario, there are four possibilities for decision making — a poor performer is recommended (false positive), a poor performer is not recommended (correct rejection), a satisfactory performer is recommended (hit), and a satisfactory performer is rejected (miss). Clearly, all coaching programs are aimed at maximizing a successful performer's chance of being recommended and to decrease the successful performer's chance of not being recommended. What is unclear is what the workshops are designed to do in the case of the poor performer. Some programs focus on more accurate portrayal of an individual's strengths and weaknesses. It is assumed that this means that the good performer will present a better case for being hired. Is the poor performer expected realistically to display a lack of qualification? This is also true for programs which target openness and honesty. On the other hand, reduction of anxiety might allow more typical performance to be available to the interviewer, resulting in an increase in score accuracy for both poor and satisfactory performers. Finally, those programs which emphasize eye contact or ideal voice loudness would seem to affect interview impression without increasing the accuracy of the decision. It seems that the effect that a coaching program has on predictive validity depends upon the specific target behaviors.

A final issue concerns generalizability. The improvement in interview behavior exhibited by an individual repeatedly coached on the same set of standard questions has limited meaning for an individual who must go into an unstandardized environment and speak with a stranger for an hour. Also, at times, the pre-test and the post-test interviews are conducted by the same person. This situation is likely to be characterized by familiarity and a somewhat contrived atmosphere which is not likely to be true in reality. Likewise, the type of criterion measure may be of concern. Frequency data, such as number of head nods or number of assertive behaviors, gleaned from studies in which the intervention is designed to increase such behaviors, convey little or no information about whether the individual will be hired. An inferential leap is required. Finally, the population from which the study sample is drawn is likely to have an effect on the generalizability of the results. Studies designed to improve the interviewing behavior of inmates, psychiatric patients, the culturally disadvantaged, or individuals with repeatedly poor interviewing performance may not prove helpful to more typical job applicants. For example, one study (Furman, Geller, Simon, and Kelly, 1979) targeted inappropriate gestures as a behavior to modify for a former psychiatric patient. This behavior is not a probable trouble spot for most interviewees.

The appearance of papers describing a variety of interviewing workshops suggests that these coaching programs have enjoyed some amount of popularity (Forrest and Baumgarten, 1975; McGovern et al. 1975; Raanan and Lynch, 1973–74; Walker, 1973–74). These papers are descriptive in nature and do not offer empirical data on changes in applicant behavior or hireability. Hollandsworth and Sandifer (1979) polled 104 individuals a year after they had been trained in the use of their coaching program. The program was rated favorably by those who had returned the questionnaire and conducted a workshop in the past year. Participants completed evaluation forms while the workshops were being conducted. Similarly, these evaluations were favorable. It would be interesting to gather consumer satisfaction data after the value of the workshop had been tested by an actual interview. Forrest and Baumgarten (1975) outlined a program involving modelling, roleplaying, videotape feedback and critique, and rehearsal. The targets were posture, eye contact, focused responses, generating questions, paraphrasing, and anxiety reduction. McGovern et al. (1975) suggested that their program, designed to increase assertiveness in job interviews, had met with some success across a population of typical job applicants. Their group intervention involved discussion, modelling, behavioral rehearsal, and feedback. Raanan and Lynch (1973–74) described a coaching program instituted at the University of Wisconsin-Milwaukee. It involved one group session in which articulation of goals, strengths, and weaknesses, effective listening, and anxiety reduction were addressed. The change techniques were roleplaying, discussion, and feedback. The authors reported positive reactions from participants immediately following the workshop. Finally, a job-search workshop was implemented at the University of Kentucky (Walker, 1973–74). A portion of the workshop involved a discussion of the job interview — what to expect and what the interviewer was looking for. This portion of the workshop was augmented due to participant interest. While not experimental, these papers suggest that interview coaching is popular and is expected to yield positive results by participants and coaches alike.

Three studies utilized a multiple-baseline approach for investigating the effectiveness of interview coaching programs. Measures of effect size cannot be determined. The criterion of interest was usually a measure of behavior frequency; contrasting any two sessions yields no relevant standard deviation because frequencies were not collapsed across subjects. Hollandsworth, Glazeski, and Dressel (1978) charted the progress of one college graduate who had demonstrated severe interviewing deficiencies. The program was designed to increase the frequency of subject-generated questions, focused responses, and attempts to maintain composure by modelling, videotaped modelling and feedback, behavior rehearsal, roleplay and feedback. Each session involved asking the subject eight standard questions, five of which were utilized for training. The remaining three questions provided information concerning whether the trained behavior was generalizing to other questions. The individual underwent twenty-four 20–40 minute training sessions, a pre-intervention interview and a post-intervention interview. The pre-test and post-test were administered by two different individuals not involved in the training and were not standardized. Frequency of the target behaviors was recorded during each training session. Results showed that, for training questions and generalization questions, target behaviors increased during the session in which the relevant training was introduced and this improvement was maintained throughout training. The improvement was slight for composure maintenance. An unobtrusive measure of the subject's socio-communicative behavior at work showed a large increase after training. Galvanic skin response was recorded during pre-test and post-test. The results suggested a reduction in experienced anxiety. It is important to note that no measure was made of the subject's hiring potential and that the target behaviors were measured only during the training sessions. Anecdotal evidence suggested that the intervention resulted in a job offer and increased confidence; however, these conclusions are tenuous. The subject had been targeted as severely anxious and verbally deficient prior to the tailor-made intervention causing generalizability to be restricted.

Furman et al. (1979) performed a multiple-baseline experiment on three formerly hospitalized psychiatric patients. The target behaviors were subject specific and included subject-generated questions, enthusiasm, and appropriate gestures. The training consisted of twenty-one 30-minute sessions, a pre-interview and a post-interview. The latter interviews were conducted by an actual job interviewer and were non-standardized. The training sessions interviews were made up of eight standardized questions. Coaching involved behavior rehearsal, videotaping, and feedback. Frequency of target behaviors was recorded during each training session. As the relevant training was introduced, the frequency of each target behavior moved in the direction predicted and was maintained throughout the training sessions. Two subjects improved on all target behaviors as well as on their rated probability of hire and overall impression. The remaining subject improved on one of three behavior frequencies and did not appear more likely to be hired. The ratings of hireability and general impression conducted during a non-standardized interview strengthened the generalizability of this study. On the other hand, the coaching programs were individualized and intended for subjects who had demonstrated unusually poor interview performance. No conclusions can be made concerning the relative contributions of different change techniques.

Kelly, Laughlin, Claiborne, and Patterson (1979) attempted to improve the interviewing skills of six former psychiatric patients. Sixteen 45-minute sessions involved a standardized interview roleplay, videotaped modelling, behavioral rehearsal, and feedback. Te coaching was designed to increase enthusiastic behavior, amount of positive information conveyed, and subject-generated questions. Unstandardized pre- and post-interviews were performed to assess generalizability. All target behaviors increased in frequency when the relevant training was introduced for all subjects. This increase was mirrored in the change in behavior frequency exhibited from pre-interview to post-interview. Finally, global ratings for characteristics such as enthusiasm, ambition, qualifications, and likelihood of being hired increased in the post-interview for all subjects.

The preceding three multiple-baseline experiments generally provide support for interview coaching interventions. No statement can be made concerning the relative contributions of different change techniques. No statement can be made with regard to coaching versus practice effects — these programs involved a large amount of interviewing practice and there is no way to tease apart the coaching and practice effects. The coaching programs were lengthy and specific. It would be interesting to see whether the global ratings remain high over time. The unusual subject populations are limiting.

We found eight experimental investigations of interview coaching. All involved a control group and at least one experimental group. Whenever the relevant data are provided, effect size will be noted. Significance of effect is always available and will be noted here.

Logue, Zenner, and Gohman (1968) randomly assigned 75 psychiatric patients to three conditions. The control group underwent a single interview and filled out an application blank. The remaining two groups underwent a single experimental session and followed the same procedure as the control group. The programmed-materials group was given written materials dealing with effective job searching and application completion. The videotape group received the programmed materials, roleplayed an interview, viewed their own interview performance and that of others via videotape, and received feedback. The target behaviors were not specified. The researchers compared two dichotomous variables across groups — whether the application blank would result in a recommendation for an interview and whether the interview would result in a recommendation for hire as rated by an independent personnel office. All differences were non-significant and, in fact, favored the control group. The authors suggested that videotaping has especially negative associations for psychiatric patients — without a preintervention interview it is impossible to move beyond conjecture. It should be noted, however, that the intervention was of short duration.

Barbee and Keil (1973) randomly assigned 64 culturally disadvantaged individuals into three groups. Every subject was interviewed for ten minutes by a personnel interviewer. Following this interview, the control subjects waited for 30 minutes and were re-interviewed by the same individual. The videotape-only group viewed a videotape of their initial interview with no comment and were re-interviewed. The videotape/feedback/behavior modification group viewed their initial interview and looked for behaviors which would be appropriate to change. This process was overseen by a trainer who provided advice and reinforced appropriate behaviors. Subject-generated questions were specifically encouraged. All conditions lasted between 30 and 40 minutes. The pre-interviews and post-interviews were rated on a number of dimensions including number of questions asked, honesty, job skills, and probability of hire. The change scores were compared across groups and the results suggested that the videotape-only group did not differ from the control group on any dimension. Effect size ranged from −.42 SD for information provided on job skills to +.37 SD for subject-generated questions. Information provided on job experience yielded an effect size closest to zero (.03 SD). The videotape/ feedback/behavior modification group demonstrated a greater increase from pre-test to post-test on asking more relevant questions (+1.17 SD) and displaying more assertiveness and initiative (+.79 SD) than the control group. In addition, they showed a greater increase from pre-test to post-test in rated ability to respond to the interviewer's questions (+.71 SD) and in likelihood of hire (+.72 SD) than the control group. On average, the videotape/feedback/ behavior modification group showed an increase of +.42 SD over the control group on pre-test/post-test change scores. This was reduced to an advantage of +.05 SD for the videotape-only group. The results of this study suggested that coaching is helpful in increasing the probability of hire as well as the frequency of some specific interview behaviors. Feedback and behavior modification were necessary in addition to videotaping in order for this improvement to become manifest. While a number of rated dimensions did not show improvement, the one that was specifically targeted (subject-generated questions) did increase.

Keil and Barbee (1973) matched 60 culturally disadvantaged subjects on sex and skill training area and randomly assigned them to two groups. Both conditions involved a pre-interview and a post-interview conducted by a personnel officer. In addition, the experimental group viewed their pre-interview performance via videotape in order to target behavior for change. Behavior rehearsal ensued with appropriate behaviors being reinforced. The pre-interview and post-interview were rated using the same scale as described in the Barbee and Keil (1973) study. The experimental group showed a significantly greater change in performance from pre-interview to post-interview than the control group on the following rated dimensions: ability to respond to interviewer's questions (1.13 SD), honesty (.94 SD), and self-confidence (.87 SD). No information was provided concerning whether these changes were in the predicted direction and there was no difference between groups in an increase in the probability of hire. Insufficient data were provided for gaining additional insight into the direction or magnitude of change scores.

Venardos and Harris (1973) performed a study with a sample of 30 individuals with poor interviewing histories and mental, physical, and emotional handicaps. The subjects were randomly assigned to three groups which met for ten hours over two days. All subjects were interviewed for 5–10 minutes before and following the intervention. Those individuals in the videotape group observed videotaped model interviews demonstrating desirable interview behaviors. This was followed by lectures, programmed materials, and discussion. The videotaped pre-interviews were shown to the group and feedback was provided. The roleplay group was not shown any videotapes. They engaged in roleplaying as well as being exposed to the lectures, programmed materials, and discussion described above. The control group took part in a series of industry tours for an equivalent period of time between interviews. The pre-interview and the post-interview were rated on 26 specific interviewing behaviors. The overall change in behavior across interviews was also assessed. Using pre-interview ratings as a covariate, the mean post-interview ratings were significantly higher than the control group for both experimental groups. The means of the experimental groups did not differ. This pattern was preserved for the change ratings.

Hollandsworth et al. (1977) randomly assigned 45 college students to a control group, a discussion group and a behavioral group. Each group participated in a standardized pre- and post-interview conducted by a blind confederate. In addition, the discussion group saw a prescriptive film and read an instructive article concerning appropriate interview behaviors. Self-diagnosis was encouraged as a springboard to group discussion. This group intervention was accomplished in one 4-hour session. The behavioral condition involved modelling, behavior rehearsal, and feedback. The target behaviors were eye contact, body expression, voice loudness, speech fluency, and appropriateness of responses. This session lasted four hours. A self-rating of anxiety was gleaned following both interviews. Eye contact, response length and interview length were timed and affect, voice loudness, explanatory skill, and honesty were rated. A frequency count of positive statements and speech disturbances was recorded. Differences in pre- and post-interview scores were assessed. The behavioral group showed a significantly greater increase in length of eye contact over the control group (+1.31 SD). The discussion group showed a significantly greater increase in speaking time, explanatory skill, and honesty than the control group (+.77 SD, +2.22 SD, and +1.03 SD, respectively). For those dimensions expected to increase in frequency, the behavioral group showed an average change score of +.44 SD more than the control group and the discussion group showed an average change score of +.90 SD more than the control group. For those dimensions expected to decrease in frequency, the behavioral group showed an average change score of .42 SD less than the control group and the discussion group showed an average change score of .05 SD less than the control group. Attention effects cannot be ruled out as accounting for these differences in change scores between the control group and the experimental groups. Also, no information was given concerning perceived hiring potential. One must assume that increased eye contact, explanatory skill, and honesty result in a greater likelihood of hire.

Keith, Engelkes, and Winborn (1977) performed a coaching study with a sample of visually impaired individuals. Subjects were matched according to severity of handicap and randomly assigned to one of three groups. Subjects in control group 1 (N = 20) reported information concerning number of methods utilized to generate job leads, number of applications completed, number of interviews completed, amount of job-search time invested, and number of jobs obtained. Individuals were also asked to complete a questionnaire which was not described. Counsellors rated the subject's employability. Following a two-month interval, these measures were taken again. The subjects in control group 2 (N = 27) underwent the same procedure without providing the information in the initial step. This was designed to assess the effects of priming. The experimental group (N = 19) followed the same procedures as control group 1 except that they also underwent a program of unknown duration during the two-month interval. The coaching program was designed to increase job-search skills including generation of job leads, résumé preparation, interviewing, and effective use of job-search time. The program consisted of self-help training materials. The experimental group obtained significantly more jobs than either control group. No SDs were provided with which effect sizes might be calculated. Because the ensuing analyses did not include the second control group, it is assumed that no significant differences were found between the post-test scores of the two control groups. Multivariate analyses of covariance were conducted comparing the experimental group and control group 1. Although it was not stated, the covariate appears to have been pre-test scores. This analysis suggested significant differences. Subsequent univariate analyses found significantly higher means for the experimental group on the following dependent measures: number of jobs obtained, questionnaire score, number of job leads obtained per week, and number of interviews obtained per week. Conclusions based upon this study are necessarily limited. The significant effect found for the questionnaire cannot be interpreted because the questionnaire was not described. Similarly, the coaching program was not clearly described. Furthermore, the training included more than interview skill training and the separate effects cannot be delineated. Finally, the subject population may not allow generalization.

Stevens and Tornatzky (1976) investigated the effect of an interview coaching program on the employability of individuals referred to a drug-abuse treatment program. Ten individuals were randomly assigned to participate in three 3-hour sessions involving discussion, roleplay, and feedback. Highlighted topics were grooming, etiquette, posture, eye contact, positive statements, enthusiasm, and application completion. The sixteen individuals in the control group simply underwent the standard drug-abuse treatment program with no special attention. Six months following the coaching program, subjects were contacted and queried concerning current job satisfaction, current employment status, rate of pay, and number of hours worked per week. Demographic data were also recorded. Ten individuals from each group completed the questionnaire. Job satisfaction did not differ significantly between the two groups although the difference between the two groups equalled .58 SD. The small sample size made significant findings difficult to obtain. Individuals in the experimental group were significantly more likely to be participating in the drug rehabilitation program after six months and less likely to be unemployed. Furthermore, the control subjects appeared to be more likely to work less than 19 hours a week and more likely to earn less than $2.09 an hour. One problem with this study is that the criteria were all self-report. It is conceivable that this introduced non-random error.

Speas (1979) investigated the effects of various coaching techniques on the interviewing performance of 56 prison inmates who were soon to be released. Each subject was pre- and post-interviewed by a confederate. In addition, one post-interview was conducted by a personnel officer approximately one week following the program. The model/roleplay/videotape group saw a filmed lecture and nine modelled interviews, participated in roleplaying, viewed all group members' pre-interviews and received feedback. The model/roleplaying group saw the filmed lecture and nine modelled interviews and participated in the roleplaying exercise with feedback. The roleplaying group engaged in the roleplaying exercises with feedback and discussion. The model group viewed and discussed the nine modelled interviews. All experimental interventions consisted of six 90-minute sessions with the exception of the model group, which was conducted in a single 5-hour session. The control group was preinterviewed and post-interviewed and received no attention in between. The interviews were rated on the following dimensions: explanatory skill, ability to answer problem questions, appearance, enthusiasm, opening and closing the interview, and the probability of hire. For only one dependent measure, opening and closing the interview, an analysis of covariance using the pre-test score as a covariate was performed because pre-test analyses suggested that the groups may have differed on this measure initially. For the remaining dependent variables, analyses of variance were conducted. All ratings of the model/ roleplay group and the model/roleplay/videotape group were significantly better than those received by the control group for the confederate post-interview. Where possible, effect sizes will be reported for these analyses. Due to some ambiguity in the presentation of the data, effect sizes cannot be calculated for opening and closing the interview scores or for the composite score for the confederate post-interview. For the model/roleplay/video group, every effect size which could be calculated exceeded a one standard deviation improvement. For the model/roleplay group, while the appearance and mannerism score increased +.93 SD over the control group, all remaining criteria enjoyed an increase of more than one standard deviation. The roleplay group rated significantly better than the control group on enthusiasm (+1.22 SD) and on a composite score (effect size cannot be determined). The model group did not differ from the control group on any dependent variable. The model/roleplay/ videotape group scored significantly better than the model group on enthusiasm. For the personnel officer post-interview, the model/roleplay/videotape group and the model/roleplay group appeared more enthusiastic than the control group (+1.60 SD and +1.56 SD, respectively) and the model/roleplay/videotape group was rated higher than the control group on opening and closing the interview (+1.43 SD). No experimental group was rated as having a higher probability of hire than any other experimental group; however, the model/ roleplay/videotape group and the model/roleplay group were more likely to be hired than the control group (+1.27 SD and +1.19 SD, respectively). Because no information was presented concerning change scores or pre-interview scores, practice effects cannot be accounted for.

In sum, there appears to be a coaching effect due to these workshop programs. Effect size measures, when they are available, indicate that the improvement in target behaviors can be substantial. Of course, the small sample sizes make these estimates unstable. Anecdotal evidence suggests that these workshops are appealing to participants and have some face validity. Longer programs and programs that involve more change techniques are more likely to produce change in the dependent measure. The interventions have been shown to bring about change, above and beyond a control group practice effect, in specific, as well as global, criteria. Feedback appears to play an important role, whether it accompanies a videotaped playback of the subject's performance or is in response to a roleplay. Programmed materials, behavior rehearsal, discussion, and behavior modification have been shown to have some positive effects. There is no consistent practice effect. These studies are characterized more by inconsistency than by consistency. Systematic evaluations of the differential prediction of various criteria, the effect of various types of coaching and the techniques utilized, and the effect upon different subject populations would provide useful information. In addition, many of the target behaviors appear to have been based upon intuitive appeal rather than empirical support — more evidence supporting these foci would be desirable. Finally, support based upon more data than interview performance assessed immediately following the intervention would increase evidence for the generalizability of the positive effect.

DISCUSSION

We undertook the task of preparing this chapter in part in an attempt to fill in gaps in our own knowledge. We noted that coaching and practice effects receive little to no attention in textbooks in the area of employee selection. This chapter opened with a partial listing of ways in which coaching and practice can and do occur in organizations; given this variety, we were troubled that summaries of coaching and practice effects in personnel selection were not available. We developed the conceptual categorization of types of coaching and practice prior to undertaking a literature review, hoping that the categorization would help us understand differences in findings across studies. While we found the categorization scheme very helpful in thinking about coaching and practice effects, in general we found much less research than we had anticipated, and thus attempts at meta-analytic syntheses of the coaching and practice literatures for each of the types of selection devices were seen as premature.

The most consistent data are on practice effects for ability testing. There certainly are differences in effect size by test and item type which merit additional attention from researchers striving to build tests which are immune to practice effects. However, ability test users should realize that, in the absence of specific data to the contrary for the particular test they are using, higher scores should be expected upon retest. No research on coaching for ability tests in employment settings was found. While both the assessment center literature and interviewing literature suggest the possibility of coaching effects, we would characterize both as focusing on non-prototypic samples. The assessment center coaching literature emphasizes single exercises, student samples, and coaching interventions not typical of the grapevine coaching that we see as most likely to occur in organizations. The interview coaching literature emphasizes work with specialized populations, such as psychiatric patients. No information on coaching or practice effects for personality tests in employment settings were found. Summaries of findings regarding coaching and practice effects for ability tests, personality tests, assessment centers, and interviews are found in the treatment of each of those selection devices, and thus we will not present detailed summaries here. We will make a number of more general comments.

First, as noted earlier, we were frustrated at the large number of retest and alternative form reliability studies which reported only the correlation between the two sets of scores. If readily available data, namely, means and standard deviations, had been reported, much more information on practice effects would be available. However, even if these data had been reported, data on practice effects in operational settings, and particularly in settings in which feedback is provided before retesting, would still be lacking.

Second, the difficulty of conducting rigorous research on coaching should be recognized. At first glance, one might think that researchers would be able to take advantage of the existence of coaching programs and simply monitor the effects of such programs. However, a major problem with such a strategy is self-selection. If the program in question is not routinely available to applicants, but rather is sought out by a subset of applicants (as in the case of college entrance exams), those seeking out the programs may differ from applicants in general in ability, motivation, or a number of other characteristics. The observed treatment effects cannot be differentiated from selection–treatment interaction effects. Random assignment of subjects to treatment and control groups is needed; thus precluding opportunistic research on existing coaching programs. It is easy to see why experimental research is difficult. When coaching is seen by at least some applicants as desirable, random assignment will prove a problem unless one draws both treatment and control groups from among those not choosing coaching of their own accord. When a coaching intervention is designed solely for research purposes, random assignment is not a problem; however, concerns about differences in participant motivation between the research participants and those participating in an operational coaching program remain.

Third, an issue worthy of attention is the accuracy of the information comprising a coaching program. In some cases, inaccurate information may have no effect on applicants' scores. For example, telling applicants to guess 'c' if they have no idea which answer to a multiple choice question is correct since test constructors put the right answer in location 'c' more often than anywhere else may be inaccurate yet harmless; if an examinee truly has no idea as to which response is appropriate, choosing 'c' is as good a strategy as a haphazard choice. In other cases, inaccurate information may hinder examinee performance. Telling applicants that test constructors avoid 'a' as the correct response to multiple choice items is not only inaccurate with regard to any competently developed test, but may impede performance if applicants adopt a strategy of avoiding 'a' unless they're certain it is the correct response.

With regard to coaching for the employment interview, information about how to behave in an interview or about what interviewers are looking for may also be inaccurate, as it is not clear that interview behavior taught in many coaching programs rests on a research foundation. As noted earlier, research showing that coaching changes applicant behavior often begs the question of whether the behavior change leads to a more favorable evaluation from the interviewer. One of us spoke recently to a campus recruiter who reported discovering an interview coaching program that provided model answers to a list of common interview questions. This was discovered when very similar responses to a question were received from two consecutive applicants; the recruiter quickly discovered that he could easily identify which applicants had and had not been coached, and he chose to reject out of hand all coached applicants. Clearly, coaching changed behavior without having the intended effect on the interviewer.

Informal 'grapevine' coaching seems to run a particularly high risk of containing inaccurate information. The hints and advice passed on from individuals who have been through an assessment center may be deficient as a result of imperfect recall, or may be completely in error as a past participant constructs general rules for behavior out of feedback specific to that participant's pattern of behavior in the assessment center. Other selection devices seen by applicants as having an element of strategy involved (e.g. interviews, personality measures) also seem prone to the possibility of inaccurate coaching lowering the construct validity of applicants' scores.

Fourth, showing that the score obtained by an applicant changes as a result of coaching or practice alerts employers to the need to be sensitive to these effects, but does not address the issue of score validity. It is unclear whether the effect is to increase scores artificially or to eliminate score deficits due to unfamiliarity with the test, anxiety, or other factors. In all likelihood, each of these possibilities is true in some settings. We found one practice study addressing the relative validity of first or second administration scores and no such studies in the area of coaching. Note that most practice effect size measures were obtained from studies aimed primarily at assessing retest or alternate form reliability. The relatively high degree of reliability reported for ability tests suggests that practice cannot have a large impact on the relative ordering of candidates and thus that the predictive validity of scores from one administration will not be dramatically different from scores on a subsequent administration.

Finally, this chapter has not considered all conceivable selection devices. We focused on major categories: paper and pencil tests, interviews, and assessment centers. These were chosen as we could find a body of published information on coaching and practice effects on each. A wide variety of other selection devices could be considered (e.g. biodata, graphology); the issues raised in this chapter will apply to other selection devices as well. We feel that this chapter has raised more issues than it has resolved and hope it will inform future research on coaching and practice.

REFERENCES

Anastasi, A. (1981) Diverse effects of training on tests of academic intelligence. In B. F. Green (ed.), *New Directions for Testing and Measurement: Issues in testing — coaching, disclosure, and ethnic bias, no. 11.* San Francisco: Jossey-Bass.

Barbee, J. R., and Keil, E. C. (1973) Experimental techniques of job interview training for the disadvantaged. *Journal of Applied Psychology*, 58, 209–213.

Bass, B. M. (1954) The leaderless group discussion. *Psychological Bulletin*, 51, 465–492.

Burroughs, W. A., Rollins, J. B., and Hopkins, J. J. (1973) The effect of age, departmental experience and prior rater experience on performance in assessment center exercises. *Academy of Management Journal*, 16, 335–339.

Byham, W. C. (1977) Assessor selection and training. In J. L. Moses and W. C. Byham (eds), *Applying the Assessment Center Method.* New York: Pergamon Press.

Cohen, S. L. (1978) Standardization of assessment center technology: Some critical concerns. *Journal of Assessment Center Technology*, 1, 1–10.

Denning, D. L., and Grant, D. L. (1979) Knowledge of the assessment center process: Does it affect candidate ratings? *Journal of Assessment Center Technology*, 2, 7–12.

Dodd, W. E. (1977) Attitudes toward assessment center programs. In J. L. Moses and W. C. Byham (eds), *Applying the Assessment Center Method,* New York: Pergamon Press.

Droege, R. C. (1966) Effects of practice on aptitude scores. *Journal of Applied Psychology*, 50, 306–310.

Dulewicz, V., and Fletcher, C. (1982) The relationship between previous experience, intelligence and background characteristics of participants and their performance in an assessment centre. *Journal of Occupational Psychology*, 55, 197–207.

Dulewicz, V., Fletcher, C., and Wood, P. (1983) A study of the internal validity of an assessment centre and of participants' background characteristics and attitudes: A comparison between British and American findings. *Journal of Assessment Center Technology*, 6, 15–24.

Forrest, D. V., and Baumgarten, L. (1975) An hour for job interviewing skills. *Journal of College Placement*, 36, 77–78.

Frank, F. D., Sefcik, J. T., and Jaffee, C. L. (1983) *The Assessment Center Process: A Participant's Workbook*. Orlando, Florida: Human Resource Publishing Company.

Furman, W., Geller, M., Simon, S. J., and Kelly, J. A. (1979) The use of a behavior rehearsal procedure for teaching job-interviewing skills to psychiatric patients. *Behavior Therapy*, 10, 157–167.

Glass, G. V., McGaw, B., and Smith, M. L. (1981) *Meta-analysis in Social Research*. Beverly Hills, CA: Sage.

Hollandsworth, J. G. Jr, Dressel, M. E., and Stevens, J. (1977) Use of behavioral versus traditional procedures for increasing job interview skills. *Journal of Counseling Psychology*, 24, 503–510.

Hollandsworth, J. G., Jr, Glazeski, R. C., and Dressel, M. E. (1978) Use of social-skills training in the treatment of extreme anxiety and deficient verbal skills in the job-interview setting. *Journal of Applied Behavior Analysis*, 11, 259–269.

Hollandsworth, J. G., Jr, and Sandifer, B. A. (1979) Behavioral training for increasing effective job-interview skills: Follow-up and evaluation. *Journal of Counseling Psychology*, 26, 448–450.

Hunter, J. E., Schmidt, F. L., and Jackson, G. B. (1982) *Meta-analysis: Cumulating research findings across studies*. Beverly Hills, CA: Sage.

Jaffee, C. L., and Michaels, C. (1978) Is in-basket performance subject to coaching effects? *Journal of Assessment Center Technology*, 1, 13–17.

Keil, E. C., and Barbee, J. R. (1973) Behavior modification and training the disadvantaged job interviewee. *Vocational Guidance Quarterly*, 22, 50–55.

Keith, R. D., Engelkes, J. R., and Winborn, B. B. (1977) Employment-seeking preparation and activity: An experimental job-placement training model for rehabilitation clients. *Rehabilitation Counseling Bulletin*, 21, 159–165.

Kelly, J. A., Laughlin, C., Claiborne, M., and Patterson, J. (1979) A group procedure for teaching job interviewing skills to formerly hospitalized psychiatric patients. *Behavior Therapy*, 10, 299–310.

Klubeck, S., and Bass, B. M. (1954) Differential effects of training on persons of different leadership status. *Human Relations*, 7, 59–72.

Krumboltz, J. D., and Christal, R. E. (1960) Short-term practice effects on tests of spatial aptitude. *Personnel and Guidance Journal*, 38, 385–391.

Kulik, J. A., Bangert-Drowns, R. L., and Kulik, C. C. (1984). Effectiveness of coaching for aptitude tests. *Psychological Bulletin*, 95, 179–188.

Kulik, J. A., Kulik, C. C., and Bangert, R. L. (1984) Effects of practice on aptitude and achievement test scores. *American Educational Research Journal*, 21, 435–447.

Kurecka, P. M., Austin, J. M., Jr, Johnson, W., and Mendoza, J. L. (1982) Full and errant coaching effects on assigned role leaderless group discussion performance. *Personnel Psychology*, 35, 805–812.

Logue, P. E., Zenner, M., and Gohman, G. (1968) Video-tape roleplaying in the job interview. *Journal of Counseling Psychology*, 15, 436–438.

Lorenzo, R. V. (1984) The effect of assessorship on managers' proficiency in acquiring,

evaluating, and communicating information about people. *Personnel Psychology*, 37, 617–634.
McCormick, B. K., Dunlap, W. P., Kennedy, R. S., and Jones, M. B. (1983) The effects of practice on the Armed Services Vocational Aptitude Battery. US Army Research Institute for the Behavioral and Social Sciences, Technical Report 602.
McGovern, T. V., Tinsley, D. J., Liss-Levinson, N., Laventure, R. O., and Britton, G. (1975) Assertion training for job interviews. *The Counseling Psychologist*, 5, 65–68.
McIntyre, F. (1980) The reliability of assessment center results after feedback. *Journal of Assessment Center Technology*, 3, 10–14.
Messick, S. (1981) The controversy over coaching: Issues of effectiveness and equity. In B. F. Green (ed.), *New Directions for Testing and Measurement: Issues in testing – coaching, disclosure, and ethnic bias, no. 11*. San Francisco: Jossey-Bass.
Petty, M. M. (1974) A multivariate analysis of the effects of experience and training upon performance in a leaderless group discussion. *Personnel Psychology*, 27, 271–282.
Powers, D. E. (1986) Relations of test item characteristics to test preparation/test practice effects: A quantitative summary. *Psychological Bulletin*, 100, 67–77.
Raanan, S. J., and Lynch, T. H. (1973–74) Two approaches to job-hunting workshops: 'Job Scene' helps students get ready for interviews, says the University of Wisconsin-Milwaukee. *Journal of College Placement*, 39, 67–74.
Sackett, P. R., and Dreher, G. F. (1982) Constructs and assessment center dimensions: Some troubling empirical findings. *Journal of Applied Psychology*, 67, 401–410.
Smith, E. P., Wing, H., and Arabian, J. M. (1985) Criterion-related validity of practice on a cognitive abilities test. Presented at the twenty-sixth annual meeting of the Psychonomic Society. Boston, Massachusetts.
Speas, C. M. (1979) Job-seeking interview skills training: A comparison of four instructional techniques. *Journal of Counseling Psychology*, 26, 405–412.
Stevens, W., and Tornatzky, L. (1976) The effects of a job-interview skills workshop on drug-abuse clients. *Journal of Employment Counseling*, 13, 156–163.
Struth, M. R., Frank, F. D., and Amato, A. (1980) Effects of assessor training on subsequent performance as an assessee'. *Journal of Assessment Center Technology*, 3, 17–22.
Teel, K. S., and DuBois, H. (1983) Participants' reactions to assessment centers. *Personnel Administrator*, 3, 85–91.
United States Department of Labor (1970) *Manual for the USES General Aptitude Test Battery*, Washington, DC. Chapter 15.
Venardos, M. G., and Harris, M. B. (1973) Job interview training with rehabilitation clients: A comparison of videotape and role-playing procedures. *Journal of Applied Psychology*, 58, 365–367.
Walker, B. J. (1973–74) Two approaches to job-hunting workshops: A useful, temporary device, says the University of Kentucky. *Journal of College Placement*, 34, 66–71.
Wing, H. (1980) Practice effects with traditional mental test items. *Applied Psychological Measurement*, 4, 141–155.

Chapter 6
RETIREMENT: A PSYCHOLOGICAL PERSPECTIVE

Jean Talaga
and
Terry A. Beehr
*Department of Psychology
Central Michigan University
USA*

Much of the literature on retirement has noted that the view of the retired as old, idle citizens of our society is misleading. The retired population of the United States is becoming younger (Beehr, 1986; Robinson, Coberly, and Paul, 1985) and the activity level of many of these individuals is thought to be quite high (Atchley, 1982a). Furthermore, the notion that there is a specific, uniform retirement age is also incorrect. There has been such an increase in longevity and simultaneous public policy changes that retirees do not fit their inactive stereotype. The 1978 amendment to the Age in Employment Discrimination Act raised the mandatory retirement age in the United States, and the European Economic Community Commission recommended in 1980 that employers institute more flexible policies to allow retirement at varying ages (McGoldrick and Cooper, 1985). Overall, the trend in the United States has been towards earlier retirement (i.e. before the age of 65). Between 1955 and 1978, the labor force participation rates of men 65 years and older dropped from 40 to 20 per cent, and the rates of men aged 60 to 64 dropped from 83 to 63 per cent (Parnes and Nestel, 1981). Furthermore, projections made by the US Bureau of Labor statistics show that the early retirement trend is likely to continue through the 1990s (Robinson, Coberly, and Paul, 1985).

These large-scale changes in retirement activities imply that the summation of many individual retirement decisions can affect society as well as the individuals involved. Psychologists rarely inspect these molar events, but they may be very important for research topics at the individual (and organization) level.

This review focuses on psychological retirement research that was published during the five-year period from 1983 through 1987. A previous review (Beehr,

1986) covered research prior to 1983 and can be used as a benchmark for comparing the results of this review to see the 'current' state of retirement research. Overall, as concluded in the previous review, it appears that two areas continue to intrigue researchers: the individual or personal causes of retirement (decisions) and the consequences of retirement for the retired individuals. Perhaps just as intriguing are the organizational and societal factors that may influence retirement (decisions) and the subsequent impact of retirement on organizations and society. Unfortunately, research in these areas is sparse.

A potential problem with defining retirement was noted in the previous review (Beehr, 1986) and is apparent. While retirement has usually been considered a dichotomous variable (retired versus not retired), some researchers and theorists have noted that there are specific types of retirement as well. These have also usually been operationalized as dichotomous variables: voluntary versus involuntary, early versus on-time, and partial versus complete retirement). A further step needed by research in the area would be to recognize and operationalize these as continuous variables (e.g. degree to which retirement is perceived as voluntary, age at retirement, and number of hours one works per week). Defining these dimensions with continuous scales might lead to new discoveries about their importance in the process of retirement. One older longitudinal study (Palmore, George, and Fillenbaum, 1982) found that the determinants of retirement varied according to some of these types of definitions, although not all of them were operationalized as continuous variables. Researchers in recent years have still tended to use dichotomies if they have studied these types of retirement.

This review was organized according to Atchley's (1982a) three phases of the retirement process: (1) the *pre-retirement phase*, focusing on attitudes towards retirement and plans (intentions) to retire; (2) the *retirement transition phase*, focusing on factors that influence retirement behavior; and (3) the *post-retirement phase*, focusing on effects or consequences of retirement. By using this supposedly complete theoretical categorization instead of simply categorizing the current literature as it was found, it was hoped that lack of research in particular areas would be discovered if that was the case.

PRE-RETIREMENT PHASE

It has long been thought that employees' pre-retirement attitudes towards the job might be related to their attitudes towards retirement. For example, if they are very positively predisposed towards the job, they may resent or fear leaving it for retired life. Conversely, if they are positive towards their work lives, they may just be the type of people who will like their life in almost any situation, including retirement. Of course, there are other options. Atchley (1982b) had found no simple relationship between work and retirement attitudes but suggested a curvilinear relationship in which people at the extremes of the occupational ladder (and therefore work-related attitudes?) would have the most favorable attitudes towards retirement.

A recent study (Kilty and Behling, 1985) of 457 professional workers revealed inconsistent results regarding the relationship between job and retirement attitudes. Two of seven work 'alienation' scales ('work gives meaning to life' and 'work is a necessity') were negatively related to anticipated enjoyment of retirement. This finding lends support to the proposed inverse relationship between job and retirement attitudes. In the same study, however, this proposed relationship was not supported in that satisfaction with one's career was positively associated with anticipated enjoyment of retirement. Also, 'work gives meaning to life' and a general measure of alienation positively predicted 'avoidance of retirement' (Kilty and Behling, 1985). The first finding lends support and the second finding fails to support the proposed inverse relationship between job and retirement attitudes.

Glamser (1976) had identified situational factors that play a role in retirement attitudes, and along these lines Kilty and Behling (1985) found that the number of sources of retirement income one could expect (e.g. public/private pensions, social security benefits, investments) was positively related to attitude towards retirement. Positive expectations regarding social involvements and career activities in retirement were also significant predictors of positive attitudes towards retirement (Kilty and Behling, 1985). One's expectations about what his or her retirement years will be like (especially expectations about one's financial situation) appear to be important determinants of pre-retirement attitudes.

The age at which people plan to retire may also be an indicator of the relative attractiveness of retirement. The population trends of the last two decades have been examined by Ekerdt, Bosse, and Glynn (1985) and Barfield and Morgan (1978). A trend towards earlier retirement was noted. In the more recent study, Ekerdt, Bosse, and Glynn (1985) examined male workers' planned retirement ages (i.e. plans to retire before 62, at 62, between 63 and 64, at 65, over 65, or never to retire) across four measurement times between 1975 and 1984. Using four waves of data from men aged 47 to 64 at each survey, they found two patterns in the distribution of these workers' planned ages for retirement. First, pre-retirees' planned ages for retirement increased between the first measurement (1975) and the second measurement (1978). Ekerdt, Bosse, and Glynn (1985) explained that this later planned age for retirement was probably due to much public discussion and national debate in the United States over the condition or the social security system and mandatory retirement policies during the 1975–78 period. This same 1975–78 pattern, however, was not apparent when measuring the variable planned retirement age as a dichotomy (i.e. plans to retire before age 65 versus at or after 65). The advantages in terms of information gained by using a multi-point scale rather than a dichotomous scale of planned retirement age are evident here (Beehr, 1986).

The second pattern found by Ekerdt Bosse, and Glynn (1985) was that the distributions of planned retirement ages remained stable from the second (1978) to the third (1981) to the fourth (1984) measurements. From 1978 to 1984 the number of cohorts at each measurement who were planning early retirement did not increase. The stability of these distributions was taken as support for the belief of some retirement researchers (e.g. Kingson, 1982) that the early retirement trend is beginning to slow down and perhaps reverse (Ekerdt Bosse, and Glynn 1985).

Planning for Early Retirement

A number of factors have been examined for their contribution in explaining people's planned age for retirement. These factors are of three major types: characteristics of the individual or personal factors, work-related factors, and environmental factors.

Regarding personal factors, in a recent study of over 800 middle-aged women, a curvilinear relationship was found between chronological age and planned age for retirement (Shaw, 1984). Women who were older planned on retiring between the ages of 62 and 64 while those who were younger planned either to retire before age 62 or at age 65. Comparing these findings with those of Barfield and Morgan (1969), which revealed an inverse relationship, it might be concluded that the relationship between chronological age and planned retirement age has changed in the fifteen years that passed between the two studies.

The difference between the Barfield and Morgan (1969) and the Shaw (1984) findings (i.e. the former showing an inverse relationship and the latter showing a curvilinear relationship between chronological age and planned retirement age) might also be explained by the way in which the dependent variable, planned age for retirement, was measured in the two studies. While Barfield and Morgan (1969) used a dichotomous measure of planned retirement age (i.e. plans to retire before 62 or not), Shaw (1984) used a three-point scale (i.e. plans to retire before 62, between 62 and 64, or at 65). Had Shaw used a dichotomous measure, those planning to retire before 62 or between 62 and 64 would have been combined and the results would have been similar to those of Barfield and Morgan. On the other hand, had Barfield and Morgan used a multi-point scale or more categories of planned retirement age, the relationship between planned retirement age and chronological age may have shifted given the added information.

A second major difference in the two studies (Barfield and Morgan, 1969; Shaw, 1984) that could explain the difference in results is the sample characteristic, sex. While Barfield and Morgan had both men and women in their samples, Shaw had only women in her sample. If there are gender differences in planned retirement age, one would expect the findings from these two studies to differ. The inconsistent results and methodological differences in these studies make it difficult to draw conclusions regarding the extent to which the relationship between chronological age and planned retirement age may be changing in recent years.

Educational level has been suggested recently as a personal factor influencing the choice of early retirement. In their study of 457 people representing four occupational groups (attorneys, social workers, high school teachers, and college professors), Kilty and Behling (1985) found that high school teachers intended to retire much earlier than any of the other three groups. Kilty and Behling explained their findings by saying that the age at which people in certain occupations entered the labor force determined the age at which they would plan to leave the labor force. Because high school teachers generally needed less formal education (for entry-level jobs) compared to the other groups, they tend to enter their professions at earlier ages. Also, many high school teachers belong to public pension programs which tend to encourage teachers into retirement after a long period of service, such as 30 years (Graebner, 1980). Early entry into their occupations along with such pension requirements would lead many high school teachers to retire in their 50s (Kilty and Behling, 1985). Older research had not supported the notion of a relationship between education and retirement age, however, while it had suggested a relationship between pension plans and early retirement. Therefore, it seems that the pension issue is the more probable of the two explanations for the teachers' plans to retire early.

Related to pensions, Shaw (1984) found that plans for retirement were strongly influenced by pensions that became available at certain ages. The women's eligibility for a pension provided a strong incentive for retiring. If the women could obtain a pension by working longer, they usually planned to continue working. Also, those women who had retirement pensions were more likely to plan to retire before 65 than those without retirement pensions. Other economic variables have been associated with planned retirement age. The Kilty and Behling (1985) study found that people with more venturesome investments (i.e. real estate, business investments, and expected income from a new career) were more likely to plan retirement at younger ages.

Health has been another personal variable that has long been associated with planned retirement age, but Shaw (1984) did not find any relationship. The study did not identify clearly the type of health measure it used, however, making it difficult to explain this finding and its discrepancy from so much consistent past research.

While numerous studies have failed to find a relationship between attitudes towards retirement and work commitment, there has been an apparent association between job-related attitudes and plans for early retirement. Kilty and Behling (1985) found that measures of work alienation were significant predictors of one's plans for retirement. People who felt that their work had little meaning, who did not take an active interest in their work, and who reported greater levels of alienation on their jobs planned to retire at earlier ages.

Regarding work-related factors affecting plans for early retirement, no recent studies were found. Examples of potential work-related factors in retirement planning that had been studied prior to 1983 include job characteristics and work-related social pressure to retire.

No recent studies of non-job environmental factors in retirement planning were found either. Social pressure from outside of the workplace is an example of such a variable. It had been a variable in at least one study prior to 1983.

Correspondence Between Retirement Plans and Actual Retirement

If information about the pre-retirement phase is to be useful in understanding the retirement process, it is important to investigate the link between pre-retirement attitudes and planning and actual retirement behavior. In a recent study using longitudinal data from 125 staff members of a large university, Prothero and Beach (1984) examined the retirement decision-making process. They proposed that the process could be viewed as a chain of predictors that begins with expectations for retirement, followed by intentions or plans for retirement, and ends with action or retirement behavior. Using chi-square analyses, they found that respondents' intentions to retire were predicted by their expectations for 78 per cent of the sample. Positive expectations for retirement were related to intentions to retire and negative expectations were related to intentions to continue working. There was also a relationship between intentions to retire and work status two years later (76 per cent of the sample had acted in accordance with their earlier intentions). Findings from this study suggest that if one's expectations about retirement are favorable, he or she will make plans for retirement and will usually follow through with those plans.

Although Prothero and Beach's (1984) results supported their hypothesized chain of predictors, the fact remains that one-fourth of the sample did not follow through with their retirement plans. Plans and intentions can change over time. Burkhauser and Quinn (1985) examined longitudinal data from 1969 to 1979 for relationships between planned and actual retirement and factors that could serve as moderators of this relationship. In 1969, respondents (aged 53 to 63) reported the age at which they planned to retire. These same respondents were interviewed every two years after 1969 about their work status and other relevant information. Based on comparisons of their planned and actual retirement ages, respondents were classified into four groups: (1) early — those who left the labor force before they planned (42 per cent of the sample); (2) on time — those who retired within a year of their planned retirement age (38 per cent); (3) late — those who retired later than their planned retirement age (13 per cent); and (4) on schedule — those who had not reached their planned retirement age and were still working (7 per cent). Retirement plans were reliable predictors for less than one-half of the sample; furthermore, the respondents were over three times more likely to retire at earlier ages than they planned rather than at later ages than they planned.

Regarding potential moderators of the relationship, those with longer tenure on their jobs were more accurate predictors of their age of retirement than were people with less tenure (Burkhauser and Quinn, 1985). Related to this, those workers who were more distant from their expected retirement age were also less accurate in their predictions. This seems logical, since it is probably easier to predict the near future than the distant future for almost anything.

Other variables found to correlate with accuracy (i.e. the correspondence between planned and actual retirement ages) were pension coverage, mandatory retirement policies, health, and social security wealth (Burkhauser and Quinn, 1985). Those with pension coverage were more accurate in their predictions and more likely to be in the late group than those without pensions. Workers subject to mandatory policies were more likely to be accurate in their plans than those not subject to mandatory retirement. Individuals who had poor health or had declining health after 1969 tended to retire earlier than planned. Respondents with greater social security wealth were more accurate in their predictions and were more likely to be in the on-time group and less likely to be in the early group than respondents with lower social security wealth. In multinomial logit estimation analyses to identify predictors of the late versus on-time and the early versus on-time groups, it was concluded that planning horizon (time until expected retirement) was the most significant discriminating predictor. Those with a longer planning horizon were more likely to retire earlier than planned and less likely to retire later than planned compared with workers with a shorter planning horizon.

Because workers' plans for retirement do not provide complete insight into their retirement behaviors, it is important to identify the variables that do influence actual retirement behavior. Some recent studies have also looked at that.

RETIREMENT TRANSITION: FACTORS THAT INFLUENCE RETIREMENT BEHAVIOR

The decision to retire is seen as a 'work–leisure' trade-off by labor economists who propose that older workers choose between work and leisure based on an assessment of their financial situation and the time they believe they should spend in the workplace and at home (Robinson et al., 1985). Research on factors influencing retirement decisions has focused on groups of people for whom retirement is voluntary, since there is no personal decision making involved when retirement is involuntary as in mandatory retirement (Beehr, 1986). Personal, work-related, and environmental factors all have potential for influencing one's decision to retire.

Because the various factors can influence one's decisions to retire simultaneously or in combination, it is sometimes difficult to separate the effects attributable to specific personal, work-related, and environmental factors. Beehr (1986) gives the example of an employee who prefers to have a certain amount of money. It is unclear in this situation whether the effects of personal or work-related factors on the decisions to retire could be separated. Although it is difficult to make these distinctions cleanly, the review follows this format.

Personal Factors

Worker characteristics and individual variables have been the major focus of research on retirement decisions and are considered the most important determinants of the decision to retire early (Robinson et al., 1985). Over the years prior to those covered in this review, it has become apparent that personal finances and health are the two most important influences on people's decisions to retire voluntarily (Beehr, 1986). Other more minor personal factors noted in that review included attitudes of various sorts, especially towards work or towards specific jobs. At times, however, the term 'attitude' was defined rather broadly — to include nearly any job-related thing measured with a questionnaire. It was also noted that predictors of retirement could logically vary with the form of retirement (e.g. partial versus complete, early versus on time). Some research has addressed factors in decisions to retire early, but the partial–complete typology has still not been examined very often.

Some recent research has focused on demographic characteristics and their ability to predict retirement decisions. Chronological age, as would be expected, has been associated with workers' decisions to retire (George, Fillenbaum, and Palmore, 1984; Gustman and Steinmeier, 1984). It is argued that retirement has become a normal phase of life (Ekerdt, Bosse, and Glynn, 1985), and people tend to expect themselves and each other to retire at or near a certain chronological age. George et al. (1984) found retirement to be related to age for both men and women. Gustman and Steinmeier (1984) used four categories of retirement (not retired, partially retired on the main job, partially retired outside the main job, and retired), to measure retirement status. They found that the probability of retirement varied systematically with chronological age. Older workers were more likely to be partially and completely retired on and outside their main jobs than were younger workers.

Gustman and Steinmeier (1984) also found that age interacted with other variables, such as social security and pension eligibility, health, and the presence of mandatory retirement provisions, to predict workers' retirement status. Similarly, Hardy (1985) found age to be predictive of retirement status because of its meaning of eligibility for social security benefits and retirement pensions. In the context of retirement decisions, age obviously has meanings other than pure number of years old an employee is.

Because availability of major retirement income is closely tied to a worker's age, the effect of age on retirement decisions may be minimal when controlling for financial variables as well as health variables which are also likely to be related to age. With a number of variables controlled including finances, health, education, job characteristics, and others, George *et al.* (1984) still found age to be a significant predictor of retirement status. This outcome probably reflects social norms in this country about appropriate times to retire from the labor force and not the effects of age, *per se*. The strongest effects of age on retirement decisions are probably via health effects and income that becomes available once a worker reaches a certain age.

George *et al.* (1984) also studied sex differences in the predictors of retirement, that is, gender as a moderator of the relationships between certain predictors and retirement decision. Using data from the Retirement Health Survey and the Duke Second Longitudinal Study, they found that variables predicting retirement for men and women were not the same. Data for both sources indicated that the only predictor of retirement for women was their age. Predictors of retirement for men included age as well as a number of other factors such as their educational and occupational status, health, income, and job tenure. These findings suggest that men and women base their retirement decisions on very different factors. Although gender may not be directly related to retirement behavior, it appears to interact with other variables to predict retirement.

Studies on the retirement decisions of women have been scarce (Gratton and Haug, 1983; Szinovacz, 1983). In the last decade, however, these studies have increased in number. Unfortunately, the majority of them have used all-female samples and researchers have compared their findings with those of past studies that have used all-male samples, in order to claim gender differences. Caution needs to be taken when comparing findings from one study with those of another due to all the possible methodological differences that may account for discrepancies in the findings. Contrary to Szinovacz's (1983) call for more studies using female samples, it is suggested here that future researchers use both males and females in their samples and analyze the data from each such study with gender as a variable that might have main or interaction effects (as in George *et al.*, 1984).

Regarding employees' marital status, Gustman and Steinmeier (1984) found that those without a spouse were more likely to report being retired. Several explanations have been offered for potential relationships between martial status and retirement decisions (e.g. see Anderson, Clark, and Johnson, 1980; Beehr 1986; O'Rand and Henretta, 1982), but these need testing.

A person's educational level is a major determinant of the occupational level at which he or she will enter the labor force, and since education influences workers' entry into the labor force, it has been suggested that it might also influence their exit from the labor force (Hardy, 1985). Recent studies examining this relationship, however, have revealed inconsistent findings. George *et al.* (1984) found that lower educational level increased the odds of men retiring, but educational level was not predictive of women's retirement status. Other studies have failed to find relationships between educational level and measures of retirement status. Using data for older white males, Hardy (1984) found that the effect of years of schooling on retirement status (i.e. being retired or not retired) disappeared when controlling for occupational categories and occupational status. Although no overall effects of educational level on retirement status were found, effects were apparent in two instances. Among professional, technical, and kindred workers a college degree reduced the likelihood of retirement. Also, among salespeople and clerical workers, a high school diploma reduced the likelihood of retirement (Hardy, 1984). Hardy (1985) also found no difference in educational level between retired and working men using three waves of NLS survey data. The main effects of educational level on retirement behavior are inconsistent and perhaps minimal according to recent studies. As suggested by the findings of Hardy (1984), the effects of educational level might be due to occupational status.

Hardy's (1984) study found that the higher the workers' occupational level, the less likely they were to be retired, but the George *et al.* (1984) study found that the effect of occupational level did not remain significant when other predictors were controlled in multivariate analyses. The failure to find significant effects of occupational level, when other variables are controlled, suggests that the relationship between occupational level and retirement status is due to other factors related to occupational status. Factors such as work commitment, job attitudes, and health have been suggested. It is possible that people in higher occupational jobs have stronger work commitment and job satisfaction, making it more difficult for them to leave their jobs (George *et al.*, 1984). To the extent that lower level jobs may be more physically demanding or more hazardous to one's health, greater numbers of people in these jobs would be expected to retire earlier because of their inability to keep up with the physical demands or because of work-related health problems (Hardy, 1985).

Another possible explanation of the occupation–retirement link is that occupational level acts as a moderator of the relationship between certain variables and retirement behavior. In a study directly examining this issue, however, Hardy (1985) found that once retirement age differences were controlled, the variables that influenced retirement behavior (i.e. health, compulsory retirement with second pension coverage, and age eligibility variables) were fairly consistent across all occupational categories. These findings, that suggest that the determinants of retirement do not vary among different occupational groups, were suggested by others (George *et al.*, 1984).

One clear predictor of the decision to retire is declining health. Over the years, as well as recently, numerous studies have indicated that poor health influences people's retirement decisions (e.g. Gustman and Steinmeier, 1984;

Hardy, 1984; McGoldrick 1983). Hardy's and Gustman and Steinmeier's studies reported this from a longitudinal study using three and four waves of data, respectively, over a number of years. Atchley (1982a) had even proposed that retirement may serve the purpose of helping the individual cope better with poor health.

George et al. (1984) found that among a panel of men over a four-year period, the more health limitations reported, the greater the probability of retirement. O'Rand and Henretta (1982), however, using the same data (RHS study) but with one less wave, found similar results for women whereas George et al. did not. Overall, however, it seems that the findings from these longitudinal studies provide strong support for the influence of health on retirement.

Another set of variables that have long been established as related to retirement are financial in nature. The George et al. (1984) study from the Duke Second Longitudinal Survey found that having higher pre-retirement income significantly increased the probability that men would retire. In other recent studies, Durbin, Gross, and Borgatta (1984) found that non-retired faculty reported greater levels of economic insecurity for retirement than did retired faculty, and George et al. (1984) found that enrollment in a pension program increased the odds of men retiring. Gustman and Steinmeier (1984), however, found no relationship between number of dependants and retirement status measured on a 4-point scale. Over the years there have been inconsistent results regarding the impact of dependants' and spouses' employment on retirement decisions, and this seems to indicate that perhaps other variables, favorableness of the family situation (Beehr, 1986) or gender for example, may be influencing the relationships in these studies. There are some previous studies of labor force participation rates suggesting that husbands and wives may make different average work choices when dependants are present in the household.

A few personal factors related to one's employment have been subject to investigation in recent years. One of these, job tenure, would seem to be an important determinant of retirement decisions in so far as it is often involved in eligibility requirement for company pension benefits. Hardy (1985) found that longer tenure on the job was associated with retirement among respondents from three waves of the National Longitudinal Surveys (NLS) in the United States. In an earlier study using the same NLS data, however, Hardy (1984) found that after other variables were controlled, including eligibility for social security and other pensions, job tenure did not have strong effects. Furthermore, George et al. (1984) found that longer tenure in the longest-held job increased the probability of retirement among a panel of men in the Retirement History Study (RHS).

Although the findings of Hardy (1984) and George et al. (1984) appear to be inconsistent, they might be explained by the researchers' measures of job tenure. The measure of length of employment on the present job (used in the Hardy study) may have different meaning from the measure of length of employment on one's longest-held job (used in the George *et al.* study). It seems likely that the effect of job tenure on one's retirement decision is probably only minimal and perhaps absent when specific income eligibility requirements are controlled.

In addition to job tenure, feelings of job alienation have been suggested recently as being related to retirement decisions. Workers' feelings of control over their jobs versus feelings of isolation and powerlessness in their jobs have been associated with retirement status. In a study comparing 74 retired faculty members with 88 non-retired faculty members from a large university, Durbin *et al.* (1984) found a significant difference between the two groups in terms of the alienation they felt on their jobs. Using path analysis techniques, they found a significant path coefficient (.43) between a seven-item measure of job alienation and retirement. This finding lent support for the authors' hypothesis that alienated faculty members tend to retire earlier than other faculty members. Further research on the connection between feelings of alienation and retirement for other occupational groups would be useful.

Besides job tenure and alienation, employees' values about work might also influence their retirement decisions. George *et al.* (1984) reported from her study that workers who reported they would not work unless necessary were much more likely to retire. These findings might be interpreted to mean employees who place less value in work itself are more likely to choose to retire early.

In summary, the recent research on personal factors predictive of retirement decisions has focused on some demographic characteristics (chronological age, financial status, gender, marital status, educational level, occupational level, health, job tenure, job alienation, and employees' work-related values). There is some support for each of these being factors in retirement decisions, although the support for some of them may be inconsistent or suggestive of moderator effects. In addition to these, the previous review by Beehr (1986) hypothesized Type A behavior and skill obsolescence as potential personal predictors. These apparently have not been studied in the interim between the two reviews.

Personal factors in the decision to retire have always been the most studied types of potential causes of retirement, and the recent research has continued that theme. Because of the relatively large number of studies that have now been conducted on this topic, there is little reason to continue performing studies with relatively weak designs. There has been a trend towards more rigorous longitudinal designs, which should be continued in order to advance our knowledge about the topic further. Also, since finances and health seem to have prevailed over the years as obvious and strong predictors of retirement, future studies might always try to measure these in addition to other potential predictor variables of interest in a specific study. That way, the challenge would be to discover variables that could predict retirement after the effects of these well-known predictors are partialed out.

Work-Related and Organizational Factors

Over the years, research on work-related or organizational variables that affect retirement decisions has been scarce compared with the number of studies that have examined the impact of personal variables, and only one such study was located from the recent literature. Beehr (1986) suggested that undesirable job characteristics may be seen as factors that 'push' workers out of their jobs and into retirement. Presumably, a worker who is experiencing an unfavorable situation on the job will be apt to want to escape from his or her unpleasant circumstances. One recent longitudinal study (Hayward and Hardy, 1985) found that opportunity to deal with others on the job decreases the probability of early retirement. This is an area in which there is a need for further research. It has been suggested that such research could investigate job characteristics such as required travel, outdoor work, and supervisory styles for their potential influence on retirement decisions (Beehr, 1986).

Part-time work options seem to have potential for influencing retirement decisions. Bosworth and Holden (1983) surveyed Wisconsin state employees who were 55 years old and older to determine under what conditions they would delay their planned retirement. Over 50 per cent of these employees said they would delay retirement if they could work part time. Another 33 per cent would delay their plans if they could continue to work full time past the mandatory retirement age (which was 65 at the time). Follow-up data were collected on these same employees after the mandatory retirement age in Wisconsin was raised from 65 to 70. One-third of the employees actually delayed their retirement given other work alternatives.

It has been suggested that part-time work offers older workers an opportunity to withdraw gradually from the workforce. It promotes greater ease in adjusting to retirement as opposed to the traditional abrupt retirement transition that workers are expected to make. For workers with minor health limitations, part-time work might offer just enough relief from full-time pressures without forcing them to retire completely. Perhaps organizations can also benefit from keeping on valuable senior workers who know the 'nooks and crannies' of the organization (Beehr, 1986) and who can help teach incoming employees 'the ropes'. More research could help to determine the validity of these suggestions.

Robinson et al. (1985) have also made many suggestions for future research in the area of work-related factors influencing retirement decisions. These include employers' policies, older employees' job performance levels, and retraining offered by employers. In addition, the previous review (Beehr, 1986) hypothesized that the degree of attainment of occupational goals may be related to decisions to retire. There are obviously many potential avenues for enlightening research in the area of work-related factors in the decision to retire. Even prior to the five-year period that was the focus of this review, there was little research on the topic. Contrary to the previous topic, effects of personal factors on retirement, there is currently so little known about the topic that even the relatively less rigorous methods such as cross-sectional studies might provide some new insight.

Environmental and Societal Factors

A number of environmental and societal factors have the potential to affect employees' retirements. Unfortunately, little empirical research has been conducted to determine the impact of these factors on retirement decisions. The lack of research is probably due, at least partially, to the difficulty of operationalizing some environmental factors such as societal norms. Also the difficulty of isolating the effects of these factors from the effects of all the other important factors that impinge on workers and their retirement decisions might be another reason for the lack of research.

The only empirical study with analyses bearing on this area during the time period reviewed was George *et al.*'s (1984) study using data from the Duke Second Longitudinal Study. That study found that the amount of time spent with friends increased the odds of men retiring. It cannot be determined, however, whether the actual amount of time interacting with friends or the content of these interactions influenced retirement behavior. More research is needed to explain this result.

This result could be related to Beehr's (1986) hypothesis that leisure pursuits in general might be related to people's decisions to retire. In addition, that review also suggested that marital and family life could have a bearing on retirement decisions. As with the impact of work and organizations on retirement decisions, this area could use much more research. As with the previous topic (effects of work-related and organizational factors on retirement decisions), although rigorous designs could provide the best information, even less rigorous methods such as cross-sectional studies could provide potentially interesting new information in this area.

POST-RETIREMENT PHASE: EFFECTS AND CONSEQUENCES OF RETIREMENT

Much of the retirement literature has focused on the problems of adjusting to the loss of one's job. Many retirement theories have been proposed to help explain the effects of retirement on the individual and subsequent adjustment to retired life, but many of these 'retirement theories' have come from general theories of aging and human development and, therefore, may not be appropriate for studying specifics of the retirement process (Beehr, 1986). Typical of these theories are continuity theory, which maintains that people behave after retirement pretty much as they did before retirement (with probably a gradual reduction of activity; Atchley, 1976); activity theory which proposes that retirees strive to remain active in order to fulfil their needs (e.g., Atchley, 1975; Friedman and Havighurst, 1954); disengagement theory, which proposes that retirement causes people to decrease their social involvement and withdraw from society (Atchley, 1975, 1976); and crisis theory, which maintains that retirement is a crisis requiring drastic adjustments (Robinson *et al.*, 1985). Many studies of the effects of retirement have implications for the validity of one or more of these theories.

An interesting sidelight to these proposals in recent years concerns the widespread use of the stressful life events scales (e.g. Holmes and Rahe, 1967), which usually list retirement as a stressful life event. There have been recent warnings about accepting this as evidence that retirement is stressful (i.e. as support for crisis theory), because retirement is not considered as a separate variable in these studies (Beehr, 1986) and because some of the scales were developed by having people rank order the impact of the events (e.g. retirement) regardless of whether or not they had ever experienced them (Matthews, Brown, Davis, and Denton, 1982). In fact, Matthews *et al.* even did an empirical study in which they had 300 recent retirees (retired one to five years) from Ontario indicate the extent to which 32 life events affected them, using a five-point scale. Respondents rated only those life events they had experienced. In terms of impact or effect, retirement was ranked 27th of 32 life events (where 1 indicated the strongest impact). These results indicate that retirement was perceived as having little effect on the lives of those experiencing it relative to many other life events such as getting married, birth of children or grandchildren, health problems, winning a major award, a big weight change, and many others. People varied widely in the impact they felt retirement had on their lives. Men were more likely to perceive retirement as a critical event than were women. More recent retirees were more likely to perceive retirement as a critical event than not-so-recent retirees, suggesting perhaps that the initial shock of retirement becomes tempered as time passes and one gets adjusted to his or her new role.

While this suggests that retired life gets better as time from the point of retirement passes, another study (Conner, Dorfman, and Tompkins, 1985) recently found a negative relationship between time since retirement and life satisfaction, and a third study (Sheppard, Beehr, and Hamilton, 1986) found duration of retirement negatively related to some types of satisfaction for retirees from some types of jobs (clerical workers and first-line supervisors) and positively related to satisfactions for retirees from other types of jobs (managers and technical/professional).

These inconsistent findings might be explained by the different dependent variables utilized in these studies: Conner *et al.* (1985) used life satisfaction as a dependent measure, and Sheppard *et al.* (1986) used retirement satisfaction as a measure of retirees' (retrospective) preferred time of retirement.

In a cross-sectional study using data from the Normative Aging Study (NAS),

Ekerdt, Bosse, and Levkoff (1985) found some support for the first two phases in Atchley's retirement model. Comparing six groups of retirees who varied in length of time retired, and controlling for other important variables such as health and income, Ekerdt *et al.* found that individuals who had been retired for 13 to 18 months reported significantly lower levels of life satisfaction and involvement in physical activities than did those who had been retired for 0 to 6 months. Also, the more recent retirees had more of a 'future orientation' (i.e. were more optimistic and enthusiastic in discussing their plans for the future) than did those retired 13 to 18 months. Ekerdt, Bosse, and Levkoff (1985) believe that their findings support the notion that the immediate post-retirement experience is marked by more enthusiasm than the later period and that some degree of 'letdown' or re-assessment is likely during the second year of retirement.

Although longitudinal data would be more appropriate for validating Atchley's phased model of retirement, the cross-sectional findings of Ekerdt, Bosse, and Levkoff (1985) have important implications. Perhaps the initial high expectations and enthusiasm that give way to later letdown and depression could be tempered by pre-retirement programs that promote realistic expectations for retirement. In their study of workers and retirees (some of whom attended a pre-retirement program and some of whom did not), Kamouri and Cavanaugh (1986) found that with increased length of time retired, retirees who did not attend the program became less satisfied with many aspects of their retirement. Retired attendees, however, remained as satisfied or more satisfied with longer retirement. In this study, the pre-retirement program may have buffered the shock that retirees seem to experience during the second year of their retirement. More research is needed to validate Atchley's model of retirement adjustment and test the impact of intervention strategies on these periods adjustment.

Overall, recent research seems to indicate that retirees are relatively satisfied with their retirement (Hooker and Ventis, 1984; McGoldrick, 1983), and some recent studies have attempted to identify the correlates or predictors of life satisfaction among retired individuals. Health and financial variables appear in the recent literature as apparent strong correlates of retirees' satisfaction (Dorfman, Kouhout, and Heckert, 1985; Hooker and Ventis, 1984; McGoldrick, 1983; Riddick and Daniel, 1984). Retirees experiencing health problems or financial difficulties tend to be less satisfied with retirement than retirees not experiencing such problems.

While health and financial predictors of retired life satisfaction have long been apparent, some other, more interesting variables have been investigated by recent research. One study (McGoldrick, 1983) reported that participation in leisure activities is related to increased life satisfaction, and another (Hooker and Ventis, 1984) found that retirees' life satisfaction was partially dependent upon the interaction between their work values and their perceptions that the activities they take part in are useful. The most satisfied retirees were those who had low work values and did not perceive their activities as useful. The least satisfied retirees were those who had high work values and did not perceive their activities as useful. McGoldrick (1983) and Dorfman *et al.* (1985) reported that the perceived quality of retirees' social contacts with family and friends were important to retirees' satisfaction.

The situation surrounding a worker's retirement may impact on his or her retirement satisfaction. McGoldrick (1983) found that people who retired from their jobs voluntarily, for example, had more positive feelings towards retirement than people who were involuntarily retired.

Although a number of studies have gone to great lengths to identify predictors of retirees' satisfaction in the name of retirement research, the use of samples consisting only or retired individuals tells us nothing about the actual impact of retirement itself. It appears not to be widely understood that in order to examine the actual impact of retirement, retirees must be compared with people of the same generation (perhaps themselves) who have not retired (Beehr, 1986). Longitudinal studies that collect data from the same individual before (perhaps during) and after their retirements are extremely valuable in studying the effects of retirement on individuals.

As Beehr (1986) indicated, retirement has not only the potential to affect the person who is retiring, but it may also affect the employing organization. For example, an organization which is seeing increased early retirement among its higher level people may be forced to move younger individuals into these positions more rapidly than it had planned. Unfortunately, organizational outcomes of retirement have been neglected in the literature. Likewise, the effect of retirement on environmental factors, such as legislative retirement policy, has not been examined in the literature yet appears to be a viable and valuable topic for research.

Impact of Retirement on the Individual

As in the past, recent studies of the effects of retirement on the retiree have been plentiful. Both the direct effects of retirement and the indirect effects of retirement (via moderator variables) have been studied widely.

Probably the most obvious effect of retirement is income reduction. A report from the US Senate Special Committee on Aging in 1982 revealed that retirement leads to a one-half to two-thirds reduction in income and consequently moves many retired individuals into low income categories (Robinson *et al.*, 1985). Using data from six longitudinal studies, Palmore, Fillenbaum, and George (1984) found that retirement had a significant negative effect on income.

The health effects of retirement have served as an intriguing area of research in the retirement literature. The stereotype of the older worker who carefully plans for retirement only to get sick and die shortly after leaving the job has contributed to the belief that retirement has negative health consequences

(Atchley, 1977). However, contrary to popular belief, the empirical research of the past has consistently failed to find negative health effects of retirement (Beehr, 1986; Kasl, 1980; Minkler, 1981). Some of the more recent studies appear to be more methodologically sound and are useful in validating the findings of the earlier studies.

Various dependent measures of health have been used in the literature. Kremer (1985) used self-reported health measures to examine the impact of retirement on 310 Israeli workers. Using a five-point scale, retirees rated their present health and pre-retirement health retrospectively. Findings indicated no change in health after retirement. The use of retrospective reports throws some suspicion on the findings. Ekerdt, Bosse, and LoCastro (1983) found that retrospective claims of improved health were not validated by longitudinal increases in self-reported health for the same individuals. Studies utilizing pre- and post-retirement health measures appear to be much more appropriate for studying health effects.

Ekerdt, Bosse, and Goldie (1983) used the Cornell Medical Index which required respondents to indicate which of 195 somatic symptoms they were experiencing. Using NAS data, they found that the level of somatic complaints did not differ between pre- and post-retirement for 171 male respondents nor did the change in level of somatic complaints differ between retirees and workers. As suggested by Streib and Schneider (1971) almost two decades ago, it seems likely that health decline is at least as likely associated with aging as with retirement.

The use of self-reported health measures may not accurately gauge one's level of physical health and the change in health that may result from retirement. Ekerdt, Bosse, and LoCastro (1983) argued that psychological variables such as workers' morale and general sense of well-being may confound self-evaluations of health. Earlier, Kasl (1980) had suggested the change that comes with the removal of work role demands may also change the whole subjective framework in which people make evaluations of their health. Kasl suggested that self-reports of health after one's retirement might be biased towards optimism.

Other recent studies have also failed to find negative health consequences resulting from retirement. Using physicians' health ratings, Ekerdt, Baden, Bosse, and Dibbs (1983) compared health changes (pre- and post-measures) of 229 male retirees with those (n = 409) of their age peers who continued to work. The results indicated no difference between retirees and workers on physical health change. Similar findings were reported when examining the effects of retirement on men's systolic and diastolic blood pressure and total serum cholesterol over a three-year span using NAS data (Ekerdt, Sparrow, Glynn, and Bosse, 1984).

Some earlier reviews had suggested that willingness to retire may be associated with slightly better health outcomes than mandatory retirement (e.g.,

Minkler, 1981; Kasl, 1980). More recent research, however, failed to find a relationship between voluntary/involuntary retirement and health effects (Ekerdt, Bosse, and Goldie, 1983; Ekerdt, Baden, Bosse, and Dibbs, 1983). Length of time retired, pre-retirement job satisfaction, social support, and marital status also had no effect on the relationship between retirement and health (Ekerdt, Bosse, and LoCastro, 1983; Ekerdt, Bosse, and Goldie, 1983).

The potential impact of workers' socioeconomic status (SES) on health outcomes of retirement has been discussed by various researchers in the past (noted by Beehr, 1986; MacBride, 1976; Minkler, 1981), but the only recent study (Ekerdt, Bosse, and Goldie, 1983) failed to find a relationship between the prestige of one's former occupation and change in somatic complaints from pre- to post-retirement. It might be argued that the differences in findings here are due to the different dependent measures of health used. Regardless, much more research is needed to examine the moderating effect of socioeconomic status, as well as many other variables (e.g. economic recession, type of pre-retirement job, Type A behavior) on health outcomes of retirement.

A large body of research has also accumulated on workers' mental health or psychological well-being. The labels attached to the dependent variables in these studies vary and include, for example, life satisfaction, retirement satisfaction or retirement attitudes, morale, happiness, and adjustment or adaptation. Although these measures appear to be different, in most studies they are used as global measures of 'well-being'. The conceptual overlap between measures such as life satisfaction of retirees and retirement satisfaction illustrates the justification for comparing studies that have used such global measures (Kasl, 1980). Some effort is made in this discussion, however, to differentiate between those studies that use global measures and those that focus on specific aspects of well-being.

In a cross-sectional study comparing female homemakers, retirees, and workers, Riddick (1985) found that women working outside the home reported greater life satisfaction than did homemakers and retirees. Unfortunately, other variables found in the literature to be important to workers' satisfaction (e.g. health, income) were not controlled in this study, making it difficult to draw conclusions about the direct effects of retirement on life satisfaction. A previous study (Atchley, 1982b) had controlled a number of variables (e.g. income, health, marital status, social status, living arrangements), and revealed a slight increase in life satisfaction with retirement among men and women. Other past studies (e.g. Beck, 1982; Streib and Schneider, 1971) had found little effect of retirement on life satisfaction, and another recent study (Palmore, Fillenbaum, and George, 1984), using data from six longitudinal studies, found that retirement status had little effect (if any) on life satisfaction and happiness when pre-retirement characteristics were controlled.

It is possible that some demographic characteristics could moderate the relationship between retirement and well-being, and a few recent studies have been looking for this type of interaction. George et al. (1984) found that gender may have a moderating effect on retirement's impact on individuals' feelings of usefulness and life satisfaction. Retirement was related to increased perceptions of usefulness and decreased life satisfaction only for men in this study. Some research from the 1970s (e.g. Streib and Schneider, 1971; Jaslow, 1976; Fox, 1977) had found that women retirees experienced greater difficulty in adjusting to retirement than men. More research is needed to determine the effects of gender on these psychological retirement outcomes.

Marital status is another demographic characteristic that has been studied recently as a potential moderator of this relationship. Based on research suggesting that work is more important to unmarried individuals than to married individuals, Keith (1985) hypothesized that the loss of work (via retirement) would have a more negative effect on the never married. Keith reasoned that because the never married lack structured family roles and the out-or-work involvement that married life can bring, they would be more strongly affected by retirement. To test the hypothesis, three groups of unmarried men and women (widowed, separated/divorced, never married) were compared on their retirement attitudes and overall happiness. Contrary to Keith's hypothesis, never married women had more positive attitudes towards retirement and were happier than formerly married women. Overall, the results failed to support the notion that retirement is more difficult for the never married.

A possible explanation for Keith's (1985) results might be that the change in marital status (which may have been recent for some) experienced by the widowed and separated/divorced groups was probably very stressful (especially in the case of widowhood), thereby affecting these individuals' feelings of happiness and attitudes towards retirement. The never married, who had not experienced the negative effects of change in marital status, did not have these unfortunate circumstances in their past to influence their reports of happiness and attitudes. In this way, change in marital status rather than current marital status may serve as a moderator of the association between retirement and well-being. Studies that have found significant negative effects of marital status change on reports of happiness in retirement (e.g. Stull and Hatch, 1984) lend credence to this assertion.

Aside from demographics, commitment to work has been proposed as an important moderator variable in the relationship between retirement and psychological well-being (Beehr, 1986). Some earlier research provided direct and indirect support for this proposition (e.g. Glamser, 1981; Thompson, Streib, and Kosa, 1960), but no recent studies have addressed the issue. Beehr's (1986) review also proposed occupational goal attainment and planning or making preparations for retirement as moderators of the relationship, but no recent empirical studies have addressed these either.

The previous discussion focused on the effects of retirement on an individual's life satisfaction and well-being. Life satisfaction and well-being encompass many aspects of life such as personal attitudes and feelings; happiness and fulfilment with leisure pursuits, social contacts, and activities; and satisfaction with family and marital relationships. Although the bulk of the research has combined some or all of the above aspects into single dependent measures of life satisfaction or well-being, a few studies have examined some these aspects separately.

In a somewhat different vein, Cassidy (1985) conducted a cross-sectional study examining the impact of both spouses' retirements on the wife's marital satisfaction. Cassidy hypothesized that women who were employed and women whose husbands were retired would experience greater role conflict and, consequently, lower marital satisfaction. Using five-item index of marital satisfaction and controlling age, health, and socioeconomic variables, Cassidy found that the employment statuses of both wives and husbands had no direct effect on wives' marital satisfaction. However, socioeconomic prestige moderated the impact of retirement on marital satisfaction. When the wife retired, her occupational level had a negative effect on her own marital satisfaction. However, when the husband retired, his occupational level had a positive effect on his wife's marital satisfaction. More studies need to be done of this potential effect of retirement.

Several recent studies have addressed the potential effects of retirement on retirees' social and leisure activities. Using data from six longitudinal studies, Palmore *et al.* (1984) concluded that overall, retirement has little effect on ones's social activities. A study by Wan and Odell (1983) revealed that retirement was associated with reduced participation in both formal and informal activities. Also, the greater the length of time retired, the greater the decline in activity. However, in this study retirement status was not nearly as important as pre-retirement activity in predicting post-retirement activity, which indicates that the impact of retirement on one's level of activity is only slight. A study examining professional activity of academics after retirement also has found continuity in level of activity from pre- to post-retirement measures (Dorfman, 1985).

Two studies have examined the effects of certain variables on the relationship between retirement and activity level. Occupation and motivational level have been suggested as possible moderators. Using retrospective reports from 1332 men, Keith, Goudy, and Powers (1984) found that the time spent with one's family did not change after retirement. However, occupation influenced the change in allocation of time in retirement, such that blue-collar workers were less likely to have increased the time spent with their families than most other groups. Salaried and self-employed professionals and businessmen were most likely to increase their involvement while farmers were least likely.

One's motivational level also may moderate the relationship between retirement and leisure activity. In a study comparing employed and retired persons, Steinkamp and Kelly (1985) found that retirees who rated high on 'challenge seeking' were significantly more involved (frequency and breadth) in leisure than those who rated low on 'challenge seeking'.

In summary, a large number of potential influences of retirement on the individual have been studied in the recent past as had been done in the distant past. Current studies focused on the effects of retirement on individuals' finances, physical health, mental health and psychological well-being such as life satisfaction, marital status, and social and leisure activities.

One of the variables that has traditionally been of great interest to researchers is health and mental health, sometimes under the heading of the stressful effects of retirement. Virtually all previous reviews of the empirical literature, including Beehr's (1986), concluded that retirement is not stressful (i.e. does not have generally deleterious effects on mental or physical health), contrary to a lot of popular conceptions. The recent research, reviewed here, again agrees with this conclusion. At this point, this proposition is probably not a good approach to future research.

Because of the relatively large amount of research in this area, for future research to be informative it needs to be rigorous and well conceived. One suggestion from Beehr (1986) was to look for potential differential effects of different types of retirement (e.g. voluntary–involuntary, partial–complete, on time–early) on individuals. This recommendation has not generally been followed yet, and is probably still a viable one.

The Impact of Retirement on the Organization

In the past, nearly all of the literature on the effects of retirement has focused on personal outcomes (Beehr, 1986). By comparison, the impact of retirement on the employing organization has been neglected in the retirement research. In reviewing the recent research for this chapter, no new studies were found on this topic. Potential research topics in this area include the possibility that large-scale retirements in an organization change the mix of skills of the remaining employees for better or for worse, change the total payroll of the organization (probably by lowering it), increase the amount of uncertainty about workings within the organization and between the organization and the environment, change the relative obsolescence of skills of the organization's employees, change the degree of perceived opportunity for promotions for remaining employees and thereby some of their motivation, and increase the difficulty of forecasting workforce needs. All of these potential effects of retirement are likely to depend on specific situations such as the types of retirement (e.g. part time versus full time), the type of industry, the relative experience and skill mix of the remaining employees, and so forth (Beehr, 1986). This list of research topics on the effects of retirements on organizations is not exhaustive. Unfortunately, examination of these effects in the recent research literature has been virtually non-existent. Industrial/organizational psychologists who have interests in both people and organizations could contribute a good deal to this untapped area.

The Impact of Retirement on the Environment

Research on the impact of retirement on the environment has been very sparse. In the past, there were a few studies focusing primarily on the effects of retirement on the retiree's immediate environment, that is his or her spouse and family (e.g., Darnley, 1975; Fengler, 1975; Kerckhoff, 1966; Szinovacz, 1980). Retirement (rates) might also have effects on society's views of retirement and retirees, the nature of desirably located retirement communities, the availability of volunteer labor for many social causes or of relatively low-paid labor in some geographical markets, and government legislation regarding retirement policies and benefits. No recent empirical research literature was located on these topics, making it an obvious topic in need of future research.

CONCLUSIONS AND RECOMMENDATIONS FOR FUTURE RESEARCH

In reviewing the research literature on retirement for an industrial/organizational (I/O) psychology review, it becomes apparent that the research on this and perhaps any topic is shaped by the personal and professional interests of the researchers. Large amounts of the literature are found in gerontological journals; very little is found in I/O journals. Presumably, the field has been more interesting to psychologists other than I/O psychologists, especially those in the developmental and gerontological subfields of psychology. As a result, most of the research has probably focused on discovering relationships and developing theories that are of interest to those fields. This might explain the focus on individual predictors and outcomes of retirement.

Given this history of retirement research, I/O psychologists probably have something of value to offer this research area simply because they are likely to approach it from a little different viewpoint. I/O psychologists' traditional dual interest in both the individual and the organization might lead them to discover predictors and consequences of retirement that others have generally not thought to look for. The organizational and work-related variables are obvious examples, but this review also suggests that a broader examination would include non-work-environmental predictors and effects as well.

This suggests that research on retirement by I/O psychologists could benefit the field by broadening the scope of predictor and outcome variables. In addition, two other topics seem particularly to beg for more research. One concerns the types of retirement — voluntary versus involuntary (or degree of perceived volition), partial versus complete (or number of hours still worked per week), and early versus on time (or age at retirement). Some studies have addressed these (especially the first and third), but most of them have used dichotomies to measure what might be essentially continuous variables.

The second content area that seems particularly ripe for good research concerns the potential gender differences in decisions to retire and reactions to retirement. In recent decades, there has been an apparent move towards more women in the workforce on a permanent basis and in types of jobs that were previously almost closed to them. As these women reach the retirement stage of their work lives, they will present society (and researchers) with a situation not encountered before. Whether they will act and react the same as males usually have at that stage is not clearly understood at present. This seems to be another area in which research could add to the information on retirement.

REFERENCES

Anderson, K., Clark, R. L., and Johnson, T. (1980) Retirement in dual-career families. In R. L. Clark (ed.), *Retirement Policy in an Aging Society*. Durham, N.C.: Duke University Press.

Atchley, R. C. (1975) Adjustment to loss of job at retirement. *International Journal of Aging and Human Development*, 6(1), 17–27.

Atchley, R. C. (1976) *The Sociology of Retirement*. Cambridge, Mass: Schenkman Publishing.

Atchley, R. C. (1977) *The Social Forces in Later Life*, 2nd edn. Belmont, CA: Wadsworth.

Atchley, R. C. (1982a) Retirement: Leaving the world of work. In F. Berardo (ed.), Middle and later life transitions. *The Annals of the American Academy of Political and Social Science*, 464, 120–131.

Atchley, R. C. (1982b) The process of retirement: Comparing men and women. In M. Szinovacz (ed.), *Women's Retirement*. Beverly Hills, CA: Sage Publications.

Barfield, R. E., and Morgan, J. N. (1969) *Early Retirement: The decision and the experience and a second look*. Ann Arbor, MI: University of Michigan Press.

Barfield, R. E., and Morgan, J. N. (1978) Trends in planned early retirement. *The Gerontologist*, 18, 13–18.

Beck, S. H. (1982) Adjustment to and satisfaction with retirement. *Journal of Gerontology*, 37(5), 616–624.

Beehr, T. A. (1986) The process of retirement: A review and recommendations for future investigation. *Personnel Psychology*, 39, 31–55.

Bosworth, T. W., and Holden, K. C. (1983) The role part-time job options play in the retirement timing of older Wisconsin state employees. *Aging and Work*, 6, 31–36.

Burkhauser, R. V., and Quinn, J. F. (1985) Planned and actual retirement: An empirical analysis. In Z. S. Blau (ed.), *Current Perspectives on Aging and the Life Cycle*. Greenwich, CT: Jai Press.

Cassidy, M. (1985) Role conflict in the postparental period: The effects of employment status on the marital satisfaction of women. *Research on Aging*, 7(3), 433–454.

Conner, K. A., Dorfman, L. T., and Tompkins, J. B. (1985) Life satisfaction of retired professors: The contribution of work, health, income, and length of retirement. *Educational Gerontology*, 11, 337–347.

Darnley, F. (1975) Adjustment to retirement: Integrity or despair. *The Family Coordinator*, 24, 217–225.

Dorfman, L. T. (1985) Retired academics and professional activity: A British–American comparison. *Research in Higher Education*, 22(3), 273–289.
Dorfman, L. T., Kouhout, F. J., and Heckert, D. A. (1985) Retirement satisfaction in rural elderly. *Research on Aging*, 7(4), 577–599.
Durbin, N., Gross, E., and Borgatta, E. F. (1984). The decision to leave work. *Research on Aging*, 6, 572–592.
Ekerdt, D. J., Baden, L., Bosse, R., and Dibbs, E. (1983) The effect of retirement on physical health. *American Journal of Public Health*, 73(7), 779–783.
Ekerdt, D. J., Bosse, R., and Glynn, R. J. (1985) Period effects on planned age for retirement, 1975–1984. *Research on Aging*, 7(3), 395–407.
Ekerdt, D. J., Bosse, R., and Goldie, C. (1983) The effect of retirement on somatic complaints. *Journal of Psychosomatic Research*, 21(1), 61–67.
Ekerdt, D. J., Bosse, R., and Levkoff, S. (1985) An empirical test for phases of retirement: Findings from the Normative Aging Study. *Journal of Gerontology*, 40(1), 95–101.
Ekerdt, D. J., Bosse, R., and LoCastro, J. S. (1983) Claims that retirement improves health. *Journal of Gerontology*, 38(2), 231–236.
Ekerdt, D. J., Sparrow, D., Glynn, R. J., and Bosse, R. (1984) Change in blood pressure and total cholesterol with retirement. *American Journal of Epidemiology*, 120(1), 64–71.
Fengler, A. P. (1975) Attitudinal orientations of wives toward their husbands' retirement. *International Journal of Aging and Human Development*, 6, 139–152.
Fox, J. H. (1977) Effects of retirement and former work life on women's adaptation in old age. *Journal of Gerontology*, 32(2), 196–202.
Friedman, M., and Havighurst, R. J. (1954) *The Meaning of Work and Retirement*. Chicago: University of Chicago Press.
George, L. K., Fillenbaum, G. G., and Palmore, E. (1984) Sex differences in the antecedents and consequences of retirement. *Journal of Gerontology*, 39(3), 364–371.
Glamser, F. D. (1976) Determinants of a positive attitude toward retirement. *Journal of Gerontology*, 31(1), 104–107.
Glamser, F. D. (1981) Predictors of retirement attitudes. *Aging and Work*, 4, 23–29.
Graebner, W. (1980) *A History of Retirement*. New Haven, CT: Yale University Press.
Gratton, B., and Haug, M. R. (1983) Decision and adaptation. *Research on Aging*, 5(1), 59–76.
Gustman, A. L., and Steinmeier, T. L. (1984) Partial retirement and the analysis of retirement behavior. *Industrial and Labor Relations Review*, 37(3), 403–415.
Hardy, M. A. (1984) Effects of education on retirement among white male wage-and-salary workers. *Sociology of Education*, 57, 84–89.
Hardy, M. A. (1985) Occupational structure and retirement. In Z. S. Blau (ed.), *Current Perspectives on Aging and the Life Cycle*, Vol. 1. Greenwich, CT: Jai Press.
Hayward, M. D., and Hardy, M. A. (1985) Early retirement processes among older men. *Research on Aging*, 7(4), 491–515.
Holmes, T. H., and Rahe, R. H. (1967) The Social Readjustment Rating Scale. *Journal of Psychosomatic Research*, 11, 213–218.
Hooker, K., and Ventis, D. G. (1984) Work ethic, daily activities, and retirement satisfaction. *Journal of Gerontology*, 39(4), 478–484.
Jaslow, P. (1976) Employment, retirement, and morale among older women. *Journal of Gerontology*, 31, 212–218.
Kamouri, A. L., and Cavanaugh, J. C. (1986) The impact of preretirement education programmes on workers' preretirement socialization. *Journal of Occupational Behaviour*, 7, 245–256.

Kasl, S. V. (1980) The impact of retirement. In C. L. Cooper and R. Payne (eds), *current Concerns in Occupational Stress*. Chichester, England: Wiley.

Keith, P. M. (1985) Work, retirement, and well-being among unmarried men and women. *The Gerontologist*, 25(4), 410–416.

Keith, P. M., Goudy, W. J., and Powers, E. A. (1984) Salience of life areas among older men: Implications for practice. *Journal of Gerontological Social Work*, 8, 67–82.

Kerckhoff, A. C. (1966) Family patterns and morale in retirement. In I. H. Simpson and J. C. McKinney (eds.), *Social Aspects of Aging*. Durham, NC: Duke University Press.

Kilty, K. M., and Behling, J. H. (1985) Predicting the retirement intentions and attitudes of professional workers. *Journal of Gerontology*, 40(2), 219–227.

Kingson, E. R. (1982) Current retirement trends. In M. H. Morrison (Ed.), *Economics of Aging: The future of retirement*. New York: Van Nostrand Reinhold Co.

Kremer, Y. (1985) The association between health and retirement: Self-health assessment of Israeli retirees. *Social Science Medicine*, 20(1), 61–66.

MacBride, A. (1976) Retirement as a life crisis: Myth or reality? *Canadian Psychiatric Association*, 21, 547–556.

Matthews, A. M., Brown, K. H., Davis, C. K., and Denton, M. A. (1982) A crisis assessment technique for the evaluation of life events: Transition to retirement as an example. *Canadian Journal on Aging*, 1, 28–39.

McGoldrick, A. E. (1983) Company early retirement schemes and private pension scheme options: Scope for leisure and new lifestyles. *Leisure Studies*, 2, 187–202.

McGoldrick, A. E., and Cooper, C. L. (1985) Stress at the decline of one's career: The act of retirement. In T. A. Beehr and R. S. Bhagat (eds), *Human Stress and Cognition in Organizations: An integrated perspective*. New York: John Wiley & Sons, pp. 177–201.

Minkler, M. (1981) Research on the health effects of retirement: An uncertain legacy. *Journal of Health and Social Behavior*, 22, 117–130.

O'Rand, A. M., and Henretta, J. C. (1982) Delayed career entry, industrial pension structure, and early retirement in a cohort of unmarried women. *American Sociological Review*, 47, 365–373.

Palmore, E. B., Fillenbaum, G. G., and George, L. K. (1984) Consequences of retirement. *Journal of Gerontology*, 39(1), 109–116.

Palmore, E. B., George, L. K., and Fillenbaum, G. G. (1982) Predictors of retirement. *Journal of Gerontology*, 37, 733–742.

Parnes, H. S., and Nestel, G. (1981) The retirement experience. In H. S. Parnes and G. Nestel (eds), *Work and Retirement*. Cambridge, Mass: MIT Press.

Prothero, J., and Beach, L. R. (1984) Retirement decisions: Expectation, intention and action. *Journal of Applied Social Psychology*, 14, 162–174.

Riddick, C. C. (1985) Life satisfaction for older female homemakers, retirees, and workers. *Research on Aging*, 7(3), 383–393.

Riddick, C. C., and Daniel, S. N. (1984) The relative contribution of leisure activities and other factors to the mental health of older women. *Journal of Leisure Research*, 16, 136–148.

Robinson, P. K., Coberly, S., and Paul, C. E. (1985) Work and retirement. In R. H. Binstock and E. Shanas (eds), *Handbook of Aging and the Social Sciences*. New York: Van Nostrand Reinhold Co.

Shaw, L. B. (1984) Retirement plans of middle-aged married women. *The Gerontologist*, 24(2), 154–159.

Sheppard, R. L., Beehr, T. A., and Hamilton, J. W. (1986) Life satisfaction and perceived quality of retired life as functions of time since retirement and type of job. In J. S. Kim and J. D. Ford (eds), *Proceedings of the 29th Annual Conference of the*

Midwest Academy of Management 1986. Columbus, Ohio: The Ohio State University, pp. 21–25.

Steinkamp, M. W., and Kelly, J. R. (1985) Relationships among motivational orientation, level of leisure activity, and life satisfaction in older men and women. *Journal of Psychology*, **119**(6), 509–520.

Streib, G. F., and Schneider, C. J. (1971) *Retirement in American Society*. Ithaca, NY: Cornell University Press.

Stull, D. E., and Hatch, L. R. (1984) Unravelling the effects of multiple life changes. *Research on Aging*, **6**(4), 560–571.

Szinovacz, M. E. (1980) Female retirement: Effects on spousal roles and marital adjustment. *Journal of Family Issues*, **1**(3), 423–440.

Szinovacz, M. E. (1983) Beyond the hearth: Older women and retirement. In E. Markson (ed.), *Older Women*. Lexington, MA: Lexington.

Thompson, W. E., Streib, G. F., and Kosa, J. (1960) The effect of retirement on personal adjustment: A panel analysis. *Journal of Gerontology*, **15**(2), 165–169.

Wan, T. H., and Odell, B. G. (1983) Major role losses and social participation of older males. *Research on Aging*, **5**, 173–196.

Chapter 7

QUALITY CIRCLES: A REVIEW AND SUGGESTED FUTURE DIRECTIONS

David D. Van Fleet
*Department of Management
College of Business Administration
Texas A&M University*
and
Ricky W. Griffin
*Department of Management
College of Business Administration
Texas A&M University
USA*

The purpose of this chapter is to review the extant literature dealing with the concept of the quality circle. Quality circles have become a common technique used by modern managers around the globe in an attempt to emulate the success of the Japanese. There is actually little evidence available as to the appropriateness or effectiveness of quality circles, however. And much of the evidence that does exist is anecdotal in nature. Thus, a review and assessment of what is known about quality circles would seem to be of some interest and value.

Given the scarcity of research which exists and the many mis-statements which appear in the literature about the origins and characteristics of quality circles, it is necessary for this review to take a somewhat different form than reviews on more mature topics. First, a brief, but carefully documented history is presented to eliminate some mis-statements which have frequently appeared in the literature. Second, the characteristics of quality circles and corresponding definitions are more carefully delineated than in previous work to assure comparability among the studies surveyed. Finally, emerging questions surrounding quality circles are discussed and the current status of quality circle theory is sketched.

International Review of Industrial and Organizational Psychology 1989
Edited by C. L. Cooper and I. Robertson © 1989 John Wiley & Sons Ltd.

INTRODUCTION

Quality circles are derived from statistical quality control. (For more on its history, see Duncan, 1959, pp. 1–8 and Littauer, 1950.) Statistical quality control began in the United States during the 1920s. Much of the formative work was done at the Bell Telephone Laboratories in the Engineering Department of the Western Electric Company (Diggles, 1922; Shewhart, 1926a and 1926b; Robertson, 1928). Shewhart's 1931 text (Shewhart, 1931) and an edited version of his lectures by W. Edwards Deming in 1938 set the pattern of statistical quality control as an operational means for attaining economic goals. Deming, a physicist who had worked during the summers of 1925 and 1926 at the Hawthorne Plant of the Western Electric Company, was employed by the Department of Agriculture. In working with the census, he was introduced to Shewhart and saw the importance of his work (Walton, 1986).

Despite this early start, however, it was not until the Second World War that statistical quality control began to be utilized by substantial numbers of corporations. A further boost came when an education program was established to help firms learn how to apply these ideas. The first program was in July 1942 at Stanford University and was planned by Eugene L. Grant, Holbrook Working; and Deming (Littauer, 1950). There were 810 organizations, only 43 of which were educational institutions, participating in these programs.

In April of 1949, a *New York Times* article heralded the positive results of using statistical quality control and noted that one result was improved employee morale (*New York Times*, 1949). A month later an article in the *Wall Street Journal* documented the success of statistical quality control in two organizations (*Wall Street Journal*, 1949). At the Bigelow–Sanford Carpet Company, for example, the results were attributed to the cooperative effort of operators, supervisors, and engineers working together.

By 1950, then, it seemed apparent that statistical quality control held great promise for organizations. To reach that promise, however, it appeared that operators and supervisors in organizations would need to be educated and involved. For some reason, management in the United States seemed to feel that the job was finished (Deming, 1982a). Statistical quality control began to become the province of experts and the involvement of operators and supervisors diminished. However, that was not the case in Japan.

QUALITY CIRCLES IN JAPAN

Much of what might be called the present 'quality circle movement' in the United States has its roots in the Japanese post-Second World War industrial rebuilding efforts. During the mid-1940s and early 1950s, these efforts were particularly intense, with the United States taking an active role. An important part of the American role involved sending lecturers, scholars, and consultants to Japan to attempt to provide both a theoretical and a practical basis for certain areas of the rebuilding efforts.

The Union of Japanese Science and Engineering

In 1947, a group of scientists and engineers led by Kenichi Koyanagi formed the Union of Japanese Science and Engineering (referred to by its telegraphic code, JUSE) (Deming, 1982a and 1982b). The purpose of JUSE was the reconstruction of Japan. JUSE, along with the Japanese government, published literature and conducted conferences and seminars on various business and industrial topics to achieve that end.

Top Management Support

One of the founders of the JUSE was Professor Ichiro Ishikawa. His discussions with the Americans who had developed the early statistical quality control programs made him aware of the need for top management support. He arranged a series of conferences for top management to enlist their cooperation in the efforts of JUSE. In 1952 Kaoru Ishikawa published a textbook, *Introduction to Quality Control*. Because of its apparent popularity, this textbook was reprinted over the next 14 years in three editions.

Teaching Techniques

In 1949, JUSE began teaching techniques of statistical quality control. To assure that their courses were the best available, JUSE invited W. E. Deming to conduct the course he had developed earlier in the United States. Deming had travelled to Japan in 1947, so Japanese statisticians were already acquainted with his work (Ross, 1986). He began conducting courses in 1950 (Deming, 1982b). During the early part of the rebuilding efforts, then, Deming became a leader among the team of educators and specialists which toured Japan. To avoid the 'burnout' which statistical quality control had experienced in the United States, Deming stressed the importance of top management commitment which he sought to attain through their involvement in conferences and programs on statistical quality control (Walton, 1986).

The 1950s

In 1954 J. M. Juran, another American professor, lecturer, consultant, and early writer on quality control began a series of lectures on the management of quality control (Juran, 1945). The apparent emphasis of his lecture series was on general management. He argued that, in addition to technical advisers, operating managers down to front-line supervisors need to understand and use statistical quality control (Juran, 1962, 1964, 1966). From this point, Juran became pivotal in the development of quality control circles both in Japan and subsequently in the United States.

Thus, by the mid-1950s, 'quality control' had gained sufficient momentum so as to be a true social movement across the whole of Japanese industry. In an attempt to dispel the image that products 'made in Japan' were of poor quality, JUSE and the Japanese government began a campaign committed to achieving 'total quality control'. That campaign included: (a) a series of nationwide radio broadcasts consisting of fifteen-minute lessons; (b) a book, *Quality Control Text Book for Foremen*, published by Ishikawa, which became a cookbook-type manual for the improvement and control of product quality; and (c) a series of nationwide television broadcasts consisting of 30-minute lectures.

Thus, four forces or factors seemed to account for the success of the quality movement in Japan during the 1950s. Those forces were: (1) experts — Japan's statisticians and engineers; (2) organization — the Union of Japanese Science and Engineering — JUSE; (3) the emphasis on education, that is, the teaching of statistical quality control techniques throughout all levels of organizations; and (4) top management understanding and support — achieved through a series of conferences (Deming, 1982a). By 1960, a fifth force had evolved — quality control circles.

THE EMERGENCE OF QUALITY CIRCLES

The move towards the formal use of quality control circles began in 1960, with the emphasis on circle formation placed on the foreman and the working crew rather than on middle or upper management. In 1962 JUSE began the journal, *Quality Control for the Foreman* (Konz, 1979). By 1967, that journal moved from a quarterly to a monthly publication (*Modern Manufacturing*, 1970; Juran, 1967). A quarterly conference on quality control was also begun at about this same time. The first formal quality control circle was registered in May of 1962 and the first quality conference for foremen was held in November of that year (Hutchins, 1980; Cole 1979). In conjunction with these events, the Japanese government designated November as quality month throughout all Japan. During November those companies with a commitment to quality were to fly 'Q' flags over their operations.

The number of registered quality control circles increased dramatically — 1000 in 1964 (Munchus, 1983); 6000 in 1966 (Juran, 1967); 12 000 in 1967 (Yager, 1981); 87 540 in 1978 (Munchus, 1983); and 125 000 in 1981 with over 1 million people involved (Wood, Hull, and Azumi, 1983). It is estimated that there are several times as many unregistered quality control circles as there are registered quality control circles. Despite this, it has also been reported that few of the largest Japanese manufacturing firms had quality circles as of the early 1980s since QC circles are regarded as a 'last step', not a first one, and should develop spontaneously and not be imposed by management (Tsurumi, 1981).

Japanese successes in quality control and the impact of international competition were recognized in the early 1960s (*Business Week*, 1962; *Steel*, 1967; Adams, 1966). It is also clear that lower level managerial personnel and, indeed, the workers themselves were recognized as critical to successful quality efforts at this time (see, for example, Lippert, 1966; Zinck, 1966a, 1966b, and 1966c). The supervisor was supposed to train workers to know about quality, take a long-range perspective, and 'change his basic approach towards the employee' (Swanson and Corbin, 1969, p. 897; see also, Budgell, 1967). Thus, it is difficult to say which country influenced which since both the United States and Japan were stressing the role of the supervisor and the importance of quality, although it does seem clear that the Japanese success was more pervasive and long term. Indeed, some seemed to forget the US practices of the 1930s and 1940s, arguing incorrectly that in the United States statistical quality control had always been by experts and from the top down (see, for example, Rubinstein, 1970).

These practices have been viewed as an acceptance on the part of the Japanese of various humanistic or participative theories of organization behavior put forward by American theorists such as Likert (1961), McGregor (1960), and Argyris (1964) (see, for example, Keys and Miller, 1984). Another view has been that the placing of the foreman and the crew at the center of quality control circles was a Japanese innovation of an American idea which originally was intended for middle or upper management.

The main emphasis of Japanese quality control circles has always been improvement of quality through the use of statistical methods, Pareto and scatter charts, cause and effect diagrams, brainstorming, and so forth (Ishikawa, 1968, 1976, 1984, and 1985). The concern for human resources was seldom if ever mentioned. The decision to involve line foremen and line workers was apparently based on the belief that they would know more about what quality improvements were needed and how they might be brought about, rather than on the belief that participation in the process would make them more satisfied or productive.

Crossing the Pacific

There is not much specific information on precisely how the quality circle concept crossed the Pacific to the United States. However, we know that the first formally registered quality control circle in the United States was at the Lockheed Missile and Space Company at Sunnyvale, California in October of 1974 (although the process began in 1973) under the direction of Wayne Rieker, the Missile and Space Division Manufacturing Manager (*Industry Week*, 1977a). We also know that Rieker was given the idea of quality control circles by a team of visiting Japanese managers, probably in early 1973, and that he and a team from Lockheed visited Japan and observed several companies with quality control circles functioning.

The original training material for Lockheed's quality control circles was translated from Japanese (Cole, 1979). Between the Japanese visit to Lockheed and the return visit of personnel from Lockheed to Japan, Rieker apparently consulted with J. M. Juran concerning quality control circles (Rieker, 1980; Juran, 1978). Upon returning to the United States, Juran formed a management consulting firm and did some writing regarding quality control generally and quality control circles specifically (Juran, 1962, 1964, 1966, 1967). By 1975 Lockheed had fifteen quality control circles in place and the company estimated that it had generated nearly $3 million in cost savings (Blocker and Overgaard, 1982; Cole, 1979; Wayne, Griffin, and Bateman, 1986). Because of extreme interest, Lockheed had to discontinue visits on the part of outsiders (Cole, 1979, 1980a).

During the 1970s, then, the quality control circle movement began to spread across the United States. It began with quality control circles being the main instrument in achieving quality control, but quickly began to be used as an organization development intervention aimed at increasing employee participation and, it was hoped, satisfaction and performance. Once they became accepted, quality circles came into widespread use in the United States.

Most of the first companies to use quality control circles were in the aerospace industry due, in large part, to their contacts with Japanese firms and their concern for quality. Hughes Aircraft Company began a pilot program in 1977, and Boeing, Honeywell's Aerospace Division, and Boise Cascade soon followed suit (*Industry Week*, 1977b). From there, the movement spread to companies in other industries such as the 3M Company, the General Motors Corporation, Ford Motor Company, General Electric, Westinghouse, Bank of America, Crucible Steel, and Pentel of America. The International Association of Quality Circles was also formed during the 1970s. During the mid-to late 1970s, the word 'control' gradually began to be dropped from the quality control circle label, leaving the presently more widely used phrase quality circles. A quality circles journal was also formed during this period.

In 1982 a New York Stock Exchange study estimated that 44 per cent of all companies with more than 500 employees had begun quality circles and that 90 per cent of *Fortune* 500 companies were using them (Lawler and Mohrman, 1985). In 1983 *Business Week* estimated that 1500 companies had reported success with quality circles. Meyer and Stott (1985) used a recent estimate to suggest that at least 500 US firms were using quality circles. Quality circles have spread to other nations, too. Their use has been reported in Australia (Wells, 1982; Smart, 1985; Duncan and McGraw, 1986), Denmark (Lund, 1987), France (Bernier, 1986), Germany (Deppe, 1987), India (Kahn, 1986), Ireland (Roche, 1985), Italy (Ferrari, 1986), Malaysia (Seng, 1984), Norway (Arbose, 1980; Aune, 1984), the Philippines (Tolentino, 1984), South Africa

(Daniel and Berry, 1984), and the United Kingdom (Dale, 1985; Dale and Lees, 1985; Hill, 1986), as well as in Brazil, China, Korea, Spain, Sweden, and Taiwan (Bank and Wilpert, 1983). Some efforts, of course, have not been successful (Dillon, 1983; Nirenberg, 1986), although many have been, and even these reports of success are anecdotal rather than based on careful research.

TOWARDS A DEFINITION OF QUALITY CIRCLES

One major problem facing researchers in the area of quality circles is that of definition. Just what is a quality circle? There has been a change in the definition of quality circles as they moved from Japan and gained prominence in the United States. Several alternative definitions or conceptualizations have been proffered.

Beginning in Japan, quality control circles were a formalized organizational structure intended primarily to improve product quality and based on the philosophy that the line worker is a valuable human resource capable of contributing significantly to the production process. The quality control movement, of which quality circles were an important part, was technologically oriented.

Juran offered an early definition of quality control circles: 'The QC Circle is a small group of departmental work leaders and line operators who have volunteered to spend time outside of their regular hours to help solve departmental quality problems' (Juran, 1967). Cole's definition is more complete:

> QC circles are small groups of employees doing similar or related work who meet regularly to identify, analyze, and solve product-quality and production problems and to improve general operations. . . . Workers are given training in a variety of statistical techniques designed to help them correctly evaluate information. The ideal size is thought to be about ten. Circles will meet for an hour, on an average of three to four times a month. Often workers will be asked to collect certain data by the following meeting. Although foremen commonly serve as leaders of the groups, workers . . . may have acquired enough skill to serve as leaders and frequently will be elected by their fellow workers (Cole, 1979).

Both of the above definitions are based predominantly on the quality circles of Japan. Though most subsequent definitions based on American experience are quite similar to Cole's definition (Marks *et al.*, 1986; Wayne *et al.*, 1986; Brockner and Hess, 1986), there are some indications of shifting emphases and philosophical differentiation in the definitions of American based quality circles.

Klein (1981) placed additional emphasis on production management and the correction of production problems in addition to the quality aspects of the quality circles. Expressing what came to be a common emphasis, especially among the practitioner oriented parts of the field, Alexander (1981) states that successful quality circles must occur in a setting where the managerial orientation is based on: (1) people building, (2) trust, (3) commitment to quality, (4) open communication, (5) supportive management, (6) patience, (7) training and development, (8) results, (9) supportive policies and procedures, and (10) shared responsibility. Munchus (1983) calls quality circles a Japanese invention with roots in motivation theory and an advocation of greater participation and responsibility for line foremen and workers.

While there are those who see quality circles as nothing more than an extension of suggestion systems (*Personnel Journal*, 1980), there seems to be a definite movement to view quality circles geared as much (if not more) towards improving quality of work life as creating a higher quality product. Indeed, most quality circle consultants frown on suggestion box schemes and report that, even when they run parallel with quality circles, teams do not submit projects for possible awards (Arbose, 1980). However, Greene (1982) conducted a study to determine the predominance of product quality as opposed to quality of work-life suggestions given by quality circle participants. He found that the suggestions on both points of view occurred in roughly equal numbers, but that suggestions geared towards product quality were much more likely to be carried out than those which dealt with the quality of work life.

Thus, it would appear that there is no precise definition of a quality circle. Some circles meet in the participants' own time (the predominant way in Japan) while others take place in company time (the predominant way in the United States). The size of the group varies although it is usually small, perhaps around ten workers. Membership is almost always involuntary and the circle generally addresses quality problems. However, especially in the United States, quality of work life and even production problems may also become concerns addressed by quality circles. Finally, the circle leaders are generally foremen, although workers are occasionally found in that role.

The main characteristics of QCs, along with those of a few selected concepts or group approaches currently being used in similar ways in many organizations, are shown in Table 1. Autonomous and semi-autonomous teams are work groups which control, within prescribed limits, their own efforts to accomplish the goals of their unit. Task forces are temporary, although usually full-time, groups with appointed members from across different organizational units to work on some particular problem. Suggestion systems, of course, do not involve groups *per se*, but they do involve many of the concepts which are found in QCs. Lernstatt is a German effort to integrate working and learning and, hence, also embodies concepts found in QC programs. Werkoverleg is the required consultation between management and workers which has been legislated by the Netherlands' parliament.

Autonomous and semi-autonomous teams are generally very similar to QCs in most ways, and they can be nearly identical except that they are

Table 1 — Characteristics of QCs and Related Groups or Programs

	Type of group					
Characteristic of group	Quality circle	Semi- or autonomous team	Task force	Suggestion system	Lernstatt	Werkoverleg
Focus						
quality	yes	some	some	some	some	some
production	some	yes	yes	some	no	yes
costs	yes	some	some	some	no	some
process	yes	some	some	some	yes	yes
training	yes	some	no	no	yes	no
motivation	yes	yes	no	yes	some	some
Composition						
small size	yes	yes	yes	no	yes	yes
mixed departments	some	some	yes	no	some	some
mixed levels	no	some	some	yes	some	yes
hierarchical leader	some	some	yes	n.a.	yes	yes
Modus operandi						
voluntary	yes	some	no	yes	yes	no
only part of job	yes	no	no	yes	yes	yes
done on own time	some	some	no	some	no	no
done on company time	some	yes	yes	yes	yes	yes
select own leader	some	some	no	n.a.	no	no
set own procedures	some	yes	no	some	yes	yes
financial incentives	some	no	no	yes	no	no

Yes = always or highly frequently present or, at least, a dominant characteristic
Some = sometimes present or a characteristic of some groups
No = never or rarely present or seldom a characteristic
n.a. = not applicable

Based on: Bank and Wilpert (1983), p. 31

full-time groupings rather than part-time ones like QCs. Suggestion systems and werkoverleg are somewhat similar to QCs in terms of focus, but each of them is drastically different from QCs in other ways. Lernstatt also shares similarities but also possesses dissimilarities. Task forces are least like QCs in most respects although they can be somewhat similar, especially in terms of group composition. Thus, the first thing researchers must do is to clarify the specific characteristics of the groups which are being studied. This will enable them and others to determine which characteristics may be more closely associated with the longer term success of QCs.

EMERGING QUESTIONS ABOUT QUALITY CIRCLES

Quality circles have been referred to as everything from a panacea with unlimited horizons to a potential source of disillusionment (Steel and Shane, 1986). In all likelihood, the truth exists somewhere between these two extremes. In the beginning, quality circles were developed largely in an atheoretical manner (whatever theory is claimed to exist was, at best, present in an implicit form or introduced *post hoc*). Some theory is beginning to be formed and some good research is beginning to be done. Still, there is much that is not known, and many questions remain as to what quality circles are, how they work, when they are effective, and what are their strengths and weaknesses as an organizational structure.

Questions of Effectiveness

There is no question that quality circles vary in effectiveness across various different settings (Varzandeh and Masters, 1988; see also Wagner and Gooding, 1987). Two questions remain to be answered: Are there situations in which quality circles are particularly effective? If so, what are they?

Although little empirical research has been done on this particular topic, there is substantial anecdotal evidence that quality circles are particularly effective when used in the context of technologically oriented quality control programs, especially in settings where the workforce is either highly educated or highly trained. This is supported by the type of firms in which Japanese quality control circles evolved and the fact that the original American quality control circles developed in the aerospace industry.

The successes reported by such corporations are overwhelming. Honeywell reported savings from over 300 QCs (Murray, 1981) of over $500 000 (Nelson, 1980) for a return on investment of six to one (*Training*, 1980). General Electric, in just one instance, achieved a $15 000 annual cost savings; Morton Chemical Company noted that one circle presented a plan to reduce material loss which saves the company about $300 000 a year; and Westinghouse is saving $636 000 annually in its purchasing department alone (Nelson, 1980).

Other savings have been cited but without detailed documentation. For instance, Dan Dewar, President of the International Association of Quality Circles, says one company saved $364 000 and another saved $157 000 (*Personnel*, 1980; Dewar, 1982). General Motors at Tarrytown, New York, improved quality while reducing absenteeism and grievances. Cincinnati Milacron reported that, in one department alone, a gauge was developed that reduced the rejection rate on an item from 50 per cent to zero (Main, 1980). Hughes Aircraft reported annual savings of $45 000 from the reduction of defects and another $48 000 from the redesign of sample boards for assembly work (*Industry Week*, 1979). Returns at Hughes have been reported to average seven to one (Arbose, 1980). When Matshushita took over Motorola, there were 1.5 to 1.8 defects per television set; after the takeover (and under the brand name Quasar), the defect rate was reduced to from 0.03 to 0.04 per set using the same employees (Juran, 1978).

However, all of these are static, anecdotal, and uncontrolled reports. It is not clear that the results are directly attributable to QCs or whether they arose, at least in part, from other changes which might have occurred. Further, it is not clear whether these are one-shot, temporary results or whether they will continue over time.

Nevertheless, quality circles have been used often in attempts to raise productivity and to improve the quality of work life (Gryna, 1981; Ingle, 1982a; Robson, 1982; Thompson, 1982; Tse, 1981). Steel and Shane (1986) propose a contingency theory of OD interventions of which quality circles is but one such intervention. Marks *et al.* (1986) report that participation in QCs influences the quality of work life, absenteeism, and productivity, although the actual outcome reported was one of preventing negative effects rather than of introducing positive effects (see Miller and Monge, 1986, for a general review of participation effects). Lawler and Mohrman (1985, 1987) argue, although without explicit empirical analysis, that QCs are not an optimal and perhaps not even an effective means of introducing participative management practices into an organization. Griffin's (1988) study, summarizing a longitudinal assessment of quality circle effectiveness, indicates that quality circles may be effective in improving attitudes, behaviors, and effectiveness.

To respond to these questions of effectiveness, research must be conducted which is experimental, longitudinal, and involves objective criteria as well as attitudinal and/or behavioral criteria.

Questions of Limitations

Within certain settings static studies have shown that quality circles are effective in the short term as a means of improving product quality (Juran, 1966, 1967), increasing productivity (Griffin and Wayne, 1984; Marks *et al.*, 1986), and improving quality of work life (Marks *et al.*, 1986). Still, there are other questions of whether quality circles as organizational interventions or as structural arrangements are susceptible to the effects of other intervening variables (see, for example, the discussion in Barrick and Alexander, 1987, and Wiebe and Zahra, 1985).

Brockner and Hess (1986) determined that quality circles are more successful when participants score high on tests measuring self-esteem. This opens the possibility (or probability) that quality circle success is contingent on intervening variables such as individual differences among participants, but more research is necessary to replicate these results.

Wayne *et al.* (1986), Meyer and Stott (1985), and Alexander (1981) have argued that quality circle success is largely dependent on the effects of such elements of the organization as its cultural, structural, or social systems (e.g. managerial orientation, personnel practices, and the nature of sub-groups). Deming (1982a, 1982b) similarly stresses that the culture of the organization must be transformed for quality circles to have a sustaining impact. This also seems consistent with some reports of success in the United States (Cook, 1982; DiGiorgio, 1981). Quality circle groups in the United States seem to lose spontaneity and become ritualistic over the long run largely because such transformation has not taken place.

In a longitudinal study, Griffin (1988) found that the beneficial effects of quality circles may tend to disappear with the passage of time. Several studies cited earlier indicate that with the passage of time, quality circle participants begin to tire of the stress, the time requirements, and the little or no extra pay. Moreover, they start to see the circles as merely another management ploy to increase productivity without increasing compensation. Cole (1980b) reports that as many as one-third of Japanese QCs are no longer making a contribution to their organizations. This suggests a major limitation of QCs which must be carefully studied in further longitudinal research to determine if all QCs display such decline or if the decline is the result of particular characteristics of certain QCs.

Questions of Focus

As part of a widespread social movement in post Second World War Japan, the quality circle phenomenon originally was strongly oriented towards the improvement of quality. Any other beneficial aspects of the practice (e.g. employee satisfaction, increased output, and better social relations) seemed to be strictly secondary to the goal of improving product quality. As it subsequently moved to the United States, the quality circle phenomenon began to emphasize general productivity and quality of work-life variables as being the main benefits of the practice (Rafaeli, 1985; Jenkins and Shimada, 1983). This, then, raises a question of focus. Should the goal of quality circles focus on the improvement of quality of production, actual productivity, or employee quality of work life, or do they function equally well in all three areas?

There is beginning to be some criticism of the idea that quality circles have often been treated as 'panaceas' for organizational difficulties. The implication is that there are situations in which quality circles are commonly used but for which they may not be the optimal or even recommended strategy. Lawler and Mohrman (1985), for example, indicate that quality circles, though often very effective, are not as useful as means of introducing participative management as are work teams. In their contingency model of OD interventions, Steel and Shane (1986) indicate that certain specific interventions, such as quality circles, may be better suited for certain specific situations. Though this point of view has some face validity, there is little empirical evidence to support it at present (Berger and Holcomb, 1985).

There have also been several implicit criticisms of quality circles on the grounds that they are used by management to improve quality and/or production while the line foremen and workers who do the actual work of the program receive no benefit from them. After the newness of the program wears off and the initial satisfaction with it begins to wane, those involved might see quality circles as exploitative or manipulative. Others argue that much of this discontent occurs because management fails to use quality circles adequately (i.e. rewarding participation, 'empowering' participants, etc.).

Certain characteristics of quality circles (i.e. that they meet for only limited times, that they are voluntary, and that they do not result in pay increases) may not include many of the aspects which some have suggested are essential for quality circle success. Thus, it is possible that new operationalizations of quality circles need to be formulated. The name of quality circles may be being given to interventions/structures which are qualitatively different from the traditional concepts of what constitutes a quality circle. There are those who note that the emphasis on QCs is on blue-collar, production workers, but that QCs may actually have great potential in white-collar areas (Richards, 1984).

Another question of focus involves motivation. The success of quality circles may depend on who is motivated (Tang, Tollison, and Whiteside, 1987). As part of the Japanese movement for quality control improvement, quality control circles have been generally thought to be very successful (Juran, 1964, 1966, 1967; Cole, 1979, 1980a). This is attributable largely to the fact that management at all levels as well as labor was motivated to participate in efforts to improve product quality.

Most of the quality circle programs in the United States are implemented by middle levels of management and prescribed downwards to the labor force — top management is insufficiently involved and committed (Baillie, 1986). Thus, US programs often lack the high motivation level across the organization which seemed to be inherent in the original quality control circles of Japan (Dean, 1985). A major explanation for this is that, as used in the United States, quality circles are either a tool or the end itself, whereas in Japan QCs are merely a part of a much larger organizational process (Weiss, 1984). Pascarella (1982, 1984) argues that QCs will have continuing value only if the organizational culture becomes based on the participation of all employees, with 'unconventional' management roles, and employing a flat structure. The impact of organizational culture on long-term QC success has not yet been addressed by any empirical research.

Here, too, good research is needed. That research must address the focus question. Do quality circles serve best when tightly focused only on quality, productivity, or the quality of work life or do they serve equally as well when they are more loosely focused so that all of these criteria are sought?

Problems

Problems involved with the use of QCs seem to be either general or specific (Goodman, 1983; Ingle, 1982b). Among the more general problems are: management inconsistency; lack of necessary skills in lower level supervisors; slow response of management to QC proposals; inadequate feedback to QC members; and turnover of key managers (Ruffner and Ettkin, 1987). Additionally, middle managers have been seen to be a major impediment to the success of QCs (Alie, 1986; Blair and Whitehead, 1984; Pascarella, 1984; Harmon, 1984; Wood et al., 1983).

The more specific problems are, of course, quite numerous. They include such things as using QCs for a 'quick fix', selecting poor circle leaders, not educating QC members and leaders, not keeping QC members informed, not keeping management informed, not using any QC ideas, QCs trying to work on problems which are too complex or long term in nature, and various forms of inter- and intra-group conflict (Ruffner and Ettkin, 1987). These factors seem to exist particularly in many government efforts to utilize QCs which uniformly led to negative results (Steel et al., 1985; Steel, Lloyd, Ovalle, and Hendrix, 1982).

Here again, though, research is needed. Why do quality circles in government organizations within the United States seem to have higher failure rates than those in private sector organizations? Are the characteristics of the QCs different? Is it the structure/process aspects of the organizations? Is the organizational culture the explanation? Work along these lines would be especially beneficial since it might quickly help us uncover causal factors between successful and unsuccessful applications of quality circles.

CURRENT STATUS OF QUALITY CIRCLE THEORY

There is much left to learn about quality circles before any definitive answers to the above questions are found. If we are to understand quality circles better, there are two things which need to be done. First, the theory which underlies quality circles needs to be more carefully specified and developed (Ferris and Wagner, 1985). Second, good research on their effects needs to be conducted (Gibson, 1981).

One of the problems with quality circle research to this point has been the lack of a viable theory of quality circles. To this point, the development, use, and evaluation of quality circles has been largely atheoretical. Given that the social sciences are generally theory-driven, there is a clear need for a theory of quality circles. Such a theory would serve to provide a unifying framework for understanding quality circles dynamics, factors that lead to their success, the identification of appropriate outcome measures to assess effectiveness, and guidelines for maintaining that effectiveness over time.

Though little explicit theory development in the quality circle field has occurred to this point, some implicit efforts at theorizing have been made. Quality circles have been seen almost universally as an OD intervention (see, for example, Yager, 1979 and 1980, and Blair and Ramsing, 1983). There are undoubtedly some theoretical constructs in OD, but because of the breadth and ambiguity of OD as a term and a general practice, the concept offers little by way of explaining the organizational structures or interventions within its parameters and offers little by way of clarification of meaning.

There are numerous areas of organizational science that may potentially provide a basis for a theory of quality circles. The literature on participative management, in particular, would be a fertile basis for conceptualization. In addition, the theory and literature dealing with task design, small group dynamics, collateral organizations, and socio-technical systems would all be relevant.

In addition, appropriate concepts and ideas from the literature on leadership, conflict, decision making, interpersonal power, communication, and interactional psychology could all be brought to bear in the development of a theory of quality circles.

Beyond theory, there is also a clear need for more empirical research. Following Griffin (1988), this research should clearly be of an experimental nature using control groups. Beyond that simple study, however, there is a clear research agenda that needs to be addressed. First, using qualitative methodologies, we need to learn more about the dynamics associated with quality circle formation and development. Why do people join? Are there some formation processes and approaches that are more successful than others?

Second, the characteristics of the quality circle groups under study must be carefully specified. This is necessary since there is considerable variation in what actually goes on in organizations under the name, 'quality circles', and since one or more of these characteristics may be particularly important to the long-term effectiveness of quality circles.

Third, we need more attention devoted to the limits of quality circles (Head, Molleston, Sorensen, and Gargano, 1986; Blair and Hurwitz, 1983). When will they not work? And why? We also need to know more about interactions between quality circles and their organizational context (Sims and Dean, 1985; Beardsley, 1986; Donovan, 1986; Gabor, 1986; Geber, 1986; Cole, 1986). Are some structures or cultures more conducive than others for the uses of quality circles?

Finally, we need to know much more about the maintenance of quality circles over time. Are they destined to have their effectiveness diminish with the passage of time? Or can they be revitalized and extended? If not, why? If so, how? Again, following Griffin (1988), this means that the research must be longitudinal and over a period of time greater than a single year (three to five years would be more likely to test this issue).

In summary, quality circles seem to have gained a significant foothold in Western industry. Like all organizational interventions, of course, they have their limits. They also seem to have considerable potential, to promote and enhance productivity and organizational effectiveness. We are just at the beginning, however. We need a carefully developed and articulated theoretical framework to further our understanding of the dynamics of quality circles. We also need high quality, rigorous research to understand better the practical side of things.

REFERENCES

Adams, C. F. (1966) Quality control and the challenges of change. *Advanced Management Journal*, **31**, 7–12.
Alexander, C. P. (1981) Learning from the Japanese. *Personnel Journal*, **60**, 616–619.
Alie, R. E. (1986) The middle management factor in quality circle programs. *SAM Advanced Management Journal*, **51** (3), 9–15.
Arbose, J. R. (1980) Quality control circles: The west adopts a Japanese concept. *International Management*, **35**, 31–39.
Argyris, C. (1964) *Integrating the Individual and the Organization*. New York: John Wiley & Sons.
Aune, A. A. (1984) The Norwegian approach to productivity and company wide quality control. *Quality Circles Journal*, **7** (4), 42–44.
Baillie, A. S. (1986) The Deming approach: Being better than the best. *SAM Advanced Management Journal*, **51** (4), 15–23.
Bank, J., and Wilpert, B. (1983) What's so special about quality circles? *Journal of General Management*, **9**(1), 21–37.
Barrick, M. R., and Alexander, R. A. (1987) A review of quality circle efficacy and the existence of positive-findings bias. *Personnel Psychology*, **40**(3), 579–592.
Beardsley, J. (1986). Beyond quality circles? *Quality Circles Journal*, **9**(3), 10–14.
Berger, L., and Holcomb, L. (1985) An empirical study of the positive side effects of quality circles. *Quality Circle Digest*, **5**, 45–50.
Bernier, L. (1986) French quality circles multiply, but with a difference. *International Management (UK)*, **41** (12), 30–32.
Blair, J. D., and Hurwitz, J. V. (1983) Quality circles for American firms? Some unanswered questions and their implications for managers. In S. M. Lee and G. Schwendiman (eds), *Management by Japanese Systems*. New York: Praeger.
Blair, J. D., and Ramsing, K. D. (1983) Quality circles and production/operations management: Concerns and caveats. *Journal of Operations Management*, **4**, 1–10.
Blair, J. D., and Whitehead, C. J. (1984) Can quality circles survive in the United States? *Business Horizons*, **27** (5), 17–23.
Blocker, H. J., and Overgaard, H. O. (1982) Japanese quality circles: A managerial response to a productivity problem. *Management International Review*, **22** (2), 13–19.
Brockner, J., and Hess, T. (1986) Self-esteem and task performance in quaity circles. *Academy of Management Journal*, **29**, 617–623.
Budgell, A. T., Jr (1967) The manager's stake in quality control. *Management Review*, **56**, 4–8.
Business Week (1962) Japan's newest quest for quality. *Business Week*, 28 July, 98–100.
Cole, R. E. (1979) Made in Japan — Quality control circles. *Across The Board*, **16** (11), 72–78.

Cole, R. E. (1980a) *Work, Mobility, and Participation: A Comparative Study of American and Japanese Industry.* Berkeley, California: University of California Press.
Cole, R. E. (1980b) Will quality circles work in the US? *Quality Progress*, 7, 30.
Cole, R. E. (1986) The 'Beyond quality circles' fad. *Quality Circles Journal*, 9 (3), 4–9.
Cook, M. H. (1982) Quality circles really work, but . . . . *Training and Development Journal*, 36 (1), 4–5.
Dale, B. G. (1985) British quality circles in operation — Some facts and figures. *International Journal of Manpower (UK)*, 6 (4), 3–10.
Dale, B. G., and Lees, J. (1985) Factors which influence the success of quality circle programmes in the United Kingdom. *International Journal of Operations and Production Management (UK)*, 5 (4), 43–54.
Daniel, R., and Berry, P. C. (1984) Quality circles in South Africa: What is happening, what seems to work, and what seems not to work/QC's in tough times. *Quality Circles Journal*, 7 (4), 17–19.
Dean, J. W. (1985) The decision to participate in quality circles. *Journal of Applied Behavioral Science*, 21 (3), 317–327.
Deming, W. E. (1982a) *Quality, Productivity, and Competitive Position.* Cambridge, Massachusetts: Massachusetts Institute of Technology, Center for Advanced Engineering Study.
Deming, W. E. (1982b) *Out of the Crisis.* Cambridge, Massachusetts: Massachusetts Institute of Technology, Center for Advanced Engineering Study.
Deppe, J. (1987) Quality circles in the Federal Republic of Germany, *Quality Circles Journal*, 10 (2), 70–74.
Dewar, D. L. (1982) *The Quality Circle Guide to Participation Management.* Englewood Cliffs, New Jersey: Prentice-Hall, Inc.
Diggles, G. L. (1922) Sampling for test purposes. *General Electric Review*, 25 (6), 379–390.
DiGiorgio, B. S. (1981) Management and labor cooperate to increase productivity. *National Research Bureau*, 43, 5–7.
Dillon, L. S. (1983) Adopting Japanese management: Some cultural stumbling blocks. *Personnel*, 60 (4), 73–77.
Donovan, J. M. (1986) Self-managing work teams — Extending the quality circle concept. *Quality Circles Journal*, 9 (3), 5–10.
Duncan, A. J. (1959) *Quality Control and Industrial Statistics.* Homewood, Illinois: Richard D. Irwin, Inc.
Duncan, R., and McGraw, P. (1986) Abandoning simple recipes and benefiting from quality circles: An Australian study. *Work & People (Australia)*, 12 (2), 22–25.
Ferrari, S. (1986) Training for quality — The Italian experience of quality circles. *Journal of European Industrial Training (UK)*, 10 (3), 12–16.
Ferris, G. R., and Wagner, J. A. (1985) Quality circles in the United States: A conceptual re-evaluation. *Journal of Applied Behavioral Science*, 21 (2), 155–167.
Gabor, C. (1986) Special project task teams: An extension of a successful quality circle program. *Quality Circles Journal*, 9 (3), 40–43.
Geber, B. (1986) Quality circles: The second generation. *Training*, 23 (12), 54–60.
Gibson, P. (1981) Short-term fad or long-term fundamental: The need for research into the quality circle process. *Quality Circles Journal*, 4, 25–26.
Goodman, P. S. (1983) Sustaining quality circles: Inherent problems, some strategies. *Quality Circles Journal*, 6, 6–8.
Greene, C. N. (1982) Effects of implementing different versions of quality circles: A field experiment. Unpublished working paper.

Griffin, R. W. (1988) A longitudinal assessment of the consequences of quality circles in an industrial setting. *Academy of Management Journal*, **31** (2), 338–358.

Griffin, R. W., and Wayne, S. J. (1984) A field study of effective and less-effective quality circles. *Proceedings of the Academy of Management*, 217–221.

Gryna, F. M. (1981) *Quality Circles: A Team Approach to Problem Solving*. New York: AMACOM.

Harmon, J. F. (1984) The supervisor and quality control circles. *Supervisory Management*, **29** (2), 26–31.

Head, T. C., Molleston, J. L., Sorensen, P. F., Jr, and Gargano, J. (1986) The impact of implementing a quality circles intervention on employee task perceptions. *Group and Organization Studies*, **11** (4), 360–373.

Hill, F. M. (1986) Quality circles in the UK: A longitudinal study. *Personnel Review (UK)*, **15** (3), 25–34.

Hutchins, D. (1980) QC circles. *Industrial and Commercial Training*, **12**, 8–15.

Ingle, S. (1982a) How to avoid quality circle failure in your company. *Training and Development Journal*, **36**(6), 54–59.

Industry Week (1977a) Talking in circles improves quality. *Industry Week*, 14 February, 62–64.

Industry Week (1977b) More companies adopt quality control circles. *Industry Week*, 1 August, 67–88.

Industry Week (1979) A quality concept catches on worldwide. *Industry Week*, 16 April, 125.

Ingle, S. (1982b) *Quality Circle Master Guide*. Englewood Cliffs, New Jersey: Prentice-Hall, Inc.

Ishikawa, K. (ed.) (1968) *QC Circle Activities*. Tokyo: Union of Japanese Scientists and Engineers.

Ishikawa, K. (1976) *Guide to Quality Control*. Tokyo: Asian Productivity Organization.

Ishikawa, K. (1984) *Quality Control Circles at Work*. Tokyo: Asian Productivity Organization.

Ishikawa, K. (1985) *What is Total Quality Control?* Translated by David J. Lu; Englewood Cliffs, New Jersey: Prentice-Hall, Inc.

Jenkins, K. M., and Shimada, J. Y. (1983) Effects of quality control circles on worker performance: A field experiment. Paper presented to the Academy of Management, Dallas, Texas.

Juran, J. M. (1945) *Management of Inspection and Quality Control*. New York: Harper & Brothers.

Juran, J. M. (1962) *Quality Control Handbook*, 2nd edn. New York: McGraw-Hill.

Juran, J. M. (1964) *Managerial Breakthrough*. New York: McGraw-Hill.

Juran, J. M. (1966) Quality problems, remedies, and nostrums. *Industrial Quality Control*, **22**, 647–653.

Juran, J. M. (1967) The Q.C. circle phenomenon. *Industrial Quality Control*, **23**, 329–336.

Juran, J. M. (1978) Japanese and western quality — A contrast. *Quality Progress*, **11**, 12.

Kahn, S. (1986) Quality circles in India: A review and assessment of the participative management movement in Indian industry. *Quality Circles Journal*, **9**(3), 51–55.

Keys, J. B., and Miller, T. R. (1984) The Japanese management jungle. *Academy of Management Review*, **9**(2), 342–353.

Klein, G. D. (1981) Implementing quality circles: A hard look at some of the realities. *Personnel Journal*, **58**(6), 11–20.

Konz, S. (1979). Quality circles: Japanese success story. *Industrial Engineering*, **11**, 24–27.
Lawler, E. E., III, and Mohrman, S. A. (1985) Quality circles after the fad. *Harvard Business Review*, **63**(1), 65–71.
Lawler, E. E., III, and Mohrman, S. A. (1987) Quality circles: After the honeymoon. *Organizational Dynamics*, **15**(4), 42–54.
Likert, R. (1961) *New Patterns of Management*. New York: McGraw-Hill.
Lippert, F. G. (1966) Responsibilities of a Supervisor. *Supervision*, **28**, 13–14.
Littauer, S. B. (1950) The development of statistical quality control in the United States. *American Statistician*, **4**(5), 14–20.
Lund, R. (1987) Industrial democracy in Denmark. *International Studies of Management and Organization*, **17** (2), 17–26.
Main, J. (1980) The battle for quality begins. *Fortune*, 29 December, 28–33.
Marks, M. L., Mirvis, P. H., Hackett, E. J., and Grady, J. F., Jr (1986) Employee participation in a quality circle program: Impact on quality of work life, productivity, and absenteeism. *Journal of Applied Psychology*, **71**(1), 61–69.
McGregor, D. (1960) *The Human Side of Enterprise*. New York: McGraw-Hill.
Meyer, G. W., and Stott, R. G. (1985) Quality circles: Panacea or Pandora's box? *Organizational Dynamics*, **13**(4), 34–50.
Miller, K. I., and Monge, P. R. (1986) Participation, satisfaction, and productivity: A meta-analytic review. *Academy of Management Journal*, **29**, 727–753.
Modern Manufacturing (1970) The secret of Japan's rise to quality fame. *Modern Manufacturing*, March, 66–68.
Munchus, G., III (1983) Employer–employee based quality circles in Japan: Human resource policy implications for American firms. *Academy of Management Review*, **8**(2), 255–261.
Murray, T. J. (1981) The rise of the productivity manager. *Dun's Review*, **117**, 64–69.
Nelson, J. (1980) Quality circles become contagious. *Industry Week*, **205**, 99 and 103.
New York Times (1949) Quality controls to reduce losses. 10 April, Section 3, 1, 6.
Nirenberg, J. (1986) Understanding the failure of Japanese management abroad. *Journal of Managerial Psychology (UK)*, **1** (1), 19–24.
Pascarella, P. (1982) Quality circles: Just another management headache? *Industry Week*, **213**(7), 28 June, 50–55.
Pascarella, P. (1984) Quality circles uncoil. *Industry Week*, 30 April, 34–40.
Personnel (1980) Productivity and morale sagging? Try the quality circle approach. *Personnel*, May–June, 43–45.
Personnel Journal (1980) Suggestion systems, An answer to perennial problems. *Personnel Journal*, **59**, 552–558.
Rafaeli, A. (1985) Quality circles and employee attitudes. *Personnel Psychology*, **38**(3), 603–615.
Richards, B. (1984) White-collar quality circles and productivity. *Training and Development Journal*, **38**(10), October, 92–98.
Rieker, W. S. (1980) Management's role in QC circles. *Transactions of the Second Annual Conference, International Association of Quality Circles*.
Robson, M. (1982) *Quality Circles: A Practical Guide*. Aldershot, Hampshire, England: Gower Press.
Roche, J. G. (1985) Breakthrough in quality education in Ireland. *Quality Progress*, **18**(1), 24–26.
Robertson, W. L. (1928) Quality control by sampling. *factory and Industrial Management*, **76**, 503.
Ross, B. (1986) W. Edwards Deming: Shogun of quality control. *FE Contents*, **2**, 24–31.

Rubinstein, S. P. (1970) New management concepts from Japan: A tale of two conferences. *Paperboard Packaging,* **55,** 44–45.
Ruffner, E. R., and Ettkin, L. P. (1987) When a circle is not a circle. *SAM Advanced Management Journal,* **52**(2), 9–15.
Seng, Y. K. (1984) Quality control circle movement in Malaysia. *Quality Circles Journal,* **7**(4), 20–22.
Shewhart, W. A. (1926a) Finding causes of quality variations. *Manufacturing Industries,* **11,** 125–128.
Shewhart, W. A. (1926b) Quality control charts. *Bell System Technical Journal,* **5,** 593–603.
Shewhart, W. A. (1931) *Economic Control of Quality of Manufactured Product.* New York: Van Nostrand.
Sims, H. P., Jr, and Dean, J. W., Jr (1985) Beyond quality circles: Self-managing teams. *Personnel,* **62**(1), 25–32.
Smart, D. C. (1985) Total quality in Kodak (Australasia) Pty. Ltd. *Practising Manager (Australia),* **6**(1), 21–23.
Steel (1967) Japanese quality moving up on US — fast. *Steel,* 19 June, 62–63.
Steel, R. P., Lloyd, L. F., Ovalle, N. K., and Hendrix, W. H. (1982) Designing quality circles research. *The Quality Circles Journal,* **5**(1), 40–43.
Steel, R. P., Mento, A. J., Dilla, B. L., Ovalle, N. K., II, and Lloyd, R. F. (1985) Factors influencing the success and failure of two quality circle programs. *Journal of Management,* **11**(1), 99–119.
Steel, R. P., and Shane, G. S. (1986) Evaluation research on quality circles: Technical and analytical implications. *Human Relations,* **39**(5), 449–468.
Swanson, L. A., and Corbin, D. (1969) Employee motivation programs: A change in philosophy? *Personnel Journal,* **48,** 895–898.
Tang, T. L. P., Tollison, P. S., and Whiteside, H. D. (1987) The effect of quality circle initiation on motivation to attend quality circle meetings and on task performance. *Personnel Psychology,* **40,** 799–814.
Thompson, P. (1982) *Quality Circles: How To Make Them Work In America.* New York: Amacom.
Tolentino, A. L. (1984) Quality control circle practices in some selected Philippine companies. *Quality Circles Journal,* **7**(4), 35–37.
Training (1980) Honeywell imports quality circles as long-term management strategy. *Training,* **17,** 91–94.
Training (1980) Quality circles: Using pooled effort to promote excellence. *Training,* **17,** 30–31.
Tse, K. K. (1981). *Harnessing Quality Circles for Higher Quality and Productivity.* Hong Kong: Industrial Relations Association.
Tsurumi, Y. (1981) American management has missed the point: The point is management itself. *The Dial* (September 1981), as quoted in W. E. Deming, (1982). *Quality, Productivity, and Competitive Position.* Cambridge, Massachusetts: Massachusetts Institute of Technology, Center for Advanced Engineering Study, pp. 84–86.
Varzandeh, J., and Masters, L. A. (1988) Quality circles: A review and new findings in union vs. non-union environments. *Proceedings of the Southwest Decision Sciences Institute.* San Antonio, Texas: SW Decision Sciences Institute.
Wagner, J. A., III, and Gooding, R. Z. (1987) Shared influence and organizational behavior: A meta-analysis of situational variables expected to moderate participation–outcome relationships. *Academy of Management Journal,* **30,** 524–541.
Wall Street Journal (1949) Improved testing plan reduces rejected items, cuts production costs. 26 May, 1, 4.

Walton, M. (1986) *The Deming Management Method*. New York: Dodd, Mead & Company.
Wayne, S. J., Griffin, R. W., and Bateman, T. S. (1986) Improving the effectiveness of quality circles. *Personnel Administrator*, **31**(3), 79–88.
Weiss, A. (1984) Simple truths of Japanese manufacturing. *Harvard Business Review*, **62**(4), 119–125.
Wells, C. (1982) Quality circles — Features of an Australian program. *Work & People (Australia)*, **8**(3), 12–18.
Wiebe, F. A., and Zahra, S. A. (1985) A longitudinal study of the impact of quality circles. *Transactions from the Seventh Annual IAQC Conference*, **7**, 175–177.
Wood, R., Hull, F., and Azumi, K. (1983) Evaluating quality circles: An American application. *California Management Review*, **26**(1), 37–53.
Yager, E. (1979) Examining the quality control circle. *Personnel Journal*, **58**, 682–708.
Yager, E. (1980) Quality circle: A tool for the '80s. *Training and Development Journal*, **34**, 60–62.
Yager, E. G. (1981) The quality control circle explosion. *Training and Development Journal*, April, 98–105.
Zinck, W. C. (1966a) The foreman and quality. *Supervision*, **28**(3), 10–12, 19.
Zinck, W. C. (1966b) The foreman and quality. *Supervision*, **28**(4), 10–12, 24.
Zinck, W. C. (1966c) The foreman and quality. *Supervision*, **28**, 20–24.

Chapter 8
CONTROL IN THE WORKPLACE

Daniel C. Ganster
and
Marcelline R. Fusilier
Department of Management
University of Nebraska at Lincoln
USA

The idea of personal control in one form or another underlies much of our theorizing in industrial and organizational psychology. For example, it is often hypothesized that individuals will be more committed to decisions that they have participated in, that they will be more satisfied and motivated in jobs that give them autonomy, that they will adopt more difficult goals if given a choice, and that they will react less negatively to stressful jobs if they have control. All of these propositions rest on some basic assumptions concerning the psychological effects of control. In this chapter we attempt to make a broad sweep of the industrial and organizational psychology and organizational behavior literatures with the intention of uncovering evidence about the effects of employee control in the workplace. This literature assesses behavioral and job performance outcomes as well as job attitudes. Moreover, there has been a great deal of interest in the effects of employee control on the general wellbeing of workers, and much of this research has been published in outlets not often frequented by I/O psychologists. Thus, in this review we devote considerable attention to this 'stress' literature as well as research in experimental and social psychology in an attempt to provide some integration of these diverse research areas.

Central to this discussion is our view that personal control is essentially a psychological phenomenon that has both environmental and dispositional antecedents. Asserting that the construct of interest is a cognition leads one naturally to a self-report strategy for operationalizing it, and indeed, this has been the dominant empirical approach in the work literature. On the one hand, this has led to problems regarding the discrimination of the control construct from its putative environmental antecedents and its attitudinal, behavioral, and health consequences. On the other hand, many management intervention techniques plausibly involve control as a central mediating variable, but few evaluations of such interventions have measured employee control beliefs. Thus, it is has been difficult to link control cognitions with objective work conditions. In this review we include those studies that measure control beliefs directly as well as studies that assess working conditions that are theoretically causal of those cognitions. Finally, we also cover studies that address relevant dispositional constructs such as locus of control, because of our interest in them as antecedents to situational control beliefs and because they may have moderating effects on the relationships between environmental conditions and employee outcomes.

Control Theories

The construct of control has been variously defined within several research traditions. From the learning theory perspective (e.g. Seligman, 1975), control is viewed as the degree of contingency between a response and an outcome. This view does not depend on a cognitive mediation of the environmental contingencies, but is operationalized as the objective response–outcome contingency facing the respondent. Rotter's (1966) model also derives from a learning theory perspective and focuses on response–outcome contingencies. In this case, however, the core concept concerns the generalized expectancies, or beliefs, of the person that important events are caused by his or her actions or controlled by powerful others or by chance. Internal locus of control, the belief that outcomes are primarily the result of one's own actions or personal characteristics, is theorized to be a stable personality factor that will generalize across many situations. Also emanating from a learning theory paradigm, Bandura's (1977) self-efficacy concept refers to perceptions of individuals regarding their capabilities to achieve different levels of performance in different domains. Such self-efficacy perceptions have been found to affect motivation, cognitions, and emotional reactions when coping with threatening events.

Control as Cognition

In his summary of the control literature, Averill (1973) proposed three types of control: behavioral, decisional, and cognitive. Behavioral control refers to the individual's ability to act directly on the environment so as to produce desired outcomes or avoid negative ones. Examples of such control include the ability to start and stop one's work when desired, the ability to speed up or slow down one's work pace, and the ability to determine the quality of the product one produces. Decisional control refers to having a choice among several possible actions, outcomes, or tasks. Cognitive control refers to one's interpretation of the environment, and this interpretation may or may not be veridical. Langer (1983) has argued that these different types of control can be distinguished from the perspective of an outside observer, but these distinctions may not be meaningful from the actor's perspective. That is, an observer can see a person as exercising behavioral or decisional control independent of his or her being conscious of it. However, from the actor's perspective no control is experienced at all unless he or she has an awareness of it. The essential point is that meaningful control, that is, control that has important psychological and behavioral consequences, consists of an active belief that one has a choice among responses that are differentially effective in bringing about an outcome. It seems important to maintain this distinction between objective and perceived control, especially given the fact that people's perceptions of their control are often inaccurate assessments of their objective control (Abramson and Alloy, 1980; Langer, 1975; Weisz, 1983).

Intrinsic Need for Control

A belief in personal control over one's environment has long been viewed as an essential aspect of human motivation. Theorists have posited that people have a basic need to achieve a mastery over their environment. For example, DeCharms (1968) asserted that 'man's primary motivation propensity is to be effective in producing changes in his environment. Man strives to be a causal agent, to be the primary locus of causation for, or the origin of, his behavior; he strives for personal causation' (p. 269). According to White (1959), behavior is 'directed, selective, and persistent, and it is continued not because it serves primary drives, . . . but because it satisfies an intrinsic need to deal with the environment' (p. 18). In Adler's (1930) view, this need for control was an 'intrinsic necessity of life itself' (p. 398). Similarly, other theorists have proposed that a need to achieve control over the environment is a basic motive, including Zimbardo and Miller (1958) and Woodworth (1958). Presumably, this propensity to perceive control over events is powerful enough to lead people to attribute such control even in situations where outcomes are totally a function of chance. Along these lines, Langer (1975) has developed a theory regarding the 'illusion of control' in which she explores the conditions that encourage people participating in a chance event to behave as if they were in a skill event.

A basic motive to have control over one's environment is consistent with studies that demonstrate the relative attractiveness of situations in which the individual has choice or control (Lefcourt, 1973). In Brehm's (1966) theory of reactance, for example, he asserts that when people feel that their freedom to choose among alternatives is abridged, an aversive state, reactance, is aroused. This reaction motivates them to take actions that will enable them to regain their freedom and sense of control.

However, the assertion of White (1959) and others that personal control reflects a basic human need has been challenged by Rodin, Rennert, and

Solomon (1980). Rodin et al. note that 'Assumptions about how control operates have been more plentiful than has empirical evidence to back them' (p. 143). Specifically, they examined two assumptions derived from White's (1959) theory: that having control is intrinsically motivating, and that being able to make a choice among alternatives enhances self-esteem. Their evidence suggests that control is attractive to the extent that it affords the individual greater opportunities to achieve desired outcomes. Furthermore, they found that giving the individual more control can make him or her less able to avoid personal attributions for bad outcomes, and in this way, control can lessen self-esteem. In sum, Rodin et al. (1980) dispute the generality of the proposition that personal control is a universally favored end; however, there is much evidence to suggest that personal control is usually seen as being instrumental to the attainment of positive outcomes. Nevertheless, Rodin et al. sensitize us to search for conditions in which control may have negative effects.

Control and Stress

Control has received a great amount of attention in settings in which the individual is required to cope with some aversive stimulus or other psychological threat. The early studies employed animal subjects and investigated the effects of having an instrumental response that enabled the animal to avoid or terminate an aversive stimulus, often electric shock (e.g. Mowrer and Viek, 1948). In general, these studies demonstrated that giving the animal behavioral control over the stimulus lessened the impact of the stress on a variety of physical symptoms, including weight loss and gastric lesions.

Much of this research has been replicated with human subjects as well. For example, Haggard (1943) found that physiological stress responses were reduced when subjects could control the onset and termination of aversive stimulation. Subsequent studies employing yoked controls suggested that it was the control itself that produced the benefit, and not just a reduction in the intensity or duration of the stimulus. This research has tested a number of different types of stressors, including both physical ones such as noise (Glass and Singer, 1972) and cold pressors (McCaul, 1980), and psychological stressors such as the administration of intelligence tests (Stotland and Blumenthal, 1964) and aversive photographs (Geer and Maisel, 1972). Many of these studies demonstrated that the belief in control itself, even if that control remained unexercised, produced significant stress-reducing impact. The effects of control perceptions, furthermore, have been found to have after-effects on task performance as well as on emotional and physiological stress. Glass, Reim, and Singer (1971), for example, exposed subjects to noxious levels of noise under one of four experimental conditions: (1) perceived control, in which subjects were led to believe that they could signal another subject to press a button that would terminate the noise; (2) no perceived control, in which the other subject possessed a control button but the subject could not communicate with him; (3) together — no button, in which neither subject could control the noise; and (4) alone — no button, in which the subject worked alone with no control. They found that subjects in the no-control conditions suffered higher levels of tension as indexed by tonic skin conductance, and that they showed relatively impaired performance on a proofreading task administered after the termination of the noise exposure session.

The experimental research literature is consistent in its demonstration of the positive effects of control for most people when they are faced with a threatening situation. However, it is interesting to note the 'executive monkey' experiments of Brady and his colleagues because they suggested that being in control might actually be more harmful than being in a passive role. Brady, Porter, Conrad, and Maso (1958) conducted an experiment in which monkeys were exposed to electric shocks while they were restrained in a chair. The 'executive' monkey could avoid the shock by pressing a lever every 20 seconds, while his yoked control sat passively and received the shocks whenever the executive monkey did. Brady *et al.* found that the executive monkeys developed gastrointestinal ulcers, whereas the passives did not. Observers were quick to note the analogy with real executives who have high levels of responsibility and control and who thus presumably suffer from high levels of job stress and its consequences. This conclusion probably did much to help popularize the notion of executive stress which suggested that high levels of decision-making responsibility could lead to ulcers and heart attacks.

However, Weiss (1968) questioned the conclusions reached by Brady *et al.* (1958) from their experiments. First, he noted that the executive monkeys had been pre-selected based on their demonstrated ability to learn avoidance responses in pre-test trials. Thus, inherent selection factors might have been associated with an increased vulnerability to the stress of the experiment. Second, and more importantly, Weiss (1971) noted that Brady's design did not provide the executive monkey with adequate feedback about the effectiveness of his coping behaviors. Working with rats, Weiss (1971) created conditions with different types of warning signal. In one warning signal condition, an audible tone preceded the onset of the shock by a few seconds. For those with control, the tone indicated that a coping response was necessary, while their yoked cohorts were merely informed that a shock might be imminent. In another condition no warning tone preceded the onset of shock, while in a progressive warning signal condition the warning signals became louder and faster as the scheduled shock neared. It was hypothesized that the progressive signals would give the animals more feedback about their responses. Stress was assessed by measuring gastric lesions and blood steroid concentrations.

As predicted, those animals with both instrumental control over the shock and a warning tone were better off than those without a control response available. The animals with both progressive warning tones and control fared the best, and those with a control response in the no-signal condition were worse off than those in the signal condition. These data suggested that working in a stress avoidance task without sufficient feedback essentially negates the benefits of instrumental control. Fisher (1985) refers to such an operating condition as 'control by avoidance', and asserts that there is little to distinguish this condition cognitively from a state of helplessness. She notes, for example, that a worker who changes his or her behavior to avoid an unpleasant consequence, such as meeting a deadline or avoiding an encounter with an angry colleague, often does not receive feedback that the behavior was effective precisely because it *was* effective. In this 'safety signal' model of control the person must maintain a state of arousal and vigilance in the absence of relevant feedback, even though he or she may have an effective coping response. This requirement to maintain high arousal prevents the individual from reaching a state of homeostasis and recovery, and thus leads to the development of stress-related disorders.

A somewhat different explanatory model was offered by Miller (1979) in the form of her 'Minimax hypothesis'. In this view, when a person perceives that he or she has control over the onset or termination of an aversive event, he or she is more likely to be confident that maximum danger can be minimized. Thus, control is a cognitive phenomenon that causes the individual to tolerate noxious situations better than one who does not perceive such personal control. There are several implications of this hypothesis for the work environment. For example, workers might tolerate a higher level of noise, working pace, or challenge if they perceive that they have some control over the onset and termination of those conditions. If the pace became too much to handle, or if the noise became too loud, they could exercise this control before the conditions became intolerable.

Learned Helplessness

Overmier and Seligman (1967) noted that after dogs had been repeatedly exposed to inescapable electric shocks they seemed to lose their ability to cope even when an escape response was made available. It was as if the dogs had learned that their responses had no impact on the shocks and this learning carried over to other controllable conditions, leading to passivity and depression. This early research spawned numerous studies that extended the paradigm to humans and explored the conditions under which such lack of control would lead to learned helplessness. Many of these studies demonstrate that exposure to uncontrollable aversive events can lead to depression and even the subject's premature death (Seligman, 1975).

Abramson, Seligman, and Teasdale (1978) later reformulated the model to include people's attributions about why they lack control in a given situation. In this model, they posit that the effects of lack of control depend on individuals' attributions about the stability, internality, and specificity of their low control. It is one thing to believe that you cannot affect the outcomes of your work because the task is inherently uncontrollable, and quite another to believe that it is uncontrollable because you have low ability and are stupid. In general, the theory proposes that control perceptions that are internal, stable, and global will have the most profound effects on depression, passivity, and lowered self-esteem.

The learned helplessness paradigm was extended specifically to the work setting by Martinko and Gardner (1982). The Martinko and Gardner model incorporates a variety of organizational characteristics such as reward systems, leadership and supervision practices, task structure, and organization structure, and proposes that they are linked to low productivity, absenteeism, and general passivity. In this 'organizationally induced helplessness' model the effects of the task environment are mediated by the worker's causal attributions regarding the internality/externality and stability of his or her control over outcomes at work. They argue that many aspects of organizational functioning foster the development of employee beliefs that their actions are not instrumental in attaining valued outcomes. For example, they cited Lawler's (1966) survey of over 600 managers who reported virtually no perceived relationship between their performance appraisals and their pay. They noted that their model has received no empirical examination in the organizational behavior literature, but that many parts of it are based on well-supported findings from other fields.

Distinguishing Predictability from Control

In most laboratory studies that examine the effects of control in the face of aversive conditions there is a confounding of predictability and control. Those coping responses given to subjects in the control condition generally make the onset of the event predictable as well. Some theorists have argued that it is the predictability inherent in control that accounts for all of its benefits (Averill, 1973). Although some of the effects of behavioral control might be explained by enhanced predictability, there is evidence that suggests that the two constructs should be treated separately. For example, Miller (1987) has found that there are dispositional differences between people in their preferred coping styles with respect to information about a threatening event, especially in situations that are perceived as uncontrollable. 'Blunters' are individuals who prefer to distract themselves from the impending event, while 'monitors' are people who prefer to focus on information about the threat. Miller (1987) reviewed research that suggests that giving more information (predictability) to individuals who are blunters may actually increase their distress. In addition, Abbott, Schoen, and Badia (1984) noted that predictability can prove to be more stressful than unpredictability when one is exposed for long periods of time to stresses of relatively low severity. Thus, it appears that the impact of predictability depends on individual differences in coping style as well as on intensity and duration of the stress exposure. This research also suggests that predictability itself will not necessarily compensate for lack of instrumental control.

Distinctions among these aspects of control in the organizational literature are most explicit in Sutton and Kahn's (1986) model. They proposed that one can distinguish between: (a) understanding how and why things happen in the organization; (b) being able to predict the occurrence, duration, and timing of events; and (c) being able to control events or processes at work. Each of these represents some meaningful aspect of control and can serve as an 'antidote' to work stress. Tetrick and LaRocco (1987) examined the main and interactive effects of these control aspects on perceived role stress, job satisfaction, and psychological well-being for a sample of 225 physicians, nurses, and dentists. The correlations of each of them with role stress, satisfaction, and well-being were quite similar. The three control variables also showed similar moderating effects, except that prediction did not moderate the relationship between role stress and satisfaction, whereas understanding and control did. Overall, these data do not make a compelling case for discriminating among these types of control. However, results from this one study do not imply that such distinctions are not important.

Summary of Experimental and Social Psychological Control Research

From the preceding discussion of control research and theory, several broad conclusions might be reached regarding the expected effects of personal control. First, the notion that personal control over one's environment represents a basic human motive, and thus is universally positively valent, is questionable. However, there is much evidence that points to the general attractiveness of situations that are perceived to be controllable. This is especially true when the situation involves choice over differentially valued outcomes or performance on a task. Second, the experimental evidence is quite convincing that holding a belief that one has control over the onset, timing, or termination of an aversive event can make the anticipation and experience of the event more tolerable. However, even in studies in which the majority of subjects showed lower stress with control, Averill (1973) noted that 10–20 per cent of the subjects often showed just the opposite reaction. Averill concluded that one must understand the meaning of the control contingency for the subject in order to predict its impact. As well as there being individual differences in desire for control, such differences as how the subject prefers to cope with an impending aversive event (monitoring versus blunting) seem to affect how control and predictability will affect emotional and behavioral responses.

Third, control may be undesirable in situations where having it would make it more likely that individuals will make internal, stable attributions for failure.

Finally, having an instrumental control response that allows one to avoid negative outcomes might be very stressful if one does not also have the necessary feedback about the effectiveness of that response. In such an instance, having control could prove more damaging over the long term than not having it.

CONTROL THEORY IN ORGANIZATIONAL SETTINGS

Despite the wealth of data produced by researchers in experimental and social psychology, conclusions from this body of research must be generalized to organizational settings cautiously. Most of the experimental studies cited above assess the effects of control in highly constrained settings in which the subject must cope with some aversive or threatening event. Whether the same effects would likely be evident with long-term exposures to working conditions (where the greatest threat might be boredom) is certainly debatable. However, we should note that field interventions to increase the control of elderly nursing home residents over their daily lives have shown some dramatic outcomes, including large reductions in mortality (Rodin, 1986).

The organizational literature contains a number of theoretical perspectives that revolve around the construct of personal control. Blauner's (1964) work on alienation, for example, highlighted the role of worker control. From his research on blue-collar workers (e.g. car assembly line, printers, textile mill workers, oil processors), he concluded that 'Alienation exists when workers are unable to control their immediate work processes, to develop a sense of purpose and function which connects their jobs to the overall organization of production, to belong to integrated industrial communities, and when they fail to become involved in the activity of work as a mode of self-expression' (p. 15). Blauner's concept of control referred to instrumental control over various dimensions of the workplace, such as pace of work, quantity and quality of production, work techniques, and freedom from direct supervision. A similar focus on the role of autonomy and control characterizes the work of other writers working in the alienation tradition, such as Shepard (1971), Sheppard and Herrick (1972), and Gardell (1971, 1977).

Participation in Decision Making

Employee participation in decision making is relevant to personal control to the extent that employees who are more involved in making decisions believe that they have more control over processes and outcomes in the workplace. In this sense participation represents a potential opportunity for the worker to exert influence. It is necessary, however, to keep the concepts of participation and control separate. Locke and Schweiger (1979) remind us that participation in the workplace has been operationalized in many ways. They noted, for example, that participation can be forced versus voluntary, formal versus informal, and direct (individual participation) versus indirect (representation on committees). Participation can also vary in degree, ranging from some degree of consultation to having full authority in making a decision. Thus, it is very difficult to generalize about the effects of participation on employee perceptions of control. It is often likely that employees may work under conditions defined as participative but perceive little actual influence on matters that concern them (Hoffman, Burke, and Maier, 1965).

Recent reviews of the participation literature (Locke and Schweiger, 1979, Schweiger and Leana, 1986, Spector, 1986) have been fairly consistent in their conclusions that employee participation in decision making is generally positively associated with job attitudes and less strongly correlated with employee performance. In Spector's (1986) meta-analysis participation correlations with job attitudes such as general job satisfaction, and satisfaction with work and pay, averaged in the high .30s (in the high .40s when corrected for attenuation from low reliability). Similarly, correlations of participation with turnover and motivation averaged −.34. However, participation's correlation with job performance averaged only .18 (.23 when corrected).

Participation's relationship to perceptions of stress and reactions to stress are also fairly modest. For example, Spector (1986) reported average correlations of −.26 and −.14 between participation and physical symptoms and emotional distress, respectively. Average correlations with perceived role conflict and role ambiguity were −.33 and −.43. The study of 23 occupations by Caplan *et al.* (1975) is also worth noting, however, because it was not included in Spector's meta-analysis and because the sample in this one study (N = 2010) is as large as the total sample of the stress studies in the meta-analysis.

The Caplan *et al.* (1975) survey measured participation with a three-item scale and focused on employee participation in decisions regarding: (1) 'things that affect them'; (2) 'the way things are done on the job'; and (3) 'what part of a task they would do'. As in previous studies, participation correlated with overall job satisfaction moderately (r = .36), but its relationships with measures of stress-related outcomes were much smaller. For example, significant correlations included those with number of cigarettes smoked (−.20), depression (−.17), and somatic complaints (−.13). Correlations between participation and anxiety, caffeine consumption, obesity, and dispensary visits were all less than .10. Participation also failed to correlate significantly with physiological stress measures such as heart rate, blood pressure, cholesterol, uric acid, cortisol, and measures of thyroid function.

As noted earlier, it is difficult to make inferences about the effects of employee control from the participation literature, because participation may or may not have a large impact on experienced control. A field experiment by Jackson (1983), however, is particularly interesting, because she not only manipulated participation in a controlled design but also assessed employee control perceptions. The study was conducted in a hospital outpatient facility, and employees were assigned either to a participation group or to a no-intervention control group. The intervention was designed to increase the amount of influence employees had over a broad range of work-related decisions. Unit heads were provided two days of training in the nominal group technique, and they were mandated by a new state requirement to hold staff meetings at least twice per month. A list of topics to address in the meetings was provided for them. Data from 95 employees at a six-month post-test and from 70 employees at a nine-month post-test showed that the intervention led to significant reductions in a measure of emotional strain. In addition, Jackson administered a 17-item self-report influence scale that tapped a broad range of issues. The intervention itself produced significant changes in this measure, explaining 8 per cent of its variance at the first post-test and 12 per cent at the second post-test. The perceived control measure also correlated negatively with the emotional strain outcome. This study, then, provides one of the few demonstrations that participation, when it results in perceptions of higher personal control over issues that matter to employees, can make jobs less stressful.

Although there is little evidence directly relating participation in decision making to employee control perceptions, participation, nevertheless, appears to be a viable strategy for augmenting control. This would especially seem to be the case when the individual has the chance to participate in decisions regarding his or her immediate job situation. Gardell (1977) noted, for example, that industrial workers report a much stronger desire for increased participation and influence over their immediate job situation than at the plant level.

Job Design Research

Worker control has also been an important characteristic for most theorists concerned with describing the components of jobs that render them satisfying and motivating. Of the six task characteristics identified by Walker and Guest (1952) in their study of assembly line workers, two were related to worker control (mechanical pacing of work and predetermination in use of tools and techniques). Some form of worker control is also a component in the lists of job design factors identified by more recent theorists such as Turner and Lawrence (1965), Herzberg, Mausner, and Snyderman (1959), Hackman and Lawler (1971), and Hackman and Oldham (1976). Control as treated in the task design paradigm can be distinguished from the participation construct in several ways. First, a worker's job can entail a high level of control over immediate processes and decisions that must be made to carry out the task, yet the worker may or may not have any opportunity to participate in decisions involving other aspects of the workplace. Second, though a worker may feel that he or she can participate in decision making, he or she may not experience a significant degree of instrumental control in any meaningful area. Control in the job design sense, however, means that the individual definitely has control, but in a specified domain—that of immediate task processes and accomplishment.

The control construct most researched in recent years is the task characteristic of autonomy. Hackman and Oldham (1976) defined autonomy as 'The degree to which the job provides substantial freedom, independence, and discretion to the individual in scheduling the work and in determining the procedures to be used in carrying it out' (p. 258). In the Hackman and Oldham (1976) model, autonomy is important because it leads to the state of 'experienced responsibility for outcomes of the work' (p. 256). Without such experienced meaningfulness the worker is unlikely to enjoy the psychological rewards of task accomplishments. This theoretical view can be contrasted with the position of Herzberg *et al.* (1959), for example, in that 'responsibility' is one of their 'motivators' because they believe that it matches a basic need that is relatively unfulfilled in most workers. Thus, the older job enrichment view is more akin to the position of the 'control as basic need' theorists (e.g. White, 1959), while the Hackman and Oldham (1976) position represents more of an instrumental formulation (e.g. Rodin *et al.*, 1980). It is important to note, however, that the latter is an interactive formulation in that autonomy is not expected to be motivating unless the worker also receives adequate feedback about his or her performance and experiences the work as meaningful. Moreover, if the feedback indicates that the worker has performed poorly, high autonomy would presumably make it more difficult for the worker to make an external attribution for the result. In that case, high autonomy would not necessarily be desired.

The job design literature has been the topic of several recent reviews (Roberts and Glick, 1981; Spector, 1986; Stone, 1986). Two of these were meta-analyses that isolated autonomy from other task characteristics and assessed its relationship with affective and behavioral outcomes. Both reviewers reported strong and consistent relationships between autonomy and various facets of job satisfaction, with growth satisfaction showing the highest correlations. Both reviewers also reported significant average effect sizes for autonomy on measures of job performance, although these were lower in magnitude than the satisfaction relationships. Spector also computed average effect sizes of autonomy on perceived stress variables, physical symptoms, emotional distress, and various behavioral outcomes such as turnover and absenteeism. In general, autonomy was significantly associated with these variables as well.

Most job design studies consist of field surveys in which employee perceptions of task characteristics have been correlated with the outcome measures. A recent study by Adelmann (1987), however, related self-report data on several facets of well-being (happiness, self-confidence, and vulnerability) obtained from a national survey to objective measures of job characteristics. Adelmann's (1987) sample consisted of 948 working men and women from a representative national survey concerning mental health outcomes in the US adult population (Veroff, Douvan, and Kulka, 1981). She aggregated the sample by occupation and constructed scales for complexity and control from DOT occupational ratings. After controlling for age, education, and income, she found control to be significantly related to happiness and self-confidence, but not vulnerability. This study avoided some of the potential methodological problems accompanying the use of self-report data (e.g. common method variance, response consistency) but also suffered the disadvantages of analyzing relationships at the occupational level. Chief among these is the potential error associated with aggregating the job characteristics data at the occupational level.

There are a few experimental studies in this literature, but most such efforts involved the simultaneous manipulation of several task dimensions (e.g. Ganster, 1980). Thus, they do not allow the estimation of the effects of autonomy, specifically, because of its confounding with such factors as skill variety and feedback. However, two laboratory experiments focused on autonomy as an experimental variable, and examined its effects on attitudinal and performance outcomes (Dodd, 1987; Farh and Scott, 1983).

The Farh and Scott (1983) experiment examined the effects of manipulated autonomy on the responses of students working on a combination of three tasks: proofreading, data coding, and grading. The autonomy manipulation consisted of allowing subjects to vary the amount of time they spent on each of the tasks and the order in which they did them. In one condition subjects were given a complete choice subject to the constraint that they work on each of the tasks at least some of the time. In the 'semiautonomous condition' subjects were allowed to choose the order of the tasks but were yoked to a subject in the autonomous condition so that they had to spend as much time on each task as their yoked cohort. In two 'non-autonomous conditions' subjects were required to spend the same amount of time in each task as their partner in the autonomous condition. They also had either to replicate the order of task choice of their yoked partner or follow a preset order. At the end of a 60-minute work period subjects completed measures of perceived autonomy and task satisfaction.

Farh and Scott found no differences across the autonomy conditions on measures of performance quality. For performance quantity, subjects in the high autonomy condition performed significantly *worse* than the low autonomy subjects. In addition, the autonomy manipulation had no impact on satisfaction. Clearly, a very restrictive operationalization of autonomy was employed here. However, subjects in the high autonomy condition reported significantly higher autonomy scores on the Job Diagnostic Survey scale (Hackman and Oldham, 1975); this scale being one of the most widely used in field research.

Several explanations might be suggested as to why the Farh and Scott (1983) experiment produced findings so at odds with the large body of field studies. First, the amount of 'control' provided the subjects concerned how they allocated their time among three fairly simple tasks. They might simply not have regarded choices among these tasks as sufficiently meaningful to produce significant affective or motivational reactions. In this regard, the situation could be likened to the experiment reported by Rodin *et al.* (1980). Subjects worked less hard to earn a choice among outcomes (different flavors in a taste rating) that were perceived to be similar than they did when they believed the outcomes would be quite different in desirability. Second, Hackman and Oldham's (1976) model predicts that autonomy will have motivating properties when it is accompanied by feedback and the task is 'meaningful'. If they are correct, then the Farh and Scott (1983) results might be explained by the general lack of feedback and meaningfulness in the tasks.

A later study by Dodd (1987) tested an interactive model like the one proposed by Hackman and Oldham (1976). Dodd assigned student subjects to one of eight versions of a word processing task. Her design consisted of a 2 × 2 × 2 factorial in which she manipulated task autonomy, variety, and feedback. In her study autonomy was operationalized more broadly than in the Farh and Scott (1983) experiment, and included control over pacing, various choices about how they performed the work, and degree of dependence on the supervisor for task-relevant information and assistance. Variety was operationalized as the number of discrete subtasks that comprised the total task. In the low variety condition, subjects edited text for spelling errors only, while in the high variety condition they checked spelling, grammar, punctuation, and mathematical errors. Subjects in the high feedback condition were provided specific feedback about the quality and quantity of performance while they worked on the task. Dodd found that manipulated autonomy had a significant positive effect on satisfaction with the task. Performance, however, was determined by an interaction between autonomy and feedback. With low levels of feedback, high autonomy had no impact on performance. Only with high task feedback did subjects in the high autonomy condition perform better than in the low autonomy condition.

It is dangerous to make generalizations about the effects of 'autonomy' on employee attitudes and performance because the construct itself has been difficult to pin down in the organizational literature. Farh and Scott (1983), for example, criticized the Hackman and Oldham (1976) definition as being inadequate for identifying autonomy as 'an orthogonal property of a job independent of skill variety and possibly other dimensions' (p. 207). Breaugh (1985) noted that most conceptual and operational definitions of autonomy confound it with the conceptually distinct construct of interdependence. He cited research by Kiggundu (1983) to show that these are empirically distinct constructs, although they are likely correlated across many jobs. Breaugh (1985) argued that we must examine subfacets of the autonomy construct, and in particular, he suggested: (1) work method autonomy or the degree of discretion and choice individuals have in doing the work; (2) work scheduling autonomy or the degree of control over scheduling and timing of work activities; and (3) work criteria autonomy or the degree of control over the criteria used to evaluate performance. Similar and more extensive lists of subfacets were suggested by Ganster (1988, in press) in discussions of control and work stress.

Bazerman (1982) argued that two critical dimensions of worker control should be distinguished: control over outcomes and control over activities. Control over activities is similar to Breaugh's (1985) work method autonomy and refers to control over the methods and activities chosen in carrying out the task. Outcome control is defined as the degree to which outcomes are contingent on performance. Bazerman's model posits that either type of control must be congruent with the individual's ability to use the control or performance will suffer. Bazerman's (1982) 'undercontrol' prediction is consistent with prior control research. However, his overcontrol prediction (that having more control than the subject can use will decrease performance) represents somewhat of a departure from traditional models. Why should too much control lead to performance detriment? Bazerman argued that if the worker is presented with an unobtainable bonus (unobtainable because the required performance exceeds his or her ability), for example, that 'there is now an additional aspect of control salient to the individual over which he or she has no control' (pp. 473–4). Rather than just being irrelevant, as expectancy theory might predict, this perception of lack of control over the bonus should lead to performance declines (perhaps because the worker's self-perceived competence has been reduced).

Bazerman reported data from two laboratory experiments that were consistent with his congruency hypotheses. However, we are not quite sure what to make of this model. On the one hand, it would seem useful to distinguish activity control from outcome control. On the other hand, the only explanation offered as to why 'overcontrol' should have adverse effects on performance essentially depends on defining it as lack of control. This brings us back to our earlier conclusion that control is important to the extent that it is perceived by the actor. How did Bazerman's (1982) subjects perceive the overcontrol experimental condition? We only know that he asked subjects two questions assessing their activity and outcome control states, and that the responses differed by experimental condition. Not knowing what these questions were prevents us from knowing whether the overcontrol subjects believed that they indeed had control over their outcomes or activities.

Summary of Autonomy Research

From the few experimental studies that isolated autonomy it is apparent that worker control interacts with other task characteristics in its effect on task performance, and perhaps with task satisfaction as well. Consistent with the experimental psychology literature, control (most specifically, choice among task alternatives) seems to acquire positive valence only in conditions in which the options are differentially desirable or where the task is significantly meaningful (in the job design sense). Making a distinction between control over activities and control over outcomes could be obviated by considering both to be control over some type of outcome. In the former case, control allows the worker to choose among activities that are more or less intrinsically satisfying, that is, the outcomes are derived from the behaviors themselves. Thus, if none of the activities, or activity sequences, is seen to be more attractive than the others, then control itself is likely to have little value.

Control's effects on task performance appear to be dependent on sufficient feedback being available concerning the appropriateness of the individual's choices. The control model at work here is probably different from that which explains control's impact on task satisfaction. Making reference to the Dodd (1987) experiment, control's impact on performance might not depend on a motivational process at all. Once an individual adopts a goal of task accomplishment (which *is* a motivational process), control and feedback are jointly necessary in a cybernetic Test-Operate-Test-Exit (TOTE) model sense (Miller, Galanter, and Pribram, 1960). That is, feedback allows the worker to make adjustments (operate) to his or her work behaviors and test these against task performance (the goal). Thus, sufficient autonomy and feedback allow the worker to execute a series of TOTE units in an efficient manner, something that could not be done without either task dimension. A lack of feedback in the Farh and Scott (1983) experiment might explain their findings relative to Dodd's (1987).

Finally, further research is needed regarding the utility of specifying different facets of job control (cf. Breaugh, 1985; Ganster, 1988, in press). Surely, control over some things at work is more important than control over others. Moreover, different types of control can take on different levels of importance depending on other circumstances of the work situation and depending on the particular needs of the worker. Assessing the effects of 'control at work' by making use of the autonomy measures that typify task design research is thus likely to have limited success, for these measures are at once too general and too narrow in focus. Autonomy measures are too general in that they index and combine several facets of control over the task (work methods, work pace, work performance criteria, independence of others, etc.). They are too narrow in that such measures do not tap the worker's control over other factors such as arrangement of the physical environment, when he or she comes to work, or whether he or she must work for that particular employer. We have more to say about control dimensions below.

Machine Pacing

Over 100 studies have been conducted that attempt to assess the effects of external pacing on various worker outcomes, including error rates and efficiency, physiological responses, and psychological stress. Much of this interest no doubt arises from the fact that over 50 million people worldwide are estimated to work on machine-paced tasks (Salvendy, 1981). Our interest in machine pacing in this review stems from the likely connection that it has with feelings of worker control. For several reasons the machine pacing literature might be expected to be particularly informative regarding the impact of worker control. First, pacing is a specific type of worker control that is conceptually straightforward. Contrasted with the concept of job autonomy in the task design literature, pacing can be clearly distinguished from other constructs, particularly those relating to other job scope dimensions (e.g. skill variety). Second, pacing is an objectively measurable aspect of the work environment. As such, researchers have the potential of assessing the impact of this type of control on various worker outcomes while at the same time they can investigate the hypothesized mediating effects of worker control perceptions. The relation of the workers' cognitive appraisals of control with this objective feature of their job can be empirically determined, rather than assumed. Third, pacing lends itself to experimental manipulation, further enhancing its researchability in inferentially strong designs. Finally, the machine pacing literature is characterized by a variety of research strategies including laboratory experiments, controlled field experiments, and epidemiological studies.

Previously we have criticized autonomy measures as being too non-specific in their assessment of worker control regarding the task itself. The complexity of this control concept is aptly illustrated by noting the complexity of the pacing construct itself, even though pacing is but one element of the broader job autonomy construct. Salvendy (1981) distinguished several types of human-paced work:

1. *Truly unpaced* The worker himself or herself determines the preferred rate.
2. *Socially paced* The peer group provides some pressure to keep pace, although management does not set a specific standard.
3. *Self-paced* Management objectives (e.g. a day rate) set a pace for the day's output. Here the worker is able to vary the pace throughout the day with the constraint of meeting the daily quota.
4. *Incentive paced* In this condition the worker may work at a pace higher than otherwise because of the financial incentives. Essentially, a monetary goal determines the worker pace.

Salvendy (1981) also lists several factors that are likely to moderate the effects of machine-paced work.

1. *Length of work cycle* The pacing begins to approximate self-pacing when the work cycle is very long. When the cycle is very short, the worker cannot vary the pace much throughout the cycle.
2. *Buffer stocks* When the worker has large buffer stocks machine pacing

begins to approximate self-pacing conditions in that interdependencies with other workers are reduced.
3. *Rate of machine pacing* Salvendy (1981) notes that the effects of the machine pacing on the worker are likely to depend to some extent on the rate that must be maintained.
4. *Continuous versus discrete pacing* In a discrete mode the line is stationary for the period of the job cycle, while in the continuous mode the line continues moving throughout the cycle. In the discrete mode the worker might have time to rest or make preparations for the next cycle.

Dainoff, Hurrell, and Happ (1981) proposed a classification of paced work that hinges on whether the worker has control over the initiation of a work cycle, its duration, or both. Completely unpaced work allows the worker to control both aspects, whereas control over neither function constitutes the most restrictive pacing condition. The Dainoff *et al.* (1981) and the Salvendy (1981) typologies thus indicate that even pacing control needs to be examined in greater complexity than its conceptual definition at first suggests. What these models imply is that the control actually experienced by the worker is the critical construct under consideration. Thus the apparent objectivity of this construct becomes compromised by taking into account the perspective of the worker. Consider Salvendy's (1981) 'incentive-paced' category. Salvendy notes: 'An incentive-paced task consists of two parts, namely the "self-paced" component and the operator's financial motivation to produce above the self-paced work' (1981, p. 7). Herein lies a conceptual difficulty with the idea of worker control. From Salvendy's machine-pacing perspective, incentive plans (e.g. piece rates) seem to have the effect of removing some of the pacing control from the worker. We might think of this as a kind of external control in the sense that the worker feels that his or her motivation to work at a particular pace is not under internal control (Deci, 1975). However, from other control theory perspectives (Bazerman, 1982; Seligman, 1975), piece rate systems seem to meet the definition of high control in that the contingencies between behaviors and outcomes are clear and direct.

Evidence regarding the stressfulness of piece rate payment systems seems more aligned with the former position (i.e. low control). For example, Timio and Gentili (1976) manipulated the payment methods for sixteen confectioners in a repeated measures design. Half of the workers started on a piece rate payment schedule then cycled to a daily pay schedule and then cycled back to a piece rate schedule, each cycle lasting for four days. The other half performed under a daily pay/piece rate/daily pay sequence. Cumulative daily measures of the excretion of adrenaline, noradrenaline, and 11-hydroxycorticosteroids showed a very large effect for the piece rate payment method, with levels of adrenaline, for example, being two to three times higher when working on piece rate. Timio and Gentili (1976) noted that the exertion levels of the workers were identical during each phase of the study, leading them to conclude that the hormonal increases reflected a 'corresponding augmentation in stress and distress' (p. 264). If the effects of piece rate were not mediated by greater exertion and work pace, were they mediated by worker perceptions of lack of control? We simply do not know. Thus, we cannot say whether this study represents a demonstration that high worker control, defined as a clear contingency between action and outcome, sometimes leads to more distress, or whether the manipulated variable, piece rate payment, really represents a loss of perceived control.

Johansson, Aronsson, and Lindstrom (1978) reported an often cited field study of work pacing effects that uses both objective assessments of pacing and self-reports of worker control. Johansson et al. classified workers in a sawmill in northern Sweden as working on high risk (n = 14) or low risk (n = 10) jobs. The high risk positions consisted of sawyers, edgermen, and graders whose work was paced by machine and involved high attentional demands. The low risk men worked as stickers, repairmen, and maintenance workers whose pace and workload were self-determined. Men in the high risk jobs exhibited a higher level of catecholamine output during the workday. They also showed a higher level of illness in the preceding year and a greater frequency of certain symptoms such as headache and slight nervous disturbance. Do these outcome differences reflect the impact of reduced personal control over work pace?

Johansson et al. (1978) examined the survey responses to a work methods questionnaire as well as the expert ratings of job content by observers. The high and low risk groups differed significantly on 21 of the expert rating factors, and these included control variables such as more autonomous work, less physical constraint, more freedom to choose order of task items, and work pace being less dependent on technology. But the low risk group also differed from the high risk group on such factors as size of work teams (smaller), size of production series (smaller), work cycles (longer), variation between tasks (more), demand for continuous attention (less), demand for precision (less), and responsibility for material and product (less).

The subjective data from the questionnaire also do not clearly show that the effects of the jobs themselves on the health outcomes were mediated through worker perceptions of control. On the one hand, individuals in the high risk group had a greater tendency to report that the workpace and noise prevented them from having contacts with co-workers. On the other hand, the high and low risk workers did *not* differ in their judgements concerning their workplace being too dependent on machines and equipment, satisfaction with their influence over the design of work procedures, or satisfaction with their general influence over work conditions. The groups *did* differ on self-reports of monotony, underutilization of ideas and knowledge, boredom, isolation, and opportunities for other employment in the area. Thus, the job groups clearly differed on a number of factors and it is impossible to isolate maching pacing, and its influence on perceived control, as the critical factor in the symptom differences between the groups.

Researchers at the US National Institute for Occupational Safety and Health (NIOSH) have also conducted a series of field studies of machine pacing, some of them focusing on machine-paced and self-paced letter sorters (e.g. Arndt, Hurrell, and Smith, 1981; Hurrell and Smith, 1981; Smith, Hurrell, and Murphy, 1981). These studies, involving thousands of workers, consistently find a variety of psychological and physical symptoms associated with the paced jobs. These include complaints such as nervousness, fatigue, heartburn, and stomach pains, as well as feelings of greater work pressure and job dissatisfaction. Smith *et al.* (1981) concluded from their study of multiple position letter-sorting machine operators that making the job self-paced might reduce the problems of perceived work pressure and reduce the high cognitive demands. However, they also noted that 'the repetitive nature of the work makes it very difficult to deal with the boredom and overall low self-esteem, and high job dissatisfaction observed' (p. 266). Again, the confounding of control over pacing with other job factors such as repetitiveness and level of workload, makes it difficult to isolate worker control as the critical variable in these studies.

Broadbent and Gath (1981) attempted to unconfound the variables of pacing control and repetitiveness, as well as cycle time. They interviewed workers in two automotive manufacturing plants and classified the jobs as being either unpaced, paced, or semi-paced. Workers in the sample were also compared on the basis of whether or not their jobs were repetitive, and on the basis of task cycle time. They found that the effects of repetitiveness were mostly on job satisfaction, whereas lack of control over pacing affected anxiety. Task cycle time had no demonstrable effects.

In general, a large body of experimental and survey research suggests that workers on externally paced jobs suffer higher levels of subjective stress and associated mental and physiological symptoms than do workers on self-paced jobs. Moreover, the presumed benefits of machine pacing in terms of higher levels of output may also be negated by the stressfulness of the working conditions (Murrell, 1963; Salvendy, 1972; Salvendy and Humphreys, 1979; Sury, 1964). The field studies have not been able to separate the effects of pacing control, *per se*, from other related factors such as repetitiveness, cycle time, and underutilization of skills and abilities. However, some controlled laboratory experiments have successfully manipulated control over pacing while controlling for variables normally confounded in field settings.

An example of a controlled laboratory experiment is provided by Johansson (1981) who assigned 30 subjects to either a 'free-tempo' or a 'paced-tempo' condition. In the free-tempo condition subjects were provided an eleven-step speed control that they could use to vary the rate of signal appearance in a choice-reaction time task. The paced-tempo subjects were each yoked to a free-tempo subject. The task itself was a complex but repetitive choice-reaction time task that included six visual and two auditory stimuli. The design thus held constant the complexity of the task, its repetitiveness, its cycle time, and all other contextual factors so that the conditions differed only in the control that subjects had over setting their workpace. Subjects were provided with performance feedback in both conditions. After three hours of work subjects were given a three-hour rest period when the experimenters could study recovery rates on the physiological variables. Following the recovery period, subjects worked on a stressful color–word conflict task in order to test after-effects of prior exposure to paced working conditions.

Measures of adrenaline and noradrenaline excretion during the work periods were taken as well as measures of subjective effort and stress. On the performance criteria of percentage correct and reaction time the paced-tempo subjects outscored the free-tempo subjects. However, the paced-tempo subjects reported higher levels of subjective effort and stress, although pacing had no apparent after-effects on the later color–word stress test. The adrenaline and noradrenaline excretion rates appeared higher for the paced-tempo subjects but these differences were not satistically reliable. Johansson (1981) concluded that the performance advantage of the paced condition was achieved at some price in worker well-being. Although the effects of pacing control seem modest here, a chronic exposure to forced pacing might be expected to produce a bigger impact. Experiments such as these demonstrate that control itself likely has some significant psychological impact, but how much of the disparity in well-being between paced and unpaced workers in field settings is uniquely attributable to this factor is unknown.

Overall, externally paced work appears to be detrimental to workers. However, it is not clear that control, that is, perceived control, is the essential intervening variable. In his review Smith (1985) concluded that the most problematic aspects of paced work were '(1) short cycle time, (2) repetitious tasks, and (3) high work pressure or production demand' (p. 62). The best evidence that control over pacing itself affects the reactions of workers comes from laboratory experiments such as that by Johansson (1981). Studies that manipulate control while also varying the levels of the variables that Smith (1985) highlights have not been done yet. It may be that, consistent with more basic experimental psychology research, control over pacing becomes important only when the other demands imposed by cycle time, repetition, or work pressure create a threatening or stressful situation.

Job Decision Latitude

The concept of job decision latitude was made prominent in the organizational literature by Karasek and his colleagues (e.g. Karasek, 1979; Karasek *et al.*

1981). Their job demands–job decision latitude model is now one of the most frequently cited theories in the occupational stress field. Karasek (1979) defined job decision latitude as 'the working individual's potential control over his tasks and his conduct during the working day' (pp. 289–90). Thus, the conceptual definition of decision latitude clearly puts it in the tradition of the job design theorists (e.g. Hackman and Oldham, 1976) as it appears very similar to job autonomy. We grant this construct its own section in this review, however, because the research addressing it has focused mostly on worker well-being, whereas job design researchers have been more concerned with job attitudes and work behaviors. In addition, even though Karasek's (1979) conceptual definition of decision latitude mirrors job autonomy, its operationalization in their research does not. We come back to this issue later.

The central proposition of the job demands–job decision latitude model is that worker well-being is determined by the interaction of job demands and latitude. Job demands are defined operationally as requirements for working fast and hard, having a great deal to do, not having enough time, and having conflicting demands. The strain experienced by the worker is expected to be high when demands are high and decision latitude is low. When demands are high but are accompanied by high levels of decision latitude, the theory predicts that new behavior patterns will be acquired and that the job is 'active'. The model is thus similar to what might be predicted from basic experimental studies in control if one thinks of job demands as potentially threatening stimuli facing the worker. In addition to the stress buffering effects of control when dealing with demanding job situations, the theory also suggests that the 'active' jobs will have regenerative effects on workers and can actually improve their well-being.

Karasek (1979) reported tests of this model with data from national surveys of workers from the United States and Sweden. The US data came from the Quality of Employment Survey (Quinn, Mangione, and Seashore, 1975) and the Swedish sample was derived from the national Level of Living Survey. Both samples included a broad and representative class of occupations. Job decision latitude in the US survey consisted of a scale composed of the following items:

1. Freedom of how to work.
2. Allows a lot of decisions.
3. Assist in one's own decisions.
4. Have a say over what happens.
5. High skill level required.
6. Required to learn new things.
7. Non-repetitious work.
8. Creativity required.

In the Swedish sample decision latitude was assessed with the following items:

1. Skill level (in years of training/education required).
2. Repetitious or monotonous work.
3. Expert rating of skill level required.

Karasek (1979) found that job decision latitude was a modest predictor of some of the outcome variables, such as pill consumption, depression, and job satisfaction. Moreover, Karasek concluded that job demands and decision latitude interacted to predict exhaustion, job dissatisfaction, and life dissatisfaction in the US data, and depression in the Swedish data. It should be noted, however, that traditional tests for interactions based on partialed product terms in regression analyses (Cohen, 1978; Cohen and Cohen, 1983) were rejected in favor of variables that reflected differences between demands and control. Thus, it is not clear that the variables truly interact to predict the outcomes.

A later study (Karasek et al., 1981) performed prospective analyses on data from the Swedish national Level of Living Surveys for 1968 and 1974. In addition to the demands and decision latitude variables measured in Karasek (1979), they also examined the impact of 'personal schedule freedom at work'. They found that skill level and job demands were each predictive of coronary heart disease indicators after controlling for age, education, smoking, and obesity. The personal schedule freedom variable was not predictive. However, in a case-control study of 22 cardiovascular–cerebrovascular deaths, schedule freedom was a significant discriminator. The interactive formulation as specified in the original model was not explicitly tested.

Later studies by Karasek and his colleagues (e.g. Alfredsson, Karasek, and Theorell, 1982; Karasek et al., 1982) examined the effects of various formulations of job demands and control by comparing the job characteristics of men with some evidence of coronary heart disease with those free of disease. In general, these findings are interpreted as supportive of the job demands–job control model. However, the interpretation of the data is complicated because of the inference method used to assign the job characteristics to the individual cases. For example, in one sample (reported in Karasek et al., 1982) data were taken from cases in the US Health Examination Survey in which a random sample of the US population were clinically interviewed and examined for the prevalence of myocardial infarction. Scores for job demands and control were assigned to each of these cases based on their three-digit census codes. Karasek et al. referred to survey data from the US Quality of Employment Survey and applied the aggregated survey responses for each occupation to the corresponding occupations in the HES data. Thus, the data really represent occupational-level analyses. It is impossible to tell how much these occupational comparisons are confounded by a host of other variables (including socioeconomic status and health behavior). Further, there is a great deal of imprecision resulting from the inability to deal with variability in the job characteristics within the occupations.

A recent analysis of data from the Framingham Heart Study (LaCroix and Haynes, 1986) examined the predictive ability of variables at the occupational and individual perception levels. Approximately 900 males and females that were surveyed in the 1960s were re-assessed for coronary heart disease after ten years. Making reference to the Karasek *et al.* (1982) classification of occupations in terms of demands and control, LaCroix and Haynes compared those in the predicted high strain occupations with those in low strain occupations. The occupational level comparisons indicated about a one and a half times higher risk for those in high strain jobs. For women, the perceptual data suggested even higher levels of risk for those working in jobs perceived to be high in demands and low in control.

The studies relating job decision latitude to coronary heart disease suffer from the limitations imposed by making secondary analyses of datasets not designed specifically to test the model. Perhaps the biggest limitation is the interpretation of the decision latitude formulations. In most of the measures of this construct in the preceding studies, items reflecting control over various workplace conditions (e.g. pacing or schedule) are combined with items reflecting skill utilization or job complexity. In this regard, the decision latitude measures are similar to Kohn and Schooler's (1973) 'occupational self-direction scale' or the combined 'autonomy' and 'variety' scales of Hackman and Oldham (1975). To the extent that any of these studies can be interpreted as demonstrating a positive impact of decision latitude on worker well-being, the same inference cannot be made about the benefits of control, *per se*. Rather, they likely reflect the influence of the more general job complexity or job scope factor.

Although the majority of studies by Karasek and his colleagues have focused on coronary heart disease as the primary outcome of interest, other efforts have examined a broader array of dependent variables (e.g. Alfredsson, Spetz, and Theorell, 1985; Theorell *et al.* 1984; Theorell *et al.*, 1985). Most of these studies sampled a broad range of occupations and made inferences about the effects of decision latitude and other work characteristics by comparing outcomes at the occupational level of analysis. The recent study reported by Karasek, Gardell, and Lindell (1987), however, employed individual level analyses and worker self-reports as the data source. There is also somewhat less diversity in social class because the sample was restricted to white-collar workers.

Karasek *et al.* (1987) analyzed surveys from a random sample of 5000 male and 3700 female full-time workers who were members of a large Swedish labor federation. The survey assessed four classes of outcome variables: (1) psychological health (depression, exhaustion, job dissatisfaction); (2) physical health (seven factors ranging from heart disease to headaches); (3) health-related behaviors (pill consumption, smoking, absenteeism); and (4) social participation (politics, sports, entertainment). In addition to the individual characteristics of age, marital status and sex, five scales measuring non-work situations (e.g. children at home, income, etc.) were also used. Six scales tapped perceived job characteristics, one of which was decision latitude (others included workload, conflict, etc.). Decision latitude was operationalized as in previous studies, incorporating items concerning ability to make decisions as well as use of skills. The analysis strategy consisted of dichotomizing all the dependent variables and computing logistic regressions separately for males and females and for different classes of predictors (e.g. work versus non-work). The authors are not clear as to why they dichotomized the outcome measures, even though many had fairly normal distributions, except to note that 'it seems easier to judge the existence of a health problem than to quantify its severity' (p. 195). For both males and females, decision latitude was significantly associated with psychological symptoms and with physical symptoms, although less strongly so with the latter. Overall, effect sizes were relatively small with job dissatisfaction being the most predictable of the outcomes. No tests were made for an interaction between demands and decision latitude, even though the latter was referred to as a 'moderator' variable.

Other Tests of an Interactive Control Model

Other researchers have tested interactive hypotheses involving demands and control, but have departed from the job decision latitude construct. Most of these studies have been cross-sectional surveys that relied on self-reports for the measurement of both independent and dependent variables. In a survey of 148 English school teachers, Payne and Fletcher (1983) measured job demands with sixteen items factored into scales for 'disciplinary demands' and 'workload demands'. Their measure of control differed from the Karasek (1979) decision latitude variable by focusing specifically on items tapping teacher autonomy over decisions at work. Job complexity and skill utilization items were not a part of the measure. As outcomes they examined psychometric measures of depression, free-floating anxiety, obsession, and somatic complaints from the Middlesex Hospital Questionnaire (Crown and Crisp, 1966) as well as a scale of minor cognitive impairments (Broadbent, 1978). Analyses of variance across subject groups formed on the basis of levels of demands, control, and social support did not uncover a significant demands–control interaction. They also constructed subtractive interaction terms of the type used by Karasek (1979), but these also failed to yield interactive effects.

Two other recent studies examined the effects of job demands and control in occupationally homogeneous populations. In a survey of 136 university clerical workers, Spector (1987) constructed a composite measure of job demands that consisted of scales for workload, role conflict, role ambiguity, and interpersonal conflict. These scales were combined into an overall index of job demands and they were also analyzed separately. Control was assessed with twelve items divided into three domains: (1) ordering of tasks and deciding how they would be done; (2) scheduling of work time, including hours of work and days off; and (3) general procedures and policies in the office. Spector tested the interactive effects of demands and control in a series of regression analyses using measures of job satisfaction, anxiety, frustration, and physical symptoms as dependent variables. The number of significant interactions barely exceeded chance expectations, and even these were not consistent with the hypothesized moderating effect of control.

McLaney and Hurrell (in press) also examined one occupational group, and thus attempted to eliminate the confounding of such variables as social class and occupational prestige with job characteristics. Moreover, their random sample of nurses from Newfoundland and Labrador was stratified on the basis of geographic location and type of employing facility. These facilities included hospitals, nursing homes, community and occupational health agencies, physicians' offices, and educational institutions. This diversity in employers should have allowed for sufficient variability in objective demands and control because of the large differences in the nature of the work and the organizational policies at these various facilities. Control perceptions were measured in four distinct domains: (1) task control (e.g. over pacing, amount of work, order of tasks); (2) decision control (e.g. over policies and procedures); (3) physical environment (e.g. over arrangement of furniture and equipment); and (4) resources (e.g., over supplies and material). These scales resulted from a factor analysis of items from a scale by Greenberger (1981), and all showed acceptable reliability.

Task demands were measured with eight different scales grouped into the categories of task demands (workload, variance in workload, cognitive demands), role demands (conflict, ambiguity, responsibility for others), and interpersonal demands (intergroup and intragroup conflict). The single outcome measure consisted of job satisfaction. Interactions were tested between both overall composite demand and control scales and between each type of demand and each type of control. Although control domains (except for decisional control) had significant main effects on satisfaction over and above the effects of demands, there was no evidence of interactions.

The Tetrick and LaRocco (1987) study, cited earlier, failed to find moderating effects for their three control scales (prediction, understanding, and control) on the relationships between role stress and psychological well-being, and between job satisfaction and well-being. Understanding and control did moderate the role stress–satisfaction relationship. However, it should be noted that, although there was evidence of interaction effects, no analyses were presented that indicated whether or not the form of the interactions fit the hypothesized model.

A study by Ganster and Mayes (1988) was designed to extend the methodology of these earlier survey studies by assessing a broader range of outcomes. These included both self-report affective measures (depression, anxiety, somatic complaints, and intent to quit) and physiological measures of strain (epinephrine and norepinephrine). Data were obtained from 306 full-time employees of a large contracting and engineering firm. The sample was occupationally diverse, with 58 per cent occupying blue-collar jobs such as electricians, plumbers, carpenters, and forklift operators. Of the white-collar segment, 60 per cent held professional or managerial positions (e.g. accountants, engineers, middle and upper managers) and the rest represented clerical, bookkeeping, and secretarial positions. Perceptions of job demands and control were obtained from a survey administered at the workplace. The demands assessment included measures of workload and variability in workload as well as measures of role conflict and ambiguity. The overall demands measure was thus conceptually similar to the constructs of Karasek (1979) and Spector (1987). The control measure combined the perceptions of control across a variety of domains, including work tasks, organizational policies, scheduling, and physical environment. The physiological measures were assayed from urine samples taken both at the beginning of the workday and at midday, with the beginning samples being used as covariates to control for off-work arousal.

Results of regression analyses revealed significant, though modest, effects of the job demands variable on the affective outcomes, although demands were not associated with the physiological measure. The main effects of control were somewhat higher than those for demands, and it correlated significantly and negatively with norepinephrine. Tests for interactions uncovered two significant effects: for intent to quit and epinephrine level. In both cases, the interactions fit the hypothesized model. That is, the impact of job demands on the outcome variable became less potent at higher levels of control. This study, then, provides partial support for the Karasek (1979) model, although the model did not fit the psychological strain variables of depression, anxiety, and somatic complaints. Following Frankenhaeuser (1979), the authors interpreted the epinephrine elevation as neuroendocrine arousal whose chronic elevation might presage the later onset of morbidity. In this sense, the findings represent some of the first evidence that the interactive formulation explains some the physiological mechanisms that intervene between job experiences and later disease development.

Finally, a laboratory experiment by Perrewe and Ganster (in press) tested the interactive demands–control model. This experiment was designed to simulate the mail sorter's job which is characterized by workload demands and repetition, and which in epidemiological field studies has been shown to be associated with physical and psychological strain (Hurrell, 1985; Hurrell and Smith, 1981). In a 2 × 2 factorial design, the level of workload demand was manipulated at high and medium levels (as determined by pre-testing), and behavioral control was manipulated at high or low levels. In this experiment, control involved a 'potential for control' manipulation, similar to the one used by Glass and Singer (1972) in their noise experiment. In the high control condition subjects were told that they could interrupt the flow of mail to be sorted if it became excessive. In addition, high control subjects were allowed other elements of task control such as rearranging the mail bins, pre-sorting bundles, and choosing between standing or sitting positions. In the high demand condition subjects were required to maintain a pace of 250 pieces per five minutes, while in the low demand condition, they had to maintain a 175-piece pace. These levels of demands were chosen on the basis of perceptual ratings of pilot subjects so as to create conditions of 'high' and 'moderate' demand. To maintain a high level of motivation, subjects were under an incentive system wherein rewards were tied to their meeting the demands of their condition. Additionally, manipulation checks in a post-experimental measure confirmed that the manipulations were perceived as intended. Outcome variables consisted of both affective measures (task satisfaction and anxiety) and physiological measures (heart rate and skin temperature). The physiological measures were taken at baseline and every five minutes throughout the work period.

The findings revealed small main effects of the demand and control variables on the affective measures, and none on the physiological variables. The only significant interaction was that between self-report measures of demands and control, and this was consistent with the model. Overall, these results provided little support for the demands–control interactive model. However, it should be noted that the manipulations employed in this study probably represented very weak approximations of the demands created in actual job conditions. Moreover, the joint effects of the factors might require longer exposures to exert their effect.

Summary

The evidence for an interactive effect of control with job stressors is relatively weak. The epidemiological findings relating coronary heart disease to occupational differences provide the most consistent, though not unanimous, support for the model. However, these data are also the most difficult to interpret in terms of worker control. The measurement of the job decision latitude construct combines control itself with what we would consider conceptually different constructs, namely, variety, skill utilization, or overall job complexity. In addition, analyses done at the occupational level are probably just too crude in their neglect of so much variability in job characteristics within the occupations.

As an illustration, consider the McLaney and Hurrell (in press) study in which they surveyed 469 nurses across a variety of employment settings. In the occupational strain classification system (Alfredsson *et al.*, 1982; Karasek *et al.*, 1982) all these nurses would have been classified in the same quadrant. In order to estimate how the variability in perceived job demands in this one occupational group compared to a more heterogeneous sampling of occupations, we compared the McLaney and Hurrell data with those of Caplan *et al.* (1975). Caplan *et al.* surveyed workers in 23 occupations ranging from machine-paced assemblers to administrative professors and physicians. The job demand variables of quantitative workload, variance in workload, and responsibility for others were measured very similarly in the two studies. The role conflict and role ambiguity variables were conceptually similar, but were measured with different scales. We computed coefficients of variation (standard deviation/ mean) for each of these variables and displayed the results in Table 1. It is apparent that there is as much variability in the sample of nurses as there is across a fairly wide range of occupations. Only in responsibility for others, a variable not included in the Karasek *et al.* (1982) formulation of demands, does there seem to be any appreciable difference in relative variability. On the one hand, these comparisons might only be suggestive of the tenuous linkage between objective work conditions and employee perceptions of them. However, the Karasek *et al.* (1982) classification of occupations (the basis for their 'objective' analyses) depends on these aggregated perceptions. On the other hand, we would presume that such characteristics as workload, role conflict, and 'hectic pace' are determined less by one's occupation than they are by the particular employment situation faced by the individual. The latter presumption is the only basis for us to hope that we could intervene (e.g. through job redesign) to make the worker's job less stressful.

Table 1 — Comparison of Coefficients of Variation for Job Demands in Single and Multiple Occupation Samples

Demand variable	Nurses[a]	23 Occupations[b]
Workload	.16	.16
Workload variability	.21	.24
Role conflict	.37	.37
Role ambiguity	.37	.41
Responsibility for others	.31	.45

[a] Computed from data reported in McLaney and Hurrell (in press)
[b] Computed from data reported in Caplan *et al.* (1975), Table IV-3, pp. 119–123

The survey studies analyzed at the individual level are considerably less supportive of the job demands–job control model. Although a reliance on employee perceptions has its own limitations, it is not clear that any resulting methodological bias should operate against the model rather than in its favor. Thus, although the model has some intuitive appeal and is gaining a wide acceptance (e.g. Baker, 1985), its empirical validity is yet to be established.

INDIVIDUAL DIFFERENCE VARIABLES

When one focuses on employee perceptions of control to explain the impact of environmental factors on employee outcomes, one is forced to deal with the possible impact of dispositional variables on both control and outcome variables. Machine pacing, performance-based pay systems, and job scope might all affect worker control perceptions. However, stable dispositional factors might also contribute to these perceptions independently of the objective characteristics of the job. In addition, other dispositions might affect how workers respond to their control beliefs. In this section we examine two dispositional variables, locus of control and Type A behavior pattern, each of which is expected to operate in one of these two ways.

Locus of Control

Locus of control (LOC) refers to a relatively stable belief that what happens to an individual is caused primarily by the person himself or herself, rather than other forces such as powerful others or chance (Rotter, 1966). *Internals* believe that they are the primary determiners of their outcomes, whereas *externals* attribute their outcomes to external forces. Because locus of control represents a 'generalized expectancy' about the relationship between one's own actions and subsequent events, we would expect internals generally to perceive more opportunities than externals for control in their work situation, quite independently of the situation itself. In this regard, we need to ask whether self-report measures of control in the workplace really are assessing anything other than the general tendency of the employee to perceive himself or herself as in control. From Spector's (1982) review of the locus of control literature, it appears that LOC does affect some control perceptions. For example, a number of studies have demonstrated that internal employees have higher expectancies about the relationship between effort and job performance and between performance and rewards (Broedling, 1975; Evans, 1974; Kimmons and Greenhaus, 1976; Lied and Pritchard, 1976; Szilagyi and Sims, 1975). There are few data, however, to show that internals are more likely than externals to perceive control over a broader spectrum of work processes (e.g. control over pacing, scheduling, work methods, etc.). Although one study reported a relationship between internal LOC and job autonomy (Kimmons and Greenhaus, 1976), another study did not (Frost and Wilson, 1983).

Theoretically, locus of control should act primarily as a dispositional antecedent of control perceptions at work. However, a number of investigators have examined the moderating, or interactive, role of LOC in the work context as well. For example, Runyon (1973) found that internals reacted more positively (in terms of satisfaction with supervision) than externals to participative leadership styles, and Cravens and Worchel (1977) found that internals were less cooperative with coercive supervisors than were externals. Both of these findings suggest that internals *prefer* work situations in which they have control, and this preference is consistent with laboratory research indicating that internals prefer tasks involving skill rather than luck (Kahle, 1980) and games where they rely on their own skill rather than someone else's (Julian and Katz, 1968).

From this same premise, Marino and White (1985) predicted that internals would find situations more stressful in which they had little freedom to react and control work conditions. They found little support for this hypothesis, however, except that internals reported more stress in response to job specificity (lack of autonomy) than did externals. Moreover, Kimmons and Greenhaus (1976) found no moderating effect for the relationship between autonomy and satisfaction, and Sims and Szilagyi (1976) found that the autonomy–work satisfaction correlation was actually higher for externals than for internals.

Although the evidence is inconclusive about the differential attractiveness of autonomy for internals and externals, the results of one study suggest that internals perform better under self-pacing conditions. Eskew and Riche (1982) created a simulated quality control inspection task in which subjects were required to rapidly scan circuit boards for defects. Some subjects were given control over the pacing (by use of a delay switch) and were matched with yoked controls who worked under the same pace but had no personal control over it. They found that internals made fewer false alarms than externals when they were self-paced, and the opposite occurred under machine pacing.

More recently, investigators have examined the moderating effects of LOC on relationships between affective relationships and behavioral reactions. Reasoning that internals would be more apt to take controlling actions, Spector (1982) hypothesized that they would be more likely than externals to leave their jobs if they were dissatisfied. Blau (1987) tested this notion with a sample of 119 nurses, surveying them for LOC, several facets of job satisfaction, and turnover intentions. Blau found that the correlations between job satisfaction (satisfaction with pay and promotions) and turnover cognitions were stronger for internals, as were the relationships between these cognitions and turnover itself.

Storms and Spector (1987) examined the relationships between 'organizational frustration' and behavioral reports of aggression, sabotage, withdrawal, and intention to quit. They hypothesized that externals would be more likely to react to frustration with aggressive or counterproductive behaviors. This hypothesis was derived from research by Allen and Greenberger (1980), who found that lowered perceived control can stimulate attempts to alter the environment through acts of destruction as a means of regaining a sense of personal control. They also referred to Taylor and Walton's (1971) conclusions that a major reason for worker sabotage is workers' attempts to exert control. As predicted, where internals and externals differed, the relationships between the frustration and behavioral variables were stronger for the externals.

In summary, there is some evidence that LOC is a dispositional antecedent of control perceptions at work, but these mainly seem to involve perceptions about behavior–outcome contingencies. Perceptions regarding broader areas of control, such as work autonomy, are uncorrelated with LOC. It thus is tenuous to assume that LOC is a general proxy for perceived situational control, though in a given situation we might expect internals to perceive that they have more control. Fusilier, Ganster, and Mayes (1987) reasoned that this tendency to perceive situations as controllable would lead internals to be more active in their coping efforts when faced with a job stressor. Accordingly, they hypothesized, and found, that role conflict was more strongly related to somatic complaints for externals than internals.

Finally, although there is some evidence that internals prefer more participative and less coercive supervision, the evidence that they generally prefer situations with more autonomy is fairly weak. LOC seems to be more important in explaining how people react behaviorally to dissatisfying or frustrating situations than it is in explaining whether they perceive the situations that way. Nevertheless, the evidence relating LOC to situational control beliefs is scant, and further work is needed that examines its relationship to other measures of worker control.

Type A Behavior Pattern

The Type A coronary-prone behavior pattern is another individual difference variable that might affect how people react to control in the workplace. (For recent reviews of Type A in the workplace, see Ganster, 1987 and Ivancevich and Matteson, 1988.) Presumably, situational demands elicit behavioral responses of Type As, including hostility, competitiveness, and aggression. Glass (1977) theorized that the primary situational determinant of this response pattern was a threat to perceived control. Evidence suggests that in laboratory settings, Type As are more likely to attempt to maintain control in a task even when giving it up to another might increase their attainment of desired outcomes (Miller, Lack, and Asroff, 1985; Strube, Berry, and Moergen, 1985; Strube and Werner, 1985). They also seem to prefer a higher level of control over environmental events (Dembroski, MacDougall, and Musante, 1984; Smith and O'Keefe, 1985).

There are only a few studies that have examined the differential responses of Types A and B to variables relevant to control in the workplace. Chesney and Rosenman (1980) administered a scale measuring perceptions of control at work to 76 male managers and also conducted the Structured Interview assessment of Type A behavior. When they trichotomized the sample on the control scale, they found that Type As in low control conditions reported more anxiety than Type As experiencing high control. Moreover, Type Bs reported more anxiety when they were in control than when they were not. Chesney *et al.* (1981) measured Type A and perceptions of the work environment on a sample of 384 salaried workers. When they split the sample on a work autonomy scale, they found that Type As had lower blood pressure with high autonomy than with low autonomy, whereas Type Bs had higher blood pressure with high autonomy.

The two previous studies provide some indication that the Type A behavior pattern might determine one's response to control at work, but in both cases less than optimal statistical methods (specifically, failure to test explicitly for interactions) make the conclusions tentative. A study by Hurrell (1985) is interesting because he examined the interaction between Type A and an objective control variable. Hurrell surveyed 5518 postal workers, 2803 working on machine-paced letter sorting jobs, and 2715 working on self-paced jobs. He reasoned that machine pacing would be interpreted as lack of control, particularly by the Type A workers. However, he found no evidence that Type As responded any more negatively (in terms of psychological strain) to pacing than did Type Bs.

Thus, the Type A behavior pattern would seem to be a likely candidate as a moderator of worker responses to control, as LOC would seem to be a likely dispositional antecedent of situation control perceptions. However, there are very few studies examining Type A–control interactions in the work context, and the results of these fail to present a clear picture.

WORKPLACE INTERVENTIONS AND CONTROL

There is no systematic body of research in which intervention attempts have been made with the specific purpose of augmenting employee control beliefs. Jackson's (1983) participation experiment is one of the few studies in which an intervention was linked to subsequent employee control perceptions. However, there are a variety of intervention approaches in the organizational literature that should have an impact on employee control, although the effects on employee perceived control have rarely been assessed. In this section we review several recent studies that touch on the control issue, though this contact is sometimes indirect.

The implementation of *quality circles* is one popular means of increasing employee participation at the level of immediate task and work processes. The goals of most quality circle applications center on generating high quality solutions to productivity problems. However, the broader goals of many of these programs concern increasing the level of job skill of the workers and making their jobs more enriched. Despite the proliferation of such programs, most evaluations of their effects consist of case study testimonials or inadequately controlled before and after designs. A recent study by Marks, Mirvis, Hackett, and Grady (1986) represents one of the better designs in this area, as well as an attempt to assess the effects of participation in the quality circle on intervening employee perceptions.

Marks et al. allowed employees to volunteer for a QC program in a manufacturing plant: 53 of 109 employees eligible did so, and the others were used as a control group. All employees were surveyed just prior to the QC start-up and again after 20 months. There was some evidence that the QC program had a beneficial effect on productivity and absenteeism. However, there was no evidence that these effects were mediated through employee control perceptions. There were only two self-report scales relevant to these perceptions — participation in decision making and personal responsibility. There was no apparent effect of the QC program on the latter, and a significant difference between the treatment and control groups on participation perceptions appeared to arise from a drop in participation scores for the control group rather than from an increase in the treatment group.

Employee involvement in the development and implementation of new computer systems is another area of control receiving some attention by practitioners and researchers. Frese (1987), for example, examined German workers whose jobs changed because of the introduction of computer technology. He found that those who had the highest control over the technological changes also reported the greatest improvement in their work situations, and suffered from the least anxiety and somatic complaints. Frese (1987) also reported that engineers showed a greater transfer of learning from their training programs to their work when they experienced high control at work. Frese thus concluded that buying expensive computers and providing extensive training would be useless unless the organization provided sufficient control to the users.

Baronas and Louis (1988) conducted an experiment in which they tried to increase the sense of control of workers whose computer systems were undergoing a major changeover. This study is unusual in that the investigators began with a control theory perspective, and designed their treatment condition so as to address specific aspects of employee control. Baronas and Louis reasoned that a significant cause of the anxiety and resistance to change that is so often experienced by users of a computer system when it undergoes a change is the threat of loss of control over their work processes. They studied employees of 35 small state government agencies that were scheduled to convert to a new computer system. Some of the agencies were scheduled to change over in the first three months of the study, and they were used as a control group (N = 43 employees). The other 22 agencies were to change over in the subsequent four months and they were slated to receive an experimental treatment as part of their changeover orientation (N = 49 employees). The treatment consisted of modifications to the standard implementation plan that was used for the control group. These changes were incorporated specifically to increase employees' sense of choice, responsibility, and predictability regarding the new computer system. Questionnaires were administered ten weeks before the change date, two weeks after, and two months after.

The results generally showed that the treatment group reported higher levels of satisfaction with the new system and that they felt that their managers had more positive attitudes about the implementation. However, there were no differences in ratings of the stressfulness of the changeover, and differences between the groups on their ratings of implementation success, although in the right direction, did not reach statistical significance. This study is interesting because it represents a conscious attempt to manipulate employee control beliefs concerning a stressful work event (the employees did report it as stressful). However, the investigators failed to document adequately the effectiveness of their intervention in terms of these beliefs. Only two items assessed the efficacy of the manipulations. The groups did not differ in their feelings regarding how much their managers encouraged participation during implementation, and the groups were only marginally different in how much they felt their opinions were listened to during the changeover. Thus, there is some question as to how effectively the hypothesized intervening variable, perceived control, was manipulated.

Flextime is another structural intervention that would be expected to increase employee perceptions of control, albeit in one specific domain. Reviews of flextime applications (e.g. Golembiewski and Proehl, 1978, 1980) indicate that they are generally viewed favorably by the participants. However, there is no convincing evidence that control perceptions are significantly affected by these programs, or even that their effects on productivity are mediated through attitudinal variables. In an experimental design with a long-term follow-up, Ralston, Anthony, and Gustafson (1985) found that a flextime intervention led to significant increases in productivity, but only for workers who shared scarce physical resources on the job. Unfortunately, they collected no data regarding employee attitudes or perceptions, but the productivity effects seemed to arise mainly from greater efficiencies and less wasted time for the scarce resource workers.

Many experimental interventions target limited areas of employee control, flextime being one example. Interventions falling under the socio-technical systems model (Emery, 1959), however, would be expected to have rather broad implications for employee control. Central to this approach is the establishment of the 'autonomous work group', although changes in other aspects of management, specifically supervisory practices, are also considered to be necessary concomitants. There are many examples of autonomous work group interventions, but so many aspects of the work situation are usually changed that it is hard to isolate the role of employee control perceptions in the whole endeavor. Moreover, many evaluations of these efforts are based on research designs that allow limited causal inference.

A relatively strong evaluation study was conducted by Kemp, Wall, Clegg, and Cordery (1983). Although random assignment to experimental conditions was not feasible, the design was relatively strong in that the investigators matched up the intervention group with three control groups. These groups were chosen to control for unique site effects and shift effects. As with most such autonomous work group programs, workers in the experimental group experienced a variety of working conditions that were different from traditional work groups. However, the intent of this intervention was to provide shopfloor workers with a high level of autonomy in carrying out their tasks. The investigators conducted time sample observations of the work groups using the Turner and Lawrence (1965) requisite task attributes (RTA) model. This assessment covers characteristics intrinsic to the nature of the tasks, such as variety, autonomy, task identity, cycle time, responsibility, and interaction opportunities. These data further demonstrated that the essential feature of the intervention concerned decision-making responsibilities, because the RTA ratings were the same across the groups, yet ratings of the level of decision-making activities showed the expected differences. This case then might represent the best approximation that we can expect to find of a condition where job demands are left relatively unchanged but employee control, through increased decision-making responsibility, is increased.

Questionnaire data concerning worker perceptions and attitudes, as well as general mental health, were taken after six months of production at the new experimental site. The groups differed as expected on measures of perceived work characteristics, supervisory styles, and group decision making. However, there was no apparent effect on mental health. Moreover, the experimental group was higher on a measure of intrinsic job satisfaction, but not on measures of motivation, commitment, and trust in management. The results of this carefully conducted and reported study suggest that decision-making control has its greatest impact on job attitudes as opposed to motivation or performance (although data on the latter were not available). The lack of significance for the mental health measures is somewhat difficult to interpret. On the one hand, they argue against the validity of decision latitude models such as Gardell's (1971) and Karasek's (1979). On the other hand, a six-month exposure to these working conditions probably does not represent a fair test of the health impact of the jobs.

Overall, there is a paucity of research that explicitly links organizational interventions with employee control beliefs. In many cases what is needed is just the addition of sound measures of employee control perceptions to the evaluation design. Such measures, for example, might have helped us understand the Baronas and Louis (1988) data, where it was unclear whether an intervention specifically designed to increase aspects of employee control beliefs succeeded in doing so. The related problem with the intervention literature is the frequent inability to separate changes in employee control from other factors that are likely affected by the intervention. Interest in targeting interventions directly at control processes seems to be just developing, however, and we expect to see more attempts at isolating the effects of control, *per se*, from other working conditions.

SUMMARY AND CONCLUSIONS

Job Attitudes

If one views participation in decision making, self-pacing of work, flextime, and job autonomy as different types of control at work, then there is much evidence that workers find control desirable. It might be premature, however, to conclude that all manifestations of employee control will have positive effects on job attitudes. First, almost all of the evidence from organizational settings is correlational. Thus it is difficult to separate the effects of control from other work characteristics, such as repetitiveness, use of skills, and overall complexity, that are almost always correlated with it. Second, apart from potential spuriousness, the effects of control on affective outcomes might to some extent depend on the level of other job characteristics. This interactive effect is predicted by at least one job design theory (Hackman and Oldham, 1976), and it might explain the failure of some studies (e.g. Farh and Scott, 1983) to find a positive impact for autonomy.

Job Performance

The impact of control on work performance is more difficult to estimate. Some control measures (e.g. participation and autonomy) generally correlate with job performance, although at a lower magnitude than with attitudinal measures. Of course, the same inferential limitations exist here as with the affective correlations. The experimental evidence, however, is far from uniformly supportive of a positive effect of control on performance. The machine pacing literature (e.g. Johansson, 1981), for example, suggests that higher control (self-pacing) can lead to lower performance. In a relatively low complexity task, giving workers more choice among task activities might also lead to lower performance (Farh and Scott, 1983). It seems likely, however, that the effect of control on performance depends on its interaction with other task characteristics such as variety, and especially feedback (Dodd, 1987).

Stress and Well-being

The basic experimental literature is most closely connected to the issue of control's impact on worker stress and well-being. Controlled studies with subjects ranging from rats to college sophomores all support the basic validity of the proposition that control beliefs can lessen the experienced stressfulness, and perhaps the negative physiological effects, of exposure to threatening events. This is a compelling proposition to transfer to the work setting, and Karasek's (1979) job decision latitude model is one translation of it. However, it has proven to be a difficult model to test. The most supportive findings are generally the result of occupational-level analyses, and even these do not really present a convincing case that control actually conditions the relationship between job demands and well-being. Furthermore, the supporting studies take a broad approach to control, and combine aspects of instrumental control with other job characteristics such as skill use and complexity. Thus, job decision latitude is not directly comparable to the instrumental control construct that the experimental researchers focus on. Those organizational researchers who have used measures more closely related to this instrumental control construct have generally not shown that control moderates the relationship between job demands and well-being. However, studies of this type are still relatively scarce, and there is some evidence that points to a moderating role of control on physiological responses, if not affective ones (e.g. Ganster and Mayes, 1988).

Directions for Research

Though the empirical support is not yet convincing, the exploration of control as a potential 'antidote' to stressful work demands is rich with possibility. It should continue to occupy the attention of organizational scholars. As we noted, control has played a prominent role in the work of personality theorists as well as experimental and comparative psychologists. Moreover, control theory has additional appeal in organizational settings because of its implications for the dual outcomes of worker well-being and job performance. The practical upshot of a theory that posits control as a buffer of job demands is that one can intervene to improve the quality of the work environment without reducing the level of the demands themselves. The plausibility of this expectation is boosted by the findings of most field studies that show virtually no correlation between measures of these two constructs. Thus, we think that field experimentation in this area is both highly desirable from a scientific standpoint and from a practical perspective. Consideration should be given to several factors if such intervention research is attempted.

First, as we noted above, there are many types of organizational interventions that have implications for employee control. Unfortunately, the effects of these interventions on employee control perceptions are rarely considered by the investigators, and when they are (e.g. Baronas and Louis, 1988) inadequate attention is given to their measurement (an exception would be Jackson, 1983). Several scales exist that address various facets of control beliefs (e.g. Greenberger, 1981; Jackson, 1983; Tetrick and LaRocco, 1987), and some writers have made suggestions about which areas of control should be addressed (e.g.

Fisher, 1985; Ganster, 1988, in press). These scales probably provide reasonable starting-off points, but researchers should give thought to the particular domains of control that are important for their particular intervention effort or setting and ensure that these are assessed in their measures.

Second, the impact that control has on workers may be direct or indirect. A direct effect of control would be postulated, for example, by theorists who propose that internal control beliefs are an essential ingredient of psychological well-being. However, control's impact may be indirect if workers use their control to alter their work demands. This 'mediating' effect of job demands to explain the impact of control on workers is not the same as the hypothesized moderating effect of control. In the latter case, control is thought to determine the appraisal of the demands as threatening or unreasonable, and thus condition the relationship between demands and worker outcomes. Such a moderating effect is consistent with findings in the goal-setting literature that show that workers have greater acceptance of difficult goals over which they have some control (e.g. Erez and Earley, 1987). The mediating role of job demands, however, posits a different causal sequence. It seems that experimental researchers have two choices. One is to control for job demands by effectively holding them constant, as with the use of yoked-control designs; this strategy eliminates the possibility of testing a mediating model. The other strategy is to allow demands to vary (as would typically occur in an action research approach), but to document carefully the changes in job demands that arise from the use of the augmented control. Either approach has promise, and the choice depends on the primary hypothesis-testing aim of the researcher.

Finally, even if we assert that the critical causal process depends on perceptions, we still need to ground these perceptions in the objective environment. Intervention studies have the ability to establish the empirical linkage between objective aspects of the work environment and worker control perceptions. Relevant dispositional variables, such as locus of control or Type A behavior, should be considered for inclusion in control experiments, because they might either contribute directly to situational control beliefs or affect the employee's reaction to the intervention. Their use thus should contribute to our understanding of the objective–subjective connection, as well as help disentangle the effects of dispositions from those of organizational factors.

REFERENCES

Abbott, B. B., Schoen, L. S., and Badia, P. (1984) Predictable and unpredictable shock: Behavioral measures of aversion and physiological measures of stress. *Psychological Bulletin*, **96**, 45–71.

Abramson, L. Y., and Alloy, L. B. (1980) Judgment of contingency: Errors and their implications. In A. Baum and J. E. Singer (eds), *Advances in Environmental Psychology*, Vol. 2. Hillsdale, NJ: Erlbaum, pp. 112–130.

Abramson, L. Y., Seligman, M. E. P., and Teasdale, J. D. (1978) Learned helplessness in humans: Critique and reformulation. *Journal of Abnormal Psychology*, **87**, 49–74.

Adelmann, P. K. (1987) Occupational complexity, control, and personal income: Their relation to psychological well-being in men and women. *Journal of Applied Psychology*, **72**, 529–537.

Adler, A. (1930) Individual psychology. In C. Murchison (ed.), *Psychologies of 1930*. Worcester, MA: Clark University Press.

Alfredsson, L., Karasek, R., and Theorell, T. (1982) Myocardial infarction risk and psychosocial work environment: An analysis of the male Swedish working force. *Social Science and Medicine*, **16**, 463–467.

Alfredsson, L., Spetz, C. L., and Theorell, T. (1985) Type of occupation and near-future hospitalization for myocardial infarction and some other diagnoses. *International Journal of Epidemiology*, **14**, 378–388.

Allen, V. L., and Greenberger, D. B. (1980) Destruction and perceived control. In A. Baum and J. Singer (eds), *Applications of Personal Control*. Hillsdale, NJ: Lawrence Erlbaum.

Arndt, R., Hurrell, J. J., Jr, and Smith, M. J. (1981) Comparison of biochemical and survey results of a four-year study of letter-sorting machine operators. In G. Salvendy and M. J. Smith (eds), *Machine Pacing and Occupational Stress*. London: Taylor & Francis, pp. 311–318.

Averill, J. (1973) Personal control over aversive stimuli and its relationship to stress. *Psychological Bulletin*, **80**, 286–303.

Baker, D. B. (1985) The study of stress at work. *Annual Review of Public Health*, **6**, 67–81.

Bandura, A. (1977) Self-efficacy: Toward a unifying theory of behavioral change. *Psychological Review*, **84**, 191–215.

Baronas, A-M. K., and Louis, M. R. (1988) Restoring a sense of control during implementation: How user involvement leads to system acceptance. *MIS Quarterly*, **12**, 111–124.

Bazerman, M. H. (1982) Impact of personal control on performance: Is added control always beneficial? *Journal of Applied Psychology*, **67**, 472–479.

Blau, G. J. (1987) Locus of control as a potential moderator of the turnover process. *Journal of Occupational Psychology*, **60**, 21–29.

Blauner, R. (1964) *Alienation and Freedom: The factory worker and his industry*. Chicago: University of Chicago Press.

Brady, J. V., Porter, R. W., Conrad, D. G., and Maso, J. W. (1958) Avoidance behavior and the development of gastroduodenal ulcers. *Journal of the Experimental Analysis of Behavior*, **1**, 69–72.

Breaugh, J. A. (1985) The measurement of work autonomy. *Human Relations*, **38**, 551–570.

Brehm, J. W. (1966) *A Theory of Psychological Reactance*. New York: Academic Press.

Broadbent, D. E. (1978) *A Questionnaire for Measuring Cognitive Failures*. Department of Experimental Psychology, University of Oxford.

Broadbent, D. E., and Gath, D. (1981) Symptom levels in assembly-line workers. In G. Salvendy and M. J. Smith (eds), *Machine Pacing and Occupational Stress*. London: Taylor & Francis, pp. 243–252.

Broedling, L. A. (1975) Relationship of internal–external control to work motivation and performance in an expectancy model. *Journal of Applied Psychology*, **60**, 65–70.

Caplan, R. D., Cobb, S., French, J. R. P., Jr, Harrison, R. V., and Pinneau, S. R. (1975) *Job Demands and Worker Health*. US Department of Health, Education, and Welfare: Publication No. (NIOSH) 75–160.

Chesney, M. A., and Rosenman, R. H. (1980) Type A behaviour in the work setting. In C. L. Cooper and R. Payne (eds), *Current Concerns in Occupational Stress*. New York: Wiley, pp. 187-212.
Chesney, M. A., Sevelius, G., Black, G., Ward, M., Swan, G., and Rosenman, R. (1981) Work environment, Type A behavior, and coronary heart disease risks. *Journal of Occupational Medicine*, 23, 551-555.
Cohen, J. (1978) Partialled products *are* interactions; partialled powers *are* curve components. *Psychological Bulletin*, 85, 858-866.
Cohen, J., and Cohen, P. (1983) *Applied Multiple Regression/Correlation Analysis for the Behavioral Sciences*. Hillsdale, NJ: Lawrence Erlbaum.
Cravens, R. W., and Worchel, P. (1977) The differential effects of rewarding and coercive leaders on group members differing in locus of control. *Journal of Personality*, 45, 150-168.
Crown, S., and Crisp, A. H. (1966) A short clinical diagnostic self-rating scale for psychoneurotic patients. *British Journal of Psychiatry*, 112, 917-923.
Dainoff, M. J. Hurrell, J. J., Jr, and Happ, A. (1981) A taxonomic framework for the description and evaluation of paced work. In G. Salvendy and M. J. Smith (eds), *Machine Pacing and Occupational Stress*. London: Taylor & Francis, pp. 185-190.
deCharms, R. (1968) *Personal Causation*. New York: Academic.
Deci, E. L. (1975) *Intrinsic Motivation*. New York: Plenum Press.
Dembroski, T. M., MacDougall, J. M., and Musante, L. (1984) Desirability of control versus locus of control: Relationship to paralinguistics in the Type A interview. *Health Psychology*, 3, 15-26.
Dodd, N. G. (1987) The interaction of autonomy, variety, and feedback to predict satisfaction and performance: A laboratory experiment. Unpublished Doctoral dissertation, University of Nebraska.
Emery, F. E. (1959) *Characteristics of Socio-Technical Systems*. London: Tavistock Institute of Human Relations.
Erez, M., and Earley, P. C. (1987) Comparative analysis of goal-setting strategies across cultures. *Journal of Applied Psychology*, 72, 658-665.
Eskew, R. T., and Riche, C. V., Jr (1982) Pacing and locus of control in quality control inspection. *Human Factors*, 24, 411-415.
Evans, M. G. (1974) Extensions of a path–goal theory of motivation. *Journal of Applied Psychology*, 59, 172-178.
Farh, J.-L., and Scott, W. E., Jr (1983) The experimental effects of 'autonomy' on performance and self-reports of satisfaction. *Organizational Behavior and Human Performance*, 31, 203-222.
Fisher, S. (1985) Control and blue collar work. In C. L. Cooper and M. J. Smith (eds), *Job Stress and Blue Collar Work*. New York: Wiley, pp. 19-48.
Frankenhaeuser, M. (1979) Psychoneuroendocrine approaches to the study of emotion as related to stress and coping. In H. E. Howe, Jr and R. A. Dienstbier (eds), *Nebraska Symposium on Motivation, 1978: Human Emotion*, Vol. 27. Lincoln: University of Nebraska Press.
Frese, M. (1987) A concept of control: Implications for stress and performance in human–computer interaction. In G. Salvendy, S. L. Sauter, and J. J. Hurrell, Jr, *Social, Ergonomic and Stress Aspects of Work with Computers*. Amsterdam: Elsevier Science.
Frost, T. F., and Wilson, H. G. (1983) Effects of locus of control and A-B personality type on job satisfaction within the health care field. *Psychological Reports*, 53, 399-405.
Fusilier, M. R., Ganster, D. C., and Mayes, B. T. (1987) Effects of social support, role stress, and locus of control on health. *Journal of Management*, 13, 517-528.

Ganster, D. C. (1980) Individual differences and task design: A laboratory experiment. *Organizational Behavior and Human Performance*, **26**, 131–148.
Ganster, D. C. (1987) Type A behavior and occupational stress. In J. Ivancevich and D. Ganster (eds), *Job Stress: From theory to suggestion*. New York: Haworth Press.
Ganster, D. C. (1988) Improving measures of worker control in occupational stress research. In J. J. Hurrell, Jr, L. R. Murphy, S. L. Sauter, and C. L. Cooper (eds), *Occupational Stress: Issues and Developments in Research*. London: Taylor and Francis, pp. 88–99.
Ganster, D. C. (in press) Worker control and well-being: A review of research in the workplace. In S. L. Sauter, J. J. Hurrell, Jr, and C. L. Cooper (eds), *Job Control and Worker Health*. Chichester: John Wiley & Sons.
Ganster, D. C., and Mayes, B. T. (1988) A field test of the interactive effects of job demands and control on worker well-being. Paper presented at the Academy of Management meeting, Anaheim, CA.
Gardell, B. (1971) Alienation and mental health in the modern industrial environment. In L. Levi (ed.), *Society, Stress, and Disease*, Vol. 1. London: Oxford University Press, pp. 148–180.
Gardell, B. (1977) Autonomy and participation at work. *Human Relations*, **30**, 515–533.
Geer, J. H., and Maisel, E. (1972) Evaluating the effect of the prediction control confound. *Journal of Personality and Social Psychology*, **23**, 314–319.
Glass, D. C. (1977) *Behavior Patterns, Stress, and Coronary Disease*. Hillsdale, NJ: Lawrence Erlbaum.
Glass, D. C., Reim, B., and Singer, J. E. (1971) Behavioral consequences of adaptation to controllable and uncontrollable noise. *Journal of Experimental Psychology*, **7**, 244–257.
Glass, D. C., and Singer, J. E. (1972) *Urban Stress: Experiments on noise and social stressors*. New York: Academic Press.
Golembiewski, R. T., and Proehl, C. W. (1978) A survey of the empirical literature on flexible workhours: Character and consequence of a major innovation. *Academy of Management Review*, **3**, 837–853.
Golembiewski, R. T., and Proehl, C. W. (1980) Public sector applications of flexible workhours: A review of available experience. *Public Administration Review*, **40**, 72–85.
Greenberger, D. (1981) Personal control at work: Its conceptualization and measurement. (Technical Report 1-1-4, University of Wisconsin-Madison; NR 170–892.)
Hackman, J. R., and Lawler, E. E. (1971) Employee reactions to job characteristics. *Journal of Applied Psychology Monograph*, **55**, 259–286.
Hackman, J. R., and Oldham, G. R. (1975) Development of the Job Diagnostic Survey. *Journal of Applied Psychology*, **60**, 159–170.
Hackman, J. R., and Oldham, G. R. (1976) Motivation through the design of work: Test of a theory. *Organizational Behavior and Human Performance*, **16**, 250–279.
Haggard, E. A. (1943) Experimental studies in affective processes: I. Some effects of cognitive structure and active participation on certain autonomic reactions during and following experimentally induced stress. *Journal of Experimental Psychology*, **33**, 257–284.
Herzberg, F., Mausner, B., and Snyderman, B. B. (1959) *The Motivation to Work*. New York: Wiley.
Hoffman, L. R., Burke, R. J., and Maier, N. R. F. (1965) Participation, influence, and satisfaction among members of problem-solving groups. *Psychological Reports*, **16**, 661–667.
Hurrell, J. J., Jr (1985) Machine-paced work and the Type A behavior pattern. *Journal of Occupational Psychology*, **58**, 15–25.

Hurrell, J. J., Jr and Smith, M. J. (1981) Sources of stress among machine-paced letter-sorting-machine operators. In G. Salvendy and M. J. Smith (eds), *Machine Pacing and Occupational Stress*. London: Taylor & Francis Ltd, pp. 253–259.

Ivancevich, J. M., and Matteson, M. T. (1988) Type A behavior and the healthy individual. *British Journal of Medical Psychology*, **61**, 37–56.

Jackson, S. E. (1983) Participation in decision making as a strategy for reducing job-related strain. *Journal of Applied Psychology*, **68**, 3–19.

Johansson, G. (1981) Individual control in a monotonous task: Effects on performance, effort, and physiological arousal. Reports from the Department of Psychology, University of Stockholm.

Johansson, G., Aronsson, G., and Lindstrom, B. O. (1978) Social psychological and neuroendocrine reactions in highly mechanised work. *Ergonomics*, **21**, 583–589.

Julian, J. W., and Katz, S. B. (1968) Internal versus external control and the value of reinforcement. *Journal of Personality and Social Psychology*, **8**, 89–94.

Kahle, L. R. (1980) Stimulus condition self-selection by males in the interaction of locus of control and skill–chance situations. *Journal of Personality and Social Psychology*, **38**, 50–56.

Karasek, R. A. (1979) Job demands, job decision latitude, and mental strain: Implications for job design. *Administrative Science Quarterly*, **24**, 285–306.

Karasek, R. A., Baker, D., Marxer, F., Ahlbom, A., and Theorell, T. (1981) Job decision latitude, job demands, and cardiovascular disease: A prospective study of Swedish men. *American Journal of Public Health*, **71**, 694–705.

Karasek, R. A., Gardell, B., and Lindell, J. (1987) Work and non-work correlates of illness and behaviour in male and female Swedish white collar workers. *Journal of Occupational Behaviour*, **8**, 187–207.

Karasek, R. A., Theorell, T. G., Schwartz, J., Pieper, C., and Alfredsson, L. (1982) Job, psychological factors and coronary heart disease: Swedish prospective findings and US prevalence findings using a new occupational inference method. *Advances in Cardiology*, **29**, 62–67.

Kemp, N. J., Wall, T. D., Clegg, C. W., and Cordery, J. L. (1983) Autonomous work groups in a greenfield site: A comparative study. *Journal of Occupational Psychology*, **56**, 271–288.

Kiggundu, M. N. (1983) Task interdependence and job design: Test of a theory. *Organizational Behavior and Human Performance*, **31**, 145–172.

Kimmons, G., and Greenhaus, J. H. (1976) Relationship between locus of control and reactions of employees to work characteristics. *Psychological Reports*, **39**, 815–820.

Kohn, R., and Schooler, C. (1973) Occupational experience and psychological functioning: An assessment of reciprocal effects. *American Sociological Review*, **38**, 97–118.

LaCroix, A. Z., and Haynes, S. G. (1986) Gender differences in the stressfulness of workplace roles: A focus on work and health. In R. Barnett, G. Baruch, and L. Biener (eds), *Gender and Stress*. New York: Free Press.

Langer, E. J. (1975) The illusion of control. *Journal of Personality and Social Psychology*, **32**, 311–328.

Langer, E. J. (1983) *The Psychology of Control*. Beverly Hills, CA: Sage.

Lawler, E. E. (1966) The mythology of management compensation. *California Management Review*, **9**, 11–22.

Lefcourt, H. M. (1973) The function of the illusions of control and freedom. *American Psychologist*, **28**, 417–425.

Lied, T. R., and Pritchard, R. D. (1976) Relationships between personality variables and components of the expectancy–valence model. *Journal of Applied Psychology*, **61**, 463–467.

Locke, E. A., and Schweiger, D. (1979) Participation in decision making: One more look. In B. Staw (ed.), *Research in Organizational Behavior*, Vol. 1. Greenwich, CT: JAI Press.

Marino, K. E., and White, S. E. (1985) Departmental structure, locus of control, and job stress: The effect of a moderator. *Journal of Applied Psychology*, **70**, 782–784.

Marks, M. L., Mirvis, P. H., Hackett, E. J., and Grady, J. F., Jr (1986) Employee participation in a Quality Circle program: Impact on quality of work life, productivity, and absenteeism. *Journal of Applied Psychology*, **71**, 61–69.

Martinko, M. J., and Gardner, W. L. (1982) Learned helplessness: An alternative explanation for performance deficits. *Academy of Management Review*, **7**, 195–204.

McCaul, K. D. (1980) Sensory information, fear level, and reaction to pain. *Journal of Personality*, **48**, 394–404.

McClaney, M. A., and Hurrell, J. J., Jr. (in press) Control, stress, and job satisfaction. *Work and Stress*.

Miller, G. A., Galanter, E., and Pribram, K. H. (1960) *Plans and the Structure of Behavior*. New York: Holt.

Miller, S. M. (1979) Controllability and human stress: Method, evidence, and theory. *Behavior Research and Therapy*, **17**, 287–304.

Miller, S. M. (1987) Predictability and human stress: Towards a clarification of evidence and theory. In L. Berkowitz (ed.), *Advances in Experimental Social Psychology*, Vol. 14. New York: Academic Press.

Miller, S. M., Lack, E. R., and Asroff, S. (1985) Preference for control and the coronary-prone behavior pattern: 'I'd rather do it myself.' *Journal of Personality and Social Psychology*, **49**, 492–499.

Mowrer, O. H., and Viek, P. (1948) An experimental analogue of fear from a sense of helplessness. *Journal of Abnormal and Social Psychology*, **43**, 193–200.

Murrell, K. F. H. (1963) Laboratory studies of repetitive work II: Progress report on results of two subjects. *International Journal of Production Research*, **2**, 247.

Overmier, J. B., and Seligman, M. E. P. (1967) Effects of inescapable shock upon subsequent escape and avoidance learning. *Journal of Comparative and Physiological Psychology*, **63**, 28–33.

Payne, R., and Fletcher, B. (1983) Job demands, supports, and constraints as predictors of psychological strain among school teachers. *Journal of Vocational Behavior*, **22**, 136–147.

Perrewe, P. L., and Ganster, D. C. (in press) The impact of job demands and behavioral control on experienced job stress. *Journal of Organizational Behavior*.

Quinn, R. P., Mangione, T., and Seashore, S. (1975) *1972–73 Quality of Employment Survey (Codebook)*. Ann Arbor: University of Michigan, Institute for Social Research.

Ralston, D. A., Anthony, W. P., and Gustafson, D. J. (1985) Employees may love flextime, but what does it do to the organization's productivity? *Journal of Applied Psychology*, **70**, 272–279.

Roberts, K. H., and Glick, W. (1981) The job characteristics approach to task design: A critical review. *Journal of Applied Psychology*, **66**, 193–217.

Rodin, J. (1986) Aging and health: Effects of the sense of control. *Science*, **233**, 1271–1276.

Rodin, J., Rennert, K., and Solomon, S. K. (1980) Intrinsic motivation for control: Fact or fiction? In A. Baum and J. Singer (eds), *Advances in Environmental Psychology*, Vol. 2. *Applications of Personal Control*. Hillsdale, NJ: Erlbaum, pp. 131–148.

Rotter, J. B. (1966) Generalized expectancies for internal versus external control of reinforcement. *Psychological Monographs: General and Applied*, **80** (Whole No. 609), 1–28.

Runyon, K. E. (1973) Some interactions between personality variables and management styles. *Journal of Applied Psychology*, 57, 288–294.
Salvendy, G. (1972) Paced and unpaced performance. *Acta Physiologica*, 42, 267–274.
Salvendy, G. (1981) Classification and characteristics of paced work. In G. Salvendy and M. J. Smith (eds), *Machine Pacing and Occupational Stress*. London: Taylor & Francis Ltd., pp. 5–19.
Salvendy, G., and Humphreys, A. P. (1979) Effects of personality, perceptual difficulty, and pacing of a task on productivity, job satisfaction, and physiologic stress. *Perceptual and Motor Skills*, 49, 219–222.
Schweiger, D. M., and Leana, C. R. (1986) Participation in decision making. In E. A. Locke (ed.), *Generalizing from Laboratory to Field Settings: Research Findings from Industrial-Organizational Psychology and Human Resource Management*. Lexington, MA: Lexington Books, pp. 147–166.
Seligman, M. E. P. (1975) *Helplessness: On depression, development, and death*. San Francisco: W. H. Freeman.
Shepard, J. M. (1971) *Automation and Alienation*. Cambridge, MA: MIT Press.
Sheppard, H. L., and Herrick, N. Q. (1972) *Where Have all the Robots Gone? Worker dissatisfaction in the '70s*. New York: Free Press.
Sims, H. P., Jr and Szilagyi, A. D. (1976) Job characteristics relationships: Individual and structural moderators. *Organizational Behavior and Human Performance*, 17, 211–230.
Smith, M. J. (1985) Machine-paced work and stress. In C. L. Cooper and M. J. Smith (eds), *Job Stress and Blue Collar Work*. Chichester: John Wiley & Sons.
Smith, M. J., Hurrell, J. J., Jr, and Murphy, R. K., Jr (1981) Stress and health effects in paced and unpaced work. In G. Salvendy and M. J. Smith (eds), *Machine Pacing and Occupational Stress*. London: Taylor & Francis, pp. 261–267.
Smith, T. W., and O'Keefe, J. L. (1985) The inequivalence of self-reports of Type A behavior: Differential relationships of the Jenkins Activity Survey and the Framingham Scale with affect, stress, and control. *Motivation and Emotion*, 9, 299–311.
Spector, P. E. (1982) Behavior in organizations as a function of employee's locus of control. *Psychological Bulletin*, 91, 482–497.
Spector, P. E. (1986) Perceived control by employees: A meta-analysis of studies concerning autonomy and participation at work. *Human Relations*, 39, 1005–1116.
Spector, P. E. (1987) Interactive effects of perceived control and job stressors on affective reactions and health outcomes for clerical workers. *Work and Stress*, 1, 155–162.
Stone, E. F. (1986) Job scope–job satisfaction and job scope–job performance relationships. In E. A. Locke (ed.), *Generalizing from Laboratory to Filed Settings: Research findings from Industrial-Organizational Psychology and Human Resource Management*. Lexington, MA: Lexington Books, pp. 189–206.
Storms, P. L., and Spector, P. E. (1987) Relationships of organizational frustration with reported behavioural reactions: The moderating effect of locus of control. *Journal of Occupational Psychology*, 60, 227–234.
Stotland, E., and Blumenthal, A. L. (1964) The reduction of anxiety as a result of the expectation of making a choice. *Canadian Journal of Psychology*, 18, 139–145.
Strube, M., Berry, J. M., and Moergen, S. (1985) Relinquishment of control and the Type A behavior pattern: The role of performance evaluation. *Journal of Personality and Social Psychology*, 49, 831–842.
Strube, M., and Werner, C. (1985) Relinquishment of control and the Type A behavior pattern. *Journal of Personality and Social Psychology*, 48, 688–701.

Sury, R. J. (1964) An industrial study of paced and unpaced operator performance in a single stage work task. *International Journal of Production Research*, **3**, 91.
Sutton, R., and Kahn, R. L. (1986) Prediction, understanding, and control as antidotes to organizational stress. In J. Lorsch (ed.), *Handbook of Organizational Behavior*. Englewood Cliffs, NJ: Prentice-Hall.
Szilagyi, A. D., and Sims, H. P., Jr (1975) Locus of control and expectancies across multiple occupational levels. *Journal of Applied Psychology*, **60**, 638–640.
Taylor, L., and Walton, P. (1971) Industrial sabotage: Motives and meanings. In S. Cohen (ed.), *Images of Deviance*. London: Penguin.
Tetrick, L. E., and LaRocco, J. M. (1987) Understanding, prediction, and control as moderators of the relationships between perceived stress, satisfaction, and psychological well-being. *Journal of Applied Psychology*, **72**, 538–543.
Theorell, T., Alfredsson, L., Knox, S., Perski, A., Svensson, J., and Wallers, D. (1984) On the interplay between socio-economic factors, personality, and work environment in the pathogenesis of cardiovascular disease. *Scandinavian Journal of Work, Environment, and Health*, **10**, 373–380.
Theorell, T., Hjemdahl, P., Ericsson, F., Kallner, A., Knox, S., Perski, A., Svensson, J., Tidgren, B., and Waller, D. (1985) Psychosocial and physiological factors in relation to blood pressure at rest — A study of Swedish men in their upper twenties. *Journal of Hypertension*, **3**, 591–600.
Timio, M., and Gentili, S. (1976) Adrenosympathetic overactivity under conditions of work stress. *British Journal of Preventive and Social Medicine*, **30**, 262–265.
Turner, A. N., and Lawrence, P. R. (1965) *Industrial Jobs and the Worker*. Boston, MA: Harvard Graduate School of Business.
Veroff, J., Douvan, E., and Kulka, R. (1981) *The Inner American: A self-portrait from 1957 to 1976*. New York: Basic Books.
Walker, C. R., and Guest, R. H. (1952) *The Man on the Assembly Line*. Cambridge, MA: Harvard University Press.
Weiss, J. M. (1968) Effects of coping responses on stress. *Journal of Comparative and Physiological Psychology*, **65**, 251–266.
Weiss, J. M. (1971) Effects of coping behavior with and without a feedback signal on stress pathology in rats. *Journal of Comparative and Physiological Psychology*. **77**, 22–30.
Weisz, J. R. (1983) Can I control it? The pursuit of veridical answers across the life span. *Life-Span Development and Behavior*, **5**, 233–300.
White, R. W. (1959) Motivation reconsidered: The concept of competence. *Psychological Review*, **66**, 297–333.
Woodworth, R. S. (1958) *Dynamics of Behavior*. New York: Holt, Rinehart, and Winston.
Zimbardo, P. G., and Miller, N. E. (1958). Facilitation of exploration by hunger in rats. *Journal of Comparative and Physiological Psychology*, **54**, 43–46.

# Chapter 9
JOB ANALYSIS

Paul E. Spector
Michael T. Brannick
and
Michael D. Coovert[1]
Department of Psychology
University of South Florida
USA

Job analysis is one of the major tools of the industrial/organizational psychologist. As is true of most of the pure industrial areas of the field, its literature has been dominated by atheoretical issues of method and use. Particularly popular has been development, evaluation, comparison, and use of both new and existing methods. Recently, however, a number of researchers have become interested in additional topics such as human judgements associated with job analysis. Such work concerns accuracy and bias in job analysis ratings and judgements, the amount and nature of information used to make ratings, and the underlying judgement process itself.

Job analysis information can affect every aspect of an organization (Hakel, 1986). Indeed, job analysis is viewed as the foundation upon which an organization's human resources are built. Ash and Levine (1980) provide a listing of some of the more popular applications of job analysis data. It includes: (1) the generation of job descriptions; (2) job classification; (3) job evaluation; (4) job design and redesign; (5) personnel requirements and specification of worker characteristics; (6) performance appraisal; (7) worker training; (8) worker mobility through career development; (9) worker efficiency/safety; (10) workforce and manpower planning; and (11) legal/quasilegal requirements and obligations. As one can see, the potential impact of job analysis information is quite pervasive. With the current state of the technology, a given method of

---

[1] The order of authorship for the second and third authors was determined by a coin flip. We thank Kathleen McNelis for her helpful comments and suggestions.

International Review of Industrial and Organizational Psychology 1989
Edited by C. L. Cooper and I. Robertson © 1989 John Wiley & Sons Ltd.

gathering job analysis data may be more suitable for one application than another.

In this chapter we will review recent research and trends in job analysis. We will begin with job analysis methodologies, summarizing research comparing various methods and the development of new methods. Included will be attempts to facilitate job analysis using computers. Considerable attention will be devoted to the work on reliability and validity of job analysis ratings. Most validity studies have concerned convergent validity, with a few researchers giving attention to potential biases. Limited work has also been done on the cognitive processes underlying job analysis ratings, particularly in terms of the nature of information people use to make judgements about jobs. Job taxonomies is another popular topic, with most of the recent work concerned with quantitative methods to build job families. Finally, interest in job evaluation, which is an application of job analysis, has been raised by the issue of comparable worth in gender related salary differences.

JOB ANALYSIS METHODOLOGIES

Since the mid-1970s there have been significant advances in the development of job analysis methodologies. These developments have largely occurred in terms of describing both the job and the worker. The trend has been towards being more exhaustive in what is examined, as well as a tendency to use multiple measures. This emphasis on obtaining more information has resulted from the increased application of job analysis information and also increased court interest in what constitutes an appropriate job analysis (Thompson and Thompson, 1982).

The major approaches for gathering job analysis data has tended to focus on either job tasks or the worker. Popular task-based methods include Functional Job Analysis (FJA; Fine and Wiley, 1971), Task Inventory–Comprehensive Occupational Data Analysis Programs (TI–CODAP; Christal, 1974), and the Department of Labor Task Analysis. Worker-oriented approaches can be partitioned into those which are behavior based versus those which are attribute based (Ash, 1982). Behavior-based approaches are the Critical Incident Technique (Flanagan, 1954), the Occupation Analysis Inventory (OAI; Cunningham, Boese, Neeb, and Pass, 1983), and the Position Analysis Questionnaire (PAQ; McCormick, Jenneret, and Mecham, 1972). Worker attribute-based approaches include FJA, PAQ, the Job Element Method (JEM; Primoff, 1975) and the Ability Requirements Scale (ARS; Fleishman, 1975). Since these techniques have been around for some time, the specifics of each will not be discussed here. The reader is referred to the original sources for detailed information, or to comprehensive overviews which can be found in Ash, Levine, and Sistrunk (1983) and Levine (1983). Although each method has contributed to our current understanding of jobs and workers, there are deficiencies in all. None can be claimed the definitive job analysis method.

Evaluation and Comparison of Job Analysis Methods

Numerous studies have specifically been designed to examine the use of several different job analysis techniques. These studies either have assessed the appropriateness of a technique for a particular purpose or have provided direct comparisons among techniques.

Through a series of five reports, Shannon and Carter (1981) examined several approaches for identifying pilot training needs under normal and adverse conditions. The primary methodology employed in the first four studies was task analysis. Generally, task analysis functioned well across a variety of training needs assessments. In a fifth study, the authors used the PAQ to translate specific tasks performed on different jobs into common tasks. These tasks were relevant to different environments, work stations, and equipment. The authors felt that the PAQ functioned acceptably for identifying common aspects of different jobs, which could be examined with the same test.

Mayo, Nance, and Shigekawa (1975) expanded the TI–CODAP survey for military officers to more than twice its normal number of tasks to examine a variety of issues. They sought to determine if the semantic characteristics of task statements could be used to ascertain job or job family attributes. More specifically, relations between verbs and nouns in task statements were examined to determine if they discriminated between different jobs. Unfortunately, it did not appear that the semantic characteristics of task statements were good discriminators. Semantic characteristics, however, have been found to have an effect on task data in a non-military settng (Coovert, 1986a). In this study, 57 task statements were written describing what individuals do daily as students. Two groupings were constructed by sorting task statements into piles based on similarity of meaning of verbs and nouns, respectively (Miller, 1969). A third grouping was obtained by sorting tasks into piles according to the same criterion, using a propositional representation (Wickelgren, 1979, 1981). A fourth grouping was obtained by having tasks grouped into scripts (Schank and Abelson, 1977). A fifth grouping was obtained by clustering items on their relative time-spent. According to response latencies, the script representation was determined to be the closest to the representation employed by individuals.

A second part of the study varied the structure of information within each of the five representations described above. Tasks were presented in one of three ways: according to the organization described above; preceded by a prime (such as instructing an individual to think of everything associated with performing a duty); or in a random order. This was done so as to assess the impact of these structures on each representation. It was predicted that priming individuals to think about certain tasks would force deeper processing of subsequent information. The effect across each of the five representations was comparable. Individuals reported spending more time on tasks when they were presented according to some structure or organization, irrespective of the overall representation. This finding suggested that it is important to present tasks in an organized fashion when asking incumbents to respond to them (e.g. indicating time spent, importance, or criticality).

Functional job analysis has been evaluated as a technique for describing jobs in such a manner that performance tests can be constructed from the resulting information (Olson, Fine, Myers, and Jennings, 1981). The job of a heavy equipment operator was successfully decomposed into tasks utilizing FJA. Performance tests and related standards were developed for the tasks through the cooperation between job analysts and incumbents. Evaluation of the approach indicated that the tests successfully differentiated between skill levels of individual operators.

Several studies by Levine and his colleagues (Levine, Ash, and Bennett, 1980; Levine, Ash, Hall, and Sistrunk, 1983; Levine, Thomas, and Sistrunk, 1988) have examined the appropriateness of alternative job analysis techniques for various organizational purposes. Based on the results of a group of empirical studies and the opinion of expert job analysts, Levine *et al.* provided several recommendations. When the purpose is to generate a job description, TI, TI–CODAP, and FJA will probably perform best, and ARS was not recommended. For job classification purposes, TI–CODAP and FJA are superior whereas the CI technique is not as desirable. The best methods for job evaluation are the PAQ, FJA, and TI–CODAP. Finally, TI–CODAP and FJA are superior if the intended use is job design. It should be pointed out, however, that these studies were concerned with established methods and not with the more recent methods described below.

Job Component Inventory (JCI)

Although a variety of job analysis scales exist, none is particularly suited to the British context (Banks, Jackson, Stafford, and Warr, 1983). Banks and his colleagues set out to develop a scale more tailored to their needs. The Job Component Inventory (JCI) targets both the job and the worker simultaneously, allowing for the matching of worker and job profiles. This serves as the basis for determining current job/skill matches for several purposes including placement, training, and job redesign. One specific use has been to redesign jobs so they can be performed by handicapped individuals.

In its present form, the JCI is composed of five components and covers over 400 features of work skills. The first component focuses on the use of tools and equipment. Twenty-six groups of items cover 220 small to large tools grouped according to function. The second section covers perception and physical requirements. Twenty-three items dealing with strength, coordination, dexterity, reaction time, and selective attention are included. The third section consists of 127 items concerning mathematics, focused on elementary algebra and trigonometry with practical applications. Communication requirements is the focus of section four, with 22 items detailing the preparation of reports and letters, receiving written communication, the use of a coding system, dealing with complaints and other aspects of interpersonal interactions. The final section deals with decision making and responsibility, with nine items covering decisions about methods, order of work, standards and related issues.

Once information profiling the worker and job is obtained, it can be presented in three different formats (Banks and Wylde, 1981). The first format is a job profile, which provides an absolute measure of skill utilization for a particular job or job group. The second format is the skill wheel, which provides a relative comparison of skill requirements (e.g. mathematics) against the average. The third format is the written sketch, which draws on the job profile and skill wheel, but also includes contextual information collected during an interview. Examples of these formats can be found in Banks and Wylde (1981).

The JCI shares aspects with the generic skills approach used in education. Not surprisingly, a primary use of the JCI is to identify and develop curriculum training content for 16- and 17-year-olds who are part of the British Youth Opportunity Program.

Four issues were considered during development of the JCI (Banks, 1988). First, its language and concepts should be at an appropriate level for job incumbents. Second, the inventory should be easily administered by trained interviewers. Expert job analysts should not be required. Third, the inventory should be comprehensive, yet not too lengthy. Fourth, the measured skills should be at a level appropriate for a wide variety of occupations and applicable for a number of purposes (e.g. curriculum development, training, and career guidance).

To date, the primary use of the JCI has been in five areas: (1) curriculum assessment; (2) careers education; (3) skill proficiency and assessment; (4) evaluation and design of training content; and (5) vocational guidance and placement (Banks, Blow, and Stafford, 1983; Banks, Jackson, Stafford, and Warr, 1983; Banks and Stafford, 1982; Banks and Wylde, 1981; Stafford, Jackson, and Banks, 1982; Warr and Banks, 1981). In the curriculum assessment area, the focus has been on evaluating skill requirements of an individual or a class. The careers education area contains job knowledge index, occupational skill profile, a model curriculum vitae, fact sheets, and exercises. Two profiles are developed for skills proficiency and assessment. The first profile contains assessment on training courses and the second contains profiles for assessment at the present point in time. One useful aspect of this is the CAN-DO checklist, which is a self-assessment instrument used at the end of training to identify mastery areas. The vocational guidance and placement area allows an individual's profile to be matched against profiles for a variety of jobs. The final application area has been the evaluation and design of training content. The JCI is used to assess similarity between jobs in order to investigate the possible structure of broad based training schemes.

One benefit of the JCI is that job requirements, individual capabilities, and training opportunities are all assessed using a common language. Additionally, the JCI profile moves the client away from preparation for one job, to preparation for jobs within a wider family (Banks and Stafford, 1982).

The JCI is also useful for differentiating between job titles within and between job families. Evidence suggests that the JCI can be administered to both supervisors and incumbents with moderate levels of agreement between raters (Kendall correlation between .40 and .71; Banks, Jackson, Stafford, and Warr, 1983). All things considered, the JCI appears to function as intended and is a welcome addition to job analysis methodologies.

Multimethod Job Design Questionnaire (MJDQ)

Job design is an area with an increased reliance upon job analysis information. The type of information required for modifying a job, however, is often much different from that required for more traditional uses of job descriptive information, such as producing a job summary. This increasing need for a variety of different types of information led to the development of the Multimethod Job Design Questionnaire (MJDQ, Campion and Thayer, 1985). The approach taken by Campion and Thayer was to develop a taxonomy of job design approaches based on the literature in four different disciplines.

The MJDQ is a questionnaire composed of items designed to measure principles of job design abstracted from motivational, mechanistic, biological, and perceptual/motor perspectives. Examples of items from each perspective are presented in Table 1.

Initial results employing the MJDQ with blue-collar production jobs have been encouraging. The scale enjoys good inter-rater reliability and agreement (Campion and Thayer, 1985), and it appears to support the relationship between the job design scales and the four theoretical job outcome components of satisfaction, efficiency, comfort, and reliability. Recently, Campion (1987, 1988) replicated the original findings on an expanded sample of professional and managerial jobs in a different work environment. Additionally, no individual differences were found to moderate the job design—outcome relationships in terms of preferences/tolerances.

In sum, the MJDQ appears to be a promising job analysis methodology. Future research will have to assess if its relevance extends beyond the job design domain.

Table 1—Examples of Multimethod Job Design Questionnaire Items

Motivational
Autonomy, responsibility, vertical loading
Intrinsic job feedback
Extrinsic job feedback
Social interaction
Task/goal clarity

Mechanistic
Task fractionalization/specialization
Specialization of materials, tools, and procedures
Task simplification
Skill simplification
Repetition/pacing

Biological
Seating
Tool design
Anthropometry
Static effort
Endurance

Perceptual/Motor
Workplace lighting—general
Control and display identification
Display visibility/legibility
Displays—information content
Control/display movement relationships

Combination Job Analysis Method (C-JAM)

One of the foremost proponents of utilizing a combination of techniques when performing job analysis has been Levine (1983). Levine argues that in order to perform a job analysis that will meet many organizational needs and be legally defensible in court, both job attributes and worker attributes must be obtained. As such, Combination Job Analysis Method (C-JAM) borrows from the task-based approach of Functional Job Analysis and TI–CODAP, along with the human attribute approach of Job Element Method.

The first step in the C-JAM technique is to have subject matter experts (SMEs) generate tasks, working first as a group to discuss the job and, then, individually to compose the task statements. An iterative process of editing and rewriting ensues until a final list is composed. After being reviewed by SMEs for adequate job coverage and accuracy, each task is rated on a seven-point scale in terms of relative time spent, difficulty, and criticality. A task importance value for each task is computed as:

Task Importance Value = Difficulty × Criticality + Time Spent.

The task importance value allows for the rank ordering of tasks within functional work areas.

Worker attribute information is gathered in much the same manner by focusing on employee KSAOs (Knowledge, Skill, Ability, and Other Characteristics). SMEs review the tasks and functional areas prior to generating the KSAOs. A rating of the KSAOs occurs in the following manner. First, SMEs indicate if each KSAO is 'Necessary for new workers' (Yes or No) and if it is 'Practical to expect' (Yes or No). Each KSAO is also rated for degree on two items: 'Extent of trouble likely' and 'Distinguish superior worker from average'. The KSAO importance rating is a combination of these four items.

The C-JAM approach is appropriate for many organizational needs to which job analysis data are applied. For those situations where the C-JAM may be too time intensive to be practical, Levine (1983) offers a modification of this approach called Brief Job Analysis Method (B-JAM).

Threshold Traits Analysis System (TTAS)

Threshold Traits Analysis System (TTAS; Lopez, 1988; Lopez, Kesselman, and Lopez, 1981) is a worker-oriented technique designed to identify those personal characteristics required to perform the functions of a specific position. A trait is considered a set of observable characteristics which distinguishes one individual from another. The TTAS considers 33 different traits to be important. These critical traits are assigned to five major groups: physical, mental, learned, motivational, and social. The first three are considered 'ability' factors and the latter two are considered 'attitudinal'.

Each trait is viewed as a construct with six dimensions (Lopez, 1988). These dimensions are relevance, level, practicality, weight, degree, and criticality. Level refers to trait complexity or intensity, and subdivides the trait into three or four segments. Practicality refers to the portion of applicants who are expected to possess a particular trait level. Weight reflects the trait's effect on overall performance, and is expressed as a percentage of the total trait configuration. Degree separates a person's possession of a trait into either unacceptable, marginal, acceptable, or superior categories. The criticality dimension conveys a type of 'make or break' quality. A trait is considered critical when a job cannot be performed satisfactorily by an incumbent who does not possess that trait. Availability describes the supply/demand ratio of each trait level in the labor market.

A threshold trait analysis (TTA) requires that supervisors, SMEs, or incumbents rate the job using the relevance, level, and practicality dimensions for the 33 traits. This is performed using both acceptable and superior job performance. A questionnaire is constructed containing the tasks/demands for the job in question. A representative sample of incumbents is used to indicate the extent to which the task or demand is part of the job. Each task or demand is linked to a particular job function which in turn is linked to a specific trait. This process is called Demand and Task Analysis (DATA). This linking allows for discrepancies between TTA and DATA to be resolved, should they arise.

A third component of the TTAS is a procedure for assessing craft knowledge or craft skill. This is termed Technical Competence Analysis (TCA). Under TTAS terminology, knowledge represents the retrieval of information. Skill represents psychomotor activity that is acquired only by practice (Lopez, 1988). TCA allows skill assessment within a job analysis.

The application of TTAS has met with success within a wide variety of organizations. It is, however, not without its critics who maintain that at times, it can be too precise, complex, and impractical (Lopez, 1988).

Specialized Approaches

Several researchers have developed job analysis questionnaires and/or methodologies targeted at specific populations. Other methods are appropriate for analyzing limited aspects of a job or incumbent.

Beardsley and Matkin (1984) developed a brief task inventory they call the Abbreviated Task Inventory (ATI). It consisted of 40 items to be utilized by rehabilitation administrators and supervisors for reporting the roles and functions of rehabilitation counsellors. The ATI represents a shortened version of the 119 item Rehabilitation Counsellor Task Inventory (RCTI; Muthard and Salomone, 1969). Factor analysis of the 40-item ATI yielded a six-factor solution with four of the factors directly comparable to factors of the RCTI. Preliminary results indicated that the ATI can be a useful tool for quickly describing the job of a rehabilitation counsellor.

A second approach took a less traditional but much needed orientation to the analysis of jobs. Given the increasing value individuals place on family and other non-work-related responsibilities, conflicts are likely to exist between time demands placed on the worker by job-related and non-job-related responsibilities. Johnson (1982) developed a scale to measure time conflicts which exist between a job and family responsibilities. The scale specifically targets job time demands which compete with the individual's time for family responsibilities. The instrument consists of fourteen items which load on three factors: flexibility in work schedule; family–work schedule conflicts; and irregular work demands. A preliminary study was performed on 381 divorced mothers. Mothers who stated that their job created difficulties in the management of family responsibilities had significantly higher responses on the first two factors. Although these findings are of interest, further work needs to be performed both in terms of scale development and generalizability on other populations.

The focus of some recent work has extended the boundaries of traditional task analytic approaches. Hakel, Hakel, and Weil (1986) sought to determine if ratings based on the results of current job analysis methods are enhanced by the addition of information concerning the social interactions inherent in jobs.

After extensive work with SMEs, Hakel developed a task inventory containing 215 task items appropriate for enlisted US navy personnel. The number of items describing the social interaction and non-social aspects of jobs were 129 and 86, respectively. A copy of the inventory was mailed to 1440 randomly selected individuals in 25 navy grades at apprentice, journeyman, and master skill levels. The sample covered the full range of social interactions.

Stepwise regression and cluster analysis were used to determine how the new task analysis method (containing social interactions) compared to more traditional approaches. Four main findings were reported. First, social interaction constructs could be reliably described and measured using a task inventory format. Second, social and non-social items were useful for predicting grade at high levels while non-social scales did not differentiate grade. Third, cluster composition differed when social information was used as the basis for the clustering, but it did not differ when non-social information was used. Fourth, the nature of the social contacts and interactions varied as a function of pay level.

The next four studies focused on jobs with a high cognitive process content. As a rule, it is more difficult to use traditional job analysis methodologies on jobs with a large cognitive component. This is because traditional approaches tend to be input/output oriented rather than designed to capture what is occurring within the incumbent's mind.

Piso (1981) adapted task analysis so that it would be appropriate for process control tasks. The general approach involved constructing a hierarchy of job goals (tasks to be performed) and subgoals which could be linked with the goals in a network structure. The operator was modelled as a feedback loop in the process control. Generally, the operator was viewed as being in either a pre-action, action, or evaluation phase at any given point in time. The phase structure allowed for temporal ordering of tasks within the network. Strengths of the approach include the ability to model operator action better as well as being able to generate hierarchical training guidelines.

Siegler (1980) reviewed the advances in task analytic techniques for studying cognitive development. One important finding of this work parallels work in an area of artificial intelligence. This is the modelling of cognition as an underlying set of rules, usually called production rules. The seminal work on this topic is Newell and Simon's (1972) book on human problem solving. Siegler demonstrated that task analysis in conjunction with theories of cognition could be used to write rules which underlie children's problem-solving behavior. The goal now is to demonstrate that the behavior of individuals at work can be modelled in the same manner utilizing task analysis and the development of productions.

One of the primary methods for gathering data to write production rules is by gathering verbal protocols. Subjects are instructed to think out loud as they solve a problem or make a decision. Ericsson and Simon (1984) provide guidance on the gathering and analysis of such protocols. Umbers (1979) applied the technique to the study of control skills utilized by gas grid operators. A large component of the job was cognitive, so the combination of verbal protocol analysis and traditional observational techniques resulted in a job analysis containing information regarding the problem-solving skills required by the operator in addition to the traditional job description. This approach could also be useful for any job with a large cognitive component.

A study which could be considered an attempt to model part of the cognitive processes of a job analyst is reported in Mallamad, Levine, and Fleishman (1980). These authors developed an instrument which leads raters through 40 binary questions dealing with whether or not an ability is required for performance on the job. These items dealt with abilities identified by Fleishman (1975) and the questions were structured into a decision diagram. The decision diagram worked well for identifying abilities required by the job only when the average score of three or more raters was used. Once the abilities were identified from the decision diagram, a questionnaire format could then be used to provide a detaailed examination of those abilities.

Measurement of Effort

Several techniques have been developed to determine the amount of physical, mental and/or subjective effort involved in a job.

Physical demands

Fleishman, Gebhardt, and Hogan (1984) conducted a series of studies to develop a general procedure for measuring the physical demands of work. A self-report rating scale was developed to rate the physical demands of various occupational and recreational tasks from 'very very light' to 'very very hard'. Dissimilar groups of males and females, some of whom were personnel specialists, performed effort ratings on a variety of tasks. Raters did not know the metabolic values of the tasks. In all cases, inter-rater agreement was high and ratings were consistent with actual metabolic costs.

Next, subjects were asked to perform tasks (e.g. move a 40 pound weight 20 feet) and then make effort ratings. Again, high agreement was reached among raters. A regression equation was developed which allowed prediction of actual physical work from physical effort ratings. These findings suggested that it is possible to substitute a perceived effort index for actual physiological measurement across a wide variety of tasks. This would allow for a reliable, valid, and yet inexpensive means of matching an individual's capacity with the requirements of a physically demanding job.

Many studies have been performed on manual material handling tasks using physiological, biochemical, psychophysical, and epidemiological information. Few studies, however, have considered multiple tasks (e.g. lift and carry or lift, carry and lower), and none of the studies using multiple tasks has utilized psychophysical modelling. Jiang, Smith, and Ayoub (1986) recently reported a study which applied 'fuzzy set' theory (Zedeh, 1965) to the modelling of tasks. This approach allows for the integration of information from many sources. It can combine both objective physiological data with subjective judgement about effort. Jiang *et al.* (1986) have found that their approach performs well when compared to traditional psychophysical methods.

A scale has been developed to evaluate job-related physical abilities (Rakimi and Malzahn, 1984). The Available Motions Inventory (AMI) consists of 71 tests evaluated on dimensions of strength, accuracy, and rate of performance. The AMI produces scores for ability, motion class, and performance prediction. The scale reflects fundamental functional output and the results of the scale are described as functional abilities. One use of the AMI has been to evaluate the physical abilities of individuals with neuromuscular impairments so that modifications can be made to an existing work setting. The current form of the AMI allows for the reliable assessment of inter- and intra-individual scores. Future versions of the AMI are planned to include the measurement of cognitive and perceptual abilities.

Subjective workload

Borg (1978) reports the results of several studies where a close correspondence was found between psychological and physiological indicators of workload. In studying physical loads, one must take into consideration factors such as emotion, motivation, the environment, as well as the sensory aspects of the job. For mental loads, one needs to consider such factors as quality of data, alternative actions, number of details, complexity, and scarcity of time. Potential moderators include social and situational factors such as task complexity and individual work values.

Vidulich and Tsang (1986) developed a bipolar scale at NASA to represent workload. The scale consists of the following nine dimensions: (1) task difficulty; (2) time pressure; (3) performance; (4) mental/sensory effort; (5) physical effort; (6) frustration; (7) stress; (8) fatigue; and (9) activity type. Comparison of the NASA bipolar scale with the Subjective Workload Assessment Technique (SWAT) (a conjoint scaling approach) consistently demonstrated lower between-subject variability than did SWAT. Each approach has associated strengths and weaknesses and would best be used in tandem.

Studies have specifically examined the approach of utilizing a secondary task as a measure of workload assessment. Wildervanch, Mulder, and Michon (1978), for example, provided an interesting demonstration of mapping the mental load involved with various driving conditions. A car was equipped with a wide angle television camera which monitored traffic in front of the car. Physiological measures from the driver were gathered simultaneously with the traffic conditions. The secondary task employed was foot tapping. As expected, as different driving conditions forced an increase in mental load, there was an associated decrease in foot tapping and an increase in the physiological measures.

Ogden, Levine, and Eisner (1979) performed an extensive literature search in order to document all secondary task studies conducted since 1964. The search yielded in 146 experimental studies. The authors surveyed each study in an attempt to quantify the best approach for selecting a secondary task within an experimental methodology. Key issues included the use of secondary tasks as a measure of workload and stress, the occurrence of constant primary task performance, and the proper choice of a secondary task. For certain studies where the desire was to determine an appropriate man/machine interface or to determine if a co-worker was required, secondary tasks were used to vary the amount of load on human capabilities. If a secondary task is purely a stress quantifier, restrictions on the task chosen as an additive load are relaxed. For each type of study, however, the inevitable decrease in primary task performance must be quantified, or at least limited to minimum acceptable levels, and a secondary task must be chosen which elicits the desired loadings. The authors provided an extensive look at the historical treatment of the issues and concluded with the suggestion that secondary tasks should be standardized. Furthermore, the authors believed that non-adaptive tasks are best suited for the measurement of subjective workload.

Brown (1978) documented the criticisms and limitations of dual task methods used to assess workload. This author was of the opinion that the secondary task should be given at a constant rate and should compete with the processing assets needed for the primary task. Secondary tasks which require different methods of input, output, or processing from the primary task will yield data biased by the locus of interference between tasks. Brown suggested that the secondary task effect may merely be reflecting changes in selective attention. Furthermore, dual tasks may not be measuring resource loading and learning since a subject is often data, and not resource, limited. Brown also believed that individual differences in personality may affect the movement of stress in unpredictable directions with the addition of a secondary task.

COMPUTER APPLICATIONS WITHIN JOB ANALYSIS

To date, the primary use of computers within job analysis has been to reduce the data analysis load on the job analyst. An example of this is the computation of task or PAQ profiles for the development of job families or the identification of compensable factors. Other uses include the production of job- or position-specific performance appraisal forms and other profiles (Coovert, 1984a, 1984b), and the generation of large human resource databases containing information necessary to make many of the decisions required by a human resource department (Coovert, 1986b). The development of such a system, however, is neither inexpensive nor quick. A review of nine geographically dispersed organizations with state of the art systems (Levine, Sistrunk, McNutt, and Gael, 1986) revealed that organizations must be prepared to spend several years and at least 1 million dollars if an automated multipurpose database is desired.

Work has recently been completed on the first phase of an artificial intelligence system developed to perform a job analysis and produce a job description (Coovert, 1986c; Coovert, Vance, and Colella, 1988; Vance, Coovert, and Colella, 1988). Coovert et al. identified several medical jobs and obtained task level descriptors from various private sector hospitals as well as from the TI–CODAP databases of the military. Working with SMEs, tasks were sorted into work activity clusters which spanned jobs. These tasks were subsequently sorted based on similarity of meaning as well as time spent. A frame-like representation (Minskey, 1975) was used to encode information about jobs into the computer. The purpose of this phase of the research was to develop a representational scheme about the various jobs which would be very similar to the representation employed by job analysts. This would allow the system to rely on various heuristics (Stefik et al., 1983) to move about the knowledge base much like an experienced job analyst would when conducting a job analysis interview. Results of the first phase of development indicated that the system performs acceptably in terms of the quality of narrative job descriptions produced and the ease of user interface. Future research should focus on extending the scope of jobs covered, generality of the heuristics, and the generation of information in addition to job descriptions. In addition, it is important to identify domains where it is appropriate to develop an artificial intelligence system (Coovert, Ramakrishna, McNelis, and Salas, 1988).

ACCURACY OF JOB ANALYSIS RATINGS

Reliability of Job Analysis Ratings

The issue of reliability of ratings conducted for job analysis has received considerable attention. Studies have generally concerned inter-rater agreement and/or test–retest reliabilities. Both reliability and validity have been investigated concurrently in several studies.

Table 2 summarizes the reliability coefficients found in twelve studies. The table indicates the type of reliability (test–retest, inter-rater agreement, or internal consistency), the type of job analysis measure, and the reliability estimate. In several studies reliabilities were provided separately for each of several dimensions. In these cases, median reliabilities are reported. As can be seen, inter-rater agreement has the lowest reliability (correlation) coefficients, ranging from .46 to .79. Test–retest reliabilities were somewhat higher, ranging from .68 to .90. Only a single internal consistency coefficient was found (r = .91).

Table 2—Test–Retest, Internal Consistency, and Inter-rater Agreement Reliability Across Studies

Reference	Type of reliability	Type of job analysis	Reliability estimate[a]
Banks and Miller (1984)	IA	JCI	.75
Cain and Green (1983)	IA	DOT	.79
Cornelius, DeNisi, and Blencoe (1984)	IA	PAQ	.52
Cornelius, Schmidt, and Carron (1984)	IA	Task Inventory	.71
Cornelius and Lyness (1980)	T–R	DOT	.68
DeNisi, Cornelius, and Blencoe (1987)	IA	PAQ	.79
Friedman and Harvey (1986)	IA	PAQ	.55
Jones, Main, Butler, and Johnson (1982)	IA	PAQ – Item	.43
		PAQ – Dimensions	.63
		PAQ Overall Dimensions	.77
Mobley and Ramsay (1973)	T–R	Attributes	.78
	IC	Attributes	.91
Smith and Hakel (1979)	IA	PAQ	.51
Taylor (1978)	T–R	PAQ Components, Single Rater	.69
	T–R	PAQ Dimensions, Single Rater	.83
	T–R	PAQ Components, Multiple Rater	.80
	T–R	PAQ Dimensions, Multiple Rater	.90
	IA	PAQ Components	.46
	IA	PAQ Dimensions	.50
Taylor and Colbert (1978)	IA	PAQ	.68
	T–R	PAQ	.78

Note T–R = Test–Retest, IA = Inter-rater Agreement, IC = Internal Consistency, PAQ = Position Analysis Questionnaire, JCI = Job Components Inventory, DOT = Dictionary of Occupational Titles.
[a]Where studies reported multiple reliabilities, medians are reported here.

Schmitt and Fine (1983) looked at inter-rater agreement on judgements of tasks written using functional job analysis from the perspectives of both correlation and rating differences. Six trained graduate students rated jobs along ten dimensions, including data level, things orientation, and mathematics. Agreement was quite variable, ranging from 25 per cent to 96 per cent across the ten dimensions. Intercorrelations among raters was better for some dimensions than others, e.g. correlations for people orientation ranged from .74 to .92, while worker instructions ranged from =.06 to .62.

Webb, Shavelson, Shea, and Morello (1981) took a different approach to the question of reliability/validity by utilizing generalizability theory (Cronbach, Gleser, Nanda, and Rajaratnam, 1972). This allowed them to explore sources of error in ratings from the US Department of Labor's General Educational Development (GED) scale. This scale is used by trained analysts to indicate three necessary educational components for any job. Sources of error in the investigation included length of job description from which ratings were made, occasions of ratings (each was done twice), and job title. Occasions accounted for little variance, suggesting good test–retest reliability. Length of job description had little effect, suggesting that limited information can result in similar ratings to those generated with more extensive information. Finally, most of the variance was attributable to job title, suggesting that the ratings were sensitive to differences across jobs.

Cain and Green (1983) also applied generalizability theory to ratings on Dictionary of Occupational Titles (DOT) scales. Reliability estimates were calculated under three sets of generalizability assumptions, with medians ranging from .70 for the most conservative to .88 for the most liberal. Some scales had better reliabilities than others, with poor reliabilities being reported for both the Things (.25 to .65) and Strength scales (.34 to .73).

Convergent Validity of Job Analysis Ratings

Most of the validity studies of job analysis instruments have been concerned with convergence among different types of raters. Commonly, expert job analysts have been compared with other raters, such as job incumbents, supervisors, or college students. Table 3 summarizes the convergent validities found in nine studies. Included are the types of raters compared, the job analysis method, and the correlations across rater types. The studies involving student raters were concerned with common knowledge effects, which are described below. In studies where multiple validity coefficients were reported, median values are presented.

Several of the validity studies were concerned with common knowledge effects in the PAQ. Interest in this topic began with Smith and Hakel's (1979) comparison of naive students with several other groups, including trained analysts. This resulted in a flurry of criticisms and replications with refinements.

Smith and Hakel (1979) had five types of judges complete the PAQ on 25

Table 3—Convergent Validities of Job Analysis Ratings

Reference	Rater type	Job analysis method	Convergent validity (correlation)[a]
Banks (1988)	I,S	JCI	.55
Banks and Miller (1984)	I,S	JCI	.72
Cornelius et al. (1984)		PAQ	.58
Cornelius and Lyness (1980)	I,S,J	DOL	.59
DeNisi, Cornelius, and Blencoe (1987)	J,St (2 conditions)	PAQ	.47
Friedman and Harvey (1986)	St (3 conditions)	PAQ	.72
	J,St (2 conditions)	PAQ	.47
Jones, Main, Butler, and Johnson (1982)	St (job description)	PAQ	.72
Sistrunk and Smith (1982)	I (2 conditions)	Task Inventory	.88
Smith and Hakel (1979)	I,S,J,St (2 conditions)	PAQ	.94

Note I = Incumbents, S = Supervisors, J = Experienced Job Analysts, St = Students, PAQ = Position Analysis Questionnaire, JCI = Job Components Inventory, DOL = Department of Labor, DOT = Dictionary of Occupational Titles
[a]Where multiple coefficients were reported, medians are provided here.

jobs. Judges included job incumbents, their supervisors, trained analysts, college students given job specifications, and college students given only job titles. Mean interjudge reliabilities were similar across judge types, ranging from .49 to .63, all statistically significant and none significantly different from one another. Convergence was high across judge categories, ranging from r = .89 to .98. Smith and Hakel concluded that the high convergence in ratings meant that the PAQ could be used by non-trained people, who had little contact with the job. They also questioned whether the PAQ was sensitive enough to detect much more than general knowledge about jobs.

Cornelius, DeNisi, and Blencoe (1984) pointed out some problems with Smith and Hakel's (1979) analysis. Most importantly, they showed how an inappropriate means of calculating agreement inflated the correlations. Furthermore, correlation itself is not a measure of agreement, as two judges can correlate perfectly, although one rates consistently higher than the other. They partially replicated Smith and Hakel's study, comparing job analysts with naive students having only job titles. The mean reliabilities were r = .89 for experts and r = .52 for students. Mean convergence between the two sources, using more appropriate statistics, was .58. Familiarity with the job correlated .58 with reliability and .48 with convergence.

Other comparisons of 'naive' and 'expert' raters have resulted in similar convergence. Friedman and Harvey (1986) compared students in three conditions: job title only, brief job description, and long job description. Convergence correlations ranged from .50 to .56. DeNisi, Cornelius, and

Blencoe (1987) compared both trained and untrained students with job analysts. The groups of students correlated .72 on average with one another, and .46 versus .47 with the experts, for trained and untrained, respectively.

A further issue raised by Cornelius, DeNisi, and Blencoe (1984) concerned the distribution of PAQ 'does not apply' (DNA) items across jobs. Each item is anchored at the low end by the response choice of 'does not apply'. For example, several items ask for ratings of 'extent of use' ranging from 'very substantial' to 'does not apply'. In this context the DNA indicates a zero response. Cornelius et al. (1984) discussed that there is considerable variation across jobs in the number of items experts reliably rate DNA. They argued that large numbers of DNA items can produce convergence correlations when naive students and job analysts agree that certain items do not apply to certain jobs. Students may be able to rate accurately obviously irrelevant items as DNA without necessarily being able to rate degree of applicability. They further argued that the PAQ may not be appropriate for jobs where many items are DNA. As evidence for this, Cornelius et al. (1984) and DeNisi et al. (1987) have noted that convergence is reduced when DNA items are eliminated. Cornelius et al. (1984) reported convergence correlations were reduced from a mean of .58 to .41 when DNAs were eliminated. Friedman and Harvey (1986) found reductions in correlations from the .50s to .40s.

Harvey and Hayes (1986) conducted a Monte Carlo study to explore the possible impact of DNA agreements between two sources on convergence correlations. They modelled the situation in which two raters agreed perfectly on all DNA items, but both gave random responses to non-DNA items. They varied the distribution shape in the random responses, the number of DNA items, and the number of judges. They found that with normal distributions, agreement on 30 DNA items produced convergence between raters of approximately $r = .50$. This is the level of agreement found in the replication studies above. They did note, however, that there will not likely be perfect agreement on DNA items when actual data are collected.

DeNisi et al. (1987) further developed the DNA idea by deriving and testing several hypotheses. They compared trained and untrained students with job analysts on a set of widely varying jobs. For students, 24 jobs were analyzed, with data available from analysts on 13 jobs. Although trends were consistent for most of their hypotheses, statistical significance failed to provide strong support. For example, they posited better reliability for the trained students. The differences were not statistically significant, although they were in the predicted direction ($r = .85$ versus .72 for trained and untrained, respectively). Correlations between each student group and job analysts were almost identical, .46 versus .47. The correlation between the number of DNA items and the magnitude of student convergence with job analysts was expected to be greater for the trained than the untrained group. Again, trends were as predicted ($r = .70$ versus .38), but the differences were not significant, based on only 13 pairs of observations per correlation. The only strong support for a hypothesis was the observed .50 correlation between the number of DNA items and the convergence between the two student groups.

The Monte Carlo results (Harvey and Hays, 1986) demonstrated that agreement only on DNA items can produce substantial convergence among sources. A comparison of analyses conducted with and without DNA items, however, does not support the notion that DNA agreement is the cause of convergence (e.g. Cornelius, DeNisi, and Blencoe, 1984; Friedman and Harvey, 1986). While correlations were reduced in both cases, they still remained in the .40s. Furthermore, elimination of DNA items is tantamount to recalculating correlations after restricting the range on the variables. Since DNA anchors one end of the rating scale, elimination of those items that tend to produce equivalent ratings at one end of the scale would be expected to reduce correlations to some extent. This would be similar to conducting a test validation study and eliminating all cases in which the individual was unsatisfactory in the job. What is interesting is that elimination of DNA items does not reduce the correlation to a greater degree. Thus there is obviously some level of agreement between sources on items beyond simple agreement about DNA.

Even if convergence was only evident in the DNA items, the artifact argument would not follow. It might well be that common knowledge is sufficient for conducting a crude analysis with limited training or direct job information. A gross screening of relevant versus irrelevant tasks could be done. Finer analyses of degree of relevance would then require more information and expertise.

While Smith and Hakel (1979) argued that naive raters are interchangeable with trained analysts, subsequent research suggests that this is not the case. A more realistic estimate of convergence is a level of correlation around .50. This suggests that college educated individuals, given little training and only a job title, have considerable general knowledge about what many jobs are like. This knowledge may be acquired in a number of ways, through both education and experience in society. We frequently encounter people in many jobs, observe them conducting their tasks, and know people who talk about their work. A certain amount of job information apparently can be gathered from people in general.

What is not clear, however, is the extent to which such common job knowledge is accurate. In other words does the agreement between students and analysts represent the overlap in veridical reports, or does it represent bias on the part of the analysts? That is, are analysts' ratings of jobs influenced by commonly held stereotypes about jobs? The research on convergence does not address this issue.

Jones, Main, Butler, and Johnson (1982) correlated PAQ ratings based on job descriptions with published ratings from the DOT. Student raters correlated well (r = .58 to .85) with the DOT. Cluster analysis based on the PAQ ratings produced meaningful job families. Jones *et al.* concluded that the PAQ can be successfully conducted using job descriptions, for at least some job analysis applications.

A limited number of studies have looked at convergence with other job analysis methods. Banks and Miller (1984) studied incumbents versus supervisors on the JCI. Sistrunk and Smith (1982) compared incumbents told to rate their own job with incumbents and supervisors asked to serve as content area experts on a task inventory. Cornelius and Lyness (1980) compared incumbents with a combined sample of supervisors and job analysts on several scales from the US Department of Labor. As can be seen in Table 3, convergence ranged from .59 to .88 in these studies.

Bias in Ratings

Part of the issue of validity concerns possible bias in job analysis ratings. Since little attention has been given to the issue of bias, it is not clear that ratings are free of it.

Smith and Hakel (1979) investigated the tendency for job incumbents to over-report doing 'impressive' tasks on their job. They had judges rate PAQ items for impressiveness and compared incumbents on the tendency to rate the impressive items higher than the unimpressive ones. Job incumbents and supervisors tended to rate high on both impressive and unimpressive items, which indicated lack of bias.

The issue of sex bias in PAQ ratings was studied by Arvey, Passino, and Lounsbury (1977). Trained students were asked to complete a PAQ on a job after viewing an interview with a supposed job incumbent. The sex of the incumbent was varied as the interview content remained constant. No evidence for sex bias in ratings was detected.

In a similar study, Arvey, Davis, McGowen, and Dipboye (1982) studied the effects of social cues on PAQ ratings. Subjects viewed interviews of supposed job incumbents, some of whom indicated the job was interesting and some of whom indicated it was not. Such cues have been shown to affect ratings of more global job characteristics (e.g. O'Reilly and Caldwell, 1979). The PAQ was found to be resistant to the effect—differences found were quite small in magnitude. The study failed, however, to replicate the effect with the Job Diagnostic Survey. A major difference between this and the successful cue studies was that observers rather than active participants were used here. Although the PAQ would seem to be resistant to social influence for observers, the same cannot be concluded for incumbents.

Some recent, as yet unpublished, data, collected by Juan Sanchez at the University of South Florida is suggestive of possible biasing effects of task attitudes. Job incumbents were asked to rate task statements on a number of dimensions, including task importance, criticality, difficulty of learning, responsibility, and time spent. He found that ratings of satisfaction with tasks were correlated with some of the scales including importance (personal communication, 18 November 1987).

Rater Characteristics

Some attention has been given to the problem of identifying the characteristics of individuals who would be accurate or inaccurate in their job analysis ratings. Green and Stutzman (1986) developed two criteria of accuracy: a carelessness index and a deviation (D) index. Several items that were obviously irrelevant to the target job were included in a task inventory. The total number of irrelevant items endorsed by the rater was the carelessness index. The D index is taken as the deviation of an individual from the mean of all raters. A total of 343 workers completed task inventories, and both indexes were calculated for each. Included, as well, were data on demographics and ratings by peers.

Results showed that the majority of raters had carelessness indices greater than zero, suggesting that most job incumbents are at least partially inaccurate in their ratings. Those who were accurate (zero carelessness scores) had greater reliabilities than those who were inaccurate. Finally, demographic characteristics and peer ratings did not predict accuracy very well. These results suggest that individuals may vary in their accuracy in completing task inventories, but they shed little light on variables that predict accuracy.

Other researchers have studied the relationship between rater characteristics and ratings. The only characteristics that seem to have had a relationship have been education (Cornelius and Lyness, 1980) and job level (Smith and Hakel, 1979). Smith and Hakel, however, argued that education might well have accounted for their results, since it was correlated with level.

No relation has been found between job incumbent performance and ratings using various job analysis methods (Conley and Sackett, 1987; Wexley and Silverman, 1978). Nor has there been found a relationship of job experience or tenure with ratings (Cornelius and Lyness, 1980; Schmitt and Cohen, 1987; Silverman, Wexley, and Johnson, 1984). In the laboratory with students rating the same jobs, small sex effects found by Arvey, Passino, and Lounsbury (1977) were not replicated in a later study (Arvey, Davis, McGowen, and Dipboye, 1982). Schmitt and Cohen (1987) found some relations of ratings on jobs with sex and race. It was not clear, however, whether males and female or whites and blacks perceived the same job conditions differently or experienced somewhat different jobs. Schmitt and Cohen speculated that employee characteristics might well lead to somewhat different task experiences. Finally, in the laboratory Arvey *et al.* (1977) found no relations between personality as assessed with the Gough Adjective Checklist and PAQ ratings.

Overall, these studies have shown that accuracy in ratings does vary across people. They say little about the sorts of individuals who are likely to be accurate or inaccurate. Only education and possibly job level have shown relations with job analysis ratings. Sex effects have been inconsistent, and those that have been found may be due to different experiences rather than bias or different frames of reference. The same may be said for race effects.

If Green and Stutzman's (1986) findings that most incumbents are inaccurate are found to be widespread, there is a need to be cautious when using such ratings. Their carelessness index would seem a useful procedure for improving the accuracy of task inventories, by eliminating inaccurate raters. For each job analyzed, several obviously irrelevant task statements could be included. Individuals who score above some predetermined criterion could be eliminated in calculating results.

COGNITIVE APPROACHES TO UNDERSTANDING THE RATING PROCESS

A limited number of studies have concerned how individuals use information to produce various job analysis ratings. One of the few efforts in this area was conducted by Sanchez and Levine (1988). This study utilized policy capturing to determine the information job raters used in making judgements of task importance. Sixty incumbents in four municipal jobs completed task inventories that asked for ratings of task importance, criticality, responsibility, difficulty, difficulty of learning, and time spent. Task criticality and difficulty of learning were most important; responsibility and time spent were least important.

A limitation of this study is that it gives no insight into the basis of the ratings on the various scales. For example, what is it about a task that leads it to be rated difficult to learn? Is it the amount of time it takes to learn the task, is it the amount of practice it takes to become proficient, or is it the degree of cognitive loading? Would a pure cognitive task and pure motor task be rated the same if both took exactly one hour to learn to proficiency? The connection between objective features of tasks and task ratings needs to be explored.

Two studies conducted by Cornelius and his colleagues were concerned with comparisons of clinical or holistic judgements and statistical or quantitative methods for making judgements. In the first, Cornelius and Lyness (1980) compared three types of judgements: a holistic based on overall ratings after studying tasks; a decomposed clinical based on overall ratings after making individual task ratings; and a decomposed algorithm based on quantitative combination of task ratings. The decomposed algorithm was superior in terms of inter-rater agreement to the other two methods. Convergent validity, however, was similar between the holistic and decomposed algorithm. Convergence was worse in the decomposed clinical condition. Cornelius et al. speculated that in the decomposed clinical condition, subjects were overloaded by having to make both task and holistic judgements.

In the second study Cornelius, DeNisi, and Blencoe (1984) found that holistic judgements of incumbents and supervisors were as accurate as discriminant analysis in classifying jobs. These two studies suggest that there is little advantage in collecting task level data and applying quantitative methods.

More work is certainly needed to test the limits of holistic judgement. It may be that many judgements can be made without having to collect detailed job analysis data. Such quantitative methods may be, as Cornelius, DeNisi, and Blencoe (1984) suggest, overkill. Situations in which detailed data are needed and situations in which holistic judgement will suffice, need to be explored.

JOB TAXONOMIES

Taxonomies are systems for clustering jobs according to common characteristics. Taxonomic work includes the development of classification structures, and also the assignment of individual elements into such structures. Structures which define job families are useful for both applied problems and theoretical research.

Various taxonomic systems have been developed in recent years. To classify jobs, researchers must make critical choices in at least two areas. First, the attributes used in classification (e.g. task statements versus incumbent ability profiles) must be chosen. Second, methods for developing the classifications must be selected. These methods can be either qualitative or quantitative. Qualitative methods are based on human judgement, and have been popular in governmental classification systems involving large numbers of jobs such as the Standard Occupational Classification Manual (US Department of Commerce, 1977), and the Canadian Classification and Dictionary of Occupations 1971 (Canada Department of Manpower and Immigration, 1973). Quantitative methods include cluster and factor analysis. In making these choices, the researchers' purposes (e.g. selection or training) are important.

Attributes Used in Classification

Many different taxonomic approaches were described at length in Fleishman and Quaintance (1984). Of particular interest are five different approaches which were emphasized by the Taxonomy Project (Fleishman and Stephenson, 1972). The first of these, called the criterion measures approach, emphasized tasks as both behavior requirements and as behavior descriptions. Teichner and colleagues (Teichner and Olson 1969, 1971) were able to classify experimental studies of learning by type of task, and to show that the relative merits of massed and distributed practice varied by types of learning task.

The information theoretic approach (Levine and Teichner, 1972, 1973) was based on a general model from information processing theory. Tasks were defined as transfers of information between a source and a receiver. This approach appears likely to be useful when analyzing human/machine systems.

The task strategies approach (Miller, 1973) defines tasks in terms of behavioral requirements. The approach analyzes tasks in four dimensions: (a) task functions; (b) task content; (c) task environment; and (d) level of learning. Miller (1973) developed a vocabulary of task functions (e.g. input select, detect, search, identify) which might be used to analyze almost any task. To date, little applied work has been done with this system.

The ability requirements approach (e.g. Fleishman, 1982) defines a task in terms of the human abilities required to accomplish the task. A large number of human abilities have been defined, and scales for rating tasks on each ability have been developed. The approach appears useful in setting performance standards, in test development, and in classifying jobs and tasks (Fleishman and Quaintance, 1984, pp. 344–6).

The task characteristics approach (Farina and Wheaton, 1973) defines tasks in terms independent from human responses to tasks. That is, tasks are defined as stimulus situations or antecedent conditions. A language was developed to describe task components, such as task goals and task responses. For each task component, task characteristics were developed. For example, for task goal, task characteristics included the number of output units, and the duration for which an output unit was maintained. This approach proved useful in predicting skill acquisition and performance levels across a number of diverse tasks.

Quantitative Methods for Job Taxonomies

Considerable attention has been given to the development of quantitative methods for determining job similarities and differences. The major use of these methods has been for taxonomic work, building clusters or families of jobs that have similar content or require similar human attributes or abilities. Much of the recent impetus for work in this area comes from the Uniform Guidelines, which allow validity generalization among similar jobs. The major problem is to determine which jobs are similar enough to assume the generalizability of validity in selection.

Several methods have been suggested to address this problem. The most frequently used method has been hierarchical cluster analysis (Mobley and Ramsay, 1973). Arvey and Mossholder (1977) were critical of the lack of statistical tests with cluster analysis and presented an analysis of variance (ANOVA) approach, based on the PAQ. Lissitz, Mendoza, Huberty, and Markos (1979), critical of Arvey and Mossholder's ANOVA, suggested the use of multivariate analysis of variance (MANOVA). McNelis (1986) applied multidimensional scaling to similarity judgements, while Cornelius, Hakel, and Sackett (1979) presented an example of three-mode factor analysis.

The basic idea in the cluster analysis procedure is to measure each of several jobs on selected dimensions taken from a job analysis, and then to apply cluster analysis to these data (Mobley and Ramsay, 1973). The result will be one or more job clusters, with members within each cluster being considered similar, and members of different clusters being considered different. The major problem with this method is the lack of a statistical criterion (i.e. significance test) for similarity (Arvey and Mossholder, 1977; Lissitz et al., 1979).

Another problem is choosing the appropriate measure of association for determining cluster membership. Hamer and Cunningham (1981) compared seven such measures, including measures of distance (Euclidean, Squared Euclidean, and Average Non-zero), angular separation (cosine of angle between vectors, product–moment correlation), and profile overlap (per cent and absolute). Judges made similarity ratings for 50 jobs from six DOT worker trait groups. Data from the OAI were cluster analyzed, using the seven measures. The angular separation measures correlated highest with the judges' similarity ratings. Judges' ratings were superior to the clustering measures in predicting DOT job group membership. Of the seven measures, again the angular separation members were superior in predicting DOT job group membership. Hamer and Cunningham (1981) suggest using multiple measures, especially when different analysts provide the ratings of different jobs.

Several examples can be found of cluster analysis being used to build job families (e.g. Mobley and Ramsay, 1973; Taylor, 1978; Taylor and Colbert, 1978). Cornelius, Carron, and Collins (1979) applied the cluster analysis approach to data from three job analysis methods to determine if the job clusters would be consistent across them. Compared were a task-oriented, worker-oriented (PAQ), and abilities-oriented method, used on each of seven foreman jobs in a manufacturing plant. Each method resulted in a different solution. The task-oriented method suggested either three or five clusters, the ability-oriented suggested three clusters, and the worker-oriented resulted in one cluster. Furthermore, the jobs grouped together in the task-oriented three-cluster solution were not the same as in the ability-oriented three-cluster solution. Cornelius et al. suggested that different job analysis methods would be appropriate for different uses. For example, a task-oriented method might be appropriate when hiring individuals who are expected to need little or no training. An ability-oriented method might be appropriate for selection when extensive training is expected.

McNelis (1986) had students make global similarity judgements between all possible pairs of fifteen jobs in three conditions: incumbent qualifications necessary, tasks required, and pay. Multidimensional scaling was applied to the judgements to identify the underlying structure of judgements. She found a different solution for each judgement condition, with three dimensions for qualifications, two for tasks, and three for pay. One dimension, working with people versus data/things, was common to all three solutions; another dimension, amount of specialized training, was common to two solutions; and three dimensions, nature of public service, prestige, and male/female, were uniquely identified. These findings support the idea that the dimension upon which judgements are made influences the nature of the resulting taxonomy.

The Arvey and Mossholder (1977) ANOVA method was based on the PAQ, although any job analysis method could be used as long as all jobs are assessed on a common set of items or dimensions. Data from multiple raters would fit an experimental design in which the different jobs would be a between-subject factor, the different PAQ scales would be a within-subject factor, and raters would be nested within jobs, that is, there would be different raters for each job. An analysis of variance would be conducted, with the major effect of interest being the job by scale interaction, indicating the degree to which jobs differed differentially across scales.

Published criticisms of the ANOVA technique revolved around three major points. First, Hanser, Mendel, and Wolins (1979), and McIntyre and Farr (1979) both expressed concerns about the statistical power of the technique. Hanser et al. (1979) were stronger in their criticism, suggesting that the use of traditional significance testing was not appropriate. They argued that in this case the Type II error would be more serious than the Type I. They noted that a Type I error falsely indicates that similar jobs are different. The result is failure to generalize validity, and unnecessary validation studies. A Type II error falsely indicates that different jobs are similar. The result is improper validity generalization, the use of invalid tests, violation of the Uniform Guidelines and poor employee selection. Both Hanser et al. and McIntyre and Farr suggest setting a lenient alpha level to increase power.

A second problem concerns the rather restrictive assumptions for repeated measures ANOVA. Homogeneity of covariance among the repeated measures and compound symmetry of the pooled within-covariance matrix are essential to maintain the theoretical alpha level. Although failure to meet assumptions can be addressed with corrections, the analyses become quite conservative and alpha levels are unknown (Hanser et al., 1979).

Finally, it has been stated that considering the different dimensions of the PAQ as levels of a within-subject variable is inappropriate (Lissitz et al., 1979; McIntyre and Farr, 1979). Lissitz et al. have recommended using multivariate analysis of variance (MANOVA) on the data collected with the Arvey and Mossholder (1977) procedure. In this case job titles would serve as levels of a between-subject variable, PAQ scales would serve as multiple dependent variables, and raters would be treated as subjects. The advantages of this procedure are that it does not require the restrictive assumptions concerning covariances among the repeated measures, and the multivariate approach provides additional procedures, such as discriminant analysis, to explore the nature of job differences. The major disadvantage is the necessity for large sample sizes. As Lissitz et al. noted, the minimum sample size must be equal to the number of PAQ dimensions plus the number of jobs. To achieve reasonable statistical power, even larger sample sizes are essential (Arvey, Maxwell, and Mossholder, 1979).

Arvey and his colleagues have answered these criticisms, suggesting yet another possible analysis (Arvey et al., 1979; Arvey, Maxwell, Guttenberg, and Camp, 1981). They addressed the power problem in two ways. First, they suggested that power is under the control of the researcher, who can increase it by adding subjects or raising the alpha level (Arvey et al., 1979). Second, Arvey et al. (1981) conducted a Monte Carlo study of their ANOVA approach to test power. They manipulated the extent of job differences from large to none, number of raters from two to eight, and violation of compound symmetry, from major violation to no violation. Power to detect differences was affected by all three manipulations, with power being sufficiently high much of the time. There were instances, however, where power was quite low, more in the detection of job main effects than for job by dimension interactions. For example, even major differences with eight raters were detected only 21 per cent of the time when compound symmetry was severely violated.

Arvey et al. (1979) argued that the repeated measures ANOVA approach was appropriate with these data. They pointed out that the scales are measured on the same metric (z-scores), allowing them to be considered as 'commensurate' (p. 534). This procedure, they noted, is quite common in profile analysis. When assumptions are met, the repeated measures approach would have more power than MANOVA. Finally, they suggested yet another approach—using MANOVA to analyze repeated measures, when sample sizes are sufficient. Otherwise, they recommend their ANOVA approach.

One demonstration has been conducted using three-mode factor analysis to cluster jobs (Cornelius, Hakel, and Sackett, 1979). This procedure allows for the analysis of three modes of data, as opposed to two (typically variables by subjects) in traditional factor analysis. Cornelius et al. used as modes job elements (modified from the PAQ), job titles, and military rank in their analysis. They found complex groupings of job families characterized by dimensions of job attributes.

Cornelius, Schmidt, and Carron (1984) compared a quantitative method of classifying jobs with a clinical judgement approach. Experts classified jobs from 30 companies into four families. Task inventory data were subjected to a discriminant analysis to derive classification functions. Upon cross-validation, the functions were shown to classify correctly 96 per cent of the jobs. Job incumbents and supervisors also made a clinical or holistic classification judgement for each job. These judgements were also accurate in 96 per cent of the cases. Cornelius et al. raised the question if statistical methods might represent overkill. It may be that individuals familiar with jobs can cluster them subjectively as well as the quantitative methods. Of course, the four families may well have been quite broad, allowing for easy judgements of membership. It is not clear that holistic judgements would do as well when families are more narrowly defined. Furthermore, jobs in the four families may in fact have been quite different from one another, even though they were similar along one or more dimensions. This may have allowed for the observed accurate classification.

One caution in the use of these quantitative methods comes from a study by Stutzman (1983). In most studies, job title or classification is used as the level of analysis, assuming reasonable homogeneity among similarly classified jobs. Stutzman tested this assumption by applying the MANOVA technique to the same job in four units of the same organization. He found considerable differences on some job dimensions, and concluded that it may be dangerous to assume all jobs with the same title are in fact the same in content.

Overall it would seem that a combination of methods, including cluster analysis, MANOVA, and discriminant analysis is probably most appropriate when exploring job similarities and differences. The results of Cornelius et al. (1979) indicate that the nature of the job analysis method is important and strongly influences the job clusters or groupings that emerge. Hence, one must pay careful attention to the dimensions along which similarities and differences are described. One should also be careful about the heterogeneity of jobs with the same title. Further work along the lines of Stutzman's (1983) comparison of jobs across units would seem appropriate.

It would further seem that the MANOVA approach, as described by Lissitz et al. (1979), would be preferred over the ANOVA. Although the problems with the ANOVA approach may not be as severe as discussed by the critics, the multivariate nature of the data would suggest the use of those methods best able to handle them, such as MANOVA and discriminant analysis.

The work described here has provided some methods for attacking the problem of job similarities, but they have seen limited use. Further work similar to Colbert and Taylor (1978) should be done to explore the utility of these methods and to answer some basic questions. For example, if one were to use the PAQ and MANOVA to build job clusters, how well would the validity of selection tests generalize to jobs both within and between clusters? What are the critical dimensions of jobs relevant to synthetic validity? Finally, can we build taxonomies of jobs or job characteristics that are relevant to training problems? Parallel questions can also be asked for other areas in which job similarities are of interest, such as salary administration, training, or performance appraisal.

Taxonomic Purposes

Taxonomic work may be quite general or narrowly directed towards a single, specific application. The intent of a taxonomic study might be to develop a tool to measure aspects of jobs which can be used for multiple purposes, such as job evaluation, personnel selection, and training. As discussed above, a study might be concerned with a single purpose, commonly validity generalization.

As with traditional job analysis, purpose should guide the choice of attributes and methods of analysis (cf. Levine, Thomas, and Sistrunk, 1988; McCormick, 1979). As the number or type of applications for the taxonomy increases, so does the difficulty of specifying appropriate attributes to measure. Two studies which attempted to integrate different approaches to job analysis illustrate the difficulties inherent in building instruments capable of a wide variety of taxonomic purposes.

Campion and Thayer (1985) used their MJDQ to classify 121 jobs. They measured each job on the four scales, as well as 35 outcome variables, which were reduced to theoretical composites of efficiency, satisfaction, reliability, and comfort. Results indicated that different job design features, as measured by each of the scales, were related to different outcomes. For example, measurements related to motivational design were negatively related to work efficiency, while measurements related to biological design were positively related to job comfort. Such results strongly suggest that a tool developed for one purpose (e.g. group jobs according to comfort) would not likely be useful for some other purpose (e.g. group jobs according to efficiency). Since the Campion and Thayer (1985) MJDQ was designed to reflect multiple approaches, it could be useful for multiple purposes related to job design.

Whitely (1985) integrated approaches based on both work content and work process. A total of 70 managers were sampled from a chemical processing plant, a hospital, and a bank. The Management Position Description Questionnaire (Tornow and Pinto, 1976) was used to measure work content. Managerial roles were assessed with a specially designed worksheet which included thirteen roles determined to distinguish among managers (Mintzberg, 1973; Stewart, 1976, 1982). Examples of process characteristics included duration of activity, categories of interpersonal contact (working with peers, boss, or those outside the organization), and purpose of activity.

Whitely (1985) constructed profiles for each manager based separately on the MPDQ and process inventories, and cluster analyzed each set of profiles. He found seven clusters of managers based on the MPDQ profiles, and six clusters of managers based on the process profiles. The convergence of clusters based on the two types of information was moderate, in that '. . . 56 per cent (39/70) of the managers in a given content cluster were located on one or two of the process clusters . . .' (p. 354). In other words, managers whose work content was very similar used different processes to accomplish their work goals. Since other information was not collected, it is not clear whether work content or process information (or both) is better suited for taxonomic work.

While a tool developed for a specific purpose need not be useful for another purpose, it is possible that a single tool can serve multiple purposes adequately. Such appears to be the case for the PAQ. The PAQ consists of items, which tap the dimensions of information input, mediation processes, work output, interpersonal activities, work situation and job context, and miscellaneous. A principal components analysis of 150 of these elements yielded five principal components, labelled Decision/communications/social responsibilities, Skilled activities, Physical activities/related environmental conditions, Equipment/ vehicle operation, and Information processing activities. The PAQ was intended to allow the analysis of virtually any non-managerial job. McCormick *et al.* (1972) showed how the PAQ can be useful in personnel selection and job evaluation. This instrument was not designed for a particular taxonomic purpose, although it was intended to be most useful for job classification, evaluation, and ability requirements estimation.

The PAQ has also been used to establish job component validity, or synthetic validity (Lawshe, 1952), a process in which job components are related to tests. The link between job components and tests allows the development of a test battery for a job from prior work component validities of the tests (Mossholder and Arvey, 1984).

McCormick, DeNisi, and Shaw (1979) reported that PAQ ratings could predict mean levels of five aptitude constructs in incumbents of various job types. Other studies have shown that PAQ ratings predict the magnitude of validity coefficients between test scores and job performance for jobs which vary on such attributes as decision making (Gutenberg, Arvey, Osburn, and Jeanneret, 1983; McCormick *et al.*, 1972). Mossholder and Arvey (1984) noted that some PAQ dimensions which do not predict mean levels of incumbent scores do predict validity coefficients.

Managerial applications

Four different managerial taxonomies are described in Table 4. As can be seen from the table, the studies differed with respect to samples of items and incumbents, and resultant dimensions. All of the authors began with different sets of tasks as well. Dowell and Wexley (1978) and Prien (1963) were focused on first line supervisory jobs, while Hemphill (1960) and Tornow and Pinto (1976) focused on general management jobs. The authors used different types of factor analysis. Two used Q-factor analysis where the data matrix is transposed so that people are columns and variables are rows. The preferred type of factor analysis for deriving task dimensions in such studies is R-factor analysis, where the matrix to be factored contains people as rows, and variables as columns (Dowell and Wexley, 1978; Tornow and Pinto, 1976). Given the differences among the studies, it is not surprising that different factors emerged across studies. The different factor structures, however, suggest common managerial functions. Common functions included organizing the work of others, supervising subordinates' work planning, and expediting production.

The general managerial studies contained factors related to working

Table 4

	Hemphill	Tornow and Pinto	Prien	Dowell and Wexley
Items	575	208	?	89
Respondents	93	489	24	251

Dimensions

	Hemphill	Tornow and Pinto	Prien	Dowell and Wexley
1.	Provide a staff service in non-operational areas	Product, marketing, and financial strategy planning	Employee supervision	Working with subordinates
2.	Supervision of work	Coordination of other organizational units and personnel	Employee contact and communication	Organizing work of subordinates
3.	Internal business control	Internal business control	Union–management relations	Maintaining efficient quality production
4.	Technical aspects with products and markets	Products and services responsibility	Manpower, coordination, and administration	Maintaining safe clean work areas
5.	Human, community, and social affairs	Public and customer relations	Work organization planning, and preparation	Maintaining equipment and machinery
6.	Long-range planning	Advanced consulting	Manufacturing process administration	Compiling records and reports
7.	Exercise broad power and authority	Autonomy of action		
8.	Business reputation	Approval of financial commitments		
9.	Personal demands	Staff service		
10.	Preservation of assets	Supervision		
11.		Complexity and stress		
12.		Advanced financial responsibility		
13.		Broad personnel responsibility		

conditions as well as task statements. The Hemphill (1960) Personal Demands factor and the Tornow and Pinto (1976) Complexity and Stress factors are examples. The general managerial studies also contained factors related to job scope, such as the Hemphill (1960) factor Exercise of Broad Power and Authority, and the Tornow and Pinto (1976) Autonomy of Action and Broad Personnel Responsibility.

The first line supervisor studies contained factors which were more specific, and in some cases absent from the general managerial studies. The first line supervisor studies had factors composed of items involving working directly with subordinates as well as organizing subordinates' work. In addition, specific factors such as Maintaining Equipment and Machinery emerged solely in the first line supervisor jobs.

Non-managerial applications

The OAI (Cunningham *et al.*, 1983) was designed to develop taxonomies applicable to occupational education and guidance. The items were developed from the following *a priori* dimensions: information received, mental activities, work behavior, work goals, and work context. The questionnaire contained 602 items used to rate 1414 jobs. Eight separate sections of the OAI were subjected to factor analyses. The factors which resulted were subjected to a higher order factor analysis, which yielded in 25 dimensions. Four of the dimensions and examples of jobs representative of the dimensions were: (a) sales, service, and public relations, such as salesperson or bartender; (b) biological/health related activities, such as dentist or veterinarian; (c) utilization and processing of numerical data, such as savings operations officer or accountant; and (d) food preparation/processing, such as short order cook or chef. The interested reader is referred to Cunningham *et al.* (1983) and Cunningham (1988) for further details on dimensions derived.

Cunningham (1988) reported several analyses relevant to the utility of the OAI as a taxonomic tool for occupational education. A cluster analysis of the 1414 jobs revealed 25 meaningful clusters. Clusters of jobs varied in the predicted direction on mental test scores of incumbents. Analyses showed that people employed in jobs high in need-reinforcement estimates measured by the OAI were more satisfied with their jobs. Those whose needs matched need-reinforcement profiles of their jobs were more satisfied than those whose needs were not matched by the need-reinforcement profiles of their jobs (Cunningham, 1988). Work is currently directed at measuring attributes of high school and college students relevant to dimensions measured by the OAI for vocational guidance (Cunningham, Slonaker, and Riegel, 1987).

A related effort to construct job families for occupational guidance was reported by Stafford, Jackson, and Banks (1984). The specific purpose was to identify job families to develop training programs for less qualified young people. The JCI was used in this research. A point of interest in the Stafford et al. (1984) paper was that the sample of jobs was obtained by following students who left school early. The target population of jobs was operationally defined as the actual jobs in which similar students were currently employed. The authors sampled 455 jobs, and were able to form six clusters of jobs from the 36 skill component profiles. The clusters were clerical work, skilled interpersonal work, operative work, unskilled manual work, intermediate skilled technical work, and skilled technical work.

A final application of taxonomic research concerns the development of job families for validity generalization (Taylor, 1978; Taylor and Colbert, 1978; Colbert and Taylor, 1978). Taylor (1978) used the PAQ to describe 76 insurance company jobs. Cluster analysis based on five overall and seventeen component dimensions yielded six job families. Taylor and Colbert (1978) used the PAQ to describe 325 insurance company jobs. In this study, principal components of the PAQ derived from the insurance company jobs were used to assign jobs to thirteen job families. The thirteen job families were reported to be more meaningful than the six job families in the prior study. Colbert and Taylor (1978) chose three of the thirteen job families identified in the prior study to test the generalizability of regression equations used in personnel selection. They found that different single predictors were significant for different job families, and that cross-validated multiple correlations were larger within job families than across job families. The magnitude of the multiple correlation across job families, however, was similar to those within job families, that is, the test batteries worked well regardless of job family. However, all job families were composed of entry level clerical jobs, so the small differences in predictability are not surprising.

Pearlman (1980) described taxonomic approaches for creating job families, especially for validity generalization. He argued that broad job families were likely to be most useful in generalizing test validity (see also Schmidt, Hunter, and Pearlman, 1981).

JOB EVALUATION

Job evaluation is the process of assigning value (e.g. wages) to jobs within organizations. In the United States, research in job evaluation began shortly after the Second World War, was abandoned for many years, and has recently become a viable research topic. The main reason for this renewed interest in job evaluation has been allegations of sex discrimination in pay across jobs, and the recent debate about comparable worth.

Methods

Numerous methods of job evaluation exist, such as the ranking method, the point method, the factor method, and regression methods based on standardized job analysis questionnaires. Hybrid methods are also used. The most prevalent in large US firms is some variety of the point method (Treiman, 1979). It has been the most commonly researched method, and it is characterized by the following steps:

1. *Choose compensable factors.* The compensable factors are the aspects of jobs (typically areas of responsibility) for which the organization pays employees. Global compensable factors are skill, effort, responsibility, and working conditions. Examples of more specific compensable factors are consequences of error, autonomy, know-how, and required education. Each job in the job evaluation study must be characterized by some standing on each of the factors.
2. *Assign points to each job on each factor.* This step involves a judgement of the degree or level of the job on each factor. For example, the judge must decide the level of education necessary to perform the job, and the severity of the consequences to the organization of error in carrying out the job. Typically, a panel of judges decides upon the compensable factors, their definitions, and specific point assignments. After the points have been assigned to each job on each compensable factor, the points are added across factors to get a total, which reflects the value of the job to the organization. The total points are intended to reflect the relative (not absolute) value of the jobs. Points need not be in currency units.
3. *Validate the system.* In the final step, the relative ordering of jobs by the job evaluation system is compared with actual wages to check whether the job evaluation system is functioning properly. In practice, a subset of the jobs (known as 'key jobs') is chosen because they are believed to be properly or fairly paid by the organization. The pay rates for the key jobs are regressed on the point values from the job evaluation system. If the system is functioning properly, the jobs should fall on a straight line. Assuming such a result, the remaining jobs can then be assigned wages through the regression equation developed on the key jobs or through an analogous system of job classification developed by personnel specialists.

Standardized methods of job analysis such as the PAQ are sometimes used for job evaluation in what might be labelled a market policy capturing approach. A group of jobs is analyzed using a single instrument. The key jobs are chosen, and a regression equation is developed where wages are values of the dependent variable, and the items or dimensions of the job analysis questionnaire are the independent variables. In essence, wages or market value choose the compensable factors and their weights through the regression procedure. The validation step should be carried out by cross-validating the regression equation to a new sample of jobs. An example of the regression approach is described by McCormick et al. (1972).

Job Evaluation and Pay Discrimination

Bias against a group of people (e.g. women) can potentially occur at each step of the job evaluation process. The choice of compensable factors can influence the relative standing of jobs on pay. A system could favor men by paying jobs that require heavy lifting but not visual acuity, for example. The assignment of points and weights to factors also allows for potential bias. As judgements are typically used to assign points to factors based on narrative job descriptions, the job evaluation panel could be influenced by characteristics of the job incumbents rather than the job itself. Several critics of job evaluation have suggested that the validation step serves to perpetuate prior discrimination because women have been segregated into a relatively small number of jobs (Eyde, 1983; Rytina, 1981). Such occupational segregation results in a large supply of labor for a small number of jobs thereby decreasing women's wages. Research has addressed each of the above steps in job evaluation.

The Choice of Compensable Factors

Only a single study has directly addressed the choice of compensable factors in possible sex bias in job evaluation. Doverspike and Barrett (1984) had four graduate students evaluate 105 male sex-typed jobs and 105 female sex-typed jobs using a fifteen-point scale method job evaluation system. The evaluation ratings were analyzed for sex bias by scale using several methods including reliability, factor analysis, partial correlation, and scale-total correlations. The authors used the results of the sex bias analyses to remove biased scales from the job evaluation system. Removal of the biased scales resulted in a 'fair' evaluation system according to each method. The authors compared the global ordering of jobs on worth estimates for job evaluation systems including and excluding the biased scales.

The factor analysis did not yield a clear decision about bias for each of the fifteen scales, although one of the three factors extracted from the correlations of the fifteen scales on the male sex-typed jobs did not match any of the three factors extracted from correlations of the scales on the female sex-typed jobs. The reliability, partial correlation, and scale-total correlation methods each allowed a verdict of whether each scale was biased. The three methods did not agree highly on inferences of scale bias. For example, the negotiating scale appeared biased in favor of men using the partial correlation method, but biased in favor of women using the scale-total method.

Doverspike and Barrett (1984) constructed job evaluation systems by eliminating biased scales separately for each method to determine the practical significance of the difference of choice of unbiased scales. They found that choice of scales did affect the relative standing of male and female sex-typed jobs on pay, but the magnitude of difference was not large.

Two other studies showed results relevant to the choice of compensable factors. The first was conducted by McCormick *et al.* (1972). The authors used the PAQ to analyze 340 jobs from 45 different organizations. The regression approach to job evaluation was used, where the dependent variable was monthly compensation. Three sets of independent variables were used in separate regressions: ratings on individual elements (items) of the PAQ; job dimension scores for the 27 job-data dimensions derived from factor analysis; and five overall dimensions. Stepwise regression was used to reduce the number of independent variables in the individual elements and job-data dimensions. Cross-validated multiple correlation coefficients for the nine individual elements chosen from 189 elements were .86 and .86. Coefficients for nine job-data dimensions were .85 and .83, and coefficients for the five overall dimensions were .87 and .83. Even though the independent variables were different in each of the regressions, the resulting correlation coefficients were quite similar. These results also suggested that the choice of compensable factors is not crucial in job evaluation.

A study conducted in South Africa by Snelgar (1982) is relevant to the choice of compensable factors. Snelgar (1982) sent job descriptions of 24 key jobs, which varied in difficulty of job content, to sixteen different organizations. The organizations used widely different job evaluation methods, including ranking, classification, point, and factor methods. Each company evaluated the 24 jobs using their own job evaluation system (the compensable factors and methods differed across organizations). The resulting point totals for jobs were correlated among the companies. Correlations between systems ranged from .93 to .99, with an average of .98. The results suggested that, for these jobs at least, the choice of compensable factors (and indeed the choice of job evaluation methods) did not matter.

The Assignment of Points

Several studies investigated the reliability in job evaluation judgements. For example, Doverspike, Carlisi, Barrett, and Alexander (1983) had ten graduate students rate twenty job descriptions of office and business personnel. Ratings were made using an eleven-point scale method job evaluation system. A generalizability analysis (Cronbach *et al.*, 1972) was computed through analysis of variance of the ratings; facets included scales, judges, and jobs. Most of the variance in ratings could be attributed to jobs, scales, and job by scale interactions. The generalizability of judges (inter-judge reliability) was generally high, both for the total points and for each of the scales. The lowest generalizability estimate across ten raters was .97.

Fraser, Cronshaw, and Alexander (1984) carried out a similar study in a large energy resource company. Three employees in employee relations rated twelve non-exempt jobs in the personnel services department. The ratings were obtained through an eight-point scale method. Again, the inter-judge reliabilities of the total points and scales were high, with the exception of the working conditions scale.

Schwab and Heneman (1986) extended the previous studies by following independent job evaluation panels in a manufacturing firm. In this study, the judges had access to more information than narrative job descriptions (i.e. they could observe the work being done and interview incumbents). Unlike the prior studies, the judges also came to consensus about the assignment of points to the jobs. Ratings of 53 jobs independently evaluated by two job evaluation panels using a ten-point scale method were compared. The correlation between total points for jobs across panels was .99. Reliabilities for each of the ten-point scales were high (r greater than .73), with the exception of working conditions ($r = .39$).

Overall, the assignment of points in the method of job evaluation appears to be very reliable. Random error due to specific judges or panels appears to be small. Reliability, however, does not rule out systematic bias. For example, judges could all agree that female sex-typed jobs should be allocated a smaller number of points than male sex-typed jobs even though job duties are identical. Several studies have addressed this point.

Mahoney and Blake (1979) had students rate 20 well-known jobs on job requirements, salary, and masculinity–femininity. The authors found a significant correlation between salary and masculinity–feminity after controlling for job requirements. Schwab and Grams (1985) investigated three sources of bias in judgements of compensation specialists: sex of evaluator, sex of incumbents, and current pay of jobs. They found that sex of the evaluator and sex of the incumbent did not affect the total worth of the job investigated. Pay, however, did affect the judgements of worth. The results suggest that knowledge of pay influenced the judges' assignment of points on the compensable factors education, experience, and complexity.

Validation

In the final step of job evaluation, salary is regressed on total points, or in the case of standardized job analysis techniques, compensable factors. Fairness in pay can be examined by comparing the regressions of salary on points separately for male and female sex-typed jobs. A significant difference in slopes and/or intercepts suggests unfair compensation practice. It should be noted that many different mathematical models have been offered as definitions of 'fairness' (e.g.

Arvey, 1979). The most commonly used model equates fairness with equality of sub-group slopes and intercepts (e.g. Arvey, Maxwell, and Abraham, 1985).

It is not clear precisely what an organization should do with regression analysis to ensure fairness. A partial list of alternatives includes: fitting regression to all the key jobs (both male and female sex-types), and then moving any jobs below the regression line on to the line by increasing pay; fitting regression lines separately for jobs of each sex-type, and then moving the lower paid jobs until the intercept terms are equal; or moving the lower paid jobs until the intercept terms are not significantly different. The latter two options differ in the expense incurred to the organization, as the last option will be cheaper to implement. Arvey (1986) discussed additional alternative courses of action.

Several articles specifically dealt with regression techniques and inferences of the fairness of compensation practices. Arvey *et al.* (1985) discussed reliability artifacts in comparable worth procedures. If two groups are characterized by identical population regressions of salary on total points, the two groups differ on mean levels of the total points, and the slope is not zero, then the estimated regression lines for the two groups will be identical only if the total points are estimated with perfect reliability. If the total point estimates are less than perfectly reliable, the intercept estimates for the two groups will differ. The slopes will be identical, but closer to zero than the true (population) slope. Thus, the finding of different intercepts for male and female sex-typed jobs may cause an unwarranted inference of unfairness. Application of the latter two options to the finding of equal slopes and different intercepts could result in an unwarranted increase in the pay of female sex-typed jobs.

Schwab and Wichern (1983) analyzed a situation in which male and female sex-typed regressions differed in intercepts such that the female intercept was lower. Female jobs were also lower in average total points. If a regression is fit to all the key jobs (both male and female sex-types), then the total slope will be higher than the slopes for either male or female sex-type jobs. More importantly, the male jobs will tend to fall below the group regression line, and the female sex-typed jobs will tend to fall above the group regression line. Application of the first option will result in an unwarranted increase in the pay of male sex-typed jobs.

Several articles were concerned with reverse regression as a technique for establishing the magnitude of bias in compensation (Birnbaum, 1979; Conway and Roberts, 1983; Roberts, 1980; Schwab and Wichern, 1983). Reverse regression is a technique in which the independent and dependent variables swap sides of the equation. Wages becomes the independent variable, total points becomes the dependent variable, and separate regressions are estimated for each set of sex-typed jobs. If certain assumptions are met, reverse regression can indicate whether random or systematic error is operating in the compensation system (Roberts, 1980; Schwab and Wichern, 1983), and give an estimate of the magnitude of sex discrimination (Goldberger, 1984). Arvey *et al.* (1985) noted that for reverse regression to yield accurate estimates of discrimination, pay must be a perfectly deterministic function of total points and sex. Given a more realistic assumption that pay is a function of total points, sex, and error, reverse regression yields biased estimates. Arvey *et al.* (1985) recommended the use of Linear Structural Relations (LISREL, Jöreskog and Sörbom, 1979) for analysis of compensation systems. The LISREL model allows a direct test of equality of regression slopes and intercepts adjusted for reliability, since it is based on different assumptions than regression. Arvey *et al.* (1985) provided hypothetical data which illustrated the superiority of the LISREL approach over the reverse regression approach.

Job Evaluation Judgements

From a purely analytical perspective, it is clear that the choice of compensable factors in job evaluation could affect the ordering of jobs on worth. The evidence on this point suggests that the rank ordering of jobs is rather impervious to the choice of compensable factors in practice. Job evaluation judgements by students, panels, and compensation practitioners are all very reliable; reliability estimates are typically above .90 and often approach perfection. Although evaluators tend to agree about the relative worth of jobs, there remains a disquieting possibility that the source of agreement among judges is based less on information about actual job activities than on common knowledge about the social standing of the job itself.

It has been shown that experienced compensation analysts use current salary in making judgements of job standing on education, experience, and complexity (Schwab and Grams, 1985). Thus ratings of female type jobs, such as clerks and secretaries may be based more on current wages than actual job content. If clerical jobs were high status, well paid jobs, it is quite possible that job evaluation systems would show that they require extensive education, skill, and know-how.

In a policy capturing study, Stang (1984) had judges estimate overall worth of untitled jobs given only job profiles which varied on the compensable factors. Each profile contained task statements indicative of responsibility on eighteen compensable factors, such as autonomy, consequences of error, and working conditions. Judges were to consider the standings on each compensable factors, and arrive at an overall worth estimate of the job represented by the profile. The judges were largely incapable of completing the task. For many judges, regression results showed that the compensable factors failed to account for variance in judgements of overall worth, and rate–rerate reliabilities were not significantly different from zero. This study suggests that people given task or activity statements have difficulty in assigning worth estimates to a job. People given job titles and narrative descriptions of jobs have no such difficulty. Future research should address what information job evaluators have and use when making judgements.

The validation step in job evaluation remains the most problematic. Comparable worth advocates have maintained that the market value (i.e. going wage rates) may be biased because of prior sex discrimination (Blumrosen, 1979; Treiman and Hartmann, 1981). The practice of assessing market value may also be problematic because the market value obtained in a given study depends on survey procedures which are not standard across organizations (Rynes and Milkovich, 1986).

SUMMARY AND CONCLUSIONS

In the past, most research on job analysis has been concerned with the development and use of methods. Much of that work continues, with both general and more specialized methods. In the past decade job analysis researchers have broadened their interests to include questions of method validity, bias, and underlying cognitive processes. Much of this work is provocative, raising interesting questions that have yet to be answered.

Job analysis ratings often show acceptable reliabilities and good convergent validities. Based on the limited research that has been done, they seem to be relatively free of gender and racial bias. Specific characteristics of individuals who make good raters have yet to be identified. While reliabilities are often high, examples can be found of low reliabilities, as well. Furthermore, work on inter-rater accuracy suggests that many individuals are inaccurate to some extent. It may be that only some individuals can give accurate ratings. The extent to which this generalizes beyond task inventories and the possible characteristics of accurate individuals needs to be explored. Furthermore, attention needs to be given to the types of ratings that can and cannot be reliably and accurately made.

The convergent validities of ratings are both encouraging and disturbing. It seems that students given job titles can provide ratings that correlate reasonably well with experienced job analysts with extensive information. It is not clear whether this 'common job knowledge' is veridical, reflecting that educated people have some knowledge about many jobs, or inaccurate job stereotypes jointly held by analysts and students. This is an important question that needs further attention.

The cognitive processes underlying ratings is another area that deserves study. It is not clear what information job analysts actually use to make ratings. This is a significant problem when trying to detect bias in job evaluation ratings. It may well be that job analysis ratings can be based on less information, thus making the process less arduous. A better understanding of the cognitive process may suggest improved ways to present information, resulting in more accurate ratings, and it also suggests limits of human judgement in tasks such as job analysis.

It seems clear that job analysis research is moving in more theoretical and interesting directions. New methods are providing additional tools more appropriate for specific situations. An expanded understanding of cognitive processes, and the introduction of computers to reduce some of the considerable effort in conducting job analysis, should both facilitate and improve job analysis methods.

REFERENCES

Arvey, R.D. (1979) *Fairness in Selecting Employees*. Reading, MA: Addison Wesley.
Arvey, R.D. (1986) Cost impact of alternative comparable worth strategies. In S.H. Taylor (Chair), *Implementing Comparable Worth*. Symposium presented at American Psychological Association, Washington, DC, August.
Arvey, R.D., Davis, G.A., McGowen, S.L., and Dipboye, R.L. (1982) Potential sources of bias in job analytic processes. *Academy of Management Journal*, 25, 618–629.
Arvey, R.D., Maxwell, S.E., and Abraham, L.M. (1985) Reliability artifacts in comparable worth procedures. *Journal of Applied Psychology*, 70, 695–705.
Arvey, R.D., Maxwell, S.E., and Gutenberg, R.L., and Camp, C. (1981) Detecting job differences: A Monte Carlo study. *Personnel Psychology*, 34, 709–730.
Arvey, R.D., Maxwell, S.E., and Mossholder, K.M. (1979) Even more ideas about methodologies for determining job differences and similarities. *Personnel Psychology*, 32, 529–539.
Arvey, R.D., and Mossholder, K.M. (1977) A proposed methodology for determining similarities and differences among jobs. *Personnel Psychology*, 30, 363–375.
Arvey, R.D., Passino, E.M., and Lounsbury, J.W. (1977) Job analysis results as influenced by sex of incumbent and sex of analyst. *Journal of Applied Psychology*, 62, 411–416.
Ash, R.A. (1982) Job elements for task clusters: Arguments for using multi-methodological approaches to job analysis and a demonstration of their utility. *Public Personnel Management Journal*, 11, 80–89.
Ash, R.A., and Levine, E.L. (1980) A framework for evaluating job analysis methods. *Personnel*, 57, 53–59.
Ash, R.A., Levine, E.L., and Sistrunk, F. (1983) The role of job-based methods in personnel and human resources management. In K.M. Rowland and G.D. Ferris (eds), *Research in Personnel and Human Resources Management*. Vol. I. Greenwich, CT: JAI Press.
Banks, M.H. (1988) Job Components Inventory. In S. Gael (ed.), *Job Analysis Handbook*. New York: John Wiley.
Banks, M.H., Blow, D., and Stafford, E.M. (1983) A vocational input to the curriculum for less-able pupils. *Remedial Education*, 18, 64–66.
Banks, M.H., Jackson, P.R., Stafford, E.M., and Warr, P.B. (1983) The Job Components Inventory and the analysis of jobs requiring limited skill. *Personnel Psychology*, 36, 57–66.
Banks, M.H., and Miller, R.L. (1984) Reliability and convergent validity of the Job Components Inventory. *Journal of Occupational Psychology*, 57, 181–184.
Banks, M.H., and Stafford, E.M. (1982) Using the job components inventory: A report

to the manpower services commission. SAPU Memo No. 528, University of Sheffield, England.
Banks, M.H., and Wylde, J. (1981) A realistic appraisal of worth skills for engineering courses within the Youth Opportunities Programme. *BACIE Journal*, 35, 130-132.
Beardsley, M.M., and Matkin, R.E. (1984) The Abbreviated Task Inventory: Implications for future role and function research. *Rehabilitation Counseling Bulletin*, March, 232-245.
Birnbaum, M.H. (1979) Procedures for detection and correction of salary inequities. In T.R. Pezullo and B.E. Bittingham (eds), *Salary Equity: Detecting Sex Bias in Salaries among College and University Professors*. Lexington, MA: Heath, pp. 121-144.
Blumrosen, R.G. (1979) Wage discrimination, job segregation, and Title VII of the Civil Rights Act of 1964. *University of Michigan Journal of Law Reform*, 12, 397-502.
Borg, G. (1978) Subjective aspects of physical and mental load. *Ergonomics*, 3, 215-220.
Brown, I.D. (1978) Dual task methods of assessing work-load. *Ergonomics*, 21, 221-224.
Cain, P.S., and Green, B.F. (1983) Reliabilities of selected ratings from the Dictionary of Occupational Titles, *Journal of Applied Psychology*, 68, 155-165.
Campion, M.A. (1987) Ability requirement implications of job design: An interdisciplinary perspective. Krannert School of Management, Purdue University.
Campion, M.A. (1988) Interdisciplinary approaches to job design: A constructive replication with extensions. *Journal of Applied Psychology*, 73, 467-481.
Campion, M.A., and Thayer, P.W. (1985) Development and field evaluation of an interdisciplinary measure of job design. *Journal of Applied Psychology*, 70, 29-43.
Canada Department of Manpower and Immigration (1973) *Canadian Classification and Dictionary of Occupations 1971* (2 vols). Information Canada, Ottawa.
Christal, R.F. (1974) The United States Air Force occupational research project. *JSAS Catalog of Selected Documents in Psychology*, 4, 61.
Colbert, G.A., and Taylor, L.R. (1978) Empirically derived job families as a foundation for the study of validity generalization: Study III. Generalization of selection test validity. *Personnel Psychology*, 31, 355-364.
Conley, P.R., and Sackett, P.R. (1987) Effects of using high-versus low-performing job incumbents as sources of job-analysis information. *Journal of Applied Psychology*, 72, 434-437.
Conway, D.A., and Roberts, H.V. (1983) Reverse regression, fairness, and employment discrimination. *Journal of Business and Economic Statistics*, 1, 75-85.
Coovert, M.D. (1984a) A user's guide for generating job analysis reports from the NTS data base. Technical Report, Organizational Research and Development, Inc., Columbus, Ohio.
Coovert, M.D. (1984b) A user's guide for generating job analysis reports from the JAQ data base. Technical Report. Organizational Research and Development, Inc., Columbus, Ohio.
Coovert, M.D. (1986a) Cognitive representations of job knowledge. In E.L. Levine (Chair), *Job Analysis*. Symposium conducted at the Annual Meeting of the Southeastern Industrial and Organizational Psychological Association, Orlando, FL.
Coovert, M.D. (1986b) Creation of the Nationwide Insurance Company's PATS Database. Technical Report, Organizational Research and Development, Inc., Columbus, Ohio.
Coovert, M.D. (1986c) Altering artificial intelligence heuristics to provide data for specific applications. In S. Gael (Chair), *Advances in Tailoring Job Analysis Methods for Specific Applications*. Symposium conducted at The First Annual Conference of the Society for Industrial and Organizational Psychology, Chicago, IL.

Coovert, M.D., Ramakrishna, K., McNelis, K., and Salas, E. (1988) How powerful should expert systems be: An examination in three domains. Presentation at the Association for Computing Machinery Conference on Human Factors in Computing Systems (CHI'88), Washington, DC.
Coovert, M.D., Vance, R.J., and Colella, A. (1988) Toward an expert system for performing task-based job analysis. Technical Report, USF-PSY-88-5-3, University of South Florida, Tampa.
Cornelius, E.T., III, Carron, T.J., and Collins, M.N. (1979). Job analysis models and job classification. *Personnel Psychology*, **32**, 693–708.
Cornelius, E.T., III, DeNisi, A.S. and Blencoe, A.G. (1984) Expert and naive rates using the PAQ: Does it matter? *Personnel Psychology*, **37**, 453–464.
Cornelius, E.T., III, Hakel, M.D., and Sackett, P.R. (1979) A methodological approach to job classification for performance appraisal purposes. *Personnel Psychology*, **32**, 283–297.
Cornelius, E.T., III, and Lyness, K.S. (1980) A comparison of holistic and decomposed judgment strategies in job analyses by job incumbents. *Journal of Applied Psychology*, **65**, 155–163.
Cornelius, E.T., III, Schmidt, F.L., and Carron, T.J. (1984) Job classification approaches and the implementation of validity generalization results. *Personnel Psychology*, **37**, 247–260.
Cronbach, L.J., Gleser, G.C., Nanda, H., and Rajaratnam, N. (1972) *The Dependability of Behavioral Measurements*. New York: Wiley.
Cunningham, J.W. (1988) Occupation Analysis Inventory. In S. Gael (ed.), *The Job Analysis Handbook*. New York: Wiley.
Cunningham, J.W., Boese, R.R., Neeb, R.W., and Pass, J.J. (1983) Systematically derived work dimensions: Factor analyses of the Occupation Analysis Inventory. *Journal of Applied Psychology*, **68**, 232–252.
Cunningham, J.W., Slonaker, D.F., and Riegel, N.B. (1987) Interest factors derived from analytically based activity preference scales. *Journal of Vocational Behavior*, **30**, 270–279.
DeNisi, A.S., Cornelius, E.T., III, and Blencoe, A.G. (1987) Further investigation of common knowledge effects on job analysis ratings. *Journal of Applied Psychology*, **72**, 262–268.
Doverspike, D., and Barrett, G.V. (1984) An internal bias analysis of a job evaluation instrument. *Journal of Applied Psychology*, **69**, 648–662.
Doverspike, D., Carlisi, A.M., Barrett, G.V., and Alexander, R.A. (1983) Generalizability analysis of a point-method job evaluation. *Journal of Applied Psychology*, **68**, 476–483.
Dowell, B.E. and Wexley, K.N. (1978) Development of a work behavior taxonomy for first-line supervisors. *Journal of Applied Psychology*, **63**, 563–572.
Ericsson, K.A., and Simon, H.A. (1984) *Protocol Analysis: Verbal Reports as Data*. Cambridge, MA: The MIT Press.
Eyde, L.D. (1983). Evaluating job evaluation: Emerging research issues for comparable worth analysis. *Public Personnel Management Journal*, **12**, 425–444.
Farina, A.J., and Wheaton, G.R. (1973) Development of a taxonomy of human performance: The task characteristics approach to performance prediction. *JSAS Catalog of Selected Documents in Psychology*, **3**, 26–27 (MS No. 323).
Fine, S.A., and Wiley, W.W. (1971) *An Introduction to Functional Job Analysis, Methods for Manpower Analysis*. (Monograph no. 4), W.E. Upjohn Inst., Kalamajo, MI.
Flanagan, J.C. (1954). The critical incident technique. *Psychological Bulletin*, **51**, 327–358.

Fleishman, E.A. (1975). Toward a taxonomy of human performance. *American Psychologist*, **30**, 1127–1149.
Fleishman, E.A. (1982) Systems for describing human tasks. *American Psychologist*, **37**, 1–14.
Fleishman, E.A., Gebhardt, D.L., and Hogan, J.C. (1984) The measurement of effort. *Ergonomics*, **27**, 947–954.
Fleishman, E.A., and Quaintance, M.K. (1984) *Taxonomies of Human Performance*. Orlando, Florida: Academic Press.
Fleishman, E.A., and Stephenson, R.W. (1972) Development of a taxonomy of human performance: A review of the third year's progress. *JSAS Catalog of Selected Documents in Psychology*, **3**, 40–41 (MS No. 320).
Fraser, S.L., Cronshaw, S.F., and Alexander, R.A. (1984) Generalizability analysis of a point method job evaluation instrument: A field study. *Journal of Applied Psychology*, **69**, 643–647.
Friedman, L., and Harvey, R.J. (1986) Can raters with reduced job descriptive information provide accurate Position Analysis Questionnaire (PAQ) ratings? *Personnel Psychology*, **39**, 779–789.
Goldberger, A.S. (1984) Redirecting reverse regression. *Journal of Business and Economic Statistics*, **2**, 114–116.
Green, S.B., and Stutzman, T. (1986) An evaluation of methods to select respondents to structured job-analysis questionnaires. *Personnel Psychology*, **39**, 543–565.
Gutenberg, R.L., Arvey, R.D., Osburn, H.G., and Jeanneret, P.R. (1983) Moderating effects of decision-making/information-processing job dimensions on test validities. *Journal of Applied Psychology*, **68**, 602–608.
Hakel, M.D. (1986) Personnel selection and placement. *Annual Review of Psychology*, **37**, 351–380.
Hakel, M.D., Hakel, L., and Weil, E.K. (1986) Evaluation of structured task analysis questionnaire as a means of analyzing social interaction characteristics of 25 Navy ratings. Technical Report, Navy Personnel Research and Development Center, San Diego, CA.
Hamer, R.M., and Cunningham, J.W. (1981) Cluster analyzing profile data confounded with interrater differences: A comparison of profile association measures. *Applied Psychological Measurement*, **5**, 63–72.
Hanser, L.M., Mendel, R.M., and Wolins, L. (1979) Three flies in the ointment: A reply to Arvey and Mossholder. *Personnel Psychology*, **32**, 511–516.
Harvey, R.J., and Hayes, T.L. (1986) Monte Carlo baselines for interater reliability correlations using the Position Analysis Questionnaire. *Personnel Psychology*, **39**, 345–357.
Hemphill, J.K. (1960) *Dimensions of Executive Positions* (Research Monograph No. 89). Ohio State University, Bureau of Business Research, Columbus.
Jiang, B.C., Smith, J.L., and Ayoub, M.M. (1986) Psychophysical modeling for combined manual materials-handling activities. *Ergonomics*, **29**, 1173–1190.
Johnson, P.J. (1982) Development of a measure of job time-demands. *Psychological Reports*, **51**, 1087–1094.
Jones, A.P., Main, D.S., Butler, M.C., and Johnson, L.A. (1982) Narrative job descriptions as potential sources of job analysis ratings. *Personnel Psychology*, **35**, 813–828.
Jöreskog, K.G., and Sörbom, D. (1979) *Advances in Factor Analysis and Structural Equation Modeling*. Cambridge, MA: Abt.
Lawshe, C.H. (1952) Personnel selection. *Personnel Psychology*, **5**, 31–34.
Levine, E.L. (1983) *Everything You Always Wanted to Know About Job Analysis*. Tampa: Mariner Publishing.

Levine, E.L., Ash, R.A., and Bennett, N. (1980) Exploratory comparative study of four job analysis methods. *Journal of Applied Psychology*, **65**, 524–535.
Levine, E.L., Ash, R.A., Hall, H., and Sistrunk, F. (1983) Evaluation of job analysis methods by experienced job analysts. *Academy of Management Journal*, **26**, 339–348.
Levine, E.L., Sistrunk, F., McNutt, K., and Gael, S. (1986) Review and evaluation of job analysis systems at selected organizations. Symposium conducted at the Annual Meeting of the Southeastern Industrial and Organizational Psychological Association, Orlando, FL.
Levine, E.L., Thomas, J.N., and Sistrunk, F. (1988) Selecting a job analysis approach. In S. Gael (ed.), *The Job Analysis Handbook*. New York: Wiley.
Levine, J.M., and Teichner, W.H. (1972) Plans for the development of a systems language. In E.A. Fleishman, W.H. Teichner, and R.W. Stephenson (eds), Development of a taxonomy of human performance: A review of the second year's progress. *JSAS Catalog of Selected Documents in Psychology*, **2**, 39–40 (MS No. 112). Cited in E.A. Fleishman and M.K. Quaintance (1984). *Taxonomies of Human Performance*. Orlando, Florida: Academic Press.
Levine, J.M., and Teichner, W.H. (1973) Development of a taxonomy of human performance: An information–theoretic approach. *JSAS Catalog of Selected Documents in Psychology*, **3**, 24 (MS No. 325).
Lissitz, R.W., Mendoza, J.L., Huberty, C.J., and Markos, H.V. (1979) Some further ideas on a methodology for determining job similarities/differences. *Personnel Psychology*, **32**, 517–528.
Lopez, F.L. (1988) Threshold traits analysis system. In S. Gael (ed.), *The Job Analysis Handbook*. New York: Wiley.
Lopez, F.M., Kesselman, G.A., and Lopez, F.E. (1981) An empirical test of a trait-oriented job analysis technique. *Personnel Psychology*, **34**, 479–502.
Mahoney, T.A., and Blake, R.H. (1979) Occupational pay as a function of sex stereotypes and job content. Paper presented at the meeting of the Academy of Management, Atlanta.
Mallamad, S.M., Levine, J.M., and Fleishman, E.A. (1980) Identifying ability requirements by decision flow diagrams. *Human Factors*, **22**, 57–68.
Mayo, C.C., Nance, D.M., and Shigekawa, L. (1975) Evaluation of the job inventory approach in analyzing US Air Force utilization fields. US Air Forces Human Resources Laboratory, Final Report, TR-75-22.
McCormick, E.J. (1979) *Job Analysis: Methods and Applications*. New York: AMACOM.
McCormick, E.J., DeNisi, A.S., and Shaw, J.B. (1979) Use of the Position Analysis Questionnaire for establishing the job component validity of tests. *Journal of Applied Psychology*, **64**, 51–56.
McCormick, E.J., Jeanneret, P.R., and Mecham, R.C. (1972) A study of job characteristics and job dimensions as based on the Position Analysis Questionnaire (PAQ). *Journal of Applied Psychology*, **56**, 347–368.
McIntyre, R.M., and Farr, J.L. (1979) Comment on Arvey and Mossholder's 'A proposed methodology for determining similarities and differences among jobs'. *Personnel Psychology*, **32**, 507–510.
McNelis, K. (1986) Using multidimensional scaling to explore biases in implicit job theories. Presented at 94th Annual Convention of the American Psychological Association, Washington, DC, August.
Miller, G.A. (1969) Psychological method to investigate verbal concepts. *Journal of Mathematical Psychology*, **6**, 169–191.
Miller, R.B. (1973). Development of a taxonomy of human performance: Design of a

systems task vocabulary. *JSAS Catalog of Selected Documents in Psychology*, **3**, 29-30 (MS No. 327).

Minskey, M. (1975) A framework for representing knowledge. In P. Winston (ed.), *The Psychology of Computer Vision*. New York: McGraw-Hill.

Mintzberg, H. (1973) *The Nature of Managerial Work*. New York: Harper & Row.

Mobley, W.H., and Ramsay, R.S. (1973) Hierarchical clustering on the basis of inter-job similarity as a tool in validity generalization. *Personnel Psychology*, **26**, 213-225.

Mossholder, K.W., and Arvey, R.D. (1984) Synthetic validity: A conceptual and comparative review. *Journal of Applied Psychology*, **69**, 322-333.

Muthard, J.E., and Salomone, P.R. (1969) The roles and functions of the rehabilitation counselor. *Rehabilitation Counseling Bulletin*, **13**, 81-168.

Newell, A., and Simon, H.A. (1972) *Human Problem Solving*. Englewood Cliffs, NJ: Prentice-Hall.

Ogden, G.D., Levine, J.M., and Eisner, E.J. (1979) Measurement of workload by secondary tasks. *Human Factors*, **21**, 529-548.

Olson, H.C., Fine, S.A., Myers, D.C., and Jennings, M.C. (1981) The use of Functional Job Analysis in establishing performance standards for heavy equipment operators. *Personnel Psychology*, **34**, 351-364.

O'Reilly, C.A., III, and Caldwell, D.F. (1979) Informational influences as a determinant of perceived task characteristics and job satisfaction. *Journal of Applied Psychology*, **64**, 157-165.

Pearlman, K. (1980) Job families: A review and discussion of their implications for personnel selection. *Psychological Bulletin*, **87**, 1-28.

Piso, E. (1981) Tasks analysis for process-control tasks: The method of Annett *et al.* applied. *Journal of Occupational Psychology*, **54**, 247-254.

Prien, E.P. (1963) Development of a supervisory position description questionnaire. *Journal of Applied Psychology*, **47**, 10-14.

Primoff, E.S. (1975) *How to Prepare and Conduct Job Element Examinations*. (Technical Study 75-1, US Civil Service Commission) US Government Printing Office, Washington DC.

Rakimi, M., and Malzahn, D.E. (1984) Task design and modification based on physical ability measurement. *Human Factors*, **26**, 715-726.

Roberts, H.V. (1980) Statistical biases in the measurement of employment discrimination. In E.R. Livernash (ed.), *Comparable Worth: Issues and Alternatives*. Equal Opportunity Advisory Council, Washington, DC, pp. 173-195.

Rynes, S.L., and Milkovich, G.T. (1986) Wage surveys: Dispelling some myths about the 'market wage'. *Personnel Psychology*, **39**, 71-90.

Rytina, N.F. (1981) Occupational segregation and earnings differences by sex. *Monthly Labor Review*, **104**, 49-53.

Sanchez, J.I., and Levine, E.L. (1988) Capturing rater policies for judging overall task importance. Presented at the Third Annual Conference of the Society of Industrial and Organizational Psychology, Dallas, Texas.

Schank, R.C., and Abelson, R.P. (1977) *Scripts, Plans, Goals and Understanding*. Hillsdale, NJ: Lawrence Erlbaum Associates.

Schmidt, F.L., Hunter, J.E., and Pearlman, K. (1981) Task differences as moderators of aptitude test validity in selection: A red herring. *Journal of Applied Psychology*, **66**, 166-185.

Schmitt, N., and Cohen, S.A. (1987) Internal analysis of task ratings by job incumbents. Unpublished, Michigan State University.

Schmitt, N., and Fine, S.A. (1983) Inter-rater reliability of judgements of functional

levels and skill requirements of jobs based on written task statements. *Journal of Occupational Psychology*, **56**, 121–127.
Schwab, D.P., and Grams, R. (1985) Sex-related errors in job evaluation: A 'real-world' test. *Journal of Applied Psychology*, **70**, 533–539.
Schwab, D.P., and Heneman, H.G. (1986) Assessment of a consensus-based multiple information source job evaluation system. *Journal of Applied Psychology*, **71**, 354–356.
Schwab, D.P., and Wichern, D.W. (1983) Systematic bias in job evaluation and market wages: Implications for the comparable worth debate. *Journal of Applied Psychology*, **68**, 60–69.
Shannon, R.H., and Carter, R.C. (1981) Task analysis and the ability requirements of tasks: Collected papers. Naval Medical Research and Development Command, Naval Biodynamics Laboratory, NBDL-81R009.
Siegler, R.S. (1980) Recent trends in the study of cognitive development: Variations on a task-analytic theme. *Human Development*, **23**, 278–285.
Silverman, S.B., Wexley, K.N., and Johnson, J.C. (1984) The effects of age and job experience on employee responses to a structured job analysis questionnaire. *Public Personnel Management Journal*, **13**, 355–359.
Sistrunk, F., and Smith, P.L. (1982) *Multimethodological Job Analysis for Criminal Justice Organizations*. Tampa: University of South Florida, Center for Evaluation Research.
Smith, J.E., and Hakel, M.D. (1979) Convergence among data sources, response bias, and reliability and validity of a structured job analysis questionnaire. *Personnel Psychology*, **32**, 677–692.
Snelgar, R.J. (1982) The comparability of job evaluation methods in supplying approximately similar classifications in rating one job series. *South African Journal of Psychology*, **12**, 38–40.
Stafford, E.M., Jackson, P.R., and Banks, M.H. (1982) School and work: A technique to help bridge the gap. *Educational Research*, **24**, 243–249.
Stafford, E.M., Jackson, P.R., and Banks, M.H. (1984) An empirical study of occupational families in the youth labour market. *Journal of Occupational Psychology*, **57**, 141–155.
Stang, S.W. (1984, August) Problems in policy capturing. In R.M. Guion (Chair), *The Measurement of Comparable Job Worth*. Symposium conducted at the meeting of the American Psychological Association, Toronto.
Stefik, M., Aikins, J., Balzer, R., Benoit, J., Birnbaum, L., Hayes-Roth, F., and Sacerdoti, E. (1983) Basic concepts for building expert systems. In F. Hayes-Roth, D.A. Waterman, and D.B. Lenot (eds), *Building Expert Systems*. Reading, MA: Addison-Wesley.
Stewart, R. (1976) *Contrasts in Management*. Maidenhead, England: McGraw-Hill.
Stewart, R. (1982) A model for understanding managerial jobs and behavior. *Academy of Management Review*, **7**, 7–13.
Stutzman, T.M. (1983) Within classification of job differences. *Personnel Psychology*, **36**, 503–516.
Taylor, L.R. (1978) Empirically derived job families as a foundation for the study of validity generalization: Study I. The construction of job families based on the component and overall dimensions of the PAQ. *Personnel Psychology*, **31**, 325–340.
Taylor, L.R., and Colbert, G.A. (1978) Empirically derived job families as a foundation for the study of validity generalization: Study II. The construction of job families based on company-specific PAQ job dimensions. *Personnel Psychology*, **31**, 341–353.
Teichner, W.H., and Olson, D. (1969) *Predicting Human Performance in Space Environ-*

ments (NASA Contr. Report CR-1370). Washington, DC: National Aeronautics and Space Administration.

Teichner, W.H., and Olson, D. (1971) A preliminary theory of the effects of task environment factors in human performance. *Human Factors*, **13**, 295–344.

Thompson, D.E., and Thompson, T.A. (1982) Court standards for job analysis in test validation. *Personnel Psychology*, **35**, 865–874.

Tornow, W.E., and Pinto, P.R. (1976) The development of a managerial job taxonomy: A system for describing, classifying, and evaluating executive possitions. *Journal of Applied Psychology*, **61**, 410–418.

Treiman, D.J. (1979) *Job Evaluation: An Analytical Review* (Interim Report to the Equal Employment Commission). Washington, DC: National Academy of Sciences.

Treiman, D.J., and Hartmann, H.J. (eds) (1981) *Women, Work, and Wages: Equal Pay for Jobs of Equal Value*. Washington, DC: National Academy Press.

Umbers, I.G. (1979) A study of the control skills of gas grid control engineers. *Ergonomics*, **22**, 557–571.

US Department of Commerce (1977) *Standard Occupational Manual*. Washington, DC: US Government Printing Office.

Vance, R.J., Coovert, M.D., and Colella, A. (1988) An expert system for job analysis: An evaluation. Paper presented at the Third Annual Meeting for The Society for Industrial and Organizational Psychology, Dallas, Texas.

Vidulich, M.A., and Tsang, P.S. (1986) Techniques of subjective workload assessment: A comparison of SWAT and the NASA-Bipolar methods. *Ergonomics*, **29**, 1385–1398.

Warr, P.B., and Banks, M.H. (1981) Taking stock of skills to meet supply and demand. *Personnel Management*, **13**, 42–46.

Webb, N.M., Shavelson, R.J., Shea, J., and Morello, E. (1981) Generalizability of general education development ratings of jobs in the United States. *Journal of Applied Psychology*, **2**, 186–192.

Wexley, K.N., and Silverman, S.B. (1978) An examination of differences between managerial effectiveness and response patterns on a structured job analysis questionnaire. *Journal of Applied Psychology*, **63**, 646–649.

Whitely, W. (1985) Managerial work behavior: An intergration of results from two major approaches. *Academy of Management Journal*, **28**, 344–362.

Wickelgren, W.A. (1979) *Cognitive Psychology*. Englewood Cliffs, NJ: Prentice-Hall.

Wickelgren, W.A. (1981) Human learning and memory. *Annual Review of Psychology*, **32**, 21–52.

Wildervanch, C., Mulder, G., and Michon, J.A. (1978) Mapping mental load in car driving. *Ergonomics*, **21**, 225–229.

Zedeh, L.A. (1965) Fuzzy sets. *Information and Control*, **8**, 338–353.

Chapter 10

JAPANESE MANAGEMENT—A SUN RISING IN THE WEST?[1]

Peter B. Smith
School of Social Sciences
University of Sussex
UK
and
Jyuji Misumi
Department of Social Psychology
Nara University
Japan

Japanese management methods have evoked steadily increasing interest in the West over the past few decades. The changing quality of that interest is reflected in the contrast between Abegglen's (1958) classic observations of Japanese factories, and the same author's more recent discussion of the evolving *kaisha* or Japanese corporation (Abegglen and Stalk, 1984). During this period Western commentators have moved from an interest in a phenomenon seen as strange and unusual, to a realization that the consequences of Japanese management are, and increasingly will be, felt throughout the world. There has also been a wide divergence of views as to whether the essence of Japanese management lies in its structures or within the processes or styles with which those structures are operated. In this chapter we shall take the view that structure and process are yin and yang—that we shall understand little about organizational behaviour if we do not take account of both structures and processes. Nonaka and Johansson (1985) lament the lack of emphasis upon 'hard' as well as 'soft' aspects of management in earlier reviews, and we aim to heed their advice. With passing time, increasing numbers of Japanese researchers are publishing their work in English as well as in Japanese, and a further aim is to ensure

---

[1]Thanks are due to the Japanese Ministry of Education Science and Culture, the British Council and the Unit for Comparative Research in Industrial Relations at the University of Sussex for grants to the first author which made possible the writing of this review, and to Toshio Sugiman, Toshihiro Kanai, and Tadao Kagono for comments and assistance.

International Review of Industrial and Organizational Psychology 1989
Edited by C. L. Cooper and I. Robertson © 1989 John Wiley & Sons Ltd.

that their work is as fully represented here as is that authored by non-Japanese. Finally, we aim to highlight and consider more fully in the concluding section, areas where the research findings do not support the conventionally accepted view as to the nature of Japanese management.

Research methods have also evolved over time with the early preponderance of case studies giving way to more systematic surveys and studies using comparative measures collected in several countries. The literature has grown to the point where this review cannot hope to be comprehensive within the space available. Emphasis will be given to studies focusing upon human resource management, while studies of methods of production, marketing, and research will only be considered where their implications for human resource management are evident.

Our review will first consider the various characterizations of Japanese management which have been advanced and how well founded they may be. Later sections will consider the evidence as to whether Japanese management is changing over time and what happens when Japanese plants open in other parts of the world. Finally, we shall consider whether the current successes of Japanese management hold lessons for us all or whether we must be content with some form of cultural relativism.

THE CLASSICAL DESCRIPTIONS OF JAPANESE MANAGEMENT

Keys and Miller (1984) propose that the distinctive qualities of Japanese management may be summarized under three heads: long-term planning, lifetime employment, and collective responsibility. Hatvany and Pucik (1981) distinguish the development of an internal labour market, definition of a unique company philosophy and identity, and intensive socialization of organizational participants. We prefer to use four, although the boundaries between the elements in such classifications are diffuse. These will be termed *time perspective*, *collective orientation*, *seniority system*, and *influence processes*. In each of these areas one may discern organizational structures, policies, and procedures which are said to be distinctive.

Time Perspective

Abegglen and Stalk (1984) propose that the strategy of the Japanese *kaisha* is to assure its long-term survival through the preservation of market share and growth in size, rather than the goals more strongly favoured by Western firms such as short-term profitability and high share values. A recently completed large-scale survey comparing Japanese, US, and European firms supports this view (Nonaka and Okumura, 1984; Kagono, Nonaka, Sakakibara, and Okumura, 1985). Responses were received from a general sample of firms in manufacturing and mining. The highest priority stated by the 277 US and 50

European firms responding was return on investment, whereas the 291 Japanese firms ranked increased market share more highly. Abegglen and Stalk suggest that the ability of the *kaisha* to take a longer term view has been partly due to the absence of a substantial threat of takeover bids. However, they make clear that this absence should be considered as much a symptom as a cause of Japanese industry's long-term perspective. If the preoccupation of Japanese management is with planning a long-term strategy which ensures the survival of the firm's organization, issues such as disposal of resources which are underutilized or the acquisition of ailing organizations are a low priority. More important is the recruitment of a loyal and skilled workforce, investment in long-term research, and the identification of distinctive markets. The data of Kagono *et al.* (1985) again support these assertions. The Japanese firms in their sample reported spending proportionately more on research into new technologies and development of new products, whereas American firms put more into improving and updating existing products. Nonaka and Johansson (1985) see extensive information search more generally as a key attribute of Japanese organizational behaviour. By continual scanning of the environment a capacity is developed to anticipate long-term developments. Information search is not simply greater, but also involves the seeking out of different types of information. For instance, Johannsson and Nonaka (1987) describe Japanese scepticism of Western market research and preference for talking to retailers and observing customers instead.

An emphasis upon long-term planning is also evident within the production technologies first popularized within Japan. Examples are the *kanban* and other just-in-time procedures which have accomplished such enormous cost savings within the automobile and electronics industries (Schonberger, 1982; McMillan, 1985). These instances, like many other recent advances in production management, have benefited from the development of increasingly sophisticated computers. As such techniques have become widely known, they have proved increasingly attractive to managements of Western firms. It remains to be seen in what way Western firms will implement just-in-time procedures. The time may come when they will not be thought of as distinctive to Japanese management.

Another aspect of time perspective which has been widely commented upon is the system of lifetime employment. By assuring employees that once they have joined the organization they are guaranteed continuing employment, it is argued that Japanese firms ensure the loyalty and security of their workforce. Research studies suggest, however, that is by no means so widespread as was once believed. Oh (1976) estimated that no more than 30 per cent of the Japanese labour force work for the same firm throughout their career, while Cole (1979) showed that rather more Americans than Japanese continue to work for their first employer. There are a number of reasons why this may be so. Most large Japanese firms utilize numerous subcontractors, and these do not enjoy security in time of cutbacks. Indeed, Oh makes it clear that lifetime employment can be effective only because of the existence of such a dual labour market, whereby the risks of recession are borne by the subcontractors—70 per cent of the goods and services required for the manufacture of a Nissan car are represented by orders to subcontractors. In textile machinery the figure rises to 90 per cent (Clark, 1979). However, it is an oversimplification to represent the labour market as a dual one. There is no definite boundary between the large first-rank companies and the others, but rather a series of hierarchical gradations (Nakane, 1970), which we shall explore in a later section.

Several other factors also restrict the extensiveness of lifetime employment. Many of the women recruited by the major firms work for only a few years before marriage. In addition, the age of retirement in Japan was most usually 55, although there is currently some tendency for it to increase. Hazama (1978) showed that within three years of first employment, 73 per cent had left small firms, many of whom would be subcontractors, while only 38 per cent had left the larger firms. Lifetime employment should therefore be thought of as a process affecting predominantly male workers within the larger corporations. We should also note that the oft-cited low figures for unemployment in Japan are computed in a different manner to those from other countries. Taira (1983) has estimated that if the US system were used, rates of unemployment in Japan would be more than doubled.

A further point of contrast is that those who stay with one firm for long periods in the West may well have exercised some choice to do so. For a Japanese within the lifetime employment system this choice is effectively absent. Lifetime employment is sometimes written about as though it were simply a guarantee of a permanent job. In understanding the system it is important to bear in mind that in exchange the employee may be expected to accept loss of the very substantial pay bonuses which Japanese firms pay when they are profitable, to work extra unpaid hours or forgo holiday entitlements, to accept an actual salary cut, to transfer to an entirely new type of work or to be assigned to another company within a related 'family' of companies. Hazama gives data from a comparative survey of workers in Japan and Britain. Asked why they took their present job, the most frequent Japanese responses were firstly the stability of the company, and secondly that there was no other suitable job. In Britain, workers cited the lack of other suitable jobs, wages, working conditions, and other reasons pertaining to the company. For British workers the stability of the company ranked ninth. The bases upon which employees are committed to a Japanese organization are thus different from those which are most frequent in the West. This has implications for the valid study of job satisfaction, and we shall return to this theme in the next section. For the present we should note that for the Japanese employee as for his employer a longer time perspective than that found in the West predominates.

Although few observational studies of Japanese managers have yet been reported, it appears that this difference in time perspective is evident even in the structuring of daily activities. Doktor (1983) found that in his observation sample, 41 per cent of Japanese managers undertook tasks which took more than one hour to carry through, compared to only 10 per cent of American managers. Conversely, 49 per cent of Americans but only 18 per cent of Japanese undertook tasks of less than nine minutes. Given that most Western observational studies of managers have shown the average transaction to last no more than three or four minutes, Doktor's data show a remarkable contrast.

Collective Orientation

The collective nature of Japanese society has been frequently discussed (Nakane, 1973). Individualistic behaviour has traditionally been seen as selfish, and within family and school it is discouraged. The work organization provides the principal locus of adult male Japanese identity, and identification with one's immediate work group of peers and superior is frequently very intense (Dore, 1973; Clark, 1979). Comparative studies reveal that Japanese employees see work as more central in their lives than do employees in ten other countries (Meaning of Working International Research Team, 1987). This study showed that it is not simply the case that Japanese employees identify more with their work, but that they draw the boundaries between what is considered to be work related and what is not in different ways. Thus, many Japanese would expect to spend substantial periods of time eating or drinking with their workmates after work and before going home. Atsumi (1979) found in his survey that 62 per cent of white-collar workers did this on two or more evenings per week. Among those from smaller firms only 26 per cent went out with their workmates that often. Employees are likely also to participate in company-organized sports, holidays, and outings. All of these activities would be undertaken in the absence of one's spouse or children. The bond between the employee and his organization and most especially his work group may thus take on some of the qualities of village life in traditional Japanese life. However, Atsumi cautions against the assumption that employees necessarily participate in all these activities simply for their own pleasure. The Japanese concept of *tsukiai* specifies one's obligation to develop and maintain harmonious relations with one's work colleagues. As Atsumi points out, the fact that employees in large firms engage in much more after-hours socializing than do those in small firms means that one cannot simply attribute the phenomenon to Japanese culture. Its meaning must lie in the culture of the large firms, the commitment they require, and the individual needs which are met by such informal contact. Further support for this view comes from the findings of the Meaning of Working International Research Team's (1987) findings. Asked to define the nature of work, Japanese were more likely than those from other countries to refer to concepts related to duty, which appeared in the Japanese version of the questionnaire as *gimu*.

Many large Japanese firms devote substantial resources to encouraging the collective commitment of their workforce. Matsushita, for instance, expects that all employees will participate each morning in singing the company song and reciting the employees' creed and seven spiritual values (Pascale and Athos, 1981). The values in question are: national service through industry, fairness, harmony and cooperation, struggle for betterment, courtesy and humility, adjustment and assimilation, and gratitude. Many other companies emphasize similar values, with most frequent emphasis upon the importance of *wa* or harmony. Commitment to the company is also fostered by extensive training programmes for new recruits, and by the fact that employees are not recruited to do a specific task but to share overall responsibility for the work of their team. Over time, those destined for senior positions are assigned to teams in each of the various functions within the organization, thus ensuring a generalist rather than a specialist view of the work to be done.

Loyalty to the firm is also fostered by a distinctive set of personnel policies. Pascale and Maguire (1980) compared policies in operation at ten Japanese plants with a matched sample of US plants. As one might expect, expenditure on social and recreational facilities per employee was more than twice as high in the Japanese companies. Pascale and Maguire also attempted to compare job rotation by comparing numbers of jobs per year of employee tenure. They found no difference, but this is most probably due to the tendency of Japanese firms not to label distinctive jobs as separate positions. Other widespread practices which encourage identification with the firm include the wearing of company uniforms and the provision of communal eating facilities. The existence of company unions rather than trade unions also aligns the interests of union and management more closely, and it is not infrequent for union officials to achieve management positions later in their career.

The concept of 'groupism' in Japanese management has been the subject of a number of Japanese-language books, some giving it a central role (Iwata, 1978), while others see it as one element among several (Tsuda, 1977; Urabe, 1978). In evaluating the function of groupism within Japanese organizations it is important to acknowledge a further Japanese distinction, that between *tatemae* and *honne*: *tatemae* refers to what might be considered ideal or correct concerning relations between two persons or groups. *Tatemae* will frequently derive from long-past events which have defined the state of relationships between the two groups in question; *honne* is what happens in practice. It is clear that the ideal values espoused by many Japanese organizations favour harmony and collective action within the organization. Detailed case studies by, for instance Dore (1973) in an electrical plant, Rohlen (1974) in a bank, and Clark (1979) in a corrugated board manufacturing company indicate that the *honne* or what actually occurs is more complex. Clark suggests that: 'perhaps one could say that in the West decision making is presented as individualistic until adversity proves it collective. In Japan it is presented as collective until it is worth someone's while to claim a decision as his own' (p. 130). In other words the basic assumption within a Western organization would be individualistic, until such time as it was desirable to share the blame around for some setback, whereas in a Japanese organization the basic assumption would be collective, unless there was some specific incentive for claiming a success as one's own. Hazama (1978) also compares the relation of the individual and the group in Japanese and Western work teams. He suggests that the difference parallels that between certain types of team sports. In baseball, for instance, the group's task is differentiated between a series of individually defined roles. Each individual's separate performance may be recorded and evaluated. A collective enterprise is carried through by a series of individualized performances, just as is the work of organizations in Western countries. In the tug-of-war, by contrast, a collective sport is undertaken which has no clear demarcation of individual roles. The team either wins or loses and no one knows which individuals contributed more or less to the result. Hazama points to the parallel between the way in which Japanese work groups do not have clearly differentiated work roles. All members are equally responsible for the success of the team's efforts.

There is substantial debate as to whether the collective orientation of Japanese primary work groups arises from the personal preferences of those who join them, or whether it is more true to say that what occurs is a matter of conformity to existing norms of harmony and solidarity. The existence of the concept of *tsukiai* provides an indication that, at the least, personal preference is enhanced by social obligation. Wagatsuma (1983) argues that commentators have certainly overstated the occurrence of harmony in Japanese society. There is clear evidence of conflict both within and between organizations. For instance Clark (1979), as part of his case study, scrutinized questionnaires which the company required employees to complete annually. He found no lack of criticisms and complaints, particularly from those who had subsequently resigned from the company. Thus the harmony of the work group may to some degree be sustained by a sense of obligation rather than by inherent pleasure in harmony. There are times at which it is acceptable for such obligations to be relaxed, such as after having a few drinks together, and criticisms made on such an occasion are treated as off the record. Leaving such occasions to one side, it is much more likely that conflict within an organization will be between teams rather than within them.

Considerations as to how far the behaviour of Japanese work team behaviour is a matter of choice or of obligation provide a vantage point from which to examine studies of the job satisfaction of Japanese employees. Western writers have usually expected that the joint impact of lifetime employment and involvement in the work group would ensure that Japanese workers were more satisfied than those in Western organizations. There are now a sufficient number of published findings reporting that, on the contrary, Japanese workers are *less* satisfied than Western workers that some explanation is required. The reported studies cover two decades of research and a variety of industries. During the 1960s, Odaka (1975) completed five studies in Japanese organizations varying from manufacturing to department stores and electricity companies. In all of these, less than half the respondents declared themselves satisfied with their work, which compares with substantially higher figures from most Western countries. Only in West Germany were lower figures reported. Around 1970, Cole (1979) compared work satisfaction of workers in Detroit and Yokohama. The Japanese were again substantially less satisfied. The more recent studies are based on large heterogeneous samples and have all repeated the same finding (Azumi and McMillan, 1976; Pascale and Maguire, 1980; Naoi and Schooler, 1985; Lincoln and Kalleberg, 1985). In the most extensive and recent of these studies, Lincoln and Kalleberg compared the job satisfaction of 4567 US employees drawn from 52 plants in Indiana with 3735 Japanese employees at 46 plants in Kanagawa prefecture. Four work satisfaction items were used and the Japanese scored lower on all items, in excess of one standard deviation on three of them. The largest difference was on the question 'Does this job measure up to your expectations?'

Several explanations are possible of lower Japanese job satisfaction. The most obvious possibility is that many Japanese work extremely long hours and do not find their pay adequate. A recent survey by Sohyo (the Japanese General Council of Trade Unions) reported that of a sample of 26 800 respondents, 76 per cent stated that they worked too hard. Asked what would be necessary for an improved lifestyle, 70 per cent cited wage increases and 62 per cent cited shorter working hours (Japan Times, 1988). Although no more than one worker in four belongs to a trade union in Japan, these figures are likely to be representative of frequent sources of discontent among non-unionized workers also. Kamata's (1983) descriptive account of shopfloor work at Toyota is consistent with this explanation. Lincoln and Kalleberg's data showed age to be much more strongly related to dissatisfaction in Japan than in America. This accords with the view that a major source of dissatisfaction in Japan is low wages among younger workers.

Cole (1970) proposes that Japanese workers are dissatisfied because they have higher aspirations for their job. High involvement and commitment lead to expectations which the organization cannot satisfy and which workers in the West would not look to their employer to satisfy. Support for this view comes from the fact that in the Lincoln and Kalleberg study the largest difference found was on the item referring to expectations.

There are difficulties in concluding that the difference in satisfaction is due to different levels of organizational commitment. Additional data in the Lincoln and Kalleberg (1985) study indicate that the Japanese sample also scored lower than the Americans on the six-item Porter Scale of Organizational Commitment. A further study by Luthans, McCaul, and Dodd (1985), using the same measure, showed that broad samples of Japanese and Korean employees both scored lower than Americans on the scale. Since both Lincoln and Kalleberg and Luthans *et al.* sampled a very wide range of organizations, their respondents will have included both those having lifetime employment with first-rank companies and those without job security—41 per cent of respondents in the Sohyo survey reported that their jobs were 'precarious'. The surprising findings obtained by these two studies may be accounted for by their confounding together those with lifetime employment and those without. An alternative possibility is that those who feel low commitment to US organizations feel freer to leave than do those in Japanese organizations. These two factors could also account for the lower Japanese job satisfaction found in the various other studies.

There is a third possible explanation of the reported differences which has to do with the difficulty of comparing mean scores on questionnaires which have been translated into different languages. While at least some of the studies under discussion used back-translation procedures to assure equivalence of meaning, one cannot control for differences in cultural norms. Japanese norms favour a modest presentation of self, while those in the United States encourage a more assertive presentation. It is quite possible that Japanese respondents would show lower mean scores than Americans on *any* self-descriptive questionnaire to which they were asked to respond. Buckley and Mirza (1985) cite a European Productivity Agency survey which showed that in 1980 only 50 per cent of Japanese described themselves as satisfied with life, compared to 89 per cent of Americans and 91 per cent of British. Lincoln, Hanada, and Olson (1981) studied Japanese-owned plants in the United States and found that Japanese-Americans employed there were less satisfied than Americans *in the same plants*. Of the explanations discussed here only the response bias explanation can account for this last finding, since presumably the conditions of employment were similar for all workers in these plants. The study by Pascale and Maguire (1980) asked respondents to compare their satisfaction with that of others similar to themselves. This way of phrasing might be expected to reduce the response bias problem to some degree, but we have no way of knowing by how much.

It is probable that all three explanations of lower Japanese job satisfaction contribute to the findings which have been obtained. For this reason it is unlikely that a definitive conclusion can be reached as to whether or not the Japanese are more dissatisfied with their jobs. In any event what is of more interest in our discussion of Japanese management is not so much the absolute level of satisfaction, but what types of structures or processes cause it to increase or decrease. We shall return to this issue when we discuss influence processes.

Seniority System

Japanese society is not only collective, but is also based upon a hierarchical status system. This is difficult for many Westerners to envisage, since in the West hierarchy is often thought of as opposite to collective activities such as participation. The Japanese language incorporates a wide variety of 'respect language', whereby it is impossible to speak to someone without making it clear whether that person is regarded as superior or inferior to oneself. The distinctions to be made are far more complex than the *tu/vous* distinction, for example, in French. Modes of address are formal and frequently refer to a person by rank rather than by name. A first-line supervisor is likely to be addressed as Mr Foreman (*hancho-san*) or Foreman Tanaka, even after long periods of working together.

The bases upon which such hierarchy is determined are numerous, including education, age, gender, and the firm one works for. The position of institutions in society, such as the firms in a particular industry or the universities in Japan, is also ordered in terms of an agreed hierarchy. One's own status is determined by the institutions one is or has been associated with combined with personal attributes such as age and gender. Wives take on their husband's status among other women. All of the above contribute to the *tatemae* of one's position relative to others, but in addition there will be factors relating not to one's own lifetime experiences but to one's family of origin.

Such processes are clearly operative also among Western business organizations, but in much more covert ways. In a business meeting or in office layout in Japan, status positions are likely to be physically represented, with high status persons furthest from the door. Behavioural differences such as amount of speaking and depth of bowing will also reflect hierarchical rank.

The management of hierarchy is exemplified by promotion procedures used within the large firms. Employee recruitment typically occurs only from school-leavers and college graduates and is followed by a substantial period of in-company training. This serves to strengthen commitment to the firm and inculcate the firm's favoured values. For about the next fifteen years, salary increases are paid regularly to all employees, with only relatively minor differentiation between high performers and low performers. This is the *nenko* system. Payment of a salary increase does not necessarily entail a change in work, but those who are destined for further promotion may be given the more interesting assignments. Thus throughout this period status differences are minimized between the members of a particular intake. Promotion beyond this point is more related to accomplishment. At the point when it becomes clear which members of a cohort are to be appointed to very senior positions, their peers may be encouraged to move to a job with one of the organization's subcontractors. By these devices, a situation is accomplished where it is rare for someone's boss to be younger than himself. It is thus possible to maintain a hierarchy of deference without confusing incongruities of age or gender. One's prospects for promotion are strongly dependent upon links with a more senior 'mentor' within the company. Assignment to a particularly senior mentor will depend upon the strength of one's prospects on entry. Wakabayashi and Graen (1984) have shown just how predictable this system makes ultimate promotion. They showed that the evaluation of the mentor–recruit relationship on entry to one of Japan's largest department store chains was a strong predictor of promotions achieved within the subsequent seven years.

In considering studies of Japanese organizational structure, it is important to bear in mind the description given above. Japanese organizations have two types of hierarchy—a seniority system for individuals, and a hierarchy of organizational ranks. The two systems do not necessarily overlap, since an organizational rank may quite frequently be left vacant. At the same time more than one person may be promoted to a particular seniority level, if their age, expertise or *tatemae* requires it. For instance in Clark's (1979) case study, 43 out of 109 ranked management positions were vacant at the time of the research. Dore's (1973) study at Hitachi gave a similar finding.

Researchers into organizational structure have mostly made use of Western measures, even though it is doubtful how far some of these may capture the aspects of organization just described. Lincoln, Hanada, and McBride (1986) drew upon the same comparative sample of organizations in Indiana and Kanagawa as has been discussed above. As they had predicted, they found that Japanese organizations had less functional specialization, that is to say fewer duties which are assigned exclusively to one individual within the organization. They also had a significantly greater number of seniority levels and a higher proportion of clerical staff. The most interesting aspect of this study was its findings concerning decision making. Respondents were asked at what level in the organization did authority rest formally for the taking of each of 37 types of decisions. They were then asked at what level these decisions were actually taken in practice. It was found that formal authority was located at significantly *higher* levels in Japanese firms than American ones, but that in practice decisions were taken at significantly *lower* levels in the Japanese firms than in the American ones. In the US firms the formal and informal locus of decisions was thus not that far apart; but in the Japanese firms the mean difference was greater than one level in the seniority system. The data thus reflect the distinction between *tatemae* and *honne* and shed light on the manner whereby a Japanese organization might appear to Western eyes to be both autocratic and participative.

The survey by Kagono *et al.* (1985) also included questions about organization structure. Within Japanese organizations, job descriptions were shown to be more general and less concrete. Power was said to be more widely shared and less systematized, particularly in respect of horizontal relationships. This survey did not distinguish between formal and informal procedures, but its findings are more in accord with Lincoln et al.'s description of decision making in practice. In these two surveys there is probably less reason to worry about response bias as a source of erroneous findings, since respondents were required to describe not themselves but their organizations.

Most researchers with interests in organization structures are interested not so much in absolute differences between Japan and the West as in whether the relationships between different aspects of formal organizational structure are the same within Japan as has been found elsewhere. Horvath, McMillan, Azumi, and Hickson (1976) examined the degree of formalization, specialization, and centralization within twelve matched trios of firms in Britain, Japan, and Sweden. Size and the degree of an organization's 'internal dependence', that is its links to parent organizations, were found to be the strongest predictors within Japan. Azumi and McMillan (1979) compared a larger sample of 50 Japanese firms with a databank of 128 British organizations. The Japanese sample scored much higher on centralization and on number of vertical levels, and somewhat higher on formalization, a measure which reflects the number of written documents used. These authors found no relationship between scores on centralization, formalization, and specialization, a finding which differs markedly from studies in Western countries. The most likely explanation for this is that the measures used in this and the preceding study, which are those developed by researchers at the University of Aston in England, fail to detect crucial aspects of Japanese organizational behaviour. As the later study by Lincoln et al. shows, there is an important distinction to be made between formal and informal decision procedures. Furthermore, the measure of specialization is defined in terms of assignment of specialist duties to *individuals*, where such specialization is much more likely to be carried through by teams in Japan.

Marsh and Mannari (1981) also made use of the Aston measures among others, but their prime goal was to compare the relative impact of size and technology as determinants of organizational structure and processes within 50 Japanese factories. They found that the type of technology employed was a somewhat stronger predictor than was size, whereas the reverse had been found earlier in Britain. In a similar study, Tracy and Azumi (1976) found that plant size and task variability were predictors of the level of automation and formalization. Lincoln et al. (1986) also studied the effect of type of technology. They concluded that the effects of technology were not, on the whole, detectably different from those in their US sample. However, on certain variables, particularly the centralization of decision making, the effects do differ. The US data show strong effects of technology type on both the formal and informal decision measures, while the Japanese data do not. Lincoln et al. conclude that variables other than technology are more crucial in Japan in this area. However, they do point out that newly emerging technologies such as highly automated process industries are precisely those in which Japan is at the forefront, and these types of plant may be ones in which it is less crucial to link supervision to technological processes. Although this may well be true, the sample used by Lincoln *et al.* spanned a wide range of technologies, and the implication of their finding is that it is not technology but something intrinsic to Japan which determines the type of decision making used. The most plausible candidate for such a cultural explanation would be the deeply rooted seniority system.

Seror (1982) attempts to specify a firmer basis upon which comparisons may be made of Japanese organizational structures and those in other countries. She proposes that before conclusions may be reached which favour universal theories of organizational structure, studies must be made that span several clearly defined cultures and show how the structures studied affect organizational effectiveness. The only study which approaches these requirements is that by Lincoln and Kalleberg (1985). In addition to the analyses within their paper that have already been discussed, these authors examine the effects of different organizational parameters upon satisfaction and commitment of employees. These are clearly not unambiguous measures of organizational effectiveness, but a study of them is none the less a step forward. Commitment in Japanese firms was found to be lower in small firms and in firms with tall hierarchies. A large span of control and low formalization was linked to positive commitment and satisfaction in the United States, but not in Japan. The implication would be that in the United States close contact with the supervisor is aversive, while in Japan it is not. A number of other differences which the authors had anticipated did not emerge. For instance there was no linkage between tenure and commitment. However, it is not clear why there should be such an effect. An employee who enters the lifetime employment system already knows the nature of the commitment he has made: there is no reason why commitment should increase with the passage of time. Lincoln and Kalleberg conclude that the differences they found in the effects of organizational structure in the two countries were rather modest. A possible reason for this may be that the effects of structures are not inherent in those structures, but in how they are interpreted and utilized in a particular cultural setting. This is a theme which we take up in the next section.

Influence Processes

The attributes of Japanese management outlined thus far delineate a system with clear positive qualities, but what may appear also to be substantial disadvantages. Japanese employers are also agreed upon the nature of these disadvantages. Hazama (1978) reports a survey made in 1967 by the Japan Federation of Employers' Associations. Among those who responded, 92 per cent agreed that lifetime employment caused employers to retain workers with inferior ability and those who were not needed, thus causing a large loss due to labour costs. Similarly, 84 per cent agreed that the seniority system led to a loss in vitality within the establishment, and 72 per cent said that the system adversely affected the morale of able workers. Whether such disadvantages are outweighed by the benefits must depend upon the manner in which the structures so far described are operated in practice. Such evidence is crucial, since when one reads descriptions of, for example, the seniority system, it is inevitable that one's reactions to it are coloured by the way in which such a system would be evaluated within one's own national culture.

Most discussions of Japanese management gave substantial emphasis to the occurrence of upward influence, particularly through the *ringi* system of decision making and through the widespread use of quality control circles. While these are certainly important and we shall discuss them shortly, it is necessary first to consider the nature of superior–subordinate relations in Japanese society. *Ringi* and quality control circles may then be seen as particular instances of a more fundamental attribute. Within Western societies a rigidly hierarchical system would most likely be one in which influence flowed down the hierarchy rather than up it. Those in high power positions would at times need to protect themselves from threats to their status from more able persons below. In Japan the position of a senior person is relatively invulnerable to such attack, due both to lifetime employment and to the fact that status derives principally from attributes which cannot be changed by others. Thus the senior manager in Japan has less reason to be threatened by suggestions from below. The traditional pattern of superior–subordinate relations in Japanese society depends upon the *oyabun–kobun* system, which derives from the parent–child relationship and now means patron–client relationship. Within modern organizations this is represented by the *sempai–kohai* or senior–junior system. This is an intense relationship of mutual obligation. The superior is expected to protect the subordinate's interests, develop his skills through training and feedback, and advance his position. The subordinate is expected to show deference and loyalty, as expressed through commitment and hard work, as well as the making of suggestions and the giving of gifts on occasions such as the New Year. The subordinate's commitment may be expressed through working extra unpaid hours, or through not taking up holiday entitlements, although as Lincoln and Kalleberg's (1985) data suggest, this may be due not so much to commitment as to an unwillingness to fall out of favour with one's superior. The superior's obligations may well extend to such matters as helping the subordinate to find someone to marry, where this is desired. The superior will be given credit for the achievements of the work team, but this will be due to the need for deference, rather than as a distinction to be made between the supervisor and his team of subordinates. It also motivates the superior to look out for valuable suggestions from subordinates. This pattern of superior–subordinate relations derives from the traditional obligations of Japanese village life, which are known as *ie* (Nakane, 1970).

The survey by Kagono *et al.* (1985) also included a series of questions about leadership styles. Japanese leaders were reported by respondents to be significantly higher than those in America and Europe on the following behaviours: strictness in applying rewards and punishments; clarifying and gathering information; adherence to the values of the current chief executive officer (CEO) or founder; conflict resolution through the use of authority; exchange of information prior to meetings; sharing of information down the line; use of a control system based upon employee self-discipline and commitment to work; long-term performance evaluation; consensus decision making; frequent informal and social exchange; commitment to change; and promotion policies from within. Few of the differences reported are surprising in view of the preceding discussion, but since the respondents were asked to describe practices within their company as a whole, their responses probably reflect *tatemae* rather more than *honne*.

The principal organizationally structured mode of upward influence within the Japanese organization is that of *ringi*. This is a procedure whereby proposals for new policies, procedures or expenditures are circulated through the firm for comment. An initial proposal is written by a junior member of the organization. The paper is then sent to all those who might be affected if it were implemented, each of whom writes comments or indicates approval with his personal seal. The document is circulated in ascending order of seniority. The above description outlines what occurs in theory. In practice, with increasing size of modern Japanese organizations, such procedures become exceedingly time consuming and a number of modifications may be noted (Misumi, 1984). For instance, the organization may use *ringi* only for important decisions, and may authorize managers at particular seniority levels to commit expenditures up to a given level without such broad consultation. Less important decisions may be handled by *ringi* among middle managers and never submitted to the highest level. It will be noted that the success of *ringi* requires a high degree of consensus among those affected. Consultation documents circulated within Western organizations are frequently criticized, negotiated over, and amended. The preferred procedure within Japanese organizations is to engage in such consultations *before* the *ringi* proposal is circulated. This informal procedure is referred to as *nemawashi*, whose literal meaning is the trimming of a tree's roots prior to its being transplanted. Only when it is clear from *nemawashi* that a proposal is likely to succeed will a written *ringi* proposal be put forward. The nearest Western equivalents, grapevine or bush telegraph, have a different connotation, since they refer to dissemination of information rather than preparation for decision. Through *nemawashi*, harmony in the organization will be preserved, but rather than being a method of decision making, *ringi* has become more a method of recording and reporting decisions already reached (Misumi, 1984).

A *ringi* decision may be thought of as the nearest which a Japanese organization will come to issuing job descriptions. The decision which is recorded will specify that certain tasks will be carried out by a particular group or groups, but it differs from a formal system of job descriptions in two senses. Firstly, it will relate to a particular task and hence will lapse when that task is complete. Secondly, it will specify the task to be done by one or more teams rather than by individuals. In practice, differential abilities and influence processes within the team may mean that one member does much more of the work than others, but *tatemae* says that all are equally responsible. The individual who does more than his 'share' will know that such industry may in the end lead to slightly more rapid promotion, but in the meantime all are equally accountable for what is done.

A further issue concerning *ringi* is the question of where the initiative comes from for the formulation of a new policy. It is often implied that the new idea derives solely from the junior member of the organization, and no doubt many ideas do so. But it must also be remembered that within the seniority system, subordinates are obligated to take note of the wishes of their superiors. Thus a superior who favours a particular initiative may drop hints to subordinates, who will then formulate a proposal in that direction. Clark (1979) reports instances where this occurred—*ringi* is thus not something apart from the rest of organizational processes. It is the product of *nemawashi*, and the fostering of both *ringi* and *nemawashi* is an integral part of the leadership processes occurring within Japanese organizations. Just as *ringi* exemplifies upward influence within the ranks of management, so does the extensive use of quality control circles and allied procedures at shopfloor level. However, QC circles will not be extensively discussed here, since they are the subject of a separate review within Chapter 7 of this volume (Griffin, 1989).

Detailed studies have been undertaken of the processes of leadership within Japanese organizations (Misumi, 1985). These have shown that leaders whose effectiveness is rated most highly are those whose behaviour is perceived as high on two functions termed P and M. These initials stand for performance and maintenance, and they parallel distinctions made by US leadership researchers between, for instance, task and socio-emotional behaviours. However, while US researchers have found that environmental contingencies require different leader styles, Misumi's studies have shown that effective leaders score high on P and M in a very wide range of organizational settings. Misumi emphasizes that although measures of P and M are factorially independent, they cannot be thought of in isolation. Within the actions of an effective manager, the exercise of the P and M functions interacts, so that the effect of each augments the other. Over a period of more than 30 years his studies have included laboratory studies, field surveys, and field experiments. Within the Nagasaki shipyards, for instance, leadership training emphasizing the need for a PM style led to very large decreases in the rate of accidents (Misumi, 1975). On the face of it, effective Japanese leader style is less environmentally contingent than are US styles, just as we reported earlier that Japanese organizational structures appear to be less driven by technology. However, in the case of leader styles, comparative studies are not yet complete which would test for alternative explanations, such as the use of different measures of leader style in different countries.

Comparative data are available from three studies which do test the linkage between various organizational processes and ratings of work satisfaction or performance. Pascale (1978a) compared matched samples of US and Japanese companies. He found that in the Japanese companies written communications were used more frequently, that there were more superior–subordinate interactions initiated from below, and that implementation of decisions was rated more highly. These last two variables were positively correlated, so that where there was more upward influence, decision implementation was better. Using the same sample, Pascale and Maguire (1980) report correlations between their one-item measures of leader style and work satisfaction which are generally low. The highest correlations with work satisfaction within the Japanese sample were for 'supervisor pitches in' (+0.23) and mean number of supervisor–worker interactions (+0.30). The equivalent correlations for the US sample were −0.15 and +0.05, but the significance of these differences is not tested. Strongly significant correlations between supervisor style and absenteeism were found in the US sample, but these were absent from the Japanese sample probably because absenteeism was very much lower there. Another relevant finding from the Lincoln and Kalleberg (1985) study was that participation in quality circles in the United States was positively linked to organizational commitment. In Japan this was less true but participation in *ringi* showed a stronger effect.

More direct tests will be required before a firm conclusion is possible, but there are certainly some grounds for the belief that the effects of leadership and of group processes more generally may differ within Japanese organizations from those found in the West.

This concludes our survey of the classical model of Japanese management. The different attributes which we have outlined are summarized in Table 1.

CHANGE AND STABILITY IN JAPANESE MANAGEMENT

In his earliest analysis of Japanese factory organization, Abegglen (1958) argued that the structures he described were derived from traditional Japanese society. It is now widely agreed that this was incorrect, not least by Abegglen himself (Abegglen, 1973). A more tenable view is that many of the distinctive qualities of Japanese management have in fact evolved over the past few decades (Dore, 1973; Odaka, 1975; Cole, 1979; Urabe, 1984). In the first section of this review Japanese management was discussed as though it were a fixed and static entity. In this section we shall consider evidence as to its diversity and rate of change. Such a type of analysis is replete with irony, since as we shall see, many of the aspects of Japanese management which have been 'discovered' by Western

Table 1—The Classical Model of Japanese Management

Attribute	Effect	Source of vitality	Difficulties
Lifetime employment	Stable tenure Job rotation Simultaneous recruitment Future abilities unknown Internal promotion	All in the same boat Can devote self to work Whole person contributes Sense of belonging	Low job mobility Small incentives to develop self Small incentives to perform well No right of dismissal
Collective orientation	Put company first Multilateral flow of information	Wish to contribute to group Sense of belonging Interchangeability of jobs Power of the group	Stress from suppression of ego needs Group process problems Unclear powers and duties
Seniority system	Gradual promotion Equitable system of promotion Job rotation	Long-term incentive Boosts collective morale Sense of belonging	'Tepid' management Promotion of low ability persons to management Elite morale low
Influence processes	Responsibilities delegated Many views sought Participative management	Flexible structure Young employee vitality Free resources utilised Shared strategy formulation	No unified control No hard-line policy Diffusion of responsibilities Time consuming

writers in recent years, have their roots in the West as much as they do in the East.

The principal difficulty in the way of analysing what is stable and what is in process of change lies in the Japanese genius for searching out new approaches, wherever they may be found and adapting them to their own purposes. It is doubtful whether there is another country in the world which has devised a system of notation for the sole purpose of incorporating into its own language words and concepts from other countries. Such a practice may in itself be no more than symbolic of Japanese enthusiasm for the importation and adaptation of technologies and procedures. None the less, the cumulative impact of such openness may have profound implications for the future of Japanese organizations, as for many other aspects of Japanese society.

Cole (1979) summarizes three views of the development of Japanese organizations. The first of these proposes, in line with Abegglen's (1958) thesis, that Japanese organizations are a unique product of Japanese cultural history. The second proposes that there are inexorable consequences of the use of specific technologies and that the structures of the modern industrial organizations of all societies are therefore destined to converge. The third alternative, which Cole himself supports, is that there may in fact be several ways in which organizations can successfully cope with the problems of production and marketing which they face. Organizational structures may therefore be expected to show some convergence, but also some diversity which is explicable in cultural terms.

The first or culturalist view has something of the status of the null hypothesis. That is to say, if studies show no evidence of change in Japanese organizations over time, its merits are enhanced, but if change is found, it is weakened. A judgement as to whether or not the changes found would require dismissal of the culturalist view, would also entail an evaluation of whether the changes found were explicable simply as a developmental stage within a unique culture, or whether they showed convergence towards the culture of other advanced industrial countries. Such judgements are by no means easy to make.

Despite such difficulties, certain facts are now well established. For instance, the system of lifetime employment for those working in first-rank companies arose after the Second World War (Cole, 1979). Between the wars there was little security of tenure, and considerable industrial conflict, sometimes violent (Urabe, 1986). The system of lifetime employment evolved out of these conflicts. Cole points out that the system is not a legally formalized one, and that in a period of expansion such as Japan has experienced since the Second World War, it may be difficult to distinguish between those who are entitled to lifetime employment and those who have merely experienced continuous employment. In the current situation, where there are already, or soon will be, substantial cutbacks in employment opportunities in such industries as coal mining, shipbuilding and car manufacture, the distinction is likely to become more explicit. Cole's (1971) survey of workers in Yokohama certainly revealed some confusion among his respondents as to the nature of their conditions of service.

There is an equal degree of uncertainty about the *nenko* system. In Cole's study at Toyota Auto Body, he found that no more than 40 per cent of a worker's pay was based upon the seniority principle, while the remainder was based upon abilities and work content. He comments that the criteria for abilities and work content were sufficiently vague that, in practice, they might well prove to be correlated with seniority. Nevertheless, since the 1960s, this and many other firms sought to include a job-based wage system (*shokumukyu*) within their criteria for determining pay. The impetus for this came from study of the personnel practices of American firms and Japanese protagonists of such changes sought to justify them by emphasizing that they are more modern (Cole, 1979, p. 130). *Shokumukyu* was found to require precise job descriptions and most firms have replaced it by an element of *shokunokyu* or payment by ability within their payment system. No evidence is available as to whether such payments do in practice conflict with the seniority system.

The *ringi* procedure has also been frequently attacked as insufficiently modern, and as we have seen its function has been changing. Takamiya (1981) reports that in 1961, 82 per cent of corporations surveyed used *ringi* for making decisions, whereas by 1969 many of these regarded *ringi* as a method for recording decisions. The other side of this picture is given by the survey conducted by Takahashi and Takayanagi (1985). They asked 299 firms by what method they took their most recent decision on a location plan for a factory, branch or office. They found that 63 per cent of the decisions were taken through *nemawashi*, 30 per cent through decision by the superior, and the remainder by conference. The firms using group-based decision methods (*nemawashi* and conference) were more likely to employ what the authors call a 'fixed size' procedure, in other words the simultaneous evaluation of a range of options. These firms tended to be those who are listed on the Tokyo Stock Exchange, and particularly those whose share performance is high. Thus this study indicates that *nemawashi* is currently most widespread among the successful first-rank companies.

The picture presented above is certainly one of change, but there is little indication that the changes which have occurred simply represent the adoption of the practices of the United States or of other industrialized countries. Cole (1979) cites several further examples of the manner in which innovations derived from the United States have been substantially amended as they are incorporated within Japanese practice. A widely known example is the manner in which the ideas of Deming on statistical quality control by staff experts were transmuted into the group-based procedure known as quality control circles. A less familiar one is the rapid adoption in the early years of this century of F.W. Taylor's prescriptions for scientific management (McMillan, 1985). The notion of work study and of production management was enthusiastically adopted, while the associated idea of performance-related pay was completely ignored. Japanese writers point out that Taylor himself was an advocate, not simply of work study but equally of 'hearty brotherly cooperation' (Mito, 1983).

The view that convergence of Japanese and Western organizations is inevitable is advanced by Marsh and Mannari (1976). Their study examined three firms manufacturing ships, electrical appliances, and *sake*. Their analyses were based both upon detailed case studies and also upon questionnaire surveys completed by the workforce of the three plants. Data collection occurred between 1967 and 1970. They found that variables such as organizational rank and work satisfaction were actually more strongly associated with 'universal' factors than with variables which might be derived from distinctively Japanese practices. For instance it was found that extra-organizational variables, such as age, gender, and number of dependents had more effect upon reward system variables such as pay than did intra-organizational variables, such as education, seniority, and rank. Work satisfaction was related to rank, age, gender, promotion chances, and the cohesiveness of the work group. Marsh and

Mannari argue that since the variables which proved the strongest predictors are not distinctive to Japan, the convergence or 'modernization' theory is more strongly supported than the cultural theory. Such a reading of cultural theories exaggerates their claims. None of the proponents of cultural theories (e.g. Abegglen, 1958; Rohlen, 1974) put forward the view that Japanese organizations have *nothing* in common with Western organizations, only the more moderate view that there are unique processes within them that have substantial importance. Furthermore, as Cole (1979) points out, it is difficult to arrive at a valid reason for classifying some predictors as 'modern' and others as 'traditional'. Marsh and Mannari think of payment by ability as modern, in contrast to the *nenko* system. However, among their respondents 48 per cent who favoured *nenko* also considered that ability should be the prime determinant of pay. Thus their respondents appear to see no contradiction between what Marsh and Mannari consider to be traditional and modern. One possible resolution of such a puzzle is that advanced above in discussing Cole's (1979) study at Toyota Auto Body. It may be that ability payments are in practice correlated with seniority ranks. In the Marsh and Mannari data, job classification certainly correlated highly with seniority (+0.77 and +0.51 for the two companies in which it was computed).

Marsh and Mannari take their argument further by suggesting that those firms with traditional Japanese emphasis will experience increasing difficulty in surviving. They support this argument by devising an index of worker performance and showing that high performance is again linked more strongly to factors such as rank, gender, and work satisfaction. However, their measure of performance was based not on actual productivity records, but upon answers to five questions, three of which had to do with the submission of suggestions for improvements. The conclusions drawn from this study are thus rather more general than the data might justify. It is difficult to draw valid conclusions about cultural differences in the absence of comparative data from different cultures. Conclusions about changes over time ideally also require data collection over some extended time period. However, the study does provide an illustration of the way in which there were substantial differences between the three firms studied, and thus contributes to the reduction of the belief that there is a single unified system of Japanese management. It does also validly demonstrate that among the sample studied the various elements postulated to make up the Japanese management system were not correlated with one another in a linear fashion. There was no particular tendency for instance for those who scored high on their measure of paternalism to express more company concerns, to have had no other previous jobs with other firms, to live in company housing, to score high on group cohesiveness or to be committed to lifetime employment. Marsh and Mannari suggest that this means that these aspects of Japanese organizations do not comprise a unified whole, but that employees participate in each one of them where they see it to be advantageous to them. This seems highly plausible.

An alternative version of the modernization hypothesis is that put forward by Dore (1973). Basing his thesis upon comparative case studies of electrical plants in Japan and Britain, he proposes that far from being backward or traditional, Japanese company organization may illustrate a form of welfare corporatism towards which other countries will converge. He reasons that since Japanese industrialization has occurred more recently than in Western countries there have been opportunities for Japan to learn from Western errors and thereby to create more advanced organizational structures. We should therefore expect more future changes in Western organizations than in Japanese ones. Cole (1979) is sceptical that Japan qualifies for 'late-developer' status, given the openness to Western ideas from the beginning of the Meiji era onwards, but acknowledges a wide range of ways in which Japanese organizations have observed and learned from Western organizations during the past century. We have noted some of these above. What are required, but have not yet been fully described, are accounts of the degree to which such innovations have been rendered into distinctively Japanese forms.

Comparative case studies of sixteen matched pairs of companies in Japan and the United States are presented by Kagono et al. (1985). They conclude that the strategies of these firms differ in five ways. The Japanese companies compared to the US ones were found to define their domain more broadly; to emphasize continuous in-house resource accumulation and development; to emphasize human resource development; to distribute risk through organizational networks; and to use inductive methods of problem solving, particularly focused upon improvement in production strategy. They conclude that both US and Japanese strategies are well adapted to certain types of market, but that each will need to change in response to continuing market change.

The most authoritative account of how such gradual transformations in Japanese firms are being accomplished is provided by Urabe (1984, 1986), the doyen of Japanese management writers. He stresses the manner in which the human and the technological innovations accomplished have been interrelated. Lifetime employment has enhanced the growth of company-specific skills. The *tatemae* of seniority has been preserved, while in practice pay differentials between senior and junior members of the organization have declined, and non-working directors have become a rarity. These changes and the payment of substantial bonuses have facilitated the convergence of management and union interests. The shift to process production increases the power of workers to disrupt production, and the trust accorded to workers by allowing them to halt a production line when necessary enhances the responsibility of their actions.

Urabe considers the potential of Japanese and Western organizations for the creation of change. He concludes that Japanese firms are well adapted to a continuous process of small incremental changes. Such changes are more likely to be the focus of resistance and negotiation in the West. Western organizations, on the other hand, may be better at making radical changes, and Urabe concludes that in this area lies a major problem for the Japanese organizations of the future. Urabe's reasoning is neatly complemented by the recent research of Yoshihara (1986), who made case studies of five Japanese firms which did accomplish successful innovations. The innovations were mostly changes into radically different markets, of which the best known is Canon. Yoshihara reports that in contrast to the popular view of Japanese firms having a 'bottom-up' system of influence, each of these firms had a strong and visible leader at the top who actively directed the innovations made. Numerous examples of the developing business strategy of specific Japanese corporations are also discussed by Itami (1987).

A major source of innovation and change in Japan as elsewhere lies in the management of research and development, and some studies of this process are now available. Kono (1986), surveyed the research facilities of 244 Japanese firms. He found that three sources of new product ideas were more frequent in the more successful firms: top management, central research groups, and divisional development teams. Westney and Sakakibara (1985) compared research and development within three Japanese and three American firms in the computer industry. Japanese researchers identified more strongly with the research administrators of their group and with the manufacturing function within their firm. US researchers gave more weight to professional colleagues and family. Promotion in Japanese labs was based upon seniority and track record, while in the United States it was based upon technical expertise and track record. Japanese researchers worked longer hours. US researchers had more choice of assignment to their next project. Kanai (1987) surveyed 49 research teams within a Japanese firm. Strong correlations were found between the leader's personal style, his network of links with other parts of the organization, and the team's performance. These studies suggest Japanese research labs share the characteristics identified in earlier sections, but also indicate that within this function as elsewhere, influence flows down the hierarchy as well as up it.

The work of Urabe and of Yoshihara confirms that substantial changes continue to occur in Japanese management practices, even though they are not necessarily convergent with Western practices. Dunphy (1987) also favours the view that these changes are the product of thought-out strategy choices by Japanese managements, rather than the inevitable consequence of culture or of technology. The work of Okubayashi (1986a, 1986b, 1987) gives some pointers as to how this process will continue in the face of further automation. He showed that the introduction of robots had not led to job losses within the firms installing them, and that unions are generally favourable to their use. His survey of 167 companies showed that automation has accentuated the division between highly skilled workers and unskilled ones. It has also led to shorter hierarchies and more decentralized decision making on production, but greater centralization of financial and personnel functions. These changes are likely to threaten wage systems based upon seniority and to pose particular difficulties for women and for older workers.

Further studies of workers have been reported which also suggest that evidence for convergence between Japanese and Western organizations is much less than might be expected, given the increasing rate of intercultural contact. The most striking evidence is that provided by Whitehill and Takezawa (1968) and Takezawa and Whitehill (1981). In this unique pair of studies, the same set of questions was posed to comparable samples of 2000 Japanese and US workers employed by eight large companies, at an interval of thirteen years. The survey included 30 questions, and significantly different patterns of response were found on every single question. The differences detected were consistent with the portrayal of Japanese management presented earlier in this chapter. The repeat survey found remarkably little evidence of convergence. Indeed on the majority of questions the gap between the United States and Japan had widened. Japanese responses showed more change than did US ones, but the strongest effect was that the attitudes of younger workers were now more similar to those of older workers.

Opinion surveys of the Japanese population have been undertaken every five years since 1953. Hayashi (1987) reports that over this period there has been remarkably little change in expressed preference for a work supervisor who 'looks after you personally', rather than one who never does anything for you that is unconnected with work. In the most recent survey, 89 per cent preferred the first of these two types of supervisor.

One other source of evidence for lack of change over time lies in the series of studies of leadership by Misumi (1985). There has been no change in support for PM theory from the earliest studies conducted in coal mines in 1963 (Misumi, 1985, pp. 22–7) to the present day.

The studies reviewed in this section provide substantial evidence of change over time in the specific practices employed by Japanese organizations. At the same time, the evidence that these changes necessarily entail the decline of those aspects of Japanese organizations which are distinctive is scant. Completed academic studies necessarily lag somewhat beyond the day-to-day life of organizations, so that one might propose that such change is present and increasing. The most substantial study indicating lack of change (Takezawa and Whitehill, 1981) was completed almost a decade ago. More recent commentators (Taylor, 1983) suggest that some at least of the younger generation shows rather different attitudes to work. Taylor notes the recent appearance in the Japanese language of 'myhomeism', a phrase used to criticize those Japanese who choose to go home after work rather than work extra hours or participate in *tsukiai*. It is also indisputable that the proportion of young to old in the population is changing rapidly, and that disrespect for one's elders, as measured by such indices as reports of assaults on schoolteachers, is on the increase. These changes, in addition to the effects of automation, are likely to place the seniority system under increasing strain during the next two decades.

However, experience to date suggests that such changes will find a mode of expression which assimilates them to Japanese culture, as has happened with some regularity over the past century. Hayashi's survey data (1987, 1988) provide the best clues as to how this will occur. He notes a decline in both those whose views are compulsively traditionalist and those who are compulsively 'modern'. The increasing trend is for respondents to state that their response to a situation would depend on the circumstances. This change in attitude mirrors the increasing pragmatism of Japanese organizations which we have already noted.

THE JAPANESE ABROAD

In recent years, a variety of economic and political pressures have led many Japanese firms to establish both manufacturing plants and sales facilities abroad. Although this process has been quite rapid, the title of Trevor's (1983) book, *Japan's Reluctant Multinationals*, conveys the impression of many observers that recent developments have been more a matter of necessity than of preference. The reasons for it have been fully explored by Ozawa (1979). He distinguishes the move into neighbouring Asian countries, primarily in search of lower labour costs, from the more recent worldwide expansion. The move towards multinational operation has been possible even for Japanese firms which are quite small, due to the existence of the giant *sogo shosha* or trading companies.

Generalizations about the performance of Japanese firms abroad need to be made with considerable caution, since not only do the reasons for setting up operations in various parts of the world vary, but so also does the manner in which firms are then staffed. Ozawa cites figures issued by the Japanese Ministry of Trade and Industry in 1971, indicating that the *average* number of Japanese nationals working within each overseas venture varied between 20 in the United States and 1 in Asia. While such differences no doubt represent an amalgam of the needs of each type of venture, and the preferences of Japanese to be stationed in particular parts of the world, they are likely to very strongly affect the degree of 'Japaneseness' of each venture.

Some studies are available of Japanese plants within Asia, but their focus is mostly general rather than specific. Ozawa indicates that the dual labour market within Japan is increasingly being replaced by a pattern where Japanese firms in other Asian countries pay very low wage rates, while more skilled work is retained within Japan. This has been encouraged by governments in Asian countries who are keen to foster foreign investment.

The loyalties of the Japanese to their in-group pose considerable problems for the Japanese abroad. They find it difficult to make contact with non-Japanese, particularly in Asian countries (Nakane, 1972). Those Japanese who do enter local networks or marry local women are thought of as having ceased to be Japanese. A wish to hire those who do understand the ways in which Japanese do business has led to preferential hiring of Japanese who already live there, especially in Hawaii and southern California. Japanese speakers are also preferred in countries where these are available, such as Korea and Taiwan. The difficulties which Japanese firms in Asia face have also included the fact they have allied themselves with the élites in some countries where those élites are unpopular, particularly in Indonesia (Ozawa, 1979). Everett, Krishnan, and Stening (1984) studied the mutual perceptions of Japanese managers and local managers working in plants in six South-East Asian countries. Factor analyses of ratings yielded three dimensions, which were termed managerial, entrepreneurial, and congenial. Japanese managers were generally rated high on the managerial factor, which included adjectives such as industrious, cautious, and honest. On the entrepreneurial factor they were rated high by Thais, Indonesians, and Hong Kong Chinese, but low by Filipinos, Malays, and Singaporeans. This factor was centred on the adjectives assertive, extraverted, and ambitious. On the congenial factor, all but the Thais rated Japanese managers low. This factor was based upon the adjectives tolerant, flexible, and cooperative. This study thus supports the more qualitative account provided by Ozawa.

Yoshino (1976) studied 25 Japanese firms operating in Thailand, and conducted some interviews also in Malaysia and Taiwan. Contrary to the figures cited by Ozawa, he found many more Japanese expatriates in post than there were in European or American firms in this area. He found this to be a consequence of Japanese mistrust in the abilities of locals to follow Japanese methods of decision making. In some plants, management was Japanese right down to the level of first-line supervisor. This pattern of staffing has one of two effects upon locally recruited management trainees. Either the locals observe that only minimal promotion is going to be available, and they therefore put in the minimum possible level of work. Alternatively, they eagerly seek out opportunities for training, including extended periods in Japan. When this is accomplished, they then leave the firm, since their level of training makes them attractive to other local firms. In both of these patterns, Japanese mistrust of the possibility of promoting local managers is enhanced. They see little prospect that locals will develop the company loyalty which a Japanese firm would expect of its employees. Negandhi, Eshghi, and Yuen (1985) discuss similar problems faced by Japanese firms in Taiwan.

Negandhi and Baliga (1979) summarize an extensive survey of 124 multinationals operating in developing countries, including 27 which are Japanese. While agreeing with Yoshino's view that Japanese firms face some difficulties in internal decision making, they found that Japanese firms had less conflict with governments and official bodies than did American firms.

Published comparative studies, with more detail of actual procedures used, focus almost entirely upon Japanese multinationals operating within advanced industrial countries. In considering these studies we need to bear in mind that not all Japanese multinationals are necessarily successful ones, despite the massive media coverage suggesting that they are. McMillan (1985) cites the case of Come-by-Change oil refinery in Newfoundland, which resulted in the bankrupting of one of the big ten *sogo shosha* companies, and of Mitsubishi Rayon, which withdrew from Canada after a thirteen-month strike. Other Japanese firms in Britain have experienced strikes, while in the United States there have been court cases alleging discriminatory hiring practices (Sethi, Namiki, and Swanson, 1984). None the less, these instances are more than balanced out by documented examples where plants have accomplished productivity levels equivalent to that of comparable plants in Japan (McMillan, 1985; Sethi *et al.*, 1984).

Fruin (1983) analyses the development since the Second World War of the Kikkoman Corporation, manufacturers of soy sauce, including their establishment of a plant in Wisconsin in 1972. He concludes that throughout this period management paid much more attention to what would work in a particular circumstance than to principle as to how things should be. Such pragmatism has proved to be a frequent attribute of Japanese multinationals, and has spawned a flood of articles in which authors enquire whether Japanese management is really distinctive at all. Kobayashi (1980) has pursued this direction by surveying 80 Japanese multinationals in comparison with 23 European and American multinationals. Respondents were asked to describe their present overseas structure and to predict how it might change in the future. Most envisaged a movement towards some type of matrix organization within a multidivisional structure. Asked which aspects of the classical Japanese approach would survive, the most frequently endorsed were (in order): joint ventures with host country firms; emphasis on market share rather than profits; joint ventures with *sogo shosha*; location close to raw materials; paternalism; lifetime employment and *ringi*. In a similar type of survey, Negandhi (1985) compared 120 US, German, and Japanese multinationals. The Japanese firms reported considerably more autonomy from headquarters. In comparison with the other multinationals they indicated that the problems they faced most frequently concerned personnel, marketing, and sales. This may not mean that they had more problems in these areas, but that they gave them greater priority.

A series of studies by Pascale and colleagues tests how substantial are current differences between American and Japanese firms operating in both Japan and the United States (Pascale, 1978a, 1978b; Pascale and Maguire, 1980; Maguire and Pascale, 1978). Fourteen American-owned units were compared with thirteen Japanese-owned units within the United States. There was a predominance of manufacturing and assembly but retailing and banking were also represented. Surprisingly few significant differences emerged. Comparing ten measures, Pascale and Maguire (1980) found only two that differed. The Japanese-owned firms spent more than twice as much per head on social and recreational facilities and they did more than twice as much job rotation. Furthermore, a larger number of differences were found between the Japanese-owned units and the comparable units owned by the same firms back in Japan. The Japanese subsidiaries in the United States were found to do more job rotation, to have supervisors who were rated more likely to listen to subordinates, and workers who were more satisfied, but also a much higher rate of absenteeism.

Some differences were also noted between the firms in the United States at managerial levels (Maguire and Pascale, 1978). Managers in the American-owned firms held larger meetings and spent more time in them, saw themselves as initiating more downward communication and receiving more upward communication. Their method of decision making more frequently involved obtaining the facts from subordinates and then deciding the matter themselves. The managers of the Japanese-owned firms more often used written communication to confirm the outcome of meetings and to request time off. They interacted more with their boss and less with their subordinates. They were more oriented towards consensus decision making, both with their subordinates and through being involved with their own boss. The personnel practices of these managers were also surveyed (Pascale, 1978b). The Japanese-owned firms had a smaller span of control at supervisor level and were more willing to allow workers to talk to one another on the job. Workers in the Japanese units reported significantly less of each of eighteen counterproductive behaviours, such as taking tools home from work. They were also stated to be more satisfied, although this is contradicted by Maguire and Pascale's (1980) report of the same data.

In summary, Pascale's project did succeed in finding a number of attributes on which Japanese-owned firms in the United States differed from locally owned firms. Most of these differences are consistent with the portrayal of Japanese management as practised in Japan. The majority of differences noted were at shopfloor level, but this may simply be because these are easier to detect. However, an equally important outcome of the project was the detection of an equally large number of differences between Japanese firms at home and abroad. This should encourage us further in the view that Japanese management abroad does not simply consist in the transposition of Japanese practices to other settings. A more active process appears to be involved, as Fruin (1983) reported, in which managements seek out what does and what does not work in a particular location.

This process of search is likely to include both the selection of worksites which appear more congenial, and the hiring of employees who will feel familiar with Japanese procedures. Lincoln, Olson, and Hanada (1978) predicted that

Japanese managers and workers would prefer organizational structures with a tall hierarchy and less horizontal differentiation into specialized groups. They found that among a sample of 54 Japanese-owned firms in America, the larger the proportion of Japanese or Japanese-American employees, the more the organization took on this form. In a subsequent paper (Lincoln, Hanada, and Olson, 1980), they showed that Japanese and Japanese-Americans were also more satisfied in organizations which had this type of structure.

A further series of detailed studies has examined some of the Japanese firms in Britain. White and Trevor (1983) studied three manufacturing firms and three banks. They report that there were marked differences in the degree to which these organizations had become noticeably 'Japanese'. The plant which had gone furthest along this path had employees who were no more satisfied than employees of other British and American-owned firms in the locality, although they did feel more secure in their jobs. Their managers were not seen as particularly oriented towards human relations. However, management was more strongly concerned with timekeeping, quality control, and efficiency generally. More meetings were held. The workforce worked hard but was willing to accept management's standards. White and Trevor propose that this was because management worked the same hours. Managers were keen to impart their expertise and wore the same clothing. Further aspects of a related study which compared the personnel practices of four manufacturers of colour televisions are reported by Takamiya and Thurley (1985). The authors propose that generalizations about Japanese management are hazardous in the light of substantial differences they found between the culture of the different companies studied. Of the two Japanese firms in the study, one was markedly more 'people oriented' than the other. None the less, both firms had considerably better productivity than the matched non-Japanese firms. Other attributes shared by both Japanese firms included dealing with only a single union and a less differentiated personnel function. The conclusion drawn from this study, as from the one by White and Trevor (1983), is that what best accounts for the superior performance of the Japanese firms is their meticulous attention to production management, their superior coordination of different organizational functions, and the management of their relations with trade unions.

The evidence discussed above derives most directly from the shopfloor level of manufacturing plants. In other types of organization and at more senior levels, it appears that it may be less easy to create a distinctively Japanese organizational climate within Western countries. White and Trevor's (1983) study indicated that although the encouragement of collective responsibility was popular among assembly-line workers, there was more reservation among the white-collar employees of Japanese banks located in London. A similar contrast is evident in a detailed case study of the operations of the subsidiaries of the YKK manufacturer of zip-fasteners in Britain and France (Davis, 1979). Although good relations with the workforce are described, an instance of conflict with secretarial staff is included. It is likely that white-collar staff would wish to retain a stronger sense of their individual skills and possible career mobility.

Yoshino (1975) suggests that one of the principal difficulties to be faced by Japanese multinationals lies in the area of decision making. There are two principal sources of difficulty. Firstly, remoteness from head office is likely to make participation in *nemawashi* particularly difficult. Yoshino argues that the creation of autonomous international divisions at least reduces this problem. This position is consistent with the data collected by Kobayashi (1980) which we cited earlier. In a more recent work, Yoshino and Lifson (1986) propose that the strength of the *sogo shosha* lies precisely in their capacity to practice a worldwide network of *nemawashi*. The second problem of multinationals concerns unfamiliarity of non-Japanese managers with *nemawashi* and *ringi*. Studies in Britain by Kidd and Teramoto (1981) and Trevor (1983) confirm that some Japanese firms in Britain do use *ringi*. Instances were found, however, where this was restricted to Japanese employees and the British managers within the plant were unaware even that the system was in use. Similar barriers between Japanese and non-Japanese are said also to exist in some firms in relation to promotion, as Yoshino (1976) found in Asia. Above a certain level, only Japanese are appointed. This means that local managers with ambition for further promotion are likely to seek posts elsewhere. The same problems will occur in more acute form within joint ventures.

Such problems will only be overcome when Japanese management is able to trust local managers to the same degree that managers trust one another. Given the strength of organizational socialization processes within Japanese organizations in Japan, this is likely to be a continuing problem. Studies by Sullivan, Peterson, Kameda, and Shimada (1981) and Sullivan and Peterson (1982) have addressed the issue. In both these studies, managers were asked to complete a questionnaire concerning a hypothetical joint venture. Japanese managers expressed greater trust in the future of the enterprise when a Japanese was in charge, and where decision making was initiated by a Japanese. This held true whether the sample was in Japan or in the United States. Where an American was in charge, Japanese managers felt that disputes should be resolved through the use of binding arbitration, but when a Japanese was in charge mutual consultation was thought preferable. American respondents showed none of these differences in preference. Sullivan and his co-workers conclude that Japanese see themselves as expert in avoiding uncertainty and conflict, but that where they are not in charge they have no confidence that similar outcomes can be achieved. Such issues become particularly important within negotiations. Miyazawa (1986) analyses the multiple pressures surrounding the establishment of legal departments within Japanese firms in the United States, on the basis of a survey of 233 firms. Crucial issues are whether the department shall include US nationals and whether it may be headed by one, particularly when seniority indicates that this should be done. Tung (1984) surveyed 113 US firms which had experienced negotiations in Japan. The parties to negotiation were reported as frequently using different negotiation styles. Failures were most frequently attributed to these differences, while successes were strongly associated with adequate prior preparation by US negotiators as to Japanese methods. A study which also addresses differences in perceived styles is that by Miyajima (1986) who asked Japanese managers in Britain to complete a test of managerial orientation and to predict how their British colleagues might complete it. The Japanese managers saw themselves as focused upon task issues, while they saw the British as more concerned with power.

A final issue concerning the experience of Japanese multinationals has to do with the processes whereby managers are prepared for overseas assignments. Tung (1987) reports a survey of European, American, and Japanese multinationals. The Europeans and the Japanese were found to have much lower failure rates, whereby managers returned home before their term was complete. Japanese multinationals were shown to be particularly thorough in their preparation of those sent abroad, both in terms of language training and of provision of prior information and of resources on arrival. Such preparation shows the same meticulous attention to detail as does Japanese production management. For instance, YKK's managers in Europe are instructed not to drive Japanese cars (Davis, 1979), as a sign of willingness to integrate with the local community. The study by Negandhi and Baliga (1979) also found Europeans and Japanese better prepared for overseas assignments, partly because they thought in terms of longer postings.

This section has shown that the experiences of Japanese corporations abroad are many and various. Only the rhetoric of popular writing could have led us to expect a uniform Japanese style to emerge everywhere, when there are substantial divergences of organizational culture even within Japan. None the less we do have evidence that Japanese-owned organizations in many parts of the world appear to function differently from those with other types of ownership. In the final section we shall discuss further how sure we can be as to why this might be so.

CULTURE AND MANAGERIAL EFFECTIVENESS

The first three sections of this review have surveyed the studies which have been made at home and abroad. A number of discussion points have been made in passing, but in this section we shall consider more thoroughly what types of conclusion the research studies permit. The issues at stake are basically three. We need to evaluate the widely held view that Japanese management is both distinctive and effective. Assuming a positive answer to this question for the moment, we need to know why this is so. Finally, we need to consider what implications our conclusions might have for managements, both Japanese and non-Japanese.

Within Japan there exists a flourishing literature known as *nihonjinron*, which seeks to distil exactly what it is about the Japanese which makes them unique. It is a truism that all ethnic groups are unique, but many Japanese believe that they are more unique than other cultural groups. In evaluating studies of Japanese management we need to be sure whether what we are considering is a particular instance of the Japanese fascination with, and perhaps even exaggeration of, their differentness, or whether there are indeed categorical differences between Japanese management and all other types of management. The studies we have reviewed make it plain that it will become increasingly difficult to argue that Japanese management is distinctive and unique. We have noted its evolution over time within Japan, and the manner in which Japanese corporations have been adept at modifying procedures and structures to align with the local needs of subsidiaries in varying parts of the world. On a broader front also, *nihonjinron* has received substantial critique (Mannari and Befu, 1982; Dale, 1986).

However, a number of more recent commentators have gone further and suggest that what characterizes Japanese management is no different from the policies which are pursued by the more progressive American corporations (Pascale and Athos, 1981). A more moderate position is that of Abegglen and Stalk (1984) and Buckley and Mirza (1985), who assert that there is no reason why Western firms cannot adopt policies and practices similar to the Japanese, even if they have mostly not done so yet.

Buckley and Mirza (1985) point out that whether or not Westerners should be in awe of Japanese management skills depends very much upon the manner in which one chooses to make comparisons with the West. While some sectors of the Japanese economy are extremely efficient, others such as agriculture and retailing are not. Still other sectors, while they may be efficient, are none the less in decline, just as they are in the West. These are industries focused upon the extraction and processing of raw materials, such as coal mining and the processing of aluminium and steel. Thus we do better to enquire not why the Japanese are such skilled managers, but why they are skilled at the management of certain types of enterprises.

Abegglen and Stalk (1984) indicate their position rather concisely in the sub-title of their book: 'How marketing, money and manpower strategy, not management style, make the Japanese world pacesetters'. Abegglen and Stalk analyse the basis upon which Japanese firms have been able to create competitive advantage within particular markets. They show that the ratio of labour costs in American and Japanese firms is directly related to *the number of separate operations required during manufacture of a product*. Where the number of operations is as high as 1500, as in car assembly, Japanese labour costs are half those of American car manufacturers. Where the number of operations is no more than ten to twenty, as in steel or paper manufacture, there is little difference in labour costs. The implication of such statistics is that Japanese firms are superior in the coordination of complex tasks. They also secure competitive advantage by restricting product variety and using large-scale facilities, both of which render coordination easier.

Although Abegglen and Stalk's lengthy sub-title dismisses management style as a source of Japanese success, this appears largely addressed towards those who suggest that analysis of management style is by itself sufficient to account for Japanese successes. Abegglen and Stalk do in fact discuss traditional Japanese management practices and assign them considerable importance. A better summary of their position might therefore be that Japanese management style is a necessary but not a sufficient explanation of the successes of the *kaisha*. While it is undeniable that Japanese firms are good at devising systems for coordinating production such as kanban, just-in-time and the like, it may well be that the collective orientation of the workforce assists in the devising and implementation of these systems. The same point could be argued with regard to the collaborative arrangements which Japanese firms sustain with banks and with trading companies.

Those who favour technologically oriented explanations of Japanese success (McMillan, 1985; Takamiya and Thurley, 1985) point to the way in which Japanese firms in Western countries can achieve equally impressive productivity, even where the workforce is almost entirely non-Japanese. There are two weak points in such arguments. The first is that most Japanese plants in the West have been open for a few years at most. One might anticipate a 'honeymoon' period for any new organization, particularly where the workforce has been newly recruited, and the production system is already tried and tested elsewhere. The YKK plant in Britain which was opened in 1967, and has frequently been written about as a success story, recently experienced an extended strike. Only passing time can show how well other plants in the West can sustain their initial successes. The second point is that most Japanese plants in the West utilize production systems which have already been designed in minute detail by Japanese in Japan. Many of the large number of assembly plants opened in Europe during the past several years in response to Common Market protectionism have been referred to as 'screwdriver' plants, that is to say that their task is only to assemble and package materials which have been designed and manufactured in Japan. While many such plants intend to make greater use of locally manufactured components, the processes of research, production design, and control remain firmly located in Japan.

It may be that rather than debating the 'hardware' versus 'software' explanations of Japanese successes, we should see them as the two faces of the same coin. It could be that the cultural context of Japan makes possible and encourages certain patterns of government, financing, research, production control and marketing and that these patterns have advantage in contemporary conditions. The firmest position from which to discuss the value of such a 'culturalist' explanation is the work of Hofstede (1980). Hofstede compared the values of managers working within a single (non-Japanese) firm located in 40 countries around the world. His analysis of the Japanese responses in his sample showed them to be particularly distinctive on two of the four dimensions used. The Japanese ranked fourth out of 40 on 'Uncertainty Avoidance', and top out of 40 on 'Masculinity'. The remaining two dimensions, 'Power Distance' and 'Individualism–Collectivism' were not wholly separable, and the Japanese scored an average ranking upon them. Hofstede's findings have been criticized for possible unrepresentative sampling, but they are none the less of great value. The classical attributes of Japanese culture are frequently portrayed as collectivism and the seniority system. Yet on Hofstede's dimensions of Power Distance and Collectivism, Japan was no more than average. The study suggests that there are numerous other countries with a more strongly collective orientation and a more hierarchical structure. On the other hand, Hofstede's data imply that Japanese are very strongly oriented towards Uncertainty Avoidance. Many attributes of Japanese management are indeed readily interpretable as attempts to reduce uncertainty, including their management of time perspective, investment in research, production and quality control systems and extensive use of *nemawashi*. However, Japanese avoidance of uncertainty is a selective process. We have seen that job descriptions are deliberately left open, and the practice of negotiation and of conflict management is enhanced by preserving areas of ambiguity (Pascale and Athos, 1981). The labelling of Hofstede's final dimension of Masculinity has been criticized. High-scoring questionnaire items loading upon this factor emphasize the centrality of work goals in the life of the respondent. If we assume that the Japanese respondents were male, it need be no surprise that they scored high here also.

In evaluating this type of culturalist explanation, we need to take account of the 'ecological fallacy', which cross-cultural psychologists have noted. That is to say, we should avoid the assumption that because a mean score on one of Hofstede's dimensions is high for Japan, all Japanese individuals or all Japanese organizations are high on that scale. What we are discussing are population *means*. No doubt, there are many Japanese who enjoy the challenge of uncertainty or who hate work, just as there are those in Western countries who seek identity collectively or favour hierarchical authority. We also need to bear in mind that Hofstede's data derive from the late 1960s, and that many commentators see evidence of increasing individualism in Japan since that time.

Further evidence relevant to the culturalist model is provided by the rapid development of the Pacific rim economies, triggered by Japanese investment. While there is substantial cultural diversity in the area, there are some common elements not shared by Western cultures. Abegglen and Stalk point out that those nations in which growth has been particularly strong have more uniform ethnic groupings and low birth rates, while those with diverse populations and high birth rates have prospered less. The high growth nations—Korea, Taiwan, Hong Kong and Singapore—share a Confucian value system, with many elements in common with Japanese modal values. As Buckley and Mirza (1985) point out, Confucian values have a long history, and cannot plausibly be used to account for recent events on their own. However, they may provide a necessary though not sufficient basis for the optimal utilization of the types of production systems which the Japanese have pioneered. Low wage levels no doubt contribute also, but these are present equally in the low-growth South-East Asian nations.

Adler, Doktor and Redding (1986) propose that the modes of thought which predominate in Pacific Basin nations and Western nations differ in quite fundamental ways. If we are to understand the operations of firms within these countries we need to investigate not simply what is done, but how it is done and why. Such a proposition may at first sound close to the *nihonjinron* type of argument, except that it is generalized to the Confucian nations of the Pacific rim. However it is based upon a detailed review of comparative studies of management, and may be helpful in summarizing what our review has found. Their suggestion is that while Western thought tends to focus upon the study of causal relations between abstractly conceptualized entities, Eastern thought focuses more upon the achievement of harmony between practical, concrete performance criteria such as quality control or sales targets. The value of this distinction between the abstract and the concrete can be illustrated through reference to Misumi's (1985) theory of leadership.

The theory proposes a distinction between the general functions of groups and organizations and the specific behaviours by which those functions are accomplished. Such a distinction has not been advanced by Western theorists. Our review has covered a number of areas in which such a distinction may prove valuable. For instance, studies of the intercorrelations of dimensions of organizational structure have shown some differences between Japan and the West. It may be that aspects of organizational structure such as centralization or formalization are indeed universal attributes of organizations, but that these attributes serve different specific functions in each cultural setting according to the meanings which attach to them. Similarly, dimensions of leadership behaviour such as task structuring and maintenance of good working relations may be universals, but the specific behaviours required to implement them in varying cultures may be entirely different (Smith and Tayeb, 1988). Thus it may be that while organizations in all parts of the world are faced with the same general problems, culture patterns in East and West encourage different patterns of specific problem solving. Growing internationalization may then reveal to us that some of these specific problem solutions have value not just within their culture of origin but much more widely.

Our argument thus leads to the view that Japanese management may indeed have lessons for Western nations, but that those lessons will need to be translated into the specific idiom of Western cultures if they are to prove applicable there. The findings to date suggest that this may prove easier in blue-collar occupational groups, and in market sectors where it is possible to retain key functions to organizational success within Japan. More substantial efforts to transplant entire Japanese organizations to Western settings are likely to encounter substantial difficulties, particularly in the areas of management decision making and promotion.

Consideration of the success of Japanese firms in the West leads us to our final discussion point: the impact of Japanese methods upon the practices of Western firms. This is most readily apparent in firms that supply components to Japanese firms in the car and electronics industries. In order to win contracts, they have been required to satisfy quality standards and delivery schedules specified by the Japanese. There has been some movement towards the development of long-term contracts between manufacturers and suppliers, with consequent reduction in the numbers of suppliers. Just-in-time systems have been widely implemented in the United States and British car industries (e.g. Turnbull, 1986). The joint venture between Honda and Rover has led to enhanced emphasis on quality within Rover (Smith, in press). Quality circles have been introduced within a wide variety of firms. On the whole the magnitude of these changes is not large, so that substantial differences most probably remain between the practices of local firms and their Japanese neighbours in Western countries, as the studies by Pascale and his colleagues showed a decade ago.

Dispassionate analysis of Japanese management is hard to come by. Japanese writers have tended either to stress its uniqueness or to foresee convergence with American practice. Western authors, on the other hand, have preferred either the view that its essentials are readily applicable in the West, or the view that it is a coercive system which would never work in the West. We have sought a middle path between these views, but it is time which will show to what degree the varying industrial cultures of the world will converge upon one another.

REFERENCES

Abegglen, J.C. (1958) *The Japanese Factory: Aspects of its social organization*. Glencoe IL: Free Press.

Abegglen, J.C. (1973) *Management and Worker: The Japanese Solution*. Tokyo: Sophia University Press.

Abegglen, J.C., and Stalk, G. (1984) *Kaisha, The Japanese Corporation*. New York: Basic Books.

Adler, N.J., Doktor, R., and Redding, S.G. (1986) From the Atlantic to the Pacific century: cross-cultural management reviewed. *Journal of Management*, 12, 295–318.

Atsumi, R.(1979) Tsukiai—obligatory personal relationships of Japanese white-collar employees. *Human Organization*, 38, 63–70.

Azumi, K., and McMillan, C.J. (1976) Worker sentiment in the Japanese factory: its

organizational determinants. In L. Austin (ed.), *Japan: The paradox of progress*. New Haven CT: Yale University Press, pp. 215–230.
Azumi, K., and McMillan, C.J. (1979) Management strategy and organization structure: a Japanese comparative study. In D.J. Hickson and C.J. McMillan (eds), *Organization and Nation: The Aston Programme IV*. Farnborough, UK: Gower, pp. 155–172.
Buckley, P.J., and Mirza, H. (1985) The wit and wisdom of Japanese management. *Management International Review*, 25, 16–32.
Clark, R.C. (1979) *The Japanese Company*. New Haven, CT: Yale University Press.
Cole, R.E. (1971). *Japanese Blue Collar: The Changing Tradition*. Berkeley: University of California Press.
Cole, R.E. (1979) *Work, Mobility and Participation: A comparative study of Japanese and American industry*. LosAngeles, CA: University of California Press.
Dale, P.N. (1986). *The Myth of Japanese Uniqueness*. London: Croom Helm.
Davis, S.M. (1979) *Managing and Organizing Multinational Corporations*. New York: Pergamon.
Doktor, R. (1983) Culture and the management of time: a comparison of Japanese and American top management practice. *Asia Pacific Journal of Management*, 1, 65–71.
Dore, R.P. (1973) *British Factory, Japanese Factory*. London: Allen and Unwin.
Dunphy, D. (1987) Convergence/divergence: a temporal review of the Japanese enterprise and its management. *Academy of Management Review*, 12, 445–459.
Everett, J.E., Krishnan, A.R., and Stening, B.W. (1984) *Through a Glass Darkly—South East Asian Managers: Mutual perceptions of Japanese and local counterparts*. Singapore: Eastern Universities Press.
Fruin, W.M. (1983) *Kikkoman: Company, clan and community*. Cambridge, MA: Harvard University Press.
Griffin, K. (1989) In this volume. Chichester: Wiley.
Hatvany, N., and Pucik, V. (1981) An integrated management system: lessons from the Japanese experience. *Academy of Management Review*, 6, 469–480.
Hayashi, C. (1987) Statistical study on Japanese national character. *Journal of the Japan Statistical Society*, Special issue, 71–95.
Hayashi, C. (1988) The national character in transition. *Japan Echo*, 25, 7–11.
Hazama, H. (1978) Characteristics of Japanese-style management. *Japanese Economic Studies*, 6, 110–173.
Hofstede, G. (1980) *Culture's Consequences: International differences in work-related values*. Beverly Hills, CA: Sage.
Horvath, D., McMillan, C.J., Azumi, K., and Hickson, D.J. (1979) The cultural context of organizational control: An international comparison. In D.J. Hickson and C.J. McMillan (eds), *Organization and Nation: The Aston Programme IV*. Farnborough, UK: Gower, pp. 173–186.
Itami, H. (1987) *Mobilizing Invisible Assets*. Cambridge, MA: Harvard University Press.
Iwata, R. (1978) *The Environment of Management in Modern Japan* (in Japanese). Tokyo: Nihon Keizai Shimbun.
Japan Times (1988) Sohyo members complain about long hours, low pay. 17 January.
Johansson, J.K., and Nonaka, I. (1987) Market research the Japanese way. *Harvard Business Review*, 65, 16–22.
Kagono, T., Nonaka, I., Sakakibara, K., and Okumura, A. (1985) *Strategic vs Evolutionary Management: A US-Japan comparison of strategy and organisation*. Amsterdam: North-Holland.
Kamata, S. (1982) *Japan in the Passing Lane: An insider's account of life in a Japanese auto factory*. New York: Pantheon.
Kanai, T. (1987) Differentiation of contrasting cosmologies among R and D personnel:

subtlety in Japanese R and D management. *Annals of the School of Business Administration, Kobe University*, **31**, 109–141.

Keys, J.B., and Miller, T.R. (1984) The Japanese management theory jungle. *Academy of Management Review*, **9**, 342–353.

Kidd, J.B., and Teramoto, Y. (1981) Japanese production subsidiaries in the United Kingdom: a study of managerial 'decision-making'. Working paper no. 203. University of Aston Management Centre, UK.

Kobayashi, T. (1980) *Japan's Multinational Corporations* (in Japanese). Tokyo: Chuo Keizai.

Kono, T. (1986) Factors affecting the creativity of organization: an approach from the analysis of the new product development. First International Symposium on Management, Japan Society for the Study of Business Administration, Kobe University, pp. 271–326.

Lincoln, J.R., Hanada, M., and McBride, K. (1986) Organizational structures in Japanese and US manufacturing. *Administrative Science Quarterly*, **31**, 338–364.

Lincoln, J.R., Hanada, M., and Olson, J. (1981) Cultural orientations and individual reactions to organizations: a study of employees of Japanese-owned firms. *Administrative Science Quarterly*, **26**, 93–115.

Lincoln, J.R., and Kalleberg, A.L. (1985) Work organization and workforce commitment: a study of plants and employees in the US and Japan. *American Sociological Review*, **50**, 738–760.

Lincoln, J.R., Olson, J., and Hanada, M. (1978) Cultural effects on organizational structure: the case of Japanese firms in the United States. *American Sociological Review*, **43**, 829–847.

Luthans, F., McCaul, H.S., and Dodd, N.G. (1985) Organizational commitment: a comparison of American, Japanese and Korean employees. *Academy of Management Journal*, **28**, 213–219.

McMillan, C.J. (1985) *The Japanese Industrial System*. Berlin: de Gruyter.

Maguire, M.A., and Pascale, R.T. (1978) Communication, decision-making and implementation among managers in Japanese and American managed companies. *Sociology and Social Research*, **63**, 1–22.

Mannari, H. and Befu, H. (Eds) *The Challenge of Japan's Internationalization: Organization and Culture*. Tokyo: Kodansha.

Marsh, R.M., and Mannari, H. (1976) *Modernization and the Japanese Factory*. Princeton, NJ: Princeton University Press.

Marsh, R.M., and Mannari, H. (1981) Technology and size as determinants of the organizational structure of Japanese factories. *Administrative Science Quarterly*, **26**, 33–57.

Meaning of Working International Research Team (1987) *The Meaning of Working*. London: Academic Press.

Misumi, J. (1975) Action research on the development of leadership, decision-making processes and organizational performance in a Japanese shipyard. *Psychologia*, **18**, 187–193.

Misumi, J. (1984) Decision-making in Japanese groups and organizations. In B. Wilpert and A. Sorge (eds), *International Perspectives on Organizational Democracy*. Chichester, UK: Wiley, pp. 525–539.

Misumi, J. (1985) *The Behavioral Science of Leadership*. Ann Arbor, MI: University of Michigan Press.

Mito, T. (1983) Japanese management principles and seniority systems. *The Wheel Extended*, Special Supplement 12, 4–8.

Miyajima, R. (1986) Organization ideology of Japanese managers. *Management International Review*, **26**, 73–76.
Miyazawa, S. (1986) Legal departments of Japanese corporations in the United States: a study on organizational adaptation to multiple environments. *Kobe University Law Review*, **20**, 97–162.
Nakane, C. (1970) *Japanese Society*. London: Weidenfeld and Nicholson.
Nakane, C. (1972) Social background of Japanese in southeast Asia. *Developing Economies*, **10**, 115–125.
Naoi, A., and Schooler, C. (1985) Occupational conditions and psychological functioning in Japan. *American Journal of Sociology*, **90**, 729–752.
Negandhi, A.R. (1985) Management strategies and policies of American, German and Japanese multinational corporations. *Management Japan*, **18**, 12–20.
Negandhi, A.R., and Baliga, B.R. (1979) *Quest for Survival and Growth: A comparative study of Japanese, European and American multinationals*. New York: Praeger.
Negandhi, A.R., Eshghi, G.S., and Yuen, E.C. (1985) The management practices of Japanese subsidiaries overseas. *California Management Review*, **27**, 93–105.
Nonaka, I., and Johansson, J.K. (1985) Japanese management: what about the 'hard' skills? *Academy of Management Review*, **10**, 181–191.
Nonaka, I., and Okumura, A. (1984) A comparison of management in American, Japanese and European firms. *Management Japan*, **17**(1), 23–29; **17**(2), 20–27.
Odaka, K. (1975) *Toward Industrial Democracy: Management and workers in modern Japan*. Cambridge MA: Harvard University Press.
Oh, T.K. (1976) Japanese management: a critical review. *Academy of Management Review*, **1**, 14–25.
Okubayashi, K. (1986a) The impacts of industrial robots on working life in Japan. *Journal of General Management*, **11**, 22–34.
Okubayashi, K. (1986b) Recent problems of Japanese personnel management. *Labour and Society*, **11**, 18–37.
Okubayashi, K. (1987) Work content and organizational structure of Japanese enterprises under microelectronic innovation. *Annals of the School of Business Administration, Kobe University*, **31**, 34–52.
Ozawa, T. (1979) *Multinationalism Japanese Style: The political economy of outward dependency*. Princeton, NJ: Princeton University Press.
Pascale, R.T. (1978a) Communication and decision-making across cultures: Japanese and American comparisons. *Administrative Science Quarterly*, **23**, 91–109.
Pascale, R.T. (1978b) Personnel practices and employee attitudes: a study of Japanese and American managed firms in the United States. *Human Relations*, **31**, 597–615.
Pascale, R.T., and Athos, A.G. (1981) *The Art of Japanese Management: Applications for American Executives*. New York: Simon and Schuster.
Pascale, R.T., and Maguire, M.A. (1980) Comparison of selected work factors in Japan and the United States. *Human Relations*, **33**, 433–455.
Rohlen, T.P. (1974) *For Harmony and Strength: Japanese white-collar organization in anthropological perspective*. Berkeley, CA: University of California Press.
Schonberger, R.J. (1982) *Japanese Manufacturing Techniques*. New York: Free Press.
Seror, A.C. (1982) A cultural contingency framework for the comparative analysis of Japanese and US organizations. In S.M. Lee and G. Schwendiman (eds), *Management by Japanese Systems*. New York: Praeger, pp. 239–255.
Sethi, S.P., Namiki, N., and Swanson, C.L. (1984) *The False Promise of the Japanese Economic Miracle*. Marshfield, MA: Pitman.
Smith, D. (in press) *Management, Technology and Culture*. London: Macmillan.
Smith, P.B., and Tayeb, M.H. (1988) Organizational structure and processes. In M.H.

Bond (ed.), *The Cross-Cultural Challenge to Social Psychology*. Newbury Park, CA: Sage.

Sullivan, J., and Peterson, R.B. (1982) Factors associated with trust in Japanese–American joint ventures. *Management International Review*, 22, 30–40.

Sullivan, J., Peterson, R.B., Kameda, N., and Shimada, J. (1981) The relationship between conflict resolution approaches and trust: a cross-cultural study. *Academy of Management Journal*, 24, 803–815.

Taira, K. (1983) Japan's low employment: an economic miracle or statistical artefact. *Monthly Labour Review*, 106.

Takahashi, N., and Takayanagi, S. (1985) Decision procedure models and empirical research: the Japanese experience. *Human Relations*, 38, 767–780.

Takamiya, S. (1981) The characteristics of Japanese management. *Management Japan*, 14(2), 6–9.

Takamiya, S., and Thurley, K.E. (eds) (1985) *Japan's Emerging Multinationals: An international comparison of policies and practices*. Tokyo: Tokyo University Press.

Takezawa, S.I., and Whitehill, A.M. (1981) *Workways: Japan and America*. Tokyo: Japan Institute of Labour.

Taylor, S.J. (1983) *Shadows of the Rising Sun: A critical view of the 'Japanese Miracle'*. Tokyo: Tuttle.

Tracy, P., and Azumi, K. (1976) Determinants of administrative control: a test of a theory with Japanese factories. *American Sociological Review*, 41, 80–93.

Trevor, M. (1983) *Japan's Reluctant Multinationals*. London: Pinter.

Tsuda, M. (1977) *Theory of Japanese Style Management* (in Japanese). Tokyo: Chuo-Keizai.

Tung, R.L. (1984) How to negotiate with the Japanese. *Californian Management Review*, 26, 62–77.

Tung, R.L. (1987) Expatriate assignments: enhancing success and minimizing failure. *Academy of Management Executive*, 1, 117–126.

Turnbull, P.J. (1986) The Japanization of production at Lucas Electrical. *Industrial Relations Journal*, 17, 193–206.

Urabe, K. (1978) *Japanese Management* (in Japanese). Tokyo: Chuo-Keizai.

Urabe, K. (1984) *Japanese Management Does Evolve* (in Japanese). Tokyo: Chuo-Keizai.

Urabe, K. (1986) Innovation and the Japanese Management System. Keynote address, First International Symposium on Management, Japan Society for the Study of Business Administration, Kobe University, 11–49.

Wagatsuma, H. (1982) Internationalization of the Japanese: group model reconsidered. In H. Mannari and H. Befu (eds), *The Challenge of Japan's Internationalization: Organization and culture*. Tokyo: Kodansha, pp. 298–308.

Wakabayashi, M., and Graen, G.B. (1984) The Japanese career progress study: a 7 year follow-up. *Journal of Applied Psychology*, 69, 603–614.

Westney, D.E., and Sakakibara, K. (1985) The role of Japan based in global technology strategy. *Technology in Society*, 7, 315–330.

White, M., and Trevor, M. (1983) *Under Japanese Management*. London: Heinemann.

Whitehill, A.M., and Takezawa, S.I. (1968) *The Other Worker: A comparative study of industrial relations in the United States and Japan*. Honolulu: East-West Center Press.

Yoshihara, H. (1986) Dynamic synergy and top management leadership: strategic innovation in Japanese corporations. First International Symposium on Management, Japan Society for the Study of Business Administration, Kobe University, pp. 353–376.

Yoshino, M.Y. (1975) Emerging Japanese multinational enterprises. In E.F. Vogel (ed.), *Modern Japanese Organization and Decision-Making*. Berkeley, CA: University of California Press, pp. 146–166.

Yoshino, M.Y. (1976) *Japan's Multinational Enterprises*. Cambridge, MA: Harvard University Press.

Yoshino, M.Y., and Lifson, T.B. (1986) *The Invisible Link: Japan's sogo shosha and the organization of trade*. Cambridge, MA: MIT Press.

Chapter 11

CAUSAL MODELLING IN ORGANIZATIONAL RESEARCH

Lawrence R. James
and
Lois A. James
School of Psychology
Georgia Institute of Technology
USA

A meta-analysis was conducted to identify general trends in the use of causal modelling in industrial–organizational psychology and organizational behavior. We prefer to refer to causal modelling as 'confirmatory analysis', and will use the general term 'organizational research' to identify the substantive areas of interest. Following a brief description of the methods employed to conduct the meta-analysis, results of the analysis are reported in three sections. The first section is designated General Information, and includes data pertaining to design issues, such as the number of studies that could be regarded as manifest (i.e. observed) variable analyses versus latent variable analyses. Data describing the extent to which attempts were made to satisfy the assumptions or conditions required to employ confirmatory analytic methods are also reported in this section.

The second and third sections of the meta-analytic results present data specific to manifest variable studies (the second section) and latent variable studies (the third section). Within each of these sections, discussion begins with issues salient to model specification and identification. Of special interest here is whether models were overidentified and thus subject to an important form of empirical disconfirmation. Reliabilities of manifest variables are then considered, followed by an overview of the types of analytic techniques used both to estimate structural (causal) parameters in the structural models and to conduct goodness-of-fit tests. The results of the latter efforts are reviewed and it is shown that most theoretical models were disconfirmed. The final subsection overviews exploratory attempts to construct models with better fits to data via specification searches.

The presentation of results of the meta-analysis comprises the bulk of this chapter. And, as we shall see, the meta-analysis is perhaps best thought of as a description of initial efforts to apply a new and complex technology in organizational research. Summary comments are presented as conclusions and recommendations. We attempted to focus on broad trends evidenced by the meta-analytic data in offering suggestions for future research. Included here are trends that are commendable and should be continued. Other trends, however, may require revision.

METHOD

Four major journals in organizational research (OR) were examined for studies that employed confirmatory analytic techniques. These journals were *Journal of Applied Psychology*, *Personnel Psychology*, *Organizational Behavior and Human Decision Processes*, and the *Academy of Management Journal*. The search for studies was bounded by a ten-year period, which extended from 1978 to 1987. Only studies that employed documentable confirmatory analytic models and methods were selected. This selection procedure eliminated studies that (a) employed confirmatory analytic techniques in an exclusively exploratory mode or (b) used analytic techniques whose status as confirmatory was, at best, equivocal. Additionally, studies were excluded from the meta-analysis if the analytic procedure was unclear or ambiguous.

A total of 52 articles were included in the meta-analysis. These articles are referenced in the appendix. Of the 52 articles, three articles had two studies which either tested different structural models or used quite different confirmatory analytic techniques to test the same structural model (e.g. manifest versus latent variables methods). The two studies within each of these articles were treated as separate analyses. The total sample for the meta-analysis was thus 55 studies.

Table 1 describes the sample of studies as categorized by journal and year of publication. These data show an imperfect trend of increasing use of confirmatory analytic methods as a function of year. This finding is not surprising given the steadily increasing dissemination of articles and texts

Table 1—The Total Number of Articles from Each Journal

	1978	1979	1980	1981	1982	1983	1984	1985	1986	1987	Total
Academy of Management Journal	1	2	1	2		2	6	2	5	3	24
Journal of Applied Psychology					4	3	1	1	5	5	19
Organizational Behavior and Human Decision Processes	1	1	1			1	2		1	1	8
Personnel Psychology	1		2				1				4
Total	3	3	4	2	4	6	10	3	11	9	55

describing the use of structural equation modelling. The majority of confirmatory analytic studies were found in *Academy of Management Journal* (n = 24; 44 per cent), followed by *Journal of Applied Psychology* (n = 19; 34 per cent), *Organizational Behavior and Human Decision Processes* (n = 8; 15 per cent), and *Personnel Psychology* (n = 4; 7 per cent).

The frequency of articles by content area is reported in Table 2. These data reflect the diverse sampling of OR domains that have been subjected to confirmatory analyses. The most popular content area was Turnover (n = 10; 18 per cent) followed by Job Satisfaction/Job Performance (n = 7; 13 per cent).

Table 2—Frequency of Articles by Content Area

	n	Percentage
Turnover	10	18.2
Job satisfaction/job performance	7	12.7
Job characteristics	5	9.1
Organizational structure	4	7.3
Goal setting	3	5.5
Stress	3	5.5
Leadership	3	5.5
Roles	2	3.6
Organizational commitment	2	3.6
Computer technology	2	3.6
Job performance/job experience	1	1.8
Altruism	1	1.8
Career management	1	1.8
Organizational policy	1	1.8
Feedback	1	1.8
Strategic planning	1	1.8
Labor unions	1	1.8
Cost containment	1	1.8
Job interview	1	1.8
Alienation	1	1.8
Decision making	1	1.8
Job preview	1	1.8
Bargaining	1	1.8

Each of the 55 studies was reviewed and scored on a set of items constructed specifically for this meta-analysis. The items fell within the following six general categories: (1) general model design (e.g. latent versus manifest variable models); (2) conditions for confirmatory analysis; (3) model specification and identification issues; (4) analytic procedures; (5) goodness-of-fit tests; and (6) specification search procedures. The specific items used to garner data from the studies are included in the tables presented throughout this report.

It is noteworthy that we generally employed only descriptive items in this meta-analysis. To illustrate, we assessed whether a study provided a rationale for the ordering of causes and effects throughout the structural (causal) model. No attempt was made to evaluate the quality of the rationale for causal orderings. With exceptions, then, we focused on descriptive items and did not attempt to evaluate specific studies in terms of substantive and/or methodological quality or merit. We had a number of reasons for adopting this approach. These reasons included: (a) we possessed neither the substantive nor the statistical knowledge to make valid judgements of merit for all studies; (b) we wanted to employ items on which the scoring was straightforward and required minimal value judgements; (c) there were too few studies to support reliable statistical inferences and thus it was considered prudent to emphasize descriptive information; and, perhaps of most importance (d) the criteria for attributing merit tend to shift in this area, in large part due to the rapid and continuous expansion of knowledge.

RESULTS: GENERAL INFORMATION

Design

Information pertaining to the general design of the studies is presented in Table 3. Of initial interest is the finding that the majority of confirmatory analyses (72 per cent) in OR employed manifest designs. A study was classified as manifest if all constructs in the structural (causal) model were represented by a single, observed variable (cf. Bentler, 1980; James, Mulaik, and Brett, 1982). A latent variable design denoted that (a) at least some constructs in the structural model were represented by multiple indicators, and (b) an attempt was made to estimate, or to set by hypothesis (e.g. fix to zero), parameters linking unobserved (latent) variables or constructs to the observed indicators as well as to one another. Latent variable designs were less popular than manifest designs, comprising only 28 per cent of the studies. More interesting is the observation that so few latent variable studies were conducted. This may reflect the comparatively greater difficulty and expense involved in developing and operationalizing a latent variable design. It is possible, however, that the benefits to be accrued from the use of latent variable designs, such as opportunities to test the construct validity of measurement procedures and to estimate structural parameters for perfectly reliable variables (cf. Bentler, 1980), will result in greater use of these paradigms in the future. This is especially likely to occur as more researchers become familiar with the rather complex statistical procedures underlying latent variable analysis.

Type of study

Studies were classified as cross-sectional if data for all variables were collected simultaneously, or essentially simultaneously. Most studies (71 per cent) were

Table 3—The General Design of the Confirmatory Analytic Studies

A. Type of model		n	%				
Manifest		39	72				
Latent		16	28				
	Total	55	100				

B. Type of study	Total (n = 55)		Manifest (n = 39)		Latent (n = 16)	
	n	%	n	%[a]	n	%[b]
Cross-sectional	39	71	28	72	11	69
Longitudinal	11	20	7	18	4	25
Panel	5	9	4	10	1	6
C. Causal direction						
Recursive	51	93	36	92	15	94
Non-recursive	4	7	3	8	1	06

[a] Percentage computed on number of manifest studies.
[b] Percentage computed on number of latent studies.

cross-sectional. (Results in the remainder of the General Information section are generally discussed for the combined samples of manifest and latent studies in order to identify general trends. Data specific to manifest and latent studies are also reported.) The logic underlying the use of cross-sectional data in confirmatory analysis is that all variables in a structural model have reached a state of temporary equilibrium, which is to say that the values on the variables have stabilized and will remain constant, or reasonably so, for a generalizable period of time. The objective of the confirmatory analysis is then to ascertain whether one or more hypothetical structural models could have generated the present state of affairs. The key to the process is that current differences among subjects on the variables are employed as surrogates for a progression of changes in a single subject that occur over time (but which stabilize periodically) (cf. James *et al.*, 1982).

A weakness of the cross-sectional design is that the ordering of cause and effect (i.e. causal ordering) may be ambiguous and open to challenge. A remedy to this causal ordering problem is to employ a design in which causes are measured prior to effects. This was the process employed in 20 per cent of the studies that used a longitudinal design. The use of 'longitudinal' here does not connote establishment of time intervals among all causes and effects. It denotes only that a time interval intervened between a cause(s) and at least one effect (typically turnover).

Panel designs comprise the third type of study found in the OR literature. A panel design is a form of cross-sectional time-series (cf. Johnston, 1984), which refers to simultaneous collection of data on presumed causes and effects on at least two occasions and for more than one subject (time-series often involve only single-subject designs). Panel designs that used only correlational methods of analysis (e.g. Kenny, 1975) were not included here. To be included, some form of structural equation analysis had to be performed (cf. Rogosa, 1980). Of the studies in the present analysis, 9 per cent employed structural analyses to analyze panel data. Most such studies were based on two variables and two waves (occasions) of measurement.

Causal direction

Ninety-three per cent of the studies were based on a recursive design, which is a model wherein all causal effects are unidirectional or asymmetric. A non-recursive design was used in only four studies. Reciprocal causation between two or more endogenous or dependent variables has not been a popular hypothesis for empirical testing. However, the possibility of reciprocal causation was often noted as a subject requiring future research.

Conditions for Confirmatory Analyses

Conditions for confirmatory analysis refer to criteria that may be used to judge whether a theoretical structural model may appropriately be subjected to confirmatory analysis (James et al., 1982). Reasonable satisfaction of the conditions suggests a well-developed, stable model that, when tested, should furnish reasonable means for confirming and/or disconfirming theoretical predictions pertaining to causal relations (conditional on adequate operationalization of variables in the model). Failure to satisfy, at least reasonably, one or more of the conditions suggests that confirmatory analysis should not be employed. If confirmatory analysis is used, then results are likely to be biased.

James et al. (1982) proposed the following seven conditions for evaluating the appropriateness of a structural model for confirmatory analysis:

1. Formal statement of theory in terms of a structural model.
2. Theoretical rationale for causal hypotheses.
3. Specification of causal order.
4. Specification of causal direction.
5. Self-contained functional equations.
6. Specification of boundaries.
7. Stability of the structural model.

We report some form of data pertaining to Conditions 1, 3, 5, 6, and 7 in Table 4. Whether a rationale for causal hypotheses had been presented, which is required for reasonable satisfaction of Condition 2, was too subjective for us to judge and thus was not included in the meta-analysis. Our *impressions* are that a rationale is always presented for key causal hypotheses in a model. However, the *extent* to which a rationale is presented for less stellar hypotheses is often oblique and difficult to ascertain (the quality of the rationale is an additional issue). Condition 4 was, in one sense, automatically satisfied by the choice of a recursive (unidirectional) versus non-recursive (bidirectional) design (see Table 3). In another sense, we might have attempted to evaluate the accuracy of the assumptions specifying causal direction. However, no attempt was made here to evaluate the quality of assumptions.

Table 4—Conditions Relevant for Evaluating the Appropriateness of a Structural Model for Confirmatory Analysis

		Total n	Total %	Manifest n	Manifest %	Latent n	Latent %
Condition 1							
a. Formal statement of theory in	yes	34	62	23	59	11	69
terms of a graphic structural model	no	21	38	16	41	5	31
b. Begin with multiple, *a priori*,	yes	5	9	3	8	2	12
models	no	50	91	36	92	14	88
Condition 3							
a. Specification of causal order for	yes	40	73	30	80	10	63
entire model	no	15	27	9	20	6	37
Condition 5							
a. Acknowledgement of self-	yes	10	18	9	23	1	6
containment	no	45	82	30	77	15	94
Condition 6							
a. Specification of boundaries—	yes	13	24	9	23	4	25
moderation analysis conducted	no	42	76	30	77	12	75
Condition 7							
a. Test of stability of model	yes	4	7	3	8	1	6
	no	51	93	36	92	15	94

Condition 1

All 55 studies furnished a formal statement of theory in terms of a verbal structural model. As shown in Table 4, 62 per cent of the studies also displayed the proposed causal model graphically via figures. The decision to rely solely on a verbal presentation of a model may or may not have been the purview of the author(s). And, indeed, a verbal presentation may have sufficed for many readers, especially for non-complex models.

More attention to another aspect of modelling appears to be needed. As shown under Condition 1 in Table 4, only 9 (09) per cent of the studies proposed two or more competing models or theories as part of the introduction to the article (and proceeded to test the competing models). James *et al.* (1982) recommended that an attempt should be made to test multiple, competing theories whenever feasible. The rationale for this recommendation was that one may place greater faith in a model that has been corroborated by empirical tests if, as part of these tests, this model has been shown to have a comparatively better fit to data than competing models. It is also noteworthy that reliance on a single model is problematic if this model is empirically disconfirmed. The next step after disconfirmation is a specification search, which, as described in greater detail later, is an exploratory attempt to build a better model. But this model can only be tested on a new sample. It is our opinion that at least some of the models developed via specification searches could have been proposed, *a priori*, as alternatives to the model of key interest (that was later disconfirmed). If indeed this was possible, then the alternative model could have been tested within the context of confirmatory, rather than exploratory, analysis on the same set of data as the key model.

Condition 3

Specification of causal order for the entire design refers to stating a rationale for the causal ordering of cause and effect for *every* causal relation in the structural model. Results in Table 4 show that 73 per cent of the studies satisfied this criterion. The other 27 per cent of the studies typically presented a rationale for the causal order for only the most salient causal hypotheses in the model. Infrequently, authors voiced uncertainty in regard to the causal ordering of some variables.

Specification of causal interval is applicable as part of the causal order question for longitudinal and panel designs. The interval between measurement of causes and measurement of effects (the measurement interval) should be the same or similar to the actual causal interval (cf. Heise, 1975; Kenny, 1979). Lack of correspondence between measurement intervals and causal intervals may result in problems such as juxtaposition of cause and effect in panel designs (Pelz and Lew, 1970). Unfortunately, our attempts to assess whether causal intervals had been specified in the longitudinal and, especially, panel studies proved to be unsuccessful. Too much subjectivity was required on our part to make a judgement of whether a rationale for a causal interval had or had not been presented. The most we might say in this regard is that many investigators could be much more explicit in their reports of why they employed a particular measurement interval.

Condition 5

Self-containment of a structural equation denotes that the equation is not subject to an unmeasured variables problem (James, 1980; James *et al.*, 1982; Simon, 1977). Technically, a structural equation is self-contained if all relevant causes for the endogenous variable are included in the equation. Self-containment is indicated *theoretically* by lack of covariation between the causal variables included in a structural equation and the disturbance term of that equation (cf. Johnston, 1984). The self-containment condition is the Achilles heel of confirmatory analysis on naturally occurring data because it is impossible to know whether the condition has been reasonably satisfied (many believe the likelihood is that it has *not* been reasonably satisfied). This is because unknown causes that are correlated with known (and included) causes will create covariation between causal variables and a disturbance term (cf. James, 1980). But one cannot assess what is unknown. The practical consequence of the unmeasured variables problem is bias in parameter estimation (cf. James, 1980). Empirically, some forms of time-series may be used to assess, and perhaps even correct, for this bias (James and Singh, 1978). Unfortunately, statistical theory and computer algorithms are only now being developed to deal with these types of models.

Given the problems known to be associated with failure to satisfy the self-containment condition, it is surprising that only 18 per cent of the studies even mentioned the condition or some euphemism for the condition. We believe that 18 per cent is a liberal figure because we assessed only whether self-containment was *acknowledged* (note, not defended) irrespective of *where* it was acknowledged (typically in the Discussion section as part of objectives for future research). This, frankly, is a sad state of affairs if for no other reason than that it furnishes the 'anti-confirmatory analysis' folks with the type of data they need to criticize the entire confirmatory effort (see Games, 1988, for an example).

Admittedly, it is troublesome to have assumptions that are likely violated to some unknown degree. On the other hand, the actual degrees of bias in parameters estimates produced by violations of the self-containment condition are also unknown, and may not be severe in well-developed models (James, 1980). But these are matters that scientists will have to judge openly. There is nothing to be gained, and much to lose, by failing to acknowledge that the problem exists. Thus, we recommend that, at the very least, researchers acknowledge the self-containment condition. Better yet would be a description of the attempts made to deal with this condition (see James, 1980, for a set of decision steps). If no attempt has been made to address this condition, then it is possible that confirmatory analysis is not a viable option (James, 1980).

Condition 6

Specification of boundaries refers to stipulating the contexts, such as types of environments and subjects, to which the structural model is expected to generalize. The empirical assumption is that the structural parameters in the structural equations are *not* contingent on values of a third or more variables. In other words, causal relations are linear and additive. If an investigator believes that the values of structural parameters will vary as a function, say, of different contexts (e.g. high versus low stress conditions) or different types of subjects (e.g. males versus females), then a moderator analysis is appropriate. Statistical treatments of moderator analysis for structural equations have been presented by Stolzenberg (1979), Schoenberg (1972), Specht and Warren (1976), Kenny and Judd (1984), and Cohen and Cohen (1983).

An evaluation of whether Condition 6 was reasonably satisfied required too much subjectivity on our part to be valid. Consequently, we assessed only whether a moderator analysis was conducted as part of the initial confirmatory analysis (tests for moderation conducted as part of a specification search were treated separately—see Table 10). Approximately one-fourth of the studies included a moderator analysis as part of the confirmatory analysis. This suggests that authors were willing to deal with the added complexity of moderator analyses, which applies especially to latent variable designs in which the moderator is a continuous variable (cf. Tetrick and LaRocca, 1987).

Condition 7

Structural models should be sufficiently stable to support causal inferences that are generalizable over a meaningful time interval. A test of the 'stationarity' of a model is the basis for inferences pertaining to stability. A model is stationary if the structural parameters are invariant over specified time intervals. A statistical test for stationarity of manifest models has been presented only recently (James and Tetrick, 1986). Only four studies (7 per cent) attempted to assess stability, and these assessments were generally based on visual inspection of estimates of structural parameters rather than a formal statistical test. Of course, only studies with two (or more) waves of data provided a means for such inspections (e.g. the panel studies).

In general, then, most studies were cross-sectional and had to rely on non-empirical means (theory, prior research) to attempt to reasonably satisfy the stability assumption.

Samples

Many of the estimation techniques used in confirmatory analysis rely on asymptotic theory to infer that estimates of structural parameters are consistent. This suggests that large samples should be utilized in confirmatory analyses. Large samples are attractive for other reasons, such as providing statistical power and reducing the likelihood of statistical problems, including failure of estimation algorithms to converge (Bentler and Chou, 1987). Unfortunately, there is no precise definition of 'large'. Some attention has been given to what might be considered a minimal sample size for latent variable models (Anderson and Gerbing, 1984; Bentler and Chou, 1987; Boomsma, 1982, 1985; Gerbing and

Anderson, 1985). In general, it appears that latent variable analyses should be avoided on samples of less than 100, although a sample of 200 or more may be required to avoid drawing of inaccurate inferences (Boomsma, 1982; Marsh, Balla, and McDonald, 1988). Bentler and Chou (1987, p. 90) suggest, however, that 'definitive recommendations are not available', and propose, as an oversimplification, ratios of 5 : 1 to 10 : 1 of sample size to the number of free parameters to be estimated (in latent variable models).

Sample sizes for the 55 studies reviewed here varied from 15 to 1474, with a mean of 284 (SD = 316) and a median of 171 (see Table 5). Although skewed, the distribution of sample sizes demonstrates that essentially 50 per cent of the confirmatory studies were based on samples of 200 or more. We believe this to be an encouraging finding in the sense that confirmatory analyses appear to be predicated on comparatively much larger samples than some other areas of OR research where large samples are a desired commodity. A key example is selection research where median sample sizes run about 68 (Lent, Aurbach, and Levin, 1971).

Table 5—Sample Sizes

	Total	Manifest	Latent
Range	15–1474	15–1474	50–1296
Mean	284	287	313.87
25th percentile	79	79	60
50th percentile	171	177	155
75th percentile	331	310	411
Standard deviation	316	317	345.8

MANIFEST VARIABLE DESIGNS

We turn now to issues that pertain to empirical tests of structural models. These issues include identification, operationalization of variables, types of analytic procedures, results of initial hypothesis tests, and specification searches. These issues differ sufficiently for manifest and latent variable models to require separate treatments. We begin with manifest designs.

Model Specification and Identification Issues

The average manifest model involved approximately ten variables, five of which were exogenous and five of which were endogenous (see Table 6). The mean number of 'free' structural parameters—that is, parameters whose values were estimated by confirmatory analysis—was approximately fifteen. The number of parameters for which values were fixed (almost always to zero) averaged close to 9.0. Interestingly, a few recursive studies had no fixed parameters in the initial structural model. This signifies that the model was just-identified and thus a 'Condition 10' form of goodness-of-fit test could not be conducted. (James *et al.*, 1982, described a Condition 10 test of fit as an assessment of whether a structural parameter fixed theoretically to zero is or is not found to be significantly different from zero in the confirmatory analysis. Condition 10 tests are often referred to as tests of overidentifying restrictions.) Most studies, however, included one or more overidentified equations and thus Condition 10 tests of fit were conducted.

Table 6—Model Specification and Identification Issues for Manifest Designs

	Range	Mean	Standard deviation
Number of exogenous variables in model	1–16	5.20	4.00
Number of endogenous variables in model	1–14	4.74	2.99
Number of free structural parameters	5–36	15.16	8.20
Number of fixed structural parameters	0–39	9.00	10.80
Parsimony Index Ratio: free parameters/total parameters	.30–1.0	.72	.23

The descriptive statistics above that refer to numbers of parameters are rather gross and subject to several interpretations. For example, a model that has only one exogenous variable may still be quite complex if it is triangular recursive (cf. Duncan, 1975; Heise, 1975). Or, having two or more fixed structural parameters does not imply overidentification in non-recursive manifest models because each endogenous variable in a non-recursive relation must have at least one instrument for the model to be just-identified (cf. James and Singh, 1978). Nevertheless, one of our concerns regarding model specification was the degree to which models tended to be overidentified, for the higher the degree of overidentification, the more easily the model is disconfirmed. Models which are more easily disconfirmed are often considered preferable to barely overidentified or just-identified models inasmuch as more highly overidentified models are also more parsimonious (James *et al.*, 1982). Furthermore, if tests of the large number of overidentifying restrictions fail to reject (disconfirm) the model, then one may have reasonable faith that the model is *useful* for explanatory purposes.

We computed an imperfect estimator of the parsimony of the manifest models by dividing the number of free parameters by the total number of parameters (i.e. free parameters plus fixed parameters). A ratio of 1.0 denotes just-identification for a recursive model (almost all manifest models were recursive; the few non-recursive models tended to be moderately to highly overidentified). Such models have no fixed parameters (or constrained parameters), and, in general, are neither parsimonious nor easily disconfirmed by Condition 10 tests. The ratio went as low as .30 for the studies reviewed here (see Table 6), which means that only about one-third of the parameters were free to be estimated. The other two-thirds of the parameters were fixed. While we have no meaningful way to interpret these ratios, having two-thirds of the parameters fixed seems to imply a parsimonious and easily disconfirmable model. The mean ratio of free to fixed parameters over studies was .72. Thus, roughly one in four parameters was fixed. We have no basis for judging whether this is, or is not, a 'good' ratio in regard to parsimony. Future research is needed to establish an interpretative base for descriptive statistics such as this.

Operationalization of Variables

Generally, the 'variables' in a structural model are latent variables, which is to say theoretical constructs that are presumed to be represented in, indeed to cause to occur, observable events. The latent variables are not directly observable. Rather, their empirical content is provided by linkages to directly measurable variables, or manifest variables. In this sense, manifest variables are often viewed as 'indicators' of latent variables (cf. Costner, 1969). When a single manifest variable (indicator) is used to represent a latent variable, we should be particularly concerned about the accuracy of this representation. Is the variable free of random measurement errors, or at least highly reliable? Is it also free of non-random measurement errors produced by such things as improper measurement procedures (e.g. aggregation bias, ceiling or floor effects, method variance—cf. Namboodiri, Carter, and Blalock, 1975)? Unreliable manifest variables and/or manifest variables that are subject to serious non-random measurement errors are likely to stimulate biased and inconsistent results in confirmatory analysis.

For the present analyses we attempted to assess the general trends pertaining to the reliability with which manifest variables were measured. This was not a straightforward endeavor because: (a) some studies did not report reliabilities; (b) some studies relied on prior evidence to support the reliabilities of variables and did not compute estimates for the data at hand; (c) for those studies that reported reliabilities, not all variables (e.g. sex, organizational size) were subjected to a reliability analysis; and (d) different estimating procedures were employed to estimate reliability. We decided to attempt to obtain a crude and imperfect indicator of whether the technical assumption of perfect reliability (for causal variables if data are in unstandardized form, and for all variables if data are in standardized form) was being reasonably satisfied by attainment of 'high reliabilities' (cf. Duncan, 1975).

There is no definition of 'high' (James et al., 1982), but we believe that most investigators would agree that a reliability of less than .70 is 'not high'. The information presented in Table 7 connotes that, for variables for which reliabilities were reported, an average of 28 per cent of the exogenous variables (per study) had reliabilities of less than .70. This statistic was computed by:

(a) obtaining the empirically estimated reliabilities for exogenous variables for each study; (b) counting the number of these reliabilities that were less than .70; (c) dividing this number by the total number of reliabilities reported for exogenous variables; and (d) computing an average of this proportion over studies and multiplying by 100 to convert to a percentage. No attempt was made to account for differences in estimation techniques, to adjust the proportions for such things as the actual number of reliabilities reported versus the total number of exogenous variables, or to weight proportions in computing the between-study mean.

Table 7—Average Reliabilities for Exogenous and Endogenous Variables for Manifest Designs

Reliability	Variables					
	Exogenous			Endogenous		
	Range	Mean	SD	Range	Mean	SD
Per cent of variables with reliability less than .70	0–100%	28%	37%	0–100%	20%	28%
Per cent of variables with reliabilities between .70 and .80	0–100%	36%	33%	0–66%	29%	27%

Note Average reliabilities computed on variables for which reliabilities were reported.

As crude as this estimate is, an average of 28 per cent seems rather high for confirmatory analytic studies. Of course, the range of 0 per cent to 100 per cent and the SD = 37 per cent signifies that no real central tendency or trend exists. Nevertheless, room for improvement appears to be generally indicated for the OR research field. The potential problem appears less severe for endogenous variables. Using procedures similar to those described above, an average of 20 per cent of the endogenous variables (per study) had reliabilities of less than .70. This estimate was computed in an analogous manner and is no less crude than that for the exogenous variables. It suggests, however, that estimates of path coefficients may be rather severely attenuated for some endogenous variables in some studies.

Estimates were also obtained for the per cent of exogenous and endogenous variables with reliabilities between .70 and .80 for each study (see Table 7). Here again the base was the number of exogenous or endogenous variables for which reliabilities were reported in each study. Examination of these data, combined with the prior reliability data, imply that, for variables on which reliabilities were reported, roughly 64 per cent of the exogenous variables in a given study and 49 per cent of the endogenous variables in a given study have reliabilities of .80 or less. These summary statistics are uneven and clear exceptions exist (in both directions). Nevertheless, OR researchers may wish to ponder the question of whether the reliability condition has, in general, been reasonably satisfied in the published studies in this area.

Analytic Procedures

Ordinary least squares (OLS) was the estimation method of choice for 90 per cent of the manifest variable studies (see Table 8). Two-stage least squares (2SLS) was adopted for three non-recursive analyses. Only one study used full-information maximum likelihood (FIML) to estimate structural parameters. We shall not attempt to present a technical, or even a non-technical, overview of the different estimation techniques, or the pluses and minuses associated with each. In fact, a comparison of methods would be premature because new information pertaining to the full-information estimation techniques, especially FIML, is being disseminated continuously in journals such as *Psychometrika* and *Sociological Methods and Research*. We suggest only that (a) whereas single-equation estimators such as OLS have a firm place in confirmatory analysis, it would be (b) worth while for investigators to familiarize themselves with techniques such as FIML (and generalized least squares or GLS) if for no other reason than to be able to enhance flexibility in choosing an analytic technique.

Table 8—Analytic Procedures Employed to Test Confirmatory Models for Manifest Designs

	n	Per cent
Estimation technique		
OLS	35	89.7
2SLS	3	7.7
FIML	1	2.6
GLS	0	0
ULS	0	0
Goodness-of-fit statistics		
Condition 9		
Significance of parameters	36	92.3
Condition 10		
Omitted parameter	13	33.3
Disturbance term regression	3	7.7
Q-statistic	3	7.7
Chi-square	4	10.3
Reported results		
Unstandardized coefficients	8	20.5
Standardized coefficients	36	92.3
(Both	5	12.8)

Note OLS = Ordinary Least Squares, 2SLS = Two-Stage Least Squares, FIML = Full-Information Maximum Likelihood, GLS = Generalized Least Squares, ULS = Unweighted Least Squares.

Goodness-of-fit tests

Almost all studies (92 per cent) reported some form of Condition 9 test. A Condition 9 test is an empirical assessment of whether estimates of structural parameters predicted by the structural model to be non-zero are indeed significantly different from zero (James et al., 1982). This is an encouraging finding because Condition 9 tests comprise a salient basis for disconfirming a model, particularly when a key, direct cause–effect hypothesis fails to be supported by a significant parameter estimate.

The remainder of the goodness-of-fit information pertains to Condition 10 tests. As discussed, Condition 10 tests refer to assessments of overidentifying restrictions. Twenty-three (59 per cent) of the 39 manifest studies conducted a Condition 10 test as part of the confirmatory analysis. The majority of these studies employed the omitted parameter technique (cf. Duncan, 1975). The three non-recursive studies utilized the disturbance term regression test suggested by James and Jones (1980). Seven studies used either the Q-statistic (cf. Pedhazur, 1982) or chi-square (cf. Hayduk, 1987) to test the overall fit of a reproduced covariance (correlation) matrix to the observed covariance (correlation) matrix.

The finding that sixteen studies did not report a test of overidentifying restrictions is in part attributable to the fact that some studies had no overidentifying restrictions to test (i.e. the models, meaning all equations, were just-identified). Other studies that did have overidentifying restriction did not report tests of these restrictions, which presumably reflects failure to capitalize on this opportunity to disconfirm the model. A problemsome finding is that some, fortunately not many, studies persisted in mixing exploratory with confirmatory analyses. We refer here to the situation where: (a) the analysis begins with a just-identified model; (b) parameters are estimated; (c) parameters having non-significant estimates are theory-trimmed (i.e. the causal paths associated with the parameters are deleted from the model); and (d) Condition 10 tests are conducted to ascertain if the paths previously theory-trimmed are still non-significant in the theory-trimmed model.

James et al. (1982) warned investigators that this process is circular and constitutes an unwarranted mixing of exploratory analysis (theory-trimming) with confirmatory analysis. The Condition 10 tests on the theory-trimmed model cannot be regarded as assessments of prior, theoretically based, hypotheses. Accordingly, in the analyses reported in Table 8, we did not include studies that utilized this procedure as members of the 23 studies that conducted Condition 10 tests.

The final data included in Table 8 concern whether results are reported in terms of unstandardized coefficients (e.g. unstandardized regression weights are used as estimates of structural parameters) or standardized coefficients (e.g. standardized regression weights are used as estimates of path coefficients). Five studies reported both standardized and unstandardized coefficients. Thirty-six studies (92 per cent), including this set of five, reported standardized coefficients (31 studies reported only standardized coefficients), whereas eight studies (20 per cent) reported unstandardized coefficients (of which only three reported unstandardized coefficients exclusively). In general, it appears that OR researchers prefer the ease of communication provided by standardized coefficients. Note, however, that there are advantages and disadvantages to both standardized and unstandardized coefficients, and the reader is referred to James et al. (1982), Long (1983a, 1983b), Bentler and Chou (1987), Hayduk (1987), Tukey (1964), and Wright (1960) for discussions of the issues.

Results of Confirmatory Analyses

As shown in Table 9, 19 per cent of the studies successfully passed the Condition 9 tests; that is, all parameters predicted to be non-zero had estimates that were significant (in the predicted direction). Five studies, or 22 per cent, passed the Condition 10 tests of overidentifying restrictions. These percentages are based on the number of studies that reported results for Condition 9 and/or Condition 10 tests, respectively. It was not possible to construct a meaningful indicator of studies that passed both Condition 9 and Condition 10 tests because a number of studies reported only the results for Condition 9 tests (see Table 8). Thus, the only general statement that is possible with these data is that approximately 75 to 80 per cent of the structural models subjected to either a Condition 9 *or* a Condition 10 test were *disconfirmed*.

Table 9—Results of Analyses for Manifest Designs

	n	Percentage[a]
Model passes original Condition 9 test	7	19.0
Model passes original Condition 10 test	5	21.7

[a] Percentages based on number of studies that reported the results of Condition 9 and Condition 10 tests, which were 36 and 23 studies, respectively (see Table 8).

This may be heartening news to those who subscribe to the logic that the primary objective of causal analysis is to reject inaccurate models (e.g. Popper, 1959). Or, such results furnish fair warning to researchers that disconfirmation is a likely product of applying a structural equation approach. Conversely, disconfirmation is not necessarily the final stage of a causal analysis because investigators have the option of switching from confirmatory to exploratory procedures. In the context of causal analysis, the exploratory follow-up to revising disconfirmed (or even some confirmed) structural models is referred to as a 'specification search' or a 'specification analysis' (cf. Leamer, 1978; Long, 1983b; MacCallum, 1986). We now turn to this subject.

Specification Searches

A specification search was conducted in 27 (69 per cent) of the manifest variable studies (see Table 10). Formally defined, a specification search refers to 'the modification of the model so as to improve its parsimony and/or its fit to the data' (MacCallum, 1986, p. 108). Specification searches are exploratory; changes are effected in the model based on observed data. It follows that changes may be capitalizing on chance associations or levels of association that will not generalize beyond the current sample (cf. Bentler and Chou, 1987). It is often recommended that data used to propose changes—that is, the data on which the specification search is conducted—should not then be used to conduct a second confirmatory analysis. In part, this point is definitional inasmuch as confirmatory analysis is designed to test *a priori* hypotheses. One may, of course, check the fit of the model generated by a specification search. The point is not whether goodness-of-fit tests should be conducted on re-specified models. Rather, the question is how such tests should be interpreted. In our opinion, they are *not* confirmatory tests. A confirmatory analysis requires a new sample, or at least a cross-validation analysis (cf. Cudeck and Browne, 1983).

Table 10—Specification Searches for Manifest Designs

		n	Percentage
Specification search conducted[a]		27	69.2
Note exploratory nature of search		6	15.4
Cross-validate model		1	2.6
	Range	Mean	SD
Number of changes made	1–10	5.9	3.6
		n	Percentage
Theoretical reason given for change:	None	21	78.0
	Some	1	4.0
	All	5	18.5
Type of changes made in specification search		n	Percentage
Theory trim		19	70.4
Free a parameter(s)		13	48.1
Change causal order		4	14.8
Change causal direction		0	0.0
Moderate		4	14.8
Introduce polynomial		1	3.7
Add new variables		1	3.7

[a] All remaining statistics in this table employ a base of 27 studies.

Interestingly, of the 27 manifest variable studies that conducted a specification search, only one study attempted to cross-validate the new model (see Table 10). In fact, only six of the 27 studies (15 per cent) explicitly noted the exploratory nature of the specification search. This is made more interesting because an average of six changes were made in the 27 re-specified models. Consistent with the general failure to acknowledge the exploratory nature of the endeavor is the finding that theoretical reasons for changes were not often given (see Table 10). Only five of the 27 studies provided a theoretical rationale for all the changes made to the causal model based on the specification search; 78 per cent of the studies (21/27 × 100) provided no rationale for change(s).

Yet, a theoretical rationale should always precede a change to a model (cf. James *et al.*, 1982; MacCallum, 1986). This is an imperfect means for attempting to avoid changes driven by chance errors. Even if a causal parameter is not deemed to be substantively critical to a model, it should not be deleted (theory-trimmed) simply because an estimate is non-significant in a particular study. That is, if there is a good reason to believe that the causal relation should be in the model, then it might be retained for future tests rather than trimmed based on contemporaneous data. Or, adding a parameter to a model via the freeing of a previously fixed (or constrained) parameter requires that one have a reasonable rationale for why two (or more) variables should be directly related. If such rationale is unavailable, then investigators may wish to consider other means for attempting to improve the fit of their model.

The actual types of changes made to the models as part of the specification search are also presented in Table 10. All percentages here are predicated on the 27 manifest studies that attempted a specification search. The most popular type of change was theory trimming (70 per cent of studies), which was followed by freeing of a previously fixed parameter (48 per cent of studies). The former changes likely reflect attempts to compensate for failing a Condition 9 test(s), whereas the latter changes were likely stimulated by failing a Condition 10 test or tests. Interestingly, 15 per cent of the studies changed some portion of the causal order. Changes in causal order were frequently supported by a theoretical rationale. Moderation was also attempted as part of the specification search in 15 per cent of the studies. Finally, one study added polynomial procedures (i.e. raising a variable to a power) to the analysis, whereas another study added an outside, previously unanalyzed, variable to the analysis.

This completes the discussion of the manifest variable studies. We shall proceed directly to a presentation of results for the latent variable studies, after which summary comments for all types of studies are offered.

LATENT VARIABLE DESIGNS

Information for the sixteen latent variable studies is reported using a structure similar to that for the manifest studies. We begin with data pertaining to model specification, proceed to discussions of operationalizations of variables, analytic procedures, and results, and conclude with an (attempted) overview of specification searches. The additional complexity of including latent variables in a structural analysis required that we address a greater number of issues here in comparison to the preceding section on manifest variable studies. On the other hand, we had only sixteen latent variable studies to analyze and discuss. These studies are perhaps best characterized as initial attempts to apply new methodological procedures in organizational research. We imply no censure for a number of the studies reviewed here could, and likely will, serve as illustrations of good methodological practice for future investigators. However, the meta-analytic data reflect some of the early struggles in initial applications of latent structural models to OR data.

Model Specification and Identification Issues

As reported in Table 11, an average of 3.2 latent variables were included in the studies reviewed here. The range was from 1 to 15, where the study with one latent variable was a confirmatory factor analysis that proposed a single underlying factor. The average number of indicators per latent variable was 2.14 (SD = 1.31). The value of 2.14 is based on a weighted average over studies and includes three studies that had but one manifest indicator per latent variable. (An estimate of reliability linked the latent variable to the single manifest variable.) Thus, the mean number of indicators to latents may be a bit low in terms of representing the average latent variable study that employed multiple indicators.

This is an important issue because many recent statistical treatments have recommended that investigators attempt to measure as many manifest indicator variables per latent variable as is possible. Three to four indicators per latent variable are often viewed as necessary to deal with identification issues, not to mention analytic issues such as convergence (cf. Anderson and Gerbing, 1984; Bentler and Chou, 1987; Boomsma, 1985; Gerbing and Anderson, 1985, 1987; James et al., 1982; Kenny, 1979). We do not wish to imply, however, that including a large number of indicators per latent variable will solve all statistical problems. Lack of careful selection of indicators may create problems (e.g. empirical underidentification—cf. Bentler and Chou, 1987), and general guidelines for establishing criteria for such things as identification are still being developed (cf. Bollen and Joreskog, 1985; Hayduk, 1987).

We noted earlier the desirability of having a parsimonious model and discussed a parsimony index for manifest variable designs. An analogous discussion now follows for latent variable models. (Note that the two parsimony indices are scaled in opposite directions.) This discussion is based on the parsimony index presented by James et al. (1982, p. 155). Briefly described, the index is the number of degrees of freedom for the model of interest, or

Table 11—Model Specification and Identification Issues for Latent Variable Models

	Range	Mean	SD
Number of latent variables	1–15	3.20	3.64
Average number of indicators per latent variable	1–5	2.14	1.31
Parsimony Index:[a] Measurement model	.33–.94	.74	.20
Parsimony Index: Total model	.10–.84	.52	.30

[a]Ratio: degrees of freedom for target model/degrees of freedom for null model.

'target model', divided by the number of degrees of freedom for a null model (typically a model that predicts that the manifest indicators have zero covariances). When this ratio is zero, it means that the target model is just-identified and is not parsimonious. Conversely, a 'high' value indicates parsimony because the target model has a large number of degrees of freedom relative to the total degrees of freedom available in the data, which is what is indicated by the denominator.

Parsimony indices were calculated separately (a) for the measurement portions of the latent variable models, which are confirmatory factor analytic models, and (b) for the total latent variable models, which are structural models overlaid on to confirmatory factor analytic models (cf. Bentler, 1980; Joreskog and Sorbom, 1979). A total model specifies relations among the latent constructs of the confirmatory analytic model using the same processes as employed to develop a structural model for manifest variable designs. The data reported in Table 11 show that the parsimony indices varied from .33 to .94 over studies, with a mean of .74 for the measurement models. The mean over the total models was .52, with a range of .10 to .84. We have no formal distributional knowledge to use to interpret these parsimony ratios. However, our experience suggests that these ratios, especially those for the total model, are somewhat low. That is, the models are not especially parsimonious.

In sum, two general suggestions provided by the data in Table 11 are (a) more manifest indicators are needed for latent variables for some studies, and (b) latent models need to be more parsimonious. These two suggestions are, of course, correlated.

Analytic Procedures

Information describing analytic procedures is presented in Tables 12 and 13. In regard to Table 12, full-information maximum likelihood (FIML) was the estimation technique of choice in all latent variable studies. LISREL (Joreskog and Sorbom, 1986) was the predominant computer program used to furnish the FIML-based estimates. Latent variables were scaled by multiple techniques depending on investigator preference and/or type of design (e.g. multiple indicator versus single indicator designs—cf. Long, 1983a; Hayduk, 1987). The matrix of observed relations typically subjected to analysis was the correlation matrix (75 per cent of studies). This created a problem for some studies because distribution-based, statistical goodness-of-fit tests (e.g. chi-square) developed for variances and covariances were conducted on estimates derived from standardized data. As noted recently by Bentler and Chou (1987, p. 90), the 'practice of substituting correlation for covariance matrices in analysis, i.e. significance tests, is only rarely justified . . .' (see also Joreskog and Sorbom, 1986; Long, 1983a, 1983b).

Table 12—Analytic Procedures Employed for Latent Variable Designs

	n	Percentage
Estimation technique		
FIML	16	100.00
GLS	0	0
ULS	0	0
Latent variables scaled by:		
1's in phi/psi matrix	8	50.0
1's in lambda matrix	5	31.2
Square root of reliability coefficient	3	18.7
Matrix analyzed		
Variance–covariance	4	25.0
Correlation	12	75.0

Proceeding to Table 13, we see that almost every study used a form of fit index that has an underlying sampling distribution, albeit some of these tests may have been applied to standardized data inappropriately. The chi-square test was a popular method for significance testing even though the susceptibility of this test to sample size has been well publicized (see Marsh et al., 1988; Wheaton, 1987, for recent discussions of this issue). The difference chi-square was utilized to contrast models in 38 per cent of the studies, and T-tests were employed to assess significance of parameter estimates in 44 per cent of the studies. (Contrary to popular opinion, as typically constituted the difference chi-square test also appears to be correlated with sample size (see Marsh et al., 1988, Table 1.)

Fit indices for which sampling distributions do not presently exist were also employed in many of the latent variable studies. A large diversity of tests was evident. In a few cases, a time factor was also evident inasmuch as some indices were not available or had not been widely disseminated when latent variable articles were written. We shall not attempt to comment on the various fit indices included in this section, one reason being that knowledge is still accumulating

Table 13—Goodness-of-Fit Indices for Latent Variable Designs

	n	Percentage
Fit indices with sampling distributions		
Chi-square	15	93.7
Difference chi-square	6	37.5
T test on structural parameters	7	43.7
Fit indices with no sampling distribution		
Chi-square/degrees of freedom	3	18.7
Coefficient of determination	2	12.5
Residual matrix	1	6.7
GFI	2	12.5
AGFI	2	12.5
RMSR	3	18.7
Normed Fit Index	7	43.8
Normed Incremental Fit Index	1	6.7
Parsimonious Fit Index	1	6.7
Overall design		
Studies that focused exclusively on measurement model	4	25.0
Single indicator models	3	18.8
For remaining 9 latent variable models		
a. Fit of measurement model assessed before proceeding to test of structural model	2	22.0[a]
b. Fit of structural model tested by nesting structural model in measurement model and using sequential difference tests	1	11.0
c. Fit of measurement model and structural model assessed simultaneously	7	78.0

[a]Percentages employ a base of 9.

regarding the statistical properties of a number of the indices. Rather, we recommend that investigators read the literature in this area before selecting 'indices' for analysis. Use of multiple indices, rather than a single index, is also recommended. Literature that was 'recent' and relevant to this issue at the time this manuscript was prepared included Anderson and Gerbing (1988), Bentler and Chou (1987), Marsh et al. (1988), and Wheaton (1987).

The final set of information reported in Table 13 pertains to data describing overall designs and analytic plans. Four studies (25 per cent) focused exclusively on measurement issues (models). As discussed, three additional studies were classified as single-indicator models. If we delete both of these sets of studies from the analysis, we have nine studies remaining on which to describe general designs for the tests of both measurement and structural models. For example, two of the nine studies (22 per cent) tested the fit of the measurement model before proceeding to assess the fit of the structural, or combined structural–measurement, model(s). Interestingly, only one of these two studies assessed the fit of the structural model via a hierarchical testing procedure wherein the structural model was nested within the measurement model (cf. Bentler and

Bonett, 1980). The other study, in concert with the remaining seven studies, tested the fit of the measurement and structural models simultaneously. We suspect that the 'tendency', where we again note the small number of studies, to conduct simultaneous tests of measurement and structural models will give way to hierarchical testing procedures in which measurement models are tested prior to structural models. At least this is the recommendation offered by several statistical treatments of this issue (cf. Anderson and Gerbing, 1988; Bentler and Bonett, 1980; James et al., 1982).

Results and Specification Searches

Our original intention was to furnish descriptive data regarding whether a latent model was confirmed or disconfirmed. We also intended to supplement this discussion with data pertaining to specification searches such as the types of changes made to latent measurement and/or structural models to improve fit and/or parsimony. After several attempts, we decided that our intentions could not be fulfilled. We found that different criteria were used by different investigators to decide whether a model had or had not been rejected. For example, an 'acceptable' chi-square to degrees of freedom ratio varied from 2 to 1 to 10 to 1, depending on the study. We also decided against attempting to impose our own criteria for confirmation versus disconfirmation of a model. This was because, as noted, statistical knowledge continues to accumulate for latent variable designs, and thus we simply could not generate an unequivocal set of standards for judging the results of the studies.

Several authors of the studies in the meta-analysis discussed the subjectivity of the various goodness-of-fit indices and refrained from stating whether their models were supported or rejected (even in a probabilistic sense). We empathize with these authors and can only suggest that the existing subjectivity surrounding goodness-of-fit tests will, hopefully, be reduced as knowledge accumulates.

Only five of the latent variable studies conducted a specification search. Our discomfort in having only sixteen latent variable studies was compounded by a sample reduction to five. Moreover, the subjectivity discussed above in regard to assessing the goodness of fit of the results of initial confirmatory analyses transfers directly to assessing the fit of results of specification searches. Thus, we did not review the data for the five studies that conducted a specification search. We do, however, recommend reviewing recent discussions of specification searches for latent variable models (cf. Bentler and Chou, 1987; MacCallum, 1986).

CONCLUSIONS AND RECOMMENDATIONS

One of the most interesting results for us was the finding that approximately 80 per cent of the structural (causal) models subjected to confirmatory analysis were disconfirmed. This descriptive and approximate statistic was based on manifest variable studies, but we suspect that it will be roughly applicable to results of confirmatory analyses based on latent variables once criteria for goodness of fit are decided upon in that area. This would seem to be a high rejection rate for studies which, for the most part, were designed to test models developed by the authors. Moreover, if the 'file drawer' issue is applicable in confirmatory analysis, then the functional rate of disconfirmation may be even greater than 80 per cent.

As discussed earlier, many theorists might suggest that an 80 per cent disconfirmation rate is an appropriate state of affairs because the objective of confirmatory analysis is to reject structural models with poor fits to data. The inference is that a model with a poor fit to data is a model that is *not* substantively *useful* for explaining causal relations among variables (cf. James *et al.*, 1982). In this context, it is interesting to speculate on the meaning of the 80 per cent rejection rate for OR models. For example, does it suggest that approximately 80 per cent of the models in OR are not particularly useful? Or, were the models subjected to confirmatory analysis an unrepresentative and especially speculative lot that had low probabilities of having good fits to data? Another possibility is that the early struggles represented in the studies reviewed here to apply complex analytic procedures to OR data had sufficient statistical problems to result in empirical disconfirmation of what might have been many useful theoretical paradigms. A related possibility is that the models tested were not so much inaccurate as they were incomplete (e.g. subject to unmeasured variables problems), and it was failure to reasonably satisfy the demanding conditions for confirmatory analysis that led to disconfirmation rather than serious inaccuracies pertaining to specific causal hypotheses.

This non-exhaustive set of possibilities is meant to stimulate investigators to consider ways in which structural models in OR might be improved. It is only after models reasonably satisfy the seven theoretical conditions for confirmatory analysis that confirmatory analytic techniques should be applied. That is, models which fail to reasonably satisfy one or more of the seven conditions have a high likelihood not only of furnishing biased parameter estimates, but also (thankfully) of being disconfirmed. This point applies irrespective of one's virtuosity with multivariate statistics and/or computers. One of the characteristics of confirmatory analysis is that statistical analyses must be preceded by strong theoretical development. Otherwise, the statistical enterprise is likely to fail. Stated alternatively, confirmatory analysis *requires* an integration of theory with statistics; the statistics must be preceded by theory.

We might now enquire what the results of the meta-analysis suggest in regard to improving models and/or statistical procedures, which includes operationalization of variables. Recommendations are as follows.

1) More attention needs to be given to the development of structural models

that reasonably satisfy the conditions for confirmatory analysis. Chief among the conditions deserving increased concentration is the self-containment condition, violation of which produces unmeasured variables problems. As noted earlier, an unmeasured variables problem, often of unknown seriousness, is likely to plague most structural models. Nevertheless, attempts should be made to include all known or projected, major or moderate, causes in a structural model (James, 1980). (It might also be noted that this recommendation applies to the causes for *all* endogenous variables in a model and not just the endogenous variables of primary interest.)

Another area in need of concentration is the establishment of causal intervals in longitudinal/time-series/panel designs. This may well require the use of exploratory procedures to compare various intervals as candidates for the most likely causal interval (cf. Heise, 1975). An associated concern is the need to test the stability of causal models. This, of course, points to the need to increase the use of longitudinal forms of designs that provide opportunities to test for stability. The panel design is the most likely candidate for enhanced use in this regard. An important contribution associated with the use of longitudinal designs is the opportunity to control causal order. This control, however, should be theoretically based and consider such factors as whether the causal relation is recursive or non-recursive.

2) The reliabilities of the variables on which confirmatory analyses are conducted should be increased. The meta-analytic results describing reliabilities of manifest variables suggested that 50 per cent or more of the exogenous and endogenous variables in a given study could have estimated reliabilities of less than .80. One ramification of this state of affairs is that a theoretically viable manifest variable model may have been erroneously disconfirmed because low to moderate reliabilities engendered biased parameter estimates. Such bias may frequently take the form of attenuation wherein estimated parameters predicted to be significant are instead non-significant (a disconfirmation based on a Condition 9 test). However, attenuation is not the only form of bias produced by unreliability in complex models. Indeed, measurement error may produce spuriously high estimates of parameters. If one such parameter estimate(s) was predicted to be zero, then we could have an erroneous disconfirmation of a model based on a Condition 10 test.

A reasonable recommendation here is to attempt to use more reliable variables in manifest variable designs. A second recommendation is to measure *multiple* manifest variables (indicators) for each construct (latent variable) in a structural model and then adopt latent variable analytic approaches. This would provide the opportunity to conduct a confirmatory analysis on a structural model that is comprised, theoretically at least, of perfectly reliable (latent) variables. It is noteworthy that every attempt should be made to measure each manifest indicator with high reliability, which is to say that latent variable approaches do not absolve one from measuring manifest indicators reliably (cf. James *et al.*, 1982).

An added benefit of latent variable models is that the measurement portion of the model may be tested for the presence of non-random measurement errors, such as systematic method errors engendered by a common response set or style (e.g. social desirability). Confirmatory tests of measurement models are, in effect, empirical assessments of the construct validity of manifest indicators. Recent advances in the use of confirmatory factor analysis to test for the presence of 'method variance' are especially applicable for OR (Schmitt and Stults, 1986; Widaman, 1985).

We have some reservations in recommending the use of latent variable approaches. As discussed, to acquire knowledge of latent variable procedures may require a concentrated effort over many months, perhaps even years depending on prior experience with multivariate statistics and structural equation analysis. This is a demanding process, although it is being simplified somewhat by more 'user friendly' computer programs and manuals such as EQS (Bentler, 1985) and LISREL VI (Joreskog and Sorbom, 1986) and by texts and monographs devoted to only moderately technical introductions to latent variable analytic techniques (cf. Hayduk, 1987; Long, 1983a, 1983b). On the other hand, we have noted repeatedly the continuing state of flux of statistical procedures in this area and the uncertainty that presently exists in regard to the accuracy and generalizability of goodness-of-fit tests. If one ventures into the domain of latent variable confirmatory analysis, then they must be willing to maintain a constant vigilance in regard to advances in statistics and methodology. A final note in regard to adoption of latent variable models pertains to recommendations made earlier in this report. Two recommendations concerning the design of latent variable studies were: (a) more manifest indicators are needed for latent variables (three to four indicators per latent variable is often recommended); and (b) latent models, particularly the structural models, need to be made more parsimonious by setting a larger number of structural parameters to fixed values (typically zero— equality constraints might also be employed, see Joreskog and Sorbom, 1986). A third recommendation was precipitated by the review of analytic procedures. This recommendation is that more attention be given to the distributional assumptions underlying chi-square tests and the goodness-of-fit assessments based on chi-square. The problem here is that tests developed for unstandardized data are being applied to standardized data. (Note, however, that the degree of bias introduced by this procedure has yet to be fully understood. Here again we see the need for future research.)

In sum, perhaps the more realistic option for enhancing the reliabilities of the variables on which confirmatory analyses are conducted is to adopt latent variable approaches. This option has much to recommend it, but it also has serious drawbacks, chief among which is the complexity of this process. In balance, however, it appears that the confirmatory analytic effort, in general, is progressing towards the use of latent models (in preference to manifest models). Consequently, complexity is not so much a drawback as a hurdle that must be surmounted if one is to keep abreast of changes in the field.

3) It is suggested that authors be much more forthcoming regarding the exploratory nature of specification searches. It is also recommended that changes in models be made in specification analyses only if statistical indicators can be supported by a theoretical rationale (cf. MacCallum, 1986). Finally, models that evolve from specification analyses should be tested using new data. Cross-validation procedures are applicable here (see Cudeck and Browne, 1983).

4) More effort needs to be given to the development of multiple, competing, *a priori*, models as part of the design of a confirmatory analysis. As discussed earlier, comparisons of theoretically viable, competing causal models reduces reliance on specification analysis and increases the faith one *may* have in making causal inferences from a confirmed model. This would appear to be an area in which recommendations could be effected readily inasmuch as multiple, competing theories are a frequent occurrence for explaining events in OR. The problem may be that investigators have simply not taken advantage of the opportunities to test competing models as they endeavored to learn new and complex techniques (that were applied to a single model). Hopefully, such opportunities will be capitalized on as investigators become more comfortable with the confirmatory techniques.

5) A final recommendation pertains to the need to study reciprocal causation. Among the benefits of confirmatory analytic techniques, as compared to exploratory techniques, are statistical procedures for: (a) estimating indirect effects in the context of mediation models (cf. James and Brett, 1984), and (b) estimating causal effects (structural parameters) in a reciprocal causative relationship (cf. James and Singh, 1978). It simply is not possible to estimate indirect effects or reciprocal effects using exploratory models and procedures such as multiple regression. The opportunity to estimate indirect effects is widely recognized and frequently attempted. Reciprocal effects are another matter. As shown here, only a few studies adopted non-recursive analyses. This is somewhat perplexing for a field that embraces causal models whose parent is often some form of open systems model that involves multiple feedback loops and reciprocal relationships.

It is possible to propose a number of additional recommendations, especially those of a rather specific nature that deal with methodology. However, we shall stop here because we wish to focus on a set of broad, policy-oriented suggestions rather than reiterate what is already available in recent methodological critiques (e.g. Bentler and Chou,,, 1987). We also wish to note that the preceding recommendations, indeed the entire review, should not be construed to imply that we are critical of attempts to employ confirmatory analysis in OR. On the whole, we believe that the OR field has performed commendably, as evidenced by such things as the willingness of OR researchers to conduct moderator analyses as part of confirmatory analysis, the use of reasonably large samples on the average, and the fact that many studies included tests of overidentifying restrictions. We expect the progression towards increased use of confirmatory analyses to endure. We also expect an escalation in the use of the more complex confirmatory methods.

Finally, there is the possibility that OR researchers will contribute innovatively to confirmatory procedures. Of special recognition here is a recent paper by Katzell, Guzzo, and Thompson (1987) in which the results of *different* studies were integrated to develop a path model relating job satisfaction to performance. The integrated model appeared to provide a more extensive and useful explanation of this relationship than any one of the separate models. Of special interest to confirmatory analysts, the integrated model included proposed values of path coefficients for all relations in that model. These values could be used to conduct tests of overidentifying restrictions in the future using procedures similar to cross-validation (cf. Cudeck and Browne, 1983). Of at least equal importance is the rationale that the development, and perhaps even tests, of complex models may require integration of theory and results from multiple studies—a form of 'confirmatory meta-analysis'.

REFERENCES

Anderson, J.C., and Gerbing, D.W. (1984) The effect of sampling error on convergence, improper solutions, and goodness-of-fit indices for maximum likelihood confirmatory factor analysis. *Psychometrika*, **49**, 222–228.

Anderson, J.C., and Gerbing, D.W. (1988) Structural equation modeling in practice: A review and recommended two-step approach. *Psychological Bulletin*, **103**, 411–423.

Bentler, P.M. (1980) Multivariate analysis with latent variables: Causal modeling. *Annual Review of Psychology*, **31**, 419–456.

Bentler, P.M. (1985) *Theory and Implementation of QS: A structural equations program.* Los Angeles: BMDP Statistical Software.

Bentler, P.M., and Bonett, D.G. (1980) Significance tests and goodness of fit in the analysis of covariance structures. *Psychological Bulletin*, **88**, 588–606.

Bentler, P.M., and Chou, C.P. (1987) Practical issues in structural modeling. *Sociological Methods and Research*, **16**, 78–117.

Bollen, K.A., and Joreskog, K.G. (1985) Uniqueness does not imply identification: A note on confirmatory factor analysis. *Sociological Methods and Research*, **14**, 155–163.

Boomsma, A. (1982) The robustness of LISREL against small sample sizes in factor analysis models. In K.G. Joreskog and H. Wold (eds), *Systems Under Indirect Observation: Causality, structure, prediction*, Part 1. Amsterdam: North-Holland, pp. 149–173.
Boomsma, A. (1985) Nonconvergence, improper solutions, and starting values in LISREL maximum likelihood estimation. *Psychometrika*, **50**, 229–242.
Cohen, J., and Cohen, P. (1983) *Applied Multiple Regression/Correlation Analysis for the Behavioral Sciences*, 2nd edn. Hillsdale, NJ: Erlbaum.
Costner, H.L. (1969) Theory, deduction, and rules of correspondence. *American Journal of Sociology*, **75**, 245–263.
Cudeck, R., and Brown, M.W. (1983) Cross-validation of covariance structures. *Multivariate Behavioral Research*, **18**, 147–167.
Duncan, O.D. (1975) *Introduction to Structural Equation Models*. New York: Academic Press.
Games, P.A. (1988, April) Invited commentary. Correlation and causation: An alternative view. *The Score*, 9f.
Gerbing, D.W., and Anderson, J.C. (1985) The effects of sampling error and model characteristics on parameter estimation for maximum likelihood confirmatory factor analysis. *Multivariate Behavioral Research*, **20**, 255–271.
Gerbing, D.W., and Anderson, J.C. (1987) Improper solutions in the analysis of covariance structures: Their interpretability and a comparison of alternative respecifications. *Psychometrika*, **52**, 99–111.
Hayduk, L.A. (1987) *Structural equation modeling with LISREL*. Baltimore: Johns Hopkins University Press.
Heise, D.R. (1975) *Causal Analysis*. New York: Wiley.
James, L.R. (1980) The unmeasured variable problem in path analysis. *Journal of Applied Psychology*, **65**, 415–421.
James, L.R., and Brett, J.M. (1984) Mediators, moderators, and tests for mediation. *Journal of Applied Psychology*, **69**, 307–321.
James, L.R., and Jones, A.P. (1980) Perceived job characteristics and job satisfaction: An examination of reciprocal causation. *Personnel Psychology*, **33**, 97–135.
James, L.R., Mulaik, S.A., and Brett, J.M. (1982) *Causal Analysis: Assumptions, models, and data*. Beverly Hills: Sage.
James, L.R., and Singh, K. (1978) An introduction to the logic, assumptions, and basic analytic procedures of two-stage least squares. *Psychological Bulletin*, **85**, 1104–1122.
James, L.R., and Tetrick, L.E. (1986) Confirmatory analytic tests of three causal models relating job perceptions to job satisfaction. *Journal of Applied Psychology*, **71**, 77–82.
Johnston, J. (1984) *Econometric Methods*. New York: McGraw-Hill.
Joreskog, K.G., and Sorbom, D. (1979) *Advances in Factor Analysis and Structural Equation Models*. Cambridge, MA: Abt Books.
Joreskog, K.G., and Sorbom, D. (1986) *LISREL VI Analysis of Linear Structural Relationships by Maximum Likelihood, Instrumental Variables, and Least Squares Methods*. Mooresville, Indiana: Scientific Software, Inc.
Katzell, R.A., Guzzo, R.A., and Thompson, D.E. (1987, October) How job satisfaction and job performance are/aren't linked. Paper presented at the Conference on Job Satisfaction, Bowling Green State University, Bowling Green, OH.
Kenny, D.A. (1975) Cross-lagged panel correlation: A test for spuriousness. *Psychological Bulletin*, **82**, 887–903.
Kenny, D.A. (1979) *Correlation and Causality*. New York: Wiley.
Kenny, D.A., and Judd, C.M. (1984) Estimating the nonlinear and interactive effects of latent variables. *Psychological Bulletin*, **96**, 201–210.

Leamer, E.E. (1978) *Specification Searches: Ad hoc inference with nonexperimental data.* New York: Wiley.
Lent, R.H., Aurbach, H.A., and Levin, L.S. (1971) Research design and validity assessment. *Personnel Psychology,* 24, 247–274.
Long, J.S. (1983a) *Confirmatory Factor Analysis. A preface to LISREL.* Beverly Hills: Sage.
Long, J.S. (1983b) *Covariance Structure Models. An introduction to LISREL.* Beverly Hills: Sage.
MacCallum, R. (1986) Specification searches in covariance structure modeling. *Psychological Bulletin,* 100, 107–120.
Marsh, H.W., Balla, J.R., and McDonald, R.P. (1988) Goodness-of-fit indexes in confirmatory factor analysis: The effect of sample size. *Psychological Bulletin,* 103, 391–410.
Namboodiri, N.K., Carter, L.R., and Blalock, H.M., Jr (1975) *Applied Multivariate Analysis and Experimental Designs.* New York: McGraw-Hill.
Pedhazur, E.J. (1982) *Multiple Regression in Behavioral Research: Explanation and prediction.* New York: Holt, Rinehart, & Winston. Pelz, D.C., and Lew, R.A. (1970) Heise's causal model applied. In E.F. Borgatta and G.W. Bohrnstedt (eds), *Sociological Methodology.* San Francisco: Jossey-Bass.
Popper, K.R. (1959) *The Logic of Scientific Discovery.* New York: Basic Book. (Originally *Die Logik der Forschung,* 1935.)
Rogosa, F. (1980) A critique of cross-lagged correlation. *Psychological Bulletin,* 88, 245–258.
Schmitt, N., and Stults, D.M. (1986) Methodology review: Analysis of multitrait–multimethod matrices. *Applied Psychological Measurement,* 10, 1–22.
Schoenberg, R. (1972) Strategies for meaningful comparison. In H.L. Costner (ed.), *Sociological Methodology 1972.* San Francisco: Jossey-Bass, pp. 1–35.
Simon, H.A. (1977) *Models of Discovery.* Dordrecht, Holland: R. Reidel.
Specht, D.A., and Warren, R.D. (1976) Comparing causal models. In D.R. Heise (ed.), *Sociological Methodology 1976.* San Francisco: Jossey-Bass.
Stolzenberg, R.M. (1979) The measurement and decomposition of causal effects in nonlinear and nonadditive models. In K.F. Schuessler (ed.), *Sociological Methodology 1980.* San Francisco: Jossey-Bass.
Tetrick, L.E., and LaRocco, J.M. (1987) Understanding, prediction, and control as moderators of the relationships between perceived stress, satisfaction, and psychological well-being. *Journal of Applied Psychology,* 72, 538–543.
Tukey, J.W. (1964) Causation, regression, and path analysis. In O. Kempthorne, T.A. Bancroft, J.W. Gowen, and J.L. Lush (eds), *Statistics and Mathematics in Biology.* New York: Hofner.
Wheaton, B. (1987) Assessment of fit in overidentified models with latent variables. *Sociological Methods and Research,* 16, 118–154.
Widaman, K.F. (1985) Hierarchically nested covariance structure models for multitrait––multimethod data. *Applied Psychological Measurement,* 9, 1–26.
Wright, S. (1960) Path coefficients and path regressions: Alternative or complementary concepts? *Biometrics,* 16, 189–202.

APPENDIX ARTICLES INCLUDED IN REVIEW

Arnold, H.J., and Feldman, D.C. (1982) A multivariate analysis of the determinants of job turnover. *Journal of Applied Psychology,* 67, 350–360.

Ashford, S.J. (1986) Feedback-seeking in individual adaptation: A resource perspective. *Academy of Management Journal*, **29**, 465–487.

Bateman, T.S., and Organ, D.W. (1983) Job satisfaction and the good soldier: The relationship between affect and employee 'citizenship'. *Academy of Management Journal*, **26**, 587–595.

Bateman, T.S., and Strasser, S. (1984) A longitudinal analysis of the antecedents of organizational commitment. *Academy of Management Journal*, **27**, 95–112.

Birnbaum, P.H. (1984) The choice of strategic alternatives under increasing regulation in high technology companies. *Academy of Management Journal*, **27**, 489–510.

Birnbaum, P.H., Farh, J.L., and Wong, G.Y.Y. (1986) The job characteristics model in Hong Kong. *Journal of Applied Psychology*, **71**, 598–605.

Curry, J.P., Wakefield, D.S., Price, J.L., and Mueller, C.W. (1986) On the causal ordering of job satisfaction and organizational commitment. *Academy of Management Journal*, **29**, 847–858.

Dewar, R.D., and Simet, D.P. (1981) A level specific prediction of spans of control examining and effects of size, technology, and specialization. *Academy of Management Journal*, **24**, 5–24.

Drasgow, F., and Kanfer, R. (1985) Equivalence of psychological measurement in heterogeneous populations. *Journal of Applied Psychology*, **70**, 662–680.

Earley, P.C., Wojnaroski, P., and Prest, W. (1987) Task planning and energy expended: Exploration of how goals influence performance. *Journal of Applied Psychology*, **72**, 107–114.

Ettlie, J.E. (1983) Organizational policy and innovation among suppliers to the food processing sector. *Academy of Management Journal*, **26**, 27–44.

Garland, H. (1983) Influence of ability, assigned goals, and normative information on personal goals and performance: A challenge to the goal attainability assumption. *Journal of Applied Psychology*, **68**, 20–30.

Glisson, C.A., and Martin, P.Y. (1980) Productivity and efficiency in human service organizations as related to structure, size, and age. *Academy of Management Journal*, **23**, 21–37.

Granrose, C.S., Portwood, J.D. (1987) Matching individual career plans and organizational career management. *Academy of Management Journal*, **30**, 699–720.

Greenhalgh, L., Neslin, S.A., and Gilkey, R.W. (1985) The effects of negotiator preferences, situational power, and negotiator personality on outcomes of business negotiations. *Academy of Management Journal*, **28**, 9–33.

Helmich, D.L. (1978) Leader flows and organizational process. *Academy of Management Journal*, **21**, 463–478.

Hill, T., Smith, N.D., and Mann, M.F. (1987) Role of efficacy expectations in predicting the decision to use advanced technologies: The case of computers. *Journal of Applied Psychology*, **72**, 307–313.

Hogan, E.A., and Martell, D.A. (1987) A confirmatory structural equations analysis of the job characteristics model. *Organizational Behavior and Human Decision Processes*, **39**, 242–263.

Hom, P.W., Griffeth, R.W., and Sellaro, C.L. (1984) The validity of Mobley's (1977) model of employee turnover. *Organizational Behavior and Human Performance*, **34**, 141–174.

Huber, V.L., and Neale, M.A. (1986) Effects of cognitive heuristics and goals on negotiator performance and subsequent goal setting. *Organizational Behavior and Human Decision Processes*, **38**, 342–365.

Ivancevich, J.M. (1978) The performance to satisfaction relationship: A causal analysis

of stimulating and nonstimulating jobs. *Organizational Behavior and Human Performance*, **22**, 350–365.
Jackson, S.E. (1983) Participation in decision making as a strategy for reducing job-related strain. *Journal of Applied Psychology*, **68**, 3–19.
James, L.R., and Jones, A.P. (1980) Perceived job characteristics and job satisfaction: An examination of reciprocal causation. *Personnel Psychology*, **33**, 97–135.
James, L.R., and Tetrick, L.E. (1986) Confirmatory analytic tests of three causal models relating job perceptions to job satisfaction. *Journal of Applied Psychology*, **71**, 77–82.
Kemery, E.R., Bedeian, A.G., Mossholder, K.W., and Touliatos, J. (1985) Outcomes of role stress: A multisample constructive replication. *Academy of Management Journal*, **28**, 363–375.
Kopelman, R.E., Greenhaus, J.H., and Connolly, T.F. (1983) A model of work, family, and interrole conflict: A construct validation study. *Organizational Behavior and Human Performance*, **32**, 198–215.
Manz, C.C., and Sim, H.P., Jr (1986) Beyond imitation: Complex behavioral and affective linkages resulting from exposure to leadership training models. *Journal of Applied Psychology*, **71**, 571–578.
Martin, T.N., Jr (1979) A contextual model of employee turnover intentions. *Academy of Management Journal*, **22**, 313–324.
Martin, T.N., and Hunt, J.G. (1980) Social influence and intent to leave: A path-analytic process model. *Personnel Psychology*, **33**, 505–528.
Michaels, C.E., and Spector, P.E. (1982) Causes of employee turnover: A test of the Mobley, Griffeth, Hand, and Meglino model. *Journal of Applied Psychology*, **67**, 53–59.
Motowidlo, S.J., and Lawton, G.W. (1984) Affective and cognitive factors in solders' reenlistment decisions. *Journal of Applied Psychology*, **69**, 157–166.
Parasuraman, S., and Alutto, J.A. (1984) Sources and outcomes of stress in organizational settings: Toward the development of a structural model. *Academy of Management Journal*, **27**, 330–350.
Podsakoff, P.M., Williams, L.J., and Todor, W.D. (1986) Effects of organizational formalization on alienation among professionals and nonprofessionals. *Academy of Management Journal*, **29**, 820–831.
Powell, G.N. (1984) Effects of job attributes and recruiting practices on applicant decisions: A comparison. *Personnel Psychology*, **37**, 721–732.
Price, J.L., and Mueller, C.W. (1981) A causal model of turnover for nurses. *Academy of Management Journal*, **24**, 543–565.
Provan, K.G. (1987) Environmental and organizational predictors of adoption of cost containment policies in hospitals. *Academy of Management Journal*, **30**, 219–239.
Raza, S.M., and Carpenter, B.N. (1987) A model of hiring decisions in real employment interviews. *Journal of Applied Psychology*, **72**, 596–603.
Schmidt, F.L., Hunter, J.E., and Outerbridge, A.N. (1986) Impact of job experience and ability on job knowledge, work sample performance, and supervisory ratings of job performance. *Journal of Applied Psychology*, **71**, 432–439.
Schmitt, N., and Bedeian, A.G. (1982) A comparison of LISREL and two-stage least squares analysis of a hypothesized life–job satisfaction reciprocal relationship. *Journal of Applied Psychology*, **67**, 806–817.
Schmitt, N., Coyle, B.W., White, J.K., and Rauschenberger, J. (1978) Background, needs, job perceptions, and job satisfaction: A causal model. *Personnel Psychology*, **31**, 889–901.
Schuler, R.S. (1979) A role perception transactional process model for organizational

communication–outcome relationships. *Organizational Behavior and Human Performance*, **23**, 268–291.

Sheridan, J.E., and Vredenburgh, D.J. (1979) Structural model of leadership influence in a hospital organization. *Academy of Management Journal*, **22**, 6–21.

Sheridan, J.E., Vredenburgh, D.J., and Abelson, M.A. (1984) Contextual model of leadership influence in hospital units. *Academy of Management Journal*, **27**, 57–78.

Singh, J.V. (1986) Technology, size, and organizational structure: A reexamination of the Okayama study data. *Academy of Management Journal*, **29**, 800–812.

Smith, C.A., Organ, D.W., and Near, J.P. (1983) Organizational citizenship behavior: Its nature and antecedents. *Journal of Applied Psychology*, **68**, 653–663.

Stumpf, S.A., and Hartman, K. (1984) Individual exploration to organizational commitment or withdrawal. *Academy of Management Journal*, **27**, 308–329.

Taylor, M.S., Locke, E.A., Lee, C., and Gist, M.E. (1984) Type A behavior and faculty research productivity: What are the mechanisms? *Organizational Behavior and Human Performance*, **34**, 402–418.

Tetrick, L.E., and LaRocco, J.M. (1987) Understanding, prediction, and control as moderators of the relationships between perceived stress, satisfaction, and psychological well-being. *Journal of Applied Psychology*, **72**, 538–543.

Walsh, J.T., Taber, T.D., and Beehr, T.A. (1980) An integrated model of perceived job characteristics. *Organizational Behavior and Human Performance*, **25**, 252–267.

Walker, G., and Weber, D. (1987) Supplier competition, uncertainty, and make-or-buy decisions. *Academy of Management Journal*, **30**, 589–596.

Williams, L.J., and Hazer, J.T. (1986). Antecedents and consequences of satisfaction and commitment in turnover models: A reanalysis using latent variable structural equation methods. *Journal of Applied Psychology*, **71**, 219–231.

Youngblood, S.A., DeNisi, A.S., Molleston, J.L., and Mobley, W.H. (1984) The impact of work environment, instrumentality beliefs, perceived labor union image, and subjective norms on union voting intentions. *Academy of Management Journal*, **27**, 576–590.

INDEX

Abbreviated Task Inventory (ATI) 289
ABI/INFORM 49
Abilities 95–7
Ability testing 155–9, 179
Accomplishment record inventory 7
Accounting 76
Accuracy determinants 54
Accuracy model 53
Achievement tests 155–9
Actor–observer biases 66
Adrenaline excretion 255
Aggregation issues 81
Alienation scales 187
Analysis of variance (ANOVA) 304, 306–8
Anxiety rating 175
Aptitude tests 152, 153, 161
Armed Services Vocational Aptitude Battery (ASVAB) 155, 157, 158
Assessment centers 160–2
Assigned role LGD (ARLGD) 165–6
Attitudes 116–17
Attribution theory 66, 80, 81
  in leadership perception 64
Attributions 116–17
Autonomous work group 269
Autonomy conditions 247–8
Autonomy of Action and Broad Personnel Responsibility 312
Autonomy research 249–50
Available Motions Inventory (AMI) 292

BARS 54
Behavioral control 236, 241, 262
Behavioral manipulation 61
Behavioral observation scales 54
Behavioral questionnaires 53
Behavioral ratings 55, 63
BOS 54

Brief Job Analysis Method (B-JAM) 288
Burnout 25–48
  causes and consequences of 36–40
  components of 42
  conceptual approach 33
  conceptual meaning of 27
  concurrent and discriminant validity 30–1
  conservation of resources in 41
  construct validity 27–34
  convergent validity 31–2
  core meaning 32–4
  definition 25
  definitional approaches 28–30
  developmental models 29, 30, 40
  eight-phase model 30
  emotional exhaustion (frequency) scale 34
  epidemiology 34–6
  future research directions 41–3
  gender differences 35
  implications of term 25
  longitudinal studies 38–40
  measurements of 40
  open systems approach 43
  prevalence of 34
  psychosomatic complaints 40
  questionnaires to measure levels of 39
  research studies 26
  rising research popularity 26
  somatic complaints 40
  stage model 29–30
  stress effects in 41, 43
  structural regression analysis 39
  theoretical model 41
  unidimensional view of 41
Burnout Index (BI) 28–9, 31, 33, 34

CANDO checklist 285

Cardiovascular diseases 42
Carelessness index 301
Catastrophe theory 80
Categorization as source of rater bias 53–4
Categorization judgements 63
Categorization processes 73
Categorization theory 62–4
  in leadership perception 64
Causal assessment 67
Causal attributions 66
Causal direction 376
Causal modelling 371–404
Causal ordering 375
Chi-square analyses 190
Closed mindedness 98
Coaching and practice in personnel selection 145–83
  definitional issues 146–7
  effects on interviewing performance 168–78
  fairness issues 149–51
  forms of 147–9
  in assessment centers 160–8
  in-basket performance 166–8
  multiple choice items 150
  reasons for examining 149–51
  summary of existing reviews 151–4
  validity issues 149–51
Cognitive antidote 66
Cognitive biases 54
Cognitive complexity 106–23
  age effects 121
  applications in I/O psychology 93–4, 122–8
  concept of 106–8
  individual differences in 94–5
  measurement techniques 110–12
  physiological concomitants 122
  research data 113–23
  Schroder theory 124–6
  stress effects in 121–2
  Streufert theory 126–8
  theory 108–10
  training 120, 123
Cognitive constructs 73
Cognitive controls 95–7, 236–7
Cognitive mechanisms 60
Cognitive orientation 60
Cognitive perspectives 49
Cognitive processes 49–91
  methodology 80–1
  theory 82–3
Cognitive strategy 96, 106
Cognitive structures 62, 63
Cognitive style 93–106
  and training or learning 103
  applications in I/O psychology 93–4, 105–6, 123–8
  category variations in 97–8
  conceptualizations of 95–7
  individual differences in 94–5
  measurement techniques 98–100
  perception 100–1
  physiological concomitants 105
  research data 100–5
  Schroder theory 124–6
  sources of differences in 104–5
  Streufert theory 126–8
Cognitive weariness 41, 42
Color-word stress test 255
Combination Job Analysis Method (C-JAM) 287–8
Communication networks 70
Communication skills 116
Complexity factor 312
Computer applications within job analysis 293–4
Computer systems 268
Conceptual similarity schema 51–2
Conceptual Systems Test (CST) 112
Confirmatory analysis
  biased and inconsistent results 383
  conditions for 376–80
  results 387–8
  samples 380–1
  structural model for 376, 377
Contrast effect 55
Control by avoidance 240
Control in the workplace 235–80
  and predictability 241–2
  and stress effects 238–40
  further research 250
  individual difference variables 264–7
  interactive model tests 259–62
  intervention attempts 267–71
  intrinsic need for 237–8
  machine pacing effects 250–5
  research directions 272–3
  stress effects 242, 271–2
  well-being effects 271–2
Control research, summary of experimental and social psychological 242–3

INDEX

Control theory 80, 236, 243–64
Cornell Medical Index 202
Cost/benefit formulation 77
Covariation 51
Creativity 117–18, 122
  assessment 103–4

Decision latitude models 270
Decision making 10–12, 75–80, 358
  contingent 76–7
  cybernetic 78–80
  participation in 243–5, 268
  strategic 74
Decisional control 236
Demand and Task Analysis (DATA) 289
Deviation (D) index 301
Dictionary of Occupational Titles (DOT) scales 296
Disciplinary demands 259
Distinctiveness information 56
Dogmatism 98
Driver Decision Style Exercise (DDSE) 112
Driver–Streufert Complexity Index (DSCI) 112

Embedded Figures Test (EFT) 99–100
Emotional exhaustion 41, 42
Epinephrine level 261
EQS 397
Executive monkey experiments 239
Exercise of Broad Power and Authority 312
Expectancy confirmation behavior 58

Factor analysis 310, 315
Feedback 68, 80, 160, 165, 166, 171–4, 177, 178, 180, 239, 248, 250
Field dependence versus independence 100–1
FIRO Awareness Scales 159
Flexibility 117–18, 122
Flextime 269
Flight Orientation Test 158
Framingham Heart Study 42, 258
Full-information maximum likelihood (FIML) 385, 391
Functional job analysis (FJA) 284

Galvanic skin response 172

General Aptitude Test Battery (GATB) 155, 157
General Educational Development (GED) scale 296
Generalizability theory 296
Generalized least squares (GLS) 385
Goodness-of-fit tests 386–8, 392, 393
Gough Adjective Checklist 301
Grapevine coaching 160–2, 180
Group behaviors 52
Group characteristics 59
Group membership 52
Group performance information 61
Group work, *see* Work groups

Halo error 51–3
Health Examination Survey 257
Hysteresis effects 80

Identification issues 381–3, 390–1
Illusory correlation 51–2
Impression formation 116
Impulsive/reflective style 102
Impulsive responses 99
In-basket performance, coaching and practice in personnel selection 166–8
Information orientation 115–16
Information processing 10–12, 49, 51, 56, 67, 69–71, 77
  limited capacity 82
  models of 83
Information systems 76
Information theoretic approach 303
Instrument Comprehension Test 158
Intelligence 104
Interactive Complexity Theory 109
Interactive demands–control model 261
Interpersonal functioning 101–2
Interpersonal perception 113–15
Interpersonal Topical Inventory (ITI) 112
Interview, *see* Selection interview

Jackson Personality Inventory 159
Japanese management 329–69
  change and stability in 345–53
  classical descriptions of 330–45
  classical model of 346
  collective orientation 333–7
  comparative case studies 350
  concept of groupism 334

Japanese management (*cont.*)
  culture and managerial
    effectiveness 359–64
  influence processes 341–5
  modernization theory 349–50
  organizational structure 339–41
  performance overseas 353–9
  promotion procedures 338
  seniority system 338–41
  superior–subordinate relations 342
  time perspective 330–3

Job alienation 196
Job analysis 5–10, 282–328
  accuracy of ratings 294–302
  applications of 282
  bias in ratings 300–1
  cognitive approaches to understanding the rating process 302–3
  computer applications within 293–4
  convergent validity of ratings 296–300
  evaluation and comparison of methods 283–4
  further research 320–1
  major approaches for gathering data 282
  methodologies 282–93
  potential impact of 282–3
  rater characteristics 301–2
  reliability of ratings 294–6
  specialized approaches 289–91
Job attitudes 69, 271
Job attributes 18
Job behavior 3, 7
Job characteristics 69–72, 257, 260
Job Component Inventory (JCI) 284–6, 300
Job decision latitude 255–9
Job demands 259, 263, 272
Job demands–job control model 263
Job demands–job decision latitude model 256
Job descriptions 69, 70
Job design 70
  research 245–9
Job Diagnostic Survey 247
Job dimensions 51
Job dissatisfaction 40
Job enrichment 69
Job evaluation 313–20
  and pay discrimination 315
  assignment of points 316–17
  choice of compensable factors 315–16
  compensation practices 317–19
  judgements in 319–20
  methods of 314–15
  reliability in 316–17
  sex bias in 315, 319
  validation 317–20
Job knowledge 51, 52
Job perceptions 70
Job performance 7, 14, 16, 271–3
Job redesign 70
Job satisfaction 69, 177, 336, 373
Job scope 312
Job taxonomies 303–13
  ability requirements approach 304
  attributes used in classification 303–4
  managerial applications 310–12
  non-managerial applications 312–13
  purposes of 308–13
  quantitative methods for 304–8
  task characteristics approach 304
  task strategies approach 304

KSAOs (Knowledge, Skill, Ability and Other Characteristics) 288

Latent variable designs 389–90
Law School Admission Test 150
Leader attributions 66
Leader behavior 61, 82
Leader Behavior Description Questionnaire (LBDQ) 60, 61
Leader–member interactions 65–7
Leaderless Group Discussion (LGD) 162–6
Leadership 118
  categories
    hierarchical nature of 63
    structure of 64
  characteristics 122
  perception 56–65
    attribution theory 64
    categorization model 62–4
    categorization theory 64
    effects of social norms and task demands 65
  questionnaire ratings 60–1
  research 59
  style
    employee centered 101
    job centered 101

theories 58–62
vertical dyad linkage model 68
Learned helplessness 121, 240–1
Learning 103
 failures in 79
Least Preferred Co-worker (LPC) 98, 118
Lewinian Person–Environment Fit Theory 36
Likert scale 161
Linear Structural Relations (LISREL) 319, 391, 397
Locus of control (LOC) 264–6
Long-term memory limitations 82

Machine pacing effects 250–5
Maintaining equipment and machinery 312
Manifest variable designs 381–9
Maslach Burnout Inventory (MBI) 28, 31–5, 38, 39, 42
Matching Familiar Figures Test (MFFT) 99–100
Meaning of Working International Research Team 333
Memory biases 55
Mental workload 292–3
Meta-analysis 151, 154, 371–404
Meta-Complexity Theory 126–8
Middlesex Hospital Questionnaire 259
Minimax hypothesis 240
Model specification 381–3, 390–1
Multimethod Job Design Questionnaire (MJDQ) 286–7, 309
Multivariate analysis of variance (MANOVA) 9, 176, 304, 306–8
Myers–Briggs Type Indicator (MBTI) 99–102, 159
Myocardial infarction 42

National Longitudinal Surveys (NLS) 195
Negative Attitude Change 39
Noradrenaline excretion 255
Norepinephrine level 261
Null hypothesis 347

OAI 312
Occupational self-direction scale 258
Operationalization of variable 383–5
Ordinary least squares (OLS) 385
Organizational research 371–404

Panel designs 375
Paragraph completion test 111–12
Parsimony index 390
Part-time work 197
Participation in decision making 243–5, 268
Pay discrimination 315
Payoff function 77
Pensions 189
Performance appraisal 50–8, 65
Performance cue effect (PCE) 59–63
Performance evaluations 53, 55
Performance manipulation 61
Performance quality 247–8
Performance ratings 51, 53, 56, 57, 284
 temporal factors in 54–5
Personal control 235
 see also Control in the workplace
Personal Demands factor 310–12
Personal responsibility 268
Personality Tests 159–60
Personnel selection, coaching and practice in, see Coaching and practice in personnel selection
Physical demands of work 291–2
Physical fatigue 41–3
Position Analysis Questionnaire (PAQ) 282, 283, 296–301, 305, 306, 309, 310, 314, 316
Predictability and control 241–2
Pre-test/post-test interviews 152, 153, 172–5, 177
Problem solving 72–5
Process models 75
Professional and Career Examination (PACE) 155, 158
Prospect theory 80
PSYCINFO 49

Q-factor analysis 310
Quality circles 213–33
 as OD intervention 224, 227
 characteristics of 225, 227
 current status of 226–8
 definition of 219–21
 derivation 214
 effectiveness of 222–3
 emergence of 216–19
 future research 227
 history 214
 implementation of 267–8
 in Japan 214–16, 224, 225

Quality circles (cont.)
  in United States   217–19, 224, 225
  limitations of   223–4
  main characteristics of   220–1
  problems involved with   226
  questions of focus   224–5
  training material   218
Quality control
  Japanese successes in   217
  management of   215–16
Questionnaires   39, 53, 60–1, 70, 161, 253, 259, 269, 270, 282, 286

Rating accuracy   53
Rating behavior   57, 58
Rating purpose   55–6
Reflection/impulsivity   99
Rehabilitation Counsellor Task Inventory (RCTI)   289
Reinforcement theory   68
Requisite task attributes (RTA) model   270
Response bias   62
Retailing, sales clerks in   3
Retirement   185–211
  age effects   187–8, 192–3
  and activity level   205
  and work commitment   189
  as stressful life event   199
  attitudes towards   186
  changes in activities   185
  correspondence between planning and actual retirement   190–1
  defining   186
  demographic characteristics   203–4
  early   188–90
  educational level   189, 193–4
  effects and consequences of   198–207
  environmental factors   198
  factors influencing behavior   191–8
  financial effects   195, 201
  future research   197, 207–8
  health effects   189, 194–5, 201–3
  impact on environment   207
  impact on organization   206–7
  impact on the individual   201–7
  job alienation effect   196
  job tenure effect   195–6
  leisure pursuits   198
  life satisfaction   199–201, 204–5
  marital satisfaction   205
  marital status   193, 204
  occupational level   194
  organizational factors   197–8
  part-time work options   197
  personal factors influencing   192–6
  planning for   188–90
  post-retirement phase   198–207
  pre-retirement phase   186–91
  related to pension   189
  role of situational factors   187
  sex differences   193
  social and leisure activities   205
  societal factors   198
  socioeconomic status   203
  sources of income   187
  spouse effects   205
  transition factors   191–8
  work commitment   194, 204
  work-related factors   190, 197–8
Retirement History Study (RHS)   195
R-factor analysis   310
Rod and Frame Test   99
Role Concept Repertory Test (REP Test)   107, 111, 113

Sales clerks in retailing   3
Scholastic Aptitude Test (SAT)   150, 152–4
Selection interview   1–23
  applicability   1
  candidate attractiveness   11
  content of   5–10
  cost effectiveness   1
  criteria of   5–10
  decision making   10–12
  effect of applicant age   9, 15–16
  effect of applicant race   15
  effect of applicant sex   9, 14–15
  effect on recruitment outcome   17–18
  impact of training programmes   13–14
  individual differences   12–17
    among applicants   14–17
    among candidates   5
    among interviewers   12–14
  information processing   10–12
  job attribute information   18
  non-verbal behavior   8–10, 18
  personality characteristics   17
  popularity of   1
  questioning strategies   8
  reliability   2–4
  research criticism   1
  simplified model of   4–5

strategies in   16
trait-type concepts   6
validity   2–4
verbal content   5–8
Self-assessment instrument   285
Self-containment condition   378–9
Self-diagnosis   175
Self-efficacy concept   236
Self-report affective measures   261
Sentence completion test   111
Situational Interpretation Test (SIT)   112
Social cue effects   69–70
Social information processing   69–72, 81, 82
Social perception model   65
Social processes   65–72
Solution development   74
Solution selection   74
Spatial ability tests   155
Spatial aptitude tests   158
Specification searches   388–9, 394
Staff Burnout Scale for Health Professionals   36
Statistical quality control   214
  teaching techniques   215
Strain measures   261
Stress effects   312
  in burnout   41, 43
  in cognitive complexity   121–2
  in the workplace   238–40, 271–2
Strong Vocational Interest Blank   10
Structural equation modelling   373
Structural models   75
Subject matter experts (SMEs)   287, 290, 294
Subjective workload   292–3
Subjective Workload Assessment Technique (SWAT)   292
Subordinates
  characteristics of   65

effectiveness of   58
motivation and training   68
Superior–subordinate interaction   65–7, 342
Survey of Interpersonal Values   159

Task demands   260
  adaptation and adjustment to   118
Task design   69
Task importance value   287
Task Inventory–Comprehensive Occupational Data Analysis Programs (TI–CODAP)   282, 283, 294
Task perceptions   69–71
Task performance   102, 119–20
Taxonomy Project   303
Technical Competence Analysis (TCA)   289
Test-Operate-Test-Exist (TOTE) model   250
Threshold trait analysis (TTA)   288
Threshold Traits Analysis System (TTAS)   288–9
Training   103, 123
  cognitive complexity   120, 123
Two-stage least squares (2SLS)   385
Type A behavior   98, 264, 266–7, 273
Type B behavior   266–7

Union of Japanese Science and Engineering (JUSE)   215
Univariate analyses   176

Work alienation   189
Work groups   58–9, 66, 70, 269, 334
Work methods questionnaire   253
Work performance   345
Work satisfaction   345
Working memory limitations   82
Workload demands   259
Workload measurement   291–3

*International Review of Industrial
and Organizational Psychology
1986*

CONTENTS

Editorial Foreword		ix
1.	**Work Motivation Theories** Edwin A. Locke and Douglas Henne	1
2.	**Personnel Selection Methods** Paul M. Muchinsky	37
3.	**Personnel Selection and Equal Employment Opportunity** Neal Schmitt and Raymond A. Noe	71
4.	**Job Performance and Appraisal** Gary P. Latham	117
5.	**Job Satisfaction and Organizational Commitment** Ricky W. Griffin and Thomas S. Bateman	157
6.	**Quality of Worklife and Employee Involvement** Susan A. Mohrman, Gerald E. Ledford Jr, Edward E. Lawler and Allan M. Mohrman Jr	189
7.	**Women at Work** Barbara Gutek, Laurie Larwood, and Ann Stromberg	217
8.	**Being Unemployed: A Review of the Literature on the Psychological Experience of Unemployment** David Fryer and Roy Payne	235
9.	**Organization Analysis and Praxis: Prominences of Progress and Stuckness** Robert T. Golembiewski	279
10.	**Research Methods in Industrial and Organizational Psychology: Selected Issues and Trends** Eugene F. Stone	305
Index		335

International Review of Industrial and Organizational Psychology
1987

CONTENTS

Editorial Foreword		ix
1.	**Organization Theory: Current Controversies, Issues, and Directions** Arthur G. Bedeian	1
2.	**Behavioural Approaches to Organizations** Fred Luthans and Mark Martinko	35
3.	**Job and Work Design** Toby D. Wall and Robin Martin	61
4.	**Human Interfaces with Advanced Manufacturing Systems** John R. Wilson and Andrew Rutherford	93
5.	**Human–Computer Interaction in the Office** Michael Frese	117
6.	**Occupational Stress and Health: Some Current Issues** Colin Mackay and Cary L. Cooper	167
7.	**Industrial Accidents** Noel P. Sheehy and Antony J. Chapman	201
8.	**Interpersonal Conflicts in Organizations** Leonard Greenhalgh	229
9.	**Work and Family** Ronald J. Burke and Esther R. Greenglass	273
10.	**Applications of Meta-analysis** John E. Hunter and Hannah Rothstein Hirsh	321
Index		359

International Review of Industrial and Organizational Psychology 1988

CONTENTS

Editorial Foreword		ix
1.	The Significance of Race and Ethnicity for Understanding Organizational Behavior Clayton P. Alderfer and David A. Thomas	1
2.	Training and Development in Work Organizations Irwin L. Goldstein and M. Jocelyne Gessner	43
3.	Leadership Theory and Research: A Report of Progress Fred Fiedler and Robert J. House	73
4.	Theory Building in Industrial and Organizational Psychology Jane Webster and William H. Starbuck	93
5.	The Construction of Climate in Organizational Research Denise M. Rousseau	139
6.	Approaches to Managerial Selection Ivan T. Robertson and Paul A. Iles	159
7.	Psychological Measurement: Abilities and Skills Kevin R. Murphy	213
8.	Careers: A Review of Personal and Organizational Research Michael J. Driver	245
9.	Health Promotion at Work Michael T. Matteson and John M. Ivancevich	279
10.	Recent Developments in the Study of Personality and Organizational Behavior Seymour Adler and Howard M. Weiss	307
Index		331